THE ROCOCO INTERIOR

THE ROCOCO INTERIOR

*Decoration and Social Spaces
in Early Eighteenth-Century Paris*

Katie Scott

YALE UNIVERSITY PRESS

New Haven & London

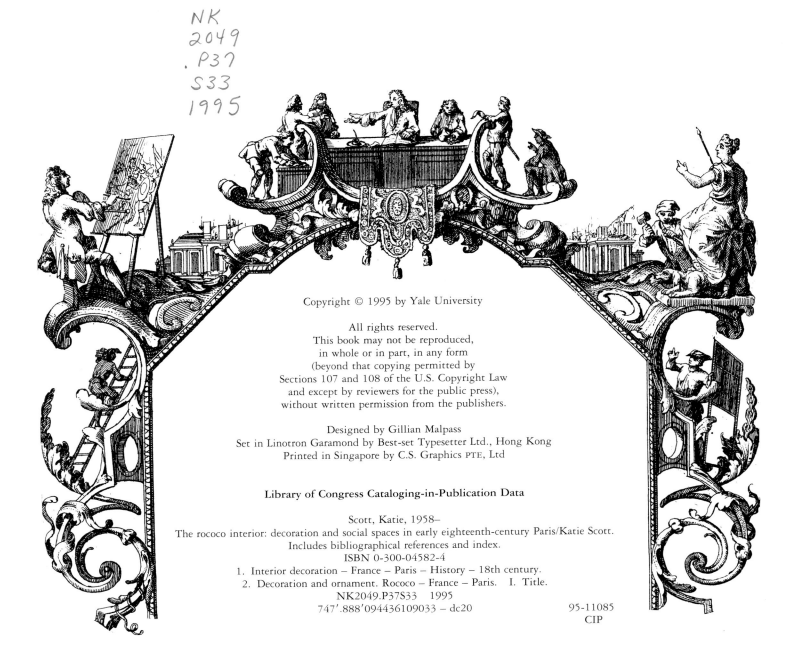

Copyright © 1995 by Yale University

Designed by Gillian Malpass
Set in Linotron Garamond by Best-set Typesetter Ltd., Hong Kong
Printed in Singapore by C.S. Graphics PTE, Ltd

Library of Congress Cataloging-in-Publication Data

Scott, Katie, 1958–
The rococo interior: decoration and social spaces in early eighteenth-century Paris/Katie Scott.
Includes bibliographical references and index.
ISBN 0-300-04582-4
1. Interior decoration – France – Paris – History – 18th century.
2. Decoration and ornament. Rococo – France – Paris.   I. Title.
NK2049.P37S33   1995
747′.888′094436109033 – dc20   95-11085
                                                                                          CIP

A catalogue record for this book is available from
The British Library

Frontispiece: Salon de la Princesse, hôtel de Soubise, Paris, *c.*1737–8.
Endpapers: Salon du Prince, hôtel de Soubise, Paris, from Germain Boffrand, *Livre d'Architecture*
Above: Nicolas Guérard, an artist's bill-head (detail), *c.*1715–19. Engraving.

For my parents

Contents

1   Natoire, detail of fig. 29.

Abbreviations, Currency and Measures

A.A.P.	Bibliothèque d'Art et d'Archéologie (Paris)
A.N.	Archives Nationales (Paris)
A.N.M.C.	Archives Nationales, Minutier Central
B.A.	Bibliothèque de l'Arsenal (Paris)
B.H.V.P.	Bibliothèque Historique de la Ville de Paris
B.M.	Bibliothèque Mazarine (Paris)
B.N.f.f.	Bibliothèque Nationale (Paris), fonds français
B.N.n.a.f.	Bibliothèque Nationale, nouvelles acquisitions françaises
I.F.	Institut de France (Paris)

The standard unit of currency in eighteenth-century France was the *livre*; a money of account. One *livre* was made up of 20 *sous*, and each was in turn made up of 10 *deniers*. Meanwhile, the silver *écu* was worth 3 *livres* and the gold *louis* 6 until after Law's System when the *écu* inflated to 6 *livres* and the *louis* to 24 *livres*.

The standard unit of measurement was the *pied* (32. 472 cm). One *pied* was equivalent to 12 *pouces*, each *pouce* (2. 706 cm) to 12 *lignes*. The *toise*, a unit of measurement frequently used in surveying, equalled 6 *pieds*.

The standard unit of measurement for textiles was the *aune* or *aulne* (118 cm).

Acknowledgements

During the years this book has taken to write I have accumulated debts of gratitude to numerous scholars both past and present. Studies of eighteenth-century decoration can proceed today with a degree of confidence only because archivists and art historians, such as the Guiffrey, Alfred de Champeaux, François Contet, George Wildenstein, Roger-Armand Weigert and, more recently, Mireille Rambaud and Bruno Pons, have made available an increasing and rich body of visual and biographical material related to the careers and works of Parisian artists, architects and artisans. I have been only too grateful to exploit their publications. But above all, though my priorities diverge sharply from those of Fiske Kimball, I could scarcely have written this book had he not first published his pioneering account, *The Creation of the Rococo*, in 1943. The chronology and nomenclature he established for the stylistic development that led from *style Louis XIV* to the *genre pittoresque* provided a framework within which I have been content to work. However, concerned, by his own admission, exclusively with the 'what?, how?, when?, where? and who?' of decoration, Kimball deliberately left uncharted the field of relationships between the rococo and the 'political, social and economic movements' of the time because he felt it could not be adequately retrieved – if indeed it could be said to have existed at all. Since the publication of Thomas Crow's *Painters and Public Life in Eighteenth-Century Paris* (1985), any such self-imposed limitation to the range of legitimate historical speculation is less easily justifiable, and it was with a mind to establishing a broader explanatory framework for eighteenth-century decoration that I embarked on the present research.

For helping me to see the potential of a subject that perhaps has yet fully to establish its intellectual credibility within art history I am pleased to acknowledge a substantial and long-standing debt to Helen Weston. Much of this book is drawn from a thesis submitted to London University in 1988 and undertaken with her supervision, encouragement and friendship. For all of these I am deeply grateful. I should also like to thank many friends and colleagues – Colin Bailey, Philip Conisbee, David Bindman, John Goodman, Sarah Hyde, David Maskill, Andrew McClellan, Neil McWilliam, Carolyn Sargenson, Michael Sonenscher and Richard Wrigley – all of whom have at various stages offered invaluable help, advice and information from which I have greatly benefited. I am particularly grateful to Thomas Crow, Tom Gretton and Alastair Laing, who, together with Yale University Press's two readers, gave a most patient and demanding reading of my thesis and made many penetrating suggestions for the improvement of that first draft. Chapters 9 and 10 owe much to the careful reading and helpful suggestions of David Solkin.

For financial support between 1980 and 1994, many thanks to the former Department of Education and Science, the Central Research Fund of London University, Christie's, the British Academy and most importantly to Christ's College Cambridge where, as a junior research fellow, I profited from the unfailing encouragement of Sir Hans Kornberg, Sir John Plumb and the fellows of the college.

For easing the difficulties of obtaining photographs I am most grateful to Annette Lloyd-Morgan of the Witt Library and Philip Ward-Jackson of the Conway Library. And I owe special thanks to James Stevenson of the Victoria and Albert Museum, Bunty King of the Wallace Collection, Rosamund Griffin of Waddesdon Manor, and the photographic services of the British Library, the British Museum, the Cooper Hewitt, the Nationalmuseum, Stockholm, the Réunion des Musées Nationaux and the Bibliothèque Nationale. For bringing the book together with exceptional editorial care, my warmest thanks to Gillian Malpass. For their patient attention to the accuracy and the consistency of the text I am pleased to thank also Celia Jones, copy-editor, and Sue Adler, indexer.

As always, I am deeply grateful to Stephen Deuchar for giving me courage, for listening to my ideas and for reading my drafts with an enthusiasm and care well beyond what his professional interest and marital duty could possibly have required of him. That he continues to share my interests and to hold my hand, even after the arrival in quick succession of our three children – Hannah, Seth and Grace – is little short of miraculous.

2 Nicolas Pineau, design for the balustrade of the main staircase of the hôtel de Mazarin, c.1737. Sanguine on paper, 50 × 37.5 cm. Musée des Arts Décoratifs, Paris.

Introduction:
The Anatomy of a Noble House

On 25 May 1736, the duc de Luynes recorded in his diary that Françoise de Mailly, duchesse de Mazarin, had paid 220,000 *livres* for a house on the rue de Varenne in the fashionable neighbourhood of Saint-Germain-des-Près, at no distance from his own hôtel.[1] This far from negligible sum had secured a portion of the original Vendôme estate upon which stood, according to the duke's intelligence, an ill-formed residence in need of immediate and extensive repair.[2] However, less than a decade later, the architect Jacques-François Blondel was able to describe the same house as a residence worthy of the greatest admiration, and a building to be ranked among the top ten models for the particular attention of his students at the Ecole des Arts.[3] During the intervening period Mme de Mazarin had evidently transformed an unpretentious home, erected originally in 1703 for Chrestien-François de Gorge d'Entraigues, into a mansion famed above all for its interior decoration.[4] The decoration represented the results of an orchestrated effort by the architect Jean-Baptiste Leroux, the sculptor Nicolas Pineau and the painters François Boucher, Jacques de Lajoue and Charles Natoire – already prominent men by the 1730s and 1740s.

Until recently it would have been virtually impossible to describe further the hôtel de Mazarin, not least because little of what Blondel had so admired survived the decision at the beginning of the nineteenth century to drive the present rue Vaneau through a good third of the building.[5] Louis Hautecoeur, on the meagre evidence of a single engraving representing one leaf of the front-door or *porte-cochère* (fig. 3) published in Mariette's *Architecture françoise* (1727–38), was thus able to indicate no more than Leroux's participation in the decoration of the building, the construction of which he mistakenly attributed to Dulin.[6] The process of reconstructing the spatial arrangement and decorative appearance of the mansion became possible only once the relevant documentation – building contracts, probate inventories, etc. – had been located and put together with surviving architectural and ornament drawings.[7] The building contracts reveal, for instance, that some of the changes effected by the duchesse de

Mazarin were immediately apparent to her neighbours and to passers-by, notably the remodelling of the street frontage which closed the lateral wings of the building and screened the *corps-de-logis* from the world beyond. The contract drawing for this screen reveals that Leroux, true to his reputation, had proposed an articulation that was conspicuous not so much for its architectonic properties or judicious handling of the classical idiom as for its decorative effect.[8] Despite the comparatively restricted space, he offered a shallow rhythm of contrasts between windows, rusticated pilasters and smooth raised panels culminating in a *porte-cochère* parenthetically framed by double consoles and crowned by an elaborate rococo cartouche (fig. 4); above all this reigned a balustrade. Passing through the doorway inscribed with the family name, visitors found themselves in a rectangular courtyard facing a three-storey house linked to the street by single-storey wings (fig. 5). Although three flights of steps serviced three different entrances to the building, the accentuation of the central bays of the main façade by means of a pediment (complete with family coat of arms), a balcony and an applied Ionic order, left those arriving by coach or on foot in little doubt either of their destination or of the social standing of the resident they hoped soon to meet.

Inside the building, space unfolded into a number of circuits of interconnecting rooms known as *appartements*. The duchesse de Mazarin's probate inventory encourages us to walk slowly through these rooms and to survey their contents with the notary's intense, even obsessive, attention to particulars. Thus, we enter the vestibule (confusingly also known as the first antechamber) which we find sparsely furnished with two large console tables painted to simulate marble, five benches, a clock and a stove.[9] The decoration consists of no more than two marble busts mounted on stone plinths. The room opens out in three directions, offering pathways to the right, up the main staircase with its baluster of forged iron designed by Pineau (fig. 2); to the left, into the dining-room; and straight ahead, into the 'white-painted saloon'. In the dining-room we find, among other things, a Flemish stove and a fireplace

4   Nicolas Pineau, cartouche for the *porte-cochère* of the hôtel de Mazarin, *c*.1737. Sanguine on paper, 42.5 × 53.4 cm. Musée des Arts Décoratifs, Paris.

3   Design for one of the leaves of the double entrance doors to the hôtel de Mazarin, after 1738. Engraving and etching. From Jean Mariette, *Architecture françoise*, 1727.

surmounted by a large mirror in a gilded moulding, and topped by a painting depicting – appropriately enough for a room of this function – 'animals, birds and a dog'.[10] Meanwhile, the white *salon*, true to its name, sports white-painted panelling, relieved only by the gilded carved frames of four large mirrors positioned above the chimney and at the centre of each of the other three walls. The most conspicuous items of furniture in the room, ten armchairs, are also white. Indeed, only two polished console tables and two *armoires* break up the relentless pallor of the room. Above the doors hang four paintings by Lajoue representing 'fishermen and landscapes',[11] while below, two diminutive bronze copies of the Marly *Fame* and *Mercury* continue the sculptural note sounded in the vestibule. The colour scheme and the iconography of this saloon suggest a *sala terrena*, a space of mediation between garden and

house.[12] As such it resembles the vestibule-cum-antechamber preceeding it, different only in its situation on the garden- rather than the courtyard-side. Indeed, the presence of a stove and an old *lit de veille* indicates that the room not only looked like an extension of the first antechamber but also functioned as one: items of furniture such as these are to be found most often where servants are constantly in attendance.

From the *salon blanc* or second antechamber we may proceed to left or right into a sequences of rooms running east and west along the garden front. To the east we discover the duchess's bedchamber, *cabinet de toilette* and a second *cabinet* (also known as La Cage), while to the west are two saloons.[13] The notary's itemisation and description of the contents quickens and expands as we progress in ascending order of importance from the vestibule to the white *salon*, and from the white *salon* to the bedchamber.[14] Moreover, the fact that Pineau started work on the panelling of the bedchamber in the same year that Mazarin acquired the house serves to confirm its importance. The principal feature of the scheme, evident from a preparatory drawing (fig. 6), consists of four large, gilded cartouches arranged at the centre of the main panels and representing the senses in the guise of four young women holding respectively a bouquet of roses (Smell), a lyre (Hearing), a lady-apple (Taste) and a telescope (Sight).[15] This allegorical theme is not taken up by the paintings above the doors which, rather than completing the sequence of senses by offering a depiction of Touch, represent instead female portraits, possibly members of the duchesse de Mazarin's family.[16] However, the pastoral note struck by the cartouches is perpetuated and even given an exotic turn by the gilded palm-tree frames which integrate the *trumeau de cheminée* and the three pier-glasses into the overall scheme. If the decoration of the *cabinet de toilette* beyond[17] includes more paintings, and if La Cage strikes an altogether

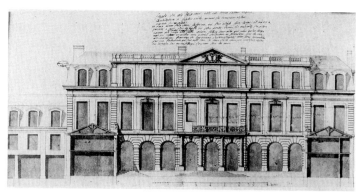

5 Jean-Baptiste Leroux, courtyard elevation of the hôtel de Mazarin, 1736. Archives Nationales, Paris.

more exotic note,[18] the bedchamber is nevertheless most handsome. A formal room, its large number of bronzes mounted on marble pedestals (including equestrian portraits of Henri IV and Louis XIV[19]) serve to impress as much by their brilliance and their value as by their invitation to exercise the one sense not represented on the walls of the room.

In the first and smaller of the two *salons* to the west of the white antechamber we discover more sculpture, including what appears to be a copy of the *Spinario*, mounted on a pedestal encrusted with 'tortoiseshell, medals and gilded bronze ornament'.[20] Once again, Pineau is responsible for creating the environment in which these objects are displayed,

6 Nicolas Pineau, *The Senses*. Cartouches for the panelling of the duchesse de Mazarin's bedchamber at the hôtel de Mazarin, *c*.1737. Pen and brown ink, 30 × 28 cm. Musée des Arts Décoratifs, Paris.

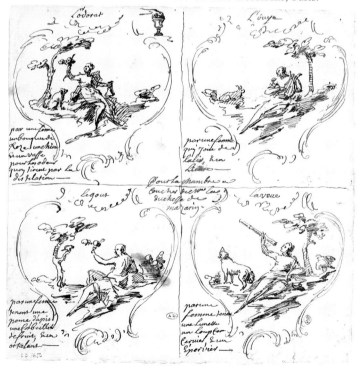

and yet again, four curved-topped mirrors placed opposite one another constitute a significant element of the decoration. They are encased in sculpted gold frames termed 'à guirlande', while the displaced palms of the bedroom take up a new location, framing the three small mythological overdoors painted by François Boucher. Though preparatory drawings survive for four works – *The Education of Cupid* (fig. 7), *Cupid and Psyche* (fig. 8), *Venus and Cupid* (fig. 9) and *Cupid and the Three Graces* (fig. 10) – all subsequently executed between 1738 and 1741, only three of the pictures were ultimately delivered (the fourth remaining in the painter's studio[21]).

Continuity is maintained in the decoration of the second and larger *salon* which merely exaggerates the features of the first. Instead of five bronzes on pedestals, there are now eight; instead of four pier-glasses, there are now seven; and instead of three small overdoors, there are now four larger ones in garlanded frames painted by Boucher's contemporary and rival, Charles Natoire. Nothing survives of Natoire's works, and we know only that they, too, depicted 'traits de fable'. As for furniture, the number of sofas, armchairs, chairs *à la reine* and console tables increases likewise, and the probate description underlines their similarity to those in the first *salon*.[22] Just as there is decorative and functional continuity along the central north–south axis of the house (that is between the vestibule and the white antechamber), so there appears to be consistency along this half of the east–west axis; but while white gives the accent to the first, gold characterises the second.[23]

The only other rooms located on the ground floor, such as the bathroom, various closets (one described for no obvious reason as 'à l'anglaise') and a chapel, are not strictly speaking part of any sequence of rooms but remain comparatively isolated spaces. The chapel, for example (whose installation required special permission from the Archbishop of Paris), is to be reached only at the end of a passage quixotically decorated with Chinese wallpaper.[24] But, in conjunction with the apartments, these rooms and corridors combine to ensure that all the duchesse de Mazarin's personal, social and spiritual needs are met on a single floor. The rest of the house – the wings and the upper storeys – is given over to the various members of her household. On the first floor, for instance, Mme de Tournelle, the duchess's cousin, enjoys a spacious apartment consisting of two antechambers, a *chambre* and a *boudoir*, the last of which is fashionably decorated by Christophe Huet.[25] The wings, on the other hand, house the service areas and provide suitably cramped quarters for the servants and the duchess's retainers.

* * *

On the surface, it seems that the documents (particularly Mazarin's inventory) have yielded more than sufficient information to render a lost monument once more accessible. According to Annik Pardailhé-Galabrun, the historical value

7   François Boucher, *The Education of Cupid, c.*1737. Black chalk heightened with white on blue paper, 19 × 40 cm. Nationalmuseum, Stockholm.

8   François Boucher, *Cupid and Psyche, c.*1737. Black chalk heightened with white on blue paper, 19.7 × 35.7 cm. Nationalmuseum, Stockholm.

9 François Boucher, *Venus Intoxicates Cupid with Nectar, c.*1737. Black chalk heightened with white on blue paper, 19.3 × 40.1 cm. Nationalmuseum, Stockholm.

10 François Boucher, *The Three Graces Playing with Cupid, c.*1737. Black chalk heightened with white on blue paper, 18.4 × 40.3 cm. Nationalmuseum, Stockholm.

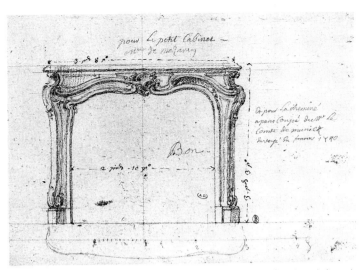

11 Nicolas Pineau, chimney-piece for the duchesse de Mazarin's *petit cabinet* at the hôtel de Mazarin, *c.*1737. Sanguine on paper, 27 × 42.5 cm. Musée des Arts Décoratifs, Paris.

of the probate inventory lies precisely in its unique capacity to restore for study the practices of everyday life by reintroducing individuals to their homes and surrounding them with their possessions.[26] Indeed, the evidential nature of the inventory, it's text latched firmly to the present, creates the inevitable impression that, by their itemised descriptions, inventories allow us to encounter the past in all its 'chaotic authenticity'.[27] Thus, experiencing the building, its decoration and contents from the notary's point of view, so to speak, encourages the use of first-person descriptions, thereby partially or completely concealing the 'otherness' of the past which, as Robert Darnton has so rightly pointed out, it behoves the (art) historian to recapture and explore.[28] The integrative effects of description — that is to say, narrative's inherent tendency to assemble and compose the dispersed fragments of history — have in the past often seemed particularly well suited to a discussion of eighteenth-century decoration, concerned as it was with the creation of unified and coherent schemes. The description of appearances seemingly brought the world of art to life. And yet that very liveliness and warmth is frequently misleading because the signification of appearances is inevitably governed by a particular rhetoric. The discourse of classical architecture and decoration demands, for instance, that its monuments be understood as independent, orderly and discrete entities, and that those lost be reconstructed in the fullness of their design. Thus, the advantages brought about by a descriptive reconstruction of an entire hôtel — in terms of a supposed familiarity with and intuitive understanding of it — must be traded off against the difficulty, also begotten of the method, of holding the 'monument' at a critical distance. The urge to see and describe *order* in decoration, and moreover to see and describe it as *natural*, as part of the internal logic of a style, is, I think, to participate unwittingly in the self-deceptions of the society for which it was deployed. Most

significantly, such participation serves to obscure the existence of conflict which was part of the process of decorative production *and* an essential constituent of its meaning.

In part I of this book, I have tried to look beneath the surface of decorative schemes in order to understand how they came into being. Instead of seeking the security of looking at complete and functioning interiors, I have deliberately substituted a piecemeal and sometimes disruptive vision of idle decorative materials immanent, no doubt, with decorative potential, but more clearly enmeshed in a set of material constraints and economic relations. In point of fact, that side of the story, the view from below, is very often present in the selfsame items used to reconstruct the appearance of lost projects. For instance. Pineau's design for the marble chimney-piece of one of the *cabinets* at the hôtel de Mazarin (fig. 11) not only provides evidence of what it looked like but also of the 'Bon' necessary in the eighteenth century to ensure a design's progression to execution, thereby revealing a trace of the hierarchical relationships that pertained between artists and clients (or architects acting for clients). In fact, it is tempting to read the configuration of notations on the drawing as illustrative of that very relationship. Pineau's 'submissive' annotations which merely provide information are located on the periphery of the motif, while Mazarin's or Leroux's activating 'Bon' stands as a necessary validation at the centre, indeed inscribed within, the design itself.[29]

Pineau's marginalia are in themselves of further interest. To the right, a second inscription picks up the title 'for the small cabinet – Mme de Mazarin' and completes it with the following: 'and for the chimney cut in Paris for the comte de Munick and despatched in February 1740'.[30] The apparent gestural spontaneity of much rococo decoration should not, evidently, be confused with irreproducibility, since here Pineau was making one design do the work of two. This indicates something about the value of time in an eighteenth-century workshop, and also suggests that the circumstances of artisanal production during the *ancien régime* do not necessarily correspond with that image of a traditional and customised practice disseminated so efficiently by capitalist nostalgia. But the identity of the client also indicates that there were limitations to the repeated use of single designs. Multiple usage presupposed the ready availability of a number of clients with equivalent and, in this instance, considerable spending power. It may also have required their relative geographical dispersal so that duplicates would remain inconspicuous.[31] More important than the particulars of this case, however, is the fact that such attention to the instrumental function of drawings helps to uncover a web of economic interests at work in a body of visual relations.

Those interests emerge particularly clearly in chapter 1 of this book. There the lines of competition between decorative artists are retraced, as are the production and marketing techniques such artists developed in order to compete effectively; furthermore, some indication is given of the relative prices charged for various skills and commodities. The result suggests that a decorative ensemble can be read as a settling of competing claims and a record of a changing economy. The parameters of the market's flexibility are later indirectly discussed in chapters 2 and 3, which deal with the institutional values and the structures of authority that shaped and placed limits on decorative development in early eighteenth-century Paris. Hence, a much larger share is there accorded to trade-guilds, their disputes and questions of labour generally, than is perhaps conventional in art-historical writing, but it seemed important to reintroduce the fine arts to their economic context and to abandon the polite assumption that eighteenth-century decoration was the work by night of insubstantial 'fairies' – as too literal a reading of Sébastien Mercier would perhaps have us believe.[32]

In order for decoration to work – to command the patronage of the great – post-Renaissance theory demanded that it should deflect attention from the technologies of its manufacture and obscure the antagonisms around which its production was organised. Thus, if the 'deconstruction' of the appearance of unity is a necessary corollary to explaining the genesis of eighteenth-century decoration, that unity must be reconstituted in order to enable a fuller understanding of its significations. In so far as part II provides at least measure of some such understanding, it does so not by building on the historical information provided in part I but by looking at the same (or comparable) visual material from the perspective of those who commissioned it – that is to say, from above. In this sense, parts I and II are complementary accounts rather than causally linked sequences in the same story.

The word 'décoration' had two meanings in the eighteenth century, as it does today. According to the *Dictionnaire de l'Académie française* (1762), it meant both the 'embellishment' that resulted from the deployment of ornament on and in a building, and the titles and 'Dignitez' conferred on 'persons in order to honour them'.[33] The relationship between these two senses of decoration is in essence the subject of part II. Prompted by eighteenth-century assertions that 'each class is distinguished not only by the degree of power or respect it enjoys, but also by a sort of *exterior appearance* appropriate to the rank it holds in society',[34] I have attempted not only to reconstruct the cultural categories that structured eighteenth-century discrimination, but also to analyse the dynamics that were thought to propel signs of distinction into action. Having thus drawn attention to the theatricality of social life during the *ancien régime*, an analysis of the spatial and behavioural relations between the nobility and the other estates and between members of the nobility itself unfolds, largely substantiated by reference to the representational and ceremonial inferences alive in the architectural discourses of the period. Through the study of ground-plans and the relational decoration of rooms, it is thus possible to establish some of the ways in which architectural space managed the lives of individuals and helped shape their perceptions of society.

Once interiors are thus notionally filled with the interplay of different lives (as they were not in our tour of the hôtel de Mazarin), they cease to be just so many flat, ornamented surfaces and regain their full three-dimensional significance. Mme de Mazarin had a range of options when she decided to buy and, if necessary, to remodel a town house. Those options and her choices – which neighbourhood?, what kind of house?, how many floors?, tapestry or panelling?, which colour?, etc. – were not pragmatic or arbitrary but informed by social convention and cultural practice. In other words, they were decisions shaped less by her personal and individual needs than by shared social and aesthetic values. In order to reconstruct this conceptual grid, Mme de Mazarin is of little use as an individual, but as a member of a social class she may play her part. Part II therefore deals in 'types' – or tokens of those types – and for that reason the text is, without apology, less picturesquely empirical. Primarily concerned with ideals, and written largely with a view to the *conjoncture* or the medium-term development of social and cultural practices, the material discussed ranges from the beginning of absolutism in the late sixteenth century to its demise at the end of the eighteenth. Thus, part II focuses on the unchanging features of architecture and ornamentation and analyses their role in the reproduction of the social and political structures of the *ancien régime*.

Taken together, parts I and II of this book suggest that early eighteenth-century decoration occupied two rather distinct neighbourhoods of history. On the one hand, it originated in a market place where it was policed by an inescapably local commercial culture. On the other, it operated in a sphere of noble domicile, in *hôtels*, where a no less parochial practice, but this time of nobility (not work), was emphatically imagined into material shape. For the most part, these separate worlds are not brought into effective conjunction in the first half of the book. The commissions that led to the creation of particular decorative schemes remain largely implicit. Moreover, when contracts are discussed they tend to be rescued as instances of a general rule at the service of an established social structure. This might seem to imply that the cultural structures of each estate (*roture* and *noblesse*) were so providentially synchronised that the things that artisans made were the very things that nobles needed. Indeed, a persuasive case could no doubt be made for regarding patronage as always contingent to some extent – that is to say, as a relationship that results not from cultural interaction (a meeting of minds as well as exchange of goods), but from the ability of consumers to minister to their own intentions by appropriating certain characteristics of artefacts and lending them new meaning.[35] This, in turn entails imagining a perfectly regulated social structure, devoid of conflict and indefinitely capable of reproducing itself. Indeed, such a synoptic and synchronic picture is perhaps conjured up by parts I and II because of the marked reliance on normative evidence, that is to say, on texts that describe what should have been rather than what was. The aim of part III is to disrupt the more-or-less comfortable certainties that have come before and, by contrast, to consider (frequently by re-using or re-addressing data and issues already introduced) the ways in which the notionally fixed representation of *ancien régime* society was transformed by events, and how the aesthetics of privilege were forced to yield before the mechanics of power.

From the perspective of part III, it seems remarkable indeed that in part II, it is apparently possible and seemingly reasonable to examine the nobility and to reconstruct its cultural character while scarcely mentioning Versailles, the seat of government. Justification for that choice rests on the fact that part II is concerned above all with the discourse on nobility, with its manifold representations, and, as such, nobility is presented as a kind of 'super-ego', a fixed, coherent, freely imagined and collectively willed idea, and not as the coerced mystification of political defeat that history teaches us it very largely was. Such projected ideas, and the ideologies to which they belong, are however, never really finished, but exist in constant dialectical exchange with the agencies of power, end-lessly seeking accommodation with the inescapable economic and political realities of the moment, and attempting to articulate rights to authority from what seem to be the most persuasive vantage points. The political landscape at the end of the seventeenth century was very different from what it had been at the beginning. Where, in the 1590s, the French nobility emerged from religious and political crisis as the glittering future victim of an absolutist policy whereby the state sought systematically to engross the competing structures of *seigneurial* power (simultaneously compensating the dispossessed by investing in a system of honour that left it socially unrivalled), a century later, in the equally fraught political climate of the 1690s, the nobility seemed, on the contrary, poised to wrest back a measure of its power and political function. By the end of Louis XIV's reign, the regime had been significantly weakened by religious bigotry (which resulted in the Revocation of the Edict of Nantes, and the loss of the commercial, industrial and maritime expertise of the fleeing Huguenots), military ambition (which culminated in the disastrous War of the Spanish Succession), financial mismanagement, and natural disaster (particularly the famines of 1693–4 and 1709–10). Moreover, in 1711–12, Louis's son, grandson and eldest great-grandson all died within a few months, leaving the crown and sceptre to the uncertain care of a sickly child. In such circumstances, it would have been surprising had there not been a resurgence of political ambition within the nobility and an intense manoeuvring for influence and position.

Part III is specifically concerned with these and subsequent changes in the political climate of the *ancien régime* and with their relation to equally significant developments in the sphere of art. Briefly, the first three chapters of part III explore the revival, around 1700, of an older, aristocratic and *salonier* culture, distinct from, and even opposed to, that of the state; the last two chart the alleged devaluation of this élite aesthetic at the hands of non-noble, or at any rate less noble, emulators

and its final demise in print culture and in the critical and public sphere of the Salon. To put flesh on this framework, chapters 6, 7 and 8 respectively focus upon genres of painting and decoration that may broadly be described as the grotesque, the pastoral and the mythological. While I shall not pretend that these categories encompass the full range of decorative projects undertaken in the early eighteenth century, they nevertheless embrace most of the more significant ones, and as such seem appropriate sights for study. The hôtel de Mazarin, for instance, bore the mark of all three decorative genres. Grotesques by Claude III Audran and his pupils were introduced to the hôtel on two separate occasions;[36] the natural world was poetically evoked by Lajoue's landscapes and by the indigenous and exotic motifs of Pineau's ornament; and Boucher and Natoire provided gallant mythological scenes for overdoors of the *salons*. However, the purpose of these chapters is not to try to refine the definition of noble taste through an exhaustive accounting (assuming such a thing were possible) of noble investment in these genres, but to analyse the satisfactions once derived from them, and to consider closely the connection between the experience of aesthetic pleasure and the exercise of social and political choice. Thus, while the grotesque appears to have offered a means of evading, notionally at least, some of the absolute proscriptions of the state, mythology encouraged a savouring of the processes and enactment of *honnête* authority. Moreover, such study highlights the complexities of social formation and brings into view rival centres of influence and ideological production, in this instance, not only within the second estate of the nobility but also at the royal court. As we shall see, the competition and interplay between such factions served to flavour aesthetic appetites and helped shape and reshape the criteria of cultural distinction. Taste is thus most evidently assertive, a claim upon the future, and not merely the passive reflection of a position occupied individually or collectively in the economy. Moreover, tastes are defined not only, or even primarily, in response to properties objectively present in material things, but in relation to the strategies and statements of preference advanced by others. The commission of Boucher's *Venus and Cupid* (fig. 9) can therefore be discussed not only as a choice of mythology, but also as a rejection of the heroic, and of the political values of magnificence which History traditionally articulated on behalf of its princely interlocutor.

If these chapters primarily describe the gains and losses made by noble idealism in its confrontation with hegemonic orations from above, chapters 9 and 10 are more obviously concerned with the nobility's response to competing discourses from below. In many respects, chapter 9 marks a return to an earlier discussion of prodigality introduced in chapter 4, but in so doing it abandons the easy moral certainties of the discourse of estates and examines the social and cultural transformations accomplished by money and the alleged transgressions of luxury. I do not, however, want to suggest that chapter 9 offers a more 'realistic' account than

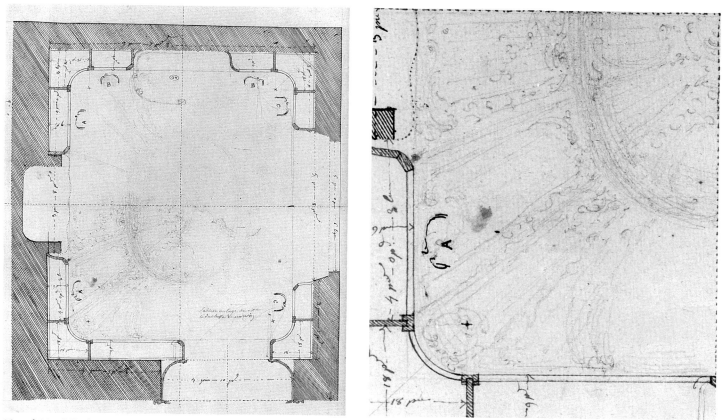

12 and 13   Nicolas Pineau, design for the ceiling of 'La Cage' at the hôtel de Mazarin, *c.*1737 (and detail). Pen, ink, red chalk and pencil on paper, 43.5 × 55 cm. Musée des Arts Décoratifs, Paris.

chapter 4. Chapter 9 is, in fact, little more concerned with assessing the evidence of *actual* social and cultural mobility than chapter 4, rather it aims to explore the perception of danger that the so-called bourgeois represented, and the response their pretentions provoked, a response that, as I hope to show, involved the nobility in repudiating that which it had formerly prized. Given that questions of luxury are invariably questions about legitimacy, I have chosen to pay particular attention to the theme of 'inappropriateness' in rococo criticism, a theme that recurs regardless of the vantage-point from which it was written. It is perhaps not surprising, in view of the almost archetypal character of the hôtel de Mazarin, that it should have acquired a certain prominence in this conflict. The mansion is the 'hôtel M***' over whose vices and virtues the comte de Saleran and another nameless amateur entered into heated debate in Bastide and Blondel's *L'Homme du monde éclairé par les arts* (1774). This text unusually provides space for both negative and positive evaluations of the same interior. Indeed, the descriptions are juxtaposed so that Saleran's condemnation of the *salon*, 'where there was little more to be seen than frivolous ornament, [and] assymetrial contours, without discretion and without choice',[37] becomes the amateur's eulogy of a building where, 'not a single straight line was to be seen', where symmetry was, 'entirely banished', and where the

decoration offered, 'delightful fantasies', which 'the magic of the mirrors', multiplied to infinity.[38] However, there was more at stake here than the simple illustration that tastes differ.

At one level, by advocating a return to the seventeenth-century tradition of decoration, Saleran was defending the interests of 'fine' artists against the intrusion of *ornemanistes* like Pineau, who had since laid claim to ceilings – the site of earlier glories of the French school – for the elaboration of their petty skills (figs 12 and 13).[39] At another level, criticism was being levelled at the patron, frequently cited as an (if not the) author of the decorative programme. Precisely those qualities that had previously guaranteed noble pedigree were now re-presented by Saleran as signs of a *common* place and ignorant culture. History was being rewritten in accordance with the new demands of the present. Chapter 10 focuses on the specific forms of misinterpretation that the rococo variously endured from the late 1730s and particularly those that occured in two separate but related fields: printmaking and criticism. However, since the interiors of the hôtel de Mazarin were never reproduced either in their entirety or in part, and since none of the decorative paintings appears to have been exhibited at the Salon, the mansion retained, Saleran notwithstanding, something of its original, noble mystique. The rococo as a style was not ultimately so lucky.

The change in orientation in part III (from structure to event) is accompanied necessarily by a revision of some of the conceptual categories examined in earlier chapters. In particular, working definitions of nobility are shown to have been nowhere near as firm as suggested in part II. In chapter 7, the contestation between the peerage and the ordinary nobility and in chapter 9, the conflicts between 'old' and 'new' — or would-be — nobles clearly reveal the eighteenth-century nobility to have been a flawed and sometimes self-contradictory order, more unified at some moments than at others, yet still working to persuade itself (and society at large) that it existed as an organic and naturally occurring entity. In point of fact, the so-called better part of society, the *honnête* or polite part, had never been equal to the order of nobility as such. The *salon*-life that unfolded with such an air of exclusivity in the Chambre-Bleue at the hôtel de Rambouillet and elsewhere in seventeeth-century Paris was not the unique performance of the *noblesse*. Barely fifty per cent of the *salonières* studied by Carolyn Lougee qualified as old nobility; the rest were a heterogeneous assortment of wealthy wives and daughters of the recently or soon to be ennobled.[40] Thus, inasmuch as the ideology of *honnêteté*, of politeness and taste, operated a principle of exclusivity, it was one that necessarily fell just short of legally defined nobility, and one that transformed the noble locutions of discourse into aristocratic ones. The classic harmony of the former was carried out and replaced by the often agonistic and conflictual inflections of the latter, carried in precisely because *honnêteté* opened up a discursive space somewhere between the official languages of estates and the economic reality of class, a space in constant need of defintion, supervision and defence.

PART I

Spaces of Production

1

The Production of Materials

'When a house is built', wrote Sébastien Mercier towards the end of the eighteenth century,

> you may say that nothing is done as yet; the fourth part of the expense is not yet over. Enter the joiner, the upholsterer, the painter, the gilder, the sculptor, the furniture-maker &c. Next mirrors are needed, and everywhere service bells must be installed. Completely decorating the inside takes three times the time employed by the bricklayers on the construction; antechambers, staircases, corridors, *commodités*, all of it is never ending.[1]

Clearly, for Mercier the most striking – if not the most shocking – features of interior decoration were its expense and the seemingly frivolous fuss which secured a boundless variety to its treatment.

Leaving aside for the time being the question of cost, a brief enumeration at this point of the materials that composed an actual eighteenth-century interior, coupled with the identification of those upon whom responsibility for its creation devolved, should demonstrate that Mercier's estimates of the volume of personnel essential to the realisation of a decorative scheme was scarcely exaggerated. Let us take the case of just one room in the hôtel de Soubise, a mansion in the Marais.[2] Decorated in the years 1737–8 under the direction of the architect Germain Boffrand (apparently as a palliative for the teenage bride, Marie-Sophie de Courcillon, for having married Hercule-Mériadec de Rohan, prince de Soubise, an octagenarian), the Chambre de la Princesse (fig. 14) provides ample testimony to the complexity of the decorative schemes Mercier might have had in mind. Here, three of the walls were encased in made-to-measure panelling prepared and assembled by one or several *maîtres menuisiers* or master-joiners.[3] They were then elaborately carved by ornament scupltors, in this instance possibly by Jacques Verberckt[4] and assistants. Such men were sometimes specialists in *lambris* but more often sculptors who worked in a variety of media from wood to stone or lead.[5] They were, therefore, invariably responsible for the plaster cornices,[6] assisted by house-painters and gilders who likewise gave a painted finish to the panelling. Into this rigid structure were fitted specifically commissioned paintings (fig.

15), in this instance an overdoor depicting *Minerva Instructing a Young Woman in the Art of Tapestry*, the work of an academician, Pierre-Charles Trémolières.[7] Mirrors were similarly inscribed in the woodwork – one separating each of the three windows, another originally above a chimney-piece and a fourth opposite. Finally, at the far end of the room, a bed-alcove, hedged in by a sculpted and gilded balustrade, was hung with red damask.[8] The installation of mirrors and the hanging of furnishing fabrics was the prerogative of Parisian upholsterers and mirror-merchants but their production might have taken place at a royal manufactory (even at some distance from the capital) and by a workforce that rarely if ever made contact with the final consumer. Hence, those who contributed to a decorative ensemble such as this, not only exercised a variety of particular skills and trades, they also experienced widely differing relations to their materials, products and clients.

WOODWORK

Towards the end of the century, the scientist and financier, Antoine-Laurent Lavoisier, judged that the building, decorating and furnishing trades of Paris annually employed an impressive 1,600,000 cubic feet of timber in pursuit of their interests,[9] by far the greatest portion of which was floated down the Seine to the timber yards at the port de la Grève where it was bought and used largely by carpenters.[10] However, from the last third of the seventeenth century a growing quantity of much finer quality timber had been arriving in Paris by road to supply the more exacting needs of joiners and panel sculptors. According to Jacques-François Blondel, panelling had originally served 'no other purpose than utility and salubrity'[11] – it ensured dry walls and consequently a healthy atmosphere[12] – but it was not long before the full potential of wood was realised (during the reign of Louis XIII, according to the joiner André-Jacob Roubo[13]), and then,

> trade made way for Art, taste replaced routine, and the custom of using panelling became a luxury which in turn

14 Chambre de la Princesse, 1737. Hôtel de Soubise, Paris.

15 Pierre-Charles Trémolières, *Minerva Instructing a Young Woman in the Art of Tapestry*, 1737. Oil on canvas, 147 × 156 cm. Archives Nationales, Paris.

introduced sculpture, gilding and mirrors into apartments . . .[14]

Various woods were used for such panelling – chestnut, lime, pine from Auvergne or Lorraine or a combination of several[15] – but for high-cost schemes oak was preferred: either imported Dutch oak or a soft French variety.[16] The latter had the advantage of few knots and a fine colour: 'light yellow scattered with small red freckles', but Roubo warned that,

> when it is of too soft a quality, it should be used only for panels and sculptural details but never for joinery, because its excessive oiliness and its short grain make it prone to cracking . . .[17]

Of whatever kind, wood for panelling was bought in planks and its price varied not only according to kind but also in relation to the thickness and width required.[18] Ornament could either be carved within the width of the panel, in which case the work might be sent along to the sculptor's *atelier* for completion (this, for example, was the practice of the Jules Degoullons workshop[19]) or it could be carved separately and

then applied to the panelling with an adhesive.[20] In some instances the choice was specified in the contract; Guillaume Dupré, for example, agreed in 1749 not only to follow in every detail the designs supplied by the architect Pierre-Noël Rousset but undertook, in addition, that none of the ornament would be of an applied variety and all of it 'executed within the thickness of the wood'.[21] Although by this date applied ornament, particularly of a kind executed in such 'new' materials as *carton* or papier-mâché[22] was beginning to present wood-carvers with increasing competition,[23] Blondel continued to affirm, well into the 1770s, that ornament integral with the support was to be preferred to all other varieties, not least because of its superior solidity.[24] This explains the disproportionately greater cost of the thicker timbers. Wide panels were expensive and sought after for similar reasons, for the greater the width the greater the possibility of uninterrupted decorative elaboration within a single field.

The divisions of labour and the distribution of earnings involved in the transformation of these raw materials into finished decorative products were rather more complex than the distinction between joinery and sculpture would seem to suggest. *Menuisiers* were responsible not only for preparing, assembling and installing panelling (fig. 16), but also for executing primary mouldings to specifications provided. Among the drawings from Pineau's workshop is a sheet of sections for the mouldings of Marguerite-Paule de Grivel d'Orrouer's *salon* at the newly built hôtel de Feuquières[25] in the rue de Varenne (fig. 17). Fitted on to the sheet are outlines of the manifold shapes and degrees of relief that the sculptor thought appropriate for the various frames and door-jambs of the room, together with polite instructions that before being executed they be shown to (if necessary, corrected) and approved by the architect Pierre Boscry.[26] It was from drawings such as these that joiners would, and possibly did, proceed. Moreover, as a plate in Roubo's *L'Art du menuisier en meubles* (1772) reveals (fig. 18), joiners also habitually blocked-out areas for sculpture: from right to left the upper pair of designs show the state of a panel designed to receive a trophy as it passed from the joiner's care into the sculptor's hands, and the lower pair illustrates the same process in the case of a *trumeau de cheminée.*

The activities of the sculptor and joiner overlapped perceptually and might well seem inextricably confused, but signicant distinctions existed between the control each exercised over their remuneration. For the most part a joiner's earnings were reckoned in measured work – that is to say they were paid at an agreed rate per unit of surface area. A sculptor, on the other hand, might employ a number of methods for evaluating his activities. For example, Henri Lambillot and Michel Lange, when submitting an invoice for their work on the Salon Doré at the hôtel de Matignon, listed, at a total cost of 240 *livres*, no less than five separate elements that combined to decorate the chimney-breast (fig. 19), of which the most expensive was a delicate trophy of musical instruments suspended from a palm above the mirror.[27] By contrast, in 1717 Pierre Juliance charged the duc de La Force by the *pied* for the ornament surrounding the mirror in his *cabinet*.[28] Then again, Louis Herpin and Jean-Martin Pelletier, a second team of sculptors employed at the hôtel de Matignon, used a combination of both systems, charging by the piece for the more elaborate motifs – 170 *livres* for a trophy above a mirror – and by the length for the twenty-three *pieds* of ornament used to frame the pier-glass, reckoned at 4 *livres*, 10 *sous*, the *pied*.[29] Juliance had only liked to charge 1 *livre*, 1 *sol*, per *pied* for his ornament, and in fact the contrast between the expense of the de La Force and Matignon schemes becomes the more marked in the final accounts: the sculptors contracted by the architect Jean Courtonne collectively submitted *mémoires* worth 18,933 *livres* while Juliance felt able to charge his client just 1,439 *livres* for the complete refurbishment of La Force's hôtel in the rue des Saints-Pères.[30]

16 *Installing Panelling*, 1772. Engraving and etching. From André-Jacob Roubo, *L'Art du menuisier en meubles*, 1772.

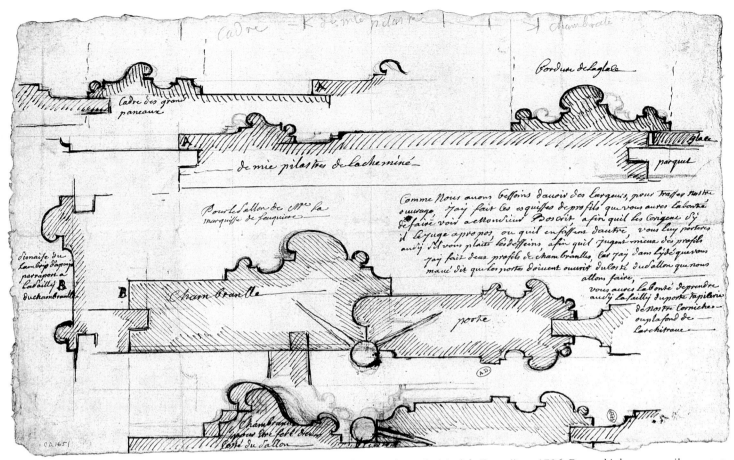

17   Nicolas Pineau, mouldings for the panelling and door casements for the *salon* at the hôtel de Feuquières, 1736. Pen and ink over pencil on paper, 27 × 43.5 cm. Musée des Arts Décoratifs, Paris.

It would be a mistake, however, to assume too readily that such a large differential necessarily reflected either the degrees of merit of the sculptors involved or an acknowledged and measurable contrast in the quality of the final products. On other occasions Juliance is known to have worked on more prestigious and lucrative commissions;[31] in this instance he simply chose not to miss an opportunity to do business, however seemingly modest. Furthermore, the final settlement was not the product of a fixed price but the result of a process of negotiation between buyer and seller, the outer limit of which was set by Juliance's *mémoire*.[32] In an economy where the sheer weight of numbers precluded the possibility of any one workshop setting the prices of primary materials, and in which primitive accounting methods frustrated the exact calculation of exchange values, price could be no more than notional and open to 'explorative' bargaining pressures.[33] Thus, variation in the cost of many decorative products was just as likely to have been the consequence of the commercial agility, not to say trickery, of particular buyers and sellers, as the measure of positive qualities inherent in the products themselves. Each transaction was thus doubly unique: in process as well as in product. It seems highly appropriate therefore, that the elaborately designed receipts published by Nicolas Guérard (fig. 21)

at the turn of the century should have so situated the painter and the sculptor (below and to the side) that their professional skills were cast as preliminary to the greater artistry of commerce by which their profit would ultimately be reckoned across the counter depicted above.

As noted in the case of the Matignon decorators, ornament sculptors tended to work in teams. Indeed Herpin and Pelletier had established a stable work association at least a year before being called to the hôtel de Matignon, an association that survived for further joint ventures at the hôtels de Bonnier and de La Vrillière in the neighbouring rue Saint-Dominique.[34] It has been suggested that the organisational structure of the Bâtiments du Roi was not a little responsible for encouraging the formation of production units of this kind, and the comment contained in a letter concerning the allocation of studios in the Louvre in 1737, to the effect that it did not seem, 'appropriate to cut back on the studios allocated to [ornament] sculptors because they were thereby assembled in a single continent, convenient for the supervision of work and the issuing of orders', would seem to endorse such a hypothesis.[35] However, the ubiquity of such associations amongst those who rarely, if ever, worked for the crown and indeed among a whole variety of other trades, implies that beyond the

16

A.J.Roubo Inv.et Del.   Berthault Sculp.

18   *Panelling Prepared Ready for Sculpture*, 1772. Engraving and etching. From André-Jacob Roubo, *L'Art du menuisier en meubles*, 1772.

20 Detail of fig. 19.

obvious convenience of the royal administrators, the habitual co-operation between certain sculptors served other, commercial interests.

In many cases these associations were formalised as partnerships before a notary. Such partnerships varied considerably in objective, duration and social structure. In 1719, for example, the sculptors Alexandre Jouasse and Jacques Loiseau entered into partnership for the time necessary to execute a commission for the decoration of the maréchal de Villeroy's house at Corbeil.[36] Their association lasted just four months.[37] By contrast, the Jules Degoullons partnership with André and Mathieu Legoupil, Marin Bellan, Pierre Taupin, Robert de Lalande and Jacques Verberckt lasted nearly forty years, during which time a son followed his father into the association and three marriages were contracted between the families of the various partners.[38] The financial management of the partnership was complicated by such an evolving membership, and additionally so by the unequal and fluctuating investment of working capital – capital essential to cover the substantial overheads of a business demanding large stocks of comparatively expensive primary materials.[39] However, the Degoullons partnership did resemble that of Jouasse and Loiseau in one respect: the association did not initially bind its members to work together without exception.[40] The first act of association pertained only to works for the Bâtiments du Roi and members were free to make their own arrangements for other commissions. Thus, in 1699 Jules Degoullons joined Louis Herpin in the decoration of the marquis de Barbezieux's château.[41] Later, like Nicolas Pineau's association with Antoine Rivet,[42] the partnership expanded to embrace all the activities of its members, but it seems nevertheless that short- and long-term partnerships were not necessarily mutually exclusive and that a sculptor might well be more than one type of partner at any one moment.

By spreading the financial risks, partnerships, of whatever kind, offered an important bulwark between the sculptors and their precarious market, dominated as it was by noble clients who rarely settled their accounts immediately or in full, and where long-term systems of credit were universal.[43] Until the 1770s clients took ample advantage of the fact that the usury laws strongly discouraged, if not effectively prevented, shopkeepers and tradesmen from charging interest on outstanding obligations, even when payment was delayed by several years.[44] To take an example, on 12 December 1742 Louise Adelaïde de Bourbon-Conti, princesse de la Roche-sur-Yon, paid Jacques Verberckt an instalment of 100 *livres* on the 1,800 *livres* still outstanding on a substantial account for works at her hôtel on the quai Malaquais executed five years earlier.[45] Moreover, if, in the same year, she did finally honour in full a debt of 35,098 *livres* owed to the joiner Gautier for works carried out between 1734 and 1741 both in Paris and at the château de Vaureal, her mason, carpenter, painters, jeweller, etc. were not to be so fortunate.[46]

On very rare occasions, however, the reverse would appear to have been the case. In 1697, for instance, Pierre Crozat ordered four pedestals, two *armoires* and two plinths from

21 Nicolas Guérard, an artist's bill-head, *c.*1715–19. Engraving.

19 Salon Doré, 1725. Hôtel de Matignon, Paris.

22 Chambre de la Princesse, 1737. Hôtel de Soubise, Paris.

Charles Boulle, and was apparently prompted to advance the cabinet-maker sufficient funds in order to ease his mounting financial difficulties and thereby, indirectly, speed up delivery of the desired pieces.[47] In the event, it took a court injunction to force Boulle to produce and install the furniture for Crozat's *cabinet* in the rue place des Victoires.[48] What may seem at first glance to have been an exceptional act of generosity, turns out therefore to have been a particularly effective means of ensuring that a verbal obligation was actually met by an enterprise visibly weakened by the irregularity and unpredictability of in-coming payments from other, less 'fortunate' clients.

In order to offset the contingencies of such an economy, many artists and artisans were encouraged into partnerships (or at least informal arrangements) with suppliers or sub-contractors so that the rhythms of credit and cash-outlays could be synchronised more effectively. Thus, for example, Verberckt was at the head of a workshop that comprised not only three assistant sculptors but also two joiners – the brothers Jean-Antoine and Jean-François Guesnon[49] – to whom he might otherwise have been obliged to subcontract work. The practice was common in other trades too. House-painters went into business with colour-merchants for the very same reasons: it eliminated or domesticated one link in the chain of credit. The ramified partnership and credit networks

in which artists were so caught, largely by the scarcity of cash in the economy,[50] combined with a variable pricing system to create a social space in which reputations bulked large. The often chronic vulnerability of individual craftsmen to expulsion by scandal from the magic circle of established or potential lenders, retailers and clients is amply illustrated by the case of the goldsmith François-Thomas Germain, who in 1766 was allegedly brought down by conspiring journeymen and fellow-competitors.[51] His under-capitalised 'general gold and silversmith store' proved satisfyingly susceptible to suggestions of personal depravity, fraud and imminent bankruptcy levelled in 'clandestine pamphlets, anonymous *libelles*' and 'foreign gazettes', as a direct consequence of which Germain was apparently relieved of his privileged workshop in the Louvre and very nearly lost his business.[52] As a safeguard against precisely such events, ornament sculptors seem often to have made their own fortunes hostage to those apparently better placed to protect them, namely architects. Thus, a royal lustre was imparted to the works of the Degoullons partnership and of François-Antoine Vassé's workshop not only by their regular employment by the crown but also because, even in private commissions, they were habitually linked with the king's First Architects: Jacques V Gabriel and Robert de Cotte. Nicolas Pineau, on the other hand, joined with Jean-Baptiste Leroux, possibly the most fashionable architect of the late 1720s and the 1730s, and in some measure staked his livelihood on Leroux's ability to guarantee them both the high level of business turnover necessary for thriving careers.[53]

It has been important to understand in detail the mechanisms that regulated a sculptor's practice, because they characterise in every important respect the circumstances governing the workshops of all those trades where various stages of manufacture were refracted through a multiplicity of separate enterprises. The role of the house-painter in further assisting the transformation of woodwork into decoration will shortly need to be addressed. For the time being, we should already be aware of how this diaspora of workshops and tasks was given co-ordination by an, as yet, poorly understood but integrative system of credit that conjoined individuals, temporarily at least, in relations of dependence. Irrespective of the avenues pursued – expert bargaining for materials or sales, short- or long-term partnerships, associations within or between trades – business acumen and managerial skills were clearly at least as important as technical proficiency or facility in design to the aspiring *sculpteur-en-bois*.

PAINTING

A manuscript notation at the head of a series of cartouches designed by Jean-Bernard Toro in 1731, possibly for the duc de Richelieu, runs as follows:

> This sculptor carved wood with such delicacy that the works he made, such as table legs, clock cases and console

tables, required no gilding, and even the varnish which might have been applied seemed unjustified; all his works were consummately finished, and he gave them all the perfection of which his genius and his fingers were capable.[54]

Although this remark specifically concerns furniture, it would seem to imply that woodwork was painted and gilded only when it was found insufficiently attractive in its natural state. A degree of support for this view is lent by the architectural treatises of Charles-Augustin Daviler and Blondel, even if both stress the quality of the wood rather than the calibre of design as a deciding factor in the choice for varnished or painted panelling.[55] As far as architects were concerned, therefore, panelling *à la capucine* offered the highest standards of work, suitable for the most exalted rooms of an hôtel,[56] for it combined fine materials with such skilled design that no further accenting of the composition was required. Yet despite the enthusiastic support of certain patrons, like the Grand Dauphin, whose apartment at Meudon was entirely fitted with varnished panelling, for the most part eighteenth-century *boiseries* were painted.[57] To achieve a successful result here a certain degree of communication between woodworkers and house-painters was required: primary contours needed to be sharpened and the secondary mouldings reduced in size, such that the layers of paint, which had the effect of deadening the relief of the former and filling out the size of the latter, did not spoil the intended effect.[58] Beyond this point, however, panel sculptors relinquished their work into the hands of house-painters, and it was they and the client who determined its final appearance.

The colourman Jean-Félix Watin called house-painting the child of necessity and luxury because it both preserved 'the most useful and everyday things', such as panelling, furniture and carriages, while simultaneously knowing 'how to render them attractive', and offering 'at modest expense the pleasures of a versatile and cheerful decoration, which, in a flash, caprice can vary, qualify and renew at will'.[59] This *peinture d'impression* was probably renewed fairly frequently, for as the painter Girard pointed out:

Decorative painting is easily prone to losing its freshness, and if it is neglected, it soon deteriorates; sun, fresh-air and damp together conspire to destroy such works, either by eroding them in part or by destroying them completely.[60]

Open fires and candle-lighting also contributed significantly to this deterioration, no more so than when, as at the hôtel de Soubise (fig. 22), a white and gold scheme was chosen, even though blue was habitually added to white in order to minimise discoloration.[61] But Girard's comments were made in a *mémoire* submitted to the Directeur des Bâtiments whom he hoped to persuade of the necessity of retaining a full-time house-painter to look after, repair and renew the *peinture d'impression* in the royal palaces, a post for which he was, of

23 *Cabinet intérieur* of Marie-Joseph de Saxe, 1748–9. Château de Versailles, Versailles.

course, ideally suited. It was evidently in his interest, and indeed in the interest of house-painters generally, to persuade clients to renew their decoration as frequently as possible: to this end the argument that schemes deteriorated within years, if not months, may have been wilfully exaggerated.

It was probably they, in conjunction with colourmen (and many painters fulfilled both functions), who promoted the fashion for polychromy in the 1740s and 1750s. As colours went in and out of favour, schemes needed to be repainted, even if the process was recommended as a means of saving on redecoration, for such schemes apparently spoiled less swiftly than those in white and gold.[62] At Versailles, the panelling for Marie-Joseph de Saxe's new *cabinet intérieur* (fig. 23), which received overdoors by Jean-Baptiste Oudry depicting the Seasons, was appropriately painted in white and green by one of the eponymous Martins, and the pastoral motifs carved by Louis Maurisan were carefully picked out in their representational colours.[63] Although this was an unusually elaborate treatment, it is clear from the inventories of painters' workshops, and from even cursory descriptions contained in invoices, that the capital's interiors were not lacking in comparable dash. In 1752, the contents of Charles-André Tramblin's studio in the Gobelins included substantial quantities of lead white, yellow ochre, Naples yellow, vermilion, carmine, red umber and Prussian blue, pigments subsequently displayed in the interiors and on the carriages of the likes of the prince de Turenne, the ducs de Biron and de Mazarin and the comtes de Stainville and de Saint-Florentin.[64] In the hands of another painter-gilder, Jacques Richot, such raw colours were transformed into the nuanced shades preferred by the eighteenth century.[65] To decorate the fields of the panelling at the hôtel de Meulan in 1749, for instance, Richot selected colours that ranged from white, light and dark blue to *petit vert d'eau* (light aquamarine), *paille* (straw), *petit gris de perle* (light pearl grey), and *ventre de biche* (doe's flank) – poetic names designed, no doubt, to appeal to a *précieuse* clientele – while the mouldings were picked out in gold or a contrasting colour.[66] The enterprise earned Richot 10,478 *livres*,[67] which, when compared with the 25,000 *livres* paid to François Le Moyne for the ceiling of the Salon d'Hercule[68] at Versailles painted more than a decade earlier, reveals the profitability of this line of work, not least because Richot was probably engaged on more than one contract at any one time. However the fashion for polychromy was short-lived, and according to Blondel it was soon despatched back 'to the confectioners' shops from where it had been taken'.[69]

The pigments used by house-painters could be bought ready-ground from colourmen[70] – for example, Claude-Philibert Cayeux regularly bought his lead white together with oil and varnish[71] from La Clef who had a shop on the rue des Princes[72] – but the exact tint used for any operation must have been mixed by the painter because pigments were combined when dry and not in suspension.[73] In the words of one writer, 'on the question of shades of colour it is impossible to determine the proportion of pigments which enter into their composition; their perfection depends upon the discernment and eye of the Artist'.[74] The successful house-painter was presumably he who offered not only a wide range of different colours but also hues that correctly anticipated – and here knowledge of new fabrics arriving on the market was particularly pertinent[75] – a market unforseen by rivals.

An alternative or additional route to success apparently lay in the development of techniques that offered advantages beyond those of standard practice. For instance, the paints used during the first half of the eighteenth century were primarily oil-based and had the inconvenience of leaving an unpleasant odour that prevented rooms from being occupied for some time after the painting had been completed.[76] However, in June 1757, the *Mercure de France* announced that Dandrillon had discovered a new method for painting panelling, one

> devoid of any hint of odour, since it employs neither oil, nor wax, nor any kind of varnish; but one which preserves the secret of imparting to the colours he uses to decorate interiors, both the polish of the *Chipolins* used up until now and the gloss of the finest varnishes.[77]

This new distemper paint *à la grecque* was tested and approved by the Académie Royale d'Architecture[78] as was the paint *à l'encaustique* invented and manufactured by Théodore Odiot which offered the same advantages.[79] However, those who specifically desired scented apartments were referred to Rigaud, Chabanne and de Lamare who, in 1751, had recently obtained permission to establish a royal manufactory, and advertised as one of their forthcoming products: '. . . scented varnishes, which perfume the apartments in which they are used; the scent is permanent [and] at the choice of those who wish to make use of it.'[80] Interested clients were encouraged to contact the firm at the office in the rue du Doyenné, beneath the arcade of Saint-Louis du Louvre.

In all three instances, manufacturers made use not only of advertising, but also of the protection of august bodies to promote their products. By granting certificates of verification to Dandrillon and Odiot, the Académie d'Architecture – which appears to have acted in respect to the building trade in a manner analogous to the Académie des Sciences' relationship to manufactures[81] – explicitly confirmed the integrity of their products. In Dandrillon's case the certificate may have been gilding the lily, because, by 1757, his reputation was already so well established that he featured in Bastide's *La Petite Maison* (1753–4); in Trémicour's circular *salon*, for instance, Mélite admired Dandrillon's skill and the industry with which he had handled 'the most imperceptible subtleties of the panelling and sculpture'.[82] Yet, since Dandrillon submitted a second product for academy scrutiny in 1758,[83] it appears that reputations were in need of repeated endorsement, and there was no better institution to perform this ritual than a royal one. Likewise, though the title Manufacture Royale brought considerable economic privileges to Rigaud and others, more important from a marketing point of view was the reputation for quality such a title connoted; for it touched every commodity produced, whether of potentially high or low unit cost.[84]

It should be clear that there were both similarities in and differences between the practices of decorative painters and sculptors. On the one hand, painters like Charles-André Tramblin felt the need of a financial partner, albeit a sleeping one, just as keenly as Degoullons or Verberckt. His workshop was also unexceptional for the differentiated activities it oversaw. Moreover, the financial management of the enterprise was like that of any sculptor's – structured by deferred payments to suppliers and long-term credit to clients, clients whose custom he obtained through a network of contacts. On the other hand, Dandrillon and Odiot seemed prepared to use stratagems rarely employed by joiners or sculptors, namely establishing brand-names and advertising. Such appeals to an unknown body of potential consumers are generally thought to be symptomatic of economies where pricing systems are sufficiently standardised that the problem for the trader lies less in the negotiation of the best possible deal in any given circumstance than in persuading potential consumers to buy at a certain price, fixed in advance.[85] There is some evidence to suggest that house-painting was indeed in the process of

24 Claude III Audran, design for a ceiling at the Ménagerie, 1699. Cabinet des Estampes, Bibliothèque Nationale, Paris.

25 Claude III Audran, design for Bacchus, for the Gobelins tapestry series, the *Portières des Dieux*, *c.*1699. Pencil, red chalk and watercolour, 37 × 24.8 cm. Nationalmuseum, Stockholm.

becoming a trade underpinned by a broad consensus over pricing. Pineau states unequivocally that house-painting was paid at a basic rate of 6 *livres* per *toise* in Paris and 8 *livres* in the country, a rate which went up by an extra 2 *livres* per *toise* if mouldings were to be picked out in a second colour.[86] In such circumstances competitive pressures could shift from the haggling between buyer and seller to the rivalry among firms.[87] However, it should be acknowledged that Dandrillon and Odiot were in a minority of two or three whose significance should not be overrated. The majority of house-painters, even those with substantial enterprises, continued to operate in a fluid market where profit was the outcome of successfully negotiated opportunities rather than calculated margins.

However, panelling offered opportunities for a treatment that exceeded the scope of the ordinary house-painter and demanded the talents of a *peintre d'ornements*. Such an artist, according to Daniel Cronström, was, 'a man who invents and arranges ornament designs', although the extent of such a person's involvement in the realisation of his designs might vary considerably.[88] In the 1690s, the decade in which Cronström made his remark, ornament was closely associated with a genre known as *arabesques*, *grotesques* or *moresques*[89] produced by the rival workshops of Jean I Berain and Claude III

Audran. In fact, Cronström initially had hopes of persuading the latter to move to Sweden because, as he explained to Nicodemus Tessin, Audran 'finds his efforts frequently thwarted . . . by Mr Berain, whom he offends'.[90] But, though competition was fierce, Audran was sufficiently employed in and around Paris not to consider a move to Stockholm for less than 2,000 *écus* per annum (an income appropriate to a modest bourgeois *rentier*[91]) worth his while.[92] Indeed, although some of Audran's most elaborate schemes were executed for the nobility[93] and not the crown, the accounts of the Bâtiments alone reveal his very substantial gains, Berain notwithstanding.

In 1699, Audran executed two ceilings for the dauphin's *chambre* and *cabinet* at Meudon, for which he was paid 6,900 *livres* and 3,000 *livres* respectively, with an additional 383 *livres* for further sundry works. In the same year he also decorated a small chamber in the princesse de Conti's apartment at Versailles for 2,500 *livres*, embarked on the decoration of no less than five ceilings at the Ménagerie worth 2,200 *livres* (fig. 24) and completed the designs for the Gobelins' *Portières des Dieux* (fig. 25) for which he was paid 7,500 *livres*.[94] In a single year, therefore, Audran's accounts totalled no less than 22,483 *livres*, though they were only met by irregular payments from the Treasury over a period of some eighteen months. Impressive though this figure may seem for an ornament painter of the kind, 'who merely designed and arranged without painting',[95] he had to meet the more regular payments to collaborators and employees who executed his designs from a sporadic and unpredictable cash-flow. This must have required a sizeable amount of disposable capital or a readily available source of credit, because, unlike many ornament sculptors, Audran does not seem to have taken partners to spread costs; instead he either subcontracted work (this was presumably the case with the gilder Desauziers and established collaborators such as Jean-Baptiste Blin de Fontenay the elder, Louis de Boullogne, Pierre-Nicolas Huilliot and Nicolas Lancret) or used the talents of the permanent members of his workshop. These included not only the house-painters Paul Chéron, Claude Guignebault and Claude III Nivelon but also future academicians serving informal apprenticeships in his studio, such as François Desportes, Jean-Baptiste Oudry, Christophe Huet and, of course, Antoine Watteau.[96] The latter two subsequently developed careers of their own in the field, although neither instituted the complex system of labour division that had been the hallmark of Audran's workshop; they preferred to execute their designs themselves.

Fully figural representations could also play their part to advantage in eighteenth-century decoration. However, since so little eighteenth-century decorative painting has survived intact in its original environment, it is difficult to appreciate the range of tasks open to artists and the versatility with which they responded to commercial opportunities. *Decoration* or decorative painting was defined in eighteenth-century dictionaries as those 'picturesque representations used in certain Celebrations and particularly in the Theatre in order to vary the scene',[97] and it is perhaps no surprise to find that many of those directly or peripherally involved in decoration either made their *débuts* at the theatre (this was apparently the case with Jacques Vigoureux-Duplessis[98] and Desportes[99]) or held semiformal positions with theatre companies.[100] The abbé Pernety claimed that French painters were indifferent decorators because they were primarily trained as 'easel painters' and that only Italians showed any real aptitude for the genre.[101] In fact many of the most successful authors of perspectives and illusionistic painting in Paris in the first half of the eighteenth century were of Italian origin. Giovanni Niccolò Servandoni enjoyed an unparalleled reputation not only for his theatre designs but also for his architectural perspectives and as a choreographer of sumptuous receptions and celebrations.[102] Moreover, in 1738 he designed a new staircase for the cardinal d'Auvergne's hôtel in the rue de l'Université (fig. 26) and filled the lunettes crowning the Ionic order of the first landing with fashionably secular depictions of nymphs surrounded by putti.[103]

However, in the sphere of domestic decoration, Paolo Antonio Brunetti, a native of Lombardy whose career spanned fifty years between 1730 and 1780, largely reigned supreme.

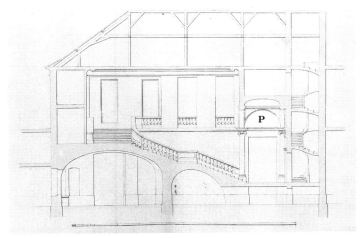

26 Giovanni Niccolò Servandoni, section of the stairwell at the hôtel d'Auvergne, 1738. Pen, ink, wash and watercolour, 29.7 × 45.5 cm. Archives Nationales, Paris.

He too provided scenery for Parisian theatre companies, notably the Comédie Française, but praise was reserved particularly for his illusionistic schemes for Paris hôtels and for châteaux in the environs of the capital.[104] One of his earliest schemes, the staircase at the hôtel de Soubise, was decorated in the same year as Servandoni's essay for Auvergne, and was to be admired, according to Dézallier d'Argenville, for 'the figures, columns, masks and other ornament [which are] so artistically painted that they trick the eye and appear as if actually in relief'.[105] A decade later he was contracted to paint the stair-well of the hôtel de Luynes (fig. 27), his only surviving work. From photographs taken before the staircase was dismantled and moved in 1899, it is clear that the ground-floor level was originally painted to simulate rusticated masonry into which niches filled with classical sculpture had been let, while an elaborate cornice stiff with heraldic emblems linked the painted walls with an otherwise empty ceiling.[106] In between, Brunetti had created the illusion of a space unfolding as an extension of the actual architecture of the landing, such that beyond the part-real, part-fictive balustrade appeared Corinthian loggias punctuated by dramatically projected antique figures on sconces, and alive with the bustle of a gaily dressed *beau-monde*, who appear, as one contemporary remarked, intent upon observing the new arrivals on the stairs.[107]

In view of the complexity of Brunetti's compositions and the sheer surface area covered, it is not surprising to discover that he relied on assistance in order to complete them with reasonable dispatch. Like Audran, he was undoubtedly responsible for the overall conception of his schemes and similarly used collaborators for the figurative work. At the height of his career in the 1740s and 1750s, Luigi Domenico Soldini and Charles-Christophe Eisen, decorative painters in their own right,[108] were among those most frequently cited by contemporary sources, but Brunetti also worked on occasion with

Natoire, with whom he probably first made contact at the hôtel de Soubise. And even for the realisation of the architectural *trompe l'œil* he used the services of at least one long-term studio assistant – the German Spourny – and his own father Gaetano, when he was in Paris.[109] Given the complex structure of Brunetti's working practice, the size of the projects he undertook and the fact that they could take years rather than months to complete, Brunetti's fees may seem superficially rather modest. The de Luynes staircase, for instance, earned him just 6,000 *livres*, paid in instalments from November 1748 to October 1750,[110] and for a similar scheme executed at Bellevue for Mme de Pompadour in 1751 he was paid 8,030 *livres*.[111] However, the accounts for the decoration of the chapel of the capital's foundling hospital reveal that Brunetti and his collaborator Natoire were paid separately: Natoire received 10,500 *livres* for his fourteen canvases and the figurative elements he contributed to Brunetti's illusionistic architecture, for which the latter was paid 9,000 *livres*.[112] It seems possible that this was Paolo Antonio's standard procedure. Rather than sub-contract work and in so doing increase his cash out-goings – he arranged separate contracts between his clients and the figurative painters whose skills he needed. Thus, when customers were slow to pay, the burden of credit was jointly borne by him and his collaborators.

While *trompe l'œil* painting may be regarded as a specialist occupation, practised by a relatively restricted number of painters,[113] a much larger percentage was involved in the production of overdoors and wall-panels, and the currently less familiar room dividers and firescreens. Natoire's *Psyche at her Toilet* (fig. 29) for instance, was apparently conceived as part of a larger series of panels which, when lowered or raised, varied the size of La Live de Bellegarde's *salon* at the château of La Chevrette.[114] Jean-Siméon Chardin's *The White Tablecloth* (fig. 30), meanwhile, is one example of the many surviving painted *devants de cheminée* that were used in the eighteenth century to block up chimneys during the summer months.[115] Painted for a dining-room, Chardin's work created the illusion of a side table tucked within the chimney, from which servants could hastily produce additional glasses, cutlery, wine and victuals. While such screens tended to be painted with a eye to subject-matter appropriate to the work's location, no theme was regarded as either visually or thematically unsuitable for overdoors and wall-panels, so that not only history painters like Natoire or still-life painters like Chardin, but even landscapists and portraitists, contributed to the field. Nor was religious painting unknown in the hôtel.

Churchmen, for obvious enough reasons, favoured devotional imagery in their apartments – the Archbishop of Besançon had a *Magdalene* and a *Woman from Samaria at the Well* above the doors in his bedchamber, and in his library the overdoors depicting scenes from the *Life of Moses* were complemented by a *Judgement of Solomon* above the chimney-mantle[116] – but it was also not uncommon in the houses of the secular nobility. In 1732, the duc d'Antin, a leading

27 Paolo Antonio Brunetti, decoration for the stairwell of the hôtel de Luynes, 1747. Fresco. Musée Carnavalet, Paris.

freemason, commissioned three decorative paintings from Natoire, *Jacob and Rachel Leaving the House of Laban* (fig. 28), *The Meeting of Jacob and Rachel at the Well* and *Hagar and Ishmael*, which he installed in his hôtel in Paris,[117] and several years later the maréchal de Noailles ordered from Pierre Parrocel fourteen wall-paintings illustrating the *Story of Tobias* and two allegorical overdoors, *Judaic Religion* and *Charity* to decorate the gallery of his property at Saint-Germain-en-Laye.[118]

Earlier in the century Parrocel's uncle, Joseph, had collab-

28 Charles-Joseph Natoire, *Jacob and Rachel Leaving the House of Laban*, 1732. Oil on canvas, 100.3 × 142.3 cm. The High Museum, Atlanta.

29   Charles Natoire, *The Toilet of Psyche*, c.1735. Oil on canvas, 198 × 169 cm. New Orleans Museum of Art, New Orleans. Purchased through the Bequest of Judge Charles F. Claiborne.

30 Jean-Simeon Chardin, *The White Tablecloth*, c.1730. Oil on canvas, 96.2 × 123.8 cm. The Art Institute of Chicago, Chicago.

orated with Gabriel Blanchard in a commission for twelve full-length portraits of the prince de Soubise's ancestors, which were, 'inscribed in the panelling between the windows' of the antechamber to the chapel.[119] In the 1720s, the comte de Toulouse likewise commissioned 'fantasy portraits' of all the admirals of the fleet, starting with Florent de Varenne, to celebrate his appointment in 1683 as an Amiral de France, and another of the kings of France, starting with Pharamond, to underscore his right to 'illegitimate' royal succession.[120] By contrast, François Castanier, whose ignoble origins were perhaps best overlooked, used portraiture to articulate his cultural rather than his biological claims to distinction. One of the rooms of his mansion in the rue des Capucines was decorated with two overdoors by Hyacinthe Rigaud, the first of which recorded the moment of Castanier's transformation from a living being into a cultural icon under Rigaud's brush, while the second represented a double portrait of Charles Le Brun and Pierre Mignard (fig. 31) which, by implication,

advanced Castanier as the inheritor and custodian of a heroic tradition, but a tradition that was redefined as artistic rather than genealogical.[121] However, if the physical immobilisation of images brought about by decoration could lend religious history and portraiture an appropriate air of symbolic permanence, one rarely equalled by the inherently mobile easel painting, there is no denying that it was not these genres but depictions of the senses, the seasons, the elements and the four times of day, together with mythological subjects, landscapes and still-life that proved the most popular subjects for decoration in the eighteenth century. And in the first half of the century, Desportes, Jean-François De Troy, Le Moyne, Lancret, Jacques de Lajoue, Trémolières, Natoire, Boucher and Oudry were among those demonstrably best equipped to produce works of this kind, some of which will be more fully discussed in later chapters.

Much more difficult to estimate is the number and identity of lesser painters operating in the field. Many of their works

31 Hyacinthe Rigaud, *Charles Le Brun and Pierre Mignard*, 1730. Oil on canvas, 130 × 140 cm. Musée du Louvre, Paris.

are lost or unidentified, and only through contracts, inventories and reports of inspection is it possible to reconstruct some of these schemes and the activities of those who created them. Characteristic of such painters was their combined practice of both house and figurative painting: the landscapists Jean-Nicolas Spayement and Damoiselet who worked at Marly at the end of the seventeenth century were apparently not strangers to distemper and whitewash.[122] Likewise, Tramblin not only painted two ceilings in yellow distemper at the hôtel Pannetier, rue des Ecus, in 1744,[123] but three years later his workshop was inspected and his eleven copies after Watteau, Lancret and Pater, probably intended as overdoors, found to

'conform in every respect to the prints'.[124] Meanwhile, between 1723 and 1724, the associates Etienne Venard and Gilles Hecquart had undertaken to paint and gild the interior of the hôtel Regnier, for which they also provided ten overdoors, but whether they divided the tasks between them or took joint responsibility for both forms of painting is unclear.[125] House-painting and painting were, then, complementary activities for which the theoretical division between liberal and mechanical art had, in many instances, little practical relevance.

Although the information to be gleaned from such documents is not, at present, equal to providing either career outlines for these painters or the basis for an iconographic analysis of lower-cost decoration, what it does offer are figures of payment against which to compare those earned by painters of reputation. It is still widely believed that the Surintendance des Bâtiments was a niggardly employer, despite the fact that artists tended to complain less about the reckoning of their due than about the delay to their payments,[126] and despite the evidence to the contrary provided by documented private contracts. For instance, the painters recruited in 1724 to paint the mythological overdoors (figs 32 and 33) for the hôtel du Grand Maître at Versailles were paid 400 *livres* for each work,[127] while Venard and Hecquart received only 186 *livres* for two overdoors of identical subject-matter with the same number of figures and painted in the same year but for a private client.[128] By the 1740s, the academician Jacques-Antoine Delaistre and the master-painter Guillaume Louviers were able to charge 100 *livres* for decorative paintings,[129] whilst the upper price of an overdoor painted for the Bâtiments had reached, 1,000 *livres*.[130] A decade later, Carle Van Loo was paid 1,200 *livres* for each of his exotic overdoors (fig. 34) for Pompadour's Turkish *salon* at Bellevue,[131] while Pierre Goussard had to content himself with just 720 *livres* for thirteen paintings (seven overdoors and six larger wall-panels)

32 François Le Moyne, *Aurora and Cephalus*, 1724. Oil on canvas, 100 × 94 cm. Hôtel de Ville, Versailles.

33 Jean Restout, *Diana and Endymion*, 1724. Oil on canvas, 90 × 75 cm. Hôtel de Ville, Versailles.

34 Carle Van Loo, *Two Sultanas Stitching a Tapestry*, 1754. Oil on canvas, 120 × 127 cm. The Hermitage, Saint Petersburg.

depicting, 'Chinese figures striking different poses, with Chinese children, houses and trees and other accessories also painted *à la chinoise* in blue cameo on a white ground', which he executed for Mme d'Arty's château de Stors.[132] Of course the difference in status and reputation, if not in ability (without surviving work there is no means of judging this last) of painters may have been, as in the case of ornament sculptors, a contributing factor in determining rates of pay for decoration.[133] However, given that the private commissions cited regularly afforded their authors just ten per cent of the value of royal commissions it is not unreasonable to assume that in many cases the crown set the upper limit to the scale of prices awarded to decorative painting. If this is correct, it is unlikely that, as is sometimes suggested, even such a successful decorative painter as Boucher could have earned as much as 50,000 *livres* per annum from this line of work – the equivalent of fifty overdoors or thirteen ten-foot canvases for tapestry at Bâtiments prices.[134] Decorative painting was certainly lucrative, but not exceptionally so. Moreover, in an unpredictable market work was not always forthcoming[135] and painters, no less than their colleagues in other areas of the decorative trades, had to develop techniques for attracting commissions.

Louis Tessier devised an appropriately artistic strategy in an effort to make one commission yield others by painting a request at the centre of his fire-screen (fig. 36) executed in 1756 for the marquis de Marigny. Among the papers addressed to the Directeur des Bâtiments, and apparently dispatched with tasteful negligence into a large Delft urn, is a slightly rumpled letter which reads as follows: 'Monsieur, Tessier, flower-painter and resident at the Gobelins manufactory, humbly begs you to grant him works [for] the

King, such as overdoors, or others . . . whatever it would please you to command of . . . his talent' – a request that was presumably designed to prick the director's generous sensibility whenever and for as long as he chose to make use of the screen.[136] For a wider but still local clientele, others, like Antoine Dieu, designed elaborate trade cards – figure 35 specifically exploits the associations between the arts, royalty and fame or reputation – but the dissemination of such publicity was, in the main, peculiar to painter-dealers with substantial retail enterprises rather than simple decorators.[137] By comparison, self-promotion through pictorial or textual advertisements in the growing number of monthly gazettes was rare.[138] However, artists did rely on the reports of successfully completed commissions published by sympathetic reviewers and editors. Thus, the *Mercure de France*'s detailed account of Parrocel's Tobias Gallery, mentioned above, and the *Journal Œconomique*'s praise of Nicolas Delobel's ceilings for the pavillon d'Aurore at Sceaux, tacitly recommended both artists for future employment.[139] Even La Font de Saint Yenne, in a work that purported to be disinterested Salon criticism, was

35 Antoine Dieu, trade card for Antoine Dieu: *Au Grand Monarque*, 1698. Engraving.

36 Louis Tessier, *The Porcelain Pot*, 1756. Oil on canvas, 76.8 × 95 cm. Private collection.

not above advancing the talent of Louis-Joseph Le Lorrain as a ceiling painter, on the strength of having witnessed his skill at the hôtel Castanier.[140]

The case of Le Lorrain is a pertinent one, for he owed a measure of his success to his association with the comte de Caylus and his deployment of the so called *peinture à l'encaustique*, invented by the amateur in imitation of the techniques thought to have been used by the Ancients.[141] The abbé Pernety certainly did not doubt the superiority of this method over oil painting, and in the article 'Ceiling' of his *Dictionnaire portatif de la peinture, la sculpture et la gravure* (1757) he reported that:

Mr Le Lorrain . . . executed in the month of March of the present year 1756, at the house of Mme du Fort, in the rue Faubourg Saint-Honoré, a ceiling painted in wax, according to the true method, which is that of Messrs de Caylus and

Majault. This work, the first executed of its kind, does great honour both to the inventors of this method of painting, and to the artist who executed it. Mr Le Lorrain is soon to execute a second ceiling in the same manner for the same residence.[142]

Pernety's reference to 'la vraie manière', the true method, not only alludes to Caylus's rivalry with Jean-Jacques Bachelier, but also is a reminder that 1757 also saw the publication of Dandrillon and Odiot's claims to practise this same technique. Encaustic painting was obviously hot property, a 'secret' which both house-painters and decorative painters vied to possess in the belief that it would attract clients. The 'artistic' component in design thus appears not to have been the only virtue to determine a sale. And it was indeed in the belief that matter not manner was of greater concern to *amateurs* of sculpture' that Laurent Hubert gave notice in the *Mercure* that, he had 'discovered the means of modelling in bronze the largest and most beautiful bas-reliefs for overdoors', a process that not only offered a new product in decoration, but, by a reduction of the amount of copper traditionally used in casting reliefs, apparently occasioned a saving of 917 *livres* on a work measuring approximately 195 × 81 cm.[143]

The very evident interest taken by eighteenth-century decorative painters in new or rediscovered techniques should not, however, be confused with process innovations – that is to say innovations that led to the lowering of production costs whilst leaving the final product largely unchanged. No evidence exists to suggest that encaustic or distemper paints were initially cheaper for either producer or consumer or that the motivation for developing them was prompted by an anticipated diminution of labour or material costs. On the contrary, the commercial advantage inscribed in these new products so far as the market-trader was concerned, was no more than the potential they offered for negotiating more advantageous deals, possibly even an official subsidy or privilege, and for importuning their regular clients, were they contractors or final consumers, for new sales. In that sense the air of modernity that seems to cling to some of the initiatives and activities of painters by comparison with, say sculptors or joiners, is largely illusory. Within the decorative arts it was left rather to the heavily subsidised or otherwise privileged royal manufactories to offer an economic culture substantially different from that of the trades.

MIRRORS, TAPESTRIES AND OTHER MANUFACTURED GOODS

Amongst the many materials used as insets to panelling in the eighteenth century, a special place was reserved for mirrors, not only because they enhanced the material range of a scheme but because their reflections amplified the space, light and ornamentation of a room.[144] In the seventeenth century mirrors were still sufficiently rare that a 124 × 65 cm mirror in a silver frame, listed in the inventory of Colbert's possessions in 1683, was valued at 8,000 *livres*, while an original painting by Raphael warranted an estimate of only 3,000 *livres*.[145] Mirror-rooms completely faced with glass, which appeared in French domestic architecture from the end of the sixteenth century, must therefore have been costly marks of distinction.[146] Moreover, although the price of mirrors dropped by approximately 30–40 per cent over the hundred-year period between 1665 and 1765,[147] the slide does not seem to have been accompanied by a parallel cultural depreciation. For example, the hôtel in the rue Saint-Honoré belonging to Adrien Maurice, duc de Noailles, scion of one of the most prestigious noble houses of France, in 1766 boasted what must have been a spectacular octagonal *cabinet des glaces* on the first floor, in which the gold and scarlet of the furnishings and the exoticism of the chinoiserie ornament were reflected ever-

more.[148] As further testimony to the consistently respectable price of mirrors and the esteem in which they continued to be held, it is only necessary to cite the example of one 280,000-*livres* mansion where, in the same year, the mirrors were valued at 14,469 *livres* – or an impressive five per cent of the whole.[149] By the 1760s mirrored wall-surfaces had, of course, long since escaped the confines of a single privileged *cabinet* and invaded every room. From the 1680s,[150] it became standard practice to surmount chimney-mantles with large vertical mirrors in sculpted and gilded frames, a custom that owed its pervasiveness largely to a single technological breakthrough: the invention of plate-glass.[151]

Until the development of the technique of moulding glass in metal trays, a process that required large furnaces and substantial quantities of readily available fuel, glass manufacturing and the production of mirrors had, for the most part, been the business of comparatively modest and dispersed enterprises, each with sovereignty over only a portion of the production process from the fusion of sand with potash to the retailing of finished goods. Nicolas Dunoyer's royal glass manufactory, established in 1665, marked the beginning of the gradual integration of these disparate activities into single firms under one management, if not under one roof, a principle of organisation that became a characteristic of the industry as a whole.[152] While the overheads of a manufactory such as Saint-Gobain (the main supplier of plate-glass in the eighteenth century) were considerable, the technique offered untold advantages of both a commercial and an aesthetic nature. First, casting glass was a much less skilled task than blowing glass, and the company could thus, in principle, respond more flexibly to demand by appropriately hiring or laying-off part of the workforce without running the risk of losing irreplaceable skills.[153] Second, the technique increased the speed of production and the size and weight of the mirrors themselves: from a maximum of 81 square cm by blowing to over 227 cm by casting. The new mirrors rendered obsolete the wood or *or-moulu* seams previously used to hold the smaller pieces in place.[154] Pier-glasses and chimney-piece mirrors, like the one designed with a frame sporting dragons and puckish and *espagnolette* heads for Peyrenc de Moras's *cabinet doré* in the place Vendôme (fig. 37), could now be moulded in only one or two pieces,[155] an advantage, however, for which clients paid dearly. If the price of smaller mirrors dropped to such an extent that by the first decade of the eighteenth century they feature in sixty-eight per cent of the working-class inventories studied by Daniel Roche,[156] the larger mirrors remained beyond the reach of all but the few. In the 1720s and 1730s, at a time when the royal treasury payed Desportes just 2,000 *livres* for each of his large canvases for the New Indies Tapestry (1738; fig. 42),[157] the wholesale price (and the Bâtiments price) of a 270 × 162 cm mirror was 3,000 *livres* – a considerable amount, given that in 1750 some three-quarters of artisanal and trade fortunes were situated between 500 and 5,000 *livres*.[158] Even after the increase in tariff for history painting in

37 Pier-glass, formerly at the hôtel Peyrenc de Moras, 1724. The Metropolitan Museum of Art, New York. Gift of J. Pierpont Morgan, 1906.

the 1750s, which raised their price to 25 *livres* the square *pied* (32.5 cm),[159] François Boucher, Jean-Baptiste-Marie Pierre, Carle Van Loo and Joseph-Marie Vien still only received 3,600 *livres* each for their canvases of 10×10 *pieds* for the Gobelins series, *The Loves of the Gods* (1757).[160]

Such apparently shaming comparisons, in so far as they may have been made at the time, elicited no more comment than did the continued high prices occasioned by the purchase of mirrors – the cost-cutting advantages of the process innovation notwithstanding. Complaints focused instead on the inability of Saint-Gobain and the sister finishing-plant in the rue de Reuilly to keep pace with demand.[161] In 1734, for instance, in a letter to 'MM of the [Royal] Glass Manufactory', the duc d'Antin, Directeur des Bâtiments, once again noted that, 'the consumption of mirrors has never been so strong', and added that, 'since you are having all the difficulty in the world in supplying your clients, I *exhort* you to redouble your efforts for the honour of your manufactory'.[162] It was generally

believed, meanwhile, that royal privilege and monopoly were obstructing the path to greater productivity, and cries for free enterprise became increasingly persistent.[163] The essence of monopoly, however, was not so much efficiency as compensation: it allowed such proto-factories as Saint-Gobain to balance the extraordinary outlays needed to set up permanent installations against comparatively stable sales to a captive market, and thus to transfer some of the investment costs to consumers.[164] In the case of Saint-Gobain, privilege was remarkably successful. By the end of the *ancien régime* the investment in the firm stood at 13.9 million *livres* and the company profits were almost unequalled.[165]

Saint-Gobain was by no means the only eighteenth-century royal manufactory with substantial fixed costs and an unusually large workforce, to provide goods for interior decoration. But, whereas Saint-Gobain had prospered fortuitously as a result of the taste for reflection – encouraged largely from outside by the building trade and widely disseminated through a myriad of fashionable prints, such as Guérard's *Cheminées nouvelles des plus à la mode* (fig. 38) – the use of tapestry was no longer guaranteed and the Gobelins, Beauvais and Aubusson found themselves having to compete for a share

38 Nicolas Guérard, design for a chimney-piece, *c*.1715–19. Engraving and etching. From *Cheminées nouvelles les plus à la mode*, *c*.1715–19.

39 (above left) Jules Degoullons
and André and Mathieu Legoupil,
detail of the frame shown in fig. 37.

40 (above right) Jules Degoullons
and André and Mathieu Legoupil,
detail of the frame shown in fig. 37.

41 Jules Degoullons and André and
Mathieu Legoupil, detail of the frame
shown in fig. 37.

42 François Desportes, *Indian Hunters*, 1740. Wool, silk and gold thread, 385 × 377 cm. The seventh design from the Gobelins tapestry series, *The New Indies*, 1735–41, woven by the workshop of Pierre-François Cozette, after 1749.

43   Panelling formerly at the hôtel Herlaut, *c.*1725. The J. Paul Getty Museum, Malibu.

in decoration.[166] Their ability to do so depended on a flexible response to demand. Floor to ceiling panelling had wrought certain changes in the division of internal space in domestic building, the most important of which, in the present context, was the reduction in proportions of many rooms.

In a memorandum written in 1780, one of the reasons given for the high-cost and low-sale figures at the Gobelins was the fact that 'the prohibitive size of the compositions . . . and the scale of their figures were such that only royal palaces could make use of them'.[167] Though the criticism was made in a report about the rival manufactory Beauvais, the explanation was thoroughly understood by the heads of the Gobelins workshops. In 1768, Michel and Jean Audran, Pierre-François Cozette and Jacques Nielson complained that in the previous year they had been compelled to turn down private commissions, 'having nothing to offer but designs of too serious a theme and with figures disproportionately large for Parisian apartments such as the tapestries of *Esther*, *Jason*, the *Vatican Stanze*, the *Old* and *New Testament*, the *Arts* and the *Indies* . . .'[168] Charles-Antoine Coypel's *Don Quixote* (1714–51) or his *Scenes from Opera, Tragedy and Comedy* (1733) might have served, but for their borders which were, 'so charged with ornament that they became expensive to produce and [in any event] are not as widely appreciated as would be happier subjects with figures approximately half life-size'.[169] The *entrepreneur*-weavers also rejected the recent *Loves of the Gods* (1757) because, or so they alleged, 'no one wants to have tapestries made for the same *salon* after masters whose manner and colour, however equal in merit, always underline the differences between them'.[170] They proposed instead that Marigny commission a series of new, oval paintings by a single painter depicting the five senses, the four times of day, the four seasons, the four elements or 'subjects taken from those comic operas that have most pleased the public'[171] – images that could be woven on a 'damasked background', at once fashionable and less expensive than the elaborate borders of a Maurice Jacques.[172] These proposals, forwarded to Soufflot for comment, apparently came to nothing and the Gobelins remained, until and even after, the end of the *ancien régime*, essentially a manufactory with a single client: the state.[173]

As the Audran report suggests, scale, design, subject-matter, execution and colour were the factors most frequently cited in administrative reports as likely to determine the saleability of tapestries. In these respects, it was Beauvais, particularly under the partnership of Nicolas Besnier and Oudry between 1734 and 1753, that reacted most sensitively to new artistic and commercial trends.[174] Aware that panelling and mirrors had become the fixed features of most decorative schemes and that few rooms could therefore accommodate six- or eight-part designs, Oudry created suites from which three or four episodes could be selected without upsetting the narrative sequence. The reconstituted room originally from the hôtel Herlaut and now in Malibu (fig. 43), which of necessity includes four Boucher tapestries from the Beauvais series, *The Story of Psyche*, in order to replace lost elements of the scheme,[175] creates, nevertheless, a reasonably accurate impression of the ways in which tapestries were used in decorative ensembles of the period, and demonstrates the extent to which designers were having to work within much more severe spatial and narrative constraints. In response to these new circumstances Beauvais produced, in effect, suites of eight thematically linked *tableaux* that could not only be combined in a variety of ways but were offered on an adjustable scale of

14 to 28 *aulnes* (or 1.65 to 3.30 m) the set.[176] The reasonably constant demand for certain compositions might, in turn, allow the manufactory to keep certain looms set up to a particular design over long periods, in itself a major saving, because tapestry looms were inordinately time-consuming to reset. Moreover, pastoral and genre subjects replaced history's 'too serious themes'; high standards of execution were ensured by a rigorous training programme for apprentices in the manufactory's school[177] and by a degree of labour division (weavers were divided into drapery, landscape, flower and figure specialists[178]); and, finally, Oudry dramatically increased the colour and tonal range of the dyed silk and woollen threads used in Beauvais weaves.[179] The result was designs more subtly calibrated and of a scale, theme and colour more in keeping with the decorative schemes of the day.

Aubusson made efforts to follow suit. In 1750, they too acknowedged the ascendancy of pastel colours in decoration and took measures to match their tapestries, upholstered furniture and carpets accordingly.[180] And if Aubusson was synonymous in the eighteenth century with *verdures* or landscapes, this did not deter them from bringing their products up to date and into line with the reigning fashion for exoticism by replacing some of the prosaic architectural motifs with wild and occasionally fantastical beasts.[181] It even prompted the manufactory's essays in chinoiserie (fig. 44).[182] Thus if, according to one report, the only essential element to manufacturing policy was that, 'turnover should prevail above all other considerations . . .',[183] sales were rarely linked directly to prices.[184] Instead, all the proposals for tapestry production invariably turned upon the introduction of new lines in goods and design[185] (the painter-partners and salaried painters retained by Beauvais and Aubusson were contracted to produce a certain number of new models each year)[186] – and upon the achievement and maintenance of exacting standards of excellence.

In so far as these integrated firms appear to have shared with the most dispersed trades an economic paradigm predicated on variety and a reputation for quality, the substantive differences between royal manufactories and artisanal workshops seem to have been financial, structural and cultural rather than commercial or ideological.[187] Integration brought increased control over both the costs and the rhythms of production, thus encouraging clear-sighted financial management, hierachical relations of production and the more or less precise calculation of the value of discounted goods. Having fixed wholesale and retail prices[188] it was then left to those who managed the firm's outlets, using all the gifts of polite persuasion that it was now essential the 'perfect tradesman' should possess,[189] to persuade retailers and final consumers to buy in a space fashioned by a new market principle.[190]

Tapestries were not, of course, the only textiles used in interior decoration. Damasks, for instance, were particularly favoured for picture rooms[191] and if the heavy brocades woven with gold and silver threads, a speciality of Parisian workshops

44   Jean-Joseph Dumont, *A Chinese Fishing Party*, *c*.1750. Wool, 320 × 300 cm. From the Aubusson tapestry series, *The Chinese Hangings*, *c*.1750. Location unknown.

45 Brocade in crimson and silver, 1731–3. Fabrique Bron et Ringuet, Lyon. Collection of the Mobilier Nationale, Paris.

46 Thomas Germain, design for a pilaster, 1733. Pen, ink and watercolour, 97.5 × 32 cm. Cabinet des Estampes, Bibliothèque Nationale, Paris.

such as Marcelin Charlier's, appeared to have fallen from favour after the turn of the seventeenth century, a recent study has shown that on occasion the Garde-Meuble de la Couronne could be a generous patron to the Lyons silk industry.[192] In 1730 orders were placed with various Lyons workshops for six different brocades (fig. 45), and although much of the cloth was destined for furniture upholstery, the Barnier enterprise also delivered eighteen fluted Corinthian pilasters, each,

> bound in gold on a crimson ground, loaded in the middle with a military trophy against which rests a shield with the arms of France, the trophy [in turn] surmounted by a helmet with laurel and other ornament [and] the whole set against a brown background, the colour of musk.[193]

Designed, surprisingly perhaps, by the silversmith Thomas Germain and measuring approximately 4.22 × 0.65 m, these extravagant pilasters – recently related to a design in the Bibliothèque Nationale (fig. 46) – were evidently much admired at court because, from 1736 they hung in the Salon de Mercure, before being moved in 1785 to the king's apartment to play their part in Jean-Démosthène Dugourc's refurbishment of the state bedchamber.[194] However, it is unclear whether the court's admiration was matched by a ready reception of such brocades and silks in the Parisian hôtels of the period. It seems unlikely, because in March 1730 the Lyons merchants complained to the controller-general of finances, Philibert Orry, that their Parisian rivals were deliberately obstructing their efforts to establish outlets in the capital.[195] Whilst competing among themselves, Parisian enterprises could apparently act together in order to alienate foreign opportunists, and indeed it was in acknowledgement of Lyons's predicament that the restitutive royal commission, outlined above, was proffered. It was probably not until the second half of the century, therefore, that silks for wall-hangings designed by the likes of Philippe de Lasalle acquired a certain *cachet*, albeit one tempered by the extravagant prices of the textiles themselves.[196]

Instead, in the early eighteenth century there was an upsurge in the production of an ever-expanding range of sometimes cheaper, mixed-media substitutes for textiles, and indeed for decorative materials of all kinds. For example, in April 1735 the *Mercure de France* published an advertisement for the work of an Englishman, Mr Levet, 'inventor of those ingenious Products which consist of a kind of cloth made of feathers'. Made only of natural materials, Levet produced tapestries for bed-alcoves and *portières* representing various exotic still-lives in garden or loosely architectural settings.[197] According to the article, he was at that very moment working on a hanging for the Duke of Leeds, 'which will represent a peacock after the design of Mr Oudry, Painter to the King', and others were encouraged to go and order similar schemes from him, at the rue Taravanne, in the faubourg Saint-Germain. In the same year, a certain Simon requested permission from the board of trade, 'to produce paper tapes-

47   Jean-Michel Papillon, wallpaper imitating cut velvet, 1742. Woodcut.

48 Pierre-Philippe Choffard, trade card of Didier Aubert: *Au Papillon*, 1756. Etching.

tries representing landscapes and *verdures*, by means of applied chopped wool'.[198] Flocked papers were, in fact, already familiar decorative currency in France by that date. According to Joachim Nemeitz, Claude III Audran manufactured flocked tapestry at the Luxembourg as early as 1727,[199] and Jean-Michel Papillon, author of some of the earliest arabesque wallpapers,[200] produced, very nearly twenty years later, a paper imitating cut velvet (fig. 47) for the japanner Guillaume I Martin, no doubt with a view to expanding the range of stock offered at the latter's shop in the grande rue du faubourg Saint-Denis.[201] However, such papers were generally imported from England,[202] and it was not until 1755 that the press felt sufficiently confident to recommend Parisian-made flocked papers. In that year the *Journal Œconomique* enthusiastically recommended the wares of Didier Aubert, 'Wood engraver, [established] at the entrance of the rue Saint-Jacques, at the sign of the Butterfly',[203] in terms that later reappeared on Aubert's elegant trade card (fig. 48). It should be noted that although Roland de La Platière substantiates the hypothesis that the relative cheapness of these papers accounted for their success,[204] entries in Lazare Duvaux's day-book reveal that these papers were eagerly sought by the very same customers who also commissioned tapestries from the Gobelins and Beauvais.[205]

The novelty and comparative rarity of the papers imported from China and the Far East were alone sufficient to ensure their outstanding success in the luxury market, aided and abetted by a mounting fascination with the exotic.[206] Most frequently applied to screens, they also featured on the panelling of many a *cabinet chinois*, such as the one in the duc de Vendôme's pavillon de Bel-Air, decorated by Michel Lange and Claude III Audran.[207] In the same spirit, Chinese and Japanese lacquer, or French imitations thereof, played an occasional part in interior decoration. Chinese lacquered screens might be broken up and inset into panelling, creating an effect not unlike Robert de Cotte's designs for the electoral palace at Bonn (fig. 50), or modern equivalents could be custom-made by a number of workshops in Paris.[208] One of the earliest of these was probably another Claude III Audran enterprise, this time at the Gobelins.[209] Letters patent issued by council decree at Versailles on 28 October 1713, 'on behalf of Pierre de Neufmaison, Claude Audran and Jacques Dagly', legitimised their establishment of a manufactory of Chinese varnish, 'to be applied to all kinds of wool and silk fabric and cloth, to leather and other flexible materials and in all colours suitable for furnishings'.[210] While the entrepreneur, de Neufmaison, supervised the daily business, and the Liégeois, Jacques Dagly, provided the technical know-how, Audran's contribution was probably limited to the supply of designs which, according to Dubois de Saint-Gelais, were 'entirely in the Chinese manner'.[211] Although this seems to have been a relatively unpretentious enterprise in both scope and kind, it is worth noting that in 1752 Charles-André Tramblin thought it worth paying 60,000 *livres* for the 'secret' of the varnish in order to continue trading under the name 'Directeur pour le roi des ouvrages de la chine à la manufacture des Gobelins', testifying once again to the perceived power of titles.[212] However, perhaps the best-known manufacturers of this kind of work were the Martin family, whose members were Vernisseurs du Roi for two generations, and ran important workshops throughout the capital.[213] One of their number, the

49 Guillaume Martin (attributed to) chinoiserie overdoor, formerly in the *cabinet chinois* at the hôtel de Richelieu 1720. Musée Carnavalet, Paris.

50   Robert de Cotte, design for a laquered room, possibly for the Elector of Cologne, 1717. Pen, ink, wash and watercolour on paper, 26.7 × 36.8 cm. The National Trust, Waddesdon Manor, Aylesbury, Buckinghamshire.

same Guillaume who was interested in wallpaper, was granted a privilege in 1730 to manufacture, 'all kinds of work in three dimensions, and in the Japanese and Chinese taste'.[214] Sadly, very few examples survive, with the probable exception of a number of isolated panels and overdoors (fig. 49), constituents originally of the *cabinet chinois* at the hôtel de Richelieu in the place Royale, and now in the Musée Carnavalet.[215]

These wallpaper and japanning enterprises are of particular interest because they seem to stand at a mid-point between the more modest artisanal workshop and the larger integrated firm. In one sense they evolved out of the first. By focusing with rare exclusivity on just one of the multiple activities or skills with which engraver or painter workshops were traditionally concerned, and by multiplying the production pattern to an unusually high power, enterprises like those of Jean-Baptiste Réveillon (of wallpaper fame) or Martin, took on all the appearance of a factory.[216] However, unlike Saint-Gobain, the Gobelins or the Lyons silk industry, the fixed and variable costs of such enterprises remained low – Tramblin's

annual expenditure on ground-rent, wages and materials barely exceeded 20,000 *livres* – and their manufacturing structure, again similar to a workshop, was composed of a heterogeneous mixture of apprentices, salaried journeymen and subcontracted or partnered master-craftsmen.[217] What distinguished businesses of this kind from the trade economy in which they were otherwise rooted, was a shift in priority away from a bespoke industry and towards the production of lines, with the result that house-style became gradually more significant than a maker's or designer's signature. Of course, by the end of the century ornament sculptors, particularly those working in plaster, had also learnt the value of serial production: François-Joseph Duret seems to have thrived on his talent for producing endless 'putti with baskets' generic overdoors and impressive lengths of neoclassical ornament, a style of course ideally suited to mass-production.[218] The importance of the shift to house-style, however, extended beyond the method of production to the manner of trading.

Consistent with the developments outlined above, increased

emphasis was placed on marketing strategies and advertising as the century drew to a close. Even 'artists' shunned neither publicity nor the charisma of new techniques as unworthy of their status, though their tactics of self-promotion were mostly indirect. From 1737 they increasingly relied on the annual or biennial Salons to display their talents – although, as shall be seen in a later chapter, the Salon ultimately functioned against the interest of decorative painting. Moreover, it is well known that the public display of products was by no means limited to academicians or to paintings.[219] The exhibition of Juste-Aurèle Meissonnier's Cabinet Bielenski (fig. 51) at the Tuileries in 1736 before its dispatch to Poland,[220] and the annual showing of Gobelins tapestries at the Fête-Dieu are familiar indeed,[221] but they were not isolated affairs. In April 1733, the locksmith Garnier had similarly opened his work-shop to a public eager to see the grills he had forged for a Capuchin church near Lisbon on the orders of the king of Portugal.[222] Meanwhile, the Garde-Meuble de la Couronne

regularly held open-days for the public, and it was on one such occasion that the brocades of 1730, mentioned above, were put on display.[223] Not to be outdone, in 1732 Aubusson sent to the capital their first tapestry woven since Jean-Joseph Dumons's appointment, where it apparently caused a stir:

> It was exhibited at the Board of Trade, next to two Gobelins pieces with extensive landscape backgrounds. Not only did it equal the competition, several renowned connoisseurs, such as Messrs de Troy, Coypel and Oudry, judged that, from an artistic point of view and taking account of the quality of the material, it was even superior.[224]

Though often less formal and invariably occasional, such displays of work counterpointed the activities of the Academy and to some extent undermined the ability of the latter to define the liberal status of art through exhibition. The Salon was not, it seems, unequivocally the site of elevated public

51 The Cabinet Bielenski, *c.*1742. (a) (facing page, left). Pierre Chenu after Juste-Aurèle Meissonnier, *Cabinet of comte Bielenski executed in 1734*; (b) (facing page, right). Pierre Chenu after Juste-Aurèle Meissonnier, *View of the Corner of the same Cabinet*; (c) (left). Maurice Baquoy after Juste-Aurèle Meissonnier, *View of the Pier-glasses of the same Cabinet*; (d) (above). Pierre Aveline after Juste-Aurèle Meissonnier, *The Painted Ceiling for the Cabinet of comte Bielenski*. Engraving and etching. From the *Oeuvres de Juste-Aurèle Meissonnier*, *c.*1738–51.

discourse on the arts; it was also a more prosaic but equally public realm of market principle. Once again, the evidence suggests that decorative painting should best be approached as an integral part of the decorative trades. Wood-sculptors, glass and textile workers, house-painters and decorative painters worked with many of the same concerns and restrictions, particularly those of location,[225] and they used many of the same strategies to compete in a market that offered sometimes modest and sometimes substantial gains.

2

The Organisation of Practice

Noël Hallé's *Education of the Poor* (fig. 53), exhibited at the Salon of 1765, and the illustration of the *High-warp Looms at the Gobelins* (fig. 54) engraved for the *Encyclopédie* (1751–72) seem to give visual expression to the notion (implicit to some extent in the sequence through which the constituent elements of eighteenth-century decoration were described in the previous chapter) that traditional workshop economies are invariably superseded and replaced by modern capitalist ones. Hallé presents an emphatically nurturing and familial environment in which the skills of one generation, be they those of a joiner or embroiderer, are patiently transmitted to a second. Ostensibly about education, then, the picture also offers a vision of a trade biologically reproducing itself and jealously guarding the patrimonies of workshop and skill from expropriation by outsiders. By contrast, the Gobelins weavers are not only anonymous, faceless even, behind the warps of the looms they work, but additionally they seem to belong to a single generational group of barely communicating social strangers, whose efforts are apparently harmonised by the only lubricant applicable, that of a common self-interest.[1]

The close kinship ties between the various members of Hallé's household seemed to preclude any such suggestion of an economic goal to which the activities he portrayed might be directed, and the close collaboration and generous pooling of resources evident in the gestures of the figures depicted were domestic virtues that effectively denied the possibility that their co-operation was potentially or actually secured by relations of exchange.[2] While the man and boy work together at a task of which they seem to have total knowledge, and over which they apparently exercise complete control, the teams of weavers at the looms seem to operate obscurely, not just because each one could only accomplish the specialised tasks for which he had been trained, but also because their horizon was limited to the section of the reverse side of the design upon which they were immediately engaged. They therefore remained largely ignorant of the final product until such time as the completed tapestry was cut off the loom.[3] Moreover, where Hallé's picture by its very medium hints at a bespoke enterprise that catered to the individual needs of its customers, the multi-copied *Encyclopédie* illustration proposed instead the

manufacture of lines whose replication was achieved by the dispassionate connivance of giant machines to which weavers were only severally attached.[4] It is, after all, the looms not the workers that the ladies and gentlemen in the foreground have come to inspect like some exotic, choreographed spectacle – one that would have been foreign to the man, apparently none other than the *père de famille*, who crosses the threshhold of his workshop seemingly unmoved by the almost cloying ambiance of natural mutuality which he rediscovers there.[5]

Surviving documentary evidence and recent historical research in fact do little to substantiate the contrasts engendered by the juxtaposition of these images. First, the guilds charged with regulating access to the sworn trades (such as joinery) rarely, and only in certain circumstances, encouraged the perpetuation of oligarchies. For the most part, the guilds, or corporations as they were called in the eighteenth century, saw no more than fifty per cent of masters' sons come into their corporate inheritance.[6] By contrast, the workshops that together constituted the Gobelins exhibited a remarkable degree of continuity. In 1662 the entrepreneur-weaver in charge of the first high-warp workshop was Jean Jans, who was succeeded six years later by his son and later still, in 1723, by his grandson, before the shop was finally ceded to another well-established Gobelins family, the Audrans.[7] Claude III Audran, himself an *habitué* of this royal manufactory in the faubourg Saint-Marcel, provided a nephew, Michel, who took over from Jans in 1732. In the same year this same Michel married Marguerite Chambonnet, the daughter of one of the manufactory's master-dyers,[8] and their son Jean followed his father behind the high-warp loom in 1771. Thus, during a period of well over a century the workshop had only two families of masters.[9]

Second, if there is no denying that a cash nexus brought the operations of the Gobelins workshops to life, there seems little reason to assume that the reverse was so in the case of the kind of independent family enterprise depicted by Hallé. A reading of the master-glazier Jacques-Louis Ménétra's autobiography amply bears out the point that in such eighteenth-century trades those emotional bonds which ideally tied father and son were in fact rarely distinct from economic relations. Ménétra

53 Noël Hallé, *The Education of the Poor*, 1765. Oil on panel, 35.9 × 45.1 cm. Private collection.

54 *High-warp Looms at the Gobelins Tapestry Manufactory*, 1762–72. Engraving. From Denis Diderot and Jean Le Rond d'Alembert, *Encyclopédie*, 1751–72.

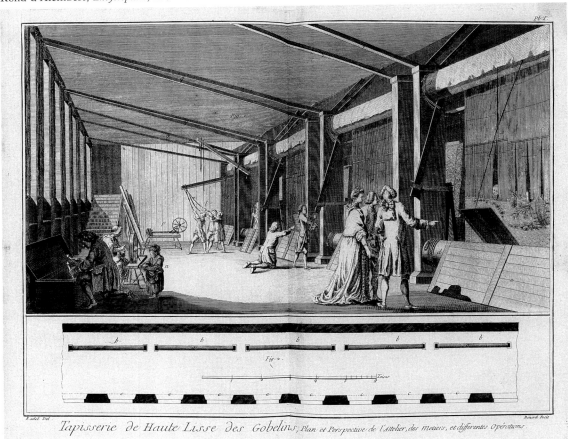

refused to return to work for his father after completing his *tour de France* in 1763 because, quite apart from the resentment he still felt about the way an inheritance left to him by his mother had been appropriated by his father, he also knew from bitter experience that the elder Ménétra's promises of adequate remuneration amounted only to so much talk.[10] Meanwhile, Jacques-Louis felt no embarrassment at employing his brother-in-law at 20 *sous* per day to help him with the job of making 120 lanterns for which he, Ménétra, was being paid 50 *sous* apiece.[11] Families, it would seem, often presented a convenient source of cheap labour precisely because kinship ties were open to economic exploitation. Differences between royal manufactories and bourgeois workshops remained, certainly, but they did not necessarily follow the familiar lines traced by contemporary art and literature.[12] Moreover, these differences, such as they may have been, were not the product of a distinction between organic and economic structures but, as we shall see, a function of the law.

GUILDS

The legally constituted body overwhelmingly responsible for the organisation and supervision of labour in eighteenth-century Paris was the guild.[13] All alternative bodies concerned with the trades, such as royal manufactories, academies or informal groups of workers under the protection of the crown or the church, were perceived by society as *privileged* organisations; in other words, bodies that had escaped corporate control through legal exemption.[14] These were the exceptions; the corporations were the rule. Since the sixteenth century, Paris had been styled the model of a *ville jurée* – a city where the majority of the trades were organised into *corps* and *communautées* or guilds[15] – and had experienced, if anything, an extension of corporate power and prestige during and immediately after the ministry of Colbert.[16] The advantages that accrued to the state as a direct consequence of the internal fiscal and juridical control of the guilds over the labour force is not relevant here,[17] beyond the fact that it was their role in the system of public finance that guaranteed them a significant place in the body politic. So long as the state continued to rely upon them for raising revenue, and it did for the best part of the eighteenth century, the corporations were able to dominate the terms in which issues of production and labour were conceived and debated.[18] Moreover, since the corporations were legally constituted by the master-craftsmen and tradesmen, under whose authority apprentices and journeymen were merely incorporated, this 'corporate idiom' expressed, by and large, the will and interests of the masters.[19] It is therefore, largely from their point of view, a point of view inscribed in the particulars of their statutes and articulated in their law-suits, that discussion of production must initially proceed.

Although the guilds presented themselves as affective

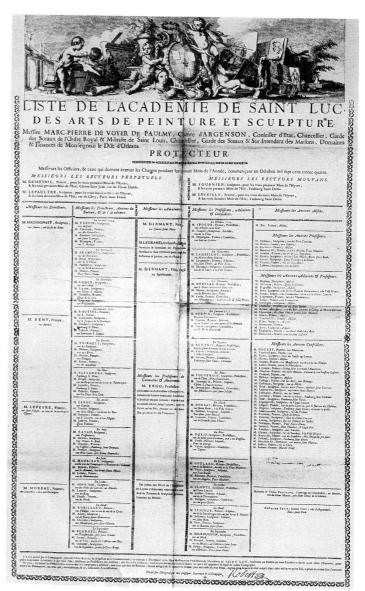

55   List of the members of the Académie de Saint-Luc, 1734. Archives Nationales, Paris.

bodies – bodies which united in mutual consideration and respect those with common interests and priorities of a commercial, social and moral nature – they were not, of course, voluntary associations.[20] In order to practise certain trades in Paris, and that included all those working in the field of decoration, it was obligatory to belong to the appropriate guild. According to Expilly, the Parisian trades were divided into 118 guilds which controlled a population of some 35,000 masters.[21] If correct, and if on average these masters employed one apprentice and one journeyman,[22] the guild population of the capital could be estimated at approximately 105,000, or twenty-four per cent of the total population.[23] Taken as a percentage of the working population the proportion would obviously be much higher. This suggests two things: first, the very extensive catchment area of the guilds, and second, com-

56 Invitation to vespers at the chapel of Saint Luke, *c*.1765. Etching.

paratively low levels of production, given that such a large number could adequately make a living in this sector of the community.[24] Thus, although a smaller and specialised subsection of the trades, those involved in the production of goods for interior decoration, undoubtedly presented a considerable body of people. The membership of the corporation of master-painters and sculptors alone was in the region of six hundred in 1742 and had more than doubled some twenty years later.[25] Marks of this guild's prosperity are to be found in the elaborately designed and engraved headers (fig. 55), which from 1730 enlivened the annual officers' lists[26] and in the attention lavished on the chapel of the confraternity. Adjacent to the corporation's office in the rue des Hauts-Moulins stood the dilapidated medieval church of Saint-Symphorian which, according to Piganiol de La Force, the guild adopted in 1704, repaired, decorated and transformed into a chapel dedicated to the Virgin and Saints John and Luke.[27] It was there that every year on 17 October the whole corporation assembled by custom and invitation (fig. 56) to celebrate the reception of new masters into an ever-expanding and apparently thriving trade. We can only assume that the prosperity of the merchant

corporations, measured once again in terms of the size as well as the wealth of the membership, must have been even greater.[28] Thus the guild, and what might be called guild culture, dominated manual work during the *ancien régime*, both by the extensiveness of its jurisdiction, the prosperity of a significant proportion of its members, and by the prestige of its ancient lineage and traditions.[29]

The guilds understood one of their primary tasks to be the maintenance of high standards of production in the trades they administered. Fine workmanship and quality goods were one of the cornerstones of corporate honour. These standards were to be achieved in a number of ways: notably by a searching system of recruitment and training,[30] but also by the legal enforcement of minimum standards of production.[31]

Although the recruiting policy of the guilds was repeatedly denounced during the first half of the eighteenth century, it was the abuses of the system, not the system itself, which were attacked.[32] Apprenticeship, journeymanship and the *chef-d'oeuvre*, or masterpiece, were generally accepted as legitimate and necessary rites of passage through which each individual had to pass in order to ensure that only the skilled acceded to the trade. The period of indenture varied from trade to trade, but five to seven years may be taken as an average minimum.[33] Once the prescribed training was completed, the individual was free to apply for membership on the submission of a masterpiece.[34] The masterpiece not only constituted the final test of the aspirant's abilities, but it also endorsed the guild's status as an institution of merit and high technical standards. However, although in theory all guilds supported the principle of the *chef-d'oeuvre*, in practice the masterpiece played a greater constitutional and ideological role in some corporations than in others. For example, it was the custom of the crown to celebrate certain important public events by awarding a number of masterships to each guild – masterships which could be bought by those who had served neither apprenticeships nor journeymanships and for whom the requirement of the *chef-d'oeuvre* was suspended.[35] In 1723 the corporation of master-painters and sculptors, for one, managed to obtain by act of the Conseil d'Etat an exemption from this custom on the grounds that, 'His Majesty's intention to perfect the Art of Painting would not be fulfilled thereby, because such receptions are obtained with cash and without demonstrable merit'.[36] In this instance it was being claimed that the honour of the guild would be compromised even by the grace and favour of the king.

Thus, training and the semi-public demonstration of ability were perceived as fundamental to the guild's ability to reproduce a highly skilled membership. But to ensure that the goods they produced were of superior quality in substance as well as in treatment, many guilds also laid down in their statutes certain minimum production requirements. In the formulation of their new statutes in 1730, the painters' and sculptors' guild found itself divided on precisely the issue of the corporation's right to enforce certain codes of practice on its members.[37] The articles in contention were XXXIX and LXIV[38] which respectively concerned the application of a kind of moulded ornament and the further application of *argent vernis* or fool's gold to embellish it. Both involved the substitution of cheaper alternatives for more expensive practices and both were to be expressly prohibited by the proposed new statutes, much to the outrage of certain members. In the case of moulded plaster, the opposition, Simon Besançon, André Tramblin and company, claimed that the issue had already been adjudicated by a court ruling handed down by the Châtelet on 21 May 1723, and as a result of which permission had been granted:

> for the use and application of *matière de composition* on Picture Frames and other such things, on the understanding that the composite material will be hard, thoroughly combined and not [solely] of plaster, and on the understanding that these masters will write on the back of the Frames, [the words] *Ouvrages de Composition*, and sign their names.[39]

The directors of the guild, however, wished to overturn this ruling. The issue had originally arisen because of complaints made by the chevalier Camilly and M. Delasseré in October 1722 about frames they had bought in good faith on the quai de Gesvres from André Tramblin and Nicolas Delaunay, assuming the ornament to have been an inherent part of the woodwork only subsequently to discover that it was in fact an applied moulding.[40] Backed by the evidence of the prosecution, the guild argued that the practice was detrimental to the public interest since the buyer could evidently be fooled by the workmanship, and, unaware of the Châtelet ruling, would not think to check for the inscription *œuvre de composition* (always assuming that the workmen responsible did indeed comply with the regulation).[41] Moreover, they found the practice prejudicial to sculpture because,

> the lack of skill required to make such works, and the modest amounts of time and money their production demand, puts those who trade in them in a position to sell cheaply [such that] Sculptors could no longer hope to gain from the time and effort they expend in the cultivation of the Art of Sculpture . . .[42]

In short, the art and careers of the corporation's one hundred and fifty ornament sculptors would be sacrificed to the interests of only a handful of would-be stuccadors,[43] and it is no surprise to discover amongst the earliest opponents of the Châtelet ruling, representatives of such prestigious Parisian sculpture workshops as those of Lange, Pelletier, Degoullons, Legoupil and Taupin.[44] The arguments had proved convincing, and at an assembly held on 21 November 1727 the guild prohibited the manufacture and sale of *ouvrages de composition*, a ban that, in the case of console tables, cornices and every other sculpted object, but with the exception of frames, was upheld by the Parlement in 1736 and registered with the new statutes two years later.[45]

The same arguments had also been advanced, but had not ultimately prevailed, for the use of false gold in the decoration of those

> Works which should last for centuries such as Church Tabernacles, Picture and Mirror Frames, Console Tables, Cornices, Panelling, & other Works in which the Public seek and expect to buy a gilding that will last as long as the goods [themselves], which is only when real gold is used.[46]

In contrast to the *caveat emptor* philosophy of so-called commercial societies, the guilds apparently saw the enforcement of their regulations as a necessary precondition of good business because only in a market where the public was assured of buying goods of high quality in substance as well as in appearance could deals successfully be struck.[47] The concerned appeal to consumer rights (not consumer choice) and the perpetuation of traditional methods of production were thus two sides of the same coin and both operated to average demand across the membership and qualify the economic leverage of particular individuals.[48] Moreover, in the manufacture of textiles, for example, as long as the number of threads in the weave, the width of the cloth and the quality of the dye were all carefully proscribed for each fabric, no manufacturer could easily obtain a cost advantage over any other while complying with the letter of the law.[49] Likewise, the significant proportion of articles among the joiners' and cabinet-makers' statutes committed to regulating methods of production for commodities as various as coachwork and painters' easels,[50] was evidently as much a means of establishing a semblance of entrepreneurial equality between members as an instrument of foreign policy. Furthermore, the regular visits by the officers of the joiners' company to verify work carried out in masters' workshops, and the public incineration of any defective work found there, were clearly designed to impress an immediate constituency as well as a local market.[51]

It is against this background of apparent technical conservatism and strict supervision that eighteenth-century concern with quality and novelty should be judged. The first, or at least a semblance of it, was in principle accepted by both producers and consumers as a prerequisite for successful trading. Moreover, since good quality was thought to ensue *a priori* from lengthy artisanal training and proven methods it was logically incompatible with *nouveauté*. Yet novelties in design and particularly in technique were attractive precisely because they were set against a background of traditional practice. The extraordinary success of chinoiserie products, either genuine or imitation, and for which designers like Bellay helpfully provided *Différentes pensées*, 'appropriate for painting on Carriages, Panelling and Screens' (fig. 57), and the vogue for *indiennage* or printed calicoes that took Europe by storm and successfully defeated repeated government injunctions against their use, are surely proof of that fact.[52] However, it would be a mistake to assume that the public stance taken by the guilds in their statutes necessarily reflected the behav-

57 Gabriel Huquier after Jacques Bellay, design for chinoiserie screens, 1735. Etching. From *Différentes pensées d'ornements arabesques à divers usages, c.*1735, plate 7.

iour of their members, or that their response to technical innovation was consistent in all circumstances and on all occasions. According to one report written in the 1770s, guild officers zealously pursued those within their jurisdiction who contravened the statutes, while themselves breaking them with impunity for the simple reason that,

> appropriate to the State of the Arts when they were [origi-nally] drawn up, they [the regulations] could hardly apply to a time when industry has been forced to follow new fashions, new techniques, new tastes.

'The taste of the comsumer', concluded this anonymous respondent to an enquiry on the efficacy of guilds, 'is the first rule of trade. One must obey it and *not* consult the regu-lations.'[53] To the extent that guild officers did indeed use their position as arbitrators to obtain unfair commercial advantages over the arbitrated within their care, it seems obvious that contradictions necessarily emerged between the ideal of economic equity (even equality) between members, promised implicitly by the statutes, and the reality of a cynically competitive hierarchy.[54] It seems likely that Besançon, Delaunay, Tramblin and company were overruled in the case of moulded ornament because they were not only outnum-bered but outranked in an assembly presided over by the powerful and prestigious panel sculptor, Pierre Taupin.[55] In order to win, Taupin had had to marshal majority support not only from his fellow officers, but also from sculptors of the rank and file, the so-called *anciens*, *modernes* and *jeunes*.[56] More-over, in so far as he obtained a mandate, the dispute became not just a contest between an office-holding élite and a corpo-rate commonality but additionally, a confrontation between the interests of the guild's sculptors and its painters – the Bezançon faction had consisted predominantly of painter-dealers,[57] determined upon sloughing off the requirement to sub-contract part of their business interests to ornament carvers. The complex web of alliances that must have resulted from these potentially counteracting occupational and status differences yielded one important concession to the appellants: the right to exercise their new technologies in the case of frame-making, an activity central to their enterprise but per-haps only peripherally significant to sculptors.[58]

In the light of the assembly's unequivocal capitulation on the question of *argent vernis* it seems reasonable to assume that if the practice encroached upon privileged commercial terri-tory it was not one which divided the membership internally, but instead, merely took liberties with neighbouring corporate domains, namely that of the gilders, and as such was properly an issue of foreign rather than domestic policy. However, faced with Guillaume Martin's application for an exclusive *privilège* for his *vernis Martin*, his rivals swiftly mobilised sufficient support amongst fellow-painters to persuade the Parlement that,

> the manufacture of Snuffboxes and Works in painted and varnished *papier moulé* was not a secret discovered by the Painter Martin, but a consequence of his Profession and Art; a more refined and more finished kind of Painting but one which nevertheless belongs equally to all Painters . . .[59]

In this instance the question was not so much whether the new technique was of sufficient quality to be admitted but whether it was sufficiently esoteric to merit protection. Indeed, it was precisely because *vernis Martin* signalled fine workmanship – very likely the outcome of the designs furnished by engravers such as Papillon (fig. 58) rather than of the materials in which they were rendered – that Martin was pressured into sharing his trade.[60] It seems then, that 'quality' functioned in corporate discourse both as a passive guarantor of the guilds' *raison d'être* and as a flexible instrument for preserving the status quo, either by disqualifying threatening innovations or by embra-cing potentially advantageous ones.

A possible explanation for the more accommodating response of painters to new technologies when compared with that of sculptors may lie in the inherent difficulty of securely defining the art of painting by traditional reference to tools and materials.[61] Paint-brushes, pigments, oils and varnishes were admissable and familiar things in any number of luxury workshops, such that painters were denied an efficient and exclusive means of policing technological development in their trade. In the case of the expanding range of house-paints and varnishes in the 1740s and 1750s, it may be significant that the right to manufacture and sell such substances was shared jointly by the master-painters and sculptors and the master-grocers. For over sixty years the two corporations were locked in a series of disputes over which could claim priority

58 Jean-Michel Papillon, design for a lacquered box, 1746. Woodcut.

to this sphere of business;[62] in the meantime, concern mounted over the apparently falling quality of pigments. The colourman De Wouters, for example, claimed that 'the sudden deterioration of paintings could only stem from the poor quality of materials in daily use'.[63] La Font de Saint Yenne, meanwhile, specifically regretted the decay of Watteau's paintings, reproached the late Trémolières for his use of unstable flesh-tints and noted that 'Economies in the use of Lapis Lazuli, which is very expensive, is one of the most common causes of [colour] alteration'.[64] He implied – and the colourman Mérimée unequivocally stated – that this was the inevitable consequence of the growing reliance of painters on ready-ground pigments, instead of preparing colours themselves in the studio.[65] Prompted perhaps by this increasingly critical climate, the Académie de Saint-Luc renewed its efforts not only to safeguard the rights of its members but also to have those of the grocers repealed; however, they founded their claim on the more persuasive grounds of public security. Many pigments were toxic, and the presence of such ingredients in a grocery, they maintained, constituted a risk to public health.[66] This last argument was not without substance, as the Convent and Hospital of the Charité estimated that between 1 January 1774 and 27 September 1775, 'two hundred and seventy-two invalids entered the hospital, as many painters as colour-grinders, suffering from gangrene . . . Of this number several have died and others have been discharged, their limbs having been amputated . . .'.[67] However, despite the risks, until the end of the *ancien régime* the painters and grocers co-existed in an atmosphere of uneasy but possibly creative rivalry as suppliers of artists' materials.

Throughout the eighteenth century such internecine disputes over economic territory were notorious and more or less inevitable because the guilds formed an intricate pattern of imbricated specialisations and overlapping claims.[68] Although in principle corporation statutes were designed to minimise friction between guilds and encourage a degree of intercorporative unity, in practice each corporation used its statutes in a more instrumental way, finding in them legal support and a vocabulary of charges for their aggression towards others.[69] For example, in 1741, threatened by the fashion for lacquerware, the *tabletiers* or toymakers drew up new statutes in which, according to the painters, they claimed the right to manufacture such goods, 'by virtue of generalised terms with double meanings', to wit, 'to mould, compose, fashion and perfect Snuffboxes, to dye them and embellish them with different colours . . . and varnish them in all manner of methods and fashions.'[70] The Académie de Saint-Luc, however, saw the imprecise terminology for what it was: a means of grasping at an illegal share of the lacquer market. The directors of Saint-Luc appealed therefore, against the registration of the *tabletiers'* statutes and, their appeal having been upheld, the toymakers were formally instructed to accept, before the registration of their statutes in 1745, a limit to their activities that would prevent future encroachment in this domain.[71] However, after registration, the *tabletiers* ignored the terms of the painters' appeal and, following a number of lawsuits, the Académie de Saint-Luc was, in turn, forced to accept that despite its legal entitlement, it could no longer enforce an exclusive right to lacquer manufacture for the benefit of its members.[72] Likewise, the upholsterers liberally interpreted article XV of their statutes, which permitted them to buy or sell, 'all kinds of Tapestries and Carpets, all kinds of Furnishing Upholstery and Furniture dependent and reliant upon their said Art',[73] and in so doing, arrogated the right to retail any commodity used in interior decoration, including mirrors, over which the mirror-merchants claimed a monopoly. A lawsuit ensued in 1739 when the mirror-merchants unsuccessfully tried to put an end to these usurpers' trade in their wares.[74] Poignant testimony to their failure is to be found in an upholsterer's trade card (fig. 59) which promises all manner of furniture, including mirrors and pier-glasses, to those who presented themselves at a shop under the apparently innocent and conciliatory sign of *Au Bon Pasteur*.

Evidently the art of drawing up successful statutes lay in the right combination of definition and imprecision: definition for those practices and commodities at the heart of a guild's identity and necessary for its survival; imprecision for peripheral tasks and concerns in order to allow expansion in new directions as opportunities presented themselves and occasion demanded. If one of the by-products of such use or abuse of the law was the perennial skirmishes between the various trades – the Académie de Saint-Luc was involved in disputes with fan-painters, engravers on metal, mercers, illuminators and bronze-founders in addition to the grocers and toymakers

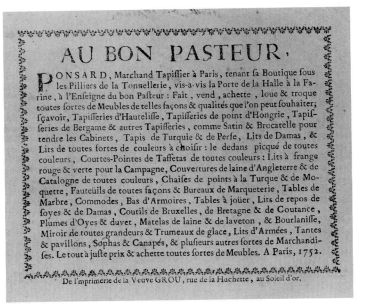

AU BON PASTEUR,

PONSARD, Marchand Tapissier à Paris, tenant sa Boutique sous
les Pilliers de la Tonnellerie, vis-a-vis la Porte de la Halle à la Fa-
rine, à l'Enseigne du bon Pasteur : Fait , vend , achette , loue & troque
toutes sortes de Meubles de telles façons & qualités que l'on peut souhaiter;
sçavoir, Tapisseries d'Hautelisse , Tapisseries de point d'Hongrie , Tapisseries de Bergame & autres Tapisseries , comme Satin & Brocatelle pour
tendre les Cabinets , Tapis de Turquie & de Perse , Lits de Damas , &
Lits de toutes sortes de couleurs à choisir : le dedans picqué de toutes
couleurs , Courtes-Pointes de Taffetas de toutes couleurs : Lits à frange
rouge & verte pour la Campagne, Couvertures de laine d'Angleterre & de
Catalogne de toutes couleurs , Chaises de points à la Turque & de Mo-
quette , Fauteüils de toutes façons & Bureaux de Marqueterie , Tables de
Marbre , Commodes , Bas d'Armoires , Tables à joüer , Lits de repos de
soyes & de Damas , Coutils de Bruxelles , de Bretagne & de Coutance ,
Plumes d'Oyes & duvet , Matelas de laine & de laveton , & Bourlanisse,
Miroir de toutes grandeurs & Trumeaux de glace, Lits d'Armées , Tantes
& pavillons , Sophas & Canapés , & plusieurs autres sortes de Marchandises. Le tout à juste prix & achette toutes sortes de Meubles. A Paris, 1752.

De l'imprimerie de la Veuve GROU, rue de la Huchette, au Soleil d'or.

59 Trade card for Ponsard: *Au Bon Pasteur*, 1752.

already mentioned[75] – on the other hand it worked in favour of a more flexible and innovative market and one better suited to respond to the vagaries of consumer choice.

Where the legislative process for collateral rivalry was protracted and the outcome uncertain, the reprisals exacted by the corporations against those who boycotted the corporative system altogether were swift. The Lieutenant-Général de Police and the guilds acted as one in their hostility to disenfranchised labour.[76] It is difficult to estimate the extent of illegal working practices but the seizures made by the painters' and sculptors' guild reveal that decorative work was on occasion carried out by black-marketeers. For example, on a tour of inspection in March 1741, the directors of Saint-Luc discovered two illegal but quite substantial workshops, one in the rue du Four and the other in the rue Saint-Germain-l'Auxerrois, run respectively by Jacques-Albert Vincenot and a certain Boquet, each of which produced oak panelling, chimney-mantles and *trumeaux*, while in an *immeuble* in the place Maubert they found a further two clandestine studios, this time the property of the painters Jean Guéret and Adrien Lebeau (called Delagery), substantially engaged in overdoor production.[77] Lest it be too readily assumed that the products made under such conditions were intended for the lower end of the market, in 1743 the *jurés* of the painters' guild visited the studio of Michel Janson, 'sans qualité', that is 'without title', who informed them that 'the overdoor he was finishing had been ordered by the architect M de Vigny for the marquis de Donnet'.[78] Royal academicians involved in commissions for distinguished clients were obviously not above subcontracting work to such artists, though in the absence of the schemes or more detailed documentation their reasons for doing so remain obscure. Did painters and panel-sculptors working outside guild regulations offer radically different products to those of

their incorporated colleagues? Or were contingencies such as availability or practicalities such as cost the pertinent considerations that led to their engagement?

While it is impossible to answer these questions in the cases of Vincenot, Boquet, Guéret, Delagery and Janson, they should be kept in mind when considering the working climate of those operating legally outside the guilds. In the eighteenth century, academicians formed the most prestigious subsection of these *privilégiés* but exemptions from corporate control dated from well before the foundation of such royal institutions as the Académie Royale de Peinture et de Sculpture. For convenience they will be divided into two kinds: first, the exemptions granted to individuals or groups of individuals – the so-called *marchands et artisans suivant la cour*, the *brevêtaires du roi* (or those with royal dispensations) and academicians – and second, the exemptions associated with certain locations of work, in this case the royal manufactories and those districts of Paris which still exercised medieval rights of asylum.

PRIVILEGED BODIES

The privileges of the *marchands et artisans suivant la cour*, established, as the title suggests, to furnish the needs of a shifting political centre, can be traced at least to the sixteenth century.[79] The artisans concerned were appointed and supervised by the Paris Provost of the Guilds, and when the court was resident in the capital or in one of the neighbouring palaces these tradesmen were entitled to open shops and trade freely in the *bourgs* and *fauxbourgs* of the city. It is difficult to determine in detail the particular advantages deriving from this courtly 'liberty', but the fact that painters as notable as Noël Jouvenet and Hyacinthe Rigaud seemingly preferred this status to the privileges that either municipal or royal academy membership could bring, tends to suggest that they were substantive as well as honorific. Although the legal battle prompted by the Académie de Saint-Luc's attempt, in 1692, to force Rigaud to commit himself either to them or the Académie Royale reveals little about the artist's motivation, it seems plausible to assume that, since there was nothing unorthodox about his painting practice, the advantage the portraitist was eager to preserve was the absence of restriction on the size of his studio.[80] Both the corporation and the Académie Royale in principle bound their members to a fixed number of apprentices, journeymen and assistants, a limitation that an ambitious and prosperous portrait painter may well have found irksome.[81]

Painters were not the only decorators to exercise the title of court artisan. The Letters Patent of 1725 which upheld the continuity of these privileges under the new monarchy of Louis XV also fixed the number of such craftsmen in each of the trades concerned. In addition to four painters, they were to include eight weaver-dyers, four joiners, two mirror-

52

merchants and two sculptors.[82] If in number these artisans seem hardly impressive, their familiarity with the taste and culture of the most exclusive clientele and the court trademark of their goods must have guaranteed them a disproportionate advantage in a luxury market where their guild colleagues could often only hope for a relationship with the final consumer mediated by a mercer or an architect. Moreover, they were guaranteed a conspicuous presence on the street, even on those commercial arteries most extravagantly bedecked with shop-signs,[83] by their exclusive right and obligation, 'to decorate their Shops and Establishments with awnings of fleurs-de-lys and with the coat of arms of the Town Hall', precisely in order that, 'they may be distinguished from all other Merchants and Artisans'.[84] Thus, although their privileges were tempered by the right of interested guilds to visit and inspect the goods produced in such workshops, these merchants and craftsmen must nevertheless have enjoyed an enviable standing with the public.

Where the advantages of court artisans perhaps amounted above all to favourable access to market information, the *brevêtaires du roi* and the academicians enjoyed more tangible commercial concessions. Supervised and protected by the Surintendant or Directeur des Bâtiments, they were entirely exempted from guild regulations. Not infrequently they were also provided with free and sometimes extensive working premises in royal buildings in the capital. In addition to the better-known ateliers of the Louvre, artists such as Audran and Parrocel were given workshops in the Gobelins and the Luxembourg Palace; others, like Oudry and later Claude-Joseph Vernet, enjoyed rooms in the Tuileries, while history painters might, like Jean Restout, simultaneously maintain studios at the Louvre and at Garde-Meuble de la Couronne in the hôtel des Menus-Plaisirs.[85] Many were granted royal pensions,[86] and they were protected from creditors by acts of reprieve.[87] The 'entrepreneurial potential' of such privileges was considerable.[88] The financial security guaranteed by privileges allowed those who enjoyed them greater flexibility in the materials and skills they deployed[89] and more opportunity to invest in expensive and exotic primary materials or to experiment with and speculate in new products.

Thus, theoretically, these producers, should have established significantly larger, more diversified and more *avant-garde* businesses with higher capital investment and larger labour forces compared to the craftsmen of the guilds. In practice, the evidence is not so clear-cut. Certainly, Audran's initiatives in flock-paper and lacquerware were born out of royal protection, but the subsequent development and growth in these two trades took place within the guild community, specifically in the workshops of the Papillon and Martin families, and in those of Didier Aubert and Jean-Jacques Arthur.[90] Moreover, few would deny the seminal role played by Nicolas Pineau (a sculptor who remained throughout his career at a distance from royal protection) in the creation of the so-called *genre pittoresque* or rococo, perhaps the most experimental and

unorthodox breakthrough in eighteenth-century design.[91] Furthermore, if information about the size and capital investment of artisanal workshops is still inconclusive, it appears that no great disparity existed between the size of those of guildsmen and those of *privilégiés*: the cabinet-maker André-Charles Boulle employed twenty-six journeymen in his studios in the Louvre at the beginning of the century,[92] while in 1748 some twenty journeymen were left stranded when the ornament sculptor and guildsman, Jean-Baptiste Robillon, went bankrupt,[93] and thirty lost their living when the carriage-painter, Antoine Vincent, died in 1772.[94] Moreover, if dowry and bride-price may be taken as indicators of the prosperity of a business, it is significant that on his wedding-day in 1701, Gilles-Marie Oppenord received 62,000 *livres* from his father, a joiner in the Galeries du Louvre,[95] compared to which the master-sculptor and *marbrier* François Le Prince settled 100,000 *livres* on his daughter when she married a grocer in 1723.[96] Thus, if the privileged sector of the luxury trades promised more expensive and innovative goods, produced in larger quantities by more advanced commercial and marketing techniques, they were not always forthcoming, and aside from their assured commissions from the crown, in the Parisian market the *privilégiés* were not so far ahead that they were in any way immune from challenges offered by their less distinguished guild bretheren.

Perhaps some of the reasons for the limited exploitation of those privileges granted to individuals may be found in a memorandum drawn up in 1762 by artists resident in the Louvre to defend the right of the painter Jean-Baptiste Pourvoyeur to be admitted into the Académie de Saint-Luc on the strength of his apprenticeship to Claude-François Desportes at the Louvre.[97] The Saint-Luc directors had dismissed the eligibility of Pourvoyeur's candidature on the grounds that he had been neither housed nor boarded by his master and could not therefore be said to have served an apprenticeship as such.[98] This claim gave rise to a lengthy dissertation on the respective nature of corporative and Louvre apprenticeships and the different cultures of the workshops in which they were discharged. According to the Louvre defendants, commensality was entirely appropriate to the relationship between masters and apprentices, because master-painters were, 'entrepreneurs in Painting of all kinds' and were therefore indemnified for the expense by setting their apprentices 'to tasks which require no talent, such as cleaning old pictures, painting trellis work, daubing pieces of woodwork', or simply running errands.[99] By contrast, how could 'the Great Artist', he who lived in the Louvre, be expected to treat his pupils in the same way, when, 'despising the unvarying pace of routine [he] extends even to his way of life the liberty of his Art'.[100] Such a man, they claimed, could not be tied to 'the minutiae of book-keeping', not least because he was no entrepreneur, having willingly forsaken such activities as too obviously beneath his dignity.[101] The superior, not to say anti-materialist, calling of Louvre art so constituted, was visually

set a limit to the entrepreneurial activities of privileged artists both *brevêtaires* and academicians. Certainly, the careers of most academicians seem positively limited by comparison with the activities of Paul Sévin, whose trade card (fig. 61) announced his talents as a painter in oil, fresco, distemper and miniature, with a facility for history, portraiture, heraldry and perspective; which declared, moreover, his willingness to design theatre scenery and decorations for religious festivities, to provide patterns for embroidery on satin, watered-silk and taffeta, and to impart with all due speed the mysteries of good draughtsmanship and painting. Finally, it advertised his standing as a dealer with a shop on the rue d'Anjou impressively stocked with two hundred paintings of all possible kinds. Boucher's artistic scope was somewhat exceptional in academic circles, yet it is only necessary to remember Audran, Tramblin, Roumier – the author of an extraordinary decorative paper (fig. 62) executed we are told with no more than a sculptor's tools – to acknowledge that Sevin was in all likeli-

61 François Ertinger, trade card for Paul Sévin: *Au Buste de Monseigneur*, c.1710. Engraving and etching.

60 Gilles Demarteau after Charles-Nicolas Cochin, *Justice Protects the Arts*, 1764. Crayon-manner etching.

articulated by Charles-Nicolas Cochin in an allegorical drawing offered to the Advocate-General Séguier, the presiding magistrate on this case, and later etched by Gilles Demarteau (fig. 60). It shows Justice and Generosity protecting Painting and Sculpture from the deleterious and besmirching attacks of the guild, personified here by the commercial vices of Envy, Jealousy and Malice.[102]

Cochin and the authors of the memorandum thus constructed an image of the artist (in this instance a painter or a sculptor, but the case was brought to court in defence of all Louvre *privilégiés*) that rendered superior skill incommensurate with business acumen. Even though it was only a rhetorical image, the possibility remains, nevertheless, that such notions

62 François Roumier, design for wallpaper, c.1727. Woodcut.

There, it seems, absence of profit almost guaranteed the presence of art. In short, the Gobelins' objective to produce 'works of art' could be achieved, perhaps only achieved, in a commercial vacuum; and acknowledgement of their intention, not demand for their products, was the sufficient condition of their success. Thus, economic privilege was exploited for status, not financial gain, because it allowed the production of goods of a 'quality' that largely precluded private demand.

If the need for a manufactory of the Gobelins sort, one whose industry enhanced 'the magnificence and dignity' of the throne,[106] was accepted by the *intendants de commerce*, steps were nevertheless taken to ensure that neither Beauvais nor Aubusson followed suit. These companies were expected to marry art with industry in just measure; at Beauvais to satisfy 'the rich' and at Aubusson to cater to 'artisans of substance' and 'the prosperous bourgeoisie'.[107] Here, quality was assigned by the price of the primary materials employed, and the best result the council of trade could therefore entertain was a successful and profitable match between design and the potential of the materials in which they were woven.[108] To this end, at Aubusson at least, the role of the weavers in policy-making was much greater than at the Gobelins, for since the manufactory was no more than a simple aggregate of independent workshops it was only on the basis of approaches made to the weavers individually that the taste of the market could be accurately gauged and accommodated.[109] The Gobelins overrode the suggestions of their merchant-weavers not by mistake but because for them quality was synonymous with art – the judgement of which was inscribed in immutable academic codes of which the weavers could in principle have no knowledge. The history of the Gobelins in the eighteenth century was, among other things, the history of the ever-increasing control of the designer over the merchant-weaver.[110] By comparison, at Aubusson, where quality was acknowledged as a physical property to which design was simply added to accelerate turn-over, entrepreneurs were treated as an essential bridgehead between consumer and management.

Ironically, privilege, so often the certificate of excellence in the luxury industry, seems to have been of greatest commercial benefit to those whose markets were primarily for low-cost goods.[111] The royal titles and statutes of Aubusson, for instance, protected them from the Paris carpet-weavers whose own regulations prohibited textile production of such inferior weaves and dyes, and Aubusson was therefore easily able to under-cut them in the market.[112] Consequently, the privileges enjoyed by Aubusson probably worked to effect results closer to those that obtained in certain districts of Paris by virtue of medieval rights of asylum than to the artistic triumphs achieved at the Académie Royale or the Gobelins.

hood a reasonably typical representative of Saint-Luc.[103] Privilege, it seems, operated in favour of tradition and specialisation as often as it may have promoted expansion, innovation and diversification.

This point is illustrated with equal force by the royal manufactories. Of the three tapestry manufactories, Gobelins, Beauvais and Aubusson, it was the first which showed the least market flexibility during the century, yet of the three, it was also the Gobelins that enjoyed the most favourable commercial terms. Beneficiary to a large government subsidy, placed exclusively under the control of the Bâtiments, directed by gifted architects and with access to the most talented designers and weavers of the day, the manufactory nevertheless ran at a loss.[104] Yet when, in 1795, the painter Anicet-Charles-Gabriel Lemonnier submitted a report to the Ministry of the Interior suggesting measures likely to transform the Gobelins into a profitable enterprise, he elicited the following response:

The Gobelins cannot be regarded as an object of Commercial speculation, experience having shown that the sale of its products can never reach a level capable of covering the cost [of production]; that if the Government has persevered in supporting this establishment it is because the art exercised there is very beautiful in itself, and serves to multiply the

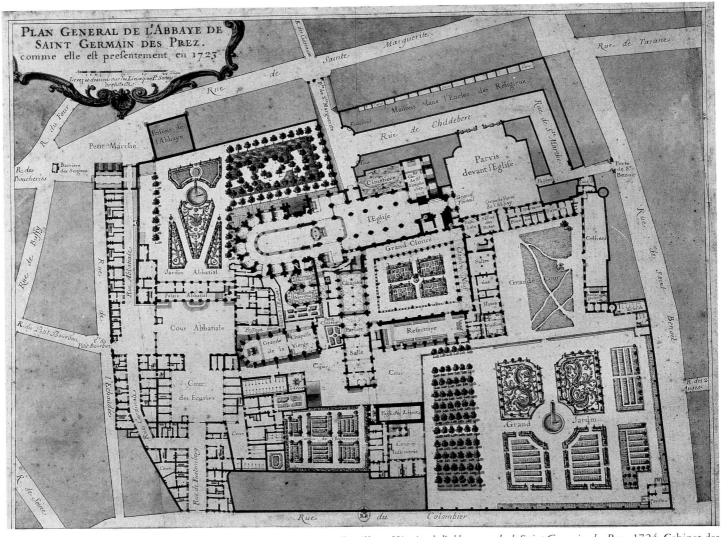

63   Map of the abbey of Saint-Germain-des-Prés, 1723. For Jacques Bouillart, *Histoire de l'abbaye royale de Saint Germain-des-Prez*, 1724. Cabinet des Estampes, Bibliothèque Nationale, Paris.

PRIVILEGED PLACES

Since, for the most part, the corporations acknowledged that the privileges enjoyed by *brevêtaires* and academicians were granted on the grounds of exceptional merit they could theoretically recognise, they rarely confronted directly the principle of royal privilege and contented themselves instead with a policy of brinkmanship levelled at specific and isolated individuals and designed to keep the scope of royal *largesse* in check. The case of 'free' trade, exercised in those enclaves and districts of the capital protected by ecclesiastical or collegiate charters, was another matter. At the beginning of the century the guilds achieved a Pyrrhic victory when, in response to their allegations of an uncontrolled proliferation of rights of asylum, a royal commission was established to review the validity of the titles variously claimed on the grounds of seigneurial, royal or ecclesiatical entitlement.[113] As a result of the review, a certain number of noble fief-holders and institutions immedi-

ately forfeited their franchises, but the more extensive and commercially threatening *lieux privilégiés*, such as the abbeys of Saint-Germain-des-Prés and Saint-Antoine, the priories of Saint-Martin-des-Champs and Saint-Denis-de-la-Chartre, and the enclosures of Saint-Jean-de-Latran, the Temple and the Quinze-Vingts emerged with their mandates not only intact but officially endorsed.[114]

In all these instances rights of asylum empowered those who lived within their limits to exercise their trade without thought or reference to corporate legislation. However, this liberation was to be had at a cost, because few of these governing bodies were in fact disposed to allow market principle free reign; on the contrary, most offered an alternative corporative life hedged in with as many, but different regulations.[115] In 1718, two years after the official enquiry, a confident Henri de Thiard, cardinal de Bissy and abbot of Saint-Germain-des-Prés,[116] judged it appropriate to re-issue the *ordonnance de police* that, in thirty-seven articles, defined the shape of liberty

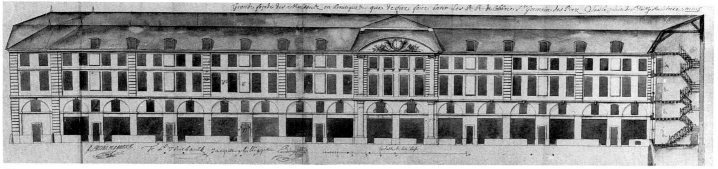

64 Victor-Thierry d'Ailly, elevation of the shopfronts for the abbey of Saint-Germain-des-Prés, 1716. Pen, ink and wash, 62 × 117 cm. Archives Nationale, Paris.

intra-muros (fig. 63). Most of the rules were designed, predictably enough, to ensure that the lay community behaved in a manner appropriate to the sacredness of the place, that they were sober in manner and dress, that they observed Christian decorum and treated church property with respect.[117] Others were of greater commercial significance: for instance, all artisans were required to register with the clerk of the abbey within three days of arrival and were bound to keep day-books.

65 Victor-Thierry d'Ailly, elevation of part of the façade of the buildings for the abbey of Saint-Germain-des-Prés, 1716. Pen, ink and wash on paper, 99 × 22.5 cm. Archives Nationales, Paris.

Moreover it was the bretheren who determined hours of access to the *enclos* and they who insisted that diocesan and local feast-days play their part in regulating the rhythms of work.[118] Since the guilds had the additional right to inspect the content of that labour, there is little reason to suppose that Joseph Bonnet, a sculptor at the Temple, or Marion a painter at the Quinze-Vingt, or Guillaume Delavergne a mason at Saint-Germain-des-Prés, implemented significantly unorthodox workshop structures or produced particularly newfangled goods.[119]

Yet, however commercially conservative these enclaves may have been, there can be no doubt of their success, in view of the energy and capital committed by the Benedictines of Saint-Germain-des-Prés and Saint-Martin-des-Champs to develop the infrastructure of their sites.[120] According to the *jurés* and *syndics* of the Six-Corps, the newly built shops and workshops, designed by Victor-Thierry d'Ailly at Saint-Germain (figs 64 and 65), were so rapidly filled 'with a large number of Individuals without titles', that they took on the threatening appearance of 'small towns rather than Enclosures'.[121] Moreover, the prosperity of individual traders is vouchsafed by the elegance and pretentiousness of the trade cards they had printed. The makers of scientific instruments Fagard and Magny (fig. 66), for instance, had cards designed by Moreau le Jeune and Charles-Dominique Eisen respectively,[122] and the distiller Noverre had recourse to the co-ordinated talents of Bosquet and Jean-Baptiste Le Bas for a composition (fig. 67) that testifies, incidentally, to the commercial potential of chinoiserie, to its exceptional ability to accelerate the turnover of any commodity, however distantly related to Cathay.[123]

The antagonism felt by the guilds towards the *lieux privilégiés* within the city limits was as nothing compared to the passions triggered by the free trade flourishing in the faubourg Saint-Antoine precisely because there, in that district beyond the Bastille, privilege was translated into commercial advantage, and the corporations' social and moral prerogatives to supervise labour were comprehensively challenged.[124] According to one journalist, 'The freedom enjoyed by the faubourg Saint-Antoine encourages daily the growth of a new branch of industry'.[125] However, the rhetoric of the free market departed in some measure from practice. Absence of

66 Charles-Dominique Eisen, trade card for Alexis Magny, *c*.1740. Etching.

67 Jacques-Philippe Le Bas after Bosquet, trade card for Noverre, *c*.1740. Etching.

restriction did not, in fact, immediately result in the install-ation of large, integrated and fixed-capital industries: to Saint-Gobain's finishing-plant on the rue de Reuilly and Réveillon's wallpaper manufactory on the corner of the rue du faubourg Saint-Antoine and the rue de Montreuil, both of which employed over three hundred workers, can be added only some ten firms whose pay-rolls exceeded fifty employees.[126] Compe-tition stemmed rather from modest, sometimes technically innovative enterprises (like that of the coach-builder François Cœullet), which were able to bring together tasks traditionally dispersed in different trades and to practise some level of labour division. Such enterprises were thus often better placed to respond promptly to evolving trends in taste.[127] But since these artisans could not deliver their work outside the privi-leged area and had to arrange for their clients to collect, it seems unlikely that important decorative schemes were ever produced in the neighbourhood. However, while the more militant corporations, such as the joiners, frequently stood guard on the perimeter of the faubourg to stem the flow of 'liberty' goods into Paris, individual masters undermined their

efforts from within by putting out work for luxuries and decorative components in the faubourg.[128] Mercers, in parti-cular, seem to have quietly but widely pursued such a *verlagssystem*, offering necessary and reliable outlets, if not actively providing materials, tools and premises, in exchange for quality products (furniture from the rue Charenton, for example) or cheaper novelties (wallpapers from the Grande rue du faubourg).[129] The liberties such masters took with guild regulations vitiated the corporations' representation of them-selves as necessary social and political institutions, and no amount of cold-war rhetoric could completely obscure the picture of two interdependent and overlapping economies.

Similarities between the worlds of the city and the faubourg were also apparent at street level because, notwithstanding the rural atmosphere of Saint-Antoine, its workshops evolved in ribbon developments akin to urban patterns in other districts inhabited by master-craftsmen. Although it is clear that *ancien-régime* Paris cannot be said to have had working-class *quartiers* as such,[130] certain urban features coincided more or less exactly with commercial neighbourhoods[131] – namely constricted, closely packed streets and small, narrow houses.[132] These features characterised the older, central districts of Paris where the urban tissue had become both dense and intractable. As a result, despite the almost feverish mobility of the artisanal population – in a period of little more than a decade Pineau moved at least four times[133] – certain parishes,[134] and more precisely certain streets, became identified with parti-cular trades, almost as if bricks and mortar generated the social continuity necessary for workshops to survive over gener-ations.[135] For example the rue and quai de Gêvres were popu-lated predominantly by goldsmiths, silversmiths, gilders and jewellers,[136] the rues Saint-Honoré, de l'Arbre-Sec and du Roule by *marchands-merciers*,[137] the pont Notre-Dame by pros-

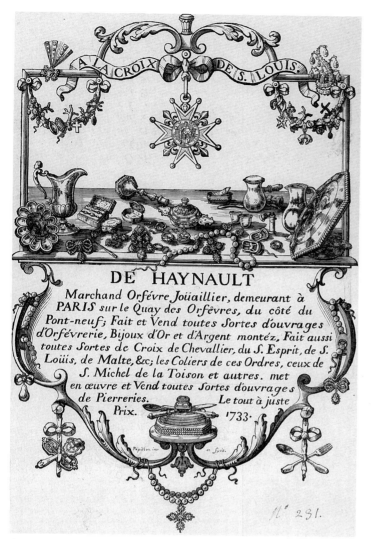

68 Jean-Michel Papillon, trade card for De Haynault: *A la Croix de Saint-Louis*, 1733. Woodcut.

69 Hubert Robert, *Studios in the Louvre*, c.1780. Wash over pencil on paper, 10.2 × 13.4 cm. Musée du Louvre, Paris.

perous picture-dealers[138] and a large proportion of the painters and sculptors of the guild chose the north–south axes of the rues Saint-Denis and Saint-Martin, plus the surrounding and interconnecting streets, as their preferred places of work.[139]

These streets constituted subjective neighbourhoods for their inhabitants, distinct from other areas of the city in terms of both their physical appearance and their social constituency.[140] Like the workshop itself, the neighbourhood offered an immediate realm of professional and social intercourse, an intercourse that undoubtedly had a bearing on patterns of production. In an economy where information about current-price, rumours of likely contracts or workshop vacancies and intimations of demand were only to be had through sociability, the neighbourhood wineshop or (in the faubourg Saint-Antoine) the local inns played a seminal role in successful trading.[141] Moreover, the density and street orientation of certain artisanal communities (for example the joiners and cabinet-makers occupied some sixty-eight, sometimes

contiguous workshops, on the rue de Cléry) must also have encouraged verbal communication on matters of technology and design.[142] Thus, while the role of prints in the introduction and dissemination of new designs was undoubtedly important, it is likely that such novelties could not have been transformed into objects unless introduced to leading workshops in significant commercial neighbourhoods.

The public, professional forum of the street stood in marked contrast to the segregated world of the *privilégiés* of the Louvre and the royal manufactories. The goldsmith and jeweller De Haynault's trade card (fig. 68), which depicts a large selection of his wares, laid out almost as if on a window-ledge, visually implies the custom that required artisans to work in their shops 'à fenêtre', in order that their activities be available to public scrutiny.[143] By contrast, Hubert Robert's wash drawing of the entrance of his studio at the Louvre (fig. 69) suggests a universe inhabited by individuals removed from one another up staircases and down corridors, and one in which works were prepared, executed and despatched in private obscurity.[144] Similarly, in the faubourg Saint-Marcel, at the bottom of the rue Mouffetard and enclosed from the public way by large and imposing buildings, was the Gobelins, sheltering an existence that seemingly had more in common with a contemplative order than with the commercial world of the capital.[145] Jean-François Blondel refused to take the elevation of the place because the lack of symmetry and order to its face apparently deprived it of artistic merit, but he did publish a ground-plan (fig. 70). There, the emphasis on the perimeter articulates the desired separation of the *artisanat* from the market, while the careful mapping of a labyrinthine sequence of inward-facing spaces not only invites the ecclesiastical simile, but acknowledges (in contrast to the Roberts' image of the Louvre) the interdependence of workshops geared to a common task.[146]

However, the monastic analogy goes beyond the mere

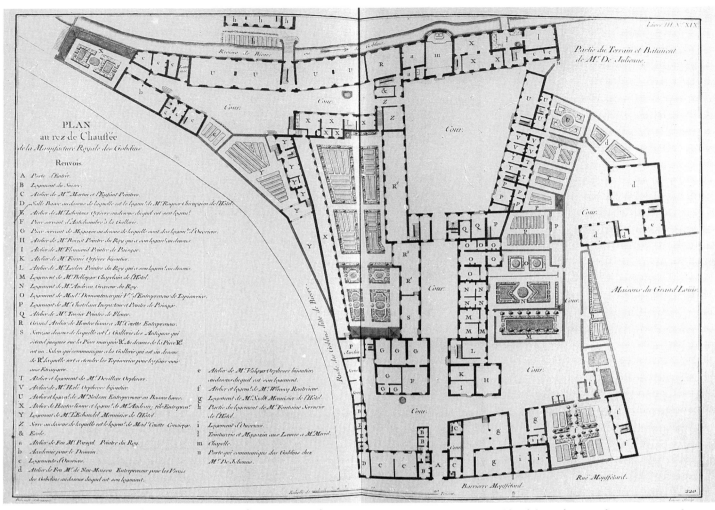

70 Ground-plan of the Gobelins tapestry manufactory, 1752–6. Engraving. From Jacques-François Blondel, *Architecture françoise*, 1752–6.

segregation of a subsection of the population from the rest. The official policy at the Gobelins manufactory was directed towards minimising contact with the outside world. Not only was every effort made to house most of the labour force, but the employees also benefited from free fruit and vegetables raised on the manufactory's communal garden,[147] and they were provided with their own taverns which offered ale at concessionary rates.[148] The discipline in the royal manufactories appears to have been strict[149] and the employees were forbidden to leave the manufactory in search of work elsewhere without authorisation (on pain of imprisonment).[150] Like Robert Darnton's printers, the Gobelins workers were truly 'a people, or rather a republic who lived separated from other nations'.[151] Moreover, like the printer's workshop, the Gobelins was structured by a hierarchically differentiated and sedentary labour-force.[152] In such a world, where masters enjoyed neither independence nor mastery, having been yoked to royal service, where apprenticeships were protracted and where (after 1750) wages were invariably delayed, sometimes for a matter of weeks, riotous insubordination was virtually

endemic, and a weaver's version of 'the cat massacre' was surely well within the logic of the situation.[153] Thus privileges, which on the one hand gave the weavers, like all *privilégiés*, the appearance of an artisanal aristocracy, self-perpetuating and separated from the commonality by physical as well as social boundaries, seem on the other hand to have fostered the very conditions of insurrection. Internal contradictions were not, therefore, exclusive to corporate bodies but fractured the organisational structures that governed eighteenth-century decorative practice as a whole. Just as the legislated rigidity of the guilds' discipline of production was more apparent than real (masters finding in their workshop plenty of scope for innovation in technique and design), so the the liberalism of the liberal or liberated arts and manufactures was less substantive than ideal. The state's purpose in establishing academies and royal manufactories consisted in part in effecting a hierarchy of labour, and it was precisely the superior, individualistic calling of 'art', as a practice theoretically beyond economic calculation and exploitation, that set limits to the commercial advantages of 'liberty'.

3

The Co-ordination of Work

Ironically, surveys of artefacts and production methods, such as the foregoing, while often arguing for shared artisanal values and similarities in institutional structure, invariably tend to highlight the particularism of the pre-industrial trades. This impression is, in part, created by the survival of a disproportionately abundant legal literature, which continues to give priority to the strident and often litigious rhetoric of the corporations, and is perhaps reinforced by our sense of historical estrangement from a world we have patently lost. Erroneous though the impression may be, it nevertheless makes it difficult to reconstruct those vertical ties of authority, dependency and reciprocal obligation that must necessarily have operated *across* as well as within trades in order to have given rise to any, modestly unified, decorative scheme. Descriptions of the constituent elements of a decorative project tend too easily to run into evocations of the total effect of the final schemes with barely a reference to the managerial stage in production, upon which the successful implementation of a programme must ultimately have depended. Indeed, the evanescence of those oral directives and imperative gestures that presumably did so much to bind the labour force to a common endeavour, has led to the assumption that co-operation resulted instead from the *naturally* synchronised task-orientation of the artisanal and artistic trades involved. Much remains to be discovered, therefore, about the social dynamics at play on the building-sites of eighteenth-century Paris.

Towards the end of his entry 'Architect', for the *Dictionnaire raisonné universel des arts et métiers* (1773), the abbé Jaubert gave sharp focus to the apparently bifurcated social structure of eighteenth-century building-sites. He noted that those 'who exhibit the greatest activity, ignore or fail to consider what effect the item they are producing will create: confusion reigns over their movements. Opperations are dispersed here and there, without order and without beauty'. In short, 'the labourers who cover the plane . . . work blind'. By contrast, 'The architect who directs so many activities sees the sense in them, and the relations between them', and when he finally dismisses the labour-force, 'that which was only an idea locked in his mind has become, by general consent, a magnificent reality'.[1] No doubt because of the uncompromising severity of Jaubert's separation of doers and thinkers (reinforced by additional contrasts between heads and hands, reason and instinct, order and disorder, vision and blindness) this description is virtually devoid of information about the channels of authority through which the architect's domination was exercised. Indeed, what is most striking about Jaubert's poetic description is the very passivity of the architect's dominion by comparison with the energy, however chaotic, of the workers. Legally speaking, the custom of Paris forbade the use of fixed contracts, that is contracts which, by ceding to the architect responsibility for supplying the required materials and for settling the necessary sub-contracts, would have yielded such unconditional control over the means and organisation of production. Instead, clients were therefore obliged to pass either notarised or private contracts with each of the separate trades involved, such that the authority of the 'author' and co-ordinator of the scheme was necessarily indirect because those executing his design were contractually empowered to organise a portion, or all of the work process themselves.[2]

To a certain extent, then, the building-site merely witnessed the extension of workshop-relations onto its terrain. To put it another way, master-artisans remained primarily responsible for the journeymen or 'employees' on site, even though they themselves might have relinquished a measure of their autonomy to a scheme co-ordinator. And lest there be any doubt on this matter, all contracts customarily committed the signatory, 'to do or have done' those works subsequently described, a phrase that conveniently covered a master's responsibility for his more-or-less sedentary force of journeymen, for the day-labourers he might have engaged at the place de Grève (the capital's most important labour-market), and for any subcontracts he might discretely have entertained.

MASTERS AND JOURNEYMEN

The relationship between journeymen and masters in eighteenth-century Paris has recently been the subject of considerable attention, as historians have sought to test the quality of the match between the ideal of corporate authority and the reality of master–journeyman relationships.[3] The corporate ideal, which owed much of its original formulation to the sixteenth-century political theorist Jean Bodin, held that the internal structure of corporations should mirror the corporate structure of society as a whole.[4] Thus, as corporations were themelves links in a political chain that extended from the hands of the monarch to the most humble constituted body, so the inner universe should reflect or reproduce this hierarchical pattern by holding masters at once responsible to their elected *jurés-gardes* and responsible for their journeymen; these journeymen subject, in turn, to the will of their masters and lastly, apprentices subordinate to the authority of both masters and journeymen.[5] Described by the Lieutenant de Police, Lenoir, as a 'chaîne domestique', this structure seemingly had the political virtue of ensuring first, the accountability of labour and second, by virtue of the ties of friendship and mutual obligation that mediated economic interests, an exceptional degree of social stability and public order.[6] In practice, however, the economy of the luxury trades militated against the realisation of even a semblance of this ideal. The seasonal rhythms of the building and decorative trades, the unpredictability of demand and the complex circuits of credit and payment, required of master-craftsmen a dependable workforce, certainly, but one also responsive to commercial realities. In other words, masters needed the flexibility to hire and fire a portion of their labour force as occasion demanded. For their part, the journeymen sought to limit the effects of these contingencies on their ability to make a living and aimed to secure the best possible terms in a makeshift economy.[7] The result was a much higher level of labour mobility than the concept of paternalist authority could easily contain, and a 'spirit of revolt' amongst journeymen that seemed almost as incomprehensible as it was shocking in view of the familial intimacy which ideally pertained in the workshop.[8]

Journeymen in the building trades were notorious *cabaleurs*[9] and if, according to one *ordonnance de police*, 'Of all those working in the Building Trade there are none as obdurate as the Journeymen Masons',[10] others, involved in the finishing trades for the construction industry, were not always more tractable. On more than one occasion Pierre-Jacques Brillon, the duc du Maine's *intendant*, felt compelled to urge the agent at Sceaux to exercise such strict control over the building-workers engaged in routine maintenance of the château as to repress their unbuttoned enthusiasm for swearing, theft and delinquency.[11] Meanwhile, in 1683 another court ruling had been issued with the purpose of putting an end both to fraudulent transactions in building materials and to disruption on the royal construction sites. It ordered that

> all those who shall be employed on His Majesty's Works, entrepreneurs, suppliers, artisans, workmen as well as day-labourers, who neglect their function, whatever it may be, or who give rise to brawls in their workshops, will be chastised and punished according to the gravity of the offence . . . up to and including the lash.[12]

The severity of the punishment notwithstanding, these successive *ordonnances* failed to secure a lasting peace and in 1747 there arose at Versailles,

> a sedition by the Journeymen engaged on works of Painting and Sculpture who asserted the right to impose terms on the Entrepreneurs of the King's Works, to fix the price, concentration and length of their *journée* and the hours at which they will start and finish their work.[13]

In response, the Académie Saint-Luc resolved, in a series of assemblies held between September and March the following year, to institute once and for all legal regulations governing the terms of journeyman employment.[14] In May 1748, a decision of the Paris Parlement brought into effect the conclusions of these deliberations. Journeymen painters and sculptors were to begin work at 6.00 a.m. and end at 7.00 p.m. with a half-hour break at 8.00 in the morning and an hour at midday; they were to be available for work at night (7.00 p.m. to midnight) between 9 September and 1 April; these so-called *veilles* were to be paid at half the daily rate; and finally, journeymen were henceforth only eligible for employment on the presentation of a *billet de congé* or certificate of leave issued by their previous employer.[15] Once again the corporation's general assemblies – *rocaille* invitations to which (fig. 71) might seem whimsically to evoke hours of leisurely reflection on the finer, aesthetic points of painting and sculpture – were the occasions at which the legal armature for the masters's control over labour was repeatedly recast and strengthened in line with changing economic and political necessities. In a sense, these regulations were a public admission that the subordination of journeymen apparently guaranteed by the corporate ethic was in fact not naturally forthcoming.

71 Invitation to an assembly of the corporation of painters and sculptors, *c*.1735. Etching.

This dispute, the regulations to which it gave rise and the journeymen's appeal afford an exceptional insight into the conditions under which decoration was carried out in eighteenth-century Paris. The *veilles* provide evidence of both the elasticity of the working day[16] – it might contain eleven hours in the winter and eighteen in the summer – and the irregularity of the decorator's year; its rhythms ideally counterpointing those of the construction industry as a whole. Peak demand occurred during the summer months and although the act laid down no tariff of wage-rates, when, in 1765, the corporation attempted to fix journeyman salaries, it was specified that they were to be paid 5 *sous* less per day in the winter season,[17] once again echoing a practice apparently standard among other construction workers, such as masons and roofers.[18] Indeed, work was so scarce in winter that immigrant journeymen-painters and sculptors habitually left for their native provinces in October, only to return to the capital the following March.[19]

By securing a statutory maximum working day of sixteen hours in the summer months and eleven and a half in the winter, the masters sought to synchronise wage-levels and the length and concentration of the working day with the peaks and troughs of the market, thus easing the burden of credit that mediated incoming returns from clients and outgoings on wages. The journeymen meanwhile, appealed against such long hours, and indeed secured an extra half hour for their midday break[20] because their interest lay in averaging the intensity of their labour so as to yield a more evenly distributed yearly income.[21] Conflicts of interest were therefore inevitable. Practice bore the marks of these perennially regenerated antagonisms between masters' time and journeymen's time in the leads and lags of the daily rates actually paid. These so distorted the calendar of seasonally adjusted salaries that the illusion of a providential synchrony between the rhythms of man's and nature's works was effectively dispelled.[22] The economy of time was thus a crucial nexus of artisanal dispute throughout the eighteenth century.

The wage was, however, only one of several components that made up the journeyman's earnings, even though it remained the most conspicuous.[23] Many journeymen were housed and fed by their masters, which secured them most of the necessities of life. Moreover, in a significant number of trades, journeymen enjoyed customary rights to a part of the materials distributed for their work.[24] Woodworkers, for instance, were unofficially entitled to *copeaux*, or the pieces of wood left over after the completion of a job – although the architect Nicolas-Marie Potain noted that in the case of parquet floors they were rarely forthcoming, 'because in these sorts of works one can use even the smallest pieces [of wood] so long as they are sound . . .'[25] By the same token, house-painters and gilders were entitled to *déchets* and *époustures*, or the silver and gold dust remaining after the decoration of an apartment, a custom that the guild tried earnestly to suppress in 1765 because it cut too deeply into masters' profits.[26] Deter-

mined opposition to all attempts of this kind to put an end to customary rights, confirms the presence of a substantial economic interest at the heart of these apparently symbolic forms. Journeymen-carpenters staged a number of stoppages between March 1698 and August 1700 in a concerted campaign to pressure the Parlement into overturning a ruling by the Conseil d'Etat that had rendered the collection of *copeaux* illegal, and in 1786 a later generation of journeymen walked off the site of the structurally fraught church of Sainte-Geneviève after the carpenters' corporation had made known its intent to substitute an extra 5 *sous* per day for the right to take wood.[27]

Although such customary rights primarily favoured their claimants they also bound them in relations of reciprocal obligation. Redeemable only on the completion of a task, such rights entailed a commitment from the journeyman, at least for the time it took to execute the project in hand. In a highly fluid labour market in which it was apparently not uncommon for journeymen in the decorating trades to work for more than one master during the course of a single day,[28] any such stabilising ritual could materially benefit the master as well as the journeyman. In the same spirit of control, mastercraftsmen also frequently made cash advances to their workers in anticipation of work carried out, thus ensuring once again that the required tasks were actually performed. Indeed, it was the advance together with customary rights, rather than any putative ideological solidarity, that ensured delivery of that obedience from journeymen extolled by those committed to maintaining the corporate system; but of course it lasted only the term it took a journeyman to work off the debt.[29]

To return once again to the occasion of the 1747 dispute at Versailles, the moment and place of its staging seem significant. Though it has been argued that many such disputes arose naturally or spontaneously from short- or long-term economic depressions, such an argument seems ultimately incapable of fully explaining the circumstances of the case.[30] The steady political hand of Cardinal Fleury and the almost austere ministry of his *creature*, the controller-general of finance, Philibert Orry, had, from 1730, set France on a path to comparative economic stability, which in turn inspired investment confidence and kept the building industry reasonably buoyant.[31] Festivities were in hand to celebrate the dauphin's marriage to Marie-Joseph de Saxe in February 1747 and the War of the Austrian Succession was effectively over – although the Treaty of Aix-la-Chapelle had yet to be signed.

However, the mid-forties also marked a time of political and artistic change. Jeanne-Antoinette Poisson, soon marquise de Pompadour, became *maîtresse en titre* in 1745 and with her rose the Pâris brothers whose hostility to Orry's stringent fiscal policies resulted in his swift dismissal in December of that year from his twin posts as chancellor of the exchequer and director of the Bâtiments du Roi.[32] He was replaced at the Bâtiments by Le Normand de Tournehem, Pompadour's uncle. One of the new director's most immediate and delicate tasks was to oversee the removal of the dauphin's apartments to the ground floor of the Palace of Versailles, below the Grande Galerie, and organise their re-decoration in time for the dauphin's second marriage. It was during the execution of this programme that the so-called sedition occurred.[33] Although there is no evidence to suggest that the journeymen-painters and sculptors downed tools in order to give greater leverage to their demands, we know that the completion of the new schemes ran two months late, and furthermore, than in the process the painted decoration of the dauphin's *petit cabinet*, which consisted of 'small cartouches and designs [in the manner] of Berain, flowers, birds etc . . .', was spoiled because it was executed in haste before the plaster had had adequate time to dry.[34] It seems likely, therefore, that the journeymen seized this particular opportunity to improve their working conditions in the knowledge that time was of the essence (a royal marriage would not wait), and in the hope that the inexperienced Tournehem, under pressure to demonstrate his fitness for an important administrative post granted through his connection with a not so popular *favorite*, might force a settlement in their favour.

It is surely no coincidence that in the same year Tournehem had to contend with a further revolt – this time from amongst the academicians, and once again over the price paid for works by the royal treasury. Orry's dual role as controller-general and director of the Bâtiments had given him the necessary authority to hold down the prices paid to painters, but once Tournehem took office, the academicians, like their humbler colleagues, saw their chance and grabbed it. Solicited or otherwise, Jean-Marc Nattier received compensation in arrears for his portraits of Mesdames de France executed in 1745 for which the new director judged him to have been insufficiently remunerated.[35] The history painters, ever sensitive to the comparative values given to portraiture and history, and backed by Charles-Antoine Coypel, forcefully requested a rise in the price of overdoors and tapestry cartoons.[36] So successful were they, that the price of Boucher's overdoors, for instance, doubled between 1744, when he executed for 1,200 *livres* three scenes depicting *Venus and Cupid* for Choisy,[37] and 1747, when his *Venus Requesting Arms for Aeneas from Vulcan* (fig. 72) and *The Apotheosis of Aeneas* for the dauphin's apartment fetched 800 *livres* apiece.[38] The decoration of the dauphin's apartment was then right at the centre of bargaining for better piece- *and* wage-rates in the 1740s. As such, it suggests first, that attention to time in labour hinged upon the need to synchronise tasks, and second, that disputes in one trade were likely to set off others in ancillary or related professions.[39] Moreover, Tournehem's statement to the effect that he hoped to promote, 'the good of painting and sculpture' by fixing piece-rates at a level to encourage, 'the King and the Individual . . . to employ those in both [the] genres [of portraiture and history painting] more often',[40] hints that clients were inclined to follow the king's lead in the prices they paid for decoration. Precisely because the rates set for the king's commissions had a currency

72 François Boucher, *Venus Requesting Arms for Aeneas from Vulcan*, 1747. Oil on canvas, 94.5 × 127 cm. Musée du Louvre, Paris.

well beyond their contractual limitation, journeymen logically looked to the workshops engaged in royal work to set a just wage. Sensitivity to the potential of time and place, to the susceptibility to pressure of those in authority and to the effects of particular decisions, was obviously essential to the achievement of favourable terms of employment.

Before moving on to broader questions of artistic authority, one last point should be made about the regulations of corporate discipline. Journeymen in general, and painters and sculptors in particular, resented and resisted the attempts of corporations to monitor their movements and judge their fitness for work through the issue of certificates of leave and, later in the century, the *livret*.[41] In an effort towards greater self-determination the journeymen painters and sculptors, some 200–400 in number, decided in the 1760s to follow the example of journeymen silk-weavers forty years earlier, and, under the protection of the Temple's rights of asylum, formed a confraternity that functioned primarily in the secular world, that is as an employment agency.[42] Rendered efficient by a formal administrative structure and by funds levied on its members, this body arrogated to itself the task of judging the fitness of masters' workshops and reserved the option of boycotting shops that, for whatever reason, did not pass muster. In 1768 specific complaints from the likes of the widow Bardou who had apparently defaulted on important contracts with Mesdames de France and for the decoration of the new hôtel de Saint-Florentin, thanks to the irregularity of her journeymen, prompted the officers of the Académie de Saint-Luc into action.[43] Early on the morning of Monday 8 May 1769, the day after the confraternity's annual feast-day, the Inspecteur de Police, Claude Bourguoin, and the commissioner, René Hughes, proceeded to arrest two *garçons doreurs* and a journeyman-painter – 'the syndics of the so-called *communauté* of journeymen-painters, sculptors and gilders'.[44] These workmen denied, however, that their aims were subversive and maintained that theirs was a confraternity established in good faith, the better to serve God, by honouring one of his saints, and the masters, by furnishing them with journeymen 'of acknowledged skill and irreproachable character'.[45] Notwithstanding the support of some masters, the directors of Saint-Luc and Bourguoin found otherwise. They classed the confraternity a clandestine association 'of secret devotions' bent on countermanding and even replacing the guild's authority; they judged its existence illegal and disbanded its members.[46]

Of more than anecdotal interest, the handling of this case suggests that masters, apparently unwilling to offer their journeymen intimacy and the level of reciprocal obligation it entailed, because to do so would have diminished their commercial competitiveness, were nevertheless equally determined that journeymen should be deprived of alternative sources of solidarity. Alienation brought its own dangers, however, because the increasing detachment of notions of patriarchal authority from the very relationships that gave them life undermined the material purchase of corporate discourse – that is, its capacity to mediate the disparate interests of masters and journeymen – to a point where an alternative form of practice became imaginable; the call for liberty, or free trade, was then made.[47]

ARCHITECTS AND OTHERS: THE AUTHORITY OF DESIGN

If the authority of master-craftsmen proved fragile at times, patrons, designers and co-ordinators of decorative schemes nevertheless continued to engage and deal with trade-workshops as if they were harmonious units of production, eschewing as far as possible all direct involvement in matters of discipline. However, since the tasks of the severally contracted masters required organisation and synchronisation, it was usual for one individual to assume overall managerial responsibility, distribute the necessary contracts or subcontracts, oversee the work and negotiate the settlement of the various *mémoires* or invoices. Contrary to Jaubert's description of the quintessential building-site quoted earlier, there was no self-evident reason why, in the case of decoration, this role should necessarily fall to an architect. Indeed, in the seventeenth century, when textiles dominated interiors, an upholsterer often played the co-ordinating role.[48] However, as decorative priorities shifted from fabrics to panelling, upholsterers experienced a decline in authority. By the end of the century most high-cost schemes had become the responsibility of the architect or entrepreneur-mason to whom the construction or the building had been entrusted.

Financial responsibility and artistic authority might or might not go hand in hand, depending on whether the architect assumed the client's responsibility for subcontracting work to the trades necessary to the project.[49] The monarchy's need constantly to re-issue indictments of fixed contracts, particularly at the turn of the eighteenth century, testifies to their popularity with clients often fearful of the potentially escalating costs of a dispersed labour force of autonomous and self-interested trades.[50] Thus, during the seventeenth and eighteenth centuries many, perhaps even most, architects in fact exercised the functions of both architect and overall entrepreneur. Financial reward, in such cases, was usually drawn from a percentage cut of each of the settled contracts or subcontracts involved in the project. These entrepreneurial architects were notorious for their sharp practice and according to one *Mazarinade*, or more accurately *Mansarade*, the venerated François Mansart's avarice had been such that he demanded fifty per cent of each account; a deduction that the workmen had only been able to meet by substituting substandard materials.[51] It was to put an end to structural failures that might inadvertently result from such malpractice, and in 1722 led to the partial collapse of the cellar vaults at the hôtel d'Aucezune (not to mention the fracturing of retaining walls and flues and the disintegration of panelling), that efforts continued to be made to enforce the ban on these so-called *marchés à forfait*.[52]

However, though architecture remained a commercial enterprise throughout the eighteenth century – speculation in building materials, construction and property lined many architects' pockets[53] – it was pursued with ever more discretion. The foundation of the Académie Royale d'Architecture in 1671 had, it is true, no more than institutionalised codes of practice and royal privileges, but the registration of the Academy's statutes in 1717 led to the transformation of the role of the architect in significant ways. For instance, the statutes expressly discouraged architects from acting as *entrepreneurs* (indeed, by 1735 it formerly prohibited academicians 'de la première classe' from so practising and in 1775 extended the restriction to those of the 'seconde classe') thus redefining the profession of architecture in terms of a legally binding division of responsibility: to the architect went care for the design, to the contractor liability for the finance.[54] Thus, when an architect offered his professional services he was henceforth to be paid differently; sometimes according to number of site-visits. Jean-Baptiste Vautran, for example, visited the site of the hôtel Vatard on the corner of the rues de Cléry and Poissonnière some 1,004 times during the course of its construction in the late 1720s, and was paid 4,000 *livres* for his trouble[55] – or approximately four times as much as the painter Delaistre received for furnishing the painted decoration for the same building ten years later.[56] More usually, the services of these designer-architects were paid by honorarium at the rate of approximately five per cent of total expenditure.[57] If conspicuous opportunities for profit were thus reduced, it should be remembered that most architects would have gained a measure of economic stability long before acceding to membership of the 'première classe', a distinction in any event restricted to the privileged few.[58] What the statutes achieved, then, was not so much a reorganisation of architectural practice, as an adjustment of architectural discourse within which the official and professional image of the architect was substantially altered. Henceforth, the architect's authority was seen to rest not on entrepreneurship but on powers of organisation and, more important still, on the ability to conceive the design of a building in all its parts.[59] It followed, therefore, that draughtsmanship was to play an increasingly significant role in determining the notional limits of authority, a transformation registered by the publication of the first treatises on architectural drawing: Buchotte's, *Les Règles du dessin et du lavis pour les plans particuliers des ouvrages et des bâtiments* (1722) and Dupain de Montesson's *La Science des ombres par rapport au dessin* (1750). Moreover, though the practice of drawing was clearly not exclusive to architecture, definitions of the 'architect' increasingly relied on references to its art. Accordingly, one contemporary writer argued that 'it is he who makes the drawings who orders all the building activity; everyone obeys him as the statutes and regulations of his corporation allow'.[60]

The architect was, indeed, by no means singularly skilled as a draughtsman. The apprenticeships of many eighteenth-century trades involved the transmission of the rudiments of technical drawing; indeed, attendance at a drawing-class was not uncommonly advanced by journeymen as a legitimate excuse for their congregation.[61] Moreover, design seems to have constituted a stage preparatory to the execution of a conspicuously wide range of artisanal practices, a liminal phase between conception and execution given particularly vivid description in Jacques-Louis Ménétra's journal. In the summer of 1764 Ménétra and fellow-glazier La Brie were engaged by a certain Elophe to produce and install stained-glass windows for the cloisters of the Petits-Pères, in the place des Victoires. 'I drew a window with a border', begins Ménétra,

> it suited the boss [but] the Brie fellow wanted the border done differently   I drew it on the ground in the cloister with white chalk   I made some remarks to him he erased part of what I had just drawn   I shoved him he shoved me back and there we were going at it when several fathers arrived along with our boss   They pulled us apart   I showed what I had done   It was approved   One father said they ought to get two other *companions*   M Elophe said that we were the *companions* most skilled at this kind of work   I said Anybody who wants to do it can do it since the father said that I am leaving   The fathers stopped me   The boss begged me   They reconciled the two of us . . . The job was done.[62]

How clearly this passage disrupts the comfortable notion of *disegno* as a polite art. Ménétra's drawings were primarily demonstrative; they were produced at his boss's request and required the latter's validation. Masons, carpenters, joiners, ornamental sculptors and painters, like glaziers, executed drawings of the same generic type – that is to say drawings for application in the medium specific to their trade, a point

apparently endorsed by the stocks of motifs and projects that have survived from Pineau's workshop and those listed in Antoine-François Vassé's inventory.[63] By comparison, architects' drawings were intentionally prescriptive. The plans, elevations and sections they elaborated, not to mention the more specific and detailed projections of interiors drawn up in their offices,[64] were described by Jacques-François Blondel as forms of communication,[65] forms that, in principle, determined the work of others. Indeed, such drawings were sometimes attached to the notarised cost-estimates passed between parties before a commission was agreed.[66] For instance, to the *devis* for the construction of the hôtel de Chanac de Pompadour (1704) were attached twenty-seven drawings by the architect Pierre-Alexis Delamair, to which the entrepreneur, mason, carpenters, marble-cutters, joiners and sculptors were expressly required to conform.[67] Likewise, in 1749, the architect Pierre-Noël Rousset provided models not only for sculptural elements of the interior decoration of the hôtel Meulan, but also for the console tables (fig. 73) that the wood-carver, Guillaume Dupré, was contracted to execute, presumably for its most lavish reception rooms.[68] The delegative function of drawings of this kind is particularly conspicuous in instances such as a design attributed to Oppenord, possibly for a chimney-mantle (fig. 74), where colour-coding – pink for a painting and blue for a mirror – was used as a shorthand means of indicating the position of certain goods and, thus, the exact areas of delegated responsibility.

Ménétra's account suggested that the distinction bewteen the architect's drawings and those of other craftsmen might perhaps be grasped from the artisan's custom of executing his on the very materials he intended to fashion, or on conveniently adjacent surfaces, rather than committing the ideas to paper.[69] Such drawings provided guidelines for his tools and a point of departure that could be verified by the architect before materials had been irrevocably committed. The *devis* drawn up in 1723 for the sculpted decoration of the

73 Pierre-Noël Rousset, design for a console table, 1749. Pen and ink on paper, 24 × 36.5 cm. Archives Nationales, Paris.

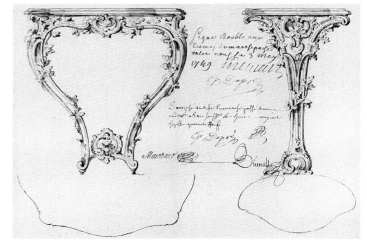

74 Gilles-Marie Oppenord (attributed to), alternative designs for a chimney-mantle, *c*.1740. Pen, brush, ink, watercolour and graphite on paper, 30.5 × 13.5 cm. Cooper-Hewitt, National Design Museum, New York. Gift of the Council.

75   Nicolas Pineau and workshop, design for a pier-glass frame, *c*.1738–40. Pen and ink over pencil on paper, 109 × 146.5 cm. Musée des Arts Décoratifs, Paris.

hôtel Peyrenc de Moras in the place Louis-le-Grand (now place Vendôme) charged the sculptors Degoullons and Legoupil to execute their work in conformity with 'the small-scale drawings provided'.[70] They were instructed, moreover, first to re-draw the designs to scale on the walls of the designated rooms so that the architect might judge the overall effect, and then to copy them a second time upon paper of identical size in order, presumably, that once approved by Jacques V Gabriel, the contours might be pricked for transfer on to prepared panels. Working cartoons of this kind rarely survive, not least because the black powdered chalk traditionally rubbed through the perforations could leave the patterns defaced. However, a design for the upper section of a mirror (fig. 75) from Pineau's workshop, executed on no less than five separate sheets pasted together, and a drawing by Claude III Audran for the wall decoration of the *salle des bains* at Bercy (fig. 76) testify to their use by a broad range of decorators working in a variety of media.[71]

Recently, charcoal drawings like those mentioned in the Peyrenc de Moras contract have come to light behind the panelling, on the masonry walls of the former hôtels Angran de Fonspertius, d'Orrouer and de Soubise, and in the Cabinet de la Dauphine at Versailles.[72] Although, in most instances, these were the detailed designs performed to the architect's purpose by would-be executants of a three-dimensional medium, in the case of the choir-stalls for the Jacobins in the rue Saint-Dominique, it was the architect, Denis Jossenay, who sketched the overall designs on the walls for the sculptor, François Roumier, to follow.[73] Given the managerial function of many such architectural drawings, they tended to be schematic and primarily concerned the general arrangement and articulation of the composition. The detail was left to be elaborated by panel-sculptors during the course of execution. Consequently, on some occasions sculptors were able to exploit the imprecision of the guidelines issued, and develop a scheme to their own artistic and financial advantage. At the Jacobins, for instance, Roumier wilfully flouted the architect's directives, ignored the commission's economic constraints and executed such extravagant trophies for the choir-stalls that he had to sue for payment.[74] But when accused, during the consequent court case, of having failed to conform to the agreed designs, Roumier argued that trophies were the kind of works, 'of which the elaboration is ordinarily left to the taste of the workman who knows how to select and compose them, according to the requirements of the space in which they . . . [are to be] placed'. Given this custom, he maintained that he could not be charged with having exceeded his brief.[75] Thus, in the absence of strict supervision and protected by the alibi of traditional practice, Roumier executed trophies to the value of 400 *livres* apiece in place of those for which an allocation of 100 *livres* had been made in the original 1723 specification.[76]

In addition to the immediate financial gain Roumier hoped to make by such licence, he was alive to the long-term value of the sight. Churches like the Jacobins offered ideal public spaces in which talents might be advertised, reputations established and thus, future commissions secured. Indeed, so keen was Roumier to exploit even the scandalous notoriety of the court case, that he catered for those who failed to cross the threshold of the Jacobins by publishing etchings of his trophies (figs 77 and 78) with yet more variations. Assuming Roumier's behaviour not to have been particularly unusual, it would seem to follow that sites of decoration were often fraught with tension as each contractor sought to negotiate or appropriate the most advantageous share of the programme. Indeed, Roumier had, according to the Dominicans at the Jacobins, not just multiplied his efforts in his allocated domain but encroached on the territory of others by producing and installing 'bas-relief sculpture stretching from the Choir-stalls to the foot of the High-Altar, even though the monks had intended that paintings should be placed there, paintings which had already been executed by one of the brothers of the monastery with all the taste for which he is known'.[77] Moreover, the actual pushing and shoving that broke out between Ménétra and La Brie over the design for the Discalced Augustinians' cloister windows were most likely endemic to situations of this kind where, despite growing optimism about the technical efficacy of geometry and mathematics, design was incapable of exactly determining the process of construction and decoration in advance.

If Michel Frémin, in his *Mémoires critiques sur l'architecture* (1702) expressed profound misgivings about the seductive character of much so-called architectural drawing, thereby suggesting an understanding on his part of design's proper use as a means of technical control, it was not until the nineteenth century that Jean Rondelet was able, with the application of Gaspard Monge's descriptive geometry, to transform architectural drawings from mimetic representations into instructions capable of compelling exact compliance from a labour force.[78] Thus, during the eighteenth century scarcely any functional distinction separated the kinds of drawings offered to patrons

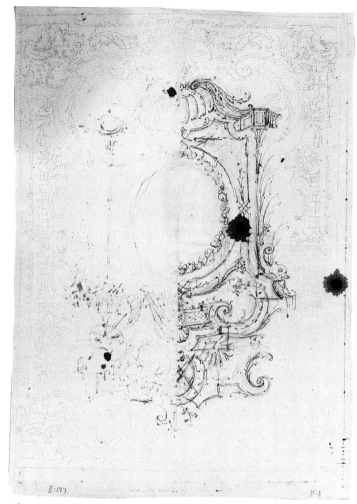

76 Claude III Audran, design for a wall decoration at the 'baths' of the château de Bercy, *c.*1715. Pen and ink over pencil on paper, 397 × 262 cm. Nationalmuseum, Stockholm.

and clients and those from which executants were supposed to proceed.[79] Often exquisitely coloured, perspectively drawn and with shadows judiciously cast to create a sense of atmosphere, these protean designs contained aesthetic information in marked excess of their function as patterns or instructions. Indeed, the pleasure to be derived from the complex mixture and handling of the graphic media (graphite, pen and ink, wash, watercolour) often negated the drawing's capacity to communicate quantitative information. Moreover, so long as a method for systematically reducing three-dimensional projections to the plane by means of an alternative and precise technique continued to evade even those most committed to establishing abstract and mathematical solutions to the practical problems of construction and decoration,[80] the authority of the architect's designs remained broadly akin to that of the history painter's. That is to say, that their power was poetic rather than technical and consisted in a privileged understanding of the aesthetic and social content of built forms.[81] Thus, even for the ostensibly enlightened generation after Claude

77 and 78 François Roumier, trophies designed for the choir-stalls at the Jacobins, *c*.1725. Etching.

Perrault (for which the symbolic, not to say sacred, value of number in determining ideal proportion was little more that the outcome of abitrary custom) the architect's tools remained active principles of the kind that had enabled Bernard Palissy in the sixteenth century to write a midnight conversation between a compass, a ruler, a plummet, a level, an astrolabe and a fixed and an adjustable triangle; a conversation in which the metaphorical significance of each instrument clearly overrides its functional purpose.[82] Unlike Jean-Jacques Lequeu's 1782 illustration of many of the same instruments for his unpublished *Architecture civile* (fig. 79) in which the compass, for instance, lies closed and idle on the edge of the draughtsman's bench, Palissy's open compass played centre-stage in a wider universe because it was responsible for 'conducting the measure of *all* things', and more importantly because it embodied the principle of good and rational conduct such that 'Men without compass are admonished, and asked to live according to its rule'.[83]

So long as the architect's domination of practice was guaranteed materially there was perhaps little reason for geometry and architectural design to develop from essentially autonomous and representational fields of signification, which building merely sought to approximate, into graphic tools capable of intervention in the very processes of construction. It seems scarcely coincidental that precisely at the time when the government was re-issuing and enforcing its ban on fixed contracts, thereby weakening the architect's entrepreneurial purchase, many of those most involved in the large urban developments of the day, such as Pierre Bullet, were attempting to functionalise geometry in order to deploy more sophisticated and accurate systems of quantity surveying and provide ready solutions to all manner of stereotomic and constructional problems.[84] In partial acknowledgement of the impossibility of calculating and transmitting the necessary information on paper, and in the local Euclidean terms available to him, Bullet insisted on practical experience as a prerequisite for good and sound architecture.[85] Indeed, for lack of the kind of scientific progress he sought, many of the arts of construction and decoration remained, throughout the eighteenth century, broadly empirical skills, or a collection of irreducible 'secrets' and knacks possessed by the workforce rather than by the architect or *entrepreneur*.[86] This explains why, for example, Elophe countermanded the dismissal of Ménétra and La Brie. He understood, where the Fathers did not, that light years separated design from execution and had quite rightly selected his workmen for their skills as *glaziers*. It seems, therefore, that

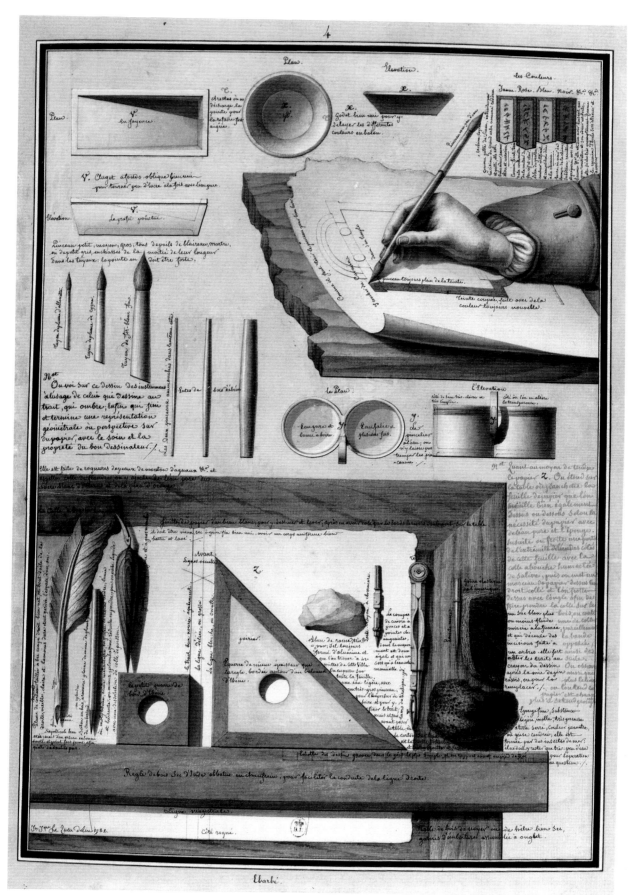

79   Jean-Jacques Lequeu, *The Architect's Drawing Instruments*, 1782. Pen, ink, wash and watercolour, 43.8 × 29.5 cm. Cabinet des Estampes, Bibliothèque Nationale, Paris.

the architect's ability to engage a workforce appropriately skilled for the job in hand, and his capacity, moreover, to communicate his requirements in the particular and colloquial jargon of the trades, were likely to be as, if not more significant in determining the desired result than his facility as a draughtsman. Indeed, André Félibien regarded nothing more important than learning the 'language' of the trades, because failure to converse invariably resulted in failure to realise.[87] Thus, if architectural discourse increasingly invoked the authority of drawing, in practice the architect's design was more effectively exacted in words.[88]

Despite this apparently obvious contradiction, the challenges most frequently levelled at the architect's authority were phrased within the terms of the discourse itself. Consequently, particular architects were singled out for disqualification on the grounds that they were incompetent draughtsmen. So inept was François Mansart apparently, that he was accused of fraudulently claiming the designs of others as his own.[89] There was similar scepticism about Jules Hardouin Mansart's ability to draw.[90] Moreover, sustained by the conviction that Jacques V Gabriel was, 'incapable of drawing the smallest scrap of ornament', Jean-Pierre Mariette no doubt felt justified in voicing his outrage that such a man had been charged with 'judging the works of *artists* placed under him'.[91] Significantly, Roubo qualified his injunction to joiners that they work to architects's models by adding,

> When I say that one should follow the tracings provided by Architects, it is only on condition that these drawings contain all the information peculiar to their function, which is sometimes very difficult to find, experience providing as it does, daily evidence that a good many of the people who dub themselves Architects possess only the title which they dishonour . . .[92]

Roubo's comment is representative of the widespread belief that the title 'architect' was being usurped by all manner of artisans, whose sole qualification was a smattering of design. Roland de Virloys, for instance, remarked that 'Today, no sooner can a man draw a little than he purports to be an architect; such temerity is not even beyond Surveyors, Joiners and other Workmen of that ilk'.[93]

To a certain extent the criticism levelled at such would-be architects was typical of a corporate mentality that not only divided workers into butchers, bakers and candlestick-makers but assumed such complete identification between artists and their trades — to the point, indeed, that in a certain tradition of visual imagery tradesmen's tools and materials invaded their very bodies (fig. 80) — that changes in profession appeared heretical.[94] So, for instance, when in 1708 Thomas Germain presented trophy designs for the choir-stalls of Notre-Dame he faced opposition not from the architect, Hardouin Mansart, but from the 'corporation of sculptors' who complained that 'he wanted to involve himself in a work which did not appear to be within his professional domain'.[95] In essence, these were

80   Nicolas II de Larmessin, *An Architect's Costume*, 1695. Engraving and etching.

disputes over commercial territory rather than arguments about social mobility. However, by the late 1740s, and in the context of increasing criticism of the rococo, such extra-curricular activities, which seemingly culminated in Meissonnier's projects for Saint-Sulpice[96] and Germain's designs for Saint-Louis-du-Louvre,[97] were damned as adventurous requisitions by ambitious artisans determined to upstage architects in their own professional sphere.

It would be a mistake to assume, however, that the discourse on drawing was always progressive and that disputes about it were invariably limited to issues of entitlement. A different tradition was perpetuated by one of Jacques Lagniet's illustrated proverbs, entitled *He Who Builds Lies* (fig. 81), a tradition hostile to the very notion of design as an intrinsically elevated and authoritative skill. In the foreground of the image sits an architect holding in his left hand a design, the product of the ruler and compass he holds in his right — the latter open to the heavens signifying his ingestion of theory. In the background, meanwhile, four men are depicted engaged on the construction of a building, apparently analogous to the one represented on the architect's paper. The immediate logic

Il nest pas au bout de ses deseins. tous les esprits ne sont pas dans une teste. Il ne fault pas bastir sur l'heritage d'autrui

60

Il fait des chasteaux en Espagne.

Il a longe un Col de grue

Cela ua par compas et par mesure

Le papier souffre tout

Suis a un coup de ——

Il se trompe a son calcul

Il met toute pierre en œuure

Il uit de regle

Qui bastit ment.   Il na pas bien pris ses mesures.
Il a pris un point trop hault, il ny trouuera pas son   conte.

I.Lagniet ex.

81   Jacques Lagniet, *He Who Builds Lies*, c.1657. Engraving. From *Plus Illustres proverbes*, c.1657, plate 60.

and relative priorities enmeshed in this spatial arrangement of foreground and background and which locates idea before object and artist before artisan seem, on closer examination, undermined at every turn by the texts which overlie and intersect with the composition and by the more subtle visual qualities of the representation itself. First, the punning title,

'Qui bastit-ment', discovers the lie at the heart of an authorial claim predicated on imagination rather than manufacture. The futility and extravagance of the intellectual exercise and the consequently excessive circulation of paper is then suggested by the slogan, 'He builds castles in the air'.[98] Meanwhile, the texts that supplement the title, together with the accompanying header and marginalia insist upon the frequent errors suffered by abstract, graphic calculation and denigrate dependence on an aged Vitruvian heritage.[99] By contrast, the traditions of the masons who 'live' rather than apply the rules of their art, are, by implication, to be found forever in the present and are put to work with such economy that nothing goes to waste.[100] The superfluity of success, expressed by the architect's marked sartorial splendour, ironically counterpoints the implied superfluity of his profession, barely emergent from error and with its back firmly turned against practice.

In the eighteenth century the hostility engendered by the subordination of the construction site to the pretensions of the architect's *cabinet* found expression in the sneering songs of protesting construction workers. In one song, current in the 1720s, labourers chanted their resentment at the humiliation of working for jumped-up masons whose science amounted to no more than the ability 'to reason/Or scribble on paper', so-called skills, for which armchair architects are unjustly rewarded with all the luxuries of a standard of living evoked by 'white bread', while the workers have to make do with the attendant miseries of 'brown'.[101] Moreover, it should be noted that the song was contemptuous not just of the 'arts' of drawing and abstract thought, but of those who sought, above all, to better themselves by recourse to them. An image such as Nicolas Guérard's *The Artisan Pulls the Devil by the Tail* (fig. 82) in which honour no less than profit is exposed as a reward of sin, is a reminder that eighteenth-century artisanal culture was still in some respects profoundly marked by a Christian tradition that identified work as Adam's curse, or the means by which mankind had to accomplish its spiritual (not its material) salvation.[102] There was, therefore, something immoral as well as pretentious about arts which, like design, allowed individuals to assume a status that was not actually theirs.

Meanwhile, if events such as the collapse of Oppenord's gallery at the hôtel Crozat[103] continued to spread scepticism about 'intellectual' qualifications, in the long run many artisans in the luxury trades, *pace* Guérard, were ultimately to find the language of art, or more specifically that dimension of its discourse that was compatible with natural law, a useful resource in professional advancement. Eighteenth-century law, which judged labour a form of property and upheld the individual's right to dispose of that 'property' at will, allowed appeals to natural rights in such cases where the plaintiffs could argue that the corporations to which they had ceded them, in exhange for civil rights, had abused their custodial function.[104] A 'liberal' art in this sense was the property of a person who exercised a natural rather than a civil right, and to

82 Nicolas Guérard, *The Artisan Pulls the Devil by the Tail*, c.1700. Engraving.

that extent 'art' and 'art theory' were frequently invoked in trade disputes and disquisitions on the mechanical arts to criticise the constraints and regulations to which individuals wished not to conform.[105] For instance (and here we return to the case for liberalism referred to earlier), the journeymen-painters and sculptors, in the appeal against the regulations introduced in 1747 to fix the terms of their employment, argued that,

it is not the same for Painters and Sculptors as for other professions, that this profession being an *Art* the Journeymen who exercise it are persons of skill distinguished by merit who cannot be confused and subjected to the same laws as Journeymen in other trades of the grossest nature.[106]

And they claimed, moreover, that given the 'artistic' demands of the work concerned, they could not be expected to have 'their attention stretched' over a working day of eleven and a half hours.[107] In this case appeals to art and the natural rights it entailed, failed to convince the court, no doubt because the directors of the corporation were able to defeat such claims by offering a definition of art to which the work of none of the *compagnons* conformed: art as a form of figurative representation.[108]

However, in the 1760s the capital's hairdressers more successfully exploited the potential of art theory in a protracted lawsuit with the wig-makers which extended into the following decade.[109] With the aim of avoiding the jurisdiction of the *maîtres-perruquiers*, the hairdressers argued in their memoranda that theirs was an art analogous to poetry, painting and sculpture. Their descriptions of hairdressing were saturated with references and allusions to chiaroscuro, composition, colour, expression, the hierarchy of genres, rules of decorum and the 'genius' apparently necessary for a successful result, in implicit contrast to the 'purely manual practice' of the wig-makers.[110] Supported by elegant Parisian society, the hairdressers finally won their case, and a decree issued at Versailles and registered by the Parlement in 1776 gave them a degree of freedom to practise undisturbed in the capital.[111] Artisans, it seems, willingly became turncoats in the proverbial and ideological battle against the supremacy of design (illustrated by Lagniet) when appeals to 'art' were seen actually and significantly to renegotiate structures of authority in their favour. In the light of frequent and instrumental elision of art and natural rights, it is perhaps not so surprising that the Académie Royale de Peinture et de Sculpture constantly encountered difficulties in establishing a normative distinction between its activities and members, and those of the guilds, particularly the Académie de Saint-Luc.

If journeymen house-painters and hairdressers could materially improve their relationship to power through appeals to art, representational painters must have been still better placed to approach and possibly challenge the apparent omniscience of the architect in matters of decoration. Draughtsmanship was as fundamental to their mimetic projects as it was to the architect's constructional purpose. In both professions, drawing implied an ability to rationalise and schematise visual perception. Moreover, if the painter's task did not necessarily entail authority over others it by no means precluded it. Indeed, in an effort to improve the quality of the Gobelins' tapestries, Charles-Antoine Coypel chose, in 1738, personally to supervise the weaving of his series, *Rinaldo and Armida*.[112] In that same year he paid at least twelve visits to the firm and insisted that work be re-woven if he found it incommensurate with the effect he had intended or with the character of the cartoons he had supplied. He accomplished the supervisory task without difficulty; he noted that in the workshops, 'they are transported {with joy} when I am satisfied and they protest that it will be made good when I criticise'.[113] The weavers, particularly those who operated the prestigious, high-warp looms, had traditionally enjoyed considerable control of the interpretation of designs, and encroachments on their artistic independence were generally registered much less politely than Coypel's experience would seem to suggest. At Beauvais, for instance, Jean-Baptiste Oudry met with outright hostility when, from 1733, he contrived systematically to dispossess the weavers of as much of the decision-making process as possible.[114] Choices of tone, colour and materials, and questions of interpretation in the transposition of a design from paint to woven-cloth were, henceforth, the privileged territory of the painter-designer, an abrogation of power no less painful for the weavers for having been perpetrated by particular men rather than by the special-purpose machines of a future industrial era.

On other occasions painters oversaw collaborative schemes. As noted in chapter 1, Audran co-ordinated the activities of painters and sculptors necessary to the realisation of his arabesque decorations; Brunetti apparently acted likewise in respect of his perspectives; François Le Moyne engaged Jacques-Charles Dutillieu to execute the flower painting for his ceiling in the Salon d'Hercule at Versailles.[115] Elsewhere, however, painters found themselves in a less enviable position. Architects sometimes subcontracted work to painters – this was probably the case at the hôtel Peyrenc de Moras where Jacques V Gabriel engaged Cassinet, an artist styled 'painter at the Louvre and of the said Gabriel', to execute the overdoors and other decorative paintings for the *grands appartements*[116] – or alternatively placed them under their direct control through the *devis*. Pierre Levé, the architect responsible for the designs of every feature (from the balconies to the chimney-pieces) of an hôtel in the cour des Chiens, also produced 'projects for the paintings', that were to be executed by 'MM Vernansal and Justina, painters'.[117] Likewise, the history painter and academician, Auger Lucas, was charged by the 'architect' Meissonnier to execute from supplied designs, four mythological compositions subsequently inserted into the panelling of the Cabinet Bielenski, although the silversmith appears to have reserved for his own talents the realisation of the ceiling depicting *Apollo on his Chariot*, known today from a gouache drawing (fig. 83) at the Cooper Hewitt.[118] Thus, although Nicolas Pineau noted on a design for the decoration of the comtesse de Midelbourg's *salon* that he could not finalise the details of the chimney-piece until the painting for it had been executed to scale,[119] it seems likely that as the designs for *lambris* evolved into increasingly intricate patterns and the shape of overdoors became ever more fanciful,[120] painters more usually found themselves at the mercy of panel sculptors – an inversion of status that they ultimately found intolerable.[121]

The attention that has recently been given to the emergence of the designer in the eighteenth century,[122] a person who, by definition, devised projects for others to execute and, in many instances, an individual with a painter's training, has tended to overshadow the fact that, by contrast with the seventeenth century, painters of the new *siècle* rarely grasped control of the conception, still less the practical organisation of complete decorative schemes. In the context of the silk, tapestry, printed-textile and wallpaper industries, dependent on the manifold but comparatively unproblematic techniques of two-dimensional pattern-making, designers certainly enjoyed a position surpassed only by the *entrepreneurs* themselves,[123] but

83 Juste-Aurèle Meissonnier, *Apollo on his Chariot*, design for the ceiling of the Cabinet Bielenski, *c.*1736. Pen, ink, watercolour, gouache, gold paint over black chalk on paper, 32.1 × 32 cm. Cooper-Hewitt, National Design Museum, New York.

on location painters experienced an erosion of their prestige and watched the extent of their contribution to decoration contract. Architects were often blamed for this state of affairs; indeed, in the seventeenth century painters already suspected architects of deliberately diminishing their role. For example, François Mansart was accused of inventing ceiling- and wall-ornament – 'Goli-fichets' and 'spiders' webs' – for the express purpose of minimising the painter's contribution.[124] Without

wishing to anticipate later discussion, it should be noted that many of the criticisms about decoration put forward by La Font de Saint Yenne and others in the 1740s, merely resurrected a well-worn – and, as seen, by no means unique – grievance on the part of painters; namely, that in the field of decoration painters were awarded an insufficient proportion of any commission and experienced a shameful lack of artistic control.

From the perspective of the makers of decoration, then, the meaning of work, articulated most tangibly by the character and quality of the creations that resulted from it, overridingly concerned the issue of authority: power to innovate within the parameters of standard practice (wax-based distemper paint, flock and printed wallpaper, *vernis Martin*, plaster ornament, fool's gold); control of the means of production (the relationship between masters and journeymen, entrepreneurs and workers, illustrated by the complex businesses of sculptors like Jules Degoullons or painters like Claude III Audran); and finally, possession and management of cultural capital (design in the dual sense of the intention to create and the means of securing that objective via professional expertise). The spaces of production were thus highly sensible of the dynamics of trade, and the artist's or artisan's appreciation of a rococo interior entailed, among other things, savouring the distance between expectation (determined by the proscriptions of conventional practice) and result (achieved, sometimes, by spirited innovations in technique or by impertinent excesses in design — Roumier's trophies, Meissonnier's *cabinets*). That meaningful gap opened up because the co-ordination of work on eighteenth-century building sites was not entirely foreseeable, owing to the fragility of the architect's authority and his inability to commodify labour into predictable and proscriptable services franchised for the job in mind. There was no resisting the ambitions of the trades, however sedulously plans and contracts were drawn up. Rococo interiors were thus original twice over, first by virtue of their composition and by consequence of the settlement of competing claims that brought them to life.

PART II

Theatres of Distinction

LE SEIGNEUR ET LA DAME DE COUR.

On qualifie du nom de Seigneur, les personnes de haute naissance, ou celles qui sont revetus des plus hautes dignités de l'etat ; pour l'ordinaire ils sont décorés de l'Ordre de leur Souverain ; il n'appartient qu'à eux d'etre très recherchés dans leurs ajustemens ; les talons rouges qu'ils portent sont la marque de leur noblesse et annoncent qu'ils sont toujours prets à fouler aux pieds les ennemis de l'Etat. Il faut distinguer du Seigneur, l'homme riche et fat qui par des dehors trompeurs cherche à surprendre le peuple toujours ebloui par l'éclat d'un habit magnifique, sans cesse on le voit ramper auprès des gens en place pour en obtenir quelque marque de distinction ; il n'est point de souplesses et d'intrigues qu'il ne se suggere pour venir à ses fins, et scait bien se vanger sur ses Vassaux des mortifications qu'il reçoit.

On entend par Dame de cour, une Femme de haute consideration, attachée à la Reine ou à quelque Princesse ; elle est toujours obligée de paroitre dans l'éclat le plus brillant, les etoffes les plus riches, l'Or, les pierreries, les Equipages les plus elegants sont de son apanage, on la distingue aisément à son air, de ces Coquettes qui la copient et même la surpassent quelquefois, la Coefure de ces dernieres varie à l'excès, tantôt elle est haute, tantôt basse ; aujourdhui en avant, demain en arriere ; on voit construit sur leur têtes des compartimens de jardins à fleurs et à fruits ; les plumes, simbole de la legereté, n'y sont point epargnée surtout dans ces derniers tems, elles ne pouvoient faire un meilleur choix pour exprimer leur vrai caractere ; enfin leur toilette est une vraie etude, on pourroit faire un assés gros Dictionnaire des mots employés pour designer chaque chose qui sert à leurs parures.

85   *A Lady and Gentleman of the Court*, 1776. Etching. From Charles Le Père and Pierre-Michel Avaulez, *Les Costumes françoises*, 1776, plate 1.

4

The Languages of Estates
and the Logic of Decoration

There is nothing original in the belief that people reciprocally interpret objects in terms of themselves – their gender, family, station, fortune – and themselves in terms of objects – skirts, castles, coats-of-arms and coronets.[1] Indeed, the notion that consumer choices articulate certain social imperatives was probably more keenly felt during the *ancien régime* than it is in post-modern society. Today we are apt to view modes of expenditure as commensurate with levels of wealth rather than position or status, and to interpret choices of goods in terms of the satisfaction they may offer to personal and psychological needs rather than to social ones. Such a perception of consumer patterns was largely alien to eighteenth-century society. For the *ancien régime*, consumption in its widest sense was not a matter of personal and private gratification but a public act of social responsibility; public because it offered itself to the scrutiny, judgement and even regulation of society; social because it customarily conformed to collectively arbitrated standards. Consequently, expenditure was rarely discussed either in terms of exchange, or in the context of the market, but instead, as a form of representation or performance that occurred with the use of marketable items, certainly, but in a place utterly distinct from the world of commerce. Thus consumption, far from standing outside the ethical order, in a bloodless sphere of logic and calculus, in fact inhabited one of its many mansions. Indeed, it is in the book 'Of Morals' in the *Traité de police* (1705–38), that Nicolas Delamare's discussion of consumption and the legal constraints within which it was necessarily practiced initially proceeds.

APPEARANCES

Delamare prefaced the history of sumptuary law, that is law regulating private expenditure, with a general discussion of luxury, in which he described and categorised consumer behaviour as either prodigal, magnificent, thrifty or modest.[2] However, he did not so much define these terms as string them out along an axis, at the extremities of which he placed two vices: prodigality and (perhaps unexpectedly) thrift. Apparent opposites, Delamare chose to emphasise their similarities. Both, he claimed, were unnatural, irrational and excessive responses prompted by vanity and pride.[3] Meanwhile, within their limits, he located two consumer virtues, magnificence and modesty, thereby implicitly investing prodigality and thrift with absolute and immutable force. The ethical stability of the last pair was, however, almost immediately compromised by the introduction of a third element to the equation: social structure. Social structure, or more specifically the categories of individuals that made up social structure, were the referents by which consumer virtues were defined. At this point, therefore, consumption lost its status as an autonomous sphere, governed by precise and universal moral codes, and was inserted into a particular social arena where norms were qualified by types of people. Magnificence, it appeared, 'was appropriate only to Princes and the Grandees of the earth', and it was distinct from prodigality in that 'it never departs from upright reason and the rules of decorum'.[4] Indeed, it was precisely because magnificence was the exclusive province of the great, that Madeleine de Scudéry argued that it should not be termed a virtue at all (virtues being universally attainable), but 'une qualité Héroique'.[5] Magnificence, therefore, defined the type of expenditure performed by princes, and *les grands*, just as modesty defined the type of expenditure practised by *les particuliers*.[6] The definitions of magnificence and modesty were, in short, little more than the definitions of those who claimed the right to exercise them, and their actions were virtuous in so far as society sanctioned those claims.

It should be clear that prodigality and thrift were not so much sins as social transgressions. They occurred at that point where expenditure was no longer commensurate with status. Since a prince was expected to be liberal, he could scarcely be prodigal, only thrifty, and since the commonality was expected to labour it could only be prodigal and not thrifty. The polar opposites were not therefore prodigality and thrift, but magnificence and thrift, prodigality and modesty. And it was entirely possible for magnificence and prodigality – or thrift and modesty – to correspond to identical levels of expenditure because meaning accompanied not real levels of expenditure, but socially related ones.

Delamare did not suggest that consumption reflected social status – it clearly did not, since there were prodigal and thrifty spenders – nor did he suggest that it should. The relationship between spending and spenders which he advanced was rather more complex, and to describe it he used a functional not a reflexive idiom. He argued that the *éclat* of grandees was 'necessary *to sustain* the rank of their birth, [and] *to imprint* respect on the People'.[7] The claim could be interpreted as a mystification of élite consumer prerogatives, however, if all that was required was greater opportunity for the dominant class to spend, their economic supremacy would have been sufficient to ensure it.[8] And if that supremacy was not individually theirs, attention would, in all likelihood, have been focused on how best to achieve it and not on consumer choices. Yet what is distinctive of much eighteenth-century 'economic' literature is its preoccupation with spending rather than earning.[9] For Delamare, it was not that consumption sustained rank in any mechanistic sense, but that it communicated, proclaimed and even celebrated its presence. Moreover, his task was to safeguard the truthfulness of this rhetoric by enforcing those laws that proscribed the use of certain things by certain people.[10] Viewed from this perspective, the sumptuary laws appeared not aggressive (that is to say, as legislation designed to wrest consumer privileges for the élite) so much as defensive. They operated to prevent the drift or devaluation of consumer currency, and thereby to protect the perceptual boundaries of rank.

In his role as Lieutenant de Police, Delamare was, of course, exceptionally concerned with the legibility of society, and sumptuary laws provided, in theory at least, a means by which to throw into greater relief the contours of social identity. In practice, however, consumer choices were regulated far more despotically and finely by the unwritten and aestheticised rules of decorum or propriety, than they were by the crude coerciveness of the law.[11] The rules of *bienséance* or decorum extended to the furthest outposts of social life, giving form and colour not only to behaviour and appearance but to property. In architecture, it demanded, according to one theorist,

> that an edifice have neither more nor less magnificence than is due to its purpose; that is to say, that the decoration of buildings should not be arbitrary, that it must always be in proportion to the rank and station of those who live in them . . .[12]

In virtual illustration of this point, the abbé Cordemoy argued that 'it would be contrary to good sense, for example, that magnificent and well formed porticoes should reign the length of markets and butchers's shops, or that superb vestibules or *salons* should announce society into tradesmen's premises'.[13] Architectural excellence thus resided, at least in part, in the match between social function and appropriate form. Indeed,

Jacques-François Blondel's concept of beauty was in many ways comparable to Delamare's 'magnificence', for though Blondel claimed that beauty could not exist without simplicity, it was not 'that poor, wretched and indigent simplicity, which revolts and repells' (the equivalent of Delamare's thrift), but the kind of simplicity, 'which puts each thing in its place and removes all which is not appropriate to the thing'.[14] Likewise, to give a final example, the abbé Laugier argued that 'a beautiful building . . . [is] one which relative to circumstances, has all the beauty which is appropriate to it and nothing more'.[15]

But if architectural treatises perennially invoked *bienséance* and defined it with condensed precision, they rarely itemised the details of its rulings. Decorum belonged germinally to the oral culture of the court and noble society and had been introduced into printed, architectural discourse only in the mid-seventeenth century.[16] The orality of decorum was inseparable from its function to unite those of a common status because its judgements were communicated through observation and practice, through 'being there', rather than at third hand. Indeed, the reconstitution of custom in a text had a distancing effect, and that which was experienced in daily life as natural, tended to become 'other' on the page: quaint, exotic, absurd. *Bienséances* in the plural were, therefore, rarely exposed to the additional dangers of print until well after the relationship between appearance and status had already become strained and self-conscious. The publishers Le Père and Avaulez, for instance, issued a series of ten engravings entitled *Les Costumes françoises* or *The different Estates of the Realm with the Dress appropriate to each Estate* (1776) (see fig. 85), of interest historically because of the 'moral and critical reflections' that accompany the plates and that ostensibly clarify the relationship between status and dress.[17] Yet ironically, the need for such exegesis not only registered the extent to which the power of sartorial representation had already withered under the pressure of exceptions, but also contributed to the system's demise by heightening the reader's sense of exclusion, as if the image belonged to history rather than actuality.

Granted decorum's lack of autonomy, its inseparability from action, it is not altogether surprising that it failed to become fully integrated into professional architectural discourse. Those who made most persuasive and assured use of the notion, were, indeed, not architects but men of letters and clergymen, such as Cordemoy and Laugier; men used to discoursing on architecture to, or perhaps even on behalf of, a polite audience. The literature of these writers, in marked contrast to the practical and commercial preoccupations of those such as Bullet and Amédée-François Frézier, focused on the pleasure of architecture, on the commodity or convenience of distribution, on the metaphorical and mimetic properties of forms and on the poetic values of proportion.[18] Moreover, the extent to which the nobility implicitly perceived this 'Vitruvian discourse', as Joseph Rykwert has christened it,[19] and the whole body of the classical tradition as peculiarly theirs, is suggested in a letter by the marquis de Lassay:

> I find all constraint, all subservience insupportable; the very slightest is painful; I *use* a Doctor, a Lawyer, an Architect as a *tool*; and for nothing would I suffer that they exert the least authority over me; I always reserve the right to judge whether that they tell me is good or bad.[20]

In the same spirit, Antoine-François de la Trémoille, duc de Noirmoutiers, though he engaged the services of the highly reputable Jean Courtonne for the construction of an hôtel on the rue de Grenelle, chose personally to determine not only the details of the decoration but also the broad outline of the plan and the very proportions of the building itself.[21] In so far as Lassay and Noirmoutiers were theory to a builder's practice, they were also the source of architectural meaning, meaning that found its point of reference not in built forms but noble bodies. Predicated on a representation of society divided into nobles and commoners, architectural propriety thus operated alongside other modes of signification to protect the visibility, honour and interests of the first. However the practice, if not the theory of civil architecture, had long since been lodged in the hands of professionals and, notwithstanding Lassay's disclaimer, society henceforth relied upon them to maintain a language of meaningful distinctions through professional consensus.[22]

That policemen and architects (among others) were in fact less than successful in their management of consumer prerogatives is evident from the eighteenth-century preoccupation, even obsession, with illegitimate spenders.[23] Those who usurped the right to splendour continued to be as vehemently denounced as those who purloined other, less ambiguous, indices of social status – such as titles and judicial privileges.[24] It appeared that to consume in a particular way was not only to display a social position, but in many ways to possess it. Indeed, symbols of status were often so confused with the subject of status that Antoine de Courtin felt it necessary to warn his readers that in certain circumstances it was as disrespectful to sit with one's back to a portrait as it was so to dishonour the person depicted.[25] The ideal of a perfect equivalence between splendour and rank led, it seems, to the identification of rank in splendour – and in so doing offered the opportunity for splendour to substitute for rank. Therein lay the threat presented by illegitimate spenders: their spending patterns could persuade others to believe that they enjoyed a social position that was not judicially theirs. What they usurped was not only the right to enjoy certain goods but, more importantly, the right to a social position expressed through those goods. Moreover, it is testimony to the degree to which material display was embedded in the eighteenth-century psyche as the very 'stuff of status' that alternative forms of discrimination were apparently slow to evolve.

Precisely because the mimetic language of distinction brooked no contradiction, admitting no ambiguity between appearance and reality, consumption was beheld as a fixed system of values. Yet the very rigidity and closure of the system made it vulnerable to spoilation. An articulate choice of goods could, seemingly, transform social structure and, by extension, manipulate the agencies of power. It was this aspect of expenditure that preoccupied Morvan de Bellegarde. Like Delamare, Bellegarde identified two modes of spending: lavish display and modest restraint.[26] But for Bellegarde these two modes did not reveal the passive acceptance of socially determined levels of spending. On the contrary, they demonstrated an active engagement with the structures of power. Of those who spent lavishly, he remarked,

> One sometimes sees at Court people who believe that it will do them no harm to hold an open table and maintain a substantial equipage, because their polite and delicate hospitality will attract to them those of merit and rank, [and] because their expenditure will do honour at Court, and will gently *force* the King to make them substantial gratuities and give them posts proportionate to their theft.[27]

This aggressive approach is contrasted with the defensive strategies employed by those 'who are persuaded that they will be able to maintain themselves in the offices to which they have risen, with greater safety and for a longer period by modesty in their expenditure'.[28] In this instance a social or political position already attained was defended by inconspicuous display – in other words, by minimising the resentment and envy that might ensue from a more emphatic expression of that position: 'their modesty is a kind of shelter within which they husband their fortune'.[29] The memory of the *affaire Fouquet* was undoubtedly still fresh and remained a tale of such cautionary power that towards the end of the eighteenth century Frédéric de La Tour du Pin thought to save himself by interrupting his pretentious projects at the château Le Bouilh.[30] Thus, if it is difficult to prove Bellegarde's assertion that courtiers armed themselves with splendour, it is evident that he was not alone in believing in splendour's force. Consumption was perceived as offering a range of paths down which socio-political objectives might be pursued. However, these objectives could only be reached with the help of others, because the power of spending depended not only on the significance it enjoyed but on the importance attached to face-to-face relationships in social and political life.

There has perhaps been a tendency to view Louis XIV's persistent drive to geld the power of feudal grandee clientship and to replace it with a venal, state bureaucracy as staging a break with an older, more intimate culture in which kinship and patronage, in short, presence, had counted significantly. And yet it is worth remembering that in matters of honour (the verification of noble titles, for instance), witnesses continued to be regarded as, *prima facie*, more reliable than documents,[31] and that in matters of shame, banishment or the expulsion of the sinful body was considered the worst kind of punishment.[32] It was precisely because statements about rank operated *between* households and not simply within them that privilege was acknowledged in action and derogation experienced as ostracism. Thus, the constant congregation of individuals (and the assessment and judgement of status through the scrutiny of behaviour, adornment and the whole theatre of display to which it gave rise) was a necessary labour for those who wished to retain their position in society.

This inspection took place at court, in the street, at religious, municipal or royal ceremonies and in the house.[33] The house in the early eighteenth century was not yet a home.[34] It was a place of retreat from the elements but not from public life, because no clear distinction divided professional and personal relationships and, in so far as these relationships may have differed, their difference was not occasioned by the choice of environment in which they were contracted. The house circumscribed a social not a familial and domestic world, and with the comparative lack of public spaces, the house long remained the principal arena for collective life.[35] The reproduction of architecture, whether by engraving or photography, has done little to preserve a sense of the sociability of built form.[36] On the contrary, it tends to transform once accessible space into impenetrable surface, or place into object. It is not simply that eighteenth-century mansions were and are generally represented as closed, their façades firmly shut (to an almost claustral degree in the case of the hôtel Desmarets, fig. 86),[37] it is that the viewpoints invariably framed by the burin and the lens serve to obscure the shape of spaces unfolding behind them. Thus, the *porte-cochère*, which was in many ways an *incipit* ('Here begins'), a point of entry for the pedestrian into a world to be experienced or re-experienced, when printed, becomes a title-page, a label, a summation of contents that holds the viewer at arms' length. Therefore, it is rather to words, and not plans, elevations and sections that one should go to recreate an impression of the house as a centre of social life. Antoine Furetière's dictionary, published towards the end of the seventeenth century, is in this respect a rich and suggestive source. For instance, as Louis Marin has shown, Furetière's spatial definition of 'place' (*lieu*) – 'private house in the city or the country' – is inseparable from the social distinctions of its use:

> the church is a sacred place; hospitals are pious places; the place of honour is the front line in battle, that is the place where there is danger to be faced and glory to be reaped.[38]

Moreover, from there Furetière was lead to consider 'place' entirely in relation to social rather than spatial structures; 'place' as position, and finally as origin or extraction ('this man comes from a good place, has connections in good places, he has made a good marriage.') Likewise, when defining the verb 'to converse', he preserved for the vernacular the semantic fullness of the Latin by drawing out the implicit meanings of 'to visit' and 'to hold learned or polite assemblies'. The noun 'conversation', furthermore, was immediately linked to those social places ('when paying a call, when out on a walk . . .')

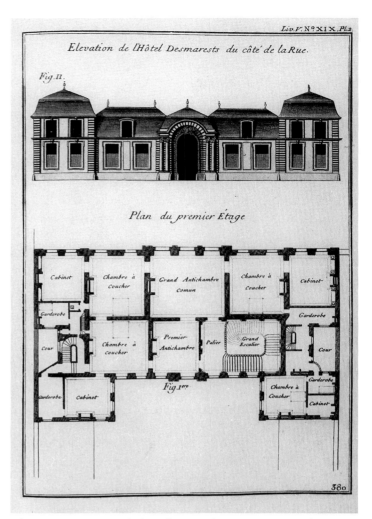

86   Street elevation and plan of the hôtel Desmarets, 1752–6. Engraving. From Jacques-François Blondel, *Architecture françoise*, 1752–6.

inseparable from polite and amiable dialogue.[39] Finally, the entry for 'house' in the dictionary of the Académie Française defined one type of residence, the *maison à bouteille*, not in terms of its architectural features but in relation to a social reality. It was, 'a small country house whose proximity to the town exposed its owner to the many expenses engendered by the visits so frequently received there'.[40] Thus, if architectural theory tended to represent domestic buildings as isolated, frigid and seemingly empty monuments, language was fraught with the commingling of spatial and social practices.

These visits were not just visits between friends for the pleasure of company but, as the Swiss traveller Béat de Muralt noted, a positive occupation.[41] They were part of the daily routine and were carried out with a level of seriousness, 'as if it were the sick who were being visited'.[42] This incessant hospitality, which filled noble houses with the constant comings-and-goings of a wide range of individuals, consisted in part of an exchange of recognition and respect.[43] Individuals visited each other in order to be present at the splendid rituals through which status was partly expressed. Magnificence thus served to keep the door of the nobleman's residence permanently ajar, when, as in the case of the hôtel d'Humières (fig. 87), it did not physically erase the threshold.[44]

THE NOBILITY DEFINED

The French nobility had not always placed such a high price on 'appearing', nor had architecture always so amiably registered signs of status. The medieval view of nobility as virtue-in-arms survived well into the Renaissance and was articulated in the decoration of the fortified entrance-way of the château de Piquigny, for instance, not by design but by the use of pompous Hebrew, Latin and Greek inscriptions extolling virtue and honour.[45] According to Guillaume de La Perrière, virtuous nobles (of whose number the lord of the château, Philibert-Emmanuel d'Ailly, was assuredly one) rose naturally to the surface of society, like the cream on full-milk.[46] Moreover, for want of their unctuous civility, he believed that society would resemble nothing so much as a defective cheese, dry, arid and lacking in sapor. Half a century or so later, Charles Loyseau's *Traité des ordres et simples dignités* (1610) compared society not to an organism but a divinely imagined mechanism, one in which nobility occured not as natural surplus but as a part in a system of adapted parts working in concert:

> Providence has established various degrees [*gradus*] and distinct orders [*ordines*] so that, if the lesser [*minores*] show deference [*reverentia*] to the great [*potiores*], and if the great bestow love [*delictio*] on the lesser, then true concord [*concordia*] and conjunction [*contextio*: the word evokes a fabric or weave in a very concrete way] will arise out of diversity. Indeed, the community [*universitas*] could not subsist at all if the total order [*magnus ordo*] of disparity [*differentia*] did not preserve it. That creation cannot be governed in equality is taught to us by the example of the heavenly hosts; there are angels and there are archangels, which clearly are not equals, differing from one another in power [*potestas*] and order [*ordo*].[47]

Loyseau's text was one from which the nobility emerged as both more and less than it had been in former times. More, because its existence was cast as essential rather than merely desirable. Less because its position was no longer self-justifying. The rhetorical harmonic of unity in diversity, of universal dependency and mutual obligation, suggested that the purpose of nobility was not so much to act as to interact. Henceforth, therefore, the discourse of nobility was no longer autonomous, but overtly or subliminally invoked its 'other' – the commonality, *peuple* or third estate.

The passage between theses two representations of society and the nobility's place within it was marked by the closing stages of the Wars of Religion and the beginning of the

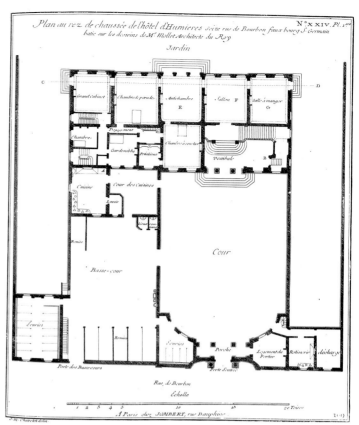

87   Plan of the hôtel d'Humières, 1752–6. Engraving. From Jacques-François Blondel, *Architecture françoise*, 1752–6.

formation of the modern state. The anti-war sentiment that emerged in the 1590s apparently served to discredit the nobility as a profession of arms, while the introduction by the state of venal office-holding had started and continued to professionalise it, in new and contentious ways. From this political and ideological crisis it appears that medieval aristocracy (government by the best) was transformed into a modern nobility (an order, estate or class defined by right of birth).[48] By so substituting pedigree for valour, to use Ellery Schalk's felicitous phrase, and ultimately etiquette for ethics, the nobility had generated a new definition of itself, one initially less vulnerable to criticism and one ostensibly less permeable to accession from below.[49] Reference to valour in noble discourse did not of course disappear – Antoine de La Roque stated in his *Traité de noblesse* (1734) that 'the Nobility is born between the arms of Mars'[50] – but it became only one of a set of features that characterised nobility henceforth.

By the eighteenth century, nobility was no longer a vocation (though it was often the consequence of one), nor did it involve the performance of particular tasks; it was an attribute, a distinction of birth.[51] It was linked to both the history and the geography of the realm: the past guaranteed noble status, and the land provided it with its distinctive titles.[52] By contrast, the third estate had no genealogy, no important past, and its particularity lay in its occupations and not in its property.[53] Estate or order was therefore a combination of somatic characteristics and pre-ordained praxis which, if it divided people irrevocably was yet capable of lending an intense feeling of ethnic identity to those of a common status group. For the nobility this was perhaps the most telling outcome of the crisis of the 1590s. Alexis de Tocqueville, when comparing aristocratic and democratic societies, noted, in the case of the former, that,

> as the classes of an aristocratic people are strongly marked and permanent, each of them is regarded by its members as a sort of lesser nation [*patrie*], more tangible and more cherished than *the* Nation.[54]

Moreover, once nobility ceased to be a matter of action and became a question of station, noblemen were necessarily compelled to distinguish the 'place' by multiplying the visual symbols of rank,[55] thus overlaying and reinforcing (with the help of the newly fashioned rules of decorum) the judicial divisions between social groups with perceptual markers, so that each estate might appeared like 'a nation within the Nation';[56] a commonwealth with its own laws, customs, language and culture.[57]

NOBLESSE OBLIGE

The days when a La Tour d'Auvergne would not have been ashamed to reside the whole year on the Turenne estates, rarely showing his face at court or in the capital were well and truly past by the close of the seventeenth century, and no amount of regret on the part of a cardinal de Bernis could alter the fact that a town house had become one of the necessities of nobility.[58] Once the crown had gained direct control of military appointments, the nobility was irrevocably drawn to seek advancement at court and at the door of the secretary of state for war in the capital in order to persue its traditional vocation.[59] Thus, although nobles continued to derive their identity and titles from their landed estates, together with a substantial measure of their revenues and political power, foreign travellers were repeatedly struck by the lack of attention they paid to these properties. Mrs Thrale was surprised to count only three country houses between Saint-Omer and Amiens,[60] and Arthur Young was persuaded that in this preference for life in the capital lay the cause of the poor state of French agriculture, because

> the nobility and gentry of large fortunes, reside the whole year in Paris, never seeing their estates except now and then possibly in a hasty party of pleasure, if at no great distance from Paris, but if in a remote province, scarce ever.[61]

'It has been thirty-two years since last I came here', admitted the maréchal de Tessé writing from his château in Normandy in 1710, 'and I find no doors, no windows, nor window-panes, except in the tower.'[62] And the same kind of interval punctu-ated the visits of the ducs de Saulx-Tavanne to their Burgundy estates after the family's definitive move to Paris in 1761.[63] The nobility, it seems, was defined in rural terms, yet sought to congregate in the towns.[64]

According to Emmanuel Sièyes, this apparent contradiction expressed the tension between two different manifestations of the nobleman's need to be distinct. On the one hand the nobleman's claim to superiority originated from and found full expression on his country estates where, in a manner of speaking, the flatness of the land around him threw his silhouette into higher profile – 'it is in the château that one senses with enthusiasm, just like art should be experienced, the full impact of a genealogical tree with spreading limbs and sprouting stem'.[65] Yet, on the other hand, the desire to participate in the prestige of the group, to shine as a member of a distinguished cast, drove him to the capital. The advantages of heightened personal prestige warred with the advantages of group superiority, and by the seventeenth century the latter was proving the stronger.[66] Paris and the court were the centres of civility and polite society; the countryside henceforth merely provided the French language with scope for insult. 'Village', according to Furetière, was coined 'out of scorn for a thing when compared to another of the same kind. He is but a village priest; a *seigneur de village*'.[67]

The nobility not only spent more time in town, they also lavished greater expense on their urban properties. Jean-François Labourdette, in his comparative study of four ducal fortunes, discovered not only a high degree of compatability in expenditure on magnificence between dukes whose wealth varied from a capital of 12 million *livres* (duc de Villeroy) to one of a modest 950,000 *livres* (duc de Lévis), but further, a consistent approach to the Paris mansion as an essential component of that splendour.[68] Indeed, it was generally supposed among the gossips that pretentious but impoverished noblemen (relatively speaking that is) were prepared to line their coffers by marrying coin in order to maintain a distinguished way of life. Thus, Henri de La Tour d'Auvergne, comte d'Evreux, accepted Marie-Anne Crozat, the daughter of Crozat *le riche* and her dowry of 2 million *livres*, and on its foundation and to Molet's designs, raised an hôtel of shameless grandeur (fig. 88) in the faubourg Saint-Honoré.[69]

Moreover, the following examples suggest that the Paris mansion was gradually evolving from a virtue made of necessity into a form of patrimony, the symbolic properties of which were close to exceeding its economic value.[70] When Charles de Lorraine-Armagnac, comte de Marsan, died in 1708 he left an estate burdened with debt and a minor, Louis de Lorraine, prince de Pons, his heir. His will instructed the executors to save three landed estates at all costs and to this effect Pons's guardian authorised the sale of a house in the rue de l'Université on the grounds that the property was not only valuable but legally alienable and cost twice as much to maintain as could be raised from letting it.[71] However, in 1720, shortly after coming of age, the prince de Pons successfully

88 Courtyard elevation of the hôtel d'Evreux, 1752–6. Engraving. From Jacques-François Blondel, *Architecture françoise*, 1752–6.

contested the sale that had taken place some ten years earlier, claiming that the hôtel was not an *acquêt* but a lineage property, equivalent in prestige to a fief, and therefore that his guardian had had no authority to dispose of it.[72] To prevent a similar alienation of property, in 1722 the duc d'Antin had taken the precautionary measure of entailing the hôtel de Travers and its contents to his grandson, Louis II de Pardaillan II de Gondrin, duc d'Epernon, on the occasion of his marriage.[73] After d'Antin's death, Epernon's right not only to the property but to all the items of decoration and furniture, the most modest inclusively, was defended against the pressing claims of creditors on the basis that the interior fittings no less than the external ornament were unique, specifically made for the house so as to match the design and colour-schemes of each room, and that they therefore formed an integral part of the family patrimony bequeathed from one generation to the next in perpetuity.[74] Here not only *immeubles* (land and houses) but *meubles* (personal property) were being presented in law as ancestral rights of a consequence in excess of their exchange value. Both examples therefore suggest that the Paris mansion, though it generated little revenue, rarely conferred seigneurial powers and constituted the kind of easily liquifiable asset perfectly placed to protect the integrity of family lands at moments of crisis, was itself gradually becoming part of the heritage which *noblesse* obliged all generations to protect from falling into the hands of strangers.

These noble houses, or 'hôtels' as they were exclusively called, were first recognised from the outside by their *portes-cochères*, often set back from the street – as in the case of Pierre Boscry's plan and elevation for the entrance-way of the hôtel d'Orrouer (fig. 89) – and inscribed with the names of their proprietors.[75] Such, indeed, was the importance of these tri-

89 Pierre Boscry, plan and elevation of the entrance-way at the hôtel d'Orrouer, 1736. Pencil and wash on paper, 18.25 × 25.5 cm. Archives Nationales, Paris.

umphal entrance-ways that when Jean Marot came to represent a view of the courtyard of, for example, Le Vau's hôtel de Bautru (fig. 90), he ficticiously destroyed screen-walls to provide, less than effectively, lines of vision to either side of a virtually inviolate *porte-cochère*.[76] That this architectural feature indulged the vanity of patrons quite as much as architects may be gauged from the comte de Matignon's decision in 1724 to entail his property on the rue de Varenne to his only son on condition that his own name and coat-of-arms, which decorated the *porte-cochère* (fig. 91) and pediments of the main house, were preserved without alteration by all future direct or collateral descendants.[77] Moreover, the exclusive right of the nobility to introduce their properties, their exclusively

90   Hôtel de Bautru, c.1660–70. Engraving. From Jean Marot, *Grand Marot*, c.1660–70.

designated 'hôtels', in this way, is suggested in a letter to Pontchartrain by the marquis d'Argenson,

> No ordinance has ever determined the rank of those entitled to afix the inscription hôtel to their dwellings; birth and status alone have established this distinction without the authority of law, and up until now I am not aware that this liberty has been greatly abused.[78]

Pompously styling the Nesmond mansion the 'hôtel de Nesmond' when to all clear-sighted *gentilshommes* it was obvi-

91   Jean Mazin, coat-of-arms for the portal of the hôtel de Matignon, 1723. Archives du Palais de Monaco.

ously a bourgeois 'mansion', was then an apparently isolated scandal,[79] but the outrage it provoked in the duc de Saint-Simon reveals the importance attached to the strict applications of nomenclature and helps to explain the nobility's sustained resistance to the introduction of street numbering – which threatened the conceptual distinction of their dwellings.[80]

The lexicographical division of houses into different social types was matched by a hierarchical typology of architectural forms. Most straightforwardly, there was a contrast of scale, but the nobility was expansive and the bourgeoisie pinched in very particular ways. For the nobility, size was partly a matter of height but predominantly a matter of surface area.[81] An hôtel was foremost an extensive horizontal structure, with an imposing façade, and able to cater to the social needs of its owner on a single floor. The most extreme opinion held that to be appropriately housed, 'one should have no one above one's head, nor be obliged to mount'.[82] Blondel thus criticised Robert de Cotte's deployment of dormer windows across the façade of the hôtel du Maine (fig. 92) on the grounds that 'to be able to discern above the apartments inhabited by masters of the first importance, the lodgings destined for mere servants', broke every rule of decorum, the transposition of architectural forms not only suggesting an inversion of the social order, but lending the building the general appearance of a *maison particulière*.[83] However, if *pavillons à l'italienne* or single-storey mansions such as the palais Bourbon (fig. 95), were comparatively rare in early eighteenth-century Paris,[84] an

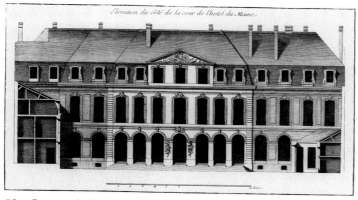

92　Courtyard elevation of the hôtel du Maine, 1727. Engraving. From Jacques-François Blondel, *Architecture françoise*, 1752–6.

93　Claude Desgotz, elevation of the château de Sablé, *c.*1715–20. Cooper-Hewitt, National Design Museum, New York.

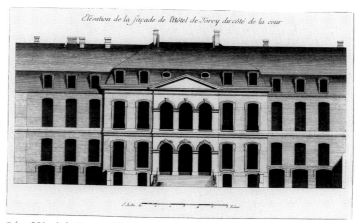

94　Hôtel de Torcy, 1727. Engraving. From Jean Mariette, *Architecture françoise*, 1727.

emphatic horizontal axis nevertheless, constituted a distinctive feature of both hôtel and château: the urban and rural dwellings of the nobility. Indeed, a comparison of the château de Sablé and the hôtel de Torcy (figs 93, 94) built respectively by Charles Desgotz and Germain Boffrand for one of the *grand Colbert*'s great-nephews, demonstrates that by the eighteenth century these two building types had become almost indistinguishable.[85] Stripped of its defensive features – moat and turrets – the château lost some of its identity and visibly merged with the hôtel.[86] Thereafter, the nobility inhabited a uniform and synthesised building-type whether in the town or the country. This ideal type made few concessions to the urban environment. Horizontal, preferably regular in shape, set back from the street at an intersection between a courtyard and a garden, the hôtel must eventually have appeared like a country house transplanted to town. The desire for a panoramic view[87] – the prospect up the Seine (fig. 96) was apparently one of the few advantages that recommended the Arsenal to the duchesse du Maine[88] – and the importance given to the garden,[89] suggest that the nobility cultivated a pastoral existence removed from the countryside. The nobleman's preferred experience of nature, indeed, was to be found in town:

> Sans sortir de la ville, il trouve la campagne,
> Il peut dans son jardin, tout peuplé d'arbres verts,
> Recéler le printemps au milieu des hivers,

95　Jean Cailleteau, called Lassurance, project for the elevation of the palais Bourbon, *c.*1722. Nationalmuseum, Stockholm.

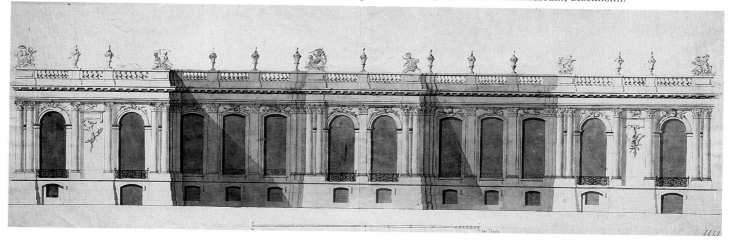

96 Philippe-Nicolas Milcent, *View of Paris from the Pavilion of Mme la Duchesse du Maine at the Arsenal*, 1736. Etching.

> Et foulant le parfum de ses plantes fleuries,
> Aller entretenir ses douces rêveries.[90]

The city offered the possibility of a rural ideal without a rustic reality. Even the country houses on the outskirts of Paris, according to one author, 'resembled the countryside and country life . . . to the same degree that dancers at the Opera resemble our shepherdesses'.[91] In their relationship to nature the nobility simultaneously distinguished themselves from the peasants who lived and worked on the land, and from the truly metropolitan classes whose livelihoods depended on direct intervention in the economy of the city.

Despite the lack of explicit and detailed practical guidelines offered by architects for the selection of a site,[92] the insertion of these country/town houses into the cityscape cannot have been undertaken arbitrarily. At the very least, certain spatial requirements had to be satisfied if the ideal hôtel was to be built. The petition submitted by the inhabitants of the faubourg Saint-Honoré in 1733 in response to a royal decree of 1724, provides an insight into the nature of these requirements.[93] The decree stipulated that, in faubourgs beyond the new city limits,[94] the construction of 'maisons à porte-cochère' and buildings of more than two storeys was to be prohibited.[95] The inhabitants of the district, most of whom had bought their lands between 1719 and 1721, protested. The substance of the faubourg's case for exemption from the new legislation rested on the nature of the area's urban tissue. In contrast to the other faubourgs affected, Saint-Honoré was, at the beginning of the eighteenth century, largely undeveloped.[96] On Turgot's plan (fig. 97) the open spaces north-west of the Madeleine and west of the hôtel d'Evreux are still clearly visible. As a result, it had been possible for buyers to acquire substantial plots of land ideally suited to hôtel construction. The distinctive feature of these plots was their wide street-fronts and their depth, a depth 'destined for front courts, service courtyards and gardens to accompany a *maison à porte-cochère*'.[97] And the sheer size of the plots available offered the possibility of building hôtels in such a manner that their architectural forms could be completely liberated from any constraints implied by the boundaries of the property.[98] Furthermore, since the area was only beginning to be developed, the plots on offer tended to be regular in shape, in contrast to the often contorted boundaries of sizeable properties in the centre of Paris which, having evolved from the patient but frequently haphazard accumulation of much smaller land-units, tested the architect's ingenuity to the limit.[99] Lastly these new plots combined depth and regularity with substantial street-frontages which, given the importance ascribed to the entrance-way, further enhanced their desirability.

If ideal for hôtel construction, these sites were, according to the faubourg's landowners and developers, completely unsuitable for other purposes. Commercial sites demanded an orientation towards the street and not a retreat from it, and if the depth of the plots alone mitigated against workshops and retail outlets, in combination with the height restriction, it also inhibited any vertical development such as the construction of tenements or *immeubles*.[100] Charles Jombert's elevation and section for the workshops and tenements on the rue Saint-Denis (fig. 98), designed for the retail hosier Jean-Claude Hude in 1734, amply demonstrate the extreme narrowness and height of such buildings when compared with hôtel architecture. Moreover, the plan for the ground floor (fig. 99) shows the exaggerated irregularity of the property. The architect had to have recourse to internal courtyards not so as to provide a space in which folk might be received, but in order merely to light the cramped accommodation locked in a dense urban mesh.[101] There was, it seems, a fundamental incompatibility between the nobleman's and the *roturier*'s relationship to the urban environment. To some extent this incompatibility arose from the differences between their respective households. The entourage of a prince or a noble was invariably extensive, including as it did not only servants but courtiers and collateral relatives,[102] and their houses were correspondingly large.

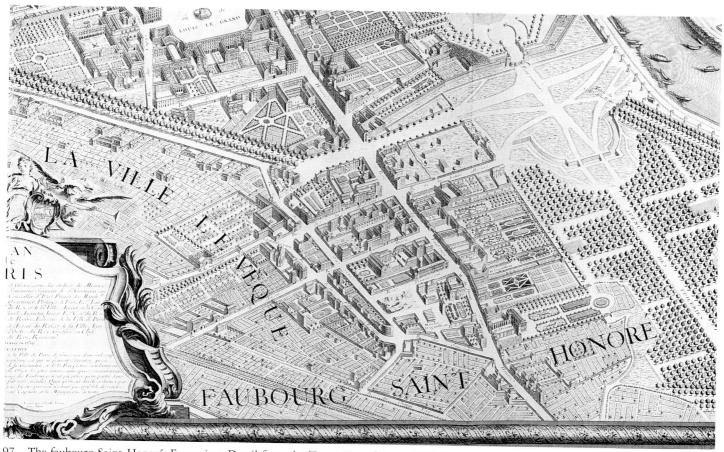

97 The faubourg Saint-Honoré. Engraving. Detail from the *Turgot Map of Paris*, 1734–9.

When, in 1732, Louise-Elizabeth de Bourbon-Condé, second dowager princesse de Conti, decided to buy the former hôtel de La Vrillière (fig. 100) she found it insufficient to accommodate her needs, and in order to install the officers essential to her household she was forced three years later to acquire the adjacent hôtel de Broglie, thus extending her domain as far as the natural boundaries created by the intersection of the rues Saint-Dominique, de l'Université and de Bourgogne would allow.[103] Further up the rue de Bourgogne the families of the artisanal, commercial and professional classes were being accommodated in just one or two rooms.[104] Artisanal and retail activities, therefore, tended to become concentrated in the older, central districts of Paris where the urban tissue was dense and inflexible, while hôtel construction could only be accommodated in new, relatively unpopulated areas where the tissue was still malleable and substantial plots could be acquired.[105]

Many eighteenth-century writers commented on the physical and social contrasts which scared the city of Paris. Germain Brice discouraged visits to the conjested *quartier des Halles*[106] and Sébastien Mercier not only likened the faubourg Saint-Marcel to a working-class neighbourhood but remarked that,

If one visits that country [*pays*], it is out of curiosity; nothing draws one there; there is not a single monument to be seen. The people do not in the least resemble Parisians those polite inhabitants of the banks of the Seine.[107]

Statistics, however, suggest that the population was distributed throughout Paris in such a way that neighbourhoods differed only in emphasis, because, as Richard Cantillon observed, noble dwellings invariably attracted about them those whose services they required.[108] Expilly estimated, in fact, that in the 1760s, 4,773 servants lived in the faubourg Saint-Germain, employed by some 1,553 noble families.[109] Furthermore, the cour des Dragons (fig. 102) in the same *quartier* offered a commercial cul-de-sac purposefully built in 1730 to the designs of Pierre de Vigny, the shops and work-shops of which were mostly occupied by scrap-merchants and coppersmiths; the adjacent rue du Sépulchre was likewise inhabited entirely by artisans;[110] whilst on the rue de l'Université the cardinal d'Auvergne and the prince de Pons found themselves rubbing shoulders with the likes of Charles Bellicard, a master-joiner, and the sculptors and marble-cutters, Jacques and Jacques-François Dropsy, father and son.[111] The petitioning residents of the faubourg Saint-Honoré

Wide streets and low-density housing gave the new faubourgs their distinctive 'aristocratic' atmosphere despite the often plebian nature of their populations. Yet for the spectator, it was primarily the three-dimensional properties of the buildings themselves, and not the urban environment, that specifically communicated status. The representational features of houses proclaimed their social destiny, and, according to Jacques-François Blondel, the architect's skill resided in his knowledge of the character appropriate to each housing type.[112] Character was a matter of convention – or rather, it arose as a result of an extension of social custom to architectural and artistic matters.[113] Convention required that, from the exterior, an hôtel should appear symmetrical.[114] Symmetry, as Perrault explained, was not just a question of proportion but also a case of resemblance;

98 Charles Jombert, elevation of an *immeuble* on the rue Saint-Denis, 1734. Pen, ink and wash on paper, 46.7 × 25.4 cm. Archives Nationales, Paris.

99 Charles Jombert, plan for an *immeuble* on the rue Saint-Denis, 1734. Pen, ink and wash on paper, 39.5 × 26 cm. Archives Nationales, Paris.

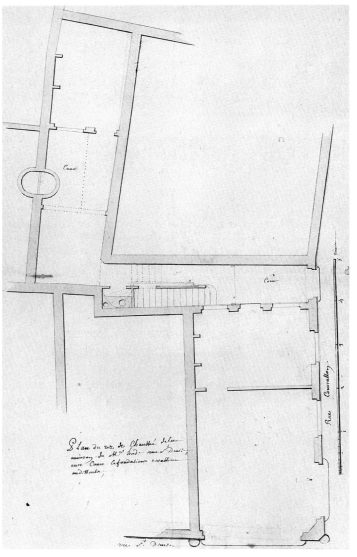

notwithstanding, it seems therefore, that the character of a neighbourhood was not determined by the exclusive presence of bourgeois or noble classes but by the subtle blend of the two, to which the presence or absence of noble households was crucial. The faubourg Saint-Germain, despite the greater number of servants and artisans in residence, counted, for the better part of the eighteenth century, as the aristocratic district *par excellence*, and its noble character was evident in its buildings and geographical layout.

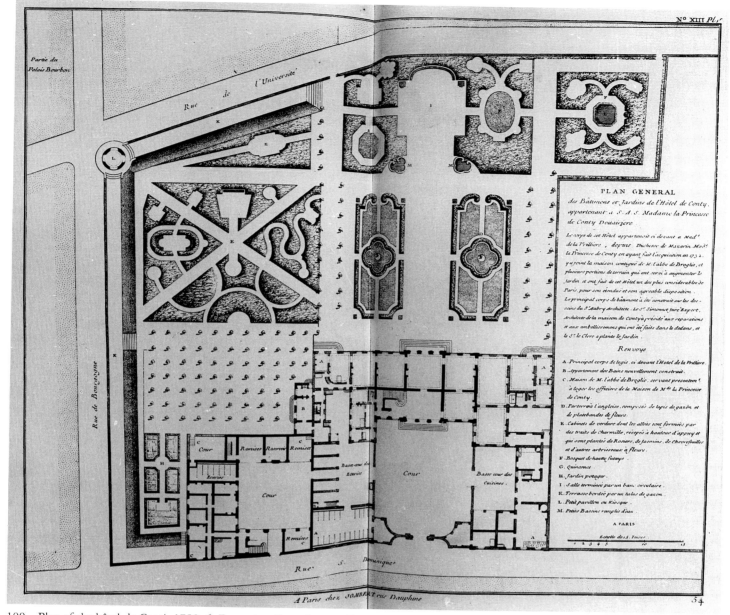

Within the image:

Partie du
Palais Bourbon

Rue de l'Université

Rue de Bourgogne

PLAN GENERAL
des Bâtimens et Jardins de l'Hôtel de Conty,
appartenant à S. A. S. Madame la Princesse
de Conty Douairiere.

Rue S. Dominique

A Paris chez JOMBERT rue Dauphine

100 Plan of the hôtel de Conti, 1752–6. Engraving. From Jacques-François Blondel, *Architecture françoise*, 1752–6.

it signifies the relationship between right- and left-hand elements, and between upper and lower, front and back ones, in scale, disposition, height, colour, number and orientation; and generally in everything which can make one thing resemble another . . .[115]

And, for the same author, it was symmetry 'which constituted a large measure of the [positive] beauty of Buildings.'[116] The symbolic significance of symmetry, from which aesthetic pleasure perhaps derived, was rooted in *ancien-régime* perceptions of humanity. According to Louis Savot, to man alone was given the unique capacity to create order and appreciate harmony:

Animals know how to select as well, sometimes better, than man the convenience of their lairs and dwellings: but bring to them the grace of symmetry they cannot, because the knowledge of order and proportion belongs only to man within the animal kingdom, who alone knows and receives satisfaction and pleasure from these things.[117]

However, man and beast were not always regarded as utterly distinct. Savot proceeds to explain that man's capacity to appreciate symmetry and proportion lay in direct relation to his humanity.[118] Since, as in Nicolas Guérard's *Born to Suffer* (fig. 101), the peasant was defined by his zoomorphic qualities – he worked like a drone and his day's labour was held as cheaply as a hen's; he was bovine for labouring so that others might eat and drink, and finally porcine for being necessary

93

yet contemptible[119] — symmetry could, accordingly, hold little charm for him. The labourer was in this sense, truly a beast of burden, comparable to 'the animals we have civilised',[120] because for the *ancien régime* it was physical work that primarily qualified the contrasts between savage and civilised, and rational and irrational.[121]

Though Guérard's print also suggests that he or she who unquestionably accepts such analogies must be asinine, testimony to the persistence of this habit of thought is to be found in a pamphlet entitled, *Sur la Nature du peuple* (1755), in which the abbé Coyer satirised the still-current prejudice of ascribing a monopoly of reason to the nobility. The female embodiment of this rational faculty, he claimed,

> is to be found lodging beneath richly decorated ceilings. She calls upon gold and silk to weave her garments. She breathes incense, and finds her appetite in *ragoûts*; and rest following upon idleness, she falls asleep upon a feather-bed. The *instinct* [of the *peuple*] knows only necessity. *Reason* attaches herself to surplus, she calculates all the degrees of esteem which proceed from it. So much from a fashionable outfit, so much from an elegant piece of furniture, so much from a fleet coach-and-four. Nothing escapes her, neither flowers from Italy, nor trinkets from the Americas, nor figurines from China, and via the infinitesimally small she reaches for the great.[122]

In this passage Coyer not only acknowledged the social power of goods but also exposed the economic infrastructure supporting and advancing the nobility's 'rational' cultural hegemony. By and large, however, 'noble reason' retained its innocence in the eighteenth century and the symmetrical patterns of the nobility's architectural projects continued to articulate the quintessential difference between civilised, enlightened leisure and instinctive, benighted labour. Symmetry was implicitly contrasted with the open-ended and asymmetrical forms of vernacular architecture, forms responsive to the internal needs of a household as opposed to the external constraints of a social and aesthetic ideal.[123]

The regularity of noble dwellings was underlined by the use of the classical orders. The orders accentuated the visual impression of symmetry by creating a pattern of traces at fixed intervals across the surface of an elevation. Symmetry and proportion could be achieved without recourse to the orders as such, but their use guaranteed the architectural objective. Consequently, the use of columns and pilasters became associated with noble housing; indeed, Blondel expressed the widely held opinion that they should be exclusively reserved for such hôtels.[124] Moreover, it seems worth noting that certain constitutionalists had, since the sixteenth century, assimilated the column, along with other architectural metaphors into their political language.[125] Columns were the support upon which the edifice of government was allegedly erected, and, in so far as the nobility constituted one of the 'pillars' of that society, its material association with the classical orders must have seemed particularly apt.[126] Thus, while the theoretical debate about the principles of proportion and the relative beauty of ratios exhausted itself, the socio-political function of the orders remained for a long time unquestioned.[127] The column and its attendant decoration was able to act as a mark of distinction quite independent of the conclusions drawn about the nature of beauty in proportion. Indeed, the fact that in constitutional thought relations of similitude seemingly existed between columns and contracts and between buildings and political arrangements suggests rather, that the customary beauty of the former could only gain in visual and literary lustre from association with the artificiality of the latter. In other words, the power of the conventional pacts that were said to have given birth to the state was capable of restoring a measure of authority to the arbitrary beauty of the classical orders when stripped of their symbolic armature. In any event, so long as columnar decoration remained the preserve of hôtel architecture it continued to embody noble status at least. From the main courtyard, the hôtel was therefore presented to the

101   Nicolas Guérard, *Born to Suffer*, c.1700. Engraving.

102 (facing page)   The former Cour des Dragons, Paris, 1730.

spectator as a unified and complete statement,[128] a visual metaphor of a graced and immutable noble estate.

However, behind these rigid and distinctively noble façades sheltered households of a decidedly more protean nature. The very extensiveness and social complexity of these households, ones that, according to Louis Audiger's manual on household management, rarely included a staff of less than some thirty people, was the object of noble pride.[129] Family members, clients and servants were caught in an intricate web of hierarchical relations, which bound them together in community and ideally made of them a microcosm of society at large. In order to describe this conjunction of unity in diversity and construct it as natural it seems scarcely coincidental that both socio-political and architectural theories should have had recourse to anthropomorphic metaphors. Just as the body and the body-politic were thought to share an inescapable resemblance, graphically caught in Abraham Bosse's frontispiece to Thomas Hobbes's *Leviathan* (1651),[130] so the particular houses that in some senses constituted the building-blocks of society, were similarly apprehended as bodies or *corps-de-logis*. From Vitruvius onwards, classical theorists explained that, just as 'one sees in a human body, that the arm, the foot, the hand, the fingers, and all other parts have their separate offices, which interact for the benefit and service of the person', so the disparate spaces that together constitute a lapidary body should, by analogy, be arranged according to similarly proportionate relations of coexistence.[131] From the 'head-point' of the main male and female apartments, rooms ideally radiated in labyrinthine patterns, offering concrete expression of the ties of intimacy or estrangement that bound dependents to their *seigneur*. On such grounds, amateurs like Laugier insisted that to be properly housed an hôtel should have no less than three courtyards: the main courtyard for the reception of visitors, and two adjacent courtyards, one for the kitchens and, beyond that, the stableyard.[132] However, a contradiction almost immediately seems to arise between this insistence on the spatial separation of social realms – there was to be no physical means of communication between the house and the stables[133] – and the kind of service we know to have obtained during the early modern period.

Servants were not only entrusted with the daily running of the household, they were also expected, when occasion demanded, to defend the interests and honour of their employers.[134] On Friday 13 June 1738 a fight broke out outside the hôtel de Soisson, the liveried servants of the prince de Carignan having apparently impugned the honour of those faithful to the prince de Conti; proof that such conflicts were indeed conflicts between noble houses, in this case Bourbon and Lorraine, is strongly suggested by the fact that the Conti livery mustered to their side the servants of the prince's sister, Mlle de la Roche-sur-Yon.[135] Establishing such bonds of loyalty, if not fealty, so that the servant almost instinctively identified with the master's interests, demanded a high degree of familiarity between master and servant and, indeed, the

living quarters provided for servants were often informal, because their contact with masters was frequent and invariably sustained.[136] It was not so much that servants *served* that counted (for personal service was extended to some degree by all members of court society[137]), but that they *worked*. As already noted, manual labour, unlike service, was regarded as ignoble.[138] Therefore, though independent living-quarters for servants may have been slow to evolve, areas where the tasks preparatory to that service were performed had long since required sharp differentiation. Not inappropriately did Louis Savot refer to the wings in which such *remises* were habitually billeted as the 'arms' of the house.[139]

Distinctions between the estates that together made up the social constituency of an hôtel were expressed, it seems, less in terms of people than functions. The only point of overlap between the 'popular' service areas and the 'noble' living quarters occurred in the antechamber, both last service-station and first room in the sequence of *grands appartements*. Moreover, it seems highly significant that it was this mediating space that so often framed accounts of social difference, transgression and contestation in the memoirs and journals of the period. Asked by the duchesse du Maine to explain the purpose of the assorted medications improperly imported in bulk by the duc de La Force, the commissioner of police, Labbé, coyly replied that they were, 'a cure for the kind of affliction to be found *not* in your chamber but perhaps in your antechamber', a response that implied that the space had been annexed to the realm of untamed, plebeian sexuality and the diseases it occasioned.[140] Moreover, the confusion and commingling of estates and social categories in this liminal zone offered not only opportunities for scandal[141] but a reference-point of insults. Charles-Henri de Malon de Bercy, formerly Intendant des Finances, was exiled in 1715, apparently not so much for his graceless surrender of the Ponts et Chaussées, but for his temerity in keeping the chancellor of king's household kicking his heels in an antechamber before receiving him with an unconscionable lack of civility.[142] Meanwhile the marquis de Courtanvaux had been prepared to surrender his life, if fate so required, in order to retrieve his honour tarnished by Captain de la Baume's assertion that he did not belong at Versailles, except perhaps in the Salle des Suisses.[143]

The efficiency of the body as body-politic and body as *corps-de-logis* metaphors to imprint a unified and harmonious shape on people's experience of inhabiting buildings and interacting with the communities they housed was never more than partial. Though symmetrical in appearance and proportionate in plan, a conceptual hiatus separated the realms of the popular and noble, despite the incessant traffic to and fro. Moreover, this division was reinforced, extended even, by a further system of overlaying relations between the sacred and the profane. To the nobility belonged the right to chapels within their dwellings[144] so that their religious observance might be maintained without participation in the social body of the (parish) church. With the exception of death, the celebration of marriage is perhaps one of the most frequent occasions for a description of a Parisian hôtel in diaries of the period. The marquis Dangeau recorded, for instance, that in 1716 the duc de la Meilleraye married Mlle de Rohan in the Rohan chapel and that the hôtel had been magnificently decorated for the occasion,[145] while the following year he related that the duc de Noailles's daughter forswore the chance to marry in the paternal oratory, decorated by Antoine Coypel, for her uncle's chapel in the archbishop's palace.[146]

The exact location of the chapel in the hôtel complex was a diocesan matter. Some dioceses required the chapel to be isolated from the residence; others were less strict and admitted a closer contact between religious and secular practices.[147] All, however, agreed that a chapel should only be placed, 'in a space whose use is not remotely indecent', that is to say, in the noble sphere removed from areas primarily associated with physical gratification.[148] However, the full significance of the chapel as a feature of the hôtel exceeded both the practical advantages of social segregation and the amplification of the moral dimension of the structure. The pre-eminence of the priesthood over the other estates and orders of the realm theoretically subordinated secular power to religious authority.[149] Thus, if the temporal and spiritual spheres were constitutionally distinct, the ideology of hierarchy combined the two, infusing political authority with a mystical aura.[150] The concepts of divine right, of the monarch's mystical body and of the miraculousness of the king's touch, are but the most familiar expressions of the sacredness of royal power.[151] Sacredness was not, however, a royal preserve; it filtered down the hierarchy and extended its grace over secular associations such as the nobility's *ordre du Saint-Esprit*. But its intensity diminished as status fell and it therefore provided its own index to rank. At the celebration of Mass the sanctity of hierarchy was ritualised in the right to precedence at the Eucharist, and in the appropriation of sacerdotal offices, such as kissing the monstrance, by the most exalted secular members.[152] Thus, the possession of a chapel and the segregation of service areas from living quarters, were more than status markers – the means of sustaining the avowed objective of social distinction; they were dominant symbols, symbols that referred to the values of sacredness and nobility axiomatic to *ancien-régime* hierarchy.

By contrast, the increasing differentiation of uses within the *corps-de-logis* seems, at first glance, to be the result of the demands of a particular way of life rather than the articulation of social beliefs. Until the eighteenth century many rooms had remained multi-functional; bedchambers were both places to sleep and spaces in which to receive; dining often took place in any available room, and so forth.[153] This lack of behavioural differentiation was a feature of the dwellings of all sectors of *ancien-régime* society,[154] but gradually noble houses seem to have drawn a measure of their distinctiveness from a more specialised distribution. According to the abbé Laugier, houses contained two types of rooms, those that fulfilled practical necessities – such as dining-rooms, closets, *cabinets*

de toilette and bathrooms – and those that catered to social requirements, such as *salles*,[155] libraries and galleries.[156] The former responded to the need for *commodité* and, by implication, were essential; the latter were merely for the 'magnificence' of *grands Seigneurs*.[157] *Commodité*, which eighteenth-century architects and architectural theorists erroneously credited themselves with having invented[158] was, therefore, explicitly contrasted with *magnificence*. Pierre Patte went so far as to associate magnificence and *commodité* with two distinct epochs in French architecture:

> Before this era, one could say of architecture, not without justification, that it was the decorated shell of one of man's most important needs; everything was committed to the exterior and to magnificence. Following the example of antique and Italian building which were taken for models, the interiors were vast and without the least convenience . . . one was housed only for the sake of appearance and the art of living comfortably and for oneself was unknown.[159]

Whereas for Delamare magnificence was the natural attribute of noble status because it was *vraisemblable* and appropriate, for Patte magnificence was unnatural and assumed. However, Patte and Delamare used the term to mean different things. Patte identifies it with a style – seventeenth-century classicism – and hence an outmoded form of splendour. Delamare, on the other hand, used magnificence as an example of the principle of appropriate display, and in so far as *commodité* distinguished the buildings of the nobility, he would have considered it a constituent of their magnificence. Patte described status symbols that seemed forced and compared them with necessities that seemed natural and therefore universal. However, 'conveniences' are no less symbolic because they are dressed up as necessities. Indeed, the power of status symbols stems from the fact that they seem to fit like a skin and not like a glove. Therefore, the whole array of rooms provided in hôtels to enhance the comfort of the inhabitants, plus the ceremonial rooms, should be considered as intrinsic to the ideal of a distinctive noble lifestyle.

Finally, not only a differentiated interior but the use of certain materials and goods for its decoration distinguished the hôtel from other habitations. First, colours were attributed symbolic values; for example, red was commonly associated with the French king and his court, and this association had its place on the statute-books. During the reign of Henri II, a royal declaration stipulated that red could only be worn by princes, princesses and the nobility.[160] Gentlemen were allowed to wear shoes with red heels to signify their rank and until the end of the *ancien régime*, only those who had been presented at court wore these famous *talons rouges*.[161] The symbolic use of red extended beyond its use in clothing; red damask remained one of the most favoured textiles for the upholstery of rooms and furniture.[162] Blue and gold, the heraldic colours of the Bourbon line were, on the other hand,

103   Jacques Lagniet, *The Empire of Reform on the Disorders of Fashion*, c.1670. Etching.

uniquely associated with the crown, and the kings of France maintained an exclusive right to dress their liveried servants in these colours.[163] Lastly, the use of gold and silver was restricted to certain estates. Since the reign of Louis XII, French monarchs had repeatedly tried to curtail the production and consumption of gold- and silverware,[164] and under Henri III the use of gilding was also brought under legislative control.[165] In order to give greater force to the law, instead of merely limiting their use to certain social strata, Louis XIV prohibited all but the church from enjoying gold and gilded goods.[166] Jacques Lagniet's print *The Empire of Reform on the Disorders of Fashion* (fig. 103) shows, on the right, a *peintre doribus* whose hand has been stayed from gilding a carriage;[167] however, the correspondence between the chancellor, Pontchartrain, and the chief of police, d'Argenson, presents a rather different picture. Only in certain instances, it seems, were transgressions of these laws pursued. In a letter dated the 28 September 1703, Pontchartrain wrote to the Lieutenenant de Police,

The king is aware that luxury is once more taking a hold in Paris, particularly where houses are concerned and he named among others, Messrs Crozat and Thévenin, who have taken the liberty of gilding their galleries, H.R.M. is greatly astonished that you pay so little attention to the implementation of the edict issued on this subject, and has ordered me most expressly to warn you that he is not at all pleased to see you give way on this matter; you should, on the contrary, put a stop to these infractions by all the means at your disposal.[168]

Antoine Crozat and Jean Thévenin were by no means alone in having the interiors of their houses gilded, but what made the liberty they took so unpardonable was their 'place' in society, their origins. These men were money-mongers, *parvenus*, and their flagrant disregard of the law, though shared by the nobility,[169] could not be dismissed. By contrast, the nobility in these same years seem to have made *orfèvrerie* and gilded

98

decoration the mark of its status and an expression of its position among the arbitrators and beyond the reach of common law.[170]

The function of certain goods as status markers was ensured not only through the control of access to them but also by the supervision of their production. Delamare noted that in 367 AD, the emperors Valentinian and Valens had taken the following measures to ensure that purple remained an imperial symbol;

> These . . . Princes selected a certain number of Dyers for the purple; they formed them into a kind of militia of unique status which could not be surrendered, and which was passed from father to son. They also allocated part of their own Palace to lodge and provide working space for these Craftsmen.[171]

The similarity between Delamare's description of imperial patronage and the French monarchy's creation of privileged artists and artisans, similarly housed at royal expense, is hard to miss. Indeed the function of the *artisans suivant la Cour* is evident in sumptuary legislation. As early as 1567 an ordinance forbade these *privilégiés* from selling their goods 'à boutiques ouvertes', to those not entitled to them.[172] The *artisans suivant la Cour* were in some senses artisans of status and to that end their clientele had to be strictly monitored. By extension, this was true of all those who worked directly under royal protection. They constituted a particular section of the monarch's personnel, and in a directive concerning the *privilégiés* of the Gobelins, Savonnerie and the Galeries du Louvre, the author noted that,

> The number of these workmen cannot be fixed, it varies according to the need the king may have for his service, and the right to augment or diminish their number according to circumstances belongs only to His Majesty.[173]

Privileged artisans did not so much earn their privileges through personal merit, as receive them in order to accommodate the needs of the crown. Bâtiments policy, which consistently encouraged the formation of artisanal dynasties, which allocated studios in the Louvre to successive generations of the same family, and which put forward for honours those whose families had faithfully served the crown,[174] gives further credence to the argument that royal protection was monopolistic in the interest of dynastic distinction. From this perspective, even the copyright privileges enjoyed by academicians seem double-edged.[175] They safeguarded not only the academicians' livelihoods but also, and perhaps more significantly, the rarity and distinctiveness of their designs. From this vantage-point it seems less surprising that privileged artists and artisans were cautious to exploit fully the commercial advantages of their privileged situation, had they even shared the modern conviction that in commercial expansion and mass-production lie the seeds of social and economic success.

At all levels of life nobles stood out from those around them. At the level of the city, their settlement patterns were distinct and contingent on a particular architectural ideal; at the level of the house, the naming, planning and decoration of their hôtels articulated the demands of a theatrically displayed *noblesse*. The aesthetic of classicism, with its rules of decorum, with its taste for symmetry and unity within diversity, offered the means by which the 'other', the ignoble, might be kept notionally at bay, whilst daily experience witnessed its reincorporation into the social fabric of the hôtel precisely because the maintenance of the noble distinction required the constant attendance of servants. Yet not all noble men and women lived in identical houses and the form of their display changed over time. How did the nobility distinguish themselves within their own 'caste', and what provided the motor for decorative renewal? These are the questions that remain to be answered.

5

A World of Distinctions

NOBLE TYPES

The content and structure of a social group invariably look different from the relative perspectives of outsiders and members. The French nobility was no exception. If, as a group, they helped construct and perpetuate an image of themselves as rightfully privileged – a splendid estate for others to contemplate – within the body of the nobility the cleavages that divided nobles one from another were profoundly felt, though not always sharply drawn. Emmanuel Sieyès, in a passage worth quoting at length, gave contemptuous expression to the nobleman's vision of his six- or seven-part society:

> In the first [class], are the *grands seigneurs*, that is to say that part of court society in which birth, high office and opulence are united. The second class comprises those presented at court [*présentés*] and known, those who appear [*paraissent*]: these are people of quality. Third in line are the presented but unknown . . . : these are people of substance [*de quelque chose*]. Fourth. In this class is to be found a mixture of the non-presented, who may nevertheless be sound [*bons*], and all the provincial *gentillâtres* – to coin an expression of theirs. In the fifth class should be placed the ennobled of some antiquity, or men of nothing. In the sixth, are relegated the recently ennobled or men of less than nothing. Finally, and so as not to forget anything, they [the noblemen] are happy to consign a seventh class to all other citizens, those who may be characterised by no more than insults. *This is how the social order appears according to the reigning prejudice, and here I am saying nothing unorthodox, except to those who do not belong to this world.*[1]

According to this representation, the nobility (roughly one per cent of a nation of some 26 million[2]) constituted a federation of highly differentiated sub-groups, in contrast to the mass of society relegated under a single, homogeneous heading. The complexity and diversity of the third estate was unrepresented, perhaps even unrepresentable, because ideologically it constituted a separate world of strangers, qualitatively and culturally distinct from the nobility. Indeed in the minds of this élite, the third estate had no culture to speak of. Germain Brice, for

instance, lamented the derogation of the once illustrious hôtel Séguier;

> It is currently the Bureau des Fermes du Roi where the Farmers General hold their assemblies. Custom duties and taxes are paid there; in a word, and without saying more, this building is frequented only by people who at best know a few basic rules of Arithmetic with which they do a good deal of business to the great inconvenience of society.[3]

Surrendering to tax-collectors the use of one of the finest Parisian mansions, and one sporting no less than two galleries and a chapel, not to mention decorations by some of the greats of the French school (namely Simon Vouet, the young Charles Le Brun and Pierre Mignard[4]) was apparently tantamount to casting pearls before swine. Brice's memory was of course socially selective. The symbolic power of the built forms of aristocratic culture had conveniently erased from his mind the uncomfortable fact that though originally erected for a duke, the hôtel Séguier owed its name and splendour to none other than a financier, however capaciously cloaked by robes of chancellery. Individual exceptions might be accommodated by such creative amnesia, but as a group financiers, though undeniably the most prestigious members of the third estate, were nevertheless perceived to inhabit a land foreign to nobility. By contrast, the differences between nobles were only ones of degree and not ones of kind. Variations in status were measured against a common scale and the distinctions between classes of nobility were in this sense quantitative not qualitative. Furthermore, to the degree that nobility was enhanced over time and through presentation at court, the internal hierarchy of the nobility was mutable and subject to competitive pressures.

According to Sieyès, in the passage just quoted, of all the characteristics with which the nobility particularly chose to qualify itself, pride of place was given to *naissance*. *Naissance* should be translated as lineage, not birth, for it was not so much a known biological event as the historical or mythical trace of a social and cultural process.[5] The most exalted birth was the one which had never taken place, the one which could not be categorically affirmed and dated, but which was immemorial, lost among the ruins of forgotten time. For these exalted few, such as the house of Montmorency, nobility was apparently theirs by right of ancient Frankish conquest and by the grace of God.[6] By contrast, a much greater number owed their noble 'birth' not to divine intervention, but to the more generous and prosaic hands of monarchs, to their bureaucratic needs and their *brevêts de noblesse*.[7] The nobility was thus divided vertically, first into ranks – in the 1660s Jean Le Laboureur's *Histoire* or *Traité de la pairie de France* had successfully invented a feudal tradition which set the peerage firmly above and apart from the rest[8] – and then once again, to established precedence within each rank according to antiquity of extraction. Thus, at the upper echelons, the social hierarchy was highly personalised; each individual finding his or her position precisely mapped on a matrix of titles and birth. In principle, the higher the rank and the longer the lineage the greater the expectation of, if not the warrant for, political power and participation in the affairs of state. To serve the crown and share in the polity was a right and duty the *noblesse* claimed as its due, and its notion of such service gave a particular focus to the idea of hierarchy in its relation to political power.

Service brought the individual directly under the patrimonial rule of the monarch and implied a personal bond between ruler and subject because, as Norbert Elias has amply illustrated, in patriarchal societies political power was grafted on to the structures of domestic authority and thus the ideal of service and *dignité* was assimilated by and expressed through the concept of kinship.[9] At the apex of the pyramidal structure of *ancien-régime* society stood the king, with below him the royal family and below them the princes and princesses of the blood, in order of their nearness to the throne. At this point the real kinship ties between the monarch and the members of his court ended and the pseudo-kinship ties began. The royal family was followed by the princes and princesses of foreign courts, the court aristocracy and the nobility, ranked in order of their progressively weaker relations to the king.[10] To be known and to be presented were the first essential steps into this familial court society; hence the emphasis on presenting, appearing and knowing in Sieyès's text. These ties of intimacy and estrangement corresponded, in the main, to the personal status of the individual concerned and could be measured in both temporal and spatial terms. Living at court and attending royal ceremonies expressed, through participation in the rituals of the monarch's daily life, a relationship with the king and a share in his power. Closeness to the royal person was equated with closeness to his status and might.[11] This analogical equation of physical proximity and political power drew the more ambitious sword and robe nobilities to court[12] and while the *séjour ordinaire du roi* remained the capital, the nobility clustered, as far as possible, in the districts immediately surrounding the Louvre.[13] The ideal nature of royal authority was centripetal, and just as the king's charisma attracted society and held individuals in various degrees of proximity to the throne,[14] so too the ideal royal capital found its shape in a series of concentric circles radiating out from the palace, each representing, respectively, the nobility in its hôtels, the third estates in its houses and lastly, on the very fringes of urban society those with neither house nor order. In such a utopian estates-city, the ideological structure of *ancien-régime* society, which privileged the perception of horizontal links of corporatism over vertical bonds of fidelity and clientage,[15] would have imprinted itself on settlement patterns and orientated housing along an axis between the centre and the periphery.

However, in fact, as noted in the previous chapter, by the eighteenth century the quartier des Halles (one of the districts adjacent to the Louvre) was no longer frequented by the second estate. Indeed, many contemporary observers registered concern at the gradual degentrification of the centre of Paris; in one instance the capital was likened to a kind of grotesque bird with 'a swallow's body and eagle's wings'.[16] Some of the reasons for the move to the periphery and the preference for suburban living have already been discussed, but the added prevalence of noble houses in the faubourgs Saint-Germain and Saint-Honoré, notably during the first half of the century, owed at least as much to the relocation of the court as it did to the requirements of the classic hôtel. The removal of the court from Paris during Louis XIV's reign favoured the areas flanking the thoroughfares to Versailles and other royal palaces. In the memorandum drawn up on behalf of the inhabitants of the faubourg Saint-Honoré in 1733, the appeal for exemption from new building restrictions had been strengthened by emphasising the ideal orientation of the district for the purposes of the court nobility.

> It almost immediately abuts the Louvre . . . It is the highway to Marly; it is adjacent to the one to Versailles: such that whereever it may be the King's pleasure to reside, one can say with certainty that there is no neighbourhood better suited to Persons whose Birth, Dignity and Functions call them to His Majesty's side.[17]

The authors concluded that the faubourgs Saint-Honoré and Saint-Germain 'are, from the point of view of location, the only two faubourgs in Paris suitable for great Houses'.[18]

Sieyès's panoramic view of noble society acknowledged that more than mere miles separated this urban nobility from country folk, and in dubbing the provincial nobility *gentillâtres* he tacitly adopted the vantage-point of the faubourgs. The wealth of buildings, theatres, salons and academies in such centres as eighteenth-century Nantes, Toulouse and Dijon is, however, a timely warning against recreating the self-deceptions of a court society committed to finding in regional culture no more than the pitiless repetition of its own demoded tastes. But, at the same time, the social and cultural contiguities that seem clearly to have existed between Paris and the provinces should not necessarily be taken as evidence of a shared identity.[19] Despite the accelerated urbanisation of the *gentilhommerie*'s (rural nobility's) cultural aspirations and spending patterns, the Renaissance ideal of autarchy remained morally and politically vital well into the eighteenth century.[20] Sobriety, discipline, independence and rational expenditure were, according to the marquis de Mirabeau, among the chief virtues that most clearly characterised country-gentlemen such as the Villièles and the Rocherolles, in contrast to their magnificent courtier cousins the Saulx-Tavannes, whose *éclat*, too often secured through the expedient of borrowing from Peter to pay Paul, seemingly dishonoured and enslaved them.[21] Magnificence, therefore, not only signified a cluster of socially specific cultural practices and, as such, constituted a key concept in the language of estates; redefined as a by-product and mainstay of absolutism it was also so polemically freighted in discourses on the nature of nobility that it effected a crucial split between true nobles and false ones, or urban courtiers and sometimes rural *honnêtes gens*.[22]

Titles, lineage and residency were by no means the only criteria by which nobility were internally differentiated, nor were they the sole factors with a bearing on royal attendance. Royal appointments and sinecures further ˙divided the nobility, in this instance into vertical orders such as the robe and the sword.[23] Sieyès, by grouping lineage with an important function, stressed that the position of even the *grands seigneurs* was contingent upon a number of factors over and above simple quality, of which office was by no means the least significant. Indeed, as the title 'logement de fonction' suggests, it was office that secured lodgings at Versailles *lateralis regis*, lodgings essential to the full flowering of noble prerogatives; only exceptionally did the king award grace-and-favour apartments.[24] Thus, for instance, before his wife's appointment as lady-in-waiting to the duchesse de Berry in 1710, the duc de Saint-Simon had lived at court thanks only to the generosity of his brother-in-law, the duc de Lorges, who was able to lend him his own suite because he and his wife were, in turn, free to poach Chamillart's (Lorges's father-in-law) rooms.[25] Such noble squatting appears to have been endemic, attesting perhaps to the resourcefulness and vitality of the nobility's *realpolitik* when confronted by royal policies that only just fell short of distorting and undermining the hierarchy of prestige and substituting a *méritocratie tempérée*. The taxonomic system that underpinned the proposal for a 1695 poll-tax, for instance, envisaged a hierarchy in which the officers of the sovereign courts and the state administration, including the financiers and tax-farmers, repeatedly outranked those merely dignified by birth, even if it was only as potentially rich sources of royal revenue.[26]

Of course, *dignité* and office were very often united, for one tended to entail the other; certain offices ennobled the holder and others were open only to those with noble status. But irrespective of the comparative authority of birth and office in relation to social hierarchy, the vertical orders within the nobility created strong force-fields of their own, both in terms of community and at the same time in the sphere of urban distribution. For example, the robe's initial preference for

those districts surrounding the Palais de Justice and its subsequent encampment in certain parishes in the Marais is well known.[27] Moreover, it was perhaps the continued prejudice for the parishes of Saint-Paul and Saint-Gervais among the many eighteenth-century epigones of these illustrious founding *robins*, at the very time when far more fashionable neighbourhoods were rapidly taking shape to the west, that had earned the Marais the reputation of a forlorn and reactionary backwater by the end of the *ancien régime*.[28] Meanwhile, as early as 1698, Brice noted that one of these westward districts, the quartier du Roule, had become a particularly densely populated neighbourhood, 'ever since Ministers of State and the businessmen who follow them everywhere, have decided to go and live there'.[29] In both instances, the settlement patterns of the ideal absolutist city were recast around the conflicting allegiances of professional culture. Where rank merely implied relative degrees of status, power (or proximity to power), splendour and office segregated, in the minds of many, the robe from the sword and ministers from courtiers.[30]

HÔTELS: ARCHITECTURE AND PLANNING

In their prescriptive writings, many architectural theorists seemingly advocated the extention of these fine social distinctions to architectural form. Jacques-François Blondel, for example, insisted that 'the rank of the property owner' should be 'the source from which the Architect determines the genre of his decoration',[31] and consequently, that built forms as a whole should offer society, 'the picture of the different orders of a policed State' in which to find its own reflection.[32] In some cases decoration was required to give tangible form to a relationship; the residences of those in line to the throne, for instance, were 'to resemble the dignity of Palaces . . .' 'One must be able to recognise in their general arrangement', continued Blondel, 'approximately the same character allocated to the residences of Sovereigns.'[33] From Blondel's discussion of the palais Bourbon it seems that palace architecture and decoration (in this case for the legitimised daughter of Louis XIV) was to be known above all for its correctness, for its exemplary character. Thus, Blondel was particularly unforgiving in his judgement of the sculptural decoration of the palace exterior, the work of Guillaume Coustou, because it audaciously gave a lead to architecture rather than settling neatly into the spaces conventionally articulated by pediment and entablature. Blondel concluded: '. . . since exterior decoration was introduced into architecture for the sole purpose of distinguishing the Palaces of *grands Seigneurs* from private houses it is essential that the former should not only be exempt from error, but also from all licence.'[34]

In other instances, Blondel maintained that decoration should give demonstrable shape to the values attached to certain social orders. The exteriors of hôtels destined for

Elevation de la principale porte dentrée de lHôtel dHumières.

Fig. 2.

Echelle

110

105   Elevation of the main entrance of the hôtel d'Humières, 1752–6. Engraving. From Jacques-François Blondel, *Architecture françoise*, 1752–6.

'Chiefs of the King's military forces' should, for example, be given

> a martial character, indicated by use of rectilinear forms, a balance of masses and voids and by a plan which, based upon the Doric order, reminds the spectator of the merit of the Heros who must inhabit them.[35]

Gentlemen were, moreover, warned against following the example of the duc d'Humières who had inadvisedly selected the Tuscan order to articulate the street façade of his residence on the rue de Bourbon (fig. 105). The ponderous rusticity of the Tuscan order was ill-suited, it seems, to expressing that urbane magnificence expected of an hôtel and a proprietor of the first rank.[36] By contrast, for the hôtels of the clergy, the Ionic order was recommended because, 'though less severe than the Doric, it announces no less the temperance which must preside in the residences of the foremost Ministers of the Church'.[37] Lastly, for the judiciary, Blondel advocated the Composite order, which thanks to its 'double aspect, both moderate and delicate' was, in his view, 'sufficiently suitable . . . for indicating the different functions attendant upon this kind of status'.[38] Thus, if the classical orders were to distinguish the hôtel from the *maison*, by the same token, the choice of order and the degree of decorative elaboration was, in principle, to distinguish the residences of the princes of the blood from those of mere nobles, and those of the marshals of France from the hôtels of the presidents of the Paris Parlement.

Evidently, the meanings of nobility articulated in jurisprudential, political, historical or genealogical writings, not to mention the host of other encomiastic texts, suffered inevitable and profound transformation when carried by the medium of architecture. The syntactic properties of construction lend themselves poorly to the semantic function required of an *architecture parlante*,[39] for proof of which we need look no further than Blondel's ultimately pedestrian reduction of the classical orders to social ones. Nobility consisted in a configuration of values, some personal, some genealogical and some vocational; and only with extreme difficulty could these be represented in coherent architectural narratives.[40] More-

over, since analysis of noble discourse must include some reference to what nobles actually said or wrote, it should be noted that rarely, if ever, did the nobility reveal any sensitivity to solecisms in the use of particular orders. Specific comments about the visual appearance of buildings are in fact rare in seventeenth- and eighteenth-century letters and memoirs.[41] The marquis de Lassay's only remark to his noble hostess, having been a guest at her house, was to suggest that she consider lowering the height of her window-sills in order to admit greater light into her apartment.[42] Ever discriminating in such matters of *commodité*,[43] Lassay, like his contemporaries, appears to have been indifferent to the symbolic values ascribed to columnar forms by professional architects such as Blondel. This perhaps suggests, that for the nobility itself these forms ultimately lacked the necessary mediating force for articulating status distinctions.

If pillars, columns and their attendant decoration can at best only allude to social values obliquely, distribution, or the internal arrangement of space is rarely representational, even in this limited sense. It constitutes a pattern of spaces variously related according to certain generative principles, and is experienced rather than read.[44] However, theorists such as Blondel, inordinately conscious of the structuring ideals of society, appear to have been eager to pursue distinction on behalf of their clients to the abstract level of the plan, and demanded that distribution arrogate the function of sign. *Convenance*, according to Blondel, required that,

> each room be located according to its purpose and according to the nature of the building, and that it have a shape and proportion relative to its function; the residence of a *particulier* should not, accordingly, be distributed in the same way as the Palace of a Sovereign . . .[45]

The difference between domestic houses was not, apparently, just a question of the type of rooms they contained but also a matter of their organisation. Sequences of spaces in an hôtel made up larger units known as *appartements*. 'An apartment', as Mme de Genlis was not the first to explain, referred both to 'a collection of several rooms, which united form a single lodging',[46] and to a social event, albeit a royal one: 'So termed . . . were general and formal assemblies of the royal family, the princes of the blood and the whole court, on the occasion of some memorable event . . .'.[47] Just as Scudéry had earlier implied that in polite speech this second meaning had all but emptied the word of its architectural sense,[48] so, contrary to expectation, Antoine Trouvain's series of engraved apartments (fig. 106), turn out to be not ground-plans or interior elevations but conversation-pieces, in which the identity and interaction of the named participants visibly outstrips in interest the character of the space in which the event takes place.[49] Moreover, this symbiosis of social and constructed forms was to characterise the spaces and distribution of the hôtel as a whole.

At a minimum, a noble dwelling was to incorporate three

104

106 Antoine Trouvain, *Quatrième Chambre des Apartemens*, 1696. Etching.

types of apartments – ceremonial, societal and personal – and the character of each was inscribed in its social function. The ceremonial rooms (or *appartements de parade*) were 'destined for the purposes of magnificence or to provide for the particular residence of the master'. There he might 'deal with matters of importance and receive people of quality'.[50] Such apartments were composed of antechambers, a *salle d'assemblée*, a *chambre de parade*, a *cabinet*, an *arrière cabinet* and several closets.[51] The purpose of the antechambers and *salle d'assemblée* was 'to receive people of distinction whilst they await the hour of the *lever* or the moment at which they might appropriately be admitted to the master's presence',[52] while the *cabinet* and *chambre de parade* were the loci of such meetings. The *cabinet* differed from the *chambre de parade*, in that the former was more-or-less equivalent to an office while the latter accommodated 'ceremonial visits'.[53] The extent to which these spaces, particularly the *chambre de parade*, were believed to occasion noteworthy events, and thus to partake of the public sphere, may however best be judged not from architectural theory but from design. For instance, Jean Le Pautre's set of model bed-alcoves published in the 1660s, instead of offering themselves exclusively as patterns, also functioned as representations, gratuitously setting the stage for momentous scenes of classical history (the deaths of Geta (fig. 107) or Cleopatra or Alexander), and suggesting thereby that the very grandeur of the place inspired the most sublime gestures of public despotism.[54] When not wrought on the battlefield, history it seems, was composed in the *appartement de parade*.

The *appartement de société*, meanwhile, comprised an antechamber, a dining-room, a *salle de compagnie*, a *salon* and several *cabinets* and closets.[55] Although certain units – notably antechambers and *cabinets* – were common to both apartments, the differing contexts changed both their ambience and function. The ceremonial apartment circumscribed an arena in which

individuals often of unequal status congregated, for whatever purpose, and the gradations in status of those present were, in a sense, ritualised. By contrast, the society rooms were rooms in which those of equal status communed for their mutual satisfaction. Thus, the rooms within the society apartments tended to provide the context for particular forms of entertainment, such as eating, conversation, gaming, music or dance, while the ceremonial apartments provided opportunities for distinction. Where the antechamber was a waiting-room within the *appartement de parade*, it doubled as a reception room, or substituted for a dining-room within the *appartement de société*.[56] Similarly, the *cabinet* was transformed from an office into a *cabinet de lecture* or a *cabinet de tableaux*, in short, a room for social intercourse of a particular kind.

The exhaustiveness of the lexicon of terms devised for describing these spaces added to the comprehensive range of geometrical forms proposed for them by eighteenth-century architectural manuals too easily promotes the idea that such places had a finalised and primarily aesthetic nature. As the following instance indicates, the identity and function of a space tended to remain flexible however prestigious its title, and was invariably open to the intentions of its occupants. In June 1722 the duc de Bourbon was forced to arbitrate in a disagreement between the gentlemen of the king's bedchamber and the officers of the royal bodyguard, provoked by the young Louis XV's habit of playing in the Galerie des Glaces at Versailles.[57] Court etiquette dictated that jurisdiction of the king's person was handed over by the gentlemen of the bedchamber to the king's bodyguard at the point when he crossed the threshold from his own chambers to the state apartment (to which the gallery was definitively attached). However, on this occasion Louis XV had effectively colonised the gallery for his personal (mis)use and since the *chambre* to which gentlemen were appointed was 'any place where the

107 Jean Le Blond after Jean Le Pautre, *On the Death of Septimus Severus, Caracalla Overwhelmed by Jealousy Murders his Brother Geta*, 1667. Engraving and etching. From *Differens desseins d'alcoves*, 1667.

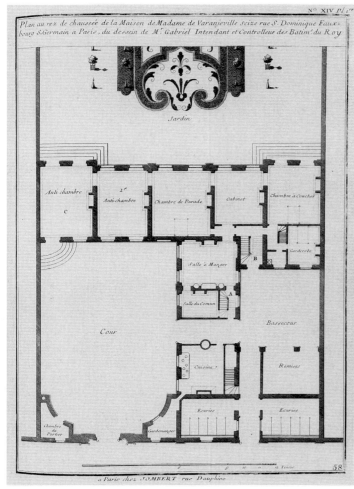

108 Ground-plan for the hôtel de Varengeville, 1752–6. Engraving. From Jacques-François Blondel, *Architecture françoise*, 1752–6.

architects were forced to improvise. At the hôtel d'Amelot (fig. 109), for instance, Germain Boffrand created an *enfilade* by blocking the axis between court and garden, thus compelling guests to turn right and 'traverse several sizeable rooms before reaching their host' in the *chambre de parade* or the *cabinet*, both situated in the far-left wing; a circuitous procedure nevertheless commended by Blondel because such 'ceremonial [was] necessary in an Hôtel of a *grand Seigneur*, though he may be the owner of an inconsiderable residence'.[60]

At an earlier date François Blondel had complained that the *enfilade* was an alien architectural form, which had evolved in Italy, for a people, 'who dedicate almost all their time and existence to ceremony and exterior show',[61] before subsequently being adopted in France. Though the comte de Tessé, for one, readily acknowledged the *enfilade's* Italian – or more particularly Milanese origin[62] – the amusement he derived from his visit to the Prince of Bozzolo arose not from the discovery of some exotic foreign custom but from the experience of a French ritual run riot: instead of two or three rooms, he traversed six or seven, instead of paying his respects once or twice he bobbed up and down like a marionette.[63] However, where Tessé hinted that such excessive ceremony merely disguised a gross lack of civility (his host having stayed in bed in order to avoid participation in the theatrical performance),

109 First-floor plan of the hôtel d'Amelot, 1752–6. Engraving. From Jacques-François Blondel, *Architecture françoise*, 1752–6.

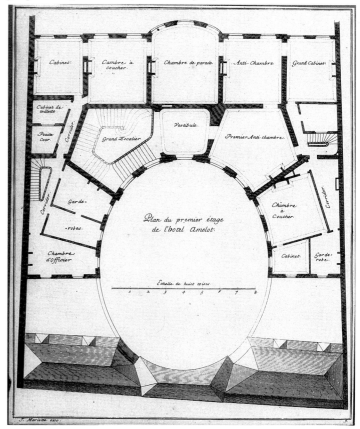

king chooses to live and where he wishes to be his particular self', Bourbon judged that shape and decoration notwithstanding the Galerie des Glaces was no gallery but a chamber. Thus, the apartment (in the social sense) to which a room belonged, consistently overrode its appearance as the primary determinent of value.

That said, the spirit of each set of rooms was usually apparent from its spatial arrangement and decoration. The *enfilade*, or linear sequence of interlocking spaces, was essential to the *appartement de parade* but merely desirable for the society rooms, so that when occasion demanded the two suites might be coupled to extend the ceremonial space.[58] The significance of the *enfilade* lay primarily in the fact that by providing an hermetic conduit through the building it also offered a gauge against which to measure distinction. Traditionally the units that constituted the *enfilade* were so arranged that when, as at the hôtel de Varengeville (fig. 108), all the doors were opened, it was possible to grasp the full length of the building and the complete scope of status at one glance.[59] When land was simply not available for such regimented unfolding of spaces,

Blondel held it responsible for the more serious crime of disfiguring the French architectural tradition. The accommodation of the *enfilade* entailed the removal of the grand staircase – pride of the architect's skill – from a central to a lateral position so that an uninterrupted axis along the width of a building could be made readily available.[64] The staircase at the hôtel de Varengeville, for instance, had been demoted to an obscure corner of the building, accessible only by inappropriate flight through the ground-floor or worse, by crossing the stable-yard.[65] The corollary to Blondel's accusation that in such instances good taste was sacrificed to social pretension was the suggestion that architecture should be subject only to the aesthetic judgement of artists and not responsive to the pressures of social life.

In a pioneering study on planning and etiquette, however, Hugh Murray Baillie argued that, contrary to architectural and literary evidence, status in French society was measured not in spatial terms (the number of rooms traversed by the visitor to reach his or her host) but in temporal terms – the exact moment at which the visitor was admitted to the master or mistress's presence.[66] The strength of Baillie's thesis lies partly in the comparison with English and German custom but, more importantly, in the ceremonial occasions he chose to discuss. He focused on group rituals, such as the king's *lever* and *coucher*, which required the mobilisation of the entire court and unfolded with customary exactitude according to a well-worn timetable, so that the exact nuance of each individual's *entrée* into the ceremony was gauged by all.[67] Yet such ceremonies, though daily, do not account for all the occasions for which the *appartements de parade* in palaces and hôtels were used. Formal visits also took place on an individual basis, and on such occasions space seems to have been more important than time in the ritualisation of status claims. Though hôtels did not necessarily contain a great abundance of rooms along a single axis, the procession through the spatial units was highly significant and occurred at both ends. It was not just a question of the number of rooms ascended by the visitor but also the extent to which the host was prepared to descend the *enfilade* to greet his guest. One eighteenth-century dictionary relates that M. de Novion, first president of the Paris Parlement under Louis XIV, when visiting Mazarin, 'penetrated as far as the last antechamber where he stopped, because cardinal Mazarin had yet to come forward to meet him'[68] and, in like manner, M. de Mesmes on a visit to cardinal Dubois, 'waited . . . until [His Eminence] came forward to greet him before moving off and entering the cabinet *with* him'.[69] Both he who called and he who received were thus aware of the exact place at which their meeting should occur, in accordance with their positions in the social hierarchy. Alternatively, ranks could be challenged and compliments or insults silently levelled by creative misuse of space and by minor transgressions of the unwritten but universally understood rules of social engagement.[70] There can scarcely be more persuasive evidence that spaces, buildings, rooms, are consti-

tutive of the social order rather than merely reflections or representations of it. The value system generated by the many and variously inflected spaces of hôtels was anchored in the motivations of a nobility who actively shaped and reproduced the social hierarchy in the rococo interiors of eighteenth-century Paris.

If the *appartement de parade* provided a hierarchical milieu within which individuals played out their social differences with the help of the sequence of sets provided, the society rooms offered an entirely different environment: the domain of sociability. The essence of sociability is interaction, not as a means to some extrinsic end, but as a goal in itself.[71] The structure of sociability is thus quite different from the structure of distinction. To maximise the levels of contact intrinsic to sociation, all those attributes likely to form barriers to interaction – such as rank, office and wealth – have to be concealed, not emphasised. Indeed, so stripped were the *habitués* of Mme de Dorcin's *salon* of all conventional marks of identity, that Marivaux's Marianne experienced difficulty defining them, and the account she gives of her introduction into their midst echoes with the sense of disorientation inevitably experienced by an outsider who wanders into a seamless and faultlessly choreographed group happening.[72] Conversation, dining, game-playing, the basic forms of eighteenth-century polite civility, were engaged in by a community of equals. It was not so much that the participants were of identical standing, but that such distinctions were suspended for the duration of the event. It seems pertinent to note here that, in contrast to the unyielding regularity with which Trouvain lined up his figures along a diagonal in the *Fourth Room*, Jean-François De Troy chose, in fashionable genre pieces such as *Reading from Molière* (fig. 110), to use a conjunctional composition, so that his figures are led to encroach upon each other's space and create a circle of overlapping and intimately enmeshed identities.

The ideological pattern of the *enfilade* was, therefore, neither necessary nor meaningful within this context; the society rooms could, potentially, be distributed in other ways. As already noted, spatial distribution is never arbitrary but is governed by systems of value. Given that the criterion informing the arrangement of society rooms was not related to the differentiated status of those who frequented them, it seems likely that the distinctive lay-out of the *appartement de société* resulted instead from the comparative importance attributed to certain forms of social intercourse. Where the logic of the *enfilade* determined that the last, or at least the penultimate room in the sequence was the most prestigious, the ideal of sociability conferred perfection on the centre, the point of ultimate confluence in a structure.[73] The pivotal importance of conversation in eighteenth-century polite society made the *salon* the generative focus of the society rooms, in some instances, closely followed by the dining-room, 'ever since the dining-table has come to be regarded as a locus of society'.[74]

The ideational structures of the *appartements de parade* and *de*

110   Jean-François De Troy, *Reading from Molière*, 1728. Oil on canvas, 72.4 × 90.8 cm. Sold Christie's, London.

société were thus quite different, even incompatible, and the incorporation of both in a building, which at the same time needed to present a unified and coherent exterior, was an unenviable task. Their separation could be effected either vertically, each being given a separate floor, or laterally in relation to the axis between courtyard and garden. The importance of a contained pathway, to modulate the gradation of personal encounters, favoured the choice of the first floor for the ceremonial apartments, since it allowed the colonisation of the staircase for processional purposes.[75] By contrast, since sociability was a matter of immediacy – Mme de Lursay, in *Les Égarements du cœur et de l'esprit* (1736–8) carefully explains to Mélicour that entry to the drawing-room could be denied to no member of polite society[76] – direct access to the *salon* and its satellite spaces encouraged a ground-floor location. By the same token, where both apartments occupied the same level, the *salon* was stationed on the short axis between court and

garden, flanked by its attendant units, and the ceremonial rooms tended to be strung out behind the courtyard façade. However, if the distribution of each type of apartment substantially followed self-regulating laws, the incorporation of both sets of rooms within the same architectural framework generated important meanings of its own. The Renaissance ideal of the *piano nobile* and the inevitable association of 'superior' with 'above' and 'inferior' with 'below' still enjoyed a certain vigour in the eighteenth century, to the advantage of the ceremonial rooms.[77] Similarly, though I have identified axis-length as primarily significant in distributional selection, within the wider context of the hôtel as a whole, the two poles, courtyard and garden, seem also to have implied a choice between engagement and retreat.[78] These additional meanings conveyed by the urban house had to be negotiated into compatability with the prevailing social vision of the eighteenth-century nobility. The greater status of the ceremonial apartments and their more obvious engagement with the world outside was tenable only so long as the house remained a public institution and admitted those of significantly unequal station to the residents. And society rooms were maintained in a subordinate, behind-the-scenes, position only so long as polite society was regarded as no more than a fraction (albeit a highly significant one) of a more universal community.

HÔTELS: DECORATION

Having established some of the principles of eighteenth-century distribution it is time to consider the ways in which interior decoration emphasised or subverted its values. Jacques-François Blondel was in no doubt about the nature of the relationship between planning and decoration: 'Distribution must be the Architect's first priority; even decoration depends utterly on an agreed plan'.[79] To this end, Blondel maintained that interior decoration should, above all else, create a unified impression, analogous in this to the exterior treatment of the hôtel.[80] Co-ordinated decorative schemes demonstrated both the architect's and the client's mastery of the universe of goods and their control of the dominant cultural paradigm.[81] The coherent decorative statement evinced a cultural competence in marked contrast to the fumbling uncertainty of those outside the orbit of polite society whose efforts produced, rather, the impression of patchwork. Thus, the family resemblances between design motifs, colours and objects was to be stressed, and only on closer inspection did the scheme reveal a subtle counterpointing in the treatment of individual rooms.[82] These variations were achieved in two ways: by proportionate elaboration and functional analogy. Just as the size and proportion of a room were indexed to its relative status,[83] so too decoration was required to reflect functional significance; the more important the room, the greater its size and the more lavish its treatment. Blondel, therefore, warned against richly ornamented vestibules, 'because it is a law of *convenance* that from the entrance of a building to the far end of the gallery, one should be able to observe a gradation in richness and magnificence proportionate to the destination and function of each room'.[84] In the *enfilade*, decoration was thus built up in stages, reaching a high point in the *chambre de parade*, the principal ceremonial reception area in the absence of a gallery.[85] Not only did ornamental design apparently evolve into ever more complex and elaborate patterns, but increasingly more costly materials were used and even the lighting effects built towards a climax.[86]

In the society rooms, the *salon* was similarly singled out for preferential treatment, but in order to effect a contrast with the other rooms, not provide a culminating point. Although *salons à l'italienne*, that is to say drawing-rooms that rose to the full height of a building, were comparatively rare in even the most substantial Parisian hôtels, more modest emphasis of

the vertical axis remained a conventional means of emphasising its centrality and importance by comparison with adjacent spaces. Instead of the drama of the Salon d'Angle at the Palais Royal (fig. 111), Mme d'Argenton, the Regent's mistress, contented herself with a more modest increase in the height of her *salon* (fig. 112), which nevertheless gave Boffrand the freedom to install a coved ceiling: a solution both architecturally valid and (intentionally or otherwise) proportionate to her status in society.[87] By and large, however, variation was achieved in these rooms by functional association; for example representational motifs might be deployed to signify the purposes for which particular rooms were used.[88] Thus, while hierarchy was established in the ceremonial suites by proportional elaboration, in the society rooms it was achieved primarily by pictorial reference to functional differences.

However, before analysing in greater depth the different treatment of the society and ceremonial rooms, it is worth briefly considering the comparative importance of the *chambre de parade* and the *salon* (and by extension, the apartments to which they belonged), judged by their respective degrees of magnificence. Such an assessment is hard to determine, since Blondel, for example, held simultaneously that the *chambre de parade* was the room 'in which is assembled the most valuable furnishings'[89] and that the *salon* was generally the largest and most elaborate room in an hôtel, likewise host to bronzes, paintings and 'expensive furniture'.[90] If, from the point of view of distribution, the ceremonial apartments should easily have outflanked the society rooms, in size and ornamentation the *salon* appears to have been winning the contest for decorative, if not societal, supremacy. Indeed, by 1714, the abbé Cordemoy confirmed that,

> At present . . . [the *salon*] is of all the rooms in a building the one over which greatest care is taken to make it the largest, the most spacious and the most highly decorated, with architectural ornament and with everything that Painting and Sculpture can offer which is both magnificent and exquisite.[91]

In short, decoration did not always support the spatial evaluations offered by planning. It sometimes qualified them.

Meanwhile, the kind of treatment prescribed for the ceremonial and society rooms was significantly different. The ceremonial apartment was not simply a living space as might be understood today, but a place of symbolic occupation, just as at court, chairs (particularly the *tabourets*) were not simply seats but symbols to be seized and positively sat upon.[92] In other words, the ceremonial apartment was an emblematic realm. Since nobility addressed itself primarily to the collective memory of society, these rooms tended to advertise the status of the owner by way of history. Though usually modestly decorated,[93] antechambers were generally hung with tapestries, and if their narrative content — the seasons, mythological or religious subjects — might appear arbitrary in

Coupe du Salon d'aligneme à l'Enfilade du grand Appartemt du Palais Royal

111   Gilles-Marie Oppenord, preliminary design for the Salon d'Angle at the Palais Royale, 1719–20. Pen, ink, and pencil on paper, 57.8 × 42.8 cm. Cooper-Hewitt, National Design Museum, New York.

Pl. XXXIV.

Décoration intérieure du Sallon de l'Hôtel d'Argenson.

Dela Marcade Sculp.

112   Section through the *salon* at the hôtel d'Argenton, 1745. Engraving. From Germain Boffrand, *Livre d'architecture*, 1745.

this context, the use of the medium alone was significant. Tapestry evoked the medieval and Renaissance lifestyle of a peripatetic court[94] and upheld the seventeenth-century taste for wall hangings.[95] In the same spirit, the costumes worn by the liveried servants present in these rooms traditionally echoed the colours of the family coat of arms and, in addition, tended to be stylised versions of the dress of a previous era.[96] Thus, the walls and the most conspicuous objects in antechambers – the servants – evoked the past of a noble ancestry. Of course, antechambers were not the only rooms to be decorated with wall hangings: Robert de Cotte's designs for the remodelling of Louis Le Vau's hôtel de Lionne (fig. 113) anticipated an important role for tapestries in the new decoration envisaged by Chancellor Pontchartrain, and focused on providing a

sculpted and panelled framework for them.[97] However, the imposing size of the rooms in which tapestries were necessarily displayed, and the distanced viewing that the scale of the figures encouraged, lent tapestried antechambers the unique function of establishing a respectful distance between visitor and master by analogy to the relationship between spectator and woven image, thus preparing strangers for the ritual structure of the hôtel.

A more direct but literal means of promoting the dignity of family lineage and the prestige of alliances, fidelities and functions was offered by the portrait. Second antechambers and *salles d'assemblée*, together with guard-rooms and presence chambers were frequently given over to 'ancestor worship' and lined with effigies of distant family heroes.[98] The intimate of

111

113 Robert de Cotte, elevation of an antechamber at the hôtel de Pontchartrain, *c*.1705. Pen, ink, wash and watercolour on paper, 15 × 22.4 cm. Cabinet des Estampes, Bibliothèque Nationale, Paris.

princes, the house of Noailles dedicated two rooms of its Paris mansion to portraiture; the guard-room was hung with six portraits of those in direct line to the throne, from Louis XIV to the ducs d'Anjou, later Philip V of Spain, and de Berry, as well as a portrait of the duc d'Orléans, while in the first-floor antechamber crowded thirteen full-length male portraits of the Noailles, up to and including the eighteenth-century field-marshal, Adrien-Maurice.[99] Moreover, the juxtaposition of antechamber and chapel within the hôtel led implicitly to the sanctification of the lives depicted and gave them an immortality in paint more palpable and perhaps more significant to the living than that offered by Christian faith.[100] Meanwhile, at the hôtel de Matignon the family's loyalty to the crown was made tangible by the congregation in the presence chamber; above the chimney-piece stood Louis XV; a marble bust of his great-grandfather on a pedestal sheltered beneath the canopy which gave the room its name, while on the walls portraits of Henri IV and François I jostled with portraits of the Matignons, notably Pierre Goubert's group portrait of the duc de Valentinois and his family. Finally, the overdoors were filled with likenesses of Louis XIII, Honoré II de Matignon, his mother, Marie de Lorraine, and Mlle d'Armagnac.[101] The compression of historical time into a genealogical present effected by this kind of chronologically negligent decorative arrangement (one occupied by a corporate community of painted past elders and living descendants) presented the viewer with a narrative that was more commendatory than commemorative and one within which pictures became active

114   Jean-Baptiste Le Paon, *The Battle of Rocroy*, 1769. Oil on canvas. Château de Versailles, Versailles.

115 Nicolas Lancret, *The Hunt Breakfast*, c.1740. Oil on on canvas, 61 × 133.5 cm. The Fine Arts Museums of San Francisco, Gift of Mrs. William Hayward.

symbols of noble right rather than the surface trace of lost identities.[102]

However, according to Louis Savot, it was the gallery that offered the environment *par excellence* for the display of 'Family trees, busts, portraits of Ancestors, [and] marks of their alliances, their ranks and their great deeds'.[103] The 'great deeds' he had in mind were, of course, primarily those actions performed on the battlefield. Savot was writing in the 1620s, at a time when the tradition of the heroic French gallery was still vital, particulary in the decoration of châteaux. Between 1631 and 1637, for instance, Claude de La Pierre executed for the château de Cadillac in Guyenne, twenty-two episodes from a projected life of Henri III, with particular attention to those heroic instances when the destinies of the king and the duc d'Epernon, patron of the scheme, were brought into felicitous conjunction. Some twenty years later, the Matignons employed Claude Vignon to celebrate eleven moments of outstanding virtue in the family's history, from the crusades to the end of the Wars of Religion, on the walls of the first-floor gallery of their château de Thorigny-sur-Vire, in Normandy.[104] Although more than a century later Louis-Joseph, prince de Condé, maintained the tradition by commissioning comparable battle pictures from Jean-Baptiste Le Paon (fig. 114) and Francesco-Giuseppe Casanova for the palais Bourbon to celebrate the glorious victories of the Grand Condé,[105] the intervening period had witnessed an eclipse of heroic galleries such as these, where the emblematic lives of particular *seigneurs* were made to demonstrate the opportune consequence of noble ideology active in society. François Blondel's endorsement of Savot's views in the 1685 edition of *L'Architecture françoise des*

bâtiments particuliers remained without effect, and early eighteenth-century galleries such as those at the hôtels Dupille and de Lassay appear more often to have functioned as extensions of the *cabinet de tableaux*.[106] As such, they generated an ambiguous space, ceremonial by size, location and traditional association, but societal by virtue of the display of cultural signs they offered as surrogates for symbols of nobility.

The decoration of society rooms was emphatically illustrative and descriptive by comparison with the *appartement de parade*. Though hunting was a noble pastime, the decoration of dining-rooms with scenes representing hunt-breakfasts or including depictions of dead game, such as Nicolas Lancret's two overdoors from a set of four (fig. 115), appear often to have been little more than a conventional reference to the fact that the product of these activities was edible, and indeed consumed within these very rooms.[107] In like manner, *jeux d'amours*, such as François Boucher's *Water* (fig. 117), were thought fitting for a *salle de billard* or *salons de compagnie* and some such decorated the *salons* at the hôtels de Montbazon and de Richelieu.[108] Evidently, representations of musical instruments were deemed suitable for music-rooms, but they might equally well substitute for gallant mythological subjects in a *salon*, when component parts of a broader allegorical scheme depicting the arts and sciences. The sculpted supports to two overdoors from panelling thought to derive originally from the hôtel Gontaud Saint-Blancart represent, for instance, instruments associated respectively with pastoral and chamber music (fig. 116) and completed a scheme that included attributes of architecture, painting, sculpture and astronomy.[109] 'Appropriateness' was the guiding principle of this type of decoration,

113

116 Panelling from the salon, formerly at the hôtel Gontaud, *c.*1740. Hôtel de Pillet-Wille, Paris.

117 François Boucher, *Water*, *c.*1740. Oil on canvas, 71.5 × 89.5 cm. Location unknown.

and appropriateness afforded a flexible and infinitely extendable lexicon of motifs; the mythological figures Bacchus and Ceres or depictions of the senses were also suitable for dining-rooms; the four seasons, the four continents, pastorals and landscapes might do quite as well for *salons*, or indeed any of the rooms in question, as they did at the hôtel de Feuquières.[110] Finally, representational motifs might be dispensed with altogether in favour of simple ornament.[111] In the absence of governing symbolic values, the rhythm of variation and change in the society apartment was therefore potentially swift.

The types of decoration respectively mooted by the *appartements de parade* and *de société* encouraged quite different ways of seeing. The sequence of contexts created in the former constituted a visual code which, if properly deciphered, furnished visitors with information and props sufficient to perform social rituals with exemplary tact. The *chambre de parade*, for instance, presented an environment divided in two by a

118   Chambre du Prince at the hôtel de Soubise, 1745. Engraving. From Germain Boffrand, *Livre d'architecture*, 1745.

balustrade. On one side, in an alcove and often raised on a dais, stood the bed, framed by tapestries, silken threads of a noble past's weaving (fig. 118); on the other side, a void opened out into a reception space circumscribed by panelled walls, often boasting heraldic emblems or sculpted monograms (fig. 120), and perhaps further embellished with portraits or allegorical personifications of noble virtues (fig. 119).[112] Offered to a knowing glance, each one provided evidence both of the ontological basis of noble status and the genealogical history of the particular household. Taken together, as part of a coherent environment structured by the contrast between alcove and room, they achieved something more. The theatre-like arrangement of space, oriented visitors towards the alcove in readiness for a performance to which they related as no more than passive spectators. The resulting axis between the bed and the door provided a contained scale along which those present in the *parterre* could arrange themselves according to rank: if asked to sit down, one should, according to Antoine de Courtin's best-selling *Nouveau Traité de la civilité* (1671), be careful 'to place onself at the bottom end, which is always the side of the door by which one has entered, just as the upper end is always there where the person of quality is stationed'.[113] Owing to the plan's additional likeness to a church or chapel, the room was overlaid with an aura of sanctity and the balus-

trade took on the function of an altar rail. In the king's bedchamber at Versailles, a valet guarded the king's bed from within the balustrade and prevented anyone from approaching it;[114] touching either the bed or balustrade was an act of desecration and was, in a noble house, grossly disrespectful.[115] The combination of plan, decoration and strategically placed objects elevated the *chambre de parade* from a bedchamber to a metaphor that perfectly aligned spatial and social frameworks. The simple oppositions between noble and common, upper and lower, sacred and profane, when grasped cognitively as well as perceptually not only enabled visitors to behave politely but involved them in the reproduction by enactment of the conceptual categories of the *ancien-régime*'s social hierarchy. As long as the content of those categories went unchallenged and undisturbed, the material environments that gave them cultural life were highly resistant to formal change.[116]

By contrast, the decoration of the society rooms was rarely interactive in this sense. Since sociability negated inherent status differences and transformed honour from a providential right into something to be negotiated, there was no call for decoration to play a symbolic part in statements about status. Instead, it occupied the margins of perception, reinforcing an ambience created independently by the activities of polite society. Courtin stressed, therefore, that it was impolite 'to

115

stare at the books belonging to a person one should respect, unless they were located in the library'.[117] By extension, while it was appropriate to study with respectful attention ancestral portraits in an antechamber or *salle d'audience*, or scrutinise and admire works of art collected in a *cabinet*, it would have been thought rude to stare fixedly at pictures decorating a *salon* or dining-room, unless expressly invited to do so. To stare and exclaim over an object in a societal space was, according to Courtin, to betray either a self-satisfied smugness or a degree of ignorance, both of which were inadmissable in polite circles.[118] In the *appartement de société*, paintings were required to blend in with the rest of the decoration not stand out from it — hence the ubiquity of easily recognisable and familiar pictorial themes, themes that were appropriate to the setting, and where possible, subjects that could either be repeated throughout a single room, such as landscapes and still-lifes, or offered an obviously linked sequence, such as the times of day, the seasons or the elements. The eye was thereby tempted not to settle for long on a single object but to sweep the room for a total impression.

It would be a mistake to infer a dissipated attention and a lack of discrimination from the refractory quality of the spectator's gaze in society rooms. There, decoration had in fact moved from a hieratic sphere into a fluid and competitive forum. The *monde* may have been constrained by its own taboos from articulating or legitimising its choices in words but the very purchases they made demonstrated a marked sensitivity to the choices of others. Hosts and hostesses vied with each other for the novel and the fashionable, because to display something suitably new was to gain a certain advantage over others.[119] The world of goods became a complex system of signs, which referred not to some extrinsic set of values but gleaned their coherence and intelligibility from one another.[120] The *tabouret*, or the chair emblazoned with the family crest, had no need to diversify or multiply, other than for the purposes of use, for the objective was achieved as efficiently by a single type as by any number of tokens; variation in form was almost redundant there. Chairs as signs, on the other hand, were infinitely variable and the significance of a *bergère* as against a chair *à la grecque* depended on the rhythms of fashion. The desirability of the one depended on the fortune of the other. Forms mutated, superseded or replaced one another as more goods entered the realm of the desirable and altered the content of the sign-system. Keeping up with the Joneses, and preferably overtaking them so as to turn back the tide of emulation, was therefore the motor force of societal display. It is not without reason, therefore, that it was the *appartement de société* and particularly its myriad *cabinets* that so often provided the context for fashion-plates (fig. 121) and other such commercial imagery.

'Novel' and 'traditional' goods were not, then, mutually exclusive nor was one more abreast of commercial realities than the other. They satisfied different cultural needs and simultaneously occupied separate spatial realms. Tapestries, *menuiserie*, antiques, Boulle furniture, formal portraits and history paintings were more often concentrated in *appartements de parade*; architectural perspectives occurred in those hôtels where the staircase was annexed to ceremony space; while *ébénisterie*, wallpapers, printed textiles and the lesser genres of painting proliferated in society rooms and pavilions.[121] The accelerated turnover of the decoration in the *appartements de société* doubtless encouraged the creation of new materials and the elaboration of new styles, but the continued presence of the ceremonial rooms at the same time ensured a stable market for less materially and stylistically adventurous commodities. Both shared, however, an orientation towards high-cost goods produced very often in comparatively small quantities for the only market that counted.

Se vend a Paris chez BEREY Graveur rue St Jacques a la Princesse de Savoye. Avec Privilege du Rey. 1697

Madame la Duchesse de Montfort.

119 (facing page top)   Cartouche representing Glory from the panelling of the Chambre du Prince, 1737–8. Hôtel de Soubise, Paris.

120 (facing page bottom)   Detail of the panelling in the Chambre du Prince, 1737–8. Hôtel de Soubise, Paris.

121 (right)   Berey, *The Duchesse de Montfort in her Cabinet*, c.1695. Engraving.

PART III

Fields of Contest

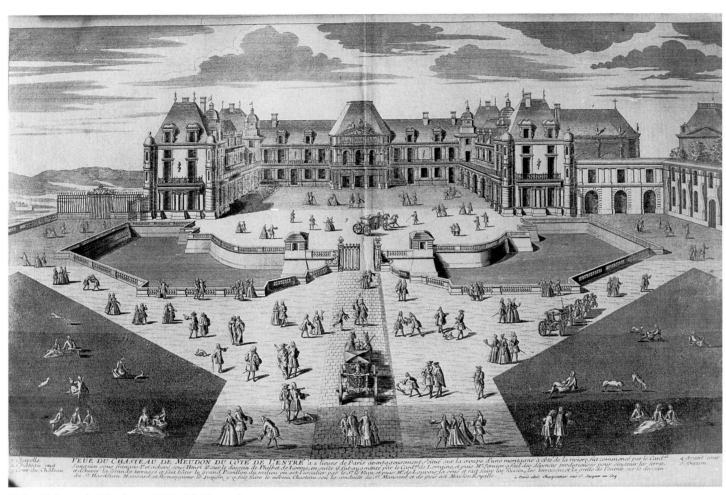

VEUE DU CHASTEAU DE MEUDON DU CÔTE DE L'ENTRE à 2 lieues de Paris avantageusement situé sur la croupe d'une montagne à côté de la rivière, fut commencé par le Card.ᵃˡ

123   Château de Meudon, *c*.1725–30. Engraving.

6

'The Nursery of Kings': Versailles and its Satellites

In 1709 Saint-Simon confided to his journal that the royal court was not one but three.[1] It had broken up along the lines of the Bourbon genealogical tree as some courtiers and ministers treasonably anticipated the king's demise and tried to curry favour with his likely successor. Mme de Maintenon, Louis's legal but unofficial wife, may have rallied those who still believed it prudent to cast in their lot with the status quo, but the factions of the Grand Dauphin and the duc de Bourgogne looked more-or-less resolutely to the future. The fragmentation of the court had also been noted, though not in so many words, at a slightly earlier date by Martin Lister who, on his journey to Paris in 1698, christened the region of the Ile de France, 'Le Berceau des Roys, or the Nursery of Kings', for the dense proliferation of châteaux belonging to the royal family to be found there, which implicitly compromised the central focus of Versailles.[2] Most important among these rural palaces was Meudon (fig. 123), a château of Renaissance origin, most recently the possession of the widowed Anne de Souvré, marquise de Louvois, but traded with the dauphin for Choisy in 1695.[3] That it immediately presented a rival attraction to Versailles is suggested by the marquis de Dangeau's entry in his diary for 18 February 1698: 'After supper the King found himself alone with M. du Maine, because Monseigneur [the dauphin], Monsieur [the king's brother, the duc d'Orléans] and the princes are all at Meudon or in Paris.'[4]

For over fifteen years Monseigneur lavished time and money reorganising, redecorating and extending the château to make it worthy of his use. Initially, attention focused on providing him with a suitable apartment, first on the ground-floor and then, from 1698 to 1699, on the first. It was the decoration of the second set of rooms, four in all, that established Meudon's fame. The elaborate marble chimney-pieces inspired by Bérain, with bronze mounts by Boulle and mirrors stretching up to the ceiling, the panelling intricately carved by Louis Nivet, the ceilings painted with grotesque fantasies by Claude III Audran and the overdoors gallantly filled with oil paintings by Coypel, La Fosse, Jouvenet or Boullogne, together allegedly struck a note of unprecedented modernity. Moreover, if

the construction and decoration of the so-called Aile des Marroniers in 1702 seemed to effect a return to more conservative artistic priorities, the interiors of the Château Neuf (fig. 124), built by Hardouin Mansart in 1706–7, once again announced decorative novelties and innovations not found elsewhere at this date.[5] The panelling by Degoullons and his workshop for the gallery of the Appartement du Roy, for instance, with its fluently carved pier-glass frames, decorated with coupled dolphins and strings of shells; the same gallery's cornice, designed as an uninterrupted sequence of arabesques with dragons, chimeras, tormenting putti and vases of flowers; the room's chimney-pieces, which anticipated those of the Regency; its console tables, which were no longer resolutely rectangular but combined curves and angles, and finally the remarkable tapestry series, the *Months in Grotesques*, designed by Claude III Audran for the dauphin's bedchamber, again seemingly conspired to set the residence and the court of a son apart from those of his father.

Meudon has, of course, long filled the role of stalking-horse in art-historical debate about the nature of artistic development at the end of the seventeenth century, perhaps not least because so little survives in the way of plans and drawings to

124 Château Neuf de Meudon, 1752–6. Engraving. From Jacques-François Blondel, *Architecture françoise*, 1752–6.

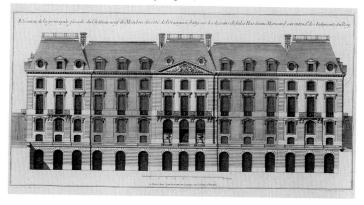

give an accurate picture of the interiors. Few would dispute that the 1680s and 1690s marked a point of departure from the orthodoxy of the *style Louis XIV*. For Fiske Kimball and Pierre Marcel, the period 1680–1720 represents a watershed between the baroque-classicism of Versailles and the later, full-blown rococo of the capital.[6] Yet, while Kimball locates the driving force of change within the state administration, at the Bâtiments du Roi, Marcel, to some extent anticipating Antoine Schnapper's views, suggests that the same decades constituted a period of artistic anarchy provoked by the collapse of the state's control over artistic practice.[7] However, Marcel and Schnapper disagree fundamentally about whether a distinction may usefully be made between Louis XIV's taste and that of his son, between Versailles and Meudon, and, more generally, between proponents of an outgoing, bigoted classicism and incoming, modern colourism; a distinction that Schnapper finally dismisses as specious.[8] All of them, however, assign a decisive role, active or passive, to the state. Recognition of Colbert's achievement in establishing a unified, sustained and politically urgent cultural policy implemented through royal patronage and the academies tends to lead, however, to the barely challenged elision of crown and court, and to the conviction that any truly alternative artistic programme must, therefore, have originated outside Versailles. However, the validity of such a monolithic construction of absolutist culture must surely remain open to question.

If, as Maurice Magendie has shown, the 'acculturation' of the nobility initially occurred away from the court, in the private *salons* of the capital,[9] by the 1660s Louis XIV had successfully effected a shift in the cultural centre of the realm by attracting *salon* society to court[10] and at the same time endorsing or founding institutions capable of directing culture for the political ends of absolutism.[11] Despite the centralising and unifying tendencies of Louis's cultural policy, a certain distinction nevertheless remained between the sociability and taste inherited from the *mondain* tradition of the *salons* and the new artistic ideology propagated through royal patronage and the academies. This distinction is discernible in the very organisation of the Maison du Roi. Until the end of the *ancien régime* the cultural life of the court was administered by two separate departments: the Surintendance des Bâtiments and the Menus Plaisirs.[12] While the Bâtiments was responsible for meeting the monarchy's needs for permanent architectural and decorative works, the task of the Menus Plaisirs was to organise court entertainments and ceremonies. In a certain sense, then, the former was charged with legitimising the ascendency of absolutism through affective images of royal supremacy and power, while the latter catered for the social life of those in the king's circle. The intended audience of the Bâtiments's activities therefore extended well beyond what Roland Barthes has called the 'inland' of court society; by contrast, the scope of the Menus Plaisirs was limited to within its enclosure.[13]

Since the Bâtiments provided the infrastructure for the Menus' schemes, there were, clearly, areas of jurisdictional overlap. However, their relationship was not always co-operative. Jean I Bérain, who held the post of Dessinateur de la Chambre et du Cabinet du Roi from 1674 to 1711, was not once employed by the Bâtiments – despite clear proof of his talents at Meudon and elsewhere, and notwithstanding the flattering dedication of his *Desseins de Cheminées* (*c*.1699) to Mansart, the Surintendant of the day.[14] It seems likely that the Bâtiments resented the amounts of revenue spent by the Menus, even though their budgets were entirely separate, and was inclined to condescend to a department that primarily concerned itself with ephemera.[15] It is rather harder to gauge the attitude of the Menus Plaisirs towards the Bâtiments. However, the nature of their respective administrative appointments may suggest something. The *surintendance* was a purchasable office at the king's disposal.[16] Colbert had, for instance, entailed the office to his youngest son Jules-Armand, marquis d'Ormoy and de Blainville.[17] Likewise, some fifty years later the duc d'Antin similarly left the now more modestly titled office of Directeur des Bâtiments du Roi to his son, the duc d'Epernon who, in the event, predeceased him.[18] The direction of the Menus Plaisirs, on the other hand, belonged in rotation to the four *Premiers gentilshommes de la Chambre du Roi*, nobles of the most sifted quality, invariably the highest peers of the realm – in short, gentlemen who could expect to outrank the *surintendants* in both status and office.[19] The duc de Luynes recognised the anomaly of d'Antin's appointment to the Bâtiments, noting that 'Before him the office of Surintendant des Bâtiments had never been occupied by seigneurs', before going on to speculate, rightly as it turned out, that the charge would revert to its former bureaucratic constituency.[20] Thus, an unshakably noble office confronted a potentially bourgeois department and tensions were surely inevitable.

It has, of course, long since been recognised that the courts of Louis XIV and his successors were socially heterogeneous, and variously composed of more-or-less indigenous grandees and migratory bureaucrats. Indeed, it may have been in partial acknowledgement of the constantly shifting nature of the court's constituency that La Bruyère chose to describe the court as a process not a place. In *Les Caractères* (1688–96), for instance, 'la ville' (the robe and wealthy bourgeoisie) and 'les grands' occupy separate chapters on either side of 'la cour' – the web of social relations in which both hoped to negotiate for favour and advancement.[21] The shared court-experience of these two groups, and the implied tendency of the former to ape the latter, is not however proof of a common cultural life.[22] Many aristocrats must have shared the chevalier de Méré's feelings of injured pride faced with the propensity of kings to call upon professionals (scientists, historians, grammarians, rhetoricians and so forth) or government officials, rather than upon 'the most *honnête* people' of the time (of whose number they counted themselves) for the council and wherewithal to fashion and increase the cultural lustre of their courts.[23] The material outcome of such resentments may perhaps be found in the outflowing of tensions between the Bâtiments and Menus Plaisirs into the patronage networks that encompassed them. The dauphin's appreciation of Bérain was apparently matched by an equal dislike of Mansart (the Surintendant and the architect officially charged with the works at Meudon), whom he would gladly have dismissed had he not feared overtly displeasing his father.[24] Monseigneur also conspicuously favoured Antoine Coypel at the very time Mansart was seeking opportunities to snatch initiatives from the Coypels in order to give them to the heir of the grand tradition, Charles de La Fosse.[25] Moreover, there is mounting evidence to suggest that the nobility not only patronised its own favourites but that it remained faithful to many of the aesthetic ideals promoted by the early *salons* in preference to the 'grand goût classique' launched through the academies and shared by 'la ville'.[26] It is possible to discern the survival of these earlier, late sixteenth- and early seventeenth-century forms of noble culture in the decorative programmes and court entertainments, inspired by the Menus Plaisirs.

125 Jean I Bérain (attributed to), designs for architects's costumes, 1700. Red chalk, pen, ink and wash, 22.7 × 15.2 cm. Nationalmuseum, Stockholm.

THE GROTESQUE

Grotesques were a form of decoration that owed their name to the cavernous, partially excavated rooms in Roman palaces and villas in which they were first discovered during the Renaissance. That this genre was grotesque adjectivally as well as etymologically, that is to say that it offered a form of decoration that was in every sense the opposite of the classical, was immediately recognised and, as I hope to show, variously appreciated. Grotesque decoration and the *ballet de cour*, for both of which Jean I Bérain provided designs in the 1680s, were introduced at the French court under François I and Henri III. They enjoyed a sustained, if low-key success throughout the following centuries, and an enthusiastic revival, particularly in the dauphin's circle, in the last decades of the seventeenth and early decades of the eighteenth centuries.[27] It is worth briefly comparing these seemingly disparate cultural phenomena, not simply because they became the subject of initiatives by the Menus Plaisirs but because they shared similar relationships with their 'audiences' despite the differences that necessarily divide the performing and the visual arts.

A significant feature of the *ballet de cour* and the later masquerade was that it entailed the participation of courtiers. The architects' costumes (fig. 125) that Bérain designed, possibly for Germain de la Barre's ballet, *Le Triomphe des arts* (1700), were intended to clothe noble flesh for a performance not only before, but of the court.[28] The visual arts, bound by the hermetic contours of their forms, are rarely credited with the potential for effecting such an immediate conjunction of the subject and the objects of cultural privilege.[29] Yet contemporary anecdotes serve to negate the commodity status proverbially assigned to works of art. Charles-Antoine Coypel implies in his account of his father's decoration of the Pavillon d'Aurore at Choisy, that the ceiling no less than the reported conversation was in some intangible way the product of the intimate and daily intercourse between the painter and the Grande Mademoiselle.[30] If in that instance 'polite commerce' benignly lit the flame of genius so often 'snuffed out by too great a solitude', its interventions, on other occasions, could be even more direct. Audran, we are reliably informed, regularly made a point of reserving parts of the composition of his grotesques 'for different subjects to be determined by the wishes of the individuals decorating their ceilings and panelling in this genre'.[31] Meanwhile, the duc d'Orléans climbed the scaffold and lent his hand to painting the ceiling of his gallery at the Palais Royal.[32] Admittedly, all these tales were told by, or on behalf of, artists whose social and professional vanity was soothed, no doubt, by the company they were said to keep. However, putting aside the relish with which the narrator reports the mad and undignified scramble that preceded Coypel's (and Orléans') excution of the *Assembly of the Gods* (fig. 126) – the central section of the ceiling of the Galerie d'Énée – as court beauties vied to audition for parts, the tale may nevertheless be trusted in so far as its contemptuous humour was anchored in a received truth; that nobility served to blur the distinctions that notionally separated production and consumption. The habits of seeing portraits in pictorial fictions, of assuming a multiplicity of hands and a community of minds at work in any decorative scheme, in short, of recognising the presence of subjects in the very symbols of their status, had the effect of belying the exchange-value of the works themselves.[33] Thus, decoration, and particularly grotesque decoration, articulated noble prestige in a manner quite different from the collecting of works of art, which, though it might also distinguish the owner, focused attention more nearly on things, on the objects of an essentially bourgeois accumulation.

126 Antoine Coypel, *The Assembly of the Gods*, 1702. Oil on canvas, 95 × 195 cm. Modello for the ceiling of the Galerie d'Enée at the Palais Royale. Musée des Beaux-Arts, Angers.

The shared character of the grotesque and the *ballet de cour* or masquerade as performance was surprisingly underscored in a letter written by Daniel Cronström to Nicodemus Tessin the younger in January 1700. 'Since my last', begins Cronström, 'I have been to see Mr Bérain to pay him. I came away with two grotesques . . . in my possession.' But the next sentence reveals that these grotesques were not, as might be expected, designs for wall or ceiling decorations, but costumes; 'Last year these grotesques were used by M. the Dauphin, and are all the more excellent for disguising both hands and feet'.[34] The use of a common nomenclature suggests the protean nature of the grotesque, ready for transfer and adaptation to any surface, while the element of disguise hints at the perceptual delusions immanent in the form. It was a kind of decorative ornament that, like court spectacles, privileged novelty, improvisation, and the *merveilleux*. In 1683 the *Mercure Galant* justified its significant failure to report in detail on the chimerical costumes created for one of the dauphin's masquerades on the grounds that they were intended 'to gladden the eye not loosen the tongue', and were, in fact, so elaborate that no painter's brush could capture their multiple *bizarrerie*.[35] Guidebook descriptions of grotesque schemes are similarly disappointing.[36] Their authors habitually excused their incapacity to give a verbal picture of the ornamental compositions on the grounds that the details were too profuse, even supposing they could describe what they could not name. Like Lemarquant in the *salon doré* at Anet, they contented themselves with simply noting that the schemes were 'in the grotesque genre'.[37] Visual impact insistently dominated narrative purpose, for although individual elements of a grotesque or pageant might be emblematically significant – for instance, the presence of Nep-

tune posed beneath a baldacchino in one of the corners of the duc de Vendôme's ceiling at Anet (fig. 127) may suggest a scheme in which classical gods were called upon to symbolise the Elements – the relationship between the components of the composition was primarily formal and metaphoric, not discursive and metonymic. In other words, relations of resemblance not representation structured the decorative field. At Anet monkeys and men, and zephyrs and dragonflies inhabited a common universe by virtue of an intrinsic, graphic (and epistemological) similitude.[38] The visual scope of a project thus invariably exceeded the putative demands of its chosen theme, and insignificant and gratuitous display outstripped the strictly meaningful.

As these introductory remarks are intended to suggest, the grotesque was, in the context of academic theory, an *agent provocateur* not least because the very boldness of Bérain's, and later Audran's designs, assured them unprecedented visual attention. In the Galerie d'Ulysse at Fontainbleau, completed by Niccolò dell' Abate under the direction of Primaticcio in the mid-sixteenth century, grotesques had been confined to the margins, where they were subtly employed to heighten the impact of the paintings they framed.[39] In such circumstances, theorists and honorary academicians such as Claude-Henri Watelet could look indulgently upon their use, on the grounds that,

since good sense does not preclude a place for a kind of aimiable unreason, which when carefully managed may serve as its ornament, [so] the Arts, sober and reserved by nature, have no less the right occasionally to derogate from the austerity of their grand principles.[40]

127   Claude III Audran, design for a ceiling at Anet, 1704. Pen, ink, wash and watercolour on paper, 41.3 × 35.5 cm. Nationalmuseum, Stockholm.

However, in the hands of late seventeenth-century exponents of the genre, the grotesque had been moved from the periphery to the centre of vision, and not only in the decoration of minor, society rooms. At the hôtel de Mailly-Nesle, one of Bérain's few documented and partially surviving commissions, both the walls and the ceiling of the *chambre du lit* (figs 128, 130) were painted with gallant patterns of golden ornament.[41] Some thirty years later, during the Regency, the duc d'Antin chose more audaciously still; he hung the royal presence chamber and *chambre de parade* at his château de Petit-Bourg, known today only from Jean Chaufourier's drawings (figs 129a, b), with grotesque tapestries, of a yet more adventurous kind.[42]

The grand scale of these social spaces made it impossible for the inherent permissiveness of the genre to be overlooked. Vitruvius, whose opening rebarbative salvoes echoed down the straights of all subsequent criticism on the subject, condemned the grotesque on at least two counts of implausibility. 'For how is it possible,' he asked rhetorically, 'that a reed should really hold up a roof, or a candelabra a pediment with its ornaments, or that such a slender, flexible thing as a stalk should support a figure perched upon it, or that roots and stalks should produce now flowers and now half-length

figures?'[43] It was as if Bérain and Audran's 'peopled scrolls' had fetched up upon a selenic landscape where none of the laws of gravity or rules of perspective applied. Along cardinal and diagonal axes airy patterns of two-dimensional strapwork, fillets and scrolls were lured into irrational conjunction with shallow, projecting stands, over-canopied with vegetal or architectural forms, thereby creating tension between surface and volume. Instead of accentuating and clarifying the tectonic structure of a room, the only proper function of decorative sculpture and painting according to the Académie Royale d'Architecture,[44] grotesques hastened to confuse the perception of volume by a complexity of pattern that settled restlessly on the supporting surfaces. The oscillation between two and three dimensions – between pattern and representation – added to the difficulty of grasping grotesque decoration in its totality, of seperating primary from secondary elements, and it intensified the beholder's sense of helpless wonder in the presense of a composition to which there was no key.

The second 'fraud' which apparently, merely added to the grotesque's charm was its mixed cast of antique and plebian, and real and fabulous characters. Bérain's grotesques and those of his followers remained sufficiently flexible within their unobtrusively symmetrical armatures, to absorb an infinite

128 (left)   Panelling for the Chambre de Parade formerly at the hôtel de Mailly-Nesle, 1686. Remounted at the château de Vernou-en-Sologne

130 (facing page)   Ceiling of the Chambre de Parade, 1686. Hôtel de Mailly-Nesle, Paris.

129a (below)   Jean Chaufourier, section of the château de Petit-Bourg, 1730. Pen, ink, wash and watercolour on paper, 63.3 × 92.1 cm. Hazlitt, Gooden and Fox, London.

129b (bottom)   Detail of the section in fig. 129a, showing the Chambre and Antichambre du Roi.

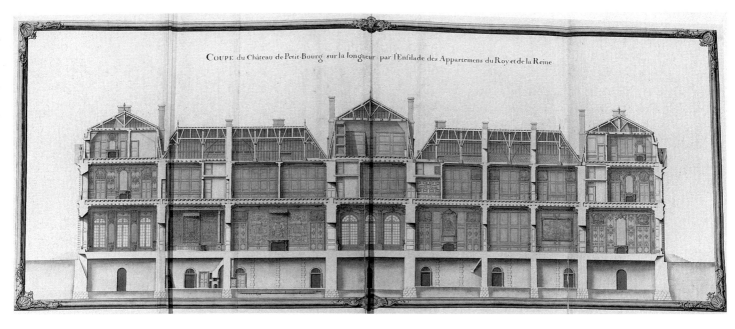

COUPE du Château de Petit-Bourg sur la longueur par l'Enfilade des Appartemens du Roy et de la Reine

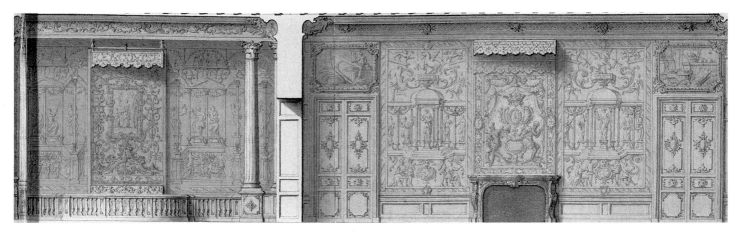

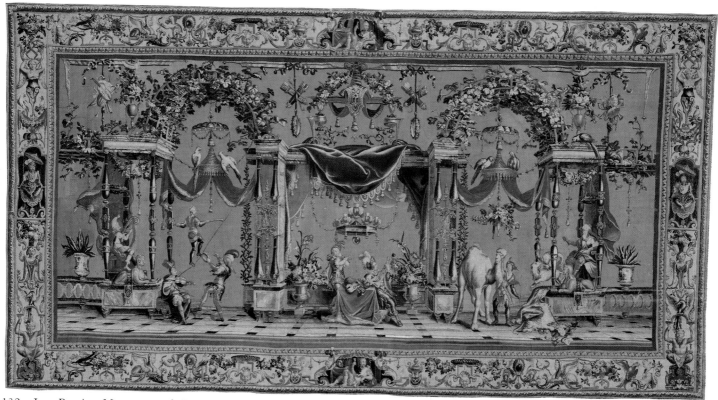

132 Jean-Baptiste Monnoyer and Guy-Louis Vernansal, *The Camel*, *c.*1700. Wool and silk, 279 × 528 cm. From the Beauvais tapestry series known as the *Bérain Grotesques*. Metropolitan Museum of Art, New York. Gift of John M. Schiff.

range of motifs and compositional variations. Though inextricably part of a long decorative tradition with its roots in antiquity,[45] the grotesque was, as Michel de Montaigne perspicaciously noted, still an evolving genre at some distance from definition.[46] Antique and sixteenth-century precedents conferred a certain respectability and prestige on the genre and offered a ready glossary of motifs, but these precedents were a point of departure – not ideal touchstones the perfection of which the modern artist could only, at best, hope to recapture. The grotesque remained an open form, and although Bérain's designs employed an almost exclusively classical and Renaissance vocabulary, his early disciples Jean-Baptiste Monnoyer and Guy-Louis Vernansal drew on the vernacular tradition of the fair-theatres for their *Tenture des grotesques*, woven at the end of the seventeenth century in the workshops of Philippe Behagle at Beauvais.[47] In *The Camel* (fig. 132) baldaquins, trophies, vases and sphinxes combine not only with exotic animals, but with tightrope walkers, fools and characters in oriental costume. Audran, in turn enriched the grotesque with hybrid animals, variations on the sphinx and the chimera, such as ribbon-necked female heads attached to winged, animal bodies or reptilian tails (fig. 133). In 1696, in the bedchamber overlooking the terrace at the hôtel de Bouillon (fig. 134), Audran had also exploited heraldry's decorative promise and potential for flattery by juxtaposing a delightfully light ducal coronet with a wreath of laurel at the mid-points above the

cornice.[48] Later still, Claude Gillot, Antoine Watteau and Nicolas Lancret explored the representational possibilities of the genre by adding characters from the *commedia dell'arte* (fig. 136), gallant pilgrims (fig. 138) and Turkish and Chinese figures (fig. 135). Classical, Mannerist and vernacular traditions were reconciled in a dream-like fiction where the associative relationship between the constituents was primarily visual not semantic.

The incorporation of new, specifically popular or 'low' motifs into the grotesque was accomplished not without consequence or meaning. The iconographic range of the genre expanded, but more importantly, the expansion to include acrobats, minstrels, monkeys and other fairground fodder (fig. 137) was accompanied by a correspondingly greater interaction between the ornamental and figurative elements. Monkeys and men are not so much framed by strapwork and scrolls as actively engaged with them. They are shown in the process of transforming the imperial acanthus and the majestic pedestal into material proper to their sport, and in so doing, they seem, almost literally, to work at the destruction of their ornamental universe. The imagery of the fair thus tended to break down the last, provisional certainties of the classic grotesque.

The significance that should be attached to this development is difficult to fathom. Low-life figures, unlike their classical counterparts, did not fit into an fixed emblematic

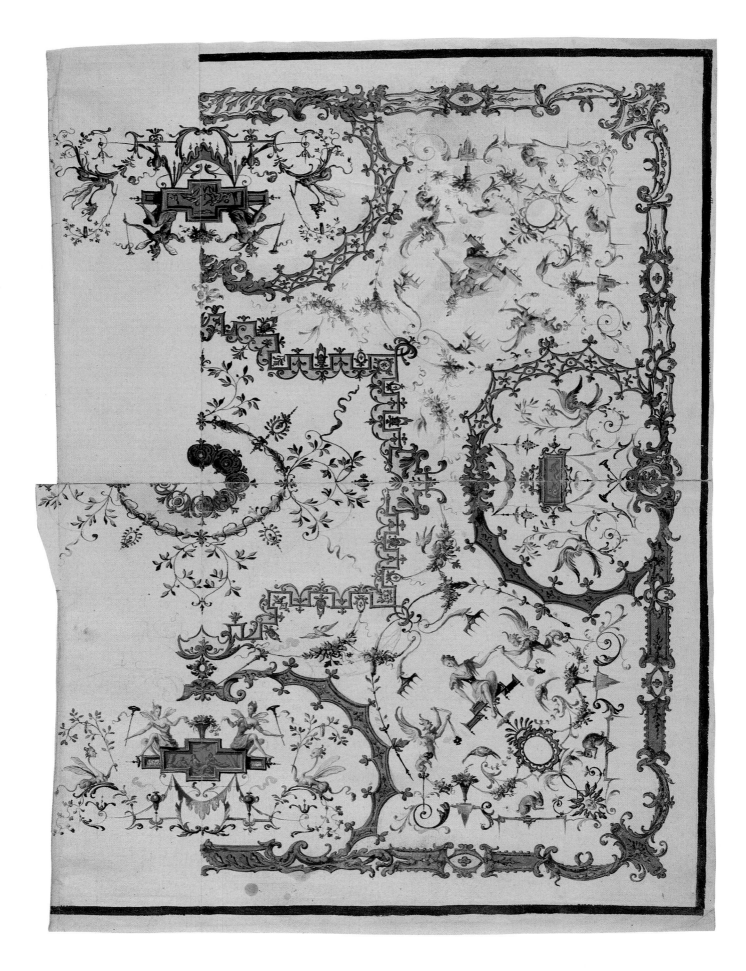

134 Claude III Audran, design for a ceiling at the hôtel de Bouillon, 1696. Pen, ink, watercolour and gold-leaf on paper, 28 × 35 cm. Nationalmuseum, Stockholm.

135 Gabriel Huquier after Antoine Watteau, *The Chinese Emperor*, c.1730. Etching.

133 (facing page) Claude III Audran, design for a ceiling, c.1700. Pen, ink, watercolour and gold leaf, 37.8 × 52.3 cm. Nationalmuseum, Stockholm.

136 Claude Gillot, design for an arabesque, c.1710. Pen and ink on paper, 22 × 26.5 cm. Kunstbibliothek, Staatliche Museen Berlin.

137 Claude III Audran, grotesques, c.1700. Sanguine and wash, 29.3 × 28.7 cm. Nationalmuseum, Stockholm.

138 Nicolas Lancret and Claude III Audran, arabesque panel formerly from the hôtel Peyrenc de Moras, *c.*1724. Oil on canvas laid on panel, 300 × 59 cm. Location unknown.

tradition of the kind that allowed Audran, more-or-less respectfully, to use the people of the pagan heavens to personify the months of the year, but instead asked to be read in relation to the changing scenes of a busy and crowded life. The Lenten fair of Saint-Germain in Paris where the tightrope walkers and buffoons featured in these designs could be met in the flesh, attracted people from all walks of life. Moreover, the abrupt conjunction of those whom the discourse of estates logically and obsessively separated was one of *leitmotifs* of literary representations of the place.[49] Thomas Crow has recently suggested that the élite's taste for 'slumming it', for the transgressive pleasures of the fairground, for the bawdy, outlandish and satiric quality of the comedies performed there, marked the nobility's return to 'a shared experience of festive life'.[50] Yet Audran's compositions clearly offer a censored vision of the *foire*. The scatalogical and sexual obscenities of so much fair entertainment are conspicuously absent, and thus while the reference to the 'low' is undoubtedly more than token, it was a 'low' that had, nevertheless, been de-natured by the artful and precious visual idiom in which it was now caught. As such, the grotesque followed the lead of other courtly arts which had also ostensibly looked to embrace the licence and salty pleasures of the street. In 1685, for instance, Bérain designed costumes for a masquerade at Versailles on the theme of the *Cris de Paris* in which courtiers were dressed-up as street-sellers and spent the evening lispingly 'trading' in delicacies of food and wine.[51] In the same year, moreover, Mme de Montespan surprised her royal lover by inverting the dignity of her apartment and recreating it as the *foire Saint-Germain*, complete with shops, tradesmen and street-players. However, if according to the *Mercure Galant*, everything there was remarkably realistic, the event was nevertheless a representation, an edited performance of life and not life itself.[52] Thus, if on the one hand, the court, or a significant faction within it, was attempting (long before reference to the fair-players or *forains* had been politicised by the banishment of the *commedia dell'arte* in 1697) to find a measure of its distinction and independence from the state by symbolically reincorporating into Versailles that which the palace as monument expressly repudiated, on the other hand, courtiers were just as committed to pasteurising the dangers of plebeian culture by reducing it to the picturesque. In that sense Montespan's fairground of a day was caught between two sets of binary oppositions; it offered itself as the contentious other side to the Hall of Mirrors, Le Brun's last word in heroic and morally improving grandeur, and as the distinguished opposite to the real *foire Saint-Germain* and its wholesale vulgarity.

Before proceding to discuss in greater detail the cultural climate into which the grotesque was received, it is, I think, worth briefly considering the process by which grotesques were invented. The creative process seems in many ways to resemble the activity Levi-Strauss called *bricolage*, that is to say, it was a process by which an existing artistic or cultural system was renewed and transformed by continual and seemingly random introduction of new elements.[53] Indeed, an anonymous and undated poem, *Sur le Dessein de l'Appartement de la duchesse du Maine à Sceaux* tells of just such myopic fumblings, as the artist's hand attempts to invent an appropriate grotesque scheme,

> Tes traits effacés mille fois
> sans aucune forme arrêté
> rendent ma carte sous mes doigts
> plus variable que protée.[54]

No one, not even Vitruvius, denied that the design and execution of grotesques required skills.[55] A ready invention, no less generous than nature's own, a sensitivity to the tastes of the moment and a sure grasp of the knacks of design were all essential attributes of the successful *ornemaniste*. It was, nevertheless, an approach to decoration that was demonstrably experiential rather than conspicuously learned. This is not to imply, however, that designers of decoration were unlettered or uneducated. On the contrary, Claude III Audran possessed an impressive library of some four hundred and fifty volumes, which included texts not only befitting his business and his faith but appropriate to his art. Moreover, the literary sources of his inspiration were no less heteroclite than the creations of his imagination; the classics, ancient history, polite letters and carnavalesque fiction were collected together in close contiguity.[56] Audran's library thus betrays a cultural horizon conspicuously less narrow and coherent than that of, say, his contemporary François Le Moyne, an academician and history painter.[57] Furthermore, Audran's approach to the world of books was very likely unsystematic and eliptical and resulted in an exceptionally rich, flexible but ultimately unprincipled and disorderly lexicon of ideas and references from which he could articulate his fantasies. In so far as the creation of grotesques could be said to exemplify a classical precept, it was by the capacity such composition shared with poetry to invent ficticious beings at will – Horace's *quidlibet audendi . . . potestas*.[58] Ironically, therefore, the grotesque's most classical heritage was also the very thing that liberated it from academic prescriptions, thereby creating professional possibilities for those deprived of any such refined education.

HONNÊTETÉ

It is not too fanciful to draw certain parallels between the 'scrap-book' compositional mode of the grotesque and the modalities of late seventeenth-century *honnête* culture, which was distinguished above all by its manner of acquisition. *Honnêteté* also derived from experience. It was an objective that aristocrats were bred to; an open-ended praxis embraced and renewed through frequenting polite society and belonging to a fellowship of taste-makers. According to Balthasar Grancian, 'tastes are formed by conversation, and one inherits the [good]

taste of others by virtue of being present in their company'.[59] Taste, as both a faculty and a body of judgements, was regarded as an indispensable facet of sociability because it implied, among other things, the rejection of obsessive interests and passions in favour of a more detached and universal curiosity.[60] It was, therefore, in conversation, games and amateur dramatics that aristocratic taste established its distinctive circuits of transmission. *Salon*-games, many of which were described in Charles Sorel's *Les Recreations galantes* (1661), included not only those designed to hone the emotive range of the language used by *honnêtes gens*, but others that ensured the assimilation of Graeco-Roman mythology and history, and the game of the Arts and Sciences rewarded those best able to formulate witty definitions of their realms.[61] In 1692, Florent le Comte reprinted with *salon* society in mind, the playing-cards designed more than forty years earlier by Stefano della Bella (fig. 139) and originally intended for the instruction of the young Louis XIV.[62] Each card in the mythological series matched an image with a synoptic account of the story depicted, to form a sugared pill; the classic means by which instruction was nobly imbibed.[63] Moreover, balls, masques and amateur theatrical performances fostered a free association between chivalric imagery, classical subjects and themes from the *commedia dell'arte*, in a manner structurally analogous to the pictorial relations active in the grotesque. Indeed, despite the tireless efforts of the Jesuit Claude Menestrier and others to rationalise and codify court ballets and to subordinate spectacle to programmatic, pedagogical discourse,[64] the *honnête* nobility apparently continued to enjoy and interpret these events in an insistently aesthetic and playful manner.

139 Stefano della Bella, *The Game of Mythology*, 1644. Etching.

140 Charles de La Fosse, *Clytie Changed into a Sunflower*, 1688. Oil on canvas, 131 × 159 cm. Château de Versailles, Versailles.

It should be clear, at this point, that any differences imputed to the respective local cultures of *honnêteté* and the state cannot rest entirely on particular selections of themes and forms (a crude contrast say, between decorative Harlequinesques, to use a convenient neologism, and stately, classical history painting) but must also take account of the distinctive manners of apprehending and interpreting a shared semantic field. The various ways in which Ovid was put to work provide a particularly eloquent testimony for this case.

Since the Renaissance the *Metamorphoses* had provided a rich and manifold source of subjects for court entertainments, garden sculpture and interior decoration. The story of the abduction of Ovid's characters by the kings of France for their own ideological purposes has frequently been related. However, less attention has been paid to the fact that the efficacy of the political metamorphosis that transformed *Clytie*, depicted by Charles de La Fosse (fig. 140) at the Trianon in 1698–9, into an exemplum of submissive courtly behaviour, depended utterly on the prior intellectual capitulation of the beholder; on his or her willingness to engage with the fiction.[65] It appears that *salon* society largely refused. Jean-Laurent Lecerf de Viéville remarked that ballets and operas owed their success with the *monde* not to their narratives and ideological content but 'to the magnificence of the spectacle', and to the luxuriousness and exoticism of the costumes.[66] In a different artistic sphere, Mlle de Scudéry's and, particularly, La Fontaine's descriptions of the park at Versailles reveal a blindness to the political equivalence of the garden and its sculpture that can only partly be explained by the incompleteness of the programme at the time of writing. For them the landscape and its monuments offered the opportunity for a pleasurable and diverting *promenade*, not a reading lesson in political acquiescence.[67]

Meanwhile, away from Versailles, the duchesse du Maine, apparently not content with ignoring or wilfully under-interpreting absolutist myths, moved beyond evasion to appropriation. In 1704, the duchess ordered Claude III Audran partially to redecorate her apartment at the recently acquired château de Sceaux. In the centre of the ceiling in the Cabinet des Muses, Audran depicted Apollo (possibly fig. 141) surrounded by grotesques (fig. 142) and at the corners, filled the pendentives with allegorical figures of epic, lyrical and pastoral poetry and satire.[68] Despite his physiognomic resemblance to a host of other Parnassian gods, enjoying comparable two-dimensional lives in neighbouring royal palaces, this Apollo was not a cipher for the duchess's father-in-law. The poetic accompaniment to the scheme suggests an altogether different and less glorious role:

> Créateur des formes nouvelles
> Germes fécond des arts ingénieux
> Principe du plaisir des yeux,
> Crayon, par des tracés fidelles
> Marques avec grâce et liberté
> Des sujets dont la nouveauté
> Cause le charme et la surprise.
> Que tout brille dans le séjour
> Où la divine Ludovise
> Doit tenir son heureuse cour![69]

Apollo was here called upon both to inspire the designer with a better discerning, and to play handmaiden to the 'divine Louisa' (Anne-Louise Bénédicte de Bourbon, duchesse du Maine) whose court had moved up-stage, to the forefront of culture, thereby apparently consigning Versailles to the virtual oblivion of the wings.

Such challenges served, if not to negate, then at least to curtail the state's claim to a monopoly of legitimate cultural expression. Indeed, the stress on the nouns 'liberty' and 'novelty' in the middle rhyming couplet of this opening stanza, draws attention at the outset to the court-nobility's struggle to escape from beneath the oppressive weight of a classical tradition inextricably yoked to a *raison d'état*. It was not simply that particular satellite courts were apparently eager to challenge the hegemony of Versailles, it was also that the ideology of taste articulated in such *milieux* promised logically to secure the transfer of the agencies of culture into their control. The alternative aesthetic mooted by the grotesque, strictly speaking neither figure nor ornament, escaped the hierarchy of genres and opened up a realm of licence which, in its perceptual appeal, by-passed intellect and addressed itself directly to the senses, to 'visual pleasure', thereby implicitly giving priority to the non-professional, untutored, amateur beholder. The qualities of grace and charm liberally invoked by the poet – significantly, qualities appropriate both to the subjects and the objects of taste[70] – were understood to defy scholarly definition. Their presence or absence, according to authorities such as Méré and Dominique Bouhours, could only be felt.[71] It

141 Claude III Audran, *Apollo*, *c.*1704. Oil on canvas, diameter 81 cm. Location unknown.

142 Claude III Audran, design for the ceiling of the duchesse du Maine's *cabinet* at Sceaux, 1704. Sanguine on paper, 31 × 24.8 cm. Nationalmuseum, Stockholm.

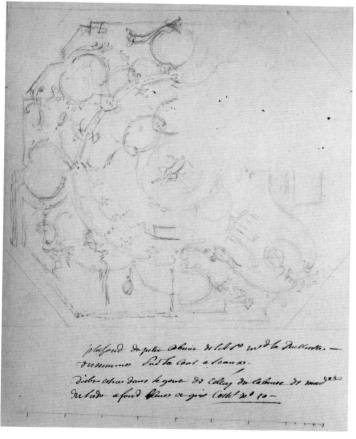

followed therefore, that these qualities were not those produced with the assistance of the minor rules of classical composition: the unities of time, place and action, and the canons of antique proportion and versification. The correct application of such rules and canons assured a deconstructable beauty reached by a discernable *modus operandi*. The effect of grace (and the attraction of the grotesque) on the other hand, eluded such analysis: 'its nature is to be incomprehensible and inexplicable.'[72] Like plebeian theatre, the grotesque offered relief from the regimentation and authoritarianism of academic culture, a deliverance whose charm appealed particularly to *honnêtes gens* eager to abandon 'rules' and 'good sense' at the door of *Arlequin empereur dans la lune* (1684, and revived in the early 1700s), in the knowledge that in so doing they distinguished themselves utterly from the scholars who found virtue only in correctness.[73] The similarities between the liberality and irreverence of the grotesque and the *comédie italienne* was acknowledged by Claude Perrault at the time. He noted the irony in the fact that Vitruvius,

> with the fine logic by which he proved that it is impossible for castles to have foundations of reeds, or for half-length animals to issue from flowers . . . succeeded far better in instructing painters in the art of these sorts of works, than in persuading them to abandon their imitation. Because it is the same as if one wanted to denounce the *comédie italienne* by arguing that nothing reasonably convincing (*vraisemblable*) was performed there and by demonstrating, with good reason (*bonnes raisons*), that it is impossible for Harlequin with his black mask to be mistaken either for the Goddess Diana or for a bunch of grapes.[74]

Bonnes raisons were impotent to dispel the charm of grotesque decoration or the fairground because fantasy and the *merveilleux* delivered these genres into a wonderland where the rules of *vraisemblance* so dear to academic theory were themselves judged inappropriate.[75] Proof of attractiveness was therefore not to be had by pointing to ineffable qualities in the works themselves, but lay instead in the subjective response of the only legitimate spectator, the *honnête homme*.[76]

But who were these *honnêtes gens* whose judgements had apparently become the new standard of taste? It is perhaps easier to start by saying who they were not. They were not the *savants*, those keepers of the canon associated with the academies and the Gallican republic of letters, centred in robe circles.[77] Indeed, such was *salon* society's repudiation of overtly learned and high-minded culture that, on one memorable occasion, the maréchal de Biron retired in shamefaced confusion after having inadvertently disclosed a capacity for translating Greek inscriptions, inappropriately superior to that of a *maître de requêtes* (a judge of appeal).[78] According to the much published Morvan de Bellegarde,

> The taste and judgement of most of those honoured with the title *Savant* is defective and unbalanced; their

conversation is pedantic and fastidious. Study sullies the mind, and warps it, unless it is redressed and polished by the society of *honnêtes-gens*. Merit is of little help to such people; because without the art of pleasing their talent becomes hoydenish and awkward.[79]

Sociability and good taste were here contrasted with study, and pleasure was opposed to skill. By implication politeness and taste were the natural and inherent accomplishments of an *honnête* aristocracy;[80] learning the mere artificial proficiency of bourgeois pedants. In so far as this latter class of social beings included ministers and royal office-holders of modest origin – Méré quite possibly had a Surintendant des Bâtiments in mind when he declared that 'under the government of a pedant, pedantry comes into fashion'[81] – there seems to have been, as Michael Moriarty has most recently pointed out, a sharp 'anti-governmental edge' to this anti-intellectualism.[82]

There has been a tendency to argue that these *honnêtes hommes*, though theoretically noble, were not courtiers either.[83] That, on the contrary, they ostentatiously held themselves apart from a 'country' infamous for conjuring the best-born into the worst sycophants and for sacrificing personal identities to the king's pleasure.[84] While it is undeniably the case that many seventeenth-century writers were critical of the society and culture of the court, and indeed contrasted its occasional barbarisms with the more exiguous standards of the polite *grand monde*,[85] it is nevertheless also true that most definitions of *honnêteté*-personified assumed his or her rightful access to the court, whether or not either chose to exercise it. Indeed, in his first essay on the subject, *De la Vrai Honnêteté*, Méré seems to suggest that in France *honnêteté* was initially lodged in those courtiers who turned the unexpected *otium* forced upon them by the peacebleness of the early years of Louis XIV's reign to the cultivation of independent forms of courtly life.[86] Moreover, his ideal *honnête homme* was a person of essentially princely virtue, summoned to his monarch's side not out of a capacity to proffer armed, judicial or bureaucratic services but because such was his 'rare' and 'noble' quality that the king unfailingly preferred his council to that of all others.[87] The difference between the *honnête homme* and the courtier was less a matter of dominion therefore, than a question of roles. The *honnête homme* baulked at assuming the courtier's habitually stooping gait in the conquest of royal favour.[88] He expected, on the contrary, to play an adjudicating role in convening a choice *grand monde*, a seemingly imaginary assembly in its global aspect, yet on closer inspection little different from a court of France purified of those 'bookful blockheads', absolute monarchs tended to judge necessary to the successful management of a modern state. In as much as *honnêté* was a quest for power, one which Donna Stanton has noted, transformed society into a metaphorical battleground,[89] its locutions were necessarily shaped by court experience and its directives implicitly acknowledged the court as the optimum field of contest because there captivation could poten-

tially mediate the royal will. In short, though it would be a mistake to subsume the *salon* into the court, it is also too simple to describe *honnêteté* as a form of compensatory escapism for a nobility in retreat. The boundaries between the two institutions were permeable and conflict arose as much within as between their respective *milieux*.

FATHERS AND SONS: VERSAILLES AND MEUDON

It seems worthwhile pursuing the notion of a significant social *fraction* given substance by *honnêteté*, to see whether its discursive reality ever assumed a more immediate and definite shape as *faction* or what contemporaries experienced as 'cabal'.[90] Endemic to the power structure of the *ancien régime*, factions were informal and sometimes mixed social groups united, temporarily at least, by common or complementary objectives. The marquis de Lassay maintained that family might, if powerful enough, substitute for faction,[91] but in truth, it looks increasingly as if great ministerial dynasties such as the Colberts or the Le Telliers acted as abiding magnets attracting to themselves shifting fields of alliances which evolved over generations.[92] By the beginning of the eighteenth century, the former, the Colberts, represented by the *grand homme*'s two sons-in-law, the ducs de Beauvillier and de Chevreuse, had invested the faction's future in the young duc de Bourgogne, second in line to the throne.[93] It is tempting to try and link the flowering of the distinctly aristocratic cultural forms discussed above, with the intensification of nobiliary claims to power advanced primarily by the members of this cabal. However, amongst the duc de Bourgogne's circle few significant patrons of grotesque decoration are to be found. For the present, the characterization of the collective taste of the de Bourgogne's circle, if indeed such there was, must remain provisional for lack of sufficient documentation, but the very meagreness of the surviving evidence suggests that neither Beauvillier nor Chevreuse, nor Jean-Baptiste Colbert, marquis de Torcy, nor Nicolas Desmarets, two further members of the group, can have been particularly renowned for their patronage of the arts. From 1681 Beauvillier and Chevreuse shared contiguous hôtels in Versailles, apparently unremarkable in either design or decoration.[94] Moreover, according to Saint-Simon, Beauvillier's way of life at Vaucresson was conspicuously modest,[95] while the decoration of the hôtel de Chevreuse in the rue Saint-Dominique was immodest only by virtue of the size of its biblical tapestries.[96] Tapestries similarly struck a traditional note at the hôtel de Torcy in the rue Neuve des Petits-Champs, and the marquess's bedchamber was hung with a dozen devotional works,[97] while the most that can presently be said about the hôtel Desmarets in the rue Saint-Marc is that it required remodelling and substantial redecoration to attain the more exacting standards of elegance demanded by its next proprietor, Charles-François de Montmorency, duc de Luxembourg.[98]

The character of the grotesque, for all its noble pedigree and aristocratic associations, seems to have been largely inimical to the ideology of the de Bourgogne cabal. The *Plans de gouvernement* or *Tables de Chaulnes* (1711), co-written by Beauvilliers and Chevreuse on the prince's behalf during the brief period of confidence when the succession looked to be theirs, is, notwithstanding an evident nostalgia for a bygone feudal age, above all a manifesto for reform. Criticism of established rule is supplemented by an agenda of corrective constitutional, administrative and fiscal measures designed to secure the greater prosperity of the realm.[99] Given that style is not only inseparable from ideology but shapes it, it seems evident that as a potential ideogram of this aristocratic policy the grotesque was lacking in one important respect: though it mocked the classical tenets of official culture its intent was neither corrective nor didactic. Indeed, its nonconformity was apparent only by contrast with the established cultural order, on which it therefore depended for its comic effect. The grotesque promoted no alternative aesthetic programme; its essence lay in harmless inversions and playful distortions of an existing language. From even the dismally few statements made by Archbishop Fénelon, de Bourgogne's tutor and the mentor of this faction, it is obvious that such visual criticism could find no place in their reformed state. A staunch defender of the ancients and a champion of Poussin, the key-note of Fénelon's policy for the arts was struck by the high-minded austerity he admired in the *Funeral of Phocion*.[100] Indeed, in the *Dialogues des morts* (c.1695) the worth of François I's traditionally vaunted achievement in spawning a rebirth of the Augustan age is brought abruptly into political focus by the uncompromising judgement of Louis XII (or rather, Fénelon): 'I would prefer that you had been known as the father of your people instead of the father of letters.'[101] Moreover, in Fénelon's novel, *Télémaque* (1699), amongst Mentor's reforms for the kingdom of Salente was an immediate retrenchment of ostentatious and gratuitous display, to which the simplicity of a pastoral existence is emphatically preferred.[102] Elsewhere, Fénelon insisted that in the case of decoration, 'One should admit in a building no element dedicated solely to ornament . . .',[103] a view surely incompatible with the grotesque, and in the case of the imitative arts he envisaged for them a primarily ethical and educational role, one which necessarily entailed a concern for content at the expense of the pleasures of form.[104] Thus, in so far as the noble ideology of de Bourgogne's cabal embraced an aesthetic vision, it was, ironically perhaps, one that had long since served Louis XIV.

Until 1711, de Bourgogne's cabal had been largely overshadowed by those of Mme de Maintenon and the Grand Dauphin, significantly closer to power, indeed, so much so in the case of the former that it was barely distinguishable from Louis's own. The Grand Dauphin, on the other hand had a settled and independent province of influence. He had adopted or been adopted by the epicurean and scepticist *salon* of the Bouillon and Vendôme families which he proceeded to transform and make his own to the extent that he introduced to it members of the royal family, notably from the houses of Condé, Conti and Orléans, never forgetting, of course, his mistress, Mlle Choin.[105] Bouillon and, particularly, Vendôme were ancient lords of decidedly profligate mien whose society must have brought zest and a spirit of release to Monseigneur's court. Something of the new flavour of licence may perhaps be gleaned from the poetry of the abbé Chaulieu and the marquis de La Fare, both lifelong members of the duc de Vendôme's notorious Paris *salon*, the *société du Temple*.[106] An irreverent, festive impulse infects much of their verse, from the roistering drinking songs to the sensual love poetry, and suggests that the dauphin may have slipped into a society determined first upon its pleasures. That it was so, is confirmed by the fact that although the dauphin's faction, no less than his son's or his step-mother's, competed for influence and lobbied on behalf of its members, the group drew up no plans for political action. Indeed, the narrow scope of the dauphin's commonplace political vision was captured with exquisite contempt by Saint-Simon in a cameo description of the prince in his Cabinet à la Capucine at Meudon, pedantically explaining to Choin the events unfolding in a series of engraved illustrations of the coronation.[107] Succession not change qualified the dauphin's ambitions and he assembled a coterie of favourites ready to move into position at the appointed time. However, after the disgrace of Vendôme and Chamillart in 1709, few of them – with the exception of d'Antin – anticipated ministerial office. They hoped only for a voice in appointments.[108]

Thus, the Meudon circle, despite the significant presence of the heir apparent, retained an overtly *honnête* atmosphere, in as much as it conspicuously pursued no more than the apparently disinterested cultural tastes of the group, and it was, appropriately, in the residences of these *habitués* that the grotesque found its natural habitat. The dauphin not only entrusted to Bérain the orchestration of masquerades and the initial decoration and furnishing of the *château vieux* at Meudon, at an earlier date (in the mid-1680s) his precocious taste for grotesques had taken shape in Jean Le Moyne le Troyen's gold and blue schemes for the Cabinet Doré at Versailles[109] and in Boulle's marquetry panelling for the adjacent Cabinet des Glaces.[110] That his weakness was enduring may be judged from the prestigious commission he extended to Claude III Audran more than twenty years later for a unique tapestry series, the *Months in Grotesques* (fig. 143) woven for the *chambre de parade* at the Château Neuf at Meudon.[111] At the same time, Audran was providing analogous schemes for other members of this satellite court, instances of which have been mentioned and illustrated above. In the 1690s, for example, Audran, assisted by Desportes, decorated rooms in the hôtel de Bouillon on the quai Malaquai (fig. 134), and in the company of Oudry completed schemes for the duc de Vendôme at Anet (fig. 127). Later, Vendôme's brother, the Grand Prieur,

143   Claude III Audran, *June*, c.1700. Wool and silk, 348 × 259 cm. The sixth design from the Gobelins tapestry series, *The Months in Grotesques*, c.1700. The Victoria and Albert Museum, London.

144 Claude III Audran, design for the ceiling for the *petite chambre à coucher* of the princesse de Conti at Versailles, 1709. Watercolour on paper, 23.1 × 34.4 cm. Nationalmuseum, Stockholm.

engaged Audran for works at the Temple, the hôtel de Vendôme and his pavilion at Clichy.[112] At Versailles meanwhile, Audran decorated the *appartement* of the princesse de Conti[113] (fig. 144) and later designed a carriage for her.[114] For the Condé branch of the family, Audran planned a dining-room ceiling for Chantilly, in the event never executed.[115] However, the duc d'Antin inherited an Audran closet originally decorated for Mlle de Charolais, also a Bourbon-Condé,[116] but it did not long survive d'Antin's ambitious projects for Petit-Bourg and was soon superseded by elaborate grotesque tapestries (fig. 129). Back in Paris, Audran covered the duchesse d'Antin's *salon de bains* with grotesques,[117] while three sanguine drawings in Stockholm record his scheme, *Les Spectacles* (c.1700, fig. 145), thought to have been executed as tapestries for Monsieur, the duc d'Orléans's apartment at the Palais Royal.[118]

The dauphin and his circle, therefore, readily espoused and promoted a form of decoration that has been described as aristocratic, and was revived thanks largely to the energies of the Menus Plaisirs. They were by no means alone in their taste; the schemes for the duchesse de Bourgogne's apartment at the

Ménagerie were undertaken in the same year as those for Meudon.[119] In 1690 the panelling for a *cabinet* and bedchamber at the hôtel de Seignelay, residence of Colbert's grandson, had been magnificently treated to Bérain's designs.[120] Moreover, besides these, the royal bastards, the duc du Maine and the comte de Toulouse, had also proved enthusiastic clients of Bérain's and Audran's work.[121] None of them, however, can be associated with a particular party at court. At the time of the Ménagerie commission the duchesse de Bourgogne was only fourteen, her husband no more than three years older, still influenced by his father and some years away from forming an autonomous circle of his own. The duchess, in any event, was notoriously flighty and happily frequented both her husband's and her mother-in-law's circles.[122] Seignelay, with his appointment as Maître de la Garde-robe in 1690 may well have found himself closer to the culture of the Menus Plaisirs than to that of the Bâtiments and the de Bourgogne faction. Du Maine and Toulouse, on the other hand, distanced themselves entirely from party intrigues at this time. Du Maine's marriage to Mlle de Charolais however, and the subsequent flowering of Sceaux,[123] had brought him abruptly into contact with the

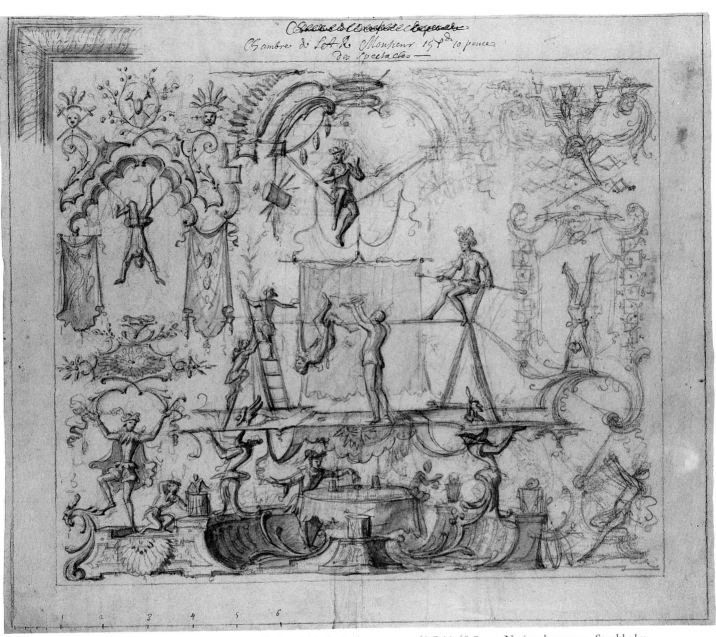

145   Claude III Audran, *The Entertainment*, *c.*1700. Red and black chalk on paper, 43.7 × 49.8 cm. Nationalmuseum, Stockholm.

taste of the Meudon circle (figs 141, 142). Therefore, if not exactly a party logo, grotesque decoration certainly seems to have had particular appeal for the members of the dauphin's new court.

Whether or not that appeal may be construed as significant depends very largely on the positive or negative answer to the question that opened this chapter, that is, can a distinction usefully be made between the tastes of Louis XIV and those of his son? François Boutard's verse description of Meudon certainly seems to suggest that the gardens if not the château offered an alternative, an escape even, from the 'inimitable model' of the 'grand Roi'.[124] On the other hand, there were, as Schnapper has concisely shown, strong similarities between

the decorative programmes of Meudon and those of Marly and the Trianon. For instance, Adam-François van der Meulen and his school provided battle paintings for the galleries of Meudon and Marly, Desportes furnished them with hunting scenes;[125] both the Trianon and Meudon accommodated a considerable number of flower paintings;[126] and a decade after the first grotesque schemes at Meudon, Louis XIV commissioned the famous *Berceau des singes* or *Nursery of Apes* (fig. 146) for Marly.[127] Marly and the Trianon were, of course, much more informal residences than Versailles or Fontainbleau, and places to which the king invited not the nation but a personal selection of guests.[128] However, acknowledgement of these pertinent facts is probably not sufficient justification for denying

146   Claude III Audran, *Nursery of Apes*, 1709. Red chalk and pencil on paper, 69.7 × 49.5 cm. Nationalmuseum, Stockholm.

that the similarities of treatment at Meudon and the Trianon were significant, and for returning to stark comparisons between the official and public culture of the state and the refined and private taste of princes. On the contrary, the similarities between Meudon and Louis XIV's lesser châteaux, particularly the Trianon, suggest that the Grand Dauphin's efforts of distinction were made specifically in relation to them, and thus, that an understanding of his cultural initiatives is only to be had in the context of a fuller analysis of these *petits palais*.

The location of the Trianon in the midst of abundant flower gardens, combined with the emphasis given to themes of nature in its figurative decoration encouraged contemporary perceptions of the Trianon as a palace of Flora, set in a kingdom of perpetual Spring.[129] Although it is tempting to take such subjects merely at face value, the iconography of the seasons had, in fact, long since served Louis to express a particular idea of his rule. In the early 1660s, Charles Le Brun's Gobelins tapestry series, *The Seasons*, and the accompanying exegesis provided by André Félibien and the Académie des Inscriptions et Belles Lettres had, under the personification of Venus, promulgated an aimiable politics of Spring to succeed the Winter's bloody Spanish exploits.[130] Boutard's ode *Trianeum* (*c*.1700) effectively extended this narrative by celebrating Mansart's pavilion as a symbol of Louis's regained continence and of his renewed willingness to extend peace and abundance to France by bringing, this time, the war of the League of Augsburg to a close.[131] In place of war, the now equinoctial king offered his people, and most particularly his court, 'games and agreable entertainments', many of them enacted, aptly enough, at his less formal residences.[132] That these gatherings, no less than their settings, more or less cynically transformed Louis's former bellicose foreign policy into vernal domestic strategy may perhaps best be judged from Madeleine de Scudéry's description of an exotic gambling party at Marly, at which the king apparently provided his guests with an impressive array of fantastic and valuable artefacts with which to wager at will.[133] By establishing himself as the unique originator of goods, Louis acutely demonstrated his power over his noble subjects, reducing their capacity for action to competition within parameters of his own devising. There was no mistaking the aggression at the heart of royal liberality; Scudéry compared the night's triumph with the conquest of the Franche-Conté.[134]

The contradiction between form and content noted by Scudéry in royal entertainments was also to be found, though somewhat differently articulated, in a series of paintings by Noël Coypel commissioned for the Trianon in 1688. They depicted episodes from the life of Hercules.[135] On first consideration, hoary Hercules scarcely seems a natural companion for Flora, nor do his repressive and self-sacrificing choices, his arduous labours and his heroic struggles readily belong to her domain. However, by largely avoiding scenes of contest and substituting pastoral and even domestic contexts for the narra-

147   Noël Coypel, *The Combat of Hercules and Achelous*, *c*.1699. Oil on canvas, 118 × 193 cm. Château de Versailles, Versailles.

tive, Coypel partially dispossessed Hercules of himself, transforming him into a more generous and aimiable fellow. Thus, in the *Combat of Hercules and Achelous for the Hand of Deianira* (fig. 147), which acknowledges the hero's manly valour, attention is focused not so much on the action but on a thing, the horn, wrenched by Hercules from his bovine adversary, and soon to become the horn of plenty. Moreover, the history and nature of the cornucopia and of abundance were subjects developed into further pictures for the series. Thus, in so far as Hercules was Gallic, he gave visual rehersal to the duplicitous nature of the right divine: destructive though apparently regenerative, chaotic though seemingly orderly, frightful though experienced as aimiable, in short Mars in the guise of Venus. In the epigrammatic words of Charpentier:

> Dans le sein de Louis loge le Dieu des armes;
> Sur son auguste front Vénus fait son séjour;
> Lors que tant de valeur est jointe à tant de charmes,
> Mortels, il faut céder par force, ou par armour.[136]

In the same way that there was no resisting the gentle violence of Spring, so the king set out to captivate his court with, in the words of Volker Kapp, a *politique du sourire*.[137]

Noël Coypel's ambitious, high-minded and intellectually demanding histories (some of which were exhibited in the Salons of 1699 and 1704, and few of which were ultimately installed at the Trianon) perpetuated the tradition of stately art more usually associated with Versailles, albeit in a more opaque and metaphorical form. Of course not all the paintings commissioned for the Trianon were as uncompromisingly academic in subject or treatment, but most, without excepting the seemingly straight-forward and decorative still-lifes of Belin de Fontenay and Antoine Monnoyer, contributed to the deployment of a Spring campaign.[138] At Meudon, the situation was rather different, not least because the absence of overall narrative coherence often diminished the thematic potential of many of the subjects represented.[139] Moreover, the mixture of commissioned paintings and works lent by the royal collection further complicated matters, creating tensions within particu-

148   Charles de La Fosse, *The Triumph of Bacchus*, 1700. Oil on canvas, 157 × 135 cm. Musée du Louvre, Paris.

149 Antoine Coypel, *Silenus Smeared with Mulberries by the Nymph Eglea*, 1700. Oil on canvas, 157 × 135 cm. Musée de Saint-Denis, Reims.

lar schemes as well as between adjacent spaces; tensions that appear sometimes, but not always, to have been creatively managed.[140] The dauphin's antechamber in the *château vieux*, for instance, was decorated with four Dionysian subjects,[141] presided over by La Fosse's magnificent and noisy *Triumph of Bacchus* (fig. 148). The godly figure of Bacchus, though not admittedly of surfeit-swelled body like Antoine Coypel's accompanying *Silenus* (fig. 149), nevertheless suggests by the imperiousness of his stance and the exaggerated proportion of his thyrsus, by the jubilant clashing of cymbals and the enthusiastic trumpeting of horns, by the satyr falling drunk and the *bacchante* half stripped, a will to revel, gourmandise and debauch of truly princely proportion. These were pastimes far removed from the province of Herculean endeavour (however charmingly edited) and majestical authority perhaps more usually associated with a future king properly mindful of his apprenticeship to power. Instead, Bacchus's cavalcade suggested a prince in his errancy; a son taking advantage of the space in the margin to be prodigal. Such an impression can only have been heightened by the grotesque ceiling, with its similarly bodily-orientated cast of classical characters, that Audran imagined and created above their heads.[142] Moreover,

it is tempting to suppose that for some visitors at least, these Bacchic scenes offered an irreverent commentary on some of the Old Masters hung about the walls. For instance, Coypel's *Silenus*, manifestly enjoying his annointing with mulberry juice by the lovely Eglea, proposed a piquantely different conceptualisation of baptism to Poussin's sacramental vision in the *Baptism of Christ* below.[143]

It would be a mistake, however, to adjust the contours of the Grand Dauphin too neatly to those of other, better-known, errant princes, to England's irrepressible Prince Hal, for example, who, under Falstaff's tutelage, riotously pursued his unprincely appetites in the inns and taverns of Eastcheap.[144] For though it is true that Monseigneur had more flesh than other men, in 1700 he was no green adolescent desperately in search of initiation, but a man of forty, and one moreover, of vacant mind and dreary vices, if Saint-Simon is to be believed.[145] It is therefore at the level of representation rather than on the scale of life that the taste of the dauphin should be interpreted. The decoration of Meudon was, it would seem, an attempt, in part at least, to lend the dauphin's seemingly endless apprenticeship a fixed and recognisable shape. In other words, it was an effort to construct for the king-in-waiting an identity at once distinct from and related to that of his father. Meudon thus became a canvas on which to project an image of prodigality richly suggestive of that liminal phase between indenture and mastery commom to all life's crafts, a prodigality in the dauphin's case perhaps rarely experienced, but 'remembered' and imparted nevertheless.

However, the decoration of Meudon also had a significance well beyond the relationship between fathers and sons. That is to say, the schemes devised by Audran, Antoine Coypel and others were meaningful in terms other than that those of familial dialogue. Bacchanals, for instance, offered more than a rejoinder to the policy of royal entertainments. According to Félibien's *Quatre Saisons* (1667), the orthodox, Lebrunian treatment of the Bacchic cult had rescued the young god from a reputation for orgiastic debauchery by stressing his resemblance to the Egyptian divinity, Osiris, thus re-presenting Bacchus as the Sun, symbol of the Ludovican 'golden century' and source of the nation's harvested wealth.[146] However, the dauphin's poet, Isaac de Benserade, offered *salon* society a more *honnête* interpretation of the legendary birth, according to which the Bacchic foetus completed its gestation in Jupiter's thigh before being entrusted to the care of nymphs. 'Telle est la Fable, en voicy le mystère', goes Benserade's rondeau,

> Estre bien né c'est une bonne affaire
> Mais tout va mal si le fruit ne meurit
> Il faut polir & les mœurs, & l'esprit,
> C'est là le point, & ce qu'on ne doit guère.
>
> A sa naissance.[147]

The reflexivity of this version of the Bacchic legend, recast it as the story about the process of refinement, and as a metaphor for the redemptive power of a taste exclusively practised by the society of *honnêtes gens*. Attention thus shifted from art and the 'authorship' of the state apparatus, to taste and the pseudo-creative activity of selectively made judgements. That *honnêteté* was an ideal that, at the turn of the century, saw profit in the spirited licences of comedy rather than in the austerely conservative endeavours of the civic hero was suggested at Meudon by the painterly exuberance with which Antoine Coypel rendered the comic hedonism of the antechamber's *Silenus* and by the festive extravagance of Audran's grotesques. Within the enclave of the state and at the interstices of the court, the Meudon faction, with the help of skills and traditions long cherished at the Menus Plaisirs, thus created and disseminated through painting and decoration a *politique du rire*, which placed them and others of society's *honnête* fraction safely beyond the reach of royal enchantment.

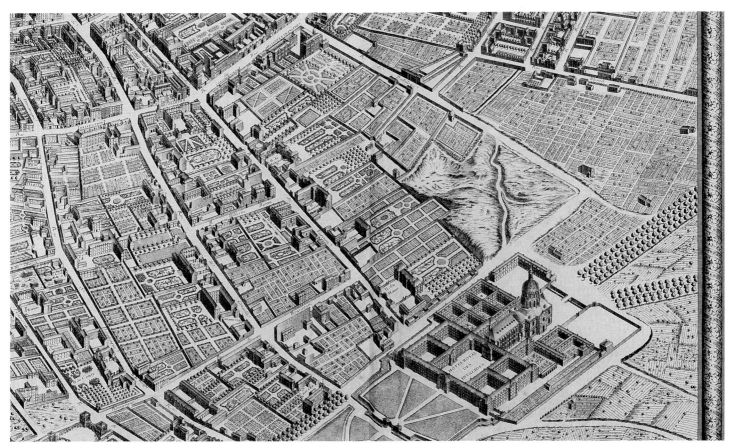

150   The faubourg Saint-Germain. Engraving. Detail from the *Turgot Map of Paris*, 1734–9.

7

Earthly Paradise on the Left Bank

Despite Louis XIV's attempts to stay the movements of his courtiers and consolidate their presence around him at or within the vicinity of Versailles, the prospect, after 1712, of an Orléanist Regency proved a stronger inducement, and the court's *grands* slipped away to Paris, if not permanently, then for increasingly frequent parties of pleasure.[1] Thus, even before the Grand Monarque had been ceremonially despatched below ground, hôtels were beginning to spring up all over the capital, particularly in the still rural, western districts of the city.[2] The Bouillon family had their mansion on the quai Malaquai, at the western end of the *rive gauche*, a section of the Seine embankment that had ostensibly been earmarked by the government for the residence of '*seigneurs*, gentlemen and other officers' of the court by an edict of July 1609.[3] It was in the streets that opened up behind the *quai* and which stretched north-westwards, towards the Invalides (fig. 150) that the old nobility and the princes and princesses of the blood (including Vendôme, the Conti and Condé) chose mostly to settle in the late seventeenth and early eighteenth centuries, thus lending the faubourg Saint-Germain its reputation for elegance and pleasure.[4] Indeed, such was the momentum of building initiatives by the second decade of the new century, that in 1725 Germain Brice felt compelled to launch an expanded version of his much-read *Description nouvelle de la ville de Paris*, to replace an earlier edition rendered obsolete by 'the extraordinary changes which have occured since the year 1717'.[5] Years later, the author of the most successful Paris guide-book of the mid-century, Piganiol de La Force, confirmed that 'never had so much building gone on in Paris and in the *Fauxbourgs* than during the minority of Louis XV'. By way of explanation, he added 'as paper money took the place of gold and silver everyone strove to give permanence to his fortune, and buildings sprang up everywhere'.[6] Thus, the social and political imperatives that had conspired to make Paris once more a capital, the place of 'pre-eminence' in the realm, were apparently supported during John Law's System (1718–20) by economic circumstances highly favourable to urban expansion and development. The combination of a relative (if momentary) depression in land value, easily available credit at low rates of interest and the effects of an inflationary policy encour-

aged, despite the soaring increase in the price of building materials, not only the architectural fantasies of a now emphatically metropolitan nobility, but also speculative housing development of a more commercial nature.[7] Moreover, it was to the decoration and redecoration of these hôtels that artists turned during a regency that could offer little in the way of official protection and patronage.[8]

However, the closing down of Meudon and then Versailles and the dispersal of the court nobility did not immediately sever the intimate connections between the manufacturers of *mondain* artefacts and their aristocratic grass-root constituency. Indeed, the social and familial alliances established by the dauphin's circle proved so enduring that the legitimate cadet branches of the Bourbon and Orléans families, plus the illegitimate Vendômes, and the foreign princes and princesses of Savoy and Lorraine may reasonably be said to have continued to play a significant role in decorative initiatives in the second and third decades of the eighteenth century.

The regent, Monsieur's son, appointed as his official architect and first painter two artists with whom he had been brought into contact through the Meudon connection: Gilles-Marie Oppenord, by the duc de Bouillon,[9] and Antoine Coypel by the dauphin.[10] Moreover, Philippe d'Orléans shared the dauphin's liking for modern Italian painting; both men owned pictures by Paolo Matteis who had visited France in 1702–5.[11] The regent's later attempt to attract Francesco Solimena to Paris to decorate a gallery at the Palais Royal and his abortive commission from the same artist, in company with Domenico Gabbiana, Benedetto Luti and Marco Antonio Franceschini, for four history paintings, testify to his continued and broad interest in contemporary Italian art,[12] an interest he apparently shared with another ex-Meudon associate, the duchesse de Bourbon-Condé, who initially selected Giardini to design her palace in the faubourg Saint-Germain.[13] Meanwhile, with Vendôme he shared an appreciation of the work of Jean Raoux and an enthusiasm for grotesques.[14] Indeed, between them, the duc d'Orléans and the duchesse de Bourbon and their circles provided Audran and his associates with a steady stream of commissions.[15] Angran de Fonspertius and the comtesse de Parabère, respectively a friend and a mistress of the regent,

151 Claude III Audran, ceiling of the *cabinet* at the hôtel Angran de Fonspertius, 1723. 21, place Vendôme, Paris.

called on Audran for the decoration of their *cabinets* (figs 151, 153) in the place Vendôme.[16] Similarly, the duchesse de Bourbon's *chef de conseil*, Peyrenc de Moras, another *place Vendômois*, engaged Audran and Lancret for the realisation of his *cabinet doré* (fig. 154),[17] while her son, Louis-Henri, duc de Bourbon, called on Audran's former associate, Christophe Huet, to create the famous *singeries* at Chantilly.[18] Furthermore, the comte de Lassay, the duchess's neighbour and artistic adviser, reserved the ceilings of two rooms in his hôtel for grotesque treatment,[19] while, at a slightly earlier date, the comtesse de Verrue, from whom Lassay inherited so many fine paintings[20] also conferred on Audran the task of decorating the ceiling of her pavilion in the rue du Cherche-Midi (fig. 152).[21] In the early 1720s the prince de Carignan, a second beneficiary of Verrue's will, and likewise renowned as a discriminating

amateur, secured the imagination and skills of Boffrand and Louis Herpin to fashion a plaster carnival of tripping monkeys, birds, masks and chimerical beasts along the cornice of his new dining-room on the ground floor of the hôtel de Soissons.[22] A decade or so earlier the same artists had united with Michel Lange under the patronage of Charles-Henri, prince de Vaudémont, and had captured in patterns for the *salon vert* at the hôtel de Mayenne ornament motifs of a kind to which the Carignan schemes have been justifiably compared.[23]

The description of these relationships is by no means exhaustive. It would be possible to pursue these princely and noble houses along their many and ever-reaching genealogical branches, hoping to accommodate the cultural behaviour of the ducs d'Estrée, de Villeroy or de Noailles, or the princes de Rohan-Soubise or de Cleremont, all variously allied to the houses of Condé, Conti and Lorraine.[24] Questions might then be raised about the closeness of the match between the contours of apparently so distinctive a taste and the constituency of its alleged patrons. However, where it was crucial for the purposes of correctly interpreting the ideological tasks performed by the grotesque in the court society of the late 1690s and early 1700s that there should have been near identity in the relation of faction and taste, by the time of the Regency the old cabals no longer fulfilled their original intentions and the interplay between rival centres of cultural production had been significantly redrawn. It can therefore, no longer be assumed that the grotesque necessarily continued to enjoy the same strategic importance in the articulation of *honnête* claims to nobiliary power. Moreover, on the death of Hardouin Mansart in 1708, the duc d'Antin had acceded to the Bâtiments and with him the *honnête* taste of Meudon had been spirited into the very centre of the state's cultural

152 Claude III Audran, ceiling for the hôtel de Verrue, *c.*1725. Fresco, 640 × 304 cm; plaster cornice, 45 cm. Musée des Arts Décoratifs, Paris.

153 (facing page) *Cabinet* at the hôtel Angran de Fonspertius, 1723. 21, place Vendôme, Paris.

policies. Thus it was, that after virtually twenty years in the wilderness Antoine Coypel was given arguably the most prestigious commission of Louis XIV's last years, the decoration of the chapel ceiling at Versailles, and that Claude III Audran came to paint his troublesome *Nursery of Apes*.[25] Moreover, just as the distinctions between the representations of state power and the pictorial enactments of *honnête* resistence were beginning to lose focus, it seems that the overt antagonism between academic and anti-academic practices, voiced in the debate over colour and line, were similarly starting to fade for lack of sufficent rehersal. Not only financial embarassment but d'Antin's relaxed approach to the visual arts seem to have contributed to a failure to keep the Academy abreast of its public duties. In particular, there was a decline in interest in theory and a creeping informality in teaching practice. Moreover, an institution so effectively dislocated from the articles of its foundation more readily accommodated painters and sculptors working in a conspicuously decorative tradition.[26]

ARABESQUES AND *FÊTES GALANTES*

Christophe Huet's painted finish to two *cabinets* at Champs for a relative of the princesse de Conti, the duc de La Vallière,[27] and Boffrand's designs for Malgrange, the duc de Lorraine's hunting lodge,[28] confirm the impression already created by Anet, Meudon, Sceaux and Chantilly, that the nobility was apt to prefer grotesques in the country, in the interiors of its *maisons de plaisance*. However, Vendôme had commissioned schemes by Audran for a pavilion at Clichy and a belvedere in the rue de Varenne, such prejudice notwithstanding. And if these architectural structures were principally suburban, known to both town and country, the hôtels of the comte de Lassay, Angran de Fonspertius and the comtesse de Parabère in the centre of Paris were fully metropolitan and also entertained grotesque fantasies in painted or sculpted form.[29] That the grotesque was not thereby stripped of its original rural context is suggested by the tendency of Audran's pupils and followers to emphasise the bucolic provenance of the genre. Around 1707–8, for instance, Antoine Watteau decorated a first-floor *cabinet* for Louis Béchameil, marquis de Nointel, a functionary of comparatively recent noble extraction, determined upon transforming a modest house on the rue de l'Université into an hôtel appropriate to his new-found prestige.[30] The eight panels and ceiling that comprised the scheme, some elements of which survive, clearly register Watteau's debt to a master in whose workshop he was still apprenticed at the time.[31] A central motif, such as Bacchus (fig. 155) is closely framed and bounded by a filigree border given structural dimension by the perspectival rendering of the platform on which the figure comes to rest. As Jacques Cailleux was the first to point out, it seems likely, given the different viewpoints of *The Faun* and *The Cajoler* (fig. 156), that the intended arrangement of panels

155 Antoine Watteau, *The Faun*, *c*.1707–8. Oil on panel, 87 × 39 cm. Private collection.

154 (previous pages) *Cabinet doré*, *c*.1724. Formerly at the hôtel Peyrenc de Moras, place Vendôme, Paris.

would have taken place on two different registers: *The Cajoler* on a lower setting and *The Faun* above.[32]

The confining and supportive role here assigned to ornament had earlier been exploited by Audran, and yet Watteau's designs reveal even at this early stage notable departures from the former's prototypes. Not only do the illusionistically projecting structures of ornament suggest a more thoroughly rational composition of space, but the absence of those monstrous violations of natural proportion that had populated Audran's ceilings with prodigious beasts and plants poking fun at their Lilliputian companions, worked to substitute a gentler whimsy in the place of Audran's robust comedy. Moreover, it is perhaps symptomatic of the unusual bodily restraint of this Bacchus that he went for so long unrecognised, mistaken for a less boistrous and self-serving faun. What these transformations seem to add up to is a loosening of the bonds that had committed the grotesque to an open-ended polemical exchange with official cultural discourse and defined it as an anti-canonical 'other'. Thus, for instance, despite the freely interpreted *comédie italienne* costumes worn by the cajoler and his sweetheart, the parodic intentions of the fair-players are no longer welcomed into the decorative context but are replaced, it seems, by a pastoral *rêverie*. The date of the panels rules out the possibility that these images articulated a response to a shift in social and political realities, as in 1707–8 the quarrelling factions at court were operating at full muster, while not until 1716 was the troupe of Italian comedians triumphantly returned to Paris as the 'players of Mgr the duc d'Orléans' to dissipate the oppositional taint their cast had picked up in the fairs.[33] Explanations for the muted, civilised challenge offered by these arabesques – a term that draws attention to their formal elegance – have therefore to be found elsewhere.

It is perhaps worth emphasising straight away that Watteau's patrons, no less than his art, differed in significant ways from Audran's. The list of Audran's known clients reads like a 'who's who' of élite noble society, and although the social parameters of his market expanded after 1710 to include financiers such as Peyrenc de Moras and Malon de Bercy, his principal activity nevertheless remained focused on the demands of grandees and the court.[34] By contrast, few gentlemen seem to have been attracted to the elegant lightness of Watteau's decorative forms or indeed the exquisite refinement of his later, landscape-cum-genre paintings, known as *fêtes galantes*.[35] With the exception of the comtesse de Verrue and possibly the comte de Caylus, it was not the *grands* who sought out Watteau, but the middling and lesser urban nobility made up of warriors like Caylus's cousin, the comte de Murcé, and Antoine de La Roque, and ennobled *robins* and functionaries such as Germain-Louis Chauvelin and Joseph-Jean-Baptiste Fleuriau, both of whom, like fellow-traveller, Nointel, commissioned decorative schemes from the artist.[36] Moreover, there is every reason to suppose that these lesser nobles were the very people for whom Watteau also created his later and more original arabesque designs, such as *The Swing* (fig. 157)

156 Antoine Watteau, *The Cajoler*, *c*.1707–8. Oil on panel, 79.5 × 39 cm. Private collection.

or *The Bower*. Indeed, his failure to break into the patronage system of élite society perhaps accounts for Watteau's early abandonment of decorative work in favour of easel painting.

Since the sixteenth century this secondary nobility, trapped between the values of an ultimately despised provincial squirarchy and the culture of an envied but often resented court aristocracy, had discovered in literary and pictorial pastoralism a vehicle capable of sustaining the projection of its hopes and frustrations.[37] Thus, although for many, the urbanisation of feudal power and the bureaucratisation of the state were precisely those indignities that had finally won them titles of nobility, in the mind's eye, it was still the conquest of *domaines*, by pecuniary means if necessary, that redeemed and qualified titles (Chauvelin was *seigneur* de Grisenoy, Fleuriau, *sieur* d'Armenoville), that evoked social conditions where status was clearly legible and, finally, that invested proprietary wealth with symbolic value.[38] However, since rural property was rarely experienced directly by men such as these (as field, pasture and woodland), there was a tendency to regard it not so much as an exploitable asset but as a distant prospect, a

landscape, the realm of a benificent and sentient social force – Nature. Moreover, it was a nature invested with precisely those qualities and values upon which nobiliary power and legitimacy depended, in contrast to the heterodox system of beliefs and priorities upheld by the genuinely urban classes.

La Bruyère noted that 'one is brought up in the town with a crass indifference to all things rural and *champêtre*'.[39] Preoccupied with commercial transactions and convinced of the innate superiority of his profession, the bourgeois was wilfully ignorant of 'nature, her beginnings, her progress, her gifts and her generosity', moreover,

> if he sometimes hears tell of the first men or the patriarchs, of their pastoral existence and their economies, he is amazed that one could have lived in such times, when there were as yet neither office-holding nor brokerage nor judges nor procurators; he cannot conceive that one could ever have done without the clerk's office, the chancery bar or the tavern.[40]

La Bruyère not only implicitly contrasted bourgeois units of

reckoning ('yardage', 'tariffed rates', 'pennies in the pound') with the gifts and *largesse* – a distinctly seigneurial concept[41] – of nature but also the social relationships they engendered. Relationships mediated by the cash nexus generated strife and exploitation and hence created a need for means of redress, the litigious 'calls to appeal', 'civil actions' and 'depositions' (apparently privileged words in the bourgeois's vocabulary) from which lawyers in turn stood to gain. Pastoral society, on the other hand, was portrayed as a good-faith economy, an economy devoid of cash exchanges but dependent instead on the gifts, services and duties of each member to the group.[42] The citizens of Bétique, like Montesquieu's Troglodytes, 'looked upon themselves as a single family'[43] bound by affective ties; essentially an idealisation of those traditional bonds of fealty apparently threatened by the burgeoning market economies of the cities.[44]

Romantic love, or a bond grounded in the complete understanding and perfect confidence that lovers have of and in each other, functioned in much pastoral literature and imagery as a metaphor for the transparency of social relations desired on a universal scale. Watteau frequently used his most emphatically verdant arabesques, in *The Swing* and *The Sparrow's Nest* (fig. 158) for instance, as settings for romantic trysts. The uniqueness of these encounters suggested by the intimacy of the action and the particular warmth of the feelings, was lent a wider application by the energy of the vegetation, which announced nature's existence as a generative principle as well as an accomplished fact and by the complex patterning of symbols of cultural and agricultural cultivation deployed in the margins. Moreover, the seeming innocence of the couples, their consciences apparently untroubled by knowledge of the boundaries of social distinction and the parameters of social convention habitually thought necessary for love's proper reception, suggested their relationships as the point of origin for all subsequent social intercourse. The credit of this originating form of relating depended on the assumed fidelity of the participants, a state of faithfulness that Watteau described in his arabesques by framing the couple, that is by isolating the lovers from further choices. It was the rustic's essential constancy, guaranteed by the candour of his expression, that marked his manner of relating as the ideal point of reference for all subsequent social contracts and as a point of contrast with a later metropolitan age, known by the sexual and, by extension, the social and political inconstancy of its citizens.[45]

If, in the *Sparrow's Nest*, Watteau worked through the immobility and contiguity of his figures to still the connotations of pursuit and flirtation associated with bird-snaring,[46] and thereby to exalt the faithful in love, in his other arabesques and *fêtes galantes* (freehand copies of which were not uncommonly made up into overdoors by others[47]) he more usually broke faith with this ideal of pastoral fidelity. All too frequently the tranquility of his pastoral scenes was unsettled by the overtly sexual connotations of the objects in the margin. The potential rhythmic equivalence of swinging and love-

making, for instance, was brought sharply to notice in *The Swing* by the ornamental 'tail-piece' featuring bagpipes whose resemblance to the male genitals was almost uncanny.[48] Moreover, in works such as *The Bower* (fig. 159) all pretence of mutual affection and respect was abandoned and replaced by rape, a forceful reminder of the irrepressibility and indiscrimination of the sexual drive set loose from moral constraints. It was left to others, to Watteau's pupils and imitators, to create less equivocal depictions of the *amusements champêtres* the nobility admired as metaphors and pursued for pleasure. Thus, an anonymous hand successfully diffused the latent eroticism of swinging in the canvas just discernable from a drawing by Nicolas Pineau (fig. 160), designed to be inscribed within a panelled scheme at the hôtel de Bonnac,[49] and Nicolas Lancret disguised all hint of physical frustration in the motif of the captured bird in his version of a sparrow's entrapment (fig. 161) executed as an overdoor for Peyrenc de Moras's *cabinet*.[50]

In the tension between the metaphorical and metonymic functions of the pastoral sign, between its capacity to promote

159 Gabriel Huquier after Antoine Watteau, *The Bower*, c.1728. Etching.

LE BERCEAU

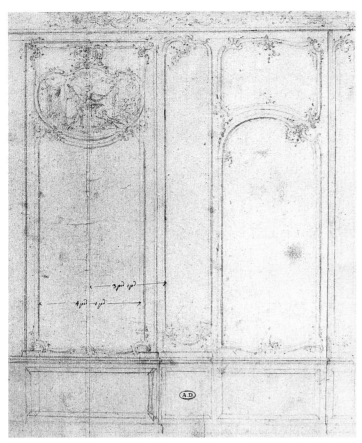

160 Nicolas Pineau, design for panelling, possibly for the hôtel de Bonnac, *c*.1732–5. Pencil on paper, 34.5 × 49. Musée des Arts Décoratifs, Paris.

obliquely noble ideology and to illustrate an aristocratic ideal, we encounter one of the fundamental ambiguities in the *champêtre* imagery of the Regency period. Since the essence of the pastoral lay not in the truthful but in the ideal depiction of rustic life, and since its characters owed their verisimilitude not to any likeness to peasants but to an analogical relationship with nobles, the genre occupied a constantly shifting position between fiction and metaphorical truth.[51] Whether in the form of outmoded seventeenth-century fashions and *commedia dell'arte* costumes favoured by Watteau, or Boucher's later *bergerie* masquerades, disguise structured the meaning of these rural scenes and, in the knowledge that the *beau monde* enjoyed dressing-up in like manner for actual *fêtes* and dramatic performances,[52] the question of the veracity of such portrayals becomes increasingly vexed. For all their deployment of theatrical costumes and props, Watteau and Lancret's *fêtes galantes* can rarely be twinned with particular performances, and their parkland settings tend to suggest that these scenes should be understood as records of the ideal reality of aristocratic leisure.[53] Moreover, since certain figures clearly announce themselves as particular, as portraits, within the *champêtre* narratives – for example, the turbanned gentleman in *Les Fêtes Vénitiennes* (1718; National Gallery of Scotland,

Edinburgh) – it may seem tempting to assume that like Honoré d'Urfé and Madeleine de Scudery's earlier *romans à clef*, such pictures depicted the narcissistic fantasies of a defeated, second-order nobility.[54] Such scenes might then be approached, to quote Nobert Elias, as recreations of 'a mimetic world in which people diguised as shepherds and shepherdesses can live out the unpolitical adventures of their hearts, above all the sorrows and the joys of love, without coming into conflict with the constraints, the commands and prohibitions of a harsher, non-mimetic reality.'[55]

161 Nicolas Lancret, *The Caged Bird*, *c*.1724. Oil on canvas, 95 × 88 cm. Musée des Arts Décoratifs, Paris.

The deployment of pastoral imagery in hôtel interiors seems at first, to support this view. In town houses, Audran's grotesques and Watteau's arabesques did not, for the most part, occupy the *grands appartements*, as they had at Meudon, but were lodged in the *cabinets* of the society apartments. Examples of such cloistering are to be found at the hôtel de Soubise, where the *cabinet vert* was as good as its name in intimacy as well as in colour, at the hôtel de Roquelaure, where, in 1742, Natoire's pastoral overdoors, apparently overcome with shyness after a brief exposure at the Salon, sought refuge in président Molé's closet,[56] and at the hôtel de Matignon, where Lancret's four overdoors depicting *jeux champêtres* were arguably given a trifle more public prominence

162 Antoine Watteau, *The Perspective*, *c.*1714–5. Oil on canvas, 46.7 × 55.3 cm. Boston Museum of Fine Arts, Boston. Maria Antoinette Evans Fund.

163 Comte de Caylus after Antoine Watteau, *Charles Le Brun's house at Montmorency*, *c.*1726–8. Etching.

by virtue of their location in the drawing-room.[57] However, to leave matters here, would I think, be to insist too strongly that figures alone signify, whether the figures in the pictures or those self-selected to look at them. Quite as remarkable as Watteau's amateur Harlequins and Columbines were the settings into which they fitted. It is generally supposed that these parklands were no less got-up or fictional than the figures, not least because the views anticipated by decades the informality of the English garden, later imported to France with so much success.[58] There is however, one exception, *The Perspective* (fig. 162), painted around 1714–15, and which from drawings, one of them etched and annotated by Caylus (fig. 163), is known to have depicted Montmorency, formerly 'the house of Mr Le Brun, F[irst] P[ainter] to the king L. XIV'.[59] Not only does the attention to topographical detail make the picture unusual in Watteau's œuvre, but the overriding sense that in this place nature was once directed along lines drawn from the centre, from the château that closes the perspective, suggests an uncharacteristic resemblance between this work and portraits of the gardens at Versailles.[60]

It has generally been accepted that the meaning of the picture is to be found in the assumed circumstances of its production, that is to say, that it should be understood as a straightforward depiction of a country estate belonging to one whose favour Watteau wished to court, namely Pierre Crozat.[61] Crozat, however, never bought the work, assuming it was offered to him, and Caylus as has been seen, remembered it as a view of Le Brun's house, not Crozat's. By now there is

no need to belabour the point that in Le Brun and his monument, Versailles, was thought to reside the essence of an absolute classical tradition. That the political implications of that linear approach to nature were readily understood is suggested by Saint-Simon's comments about the gardens surrounding Louis's suburban palace: 'There it gave the king pleasure *to tyrannise* Nature and *to tame* her by expending art and money . . . One feels repelled by the constraint that is everywhere imposed upon Nature.'[62] However, in Watteau's picture the exaggeration of the perspectival strength once used by a giant's hand to lay down such gardens, has so overgrown the orthogonals that the trees seem to obstruct rather than ease a passage to the gutted space beyond a conspicuously fragile, almost temporary looking, classical façade.[63] Moreover, many of the figures, far from registering the constraints tyrannously imposed upon their world, feign ignorance of the view designed for their entrapment (those most at risk apparently preferring the sight of their own watery reflections), while the only determined gesture struck in the picture points to an exit to the left.

French theorists, as disparate in their views as Roger de Piles, the champion of colour, and Henri Testelin, the tireless defender of Le Brun, were inclined to agree that the function of perspective was principally to facilitate the legibility of a pictorial narrative by so judiciously aligning the point of central perspective with the object or action of the composition's primary focus, that the spectator was enlightened in a single, instantaneous *coup d'œil*.[64] On the surface, *The Perspective*

Oppenord inv.

Huquier Sculp. et ex. rue des Matharine C.P.R.

164 and 165   Gabriel Huquier after Gilles-Marie Oppenord, designs for *salons*, *c.*1748. Etching.

Oppenord inv.

Huquier Sculp. et ex. rue des Matharine   C.P.R.

promises no less, but where the diagonals converge is found only a carcass; an empty centre. It would perhaps be a mistake to insist too strongly that this painting, notwithstanding its title, should be approached with an eye for the discreet expressions of revolt built into the very structure of the image; however, the work usefully raises the suggestion that ideological work is accomplished no less efficiently by the apparently objective and abstract mechanics of perspective and composition, than by the interpretation and management of subject-matter. The more conspicuously staged compositions of two of Watteau's contemporaries, Gilles-Marie Oppenord and Jacques de Lajoue, might be approached with this issue particularly in mind. In Oppenord's engraved projects for the decoration of *salons* and *cabinets* (figs 164, 165), for instance, what is striking is not only that the elevations are so ambiguously punctured that it is virtually impossible to decipher whether we are staring at a representation or looking out on to a space beyond;[65] it is also that such compositions wilfully occlude the point of perspectival confluence, and therefore the moment of significant conjunction, precisely to withhold from the viewer an explanation where he or she would most expect to find it. Moreover, such games were played in three as well as two dimensions. Architects manipulated and exaggerated the effects of parallax by combining mirrors, painted perspectives and fenestration in such a way as to surprise and disorientate[66] – at Bastide's *Petite Maison*, the scene of an *ingénue*'s seduction, to quite devastatingly immoral effect.[67]

Meanwhile, the theatrical illusionism of Lajoue's landscapes, which probably owed more than a passing resemblance to Servandoni's theatre backdrops,[68] at one level, simply connoted that dimension of performance quintessential to noble leisure, already familiar from Watteau's *fêtes*. However, the oblique angle of many of his spatial projections promoted a highly self-conscious use of perspective, literally a point of view, so that at another level, these parkscapes worked beyond the compass of their frames to expose the relativity of the universal claims pronounced by a unitary but spent classical order. To put it another way, Lajoue's use of dramatic angles served to alert the viewer to his perspective or purchase on the world and suggested, moreover, that any system of representation that purported to reconcile all interests in a common and absolute view was founded on deceit. Thus, the most striking difference between Watteau's cosmetically tamed *Perspective* and Lajoue's *Fountain in a Park* (fig. 166), one of two overdoors executed in the 1720s, possibly for the duc de Gesvres's château de Maillebois,[69] derives from Lajoue's decision to reverse the direction of the pyramid of vision and locate the focal point in the body of the spectator rather than at the centre of the picture. The result is a cloven composition, fragmented by orthogonals running away in different directions, leaving a centre foreground occupied by an irrationally designed fountain and cluttered with seemingly gratuitous trivia (a pair of dogs, a vase, a broken column perched precariously across a section of frieze) captured with *tour de force*

166   Jacques de Lajoue, *Fountain in a Park*, *c.*1738–40. Oil on canvas, 190 × 140 cm. Location unknown.

illusionism. The relationship between foreground and background has effectively been reversed, with accessories that should have been marginalised as decoration and setting brought forward for attention. Like Watteau's *fêtes* which, according to Caylus, lacked 'focus' because no overriding passion or intention unified their dramatic action,[70] Lajoue's compositions neutralised narrative by rendering the figures incapable of detaching themselves from the backdrop, for lack of those laws of composition that had formerly announced the meaningful presence of the cast, simply by allowing all diagonals to converge upon them. Instead of playing a role, hero or villain, the figures merely enjoy a negotiated identity within a non-hierarchical pictorial space.

Lajoue's paintings therefore, seem to rely no less heavily than Watteau's on the competence of the spectator. Indeed, it is possible that one of the primary functions of paintings such as these, was to advertise the power of the viewer, specifically the patron, to effect a mental reconciliation of the particularistic elements of the work that the painter had seemingly abandoned in artful chaos. Sébastien Le Clerc, in the forward to his often-republished *Pratique de la géométrie* (1669) had done much to emphasise the empowering nature of perspective and had underlined through illustration (fig. 167) as well as in words, its suitability as a skill for the nobility.[71] Moreover, by making perspective an end in itself, into an illusion controlled and understood from a privileged point of view, Lajoue transformed the pastoral's latent nostalgia into a discourse with a purchase on reality. To put it more broadly, it seems that these landscapes represented, in their different ways, not the reactionary yearnings of a marginalised and alienated nobility for a lost golden age, but the noble aspiration to a regenerated natural and social order unified and stabilised by an aristocratic gaze.

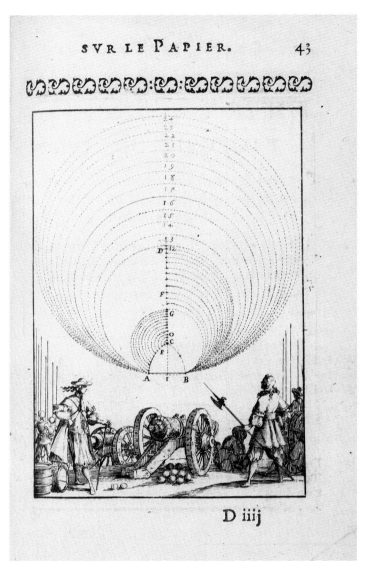

167 Sébastien Le Clerc, *Artillery Officer and Soldiers*, 1669. Etching. From Sébastien Le Clerc, *Pratique de la géométrie sur le papier et sur le terrain*, 1669.

It surely cannot be by chance that the pastoral should have apparently recovered its status as 'landscape of restoration' at the very time that the political imagination of the nobility was bodying forth its most ambitious plans for the reconstitution of a noble civic order.[72] Moreover, the expansion of the Regency council through the creation of a system of advisory colleges, collectively known as the Polysynodie, suggested to nobles that the regent was prepared in principle, and if only at first, to draw them into government, and in so doing, hand them opportunities to privatise the state (so to speak) by investing it with their own class interests.[73] At a time when political augury was impossible to divine, these concessions must have suggested to many that Virgil's wish, expressed in the fourth *Eclogue*, that these 'woods' should be 'worthy of a consul' was a hair's breadth from fulfilment. The second estate

had, therefore, every reason for genuine political optimism. However, at the same time, the dynastic uncertainties begotten of Philip V's enforced renunciation of the French throne and Louis's gift of successorial rights to his legitimated sons propelled the Regency into a crisis that split the nobility, fragmenting it into competing factions each claiming that matters pertaining to the unwritten French constitution were properly theirs to resolve.[74] The *affaire du bonnet* (1715–16) and the *affaire des princes* (1716–17), as these disputes were called, set the dukes and peers against the untitled (non-ducal) nobility. While the former called upon the regent to confirm their necessary presence in the Grande Chambre of the Paris Parlement on occasions of constitutional importance, the latter, for the first time since the Fronde, gathered in assemblies, drew up petitions, scripted pamphlets and insisted that issues relating to regencies and the succession could be decided only by the 'nation' convoked in Estates General.

If both sides were hoping to exploit the uncertainties of Orléans's fate in order to regain lost political territories, particularly significant with respect to *champêtre* ideology was the impulse to form new accommodations provoked by these disputes. Though little is known about the number and constituency of the assemblies of the nobility, Saint-Simon's splenetic reference to their members as no more than 'a heap of *safraniers*', who 'styled themselves nobles but three-quarters of whom would have had difficulty in proving it', confirms their self-representation in pamphlets as a legally defined order that admitted no distinction between sword and gown, or old nobility and new.[75] If not necessarily active participants in these quarrels, it would have been this nobility, bound by common interests yet loyal to the crown, that would surely have harvested the sympathies and support of a Nointel, a Chauvelin, a Fleuriau d'Armenonville, or indeed those of the young Antoine-Louis Rouillé, comte de Jouy, whose hôtel in the rue des Poulies belatedly received *fête galante* overdoors by Watteau or Lancret and landscapes by Lajoue that were fitted into painted and gilded panelling sculpted by Pineau.[76] For a time at least, it may be possible to talk of a shared élite culture, one from and through which the nobility sought to make good an aesthetic ideal by substituting political for poetical truths.

The unusual power of Watteau's contribution derived perhaps from the tension between an enchanted and almost ethereal pastoral will, which refused to reduce the natural world to inanimate matter, to an economic fact, and the incipient immorality of a nobility for whom the pleasures of the countryside lay not least in an evasion of the constraints of court discipline and its manifold *bienséances*.[77] That this contradiction had a place in life as well as in art is suggested by the comte de Téssé's arch remark to the princesse des Ursins in 1713, the year in which the abbé de Choisy's abridged edition of *L'Astrée* was published, in which he states that 'our young ladies of today are more knowing in their *entresols* than the shepherdesses of Lignon were in their woods'.[78] The aristocratic will to power thus visibly contained the seeds of its own undoing.

PASTORALS AND LANDSCAPES

The idea that Watteau handed over the golden bough to the young François Boucher, who proceeded casually to strip the pastoral of its emotional and intellectual complexity leaving little more than a sophisticated husk, remains stubbonly current, despite Alastair Laing's recent publications, which have set out to explain the nature of this supposed impoverishment.[79] Attention to the subjects of Boucher's contemporary pastorals suggests that the difference lies in a changed relationship between the image and social practice. In place of the rich and constantly shifting significations of metaphor, Boucher substituted a specific and exhaustive modern literary reference. Thus, instead of using theatrical costumes to describe the conditions and quality of aristocratic leisure, the dress of Boucher's shepherds and shepherdesses in works such

as the *Gallant Shepherd* (fig. 168) – an overdoor painted in around 1738 for the *salle d'audience* at the hôtel de Soubise – referred the spectator to a text, just as one of the tapestries which hung alongside, *The Charlatan and the Peep-Show* (1739; fig. 169), notwithstanding its classical ruins, probably represented two scenes from Panard and Favart's *La Foire de Bezons*, performed at the Foire Saint-Laurent in 1735.[80] The relationship between Boucher's pastorals and Charles-Simon Favart's plays was one of illustration, and the transformation of the Opéra-Comique's repertoire in the late 1730s and 1740s[81] therefore also brought about a parallel modification in its visual equivalent. Honoré d'Urfé in his *romans-à-clef* had held out a mirror to nobles and encouraged them to recognise themselves in the allegorical portraits he devised;[82] almost a century later Watteau, perhaps no less successfully, offered nobles a rural metaphor of their pretentions to aristocracy,[83] but with Favart and Boucher analogy broke down. Favart's rustics certainly no more resembled the French eighteenth-century peasantry than d'Urfé or Watteau's, but on the other

168   François Boucher, *The Gallant Shepherd*, 1738. Oil on canvas, 147 × 198 cm. Archives Nationales, Paris.

169   François Boucher, *The Charlatan and the Peep-Show*, 1739. Wool and silk, 324 × 417 cm. From the Beauvais tapestry series, *The Fêtes Italiennes*, 1736. Location unknown.

hand they were not ciphers for noblemen. Indeed, in *Ninette à la Cour* (1756), Favart used the attempted seduction of the naive and innocent heroine by the worldly seigneur, Prince Astolphe, to promote the positive virtues of humble village life at the expense of the knavish and perfidious existence of a courtly élite.[84] Thus, Favart's *Les Vendanges de Tempé* or *La Vallée de Montmorency*, a pantomime first performed in 1745, no doubt expanded the range of available subjects from which the painter and patron might devise a scheme[85] and added that air of topicality at the core of the fair-theatres' success; but at the same time it restricted the semantic range of the pastoral, limiting its connotations to the parameters of the bucolic text. Of Boucher's *Summer Pastoral* (Wallace Collection, London) and *Autumn Pastoral* (fig. 170), commissioned around 1749 by Trudaine de Montigny for the decoration of his château at Montigny-Lencoup,[86] for instance, the first possibly portrays the cousins, Babet and Lisette in an imaginary scene, while the second depicts a subject directly adapted from scene VI of the pantomime in which the shepherd gallantly feeds Lisette with a bunch of grapes.[87] Neither are fully comprehensible without certain knowledge of Favart's text. In this respect such pictures bore a closer family resemblance to 'ancient' pastorals

inspired by Longus's *Daphnis and Chloe*, such as Natoire's overdoors for the hôtel de Roquelaure (figs 171, 172), or indeed Boucher's decorative celebration of the lovers in the Wallace Collection (fig. 173), than they do to Watteau's modern *fêtes galantes* from which they are too often thought to derive.[88] The dialectical structure of the pastoral which had injected life into the ongoing dialogue between representation and social life had effectively been broken, and the *fête champêtre* was seemingly turned out to pasture in a charming and complaisant world of make-believe.

The erosion of the pastoral metaphor and the displacement of historicised idylls by either literary fiction or comic realism has been attributed in part to a shift in intellectual concerns away from interpretation and towards definition.[89] Marivaux's *Télémaque travesti* (1735) forcefully exposed the extent of the breach between Fénelon's carefully circumscribed agrarian nirvana and the reality of French rural society to which it purported to refer.[90] Moreover, though some, like Desmahis, claimed to have encountered 'Celadons and Astrées' dancing to the strains of a flute on the outskirts of the forest of Saint-Germain,[91] most travel literature of the first half of the eighteenth century testified, on the contrary, to the brutality

170   François Boucher, *Autumn Pastoral (Les Raisins Pensent-ils au Raisin?)*, 1749. Oil on canvas, 147 × 198 cm. Wallace Collection, London.

171 Charles-Joseph Natoire, *Pastoral Scene*, c.1742. Oil on canvas, 90 × 100 cm. Hôtel de Roquelaure, presently the Ministère de l'Equipment, Paris.

172 Charles-Joseph Natoire, *Pastoral Scene*, c.1742. Oil on canvas, 90 × 100 cm. Hôtel de Roquelaure, presently the Ministère de l'Equipment, Paris.

of life in the country. The double existence led by the pastorals of Fontenelle and his contemporaries, pretending to freedom and plenty on the one hand, while decently obscuring the pain, toil and oppression of actuality on the other, was, by the 1730s and 1740s, becoming an unsustainable hypocrisy. In *Le Siècle pastorale* (1748), the poet Gresset was moved to deny that the world invoked by the pastoral had ever had substance, even in some distant, antedeluvian age.[92] Moreover, two small pictures by Boucher depicting a young shepherdess with her dog and the Indian queen Golconda crossing a bridge, which decorated a ground-floor room at the hôtel de Lamoignon, suggest a surprising sensitivity on the part of this painter to the terms of the debate, since the first apparently played poverty to the second's plenty.[93]

According to the abbé du Bos, the pastoral could survive

173 François Boucher, *Daphnis and Chloe*, 1743–5. Oil on canvas, 109.5 × 154.8 cm. Wallace Collection, London.

this crisis in verisimilitude only by deflecting attention from shepherds and shepherdesses and refocusing it on the landscape.[94] Though poets and painters were apparently slow to respond to this suggestion – in 1744 Mariette still felt justified in lamenting the neglect of landscape painting[95] – visual depictions of the French countryside significantly gave a lead to developments in poetry. Eighteenth-century inventories and picture sales suggest that the decorative value of landscape was greatly appreciated. Thirteen of the fifteen overdoors that had formerly decorated the hôtel de Tallard, and were auctioned with the duke's collection in 1756, were landscapes, two of them by Allegrain.[96] In the early 1720s, Louise-Julie de La Tour d'Auvergne, princesse de Montbazon, chose landscapes to crown the doors of the first antechamber in her newly built hôtel in the grande rue du faubourg Saint-Honoré,[97] while the marquise de Feuquières similarly opted for landscapes in the decoration of her two successive hôtels on the rue de Varenne.[98] In 1738, the very same year Pineau was engaged on the panelling for the second of these residences, Boucher and Trémolières each produced a *Rustic Landscape* (fig. 174) to complement the sculpted cartouches of the princesse de Soubise's *cabinet vert* (figs 175, 176).[99] Notwithstanding Boucher's known study of the Beauvaisis *sur le motif*, these landscapes were imaginary and generalised depictions, and it was perhaps only the absence of classical ruins that lent them the appearance of genuine provincialism.[100] However, if more convincing peasants now replaced the noble or stage rustics of the pastoral, these landscapes continued to perpetuate an idyllic belief in the benefits – 'Peace, gentle rest, strength and health'[101] – of a simple, yet humble, country life. The mill stationed in the left background of Boucher's work suggests at first an appetite for Georgic scenes, but the figures offset by the overwhelmingly fecund vegetation in the centre, are the

175   Jacques Verberckt (attributed to), cartouche with *The Two Cocks and the Partridge*, detail of the panelling from the *cabinet vert* formerly at the hôtel de Soubise, *c*.1738. Remounted at the hôtel de Rohan, Paris.

176   Jacques Verberckt (attributed to), cartouche with *The Bear and the Honey-Bees*, detail of the panelling from the *cabinet vert* formerly at the hôtel de Soubise, *c*.1738. Remounted at the hôtel de Rohan, Paris.

very same cowherds and shepherdesses of lyrical poetry, their occupations only marginally extended by Trémolières's introduction of a fisherman. The effect of this palimpsestic enterprise, by which the pastoral was made over as landscape through the simple diminution of the scale of the figures, was to eliminate the dynamism of the *champêtre* offensive and to put in its place an amiable rustic defence, a palliative without power to impell or induce society (in both its restricted and general senses) to return to a feudal ideal that the *fête galante*, if not the pastoral, had so persuasively conjured up.

From the festive irreverence of Audran's grotesques to the political quietism of Boucher's landscapes, the pastoral had been caught in a process of constant redefinition and accommodation. Indeed, it was perhaps this quality of inherent instability that most conspicuously set the genre against the immutable codes of the academic tradition.[102] Moreover, it was not simply that pastoralism arrived variously got up, it was also that a single visual cue might, at different times, sustain more than one interpretation. For example, by the 1720s the spirit of arrogant optimism that had emboldened the duchesse du Maine to establish a rival court at Sceaux and, under the direction of Audran, to transform the *petit appartement* of the Colbert country estate into an enchanting 'grotesque' parody of Versaillais culture, had evaporated, to be replaced, in the duchess's mind at least, by the genius of exile and expropriation. In a letter to Hénault sent from Normandy in 1726, du Maine wrote of her pain at having been transported from beneath the trellised canopy of her other Eden (fig. 177) – the realm of birds, monkeys, sprites and more prosaically-occupied gardeners – into the 'age of iron'. 'Instead of the sound of the flute and the bagpipes to which I am accustomed', she continued,

177 Claude III Audran, design for a ceiling at Sceaux, *c*.1704. Pencil and wash on paper, 25 × 29.2 cm. Nationalmuseum, Stockholm.

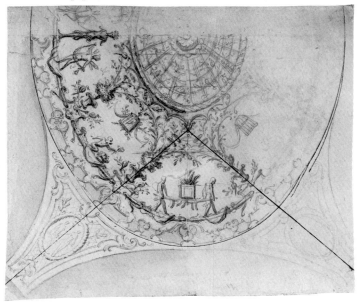

I hear only the explosive noise of drums, kettledrums and trumpets. Instead of the peaceable dances of our shepherds under the elm trees' shade, I am offered the spectacle of exploding bombs and frigates engaged in battle; finally, instead of floral crowns, garlands and romances hymned in my honour, I am saluted by canon fire.[103]

And yet it was her earlier willingness not only to envisage such military conflict in order to replace Orléans with a Spanish regent, but actively to participate in the so-called Cellamare conspiracy which had, in fact, earned her the exile from power she now thought to celebrate.[104] To a certain extent, in the story of her political life the fortunes of the nobility as a whole may also be read. The chronological coincidence of the emergence of literary pastorals and rustic landscapes with the advent of the unofficial ministry of cardinal Fleury suggests that the nobility's optimism of the Regency years had dissipated in the light of new political realities, and that the form of their ideology had consequently transformed itself from positive analogy and statements of things as they are, and could be, to passive fictions and nostalgic evocations of things as they might, or should have been. Virtue had quietly moved house from history to fiction.

NATURAL AND ARTIFICIAL CURIOSITIES

Perhaps the most striking characteristic of the ornamentation that accompanied the pastoral imagery discussed above is that it tended very obviously neither towards the grotesque nor towards the ideal. Expanding upon the swags and baskets of flowers long familiar to the French decorative tradition, Nicolas Pineau had provided the *chambre de parade* at the hôtel de Roquelaure with more studied and near-sighted representations of flowers and fruit (fig. 178) to complement Natoire's overdoors, and in the *salon* had set the cooing of gallantly paired doves at the base of the wider panels (fig. 179) to counterpoint the music evoked by the trophies of rustic musical instruments suspended above. Moreover, perhaps with greater originality, Pineau and other *ornemanistes* active in the 1720s and '30s had set their sights at Neptune's realm: an overdoor in the *grand cabinet* at the hôtel d'Evreux (fig. 180), for instance, possibly by Michel Lange, depicts Venus, accompanied by putti, emerging from the waves in an appropriately shelly chariot, and protected by a canopy suspended above her head from the grasp of a scallop shell. Such ornament offered a 'naturalism' that, on the surface at least, seemed to owe more to *curiosité*, to the taste for collecting natural history, than to either the comic or lyrical genres of literature.

The nobility had, in fact, taken an active interest in natural history and philosophy at least since the days of Théophraste Renaudot's short-lived scientific debating society, the Bureau d'Addresses (1633–42).[105] By the early eighteenth century the *monde* fairly throbbed with enthusiasm for Nature's particulars, notwithstanding the fact that scientific inquiry was gen-

178 Nicolas Pineau, fruit and flowers, detail of the panelling of the bedchamber at the hôtel de Roquelaure, *c*.1733. Hôtel de Roquelaure, presently the Ministère de l'Equipment, Paris.

179 Michel Lange (attributed to), Venus and putti, overdoor from the panelling of the Salon d'Angle at the hôtel d'Evreux, *c*.1719–20. Palais de l'Elysées, Paris.

180 Nicolas Pineau, paired doves, detail from the panelling in the *salon* at the hôtel de Roquelaure, *c*.1733. Hôtel de Roquelaure, presently the Ministère de l'Equipment, Paris.

erated primarily by a body of professional individuals generally excluded from polite society.[106] Empiricism had, by the turn of the century, gone a long way to transforming the material world into a place that was profoundly knowable through observation, a commonplace, sensory skill in which the noble amateur believed himself as well, if not better endowed than the bourgeois professional. Moreover, it was, as I hope to show, through the fashionable exploitation of some of the new discoveries in science that the *honnête* élite perhaps most persuasively sought to preserve and perpetuate a measure of its traditional pastoral idealism, by articulating it in a particularly modern idiom.

Among the most remarkable collectors of curiosities and amateurs of science of the first half of the eighteenth century was Joseph Bonnier de la Mosson, a colonel in the dragoons who, after the death of his father in 1726 inherited both the lucrative post of treasurer of the estates of Languedoc and a mansion, the hôtel du Lude, in the rue Saint-Dominique.[107] Bonnier continued the decorative initiatives of his father and in 1734 Jacques de Lajoue delivered one of several overdoors (fig. 181) commissioned for the decoration of a first-floor apartment, where the amateur's remarkable collections of natural and artificial scientific phenomena had been duly installed.[108] For a long time the picture was thought to offer a faithful record of the physic and mechanic cabinet, on the grounds that many of the instruments and models described in Bonnier's sale (1744) seemed to correspond almost exactly to the painted specimens arranged along the shelves depicted.[109] If closer study of these accessories has since suggested a finer balance between record and invention, then it is perhaps not surprising further to discover that the composition resembles Sebastien Le Clerc's frontispiece (fig. 182) to the *Mémoires pour servir à l'histoire des plantes* (1671) at least as much as it records the appearance of the interiors themselves, known from a series of drawings (fig. 183) made in 1739–40 by Jean Courtonne.[110] Both compositions are dominated by a double arch which

181 Jacques de Lajoue, *The Cabinet of Physical Sciences*, 1734. Oil on canvas, 119 × 152 cm. Sir Alfred Beit Foundation, Russborough.

divides the pictorial space into foreground and background and more strikingly, into left-hand and right-hand halves. Moreover, both depictions offer a view through the right-hand opening to a distant, arcaded masonry building in the process of construction. At the central pier, however, Lajoue at once wittingly replaced Le Clerc's skeletal evidence of the passage of Time with an instrument of comparable dimension by which to measure it, and, elegantly substituted the coat of arms of a particular man (just discernable sandwiched between Pegasus and the clock) for the osteological symbol of *homo sapiens*. Since Lajoue thus appears not just to have borrowed from Le Clerc but also to have played games with the meanings of the original image, it may be possible provisionally to suggest an interpretation of *The Cabinet of Physical Sciences* amplified by comparison with the frontispiece.

At one level, Le Clerc offered his readers a portrait of courtiers and of the capital's academicians of science grouped around a flamboyantly confectioned Louis XIV, and a more austerely clad Colbert as they entered the rooms of the Académie Royale des Sciences on the rue Vivienne.[111] However, the refusal to apotheosise the king by setting him apart from and above his subjects, and the withholding of special privileges from portraiture, evident from Le Clerc's equal attention to the backs and the fronts of bodies, suggests that on another level the image depicted an event, an action, and one invested, moreover, with an importance beyond the local prestige occasioned by the reception itself.[112] The twinned figures of the minister and the king and the non-hierarchical delineation of scientists may be read, as Erica Harth has recently suggested, in terms of a narrative of the advantageous reciprocities between state and Academy as a result of which the nation progresses along the path to glory.

The near identity of the views through Le Clerc's window and from Lajoue's later interior (a prospect of the Observatoire

Royale located, in reality, some miles away) would seem to suggest that a case was being advanced *chez* Bonnier for regarding the spaces of the Academy and of the *cabinet* as interchangeable, or even coterminous. However, if to those in the know this subtle elision afforded the *cabinet* an unforseen measure of public status, it was a status almost immediately withdrawn by the evident discontinuity between the social constituencies visually circumscribed by these pictorial places. Instead of the productive and public interaction of scientists and statesmen, Lajoue offered a celebration of the scientific isolate formed for contemplation. Significantly, Bonnier de la Mosson, unlike his contemporary Pajot d'Osenbray or his brother-in-law, Michel-Ferdinand d'Albert d'Ailly, the duc de Picquigny, was himself never elected a member of the Académie Royale des Sciences, and the status of his hôtel as a legitimate place for the display of scientific knowledge depended, therefore, on his quality as a nobleman, however recently attained, and on the value of his collection.[113]

The nature of the *honnête* version of Academy offered by Bonnier's cabinet of curiosities was poetically suggested in Lajoue's work by the inhabitants of the realm beyond the cornice. Pegasus conjures up *mouseion* or the seat of the Muses on Mount Helicon, where with one stamp of those plunging hooves he created a fountain for the refreshment of the nine arts. The *cabinet* reaped a union of arts and sciences from Pegasus's inspiration, a survival of the encyclopedic unity of the sixteenth-century Pleiade, given a harsher and more pragmatic thrust by the combined intervention of Mercury and Minerva, seen breaking through the cornice in the room beyond. Thus, at the level of display not only do instruments and antiquities inhabit a common realm, but the actions of the crane on site and the model lifting-mechanisms on the shelves seem abstractly to mimic Boreas's sculpted elevation and abduction of Oreithyia on the pedestal above the Sage.[114] At the level of the collection, meanwhile, Bonnier had, for instance, reserved a place for fancy turning, a particularly noble hobby, having apparently amused people of quality since the seventeenth century.[115] It was an art that both met the exacting scientific requirements of clock and instrument making and yet entertained the aesthetic fancy with virtuoso displays of ornamental turning in ivory, amber, precious metals and exotic woods.[116] Finally, at a social level, Bonnier was a member of the briefly influential Société des Arts, a social gathering that, at its twice weekly meetings at the hôtel du Petit Luxembourg, temporarily disguised the growing functional distinction between the amusements of the *salon* and the learning of academies, by encouraging a polite commerce between scientists, artists, men of letters and men of taste in order that the secrets of nature exposed by science might serve as models for novelties in art.[117]

Appropriately, Lajoue (also probably a member of the society) chose in his overdoor to erase of the physical threshold between the realm of theoretical, academic, speculation in the laboratory and the world of practical application outside which

182   Sébastien Le Clerc, *Louis XIV being shown the Académie des Sciences by Colbert*, 1671. Engraving and etching. From Claude Perrault, *Mémoires pour servir à l'histoire des plantes*, 1671.

in Le Clerc's frontispiece could not be scaled. Moreover, the rapt attention of the Sage upon the scene outside (and not on the book propped on his lap), and the shaft of light that enters the *cabinet* and seems to illuminate his intelligence, together imply an inversion of the respective values of system-building and observation seemingly implicit in the spatial arrangement of foreground and background. By comparison with Lajoue's hymn to a gentlemanly ideal of singular, leisurely contemplation, Le Clerc's academicians seem to promote an introverted collective culture of professional scholarship, cut-off by self-imposed parapets from the aesthetic spectacle of nature and uniquely preoccupied with parochial scientific problems. Lajoue's library overdoor (fig. 185) might temper the contrast since its meaning is more equivocal. Again, one of the foreground figures twists round to face nature but his companion concentrates on study. However, the figure perched high on a ladder reading a book is situated on the very threshold between erudition (library) and natural spectacle (garden) and the extent of the latter's intrusion into the world of abstract speculation is underscored by the gargantuan materiality of the globe.[118] The attempts of the Académie Royale des Sci-

183 Jean Courtonne, Bonnier de la Mosson's physical sciences cabinet, 1739–40. From *Recueil des dessins des cabinets de curiosités de M. Bonnier de la Mosson*, 1739–40. Bibliothèque d'Art et d'Archéologie, Fondation Jacques Doucet, Paris.

ences to foreclose on all alternate avenues of scientific discourse and experimentation, partly by means of a visual disqualification which in Le Clerc's frontispiece denied the cabinet of curiosities space on the public stage, were partially thwarted therefore, by the implicit nobiliary reconstruction of their ambitions as corporate interests dressed up by the privilege of royal dispensation.[119]

The fact that some visual imagery continued to occlude the divisions between the various branches of knowledge introduced and increasingly exaggerated by the professionalisation of intellectual life testifies to the extent to which even the Academy's purchase on reality remained trapped within a representational paradigm that classically combined instruction with pleasure. In Le Clerc's plates (fig. 186) for the *Mémoires pour servir à l'histoire naturelle des animaux* (1671–6), for instance, anatomical drawings were combined with picturesque scenes of the animals in their natural habitat, yet the scientifically uninformative vignettes occupy more than fifty per cent of the field, and the objective truth of the anatomical descriptions is at first glance comprehensively undermined by the *trompe-l'œil* scrolls on which they are delineated.[120] However, the purpose of the image's sophisticated illusionism was apparently epistemological rather than aesthetic. In the preface, Perrault explained that this 'natural painting' was designed 'to show things as we have seen them, as in a mirror, which puts nothing of itself into the image and represents only

that which was presented to it'.[121] In other words the 'realism' of the far from extraneous vignettes served to guarantee the truthfulness of the anatomical exegesis effected above by suggesting to readers that they were actively witnessing and not passively contemplating evidence put before them. However, despite the objective function Perrault claimed for the illustrations, their conspicuous artistry nevertheless advertised links with the tradition of science-as-spectacle, with science as a re-creation or dramatic re-presentation of natural phenomena,[122] thereby frustrating the attempts of non-noble professionals to effect complete control over this area of knowledge.

If the division between the Academy and the *cabinet* willed by the former and resisted by the latter was never absolute, the elision of art and science effected in a cabinet of curiosities was nevertheless manifestly different from that articulated by academic discourse. At one end of Nicolas Grollier de Servière's *cabinet*, for instance, hung a mirror which, when so closely approached that the frame was touched, miraculously replaced the flattering reflections of glass, first with a *vanitas* painting of a skull, and then by a plastic, grimacing head from whose mouth issued alarming shrieks.[123] This was just one of the many mechanical wonders which at the press of a button unlocked the high-minded decorum of the laboratory to expose, just behind the surface, a necropolis with doors on to the walking dead, or a sort of spontaneous theatre complete

with mechanical cast (a corpse, an Amazon and a mouse) and moving 'sets' changed by self-opening cupboard doors.[124] Likewise, the engineer Alexis Magny made a robotic Swiss guard for Bonnier to open and close the door for visitors to the *cabinet mécanique*.[125] In other instances the dramaturgy of science was seemingly engendered by natural phenomena alone.[126] In one of a sèries of thirteen small paintings commissioned by the duc de Picquigny for the decoration of his natural history cabinet in the rue du Bac, and today known through prints, Lajoue depicted a chemist at work in an al-chemical chamber surrounded by stuffed companions apparently no less lively than he (fig. 184).[127] In an atmosphere charged with incipient violence, a stoat squared up to a rhinocerous's head, a long-legged spider of prodigious size stalked the chimney-breast, and in the very nick of time, a mole flying in through the right-hand arcade escaped the snap of a crocodile's jaws.

The arrangement of actual specimens in concrete spaces did little to redress the promiscuity of such heteroclite collections of curious things. Courtonne's drawing of Bonnier's natural history room (fig. 189) shows an array of glass-fronted cases, but the flora and fauna have slipped their cages to climb all over the panelling, so that it is often impossible to distinguish between sculpted representations of serpents, stags's heads, horns, coral, sponges and shells and the specimens them-selves.[128] Logic might look for a progression through the elements of water, earth and air in the vertical order of things but the lowest drawer to the left of the left-hand chimney-

piece contained mice and lizards at play with shells on a sea-bed, picking the teeth of long buried whales, and close to the ceiling an exotic-looking bird perched on a coral tree. Moreover, nothing can find its authentic place while some-thing remains to defy categorisation as such. And here, along the inside edges of the mirrors sprang unicorns, with horns, issuing from forehead and mouth, of a length immodestly to

184   Charles-Nicolas Cochin after Jacques de Lajoue, *The Chemist's Laboratory*, *c.*1737–45. Etching.

171

185 Jacques de Lajoue, *The Library*, 1734. Oil on canvas, 119 × 152 cm. Sir Alfred Beit Foundation, Russborough.

scratch the cornice. Their presence is a reminder that monsters and prodigies were the stuff of escapist travel literature and chivalric romance; Rabelais's Pantagruel was, after all, scion of a house of giants.[129] Thus, for a brief moment, before being completely undone by science, these late *wunderkammern* seem to have been host to a tense conviviality between fantasy and reason and fable and history. Moreover, the epistemological virtues of a continued equivalence of representation and object, advertised by such laymen as Guyot to bolster the sale of 'the rarest shells *either painted or real*',[130] but sustained equally by professional science, was a gambit that indirectly encouraged the proliferation of shells, palm-trees, garlands, birds and all manner of naturalistic motifs in sculpted ornament from the 1720s, as the aristocracy sought to satisfy an enthusiasm for pastoralism seemingly modernised and expanded by science.[131]

Garlands and trophies of the seasons and elements had of course long since been part of the decorator's stock-in-trade, though both were brought to greater prominence during and immediately after the Regency;[132] the garland enjoyed the distinction of traversing not only panels but mirrors and pictures too.[133] Similarly, the palm-tree had been used for decorative purposes in the seventeenth century, though primarily in pageantry, and it was not until the late 1720s and early 1730s that it graced domestic interiors, to particularly striking effect at the palais Bourbon and the hôtel de Villars, before transferring to the more exotic clime of Bonnier's chambers.[134] Above all it was the shell that added a note of novelty to the interior decoration of the 1730s. Since the Renaissance, shells had been an important component of grottoes[135] from where the term *rocaille* or rococo ultimately derives,[136] but the influx of shell motifs into the decorative repertoire of the early eighteenth century owed at least as much to the expanding market for conchology as it did to these watery caverns.[137]

186 Sébastien Le Clerc, *The Lion*, 1671–6. Engraving and etching. From Claude Perrault, *Mémoires pour servir à l'histoire naturelle des animaux*, 1671–6.

187 F. de Bakker, *Sample Drawers of Shells*, 1735. Engraving and etching. From Albert Seba, *Locupletissimi rerum naturalium thesauri accurata descriptio et iconibus artificiosissimis expressio per universam physices historiam*, 1735–65.

Edme-François Gersaint's natural-history sales of specimens bought in The Netherlands for auction in Paris in 1735 and 1736 caused a sensation. From the outset, treatises on shells had underlined their variety, singularity and visual appeal. The ostensibly scientific plates of Albert Seba's internationally renowned collection (fig. 187) visibly exploited the naturally decorative properties of the shells,[138] while, earlier, Buonani had entitled his highly popular picture-book of molluscs *Ricreatione dell'occhio et della mente* (1681), a phrase later re-used by Gersaint to flag his sales.[139] Indeed, Gersaint's promotional publicity in the pages of the *Mercure* made little of science, maintaining instead an overtly aesthetic sales pitch. He remarked of his 1735 collection,

188 Nicolas Pineau, design for a chimney-piece, *c.*1735–45. Pencil, pen and ink and grey wash on paper, 29.7 × 23.4 cm. Kunstbibliothek, Staatliche Museen, Berlin.

> There are {here}, singular accidents, in which Nature appears to take her sport, sometimes by an outlandish and limitless bizarrerie, sometimes by a symmetry so precise and well judged that the most refined Art could not equal it.[140]

Again, in 1736 he noted the decorative potential of large shells, which he claimed were suitable for garnishing 'the tops of Cabinets or small Tables and Cornices'.[141] Predictably, the vulgar fever to consume spawned by this Dutch trade, was the

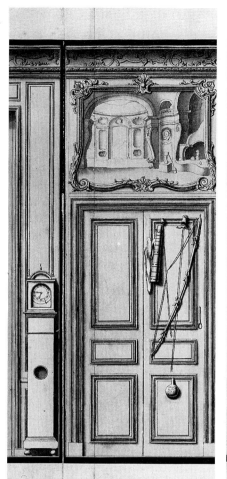

189   Jean Courtonne, Bonnier de la Mosson's natural history cabinet, 1739–40. From *Recueil des dessins des cabinets de curiosités de M. Bonnier de la Mosson*, 1739–40. Bibliothèque d'Art et d'Archéologie, Fondation Jacques Doucet, Paris.

great unmentioned in the noble response to shells. In a letter to the marquise de Bouzoles, for instance, the marquis de Lassay explained that the remarkably beautiful shell he was about to offer her came into his possession, not under the hammer, but from a nereid who handed it to him at sundown on a deserted beach with the words, ' "Here is the Shell which once housed Cleopatra's pearl, give it to her whom you love the best" '.[142] The gallantry of such a gesture was given independent visual expression in a decorative drawing by Pineau (fig. 188) in which the projected painting to crown the chimney-piece depicted a young woman receiving nature's gifts from a Triton's hand. It is therefore perhaps not too fanciful to suggest that the success of *rocaille* designs, such as Boucher's *Nouveaux morceaux pour les paravents* (1737), stemmed from the combined satisfaction they afforded to the thirst for scientific novelties and the demands of natural sentiment.[143]

The step from *lussus naturae* to exoticism was a small one. In the duc de Sully's cabinets arranged on the *piano nobile* of another hôtel in the rue Saint-Dominique, not only was time

suspended in order that antiquities, natural and artificial (fossils and Egyptian mummies), might metaphorically rub shoulders with nature's more recent novelties, but suspended too was the notional unity of place, such that the New World cohabited with the Old offering a summation or microcosm of the universe complete.[144] North and South were brought together by the conjunction of a dense hanging of studies of exotic animals, reptiles and butterflies and a serried rank of marble busts of ancient emperors displayed above Sully's collection of shells, while East and West made contact more intimately still when the duke chose to house portions of his collection in Chinese lacquered cupboards in the *grand cabinet*.[145] Chinese *cabinets* had, of course, been fashionable for some time. Lister had been particularly impressed by Saint-Cloud, Monsieur's country residence, where he had discovered a 'fine Sett of Closets',

furnish'd with a great variety of Rock Crystals, Cups, Agats upon small Stands, and the sides of the Rooms . . . lined with large Panes of Looking-glass from top to the bottom,

with Japan Varnish and Paintings of equal breadth intermix'd, which have a marvellous pretty effect. The other Room had in it a vast quantity of Bijou, and many of very great price; but the Siam Pagods, and other things from thence, were very odd.[146]

The 'oddity' of the Siamese pagodas or Chinese figures mirrored the singularity of crystals or shells, and underlined the often abrupt conjunction effected between nature 'wrought' and nature 'caught'.[147] Conjoined by an attributed relationship construed as essential and disclosing patterns of analogy between all curious things, the reception of distant artefacts into the *wunderkammer* bespoke a reification of cultural differences. Licensed to whet appetites by their novelty, these exotic predicates of a culture unseen availed themselves not as indices by which Paris might measure its distance from Cathay, but as witty emblems of exoticism to be refigured by the local idiom and enjoyed; in the case of porcelain, by encasing *famille rose* or celadon (which owed its name to a resemblance to Honoré d'Urfé's shepherd) in rue Saint-Honoré *or-moulu* mounts.[148]

A passage from Perrault's *Parallèle des anciens et des modernes*

(1688–97) suggests that this objectification and domestication of alien cultures might also have been a conspicuous feature of Colbert's projected decoration of the Louvre, planned in the 1690s to include a sequence of rooms representing the nations of the world through objects, furnishings and national styles.[149] The ostensible purpose of the scheme was to offer visitors the courtesy of finding themselves at home when actually abroad. However, the project seems to have been rather more strategic than the seemingly gratuitous displays in Parisian *cabinets*, inasmuch as its design offered a vindication by plenitude of Colbert's colonialist and mercantilist policies.[150] The exhibited foreign goods, bounty from conquered territories, would have functioned as trophies of ministerial enterprise exercised through the Compagnie des Indes, and as testimony to the scientific advances made by the Académie Royale des Sciences in mathematics, mechanics and astronomy which collectively improved the arts of navigation and cartography to the point where the originating place of these things assumed a measurable distance from the royal palace, and therefore appeared objectively and geographically remote. Although Louis de Pontchartrain's reforms of the Académie Royale des Sciences in 1699 removed the company's implementive role in foreign exploration and left it a diminished advisory function primarily in the fields of technology and manufacture, the politics of royal science remained wedded to economic ends.[151]

Unlike the Académie des Sciences the *salons* and *cabinets* of the *honnête noblesse* were primarily concerned with the biological sciences, in natural history, chemistry, botany and anatomy.[152] Moreover, by embracing a concept of nature that still celebrated the noble experience of the unity of art and science and the old and new worlds, the nobility sought to further their own social and political ends. Noble 'encyclopedism' promoted the competences of the élite for whom science was not yet something to be done or produced so much as taste to be claimed and displayed. In so far as amateurs such as Bonnier used their laboratories, they did so to rehearse or re-enact experiments long since proven by professionals. The object was not so much to understand the operations of science as to perform and enjoy them, in exactly the same way that the nobility rehearsed the popular culture of the fairs or the exotic culture of the Far East in order to hold worldly wonders in theatrical proximity.[153] To that extent the commodities secured by royal policy were the very means by which the nobility continued to satisfy its own political ends of distinction.

8

Paris–Versailles:
The Eclipse of the Heroic Decorative Mode

The arts of the grotesque and the pastoral operated at the edges of the field of artistic endeavour as constituted by the Académie Royale de Peinture et Sculpture and as defined by the theory of the hierarchy of genres. History on the other hand, and most particularly heroic history, lay at its very centre. During the *ancien régime* the discourses of history and of heroism necessarily involved dialogue with the state because absolute sovereigns made absolute claims on the valour of their subjects and thereby ensured that all history was royal by nature. Thus, to begin to understand the traditionally recognised decline in the heroic mode of painting and decoration at the end of the seventeenth century and its replacement in the Parisian culture of the eighteenth by a taste for gallantry, it is necessary to return to Versailles and to a consideration of the offical artistic culture of the state as it related to that of the capital.

OPPOSITION TO LOUIS XIV AND ABSOLUTIST NOTIONS OF HISTORY

The eighteenth century inherited, more or less intact, a literary conception of history[1] which variously combined chronology, hagiography, legend and myth, not in an effort to recover the past but for the purpose of edifying those with a preordained place in present and future heroic discourse, namely the princes of the church and state and the peers and nobles of the realm.[2] The exemplary mould of seventeenth- and early eighteenth-century historical genres tended to recreate the past as a place to be visited selectively rather than a continuous process to which the present was irrevocably connected. Thus, in Jean Desmarets de Saint-Sorlin's widely read epic poem *Clovis*, republished five times between 1657 and 1673, the sorceror, Auberon, invites the king to his enchanted palace and introduces him into an historic gallery where the heroic deeds of their ancestors from the Trojan wars to the conquest of Childeric are displayed about the walls. Spatial metaphors operated at more than one level: at the same time as

the fictional Clovis was admitted to the past across the threshold of a gallery, the actual king, Louis XIV, to whom the poem was dedicated, was presented with a book-as-gallery which he was invited to enter to see the *tableaux* of the royal past illustrated in the images and text of Clovis's life.[3] Moreover, a further parallel operated between the magician's acknowledgement in book 2 of the incompleteness of his scheme and his prophecy that 'Dans ces quadres restans, encor vides d'histoires,/Magnanime Clovis, se peindront tes victoires', and the intervention of the authorial voice in the dedicatory epistle to predict that Louis likewise would win his epithet 'The Great'.[4] Indeed, in the frontispiece of the *Almanach royal* of 1699 Louis was represented (fig. 190) indicating to his heirs, particularly the duc de Bourgogne, the very manner in which he had done so in the architectural projection of his own story.

The pedagogic substance of the past was clearly not focused indiscriminately; it acted as guardian to the values of monarchy, and to that end it circumscribed the options of legitimate political action for future incumbents. History was a privileged narrative and, one moreover, traditionally active as both council and tribunal to kings – 'as she [Clio] has her Theatres and her Thrones . . . she also has her scaffolds and her wheels . . .',[5] warned the historian, Pierre Le Moyne.[6] Yet if, during the first half of the seventeenth century Desmarets's patron Richelieu had commissioned histories with which to win polemical struggles with competing power-bases both at home and abroad, the inauguration of Louis XIV's personal rule heralded the dispach of history-as-judge in favour of a less critical assentor.[7] The Sun King's unprecedented drive to consolidate and expand central authority logically ruled out the possibility of historical legitimation. Indeed, Jean Chapelain's discussions with Colbert in 1663 spelled out the perils of history for an absolutist state, because 'if it [history] does not explain the causes of the things narrated, if it is not accompanied with reflections and documentary evidence, it is no more than a simple account, devoid of force and dignity', and yet if it did explain motives and hazard judgements it not only jeopardised national security but demystified the sacred processes of rule.[8] Thus, under the joint stewardship of Chapelain and Colbert the state was increasingly guided away from history and towards glorifying, proleptic fictions, in the form of literary panegyrics and their visual equivalents – medals, monuments, pictures and tapestries.[9] To this end, the revision of the statutes of the Académie Royale de Peinture et de Sculpture in 1665 expressely included an article that bound students forthwith to submit drawings of 'a general subject on the heroic actions of the King' for an annual competition,[10] while Charles Perrault enjoined the Premier Peintre, Le Brun, to ensure to remember,

> . . . qu'à jamais ta main laborieuse
> Poursuive de Louis l'histoire glorieuse,
> Sans qu'un autre labeur, ni de moindre tableaux
> Profanent désormais tes illustres pinceaux . . .[11]

The result was a visible and visual detachment of the cult of monarchy from the history of the nation, to the extent that monarchy appeared to occupy a remote temporal and spatial reality qualitatively different from the commonplace actuality of society.[12] Louis, the state incarnate, its sacred centre and its universal principle,[13] defied both time and place, because in him all past and future French kings and kingdoms were forever present.

On 22 December 1667, a decree issued by the king's council outlined a project for engraving exterior views of the royal monuments and palaces, representations of the paintings, sculpture and tapestries made to furnish them and records of the antiquities and works of art gathered in the Cabinet du Roi.[14] These prints were destined for binding together in splendid folio editions for distribution among fellow sovereigns, to foreign ambassadors and other important visitors to the French court. In this manner French propaganda entered an international court economy as a political commodity to be circulated and exchanged. It was, initially perhaps, the nature of the European response that partially eclipsed the glory of France and endangered the national stock of heroic imagery. Starting with the Dutch war (1672–8), caricatures, pamphlets and articles in the periodical press overtly hostile to the means as well as the ends of Louis's foreign policy flooded out of The Netherlands into neighbouring regions. Likewise, some thirty years later, the beginning of the war of the Spanish Succession (1701–3) witnessed the publication in Amsterdam of a series of Dutch satires directed at the opponents of William III, collectively titled *Aesopus in Europa* and accompanied by etchings by Romeyn de Hooghe.[15] One of them in particular, *Ptolemy, Copernicus and Mercury in Parnassus, Speaking about the Sun and the World* (fig. 191), invited sustained intellectual amusement at the deflation of Louis's cosmological disguise. The etching represents a shrunk and halting king, his youthful, Apollonian mask uselessly slipped about his neck, riding a chariot that on closer inspection turns out to be a closed stool driven across the heavens at hysterical pace by Mme de Maintenon. Visually, the print exploited the gap

190 Nicolas III de Larmessin, *The Peace-loving King in the Midst of his Family*, 1699. Etching and engraving. Headpiece for the *Almanach Royale*, 1699.

between Ludovican poetics and politics by demonstrating that when Apollo actually came into abrupt contact with reality, instead of smoothly landing on allegorised territories located, for instance, at the four corners of Charles de La Fosses's ceiling in the Salon d'Apollon at Versailles, the wheels of his chariot shattered under the pressure of England (the unicorn) and the reins fell ultimately into the hands of Germany (the eagle) and The Netherlands (the lion). The text, meanwhile, opened with a heated discussion between Ptolemy and Copernicus about the dynamics of the cosmos, with the former citing as proof of his theory that the earth was stationary while the sun moved, that, 'the French Sun has shown his beams on the Alps, the Po, the whole of Italy, the Mediterranean, and has gone round the world in one day, over the South Sea and back again'.[16] With Copernicus understandably unmoved, Mercury was brought in to arbitrate. He promptly agreed with both sides, on the one hand acknowledging Louis's solar ambitions and on the other, predicting the end to his revolutions when other stars in their courses fought to fix him and set the Earth once more in motion.[17] What the text adds to the ridicule of ornamental mythology well enough accomplished by de Hooghe is a satire on the wilful false-consciousness of a heliolithic nation adrift in an otherwise modern, scientific world which had long since demoted the sun to the rank of a common star: in other words *Nunc* and not *Nec pluribus impar*.[18]

There was, of course, as much a conflict of medium as of interest between such cheap and secretly distributed caricatures[19] and the vast, public decorative schemes triumphantly elaborated during the 1670s and 1680s by Le Brun and his school in the Grand Appartement and the Galerie des Glaces at Versailles. The vulgar medium of print moved to compromise the overwrought verisimilitude of high culture as well as to score particular political points. Of greater concern to the French, however, were those more limited propaganda wars fought on a shared cultural territory, notably in numismatic history.[20] Medals, because of their material incorruptibility, were traditionally regarded as constitutive as well as merely reflective of history, that is to say that, because the evidence

192   Jan Smelting, *The Fall of Icarus or the Battle of Turin*, 1706 Silver. British Museum, London.

193   Jan Smelting, *Louis XIV Returning to Versailles*, 1693. Pewter. British Museum, London.

191   Romeyn de Hooghe, *Ptolemy, Copernicus and Mercury in Parnassus, Speaking about the Sun and the World*, 1700–2. Etching. From *Aesopus in Europa*, 1700–2, plate 20.

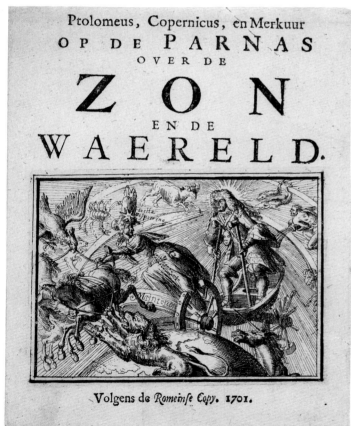

they provided was judged primary and incontrovertible, medals were credited with a historicity quite different to the merely discursive validity of literary texts.[21] Satire in this field was therefore particularly to be feared. However, instead of using excoriative strategies to expose the corrupt mechanics of myth in the manner of de Hooghe,[22] Dutch, German and English medallists chose to match the flushed confidence of the *Médailles sur les principaux evénements du règne de Louis le Grand* (1702) with conceits played upon the iconographic similitude between myths. Thus, in the case of charioteering, Jan Smelzing was one among many to enjoy the obvious and natural confusion of Apollo with Phaeton, his overweening fan (fig. 192), but perhaps unique in harnessing the joke to the moment of maximum political impact.[23] On another occasion, Apollo had seemingly been highjacked by the character of Paris (fig. 193) who, during the war of the League of Augsburg (1687–97), 'came and saw but did not conquer' Namur, and was depicted thereafter being drawn back to Versailles in immodest haste by three court Graces, very possibly the king's mistresses, Mesdames de La Vallière, de Montespan and de Maintenon, who made frequent and similar interventions in

Guerriers, si vous courez défendre vos Murailles,
Partez, et s'il le faut brillez dans cent Batailles :
Mais, si vous ne voulez qu'errer en Conquerans,
Ne portez pas plus loin vos Projets effraians.

LA PASSION
de la Guerre,
Exprimée par des Satires
Guerriers.

Qu'attendez-vous du Sang que vous allez répandre?
De nos Champs désolez, de nos Villes en cendre?
Fleaux de l'Univers, Heros, êtes-vous nez,
Pour ne faire icy-bas que des Infortunez?

A Paris chez Audran, graveur du Roy, à l'Hôtel Royal des Gobelins. Avec Privilege du Roy.

194   Jean Audran after Claude Gillot, *The Passion of War*, c.1727. Engraving and etching.

caricatures of the period.[24] Like caricatures and subversive pamphlets, medals such as these were smuggled into France, but the fact that they were minted in gold and silver as well as baser metals suggests that they functioned as expensive and enduring jokes offered for safekeeping only to a comparatively narrow market of highly cultured court élites. Indeed, by 1690 two had quite inappropriately made their way into the royal collection.[25] With unbounded wit and no loss of aesthetic decorum, royal mythology was thus turned on its head, and although it is impossible to gauge exactly the effect the counterfeited myths had on the currency of fable, there can be little doubt that they were designed further to encourage indigenous resistance to the symbolism of divine right.

Almost from the outset, the war of the Spanish Succession had raised legitimate doubts in France about the motivation of Louis's foreign policy.[26] The exorbitant financial cost of the campaigns to a depleted taxpaying population and the unprecedented carnage of Malplaquet (1709) seemed all the more indefensible in light of Louis's apparent pursuit of dynastic rather than national interests.[27] However, unlike foreign critics and satirists, French *donneurs d'avis* held back from mocking Louis's peacock pride, preferring to hold up, for quieter political reflection, pictures of the miseries and neglect of France, in the hope of forcing recognition of the disjunction in fortunes between the actual and formal kingdoms. The most

searching revision of the complacent tautology that by right divine the king could never govern wrong sprang from the circle around Mme de Maintenon, within which conspired members of the Le Tellier clan including, ironically perhaps, certain marshals of France, and was penned most cogently by the great military engineer, Sebastien le Prestre de Vauban.[28] A conspicuous theme of Vauban's banned *Projet d'une dîme royale* (1707) was that the 'greatness of kings' was to be measured by the number and prosperity of their subjects, an argument that necessarily and unusually attached 'gloire' to the promotion and preservation of peace.[29] The very morality of heroism was thereby placed in jeopardy. Indeed, fuelled by Jansenist theology, which for over half a century had rallied a powerful current of opposition to absolutism – and to which incidentally, a number of the Le Tellier faction were overtly sympathetic[30] – criticism rained down on those who resolved to make themselves instruments of royal might, and delivered to the eighteenth century the parody of war as a lasting pictorial genre. Thus, Claude Gillot's *La Passion de la guerre exprimée par des satires guerriers* (fig. 194), though published well after the Peace of Utrecht (1713–15), was nevertheless accompanied by the following verses:

Guerriers, si vous courez défendre vos murailles,
Partez, et s'il faut briller dans cent Batailles;

Mais, si vous ne voulez qu'erRer en Conquèrans,
Ne portez pas plus loin vos Projets éffraîans,
Qu'attendez-vous du sang que vous allez répandre?
De nos Champs désolez, de nos Villes en cendres?
Fléaux de l'univers, Héros, êtes vous nez,
Pour ne faire icy-bas que des infortunez?[31]

However, the image itself revealed none of the distress alluded to in the verses and only 'satirised' the would-be tyrant by presenting him as a pun clothed in imperial Roman armour. Likewise, in *The Apes of Mars* (fig. 195) Watteau, Gillot's one-time pupil, resorted to the now familiar tactics of the grotesque to rattle the sublime confidence of the god of war.[32]

196 Gabriel Huquier after Jacques de Lajoue, cartouche, 1735. Etching. From *Livre de cartouches de guerre dédié à monseigneur le duc de Mortemart*, 1735, plate 7.

197 Pierre-Edmé Babel, cartouche, c.1738–48. Etching. From *Cartouches décorés d'une fontaine en pyramide*, c.1738–48, plate 5.

195 Jean Moyreau after Antoine Watteau, *The Apes of Mars*, 1729. Etching.

And if Watteau used the figures in the margins to challenge the meaning of the central motif, the designers of rococo cartouches, such as Toro, Lajoue (fig. 196) and Pierre-Edmé Babel (fig. 197), by leaving the centre of their compositions void and concentrating their creative powers on a surrounding arrangement of history's hackneyed *ornements reçus*, inverted the hierarchical relationship of image and frame, and tacitly condemned the superior authority of heraldry.[33] However, grotesques and cartouches, no matter how anti-heroic, effectively negated the central premise of Dutch and English

caricature – that a particular person bristling with identifying devices, was alone responsible for the present state of affairs – because, with familiar sleight-of-hand, French criticism was safely levelled at a role and not at the person who had the temerity to abuse it.

The decorative realisation of these patterns of parody in society rooms (the duc du Maine, for instance, appears to have enjoyed a *cabinet* on the walls of which valorous monkeys duelled for their honour[34]) curtailed their political function in the interests of polite pleasure. Theirs was not the bitter unmasking of the horrors of war pursued by Marivaux in the *Iliad travesti* (1715):

> Notre fils est mort à la guerre;
> Quant au reste de sa misère,
> Ecorchures et nudité
> Reins fracassés et cul crotté
> Ventre troué, perte d'entrailles
> Ce sont les suites des batailles . . .[35]

Nor did the antics of satyrs and monkeys or the asymmetrical gavotte of symbols lead to Marivaux's inexorable conclusion that '. . . bêtise est d'estimer grands / De malheureux tueurs de gens.'[36] Marivaux's travesty was satirical in as much as his criticism was directed against traditional values from the vantage-point of an alternative moral ideal, one with different and implicitly superior standards and stars – 'Moi, je dirai qu'un chirugien / A ces héros ne cède en rien'[37]. By contrast, though Watteau's apes were depicted igniting the cannon upon which the edifice of heroism was supported in order cheerfully to destroy it, their revolution was fashioned in a noble cultural style which by itself forstalled outright conspiracy, limiting it to a flirtation with violence and thereby preventing an implosion of the aristocratic ideal of the profession of arms.

Significantly, in view of the recent conflict over Spain, the literary text that inspired the most sustained visual ridicule of military valour in the early eighteenth century was Cervantes's *Don Quixote*, translated by Filleau de Saint-Martin at the end of the previous century [38] and woven from 1714 in highwarp to cartoons by Charles-Antoine Coypel. Coypel's Manchagan knight was not the monstrously insane Louis of political satire[39] but a picaresque anti-hero whose actions, despite the purity of his intention and its valorous execution aboard a silly ass (fig. 198), provoked spectacular catastrophe to public delight. Inasmuch as Quixote's errors were clearly the consequence of delusions caused by his incapacity to distinguish the ideal projection of chivalry in literature from the real world of violence, they were not moral transgressions and therefore neither were they exemplary or historical acts.[40] Indeed, the apparently unalloyed pleasure to be had at the prospect of the knight-errant, massacring in earnest, for the sake of the puppets Don Galiferos and the fair Melisandra (fig. 199), above the wainscot in the *appartements de parade* at the hôtels d'Antin or de Charost,[41] stemmed

from Quixote's position, narratively and visually, on the indecorous border separating an epic world of classically enclosed forms and a comic plain of grotesques and ornaments as yet unscored by rational definition.[42] The conflictual dialogue between official and oppositional cultures was thereby internalised. Moreover, the neutralising result was upheld by the chivalric commitment of a hero whose satire of the bellicose play-acting of a Mars or an Alexander was not of his own intending, and served merely to ridicule the ideal of heroism from within instead of laying siege to it from abroad.

It was perhaps the self-conscious theatricality of many of Coypel's compositions that did most to withdraw attention from the satirical potential of the eponymous hidalgo and re-direct it towards the problematic interplay between resemblance and representation; a semantic ambiguity that had earlier proved so rich in the production of political meanings in medals. For example, in *Quixote at Don Antonio's Ball* (fig. 200), designed in 1731, the curtain rises on a performance of the minuet introduced and accompanied by a court musician in the left foreground. The purpose of the curtain in episodes lacking the conspicuous dissimilitude of flocks and armies or taverns and châteaux, was to remind the spectator that no matter how commodious the illusion, Quixote was himself no more than a semblance, a phantom-sign chasing proof of his own identity.[43] Where the gallery lodged representations of Clovis's actual deeds, preserving them as proof-stones of history, Quixote took the stories from their frames and embarked on an heroic quest in search of those things that, by analogy, would allow him to rehearse the text and enact its authenticity. The extent to which the spectator is party to Quixote's endeavour and subject to the same delusions is suggested by the door open in the background. This gratuitous detail of a patch of sky contradicts the distinction between the spaces of representation and reality, confidently policed by the recumbent guitar player, because the land actually beyond the boards is back-stage, not the street. Thus, having retreated before the superstitious faith in epic truths to an enjoyment of their hollow forms, the viewer is forced back to acknowledge that the pleasure induced by mistaking a charade for a performance was itself founded upon deceit.

Quixote's cruel betrayal by analogy must have struck home with a generation regularly assaulted by the rhetoric of grandeur, and from the 1680s increasingly conscious of the coersive tactics of a pseudo- or *trompe l'œil* history that preempted criticism.[44] Against the crown's continued deployment of strategies of apotheosis which stressed the unquestioning duty of subjects to their king,[45] the new criticism presented an account of the past that emphasised the obligations of the sovereign to his people.[46] Moreover, the yardstick for measuring the contractual sufficiency of the king's actions wielded by reformed historical discourse, hot off Dutch presses, was empirical truth.[47] Historians such as Henri-Philippe de Limiers and Pierre Bayle identified two important preconditions of

198 Charles-Antoine Coypel, *Don Quixote Guided by Folly and Inflamed with Extravagant Love of Dulcinea Sets Out as a Knight Errand*, 1717–19. Wool and silk, 348 × 131.5 cm. The first episode from the Gobelins tapestry series, *Don Quixote*, woven by Jean Jans fils and Jean Lefebvre fils, 1715–19. Location unknown.

199 Charles-Antoine Coypel, *Don Quixote Attacks Marionettes he Believes to be Moors in Defence of the Fugitive Lovers*, 1717–19. Wool and silk, 344.5 × 128 cm. The ninth episode from the Gobelins tapestry series, *Don Quixote*, woven by Jean Jans fils and Jean Lefebvre fils, 1717–19. Location unknown.

200　Charles-Antoine Coypel, *Don Quixote at Don Antonio's Ball*, *c*.1751. Wool and silk, 375 × 547 cm. The twenty-fifth episode from the Gobelins tapestry series, *Don Quixote*, woven by Pierre-François Cozette, *c*.1751. Location unknown.

historical writing: first, the elimination of religious, national and political bias[48] and second, the repudiation of the maxims, harangues and reflections of Renaissance exegesis, which had formerly knit the past together in an unbroken web of commentary cut loose from the events themselves.[49] Historians should henceforth adopt a plain language of such transparency that the author was metaphorically swallowed up by his words and disappeared behind them.[50] Such views found ready acceptance in France, and Fénelon understood, perhaps better than many, that for history to continue to offer 'the most solid moral truth' without appearing to preach,[51] its signs must, more successfully than Quixote's, reach out beyond the realm of analogy and resemblance and touch the world of things and events.[52] The engendered modification of the structure and terms of historical thinking profoundly challenged the viability of epic forms from the end of Louis XIV's reign.

From the point of view of the visual arts, the Dutch war, for instance, had been as much a battle of genres as a conflict in arms. In 1672 Adam-François van der Meulen received a royal commission to paint the *Crossing of the Rhine* (fig. 201) in which the king was depicted astride a high and prancing horse directing events above the thunder of cannon, with a view of Tolhuis, a place of one of Louis's greatest victories, in the distance.[53] Meanwhile, the following year saw publication in The Hague of a book attributed to Abraham van Wicquefort, one of de Hooghe's engravings for which (fig. 202) illustrated a once comfortable Dutch interior in the village of Bodegrave or Swammerdam, overrun by French beserkers.[54] Corpses, some of them dismembered, abound in the foreground while the eloquently passive feet of the menfolk, felled at the knees by fire, protrude innocently from the chimney. Whilst the cottage is being put to the torch, a woman in the left background is savagely raped across the carcass of a heifer.[55] This, according to van Wicquefort and de Hooghe, was the unvarnished truth of the Dutch campaigns, told in the minute record of the genre painter's witnessing eye and not sung in the censored forms conjured by the history painter's universalising mind. It was, in fact, a history of unbridled passions unleashed in the private spaces of the common people and not the story of rational actions unfolding upon the public stage. Truth abided, therefore, not just in the character of the medium that carried it but also in the kind of places in which

201   Adam-François van der Meulen, *The Crossing of the Rhine*, 1672. Oil on canvas, 49 × 111 cm. Musée du Louvre, Paris.

it was spoken. It was a secret history to be ferreted out from the hidden spaces behind the scenes in order to expose that which officially sanctioned representations before the curtain wilfully obscured. It was doubly secret, moreover, because it purported to reveal those motives behind historical events, knowledge of which Chapelain and Colbert had judged so prejudicial to public order. Just as lust, anger and pride visibly activated Louis's troops in de Hooghe's print, the popular and scandalous *nouvelles* of Courtilz de Sandras and his imitators invariably and repeatedly demonstrated that concupiscence not virtue motivated princes and oiled the machinery of state.[56] The immediate and vulgar history of the passions[57] played out in intimate *boudoirs* and *cabinets* thus came forward to demystify and challenge the remote, petrified story of mimetic actions hung about the heroic gallery.

202   Romeyne de Hooghe, *The Sacking of a Dutch Town*, 1673. Etching. From Abraham van Wicquefort, *Avis Fidelle aux veritables hollandois*, 1673.

It was in the context of this varied and international demonstration that the arsenal of state propaganda contained nothing more than glosses to deceit,[58] that even such defenders of absolutism as the abbé Banier argued for the repeal of such mythic history, readily acknowledging that 'that which is fabulous does not increase the glory of great men, [but] serves at the most to diminish the credibility of certain facts'.[59] Of the same mind, Du Bos rejected the allegorical and mythological admixtures to history painting[60] in Rubens's Medici cycle, for instance, and called instead for a painted history that would follow the same critical exigencies as the new Clio and was therefore truthful and plausible for a secular and critical public.[61] It remains to be discovered whether during the first half of the eighteenth century his voice was ever heard.

GALLERIES: THE DECLINE OF HEROIC THEMES

No sooner had his father, Monsieur, died in 1701 than the future regent, Philippe d'Orléans embarked on a thorough refurbishment and redecoration of the Palais Royal.[62] Externally the palace remained unchanged (fig. 203), but the surface austerity of Jacques Le Mercier's façades rapidly became a screen behind which sheltered the infamous Appartment des Roués where the regent allegedly gathered around him young bucks from the better noble houses, free-thinkers, opera singers and women of demi-virtue in a relentless campaign of pleasure that quickly earned the Regency a reputation for scandal.[63] Before then, however, and within little more than a year of his father's death, Philippe d'Orléans had summoned Antoine Coypel to the *grand appartment* to decorate with scenes

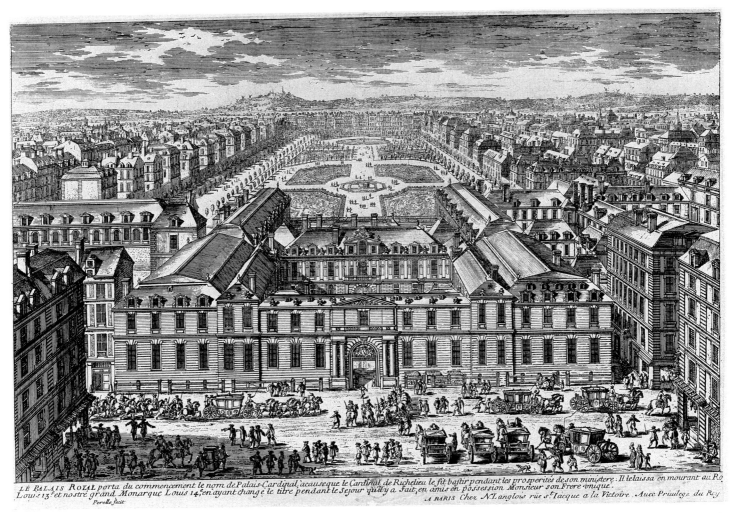

LE PALAIS ROYAL porta du commencement le nom de Palais-Cardinal, acause que le Cardinal de Richelieu le fit bastir pendant les prosperités de son ministere. Il le laissa en mourant au Roy Louis 13.e et nostre grand Monarque Louis 14, en ayant changé le titre pendant le Sejour qu'il y a fait, en a mis en possession Monsieur son Frere unique.
A PARIS Chez N. Langlois rüe s.^t Iacque a la Victoire. Auec Priuilege du Roy
Perelle fecit.

203   The Palais Royal, *c.*1690. Etching.

from the *Aeneid*, first the ceiling and then the walls of the 'new' gallery, erected parallel to the rue de Richelieu sometime between 1698 and 1701 by Hardouin Mansart.[64] The vault was completed in 1705, while the seven wall-pictures commissioned in 1715 to decorate the blind elevation backing on to the street were finished within three years.[65] Meanwhile, starting in 1714, Oppenord, Mansart's successor as Orléans's first architect, turned his hand to replacing his predecessor's probably modest decorative works with his own much more lavish schemes of gilded ornament, most strikingly at the far end of the gallery (fig. 204) where he designed into a shallow elipse a chimney-mantel, set above with a mirror of prodigious size.[66] Flanked on either side by pairs of Corinthian pilasters between which rose impressive military trophies, the design culminated at frieze level in two winged Victories supporting a cartouche inscribed with the arms of Orléans, above which the ducal coronet broke through the cornice to lodge itself in a shell.

At the same time, Orléans's two legitimated cousins, the duc du Maine and the comte de Toulouse were committing themselves to similarly ambitious decorative programmes.

Germain Boffrand had been at work at the Arsenal, on modifications to the lodgings of the Grand Maître de l'Artillerie[67] since 1712, and the surviving drawings[68] for the projected decoration of the *salon* probably date from no later than 1715–17. The elevation of the window side (fig. 205) clearly indicates that if more modestly proportioned and different in function to the Galerie d'Enée, this room was nevertheless conceived on the same heroic scale. Indeed, above the central window two winged figures, not unrelated to Oppenord's Victories but here personifications of History and Fame, accompanied a roundel sporting the interlaced 'A's and 'L's of Louis-Auguste de Bourbon, duc du Maine. At the opposite end of Paris, meanwhile, the comte de Toulouse had, in 1713, bought François Mansart's famous hôtel de La Vrillière. Five years later Robert de Cotte and Antoine-François Vassé had finished transforming the gallery (fig. 207), into a celebration in ornament of Toulouse's public functions as Amiral de France, Grand Veneur and, from 1715, Chef du Conseil de la Marine – and, by default, into an illustration in pictures of the count's apparently exquisite taste.[69] Echoes of the Palais Royal abounded, most conspicuously in Vassé's third project for the

186

chimney-piece (fig. 206), set once more within coved panelling, flanked by pilasters and trophies on either side and crowned by a coat of arms, although in this instance the figure of Fame is conspicuously smaller in proportion to the device she heralds. In a climate notably suspicious of grandiloquence, each of these three schemes attempted variously to reconstruct or rehabilitate the great tradition according to their several capacities and purposes. Inasmuch as all three were substantially conceived and possibly executed in the heat of the *affaire des princes* (1716–17), a dispute that effectively pitted the constitutional pretentions of the royal bastards du Maine and Toulouse against the established authority of the regent,[70] it may be appropriate to consider them, moreover, as cultural statements shot across each other's bows.

Of the three, the Arsenal appears in many ways to have been

206 Antoine-François Vassé, design for the chimney-piece end of the Galerie Dorée at the hôtel de Toulouse, *c.*1713. Nationalmuseum, Stockholm.

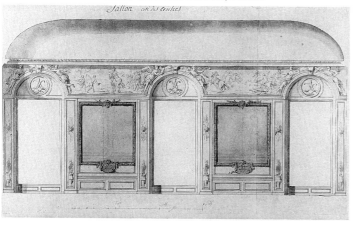

204 A view of the gallery of the Palais Royal, facing the fireplace, *c.*1771. Etching. From Jacques-François Blondel, *Cours d'architecture*, 1771–7.

205 Germain Boffrand, design for a *salon* at the Arsenal, *c.*1715–17. Pencil, pen and ink, grey wash and watercolour on paper, 35.8 × 58.5 cm. Kunstbibliothek, Staatliche Museen, Berlin.

iconographically and stylistically the most conservative. Its insistent bellicosity, though clearly encouraged by the nature of the building and the identity of the patron, nevertheless seems to recall certain features of Versailles and Marly. Boffrand, like Mansart at the Pavillon Royal, reserved a special place for personifications of princely virtues.[71] At the far end of the *salon*, above a chimney-piece and mirror, Boffrand planned to station Bellona, perched upon the cornice, sword raised to quell her prisoners and surrounded by standards yielded on the field of battle,[72] while above an adjacent doorway (fig. 208), a projected Mars would have leant upon his shield in contemplation of the martial trophies, including a cannon, likewise ringed about him. The six arcades composed of doors, windows and mirrors were to be linked by a broad frieze, apparently depicting the battles of Alexander,[73] while below, Boffrand anticipated a series of four paintings encased in comparatively austere, rectangular frames and accompanied by explanatory cartouches seemingly fashioned from the hide of the Nemean lion. No evidence there of a retreat before an iconography devalued by a father's encomiastic exploitation. Indeed, the arrangement of the figurative components within panelling divided into simple rectilinear or circular shapes with plane mouldings, and punctuated only by anonymous

207   The Galerie Dorée, 1713–18. Hôtel de Toulouse, presently the Banque de France, Paris.

pilasters decorated with smoking votive burners and diminutive trophies, further conspired to attach the scheme to the official idiom of Louis XIV, rather than the oppositional culture that the duchesse du Maine had earlier been exploring through grotesques at Sceaux.

The remodelling of the Arsenal was planned when the duc du Maine was in the ascendency – both domestically, in his father's affections, and politically, by his father's patronage. Starting with a declaration on 5 May 1694, Louis XIV had proclaimed for du Maine and the other royal bastards a rank midway between the princes of the blood and the dukes and peers.[74] With the loss of so many of his direct descendents, he had then proceeded by edict of July 1714 to arrogate for them the right to royal succession should all legitimate blood fail, and lastly, by declaration of 23 May 1715, he had conferred upon them the rank of *prince du sang*. It was the legality of these rights and titles, contested by the legitimate house of Condé in an opening petition presented to the regent in 1716,

that constituted the matter of the *affaire des princes*. While the duc de Bourbon-Condé, his brother the comte de Charolais and his cousin the prince de Conti maintained that Louis XIV had violated the fundamental law of the kingdom forcibly to admit his bastards to the royal succession and that the regent should therefore immediately repeal the legislation of 1714–15, du Maine, Toulouse and their pamphleteers sought to prove by recourse to historical precedent the admissability of bastardy to the throne and hence the legitimacy of Louis's laws. There can be little doubt that the projected decoration of the Arsenal also bespoke a consciousness of successorial rights, though the visual evidence is insufficient to establish whether it would have done so with pre-1715 complacency or post-1716 tenacity – assuming indeed, that such fine distinctions may appropriately be made. As already noted, the duc du Maine's participation in the history of the nation was to be repeatedly alluded to by the decorative deployment of his monogram and symbols of war; moreover, if the paintings

188

Sallon coté opposé aux croisées.

intended for the room were to have been of a battling kind, it seems likely that they would have recorded the duke's military campaigns.[75] Moreover, the frieze, though it was to illustrate a Greek *exemplum* and not the episodes from the Frankish past deployed in the pamphlet campaign,[76] and though it placed its edifying pattern in an upper register rather than in a literally supportive role as a precedent, would nevertheless have functioned to provided du Maine with tangible proof of his descent from the same mythical genealogy as his father, stretching back to the patriarchs of antiquity.[77]

By comparison, the Galerie Dorée at the hôtel de Toulouse was less programmatically explicit and iconographically reductive. Apart from Louis-Alexandre's monogram tucked discreetly into scallop-edged cartouches on the inside of the pair of niches at either end of the gallery, perhaps only the selection of 'royal' artists to design and execute the scheme betrayed a conspicuously Bourbon inheritance. The Premier Architecte, de Cotte, along with Vassé, the Dessinateur Général de la Marine, devised for the hôtel de Toulouse an articulation of the gallery elevation, distinctive above all for the contours of the frames that served to dispatch into panelling the *seicento* La Vrillière pictures acquired by Toulouse along with the house.[78] If, in the eyes of contemporary Parisians, the design did not obviously derive from royal prototypes,[79] it became, however, a characteristic arrange-

208 Germain Boffrand, design for a *salon* at the Arsenal, *c*.1715–17. Pencil, pen and ink, wash and watercolour on paper, 36.8 × 59.5 cm. Kunstbibliothek, Staatliche Museen, Berlin.

209 Antoine-François Vassé, design for trophies, *c*.1713–14. Black chalk heightened with white on blue paper, 34.2 × 40.5 cm. Cabinet des Estampes, Bibliothèque Nationale, Paris.

ment, variations upon which were used by the king's works during the following reign.[80] Notwithstanding the fact that three of the original collection of twelve canvases were withdrawn from the gallery and the remaining canvases substantially altered in response to the new setting,[81] neither thought nor resolution seem to have been given to commissioning contemporary or allegorical history pictures that might have been more in keeping with Vassé's projected ornament. The new scheme therefore arose out of the constituents of the old. According to Sabine Cotté's reconstruction, it seems that the paintings had originally been arranged at regular intervals above a *lambris à hauteur*.[82] Surrounded by painted and gilded stucco alternately fashioned by Gerard van Obstal into smoking votive burners, putti with ensigns spread, triumphal trophies and imperial eagles, these pictures had thus been stilled beneath a mythological sky frescoed by François Perrier and immediately above a relentless row of Roman busts poised along a cornice. Although these disparate painted and sculpted elements never advanced a coherent narrative, an odour of grandeur nevertheless stole over the scheme bringing into felicitous conjuction Apollo's gilded realm with the golden age of ancient Rome, and linking by a thread of heroic ornament the different times and hours of antique glory.

De Cotte and Vassé's substitutive scheme all but snuffed out the former power and authority of these Roman *exempla* by breaking down the ornamental syntax of fame and building from it an abstract rhythm of Composite pilasters, arcades and frames which drew the physical surfaces of the scheme into satisfying tension but left images isolated one from another. Moreover, the proliferation of maritime and hunting emblems (one project for the trophies (fig. 209) also envisaged pictorial scenes of a harbour and a chase) only added to the obfuscation of the original programme. For, although Vassé attempted simultaneously to fulfil the patron's emblematic needs and to relate wall and vault by bringing some of the gods and goddesses off Olympus and distributing them along the cornice (fig. 210), devices such as the ship's prow breaking through above the chimney-piece appeared iconographically incongruous, notwithstanding its fellowship of Tritons. Most disturbing of all were the cartouches that Vassé designed to accompany the pictures. Such cartouches, if not supporting descriptions of the pictures above (as envisaged for the Arsenal or realised in the engravings of the Galerie Dorée[83]) generally repeated, in a lower case, the subjects of their painted companions; but there the cartouches alternately represented maritime and venery myths – Orion, surrounded by exquisitely fashioned treasures of the sea (fig. 211) or Hercules with the head of the Erymanthian boar (fig. 212) – and were completely at odds with the pictorial themes they appeared to complement.[84] The absence of thematic reinforcement between the various figurative elements of the room diminished the iconographic impact of Vassé's ornament and denied it the heroic leverage latent in the Arsenal solution.

However, the Galerie Dorée perhaps owed its long-term

211   Antoine-François Vassé, cartouche with Orion, from the panelling of the Galerie Dorée at the hôtel de Toulouse, 1713–18. Banque de France, Paris.

212   Antoine-François Vassé, cartouche with Hercules and the head of the Erymanthian boar, from the panelling of the Galerie Dorée at the hôtel de Toulouse, 1713–18. Banque de France, Paris.

success and survival to this very lack of congruity. The collection of seventeenth-century masterpieces by Guercino, Guido Reni, Nicolas Poussin and others, created an atmosphere markedly different to what we know, for example, of the comte de Seignelay's *grand cabinet*, which otherwise deployed – to Boffrand's design – analogous maritime motifs in commemoration of the Colberts' devoted service to the royal navy.[85] Setting aside for an instant the types of room concerned, the distinction between the two schemes seems to have amounted above all to the difference between geographical charts and Old Masters. The twenty maps that hung in Seignelay's 'temple of memory', must have lent a professional and learned edge to the poetic fancy of tritons and dolphins disporting along the cornice; by contrast, the marginal ornament in the Galerie Dorée was never a decorative sediment deposited by the main objects of attention, but a symbolic reminder of the rank and means by which the hôtel de Toulouse had been secured as an exemplary centre of polite civilisation (signified by pictures above all) to rival the Palais Royal. Closer then, in generative principle to the decoration of Louis XIV's *grand appartement* at Versailles, where the rooms were hung with a collection of predominently *seicento* Italian works until the end of the *ancien régime*,[86] it might be argued that, at the Galerie Dorée, possession of the trophies of a princely culture was being advanced as nine points of a judicial and moral entitlement to that rank.

210   The Galerie Dorée, 1713–18. Hôtel de Toulouse, presently the Banque de France, Paris.

191

213 Nicolas Pineau, pier-glass, from the gallery of the hôtel de Villars, 1732. The National Trust, Waddesdon Manor, Aylesbury, Buckinghamshire.

Of the bastards' schemes, it was undoubtedly the hôtel de Toulouse that proved representative of the heroic schemes erected in the hôtels of the early eighteenth-century nobility. *Habitués* of the *vieille cour*, like the duc de Villars, loyal to du Maine and Toulouse, proved belated devotees of the disintegrative structure and periphrastic logic of an ornamental epic genre, circulated discreetly about the edges of things. In 1730 Villars, a French marshal, decided to add a gallery to his hôtel in the rue de Grenelle for which Pineau provided the panelling in the following years.[87] Here the spaces between the arcades were filled with pier-glasses and the contribution of painting to the overall appointment of the room was both less substantial and less high-minded than at the Galerie Dorée. History painting was displaced by copies of seventeenth-cen-

tury half-length female figures (fig. 213),[88] encased in florid triangular frames above the mirrors, and if the double doors at the west end supported representations of the marshal's batons, only one of the four elaborate cartouches that traversed the cornice made any further allusion to the patron's military career.[89] The 'representational' function of the gallery, compromised at the hôtel de Toulouse by the room's other role as a *cabinet de tableaux*, had in this instance all but disappeared. Indeed, the delicate balance effected at the hôtel de Toulouse between, on the one hand, the need to seize the tradition of the *grand siècle* in order to articulate an entitlement to power and, on the other, the need to avoid the ridiculed and despoiled forms of its language, had finally collapsed into a playful display of martial rhetoric in all its garrulous but impotent variety. Appropriately therefore, it was in the *salon* of the petit hôtel de Villars, built shortly after the Treaty of Radstadt (1713), negotiated by Villars, that the duke most fulsomely acknowledged his professional accomplishments by means of military trophies and crossed marshal's batons.[90] However, trophies alone – no matter how impressive – could scarcely compensate for the departure of the exemplary narrative, customarily afforded by figurative sculpture and painting, particularly when they were suspended, as they were at the hôtel de Villars, from delicate, fluttering ribbons, and when the laurel of Fame tended to become entangled with garlands and shells of a decidedly pastoral nature. Furthermore, valorous trophies rarely enjoyed complete mastery of a space; panelling at the Metropolitan Museum of Art (fig. 214), thought originally to have come from the hôtel de Varengeville, was indiscriminately sculpted with trophies of fame and glory (figs 215, 216) and others invoking the seasons, music, poetry, gardening and commerce (figs 217, 218).[91] The discourse of violence intrinsic to heroic action had been domesticated and transformed into a polite conceit of the spoils of conquest;[92] moreover, the transfer of such trophies from the gallery to the *salon* implies that allusions to the nobility's preferred profession were perhaps best kept for its *semblables* and not paraded in the more public spaces of the residence, where they might risk mockery from a less self-deceiving public.

It would be quite inaccurate, however, to suggest that (like the grotesque) this unpicked and ornamental epic genre circulated predominantly within a closely sutured faction. Villars's *salon* was probably inspired by the earlier, mid-1720s decoration of a drawing-room at the hôtel d'Evreux, for which Michel Lange had sculpted magnificent trophies (fig. 219) of antique instruments of battle.[93] Given his lineage, Henri-Louis de La Tour d'Auvergne, third son of the duc de Bouillon, would very likely have fetched up on the same side as the legitimate princes who effortlessly rallied the support of a peerage still smarting at the insult of their abrupt demotion to a rank below Louis's illegitimate sons.[94] Moreover, though not actually listed among the duc de Bourbon's so-called regiment, 'encamped' from 1720 at the place Vendôme, the better

214 *Salon*, formerly at the hôtel de Varengeville, *c.*1735–40. Metropolitan Museum of Art, New York. Acquired with funds given by Mr. and Mrs. Charles Wrightsman, 1963.

to speculate in government stocks and bonds, Evreux certainly profited no less than Bourbon's vassals by loyal investment in the regent's financial experiments.[95] At the same time, Louis-Charles-Auguste Fouquet de Belle-Isle, hero of the siege of Lille and later duke and field marshal, had himself built an hôtel on the rue de Bourbon, yet so noble and heroic a life as his marked the decoration of his house only upon its ornament – the familiar trace of palms, laurel and trophies.[96] Since Belle-Isle was a leading figure in the duc de Chaulnes's cabal, which from 1722 worked for the downfall of the first minister, cardinal Dubois, it should be evident that, during the Regency, nobles of a wide political and cultural cast[97] indulged a common taste for gelded glory, its exemplary force cut away by satire and strife.

Ironically, whereas the bastards had been led by physiological necessity to couch their 'radical' political claims in an often suspiciously orthodox cultural style,[98] the regent, whose personal and constitutional legitimacy was much less obviously in doubt, was theoretically at liberty to mobilise greater originality in the decoration of the Palais Royal. However, the apparently novel decision, taken at a time when none entertained thoughts of a Regency – but fully endorsed by the later campaign of 1715–17 – to enliven the gallery with episodes from the decoratively unexploited *Aeneid* (fig. 221), seems on reflection more conservative than innovatory, inasmuch as choice settled on a classical epic. Indeed, though Virgil's poem had never furnished the subject of a royal programme, dedicatory epistles to French editions of the text reveal that the

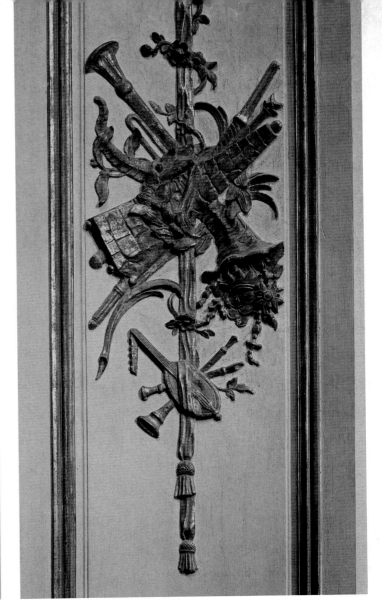

215 Trophy of Fame, from the panelling of the *salon* of the former hôtel de Varengeville, *c*.1735–40. Metropolitan Museum of Art, New York.

216 Trophy of Glory, from the panelling of the *salon* of the former hôtel de Varengeville, *c*.1735–40. Metropolitan Museum of Art, New York.

tale was thought particularly fitting for princes. For instance, in 1655 Michel de Marolles dedicated his princely folio translation of the *Aeneid*,[99] which he described as 'a most beautiful peincture', to the young Louis XIV, first because he believed that the semi-divine hero perfectly represented 'the greatness of his [Louis's] extraction, which draws its origin from the most glorious blood-lines of the universe', and second because in Aeneas was found the portrait of the consummate prince, at once valorous and civilised.[100]

Later translations, such as that by the poet Segrais in 1686, steadily reprinted in cheaper, octavo editions well into the eighteenth century, continued to propound flattering analogies between the Virgilian past and the Ludovican present. However, where Marolles had held out the Trojan Aeneas that his movements might serve as arguments and ideas to a young king at the inauguration of his reign, Segrais, writing when a nation's hopes had largely been fulfilled, emphasised instead the comparison between contemporary French society and the civilisation that gave the *Aeneid* life. Indeed, Segrais argued that a reincarnated Virgil would have recognised in Louis XIV a prince superior to Augustus because 'whilst Augustus's victories ended only in establishing an illegitimate authority, V[otre] M[ajesté] has no more than amplified the glory of the most just and the foremost Monarchy on earth'.[101] The link between this particular brand of literary encomium and the theories of royalist *modernes* has recently been recognised, particularly in the case of Charles Perrault who expressly rejected the view that the perfection of western culture had been reached in antiquity and argued that the greatness of Louis XIV's reign so surpassed the achievements of an Alexander or an Augustus that it could not be meaningfully enhanced by analogy with theirs.[102]

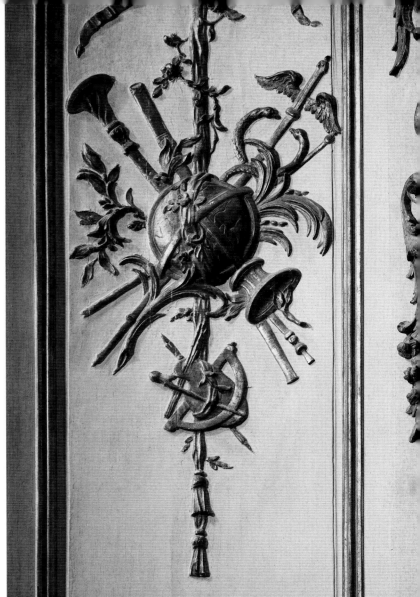

217   Tropy of Gardening, from the panelling of the *salon* of the former hôtel de Varengeville, *c.*1735–40. Metropolitan Museum of Art, New York.

218   Tropy of Commerce, from the panelling of the *salon* of the former hôtel de Varengeville, *c.*1735–40. Metropolitan Museum of Art, New York.

In the same way, but not necessarily for the same reasons, there can be little doubt that at the Palais Royal Aeneas was not intended as a cipher for Philippe d'Orléans and that, for example, the Trojan prince's single-handed victory over the Rutulians, was innocent of analogy with Philippe's daring campaigns on the Iberian peninsula. Women of the court may well have volunteered as models for Coypel's ceiling but they were not assigned roles in an allegorised narrative.[103] In the absence of such coded resemblances, Coypel's paintings have tended to be approached as illustrations, in other words as a measured and academic translation of Virgil's text into appropriate visual forms, which together comprehensively animated the tale from the sacking of Troy (fig. 220), a prelude to the *Aeneid* recounted by the hero at Dido's feast in book 2, to the combat between Aeneas and fierce Turnus in Latium, narrated in book 12. And yet, the arrangement of the pictures in the

gallery alone militated against a straightforward 'reading' of the poem and created a confusion that the circumstances of the commission can only partly explain.[104] Acknowledging, in the first instance, that the wall paintings may not have been planned from the outset and that the vault was therefore conceived as an autonomous and coherent unit, it is nevertheless apparent that Coypel's disposition of events does not follow Virgil's. A crib translation would have meant locating the lost canvases, *Mercury Urging Aeneas to Abandon Carthage*, and *Juno Arousing Allecto from the Underword*, side by side to the right of the central opening, while instead they each enjoyed a slipped position at either end of the gallery. Though scant visual evidence survives to justify these compositional liberties, it seems likely that Coypel settled on opening with *Mercury and Aeneas* because of the opportunity it gave him to introduce the hero at the very threshold of the room,[105] while

195

219   Michel Lange, trophies, from the panelling of the Grand Salon at the hôtel d'Evreux, 1720–2. Palais de l'Elysée, Paris.

Allecto perhaps naturally found her place above the chimney-piece because her mission to set peace-treaties ablaze and whip up discord with her firebrands made fire an element to which she was conspicuously attached, though her purpose was arson, not a cheerful hearth.

Coypel's Galerie d'Enée was clearly not a literal illustration of the text because the painter so obviously exceeded the commission. Not only did he rearrange events but he omitted completely certain episodes while elaborating others in a visual paraphrase of a poem noted for its distinctive focus and handling.[106] Through variation in the dimensions of the scenes, for instance, Coypel provided emphasis to the tale as well as affording rhythm to the programme. At the centre of the vault and at the midpoint of the gallery wall, Coypel stationed his two largest compositions, *Venus Appealing to Jupiter on Aeneas's Behalf* and *Aeneas in the Underworld*, works that, in a number of ways, brought these separate architectural planes into conjunction, thereby providing some much needed unity to an often incoherent scheme. The 1719 edition of the *Curiositez de Paris* reveals that the frame of *Aeneas in the Underworld* was particularly elaborate.[107] Instead of the modest references to Aeneas's famous armour crowning the other wall paintings, the frame of the centrepiece offered a 'carpet of ornament', which two large and gilded figures, sculpted in relief and personifying Time and Fame had just finished raising in order to reveal the realm below. On a formal level these allegorial figures found ready analogues in the caryatids, *ignudi* and, especially, the winged Victories that similarly framed the *quadri riportati* above, but more importantly, through their position on the cornice they were able to suggest that at a thematic level both compositions were concerned with prophecy. Indeed, in these two paintings Coypel balanced the offices of the mother against the services of the father with a symmetry scarcely justified by the text, and gave their care a narrative significance that ultimately undermined the personal achievement of the poet's hero.

Response to such free interpretations of the epic were mixed. Germain Brice was among those generous with their praise; he found Coypel's creative interpolation of images 'admirable' and the communion between the terrestial and celestial planes 'ingenious'.[108] On the other hand, Le Rouge, the presumed author of the *Curiositez de Paris*, regretted the absence of a stricter respect for the chronological sequence of the legendary events and felt an obligation to make good Coypel's errors by providing his readers with a route map of scenes numbered as they appeareared in Virgil's original.[109] Likewise, while Brice favoured Coypel's sometimes daring handling of perspective and his powerful colourism, Le Rouge, apparently speaking in the name of connoisseurs, denounced the brilliant draperies, the blushed flesh and the draughtsmanship as inappropriately closer to Rubens than the marbled remoteness of antiquity.[110] Though their judgements conflicted, both recognised in Coypel's gallery a 'modern' imitation of Virgil's tale, one less concerned with accuracy of

220 Antoine Coypel, *Aeneas and Anchises*, 1715–17. Oil on canvas, 387 × 190 cm. Musée Fabre, Montpellier.

illustration than with capturing in a three-dimensional space the essence of the poem in an idiom with contemporary resonance. In this sense the gallery not only cleaved to the side of the *Rubénistes* but lent its support to Houdart de La Motte and the *modernes* in the not unrelated quarrel over Homer that raged between 1713 and 1716.[111]

By comparison with the programmes of du Maine and Toulouse, the regent's gallery seemed to break much more

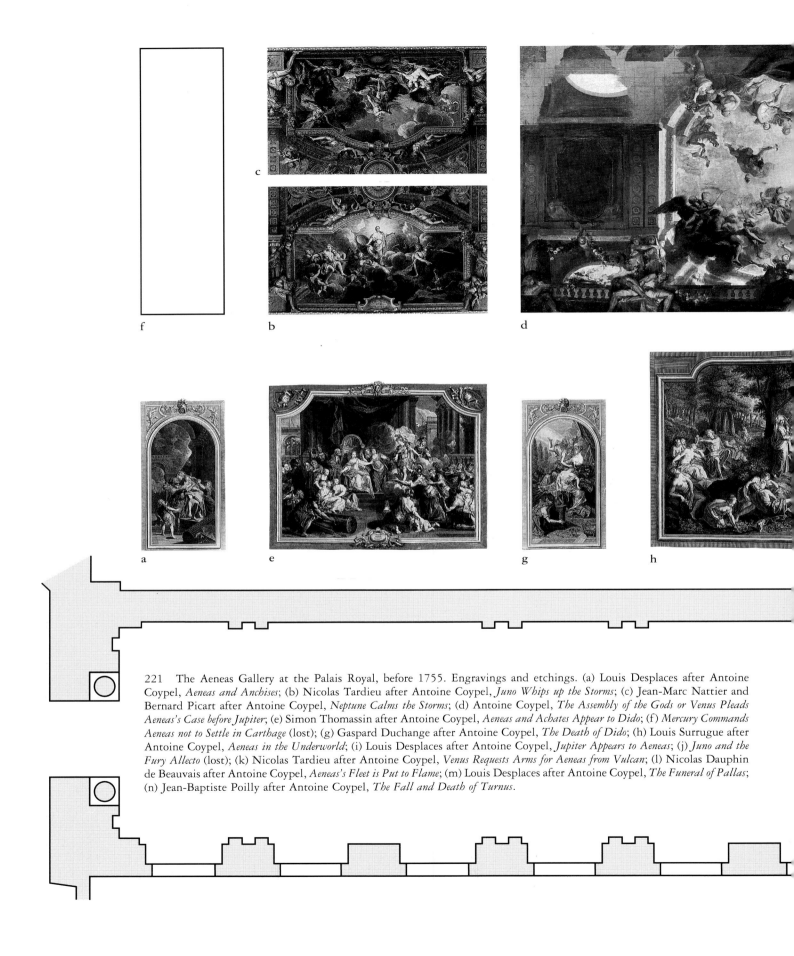

221 The Aeneas Gallery at the Palais Royal, before 1755. Engravings and etchings. (a) Louis Desplaces after Antoine Coypel, *Aeneas and Anchises*; (b) Nicolas Tardieu after Antoine Coypel, *Juno Whips up the Storms*; (c) Jean-Marc Nattier and Bernard Picart after Antoine Coypel, *Neptune Calms the Storms*; (d) Antoine Coypel, *The Assembly of the Gods or Venus Pleads Aeneas's Case before Jupiter*; (e) Simon Thomassin after Antoine Coypel, *Aeneas and Achates Appear to Dido*; (f) *Mercury Commands Aeneas not to Settle in Carthage* (lost); (g) Gaspard Duchange after Antoine Coypel, *The Death of Dido*; (h) Louis Surrugue after Antoine Coypel, *Aeneas in the Underworld*; (i) Louis Desplaces after Antoine Coypel, *Jupiter Appears to Aeneas*; (j) *Juno and the Fury Allecto* (lost); (k) Nicolas Tardieu after Antoine Coypel, *Venus Requests Arms for Aeneas from Vulcan*; (l) Nicolas Dauphin de Beauvais after Antoine Coypel, *Aeneas's Fleet is Put to Flame*; (m) Louis Desplaces after Antoine Coypel, *The Funeral of Pallas*; (n) Jean-Baptiste Poilly after Antoine Coypel, *The Fall and Death of Turnus*.

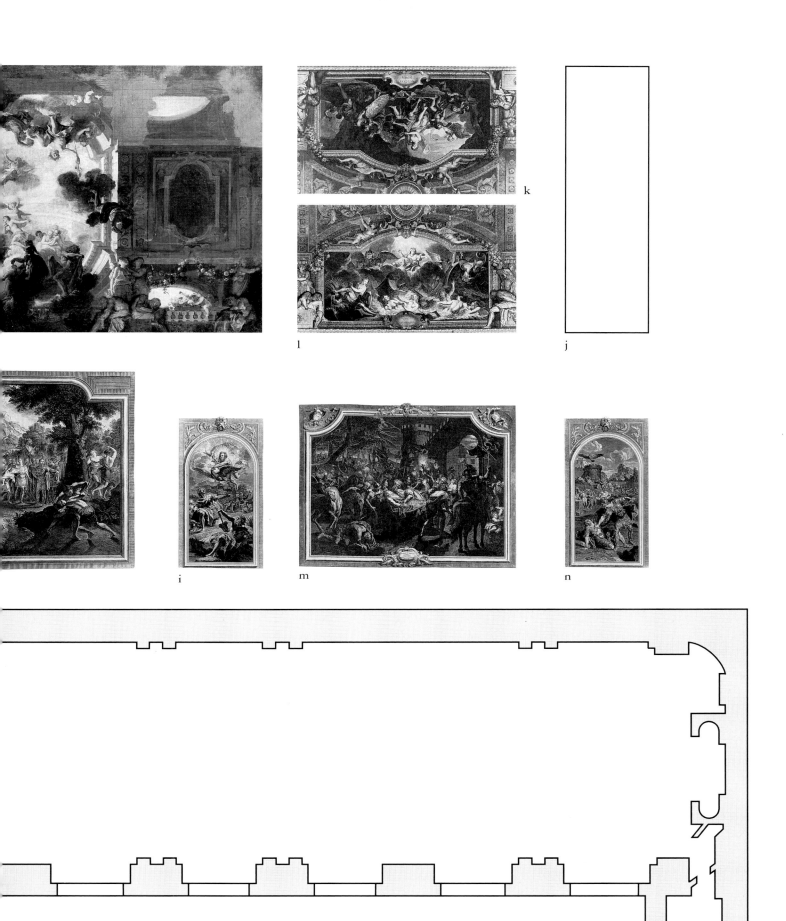

k

l

j

i

m

n

cleanly with the past. Not only was Coypel's painted *Aeneid* never populated with the political and eulogistic intentions usually at work in such heroic schemes, but the ornamental decoration eschewed, even in the modest spaces of the margins, extravagant references to the patron's status and credentials for power. The past, whether history or legend, was effectively depersonalised; it no longer functioned as the privileged mirror or portrait of history-makers (princes, nobles and ministers) but offered a generic and 'democratic' discourse whose moral injunctions were there for society at large to heed. Insofar as spectators were therefore referred back to their own conduct and to their own experience, this scheme seems to announce a new history painting, one of a kind Du Bos could have admired and one whose publicity depended not only on the space it occupied but on its ability to address an audience collectively. Thus, when in 1733 Le Moyne came to paint the ceiling of the Salon d'Hercule at Versailles and invited spectators to recognise in his Hercules not the Gallic prince of former times but the image of the perfect citizen, he was in many ways completing a restructuring of history initiated by historians in The Netherlands and by a painter with a Flemish touch.[112] To take the comparison of the three princely schemes one final step, the genealogical consciousness at the heart of the Arsenal and the de Toulouse programmes qualified their seats as particular, and public, only insofar as their claim as royal heirs was upheld. The civic oratory of the Palais Royal scheme, on the other hand, construed the gallery as a public space without qualification, indeed as the only public space in which legitimate members of *gouvernement* could gather. Proof of the different significations of these places emerged most fully, however, only in the wake of the settlement of the *affaire des princes*, when du Maine's and Toulouse's residences were exposed as spaces of conspiracy from which their owners swiftly took their leave.

However, the Galerie d'Enée should not be seen just in terms of the completeness of its erasure of the Maecenas. Though the demise of analogy curtailed the extent to which the virtues of the patron might be directly expressed through a hero's actions, the overt concern with the poetics of history — with its formal properties — provided a spectacle by which that person's learning, taste and *honnêté* might be fully beheld.[113] Moreover, the erosion of active moral virtues by softer, interactive social values is discernable in the internal structure and significations of Coypel's gallery as well as in its external relations as property attributed to a particular individual. To begin with, Coypel's rearrangement of the sequence of events, whether intentional or circumstantial, ultimately served to blur the sharp outline of the narrative progress and obscure the necessity of Aeneas's actions in fulfilment of his divine quest. Indeed, it might be argued that only in the first and last scenes does the protagonist clearly exhibit the physical and moral strength characteristic of a hero's high-minded interventions on the public stage. On the whole, the portrayal of emotion in response to given actions, rather than the execution of the heroic deeds themselves, seems to have preoccupied the painter more nearly. Consider, for example, the story of Dido and Aeneas, widely acknowledged at the time as one of the finest passages in the *Aeneid* and, of all the books, the one most often translated into French verse.[114] Coypel avoided depicting the moment of agonised fortitude when Aeneas takes his leave of Dido and Carthage, a subject keenly rendered during the previous century,[115] and instead chose to depict separately the two events that bracketed the farewell: Aeneas receiving his marching orders according to Jupiter's wish and Dido finding in death (fig. 222) carrion comfort for her lover's betrayal. The isolation of the former outside the original narrative flow could not help but rob it of much of its moral vigour and justification, whereas the juxtaposition of scenes of Dido's prompt and expansive welcome to Aeneas and Achates with the fatal outcome of her too generous hospitality surely encouraged sympathy for the victim of the Trojan's uncompromising ambition. At an earlier date, Segrais had already noted a swelling tide of opinion that, fuelled perhaps by admiration for Ovid's seventh *Heroides*, judged rude and perfidious Aeneas's treatment of the siren queen.[116] Moreover, he diagnosed the pressing need to defend Aeneas's attachment to a higher, civic duty as an eloquent symptom of the yawning corruption of contemporary French mores. The queen's excess of passion was now, it seems, more willingly forgiven than the hero's absence of consideration and polish. Thus the passional theory of human personality advanced in pornographic and topical detail by satirical *nouvellistes* mentioned earlier, was supported no less by a new generation for whom love represented not a weakness but a calling to culture.

THE TRIUMPH OF SEDUCTION:
MYTHOLOGIES GALANTES

Politeness, unlike arms, was an ideal of 'being' rather than 'becoming', and the contradictions and tensions between the will to culture and the will to valour were explored more fully in the decoration of aristocratic residences in the following decades. The irreconcilability of the pursuits of pleasure and fame was the *leitmotif* of another Odyssian tale, the story of Telemachus, which some twenty years after the completion of the Galerie d'Enée inspired six of Natoire's twelve paintings for the gallery at Philibert Orry's château de La Chapelle Godefroy.[117] There, despite Mentor's civic council alluded to in an overdoor (fig. 223), council which initially coloured Telemachus's reaction to the sexual freedom, the *mollesse* and luxury of the island's natives, the hero gradually found himself becoming accustomed to the ways of the flesh:

I felt myself weakening day by day; the sound education I had received scarcely supported me still; all my good intentions melted away, I no longer had any strength to resist the

222 Antoine Coypel,
The Death of Dido,
1715–17. Oil on
canvas, 387 × 190 cm.
Musée Fabre,
Montpellier.

wickedness which pressed in upon me from all sides; I was even sickly ashamed of virtue . . .[118]

In the book, Telemachus, who like all heroes properly belonged to the fulfilment of his quest, briefly succumbed to a nearer and apparently more desirable goal: the conquest of pleasure, an isle presided over by Cupid and Calypso and depicted in another overdoor, pair to *Mentor and Telemachus*. However, the allegorised role Fénelon entrusted to Calypso and Mentor did not emerge so clearly in contemporary depictions of the text (and here La Chapelle Godefroy was no exception), which generally forsook pedagogical contrast for a poetic evocation of Calypso's isle as the realm of love – a necessarily different social and moral polity to that governed by civic heroism, if not an obviously inferior one.[119]

Coupled with the ethical polarities structuring Fénelon's tale was a disparity in the dynamics and orientation of love and heroism. In the first of the two larger canvases of Orry's series Calypso was shown having attracted and captured Telemachus (fig. 224), while in the second, nymphs inspired by Cupid's torch hastened to set ablaze the captive's ship in order to preempt further movements outwards into the public sphere. Where heroism, exemplified in the gallery by a pendant series, the *History of Clovis* (1735–7), was active and demanded a hero's personal but selfless intercession in the events of the world beyond the self – Natoire significantly chose to focus Clovis's life around the *Battle of Tolbiac* and the *Siege of Bordeaux* (fig. 225) – love was perceived as drawing its victims in

224 Charles-Joseph Natoire, *Telemachus on the Isle of Calypso*, c.1739. Oil on canvas. The Hermitage, Saint Petersburg.

upon themselves, precluding all movement beyond a selfish interaction with or a passive contemplation of the subject desired.[120] The implication of Telemachus's (and Aeneas's) brush with eroticism ought therefore to have been that *salon galanterie*, should it become a hero's *raison d'être* instead of his occasional pleasure, threatened the moral justification of his superiority by bringing about a 'fall of public man'.[121] Such a whispered warning may have echoed through the Galerie d'Enée where the Carthaginian episode was contained and framed within a larger epic plan, but at the château near Nogent-sur-Seine Telemachus's adventures with Calypso constituted the only subject of the tale, and though offset by the deeds of the noble Clovis, both sides quantitatively emerged as equally viable alternatives. Moreover, the vanquished Telemachus, like other victims of Venus, such as those depicted by Antoine Coypel in 1708 on the *salon* ceiling at the hôtel d'Argenton,[122] showed none of the moral turpitude or spiritual anguish appropriate to such a fall. On the contrary, they exhibited a seemingly joyous and optimistic capitulation to love's authority. In the case of the *Triumph of Venus over the Gods* perhaps this was only to be expected, executed as it was in the residence of one of the regent's mistresses. However, the erotic mythology of the rococo period was no less widely known for its slack moral will – from which it must be concluded that where the visual arts acknowledged the traditional discord between love and heroism, by the reign of Louis XV they invariably did so in praise of the former.

Between the opening of the Galerie d'Enée and the completion of the gallery at La Chapelle Godefroy, the political and economic fortunes of France had not only stabilised but improved considerably. Cardinal Fleury, Bishop of Fréjus and first minister in all but name from 1726, had followed the ambitious experiments of the Regency with a return to more orthodox and popular policies aimed at securing lasting

223 Charles-Joseph Natoire, *Mentor and Telemachus*, 1740. Oil on canvas, 140 × 131 cm. Musée des Beaux-Arts, Troyes.

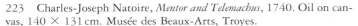

détente both at home and abroad.[123] With subtle diplomacy he manoeuvered French national interests away from the temptation of military solutions, particularly conflicts of a scale seriously to jeopardise the controller-general Orry's effective but slow administrative efforts towards economic recovery.[124] So successful was Fleury and his personnel of unusually young and able ministers and secretaries of state,[125] that, in the opinion of one historian, there followed in the 1730s a period in French history that, 'for some sections of society at least was the golden age of the *ancien régime*'.[126] Though Alfred Cobban certainly had financiers, merchants and industrialists particularly in mind, the court nobility may also be accounted among the significant beneficiaries of the ministry, although their gains were economic rather than political.[127] In fact, the political dialogue between monarchy and nobility reopened by

Philippe d'Orléans had become increasingly strained and one-sided as the Regency unfolded and the dream of a power-sharing, aristocratic monarchy was finally dispelled by Louis XV's declaration on 16 June 1726 that, like Louis XIV before him, he would forthwith personally take up the mantle of government.[128] Moreover, Fleury, as befitted his conservative nature, was careful to return politics to its pre-Polysynodie structure, ensuring no direct links between those holding ministerial office and the well-established court nobility. By this means, the cardinal won independence from competing factions at court, helped not a little by the birth of a dauphin in 1729, which quashed once and for all the pretensions of the 'Spanish party', a label here collectively used to refer to those who had continued to rally opposition to the young king after the regent's death, by looking to Philip V as

225   Charles-Joseph Natoire, *The Siege of Bordeaux*, 1737. Oil on canvas, 266 × 300 cm. Musée des Beaux-Arts, Troyes.

a potential alternative and successor in the event that Louis XV should die without issue.[129] The court was of course never without its factions, but for a time at least Fleury commanded sufficient control to mute opposition within the court. It may seem appropriate during this period of virtual peace, when advancement was once again no longer to be sought through counsel or on the battlefield but entirely by way of social relations at court, that the discourse of power became deeply figured with erotic codes.

Peter Brooks has amply and richly demonstrated that, in 'novels of wordliness', *libertinage* functioned as a paradigm for the search for authority through knowledge.[130] For instance, each love affair entered into by male characters in Crébillon's novels, by increasing the scope of their experience, extended the range of their control over *salon* gamesmanship. Thus, love and valour may have differed in their agencies of domination and in their interpretations of human psychology, but their objectives were invariably the same: conquest. Indeed, in Boucher's *Venus Requesting Vulcan to Make Arms for Aeneas* (1732; Musée du Louvre, Paris), which with its pendant decorated the lawyer François Derbais's billiards-room, sex and arms have become visibly so interdependent as sources of power that Aeneas's weapons appear literally forged by the flames of passion.[131] Moreover, when Méré, not unlike Boucher, suggested to *honnêtes gens* that, in order to achieve the most worthwhile superiority, 'one should not wish to win at any price, but like heroes, in a manner pleasing even to the vanquished',[132] he did so acknowledging by his use of idiom the formal similarities between the spheres of pleasure and violence. However, to imply similarity is of course not to judge things identical. Later, in the 1730s, Jean-Baptiste Rousseau was among those poets to explore more fully the contradictions and complexities in the relationship between these twin divinities through Venus's ultimate preference for Adonis over Mars. True to his nature Mars was, it seems, too violent and domineering a lover, one whose jealous heart was satisfied with nothing less than possession. Before long Venus was lured away by the more subtle and aimiable Adonis, from which the author drew the following lesson:

> On oublie aisément un amour qui fait peur,
> En faveur d'un amour qui flatte.
> Que le soin de charmer
> Soit votre unique affaire.
> Songer que l'art d'aimer
> N'est que celui de plaire.
>
> Voulez-vous, dans vos feux
> Trouver des biens durables?
> Soyez moins amoureux;
> Devenez plus aimables.[133]

It is perhaps worth noting that in contemporary depictions of Venus and Adonis, for example François Le Moyne's version acquired by count Tessin in 1729, the captivation of the goddess by love and her subsequent powerlessness to prevent her lover's fatal departure contrast similarly with the supreme potency of her influence when depicted with her estranged husband Vulcan or her erstwhile lover Mars.[134]

Few, meanwhile, would have argued with Boullainvilliers's claim that 'there is no greater distinction among men than that between victor and vanquished',[135] but the savagery that was said to have secured and authenticated aristocratic superiority during the Frankish conquest was, it seems, no longer sufficient to maintain it. In politics as in art, the fiction of love and *honnêté* had become equally important instruments of repression in the post-Fronde era. In the cause of distinction, brute force had ceded to pleasing cunning as physical attrition gave way to psychological warfare, but the tactics remained the same: to divine the weaknesses and susceptibilites of others while remaining opaque to their conjectures. With this *mondain* preoccupation with the concealment of self-interest in mind, it may be possible to discern, in part, the specific historical acuity of much eighteenth-century *mythologie galante*.

Ovid's *Metamorphoses* had provided a rich compendium of subjects for the visual arts under Louis XIV,[136] and if its popularity with patrons and artists apparently waned after 1700, the more pertinent difference between seventeenth- and eighteenth-century uses of this source lies surely in the episodes favoured. The subjects chosen for the decoration of the ground-floor apartments of the palais des Tuileries, for instance, were those most clearly 'allégoriques du Roi',[137] and expressive of the speed of his vengeance against those who threatened his sovereignty and that of his descendants (Apollo and the Cyclops), or those determined to usurp his authority (the Fall of Icarus) or his grandeur (Midas).[138] Eighteenth-century selections from Ovid tended to avoid the more obviously didactic tales[139] and generally resisted the custom of allegorisation — except perhaps where myths could be called upon to exemplify the Elements or the rhythms of nature. Watteau, for instance, following La Fosse's initial idea, used the budding desire of Zephyr and Flora to capture the rousing spirit of spring in one of a series of four overdoors painted around 1716 for Pierre Crozat's dining-room in the rue de Richelieu.[140] Across the river and some ten years later, Le Moyne decorated the *grand salon* at the hôtel Peyrenc de Moras, home to another ennobled and conspicuously cultivated financier, with stories taken from the *Metamorphoses* but fashioned this time to illustrate the four times of day. The loves of Aurora and Cephalus and Diana and Endymion respectively opened and completed the cycle, while noon had conjured a scene of *Venus Showing Cupid the Power of his Arrows* (fig. 226), and evening had evoked *Diana Returning from the Hunt*.[141] In both schemes, metaphor had provided a decorous alibi for the depiction of potentially erotic adventures. Notwithstanding the repeated and defensive declarations of Ovid's eighteenth-century translators that his poetry needed its crude sensuality disguised or, better, utterly polished away,[142] many

226 François Le Moyne, *Venus Showing Cupid the Power of his Arrows*, c.1729–30. Oil on canvas, 109 × 164 cm. Musée Rodin, Paris.

patrons dared to enjoy mythology bare of justifying allegorical glosses, confident in the knowledge that amorous licence would be rendered in a stylistic code, itself sufficiently elevated to defy outright criticism.

Regrettably, probate inventories rarely provide precise information about the subjects of decorative paintings, though it is known that the hôtels de Carignan, de Mazarin, de Montbazon and de Verrue, among many others, were variously embellished with *sujets de fable*.[143] However, one exceptional example survives, the decoration of the hôtel de Soubise, an hôtel remodelled and considerably enlarged, initially by Pierre-Alexis Delamair and then by Boffrand, for one of the foremost noble families of the realm. The sculpted decoration of the *chambre de parade* (fig. 227), belonging to the princesse de Soubise, and situated on the first floor, included sculpted depictions of the coupled joys of Venus and Adonis and of Semele and Jupiter in the medallions at the centre of the wall-panels, a cartouche portraying Hebe in one of the angles of the ceiling and, seated along the cornice, stucco figures of Bacchus and Ariadne, Pallas and Mercury, and Venus and Mars.[144]

However, more telling were the images in which surrender was assured by the disguised or veiled approach of the suitor, such as *Diana and Endymion* (fig. 228) which occupies the space above the bed, the fables of Danaë (fig. 229) Leda and Ganymede in the remaining three ceiling cartouches and the *Rape of Europa* (fig. 230) in a wall medallion. All these stories exploited effects that yielded to sight (a fundamental reason, no doubt, for their pictorial success) and told of the ingenuity and guile of lovers who clothed themselves in shapes that soonest might deceive those they tricked to conquer. Love, it seems, was the product of perception, and Cupid ruled eyes to triumph over hearts. However, the subject that perhaps most perfectly encapsulated the *honnête* obsession with the form of conquest was the fable of Mercury and Argus (fig. 231), told in the last wall-medallion, for there Argus even invited Mercury (seen strolling in the background) to tell the tales and play the sleep-inducing pipes that were to bring about his downfall, thus illustrating Méré's maxim that civilised victory secured the voluntary collaboration of the vanquished in their own defeat. From the certainty of painful retribution announced at

227   Chambre de la Princesse, *c*.1737. Hôtel de Soubise, Paris.

the Tuileries we have moved to the promise of a pleasurable and unwitting capitulation at Soubise.

    The story of Cupid and Psyche (1737–9),[145] told by Natoire in eight canvases in the adjacent oval *salon* at the hôtel de Soubise (fig. 232), initially repeated the same lesson.[146] The first two pictures portrayed the despairing Psyche who, unable to fix a suitor, was exposed by her father on a deserted rock in fulfilment of Apollo's prophecy that the king should abandon all hope of a 'son-in-law of mortal kind' and settle for a 'cruel monster'.[147] However, Zephir came to Psyche's aid and conducted her to the palace of Love, which she entered having been seduced by the genius of the place and the welcome of nymphs who offered her garlands. It was in this place, at nightfall, so the story goes, that Cupid came under the cover of darkness and consummated their union, extracting from Psyche a promise never to seek to know his identity. Inasmuch as Psyche is little more than an object of erotic possession, the nature of her relationship to Cupid was equal to those of Europa or Leda to Jupiter already mentioned, and might be labelled a slave relationship because she blindly submits to Cupid's despotic authority. Psyche's confinement in this kind

228   Michel Lange (attributed to), *Diana and Endymion*, detail from the cornice of the Chambre de la Princesses, *c*.1737. Hôtel de Soubise, Paris.

229 (facing page)   Michel Lange (attributed to), *Danaë*, detail from the cornice of the Chambre de la Princesse, *c*.1737. Hôtel de Soubise, Paris.

of harem was achieved not by force but by the fiction spun by Cupid that her happiness depended on an ignorant submission. It was Cupid's knowledge of the situation, his ability to define Psyche and gauge her emotional vulnerability, that gave him mastery, and no doubt pleasure in the exercise of that power. However, as Duclos astutely surmised, infidelity was built into the libertine's will to power,[148] for his authority, like that of the military hero's, was cumulative and guaranteed only by a succession of victories.[149] His victim's only chance of escaping repression lay in redressing the balance of knowledge by uncovering, in turn, her partner's susceptibilities and by penetrating his psychological motives in order to redirect them to her own advantage, namely by securing a commitment. The episode of *Psyche Showing her Gifts to her Sisters* (fig. 233) marks the moment of the heroine's grudging *prise de conscience*. Persuaded by her more wordly and experienced sisters, she determines to discover her lover's identity. Then followed the famous and most frequently depicted scene of the story; Psyche lights her lamp and the illumination of Cupid is her own enlightenment (fig. 235). However, her new-found

knowledge initially accomplishes what her ignorance had promised; Cupid departs, leaving her violated and suicidal. Nymphs effected a timely rescue and having been saved from drowning in the fifth scene, Psyche is then delivered into the care of shepherds. Psyche's sojourn in Arcadia (fig. 234) was an episode in the Apuleian myth considerably elaborated by La Fontaine in his highly successful version of the tale, the likely source for Natoire's scheme. Like the poet, the painter depicted a peaceable interlude furnished with a goat, sheep and appropriate pastoral activities (a shepherdess holds a distaff, while by her side lies evidence of basket-making) but devoid of dramatic action to move the story along. The unwarranted attention accorded to this scene by both La Fontaine and Natoire suggests that pastoralism held a specific and more important significance for their audience, and that in Arcadia were to be found the moral codes that would ultimately lead to the successful resolution of this contest of wills. The theme of romantic love in Arcadia stood for the values of mutual trust and fidelity invested in an ideal of traditional, pre-mercantile society, where the absence of competition in human relation-

230 Jacques Verberckt (attributed to), cartouche with the Rape of Europa, detail from the panelling of the Chambre de la Princesse, *c*.1737. Hôtel de Soubise, Paris.

231 Jacques Verberckt (attributed to), cartouche with Mercury and Argus, detail from the panelling of the Chambre de la Princesse, *c*.1737. Hôtel de Soubise, Paris.

232   Salon de la Princesse, *c*.1737–8. Hôtel de Soubise, Paris.

ships secured the transparency of intentions. It was only in such a context that Psyche could apparently hope to sunder the chain reaction of conquest and inconstancy implied by Cupid's behaviour.[150] Thenceforth, Psyche, insensible with fright, was, in the penultimate scene, brought before Venus, at which point a repentant Cupid appeals for the goddess's clemency and blessing[151] and, once secured, Psyche is raised up at last to Olympus in the arms of her beloved.

The vigour of the myth and the root of its outstanding popularity as a subject for decorative painting in the first half of the eighteenth century stemmed perhaps from its narrative and moral symmetry. Ovid's *Metamorphoses* offered tales of disguised conquest and transfigurative deliverance but no instances of resolution to the prolix sexual power-games of gods and mortals. Psyche, from the moment she entered the palace of Love, relinquished all possibility of evading subjugation. Unaware of Cupid's intent, she could not in the manner of Syrinx – depicted for instance by De Troy[152] – adopt a disguise capable of defeating her suitor's advances. The element of surprise won Cupid the first round, and Psyche had

to find other means of retrieving a measure of control, a step that exceeded the narrative scope of the Ovidian tales. A further significant factor of the myth was Psyche's aim to achieve reciprocity. Unlike the seventeenth-century *précieuse* heroine Omphale – also memorably depicted in the eighteenth century by Le Moyne and Boucher[153] – Psyche did not overturn the dominion of male subjectivity, thereby debasing and ridiculing the hero, but sought merely to equal Cupid's ability to fashion history. What the story of Cupid and Psyche seemed to question was not the authenticity of chauvinist perceptions of history,[154] but the necessity or even desirability of authority centralised in the hands of a single individual. The political implications of such an interpretation are tantalising indeed, particularly given the divinity of Cupid and the humanity of Psyche, perhaps a last, fading echo of a desired relationship between monarch and citizenry disallowed by divine right.[155] In any event, the story undoubtedly implied that the pursuit of self-interest was not invariably at the cost of the prosperity of others but could, in fact, accomplish a balance of individual needs from which would emerge a superior universal inter-

233 Charles-Joseph Natoire, *Psyche Showing her Gifts to her Sisters*, 1738. Oil on canvas, 162 × 318 cm. Hôtel de Soubise, Paris.

234 Charles-Joseph Natoire, *Psyche in Arcadia*, 1738. Oil on canvas, 162 × 318 cm. Hôtel de Soubise, Paris.

235   Charles-Joseph Natoire, *Cupid and Psyche*, 1738. Oil on canvas, 172 × 260 cm. Hôtel de Soubise, Paris.

est.[156] From an obscure and dishonourable affair, Psyche, once she asserted her own interests, acceded to a heavenly marriage.

The decoration of the *salon* at the hôtel de Soubise was remarkable in a number of ways, not least for the sustained elaboration it offered of a single legend. The narrative unfolded in a measured sequence of easily intelligible forms, suggesting that, like a history, there was a lesson to be drawn. Although the decoration of drawing-rooms and *cabinets* more commonly sported synoptic depictions of coupled joys, in themselves scarcely suggestive of action – never mind instruction – the Psyche cycle seems to indicate that beneath these

seemingly hackneyed and frivolous rehearsals of divine passion lies a more complex articulation of social and political concerns. The crisis of the last years of Louis XIV's reign had compromised the verisimilitude of history – that is, its claim to a higher truth – and cut loose mythology from its mooring at the centre of royal apotheosis. Prey to the manipulations of a noble and *mondain* society determined to regain lost political ground, myth became a vehicle both for exposing the underside of the *raison d'état* and for exploring the nature of influence alive in a court society.

Veuë et Perspective de la Place de Louis le Grand
Fait par Aveline sur le Petit Pont

236   Pierre Aveline, view of the place Vendôme, *c.*1700. Etching.

9

Counterfeit Culture on the Right Bank

FINANCIERS AND THE FAUBOURG SAINT-HONORÉ

One of the widely repeated complaints of Louis XIV's reign was that the brilliance of his splendour not only eclipsed the glory of every other estate in the realm, but that it reduced all members of society to a common and equal obscurity.[1] Given the acknowledged social function of decoration it is easy to understand why the nobility should have been eager to take revenge for this real or supposed humiliation in the very interiors of their mansions by endeavouring simultaneously to set itself apart from the royal court above and from the host of new men below, deliberately multiplied by Louis XIV's increasingly desperate fiscal policies.[2] A measure of the political antagonism that was long to sustain this cultural ambition may perhaps be gauged from the snatches of verse that circulated about the streets of Paris in the wake of the 1699 unveiling of François Girardon's bronze equestrian statue of the king[3] in the yet to be built place Louis-le-Grand:

> A la Place Royale on a placé ton père,
> Parmi les gens de qualité,
> On voit sur le Pont-Neuf ton aïeul débonnaire
> Près du peuple qui font l'objet de sa bonté,
> Pour toi des partisans le prince tutélaire
> A la Place Vendôme entre eux on t'a placé,[4]

The most striking aspect of this comparison of the three Bourbon monarchs from which Louis XIV emerged so unfavourably, is that judgement was meted out by allusion to the distinct urban and social morphologies in which political culture had seemingly and variously taken shape. The seventeenth-century place Royale, or des Vosges – 'où n'habite / Que mainte personnes d'élite'[5] – had, by the early eighteenth century, been matched by a competing sphere of influence (if not prestige) in the shape of the place Louis-le-Grand, or Vendôme. Indeed, though originally conceived as a vast public forum behind the noble façades of which would have prospered the royal library, the academies and other such public bodies,[6] difficulties at the exchequer caused by the escalating costs of the Spanish war had forced the king to abandon the project

and elicit instead from Hardouin Mansart a second, more modest plan for an octagonal square, and one, as the verses accused, enclosed on all sides by the private residences of the merely wealthy.[7] So deep, in fact, was the depression of the 1690s and early 1700s that only gradually were plots bought and houses built – the first, finished in 1702–3, belonged to Antoine Crozat, 'le riche' and was erected to the plans of Pierre Bullet.[8] Despite the slow start, however, the place Vendôme and the immediate neighbourhoods of Saint-Honoré, the Palais Royal and Montmartre emerged soon enough as the centre of financier high society to challenge the gilded enclave the nobility had simultaneously been developing on the opposite bank of the Seine.

Perhaps because of the imposed uniformity of Hardouin Mansart's façades (fig. 236), contemporaries were apt more readily to comment on the character of the interiors. It was in them that Germain Brice, for one, discovered a proliferating 'counterfeit' culture – one so-called because the third estate allegedly sought no more than to replicate the taste of *grands seigneurs*.[9] Description thus inclined towards generalisation – Crozat's mansion was noted for the quantity and variety of its richly decorated rooms,[10] those of Amboise Besnier and Nicolas Jérôme Herlaut for their *commodités* and highly fashionable charms.[11] However, thanks to surviving documents and drawings and one anonymous pamphlet, the house of the infamous Paul Poisson de Bourvallais emerges rather more distinctly. The provincial son and grandson of notaries from Laval, Bourvallais had early moved to Paris where, with the protection of chancellor Pontchartrain, he had quickly amassed a fortune, thanks primarily to lucrative army contracts. In 1706, at the height of his influence, this 'seigneur de nouvelle fabrique' left apparently mournful accommodation in the rue des Petits-Champs[12] for more triumphant apartments in a house at the centre of the west side of the square. Built originally for the tax-farmer Alexandre Lhuillier by Jean-Baptiste Bullet de Chamblain, it may be assumed to have been decoratively more or less complete when Bourvallais purchased it, since included in the sale were mirrors, paintings and the panelling into which they were set.[13] That Bourvallais nevertheless chose to improve upon the original is suggested by Brice's description of the property in successive editions of his Paris guide-book and by the evidence among the owner's papers of outstanding debts to various decorative artists.[14] Moreover, according to the pamphlet entitled *Médailles sur la Régence* (1716) the decoration of the rooms was not only 'magnificent' but the furnishings 'superb'.

> They are changed with every season. The tapestries are of velvet or woven in high-warp and highlighted in gold and silver. There are *canapés* upholstered in *petits-points* . . . and embroidered beds, mirrors of the largest size; [and] an amazing variety of clocks, console-tables, statues and miniatures: in short everything is so splendid and tasteful that those who have seen inside readily agree that it has no equal in Paris.[15]

By contrast with descriptions of such extravagance, liberally peppered with superlatives, the drawings that may tentatively be attributed to this redecoration – an elevation for a room on the ground floor (fig. 237) and a pier-glass design for the *grande chambre* (fig. 238) – seem remarkable for their sobriety and attachment to the formal prejudices of the seventeenth century. Only the shell motif lends a minor note of modernity to an otherwise cautious ensemble.

Closer attention to the nuances of contemporary comment suggests that the acknowledged novelty of bourgeois upward social mobility was rarely thought to have been matched by

238 (right) Jean-Baptiste Bullet de Chambelain, design for a pier-glass for the hôtel de Bourvalais, *c.*1706–9. Nationalmuseum, Stockholm.

237 Jean-Baptiste Bullet de Chambelain, design for panelling for the hôtel de Bourvalais, *c.*1706–9. Nationalmuseum, Stockholm.

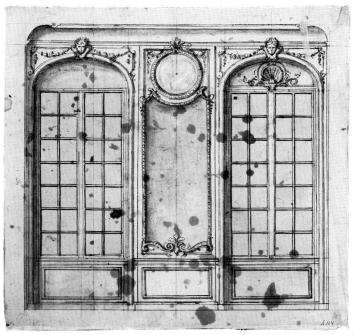

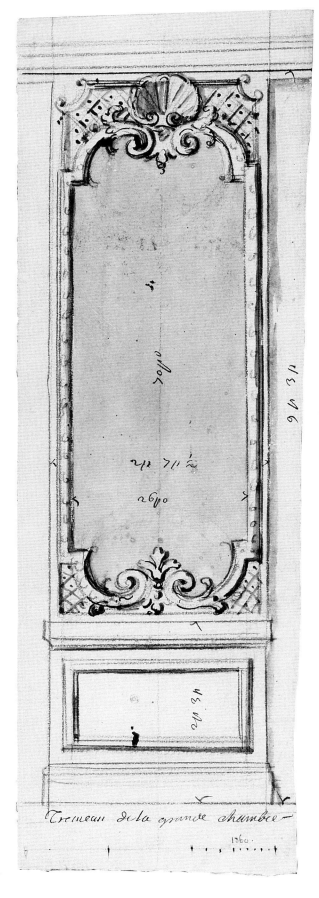

214

cultural innovation, but was perceived instead as merely passively reflected in the accumulation of a multitude of things.[16] Bourvallais, for instance, brought with him to the place Vendôme a collection of some seventy-five paintings which were displayed in five contiguous rooms on the ground floor.[17] This balanced selection of Italian, Netherlandish and French masters initially stunned the author of the *Médailles sur la Régence* by its sheer number of Raphaels, Rubenses and Poussins, and by the bronzes, alabaster vases, Chinese commodes, Far Eastern porcelain, crystal and engraved gems that accompanied them.[18] The naming of names and the listing of things in such accounts echoed the apparently obsessive determination of new men to grasp the full encyclopaedic range of noble cultural signs. Moreover, it is clear from a brief survey of the commissions of Bourvallais's *semblables* that financiers generally selected the same authors in design, wood-sculpture and painting as the nobility. In 1714, Oppenord, the regent's official architect, had redesigned the interiors of the hôtel de Pomponne for the receiver-general, Michel Bonnier (fig. 240),[19] and five years later decorated a new *salon* at the hôtel d'Assy for the tax-farmer Jean-François Masson.[20] Likewise, Nicolas Pineau, creator in the 1730s of the *salons* at the hôtels de Villars and de Mazarin, in the 1740s decorated with lavish trophies (fig. 239) Etienne Bouret's famous hunting lodge at Croix Fontaine.[21] Moreover, for another tax-farmer, d'Augny, he created a *salon* complete with overdoors by Huilliot, Pierre, Le Lorrain and Boucher.[22]

240 (right)   Gilles-Marie Oppenord, designs for chimney-mantles for the hôtel de Pomponne, *c*.1714. Pen and brown and black ink, and black chalk, 76.6 × 27.5 cm. Cooper-Hewitt, National Design Museum, New York.

239   Nicolas Pineau, design for a hunting trophy for the hunting lodge at Croix Fontaine, *c*.1745. Pen and ink on paper, 18 × 23 cm. Musée des Arts Décoratifs, Paris.

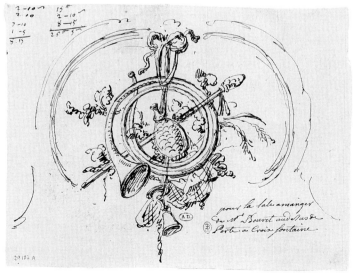

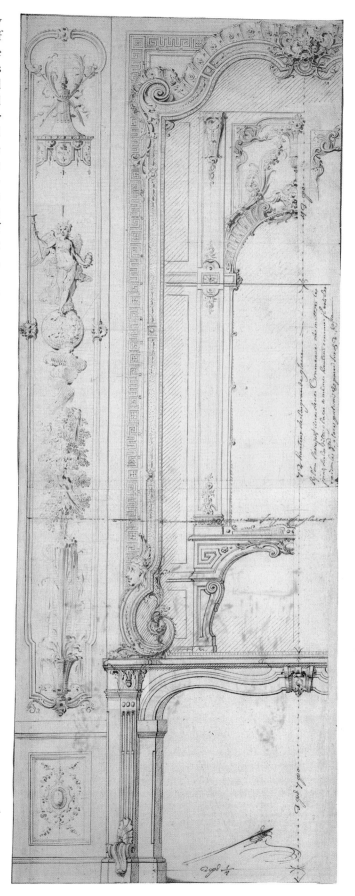

Pineau, Le Lorrain and Boucher also contributed to the embellishment of the hôtel Castanier,[23] the show-case of the Directeur de la Compagnie des Indes in the rue des Capucines. Indeed, Boucher proffered his services to distinguished aristocrats and wealthy money-mongers with equal liberality; from the prince de Soubise[24] and the ducs de Penthièvre[25] and de Richelieu[26] to d'Augny and one of Crozat's heirs, Crozat de Tugny.[27]

Natoire's clients similarly ranged from the *haute noblesse* – to the Psyche series for Soubise can be added overdoors for the ducal hôtels of d'Antin,[28] Mazarin[29] and Montmorency-Luxembourg[30] – to tax-farmers, notably Marin de La Haye[31] and to financiers such as Grimod du Fort, for whom he provided not only overdoors but the tapestry series, *The Adventures of Don Quixote* (1735–44), which decorated the château d'Orsay.[32] Moreover, not only did financiers court the signatures of the most renowned painters, sculptors and architects for the decoration of their houses, they also showed a predisposition to favour the same types of things as the nobility. Thus, *mythologies galantes* demonstrably appealed not only to the prince de Carignan[33] but also to Samuel Bernard,[34] Peyrenc de Moras[35] and Michel Ollivier de Senozan.[36] Pastorals by Natoire found a place at the hôtel de Lambert[37] just as ones by Boucher had at the hôtel de Berighen;[38] and the taste for chinoiserie, oriental lacquer and Chinese porcelain seduced the financier Jean Thévenin,[39] the contrôleur-général Bertin[40] and the tax-farmer François de Beaumont,[41] just as they had the residents of the faubourg Saint-Germain. These examples would therefore seem to confirm the view according to which new cultural forms are always imposed downwards through the social structure and thus, notwithstanding the innovative economic initiatives by which new men rose into the lower echelons of the second estate, that social gains were and are invariably articulated mimetically.

However, it was perhaps the very slavishness of these imitations that, in the opinion of some, brought about a subtle alteration to the original. The fetish for noble things, for the multiple signs of aristocratic cultural practices, seemingly transformed those same practices into commodities. For example, the right to hunt was a highly prized privilege of nobility; it belonged exclusively to *seigneurs hautes justiciers*[42] and the royal hunt provided the occasion at which gentlemen were formally presented to the king for the first time.[43] A more fitting reference to the titles of ancient feudal *noblesse*, conferred by the *seigneurie* – never mind that for financiers it was purchased not entailed – would have been hard to find; and depictions of game evoked that aura of seigneurial justice that still clung to the ownership of land despite the extensive erosion of the feudal system by money substitutes for dues and the free salability of fiefs.[44] Now, if recent and would-be nobles were apparently reluctant sportsmen,[45] always assuming they had the exacting credentials for so being, they were certainly not so reticent in their appetites for representations of the fruits of the hunt. For instance, Oppenord's panelling for the

Bonnier residence in the place des Victoires (sections of which survive, along with Oppenord's drawings) sported at the centre of the main fields, large, naturalistic standing trophies (fig. 241), which combined instruments of the chase elegantly suspended from trees with the dead victims of their aim and furred and feathered agents of pursuit. The affinity between Oppenord's compositions and the work of contemporary animal painters, particularly François Desportes, is abundantly clear, and it is surely appropriate that the painter as well as the architect became favourites in financial circles. Bankers, in particular, seem to have had a weakness for Desportes's talents; in the pavilion of Samuel Bernard's château de Coubert-en-Brie no less than thirteen pictures of game of various shapes and sizes, possibly his, were inset into panelling.[46] With greater certainty moreover, we may count the bankers Hogguer,[47] the Pâris de la Montagne, Duvernay and de Montmartel[48] and the Contrôleur-Général des Finances Nicolas Desmarets among Desportes's most enthusiastic patrons.[49] Likewise, Desportes's long-term successor, Jean-Baptiste Oudry, found little difficulty catering to princes of the blood, like the duc de Bourbon,[50] the old nobility such as

241 Panelling from the dining-room, formerly from the hôtel de Pomponne, *c.*1714. Musée des Arts Décoratifs, Paris.

242 Jean-Baptiste Oudry, *Still Life*, 1742. Oil on canvas, 227 ×
151 cm. Palais de Rohan, Strasbourg.

dependents. It was thus a constituent of feudal *largesse*. Moreover, so long as the practice of hunting remained bound to
notions of justice, the depiction of the bounty of the chase
invariably tended to dominate views of pursuit, such that only
when hunting vacated its place in a judicial system to take up
a new position amongst rights of property did the sportsman
finally appear on the horizon chasing over those acres of land
upon which his privilege then depended.[56] However, before
this emancipation of hunting, those whose economic values
were often demonstrably opposed to the survival of feudal
interests were, as we have seen, nevertheless fascinated by
depictions of one of feudalism's most ancient customs. Perhaps
for them a still life with game did not readily conjure up the
nexus of reciprocal obligations and material relations constitutive of the sport, but existed instead as an object of inherent
aesthetic and social power, the possession of which linked
them indisputably to an anonymous market of other noble
consumers. Moreover, the satisfying community of taste
thereby implicitly achieved obscured the fact that as the
material culture of the nobility stole downwards through the
social hierarchy it suffered a progressive disintegration of its
discursive structure. Jacques-Samuel Bernard's *Still Life* may
be used as a metaphor for this process since the attributes of
the arts therein (albeit literary, sculptural and musical ones)
draw attention to the formal qualities of the things depicted,
to such an extent indeed, that the feudal relations potentially
connoted by the dogs and game-bird in the foreground are
silently and effectively concealed beneath a glowing surface of
imitation.

Irrespective of how illusory the integrative function of taste
may actually have been, the arts were clearly perceived as
socially redemptive, that is to say, as capable of refining the
vulgar and delivering them up into high society. Appropriately enough, therefore, the theme of the arts and sciences
enjoyed marked popularity in interior decoration, notably it
seems, with those eager to provide tangible evidence of cultural merit to help cushion the response to their rising social
status. Of particular importance was the interior conceived,
planned and overseen by Charles Perrault and known as the
Cabinet des Beaux-Arts,[57] a scheme which, though not long to
survive (the building in which it was housed having to make
way in 1685 for the development of the place des Victoires),
owed its lasting influence to its publication in 1690 as a series
of prints with accompanying text.[58]

The ceiling (fig. 243) consisted of eleven compositions, each
the work of a different painter, set into a sculpted framework.
The centre was occupied by three canvases: *Apollo
and the Muses* by Charles de La Fosse, with Jean-Baptiste
Corneille's *Mercury* and Louis de Boullogne's *Minerva* to either
side. Distributed around the periphery, meanwhile, were eight
oval allegories of the Arts and Sciences,[59] anchored at the
corners by three-dimensional *genii* and interspersed with
sphinxes which, according to Perrault's text, signified that the
arts 'do not reveal their secrets to everyone'.[60] The iconography

Beringhen[51] and also to comparative newcomers like Louis
Fagon,[52] Rouillé[53] and Jacques-Samuel Bernard,[54] for whom,
in 1742, he painted a pair of large dining-room pictures, the
one depicting a dog chasing duck across water, while the other
(fig. 242) more unusually combined evidence of the hunt with
the peaceable attributes of the arts.

It may seem odd, since hunting connoted nobility so
plainly, that depictions of the sport itself were rare.[55] The
explanations generally forwarded for the preference for depictions of the fruits of the hunt rather than the actions of the
chase, cite the powerful grip of the Dutch and Flemish
traditions. However, while such traditions may have been a
contributing factor they do not adequately account for the
restricted and almost iconic treatement of venery subjects.
Additionally, one might take note of the nature of the hunting
privilege: to hunt was a right of justice which expressed the
lord's duty and power to provide for his vassals and other

217

of the decoration thus specifically drew attention to the exclusivity of high culture, one made more partisan by the intellectually complex symbolism of the personified arts and by the designation of the space as a *cabinet*. Moreover, after a short digression on the nature of art, Perrault announced that his sole criterion in selecting his eight Muses had been to indulge a personal preference within the parameters of those arts worthy of being loved and cultivated by that rare and exacting creature, the *honnête homme*.[61] However, if certain aspects of the scheme indeed operated to exclude the uniniti-

243 Jean Dolivart after Charles Perrault, *Ceiling of the Cabinet des Beaux-Arts*, 1690. Etching.

ated on the grounds of aesthetic and intellectual incompetence, others, combined with Perrault's own remarks, may have proffered some much needed encouragement to bourgeois cultural pretenders. First, the published explanation of the scheme was dedicated to Louis Boucherat, the Chancelier de France, not himself of conspicuously noble extraction; moreover, the dedicatory epistle made much of the judicious role played by the arts in balancing the onerous burdens of public duty with profitable moments of retirement,[62] suggesting it would seem that the arts far from being the exclusive province of the leisured class were properly accessible to office-holders of all kinds, financiers no less than ministers or magistrates. Second, the scheme was conceived as a tribute to the achievements of its own century, not from any lack of respect or admiration for the ancients but out of the conviction that the modern era had equalled if not surpassed the ages of Alexander and Augustus.[63] In the broadest sense this implied that for society as for culture change and innovation even in the social structure were not only acceptable but possibly even desirable. More specifically, modernity ostensibly demanded much less of its spectators in the way of connoisseurship and erudition, thereby opening out this refined *cabinet* into a wider forum where the *nouveaux riches* as well as the *anciens nés* might comfortably find a place. In short, Perrault's Cabinet des Beaux-Arts seemed to create a cultural space for newcomers, both collectively and individually.

The discreet, even unwitting, invitation to commoners to take up a place in polite society was accepted in full measure some twenty years later by Pierre Crozat, Antoine's younger and only slightly less wealthy brother, who moved to a mansion built for him by Jean-Sylvain Cartaud on the rue de Richelieu in 1704,[64] and proceeded to inaugurate what

244 Gérard Audran after Claude II Audran, *Painting*, 1690. Etching.

emerged as arguably the most influential cultural circle of the early eighteenth century.[65] The task of decorating the ceiling of the first-floor gallery, the mansion's most important reception room, was entrusted yet again to La Fosse.[66] Moreover, the

245   Charles de La Fosse, *The Birth of Minerva*, *c.*1704–7. Oil on canvas, 77 × 95 cm. Musée des Arts Décoratifs, Paris.

continuity with the Cabinet des Beaux-Arts did not end there, inasmuch as the fresco composition that La Fosse completed in approximately three years similarly broached the theme of the arts and sciences. There were, however, also notable differences between the two schemes. If Perrault had allowed personal whim to play some part in devising his ceiling, ultimately, the *cabinet* served to proclaim not his taste but the triumphant patronage of Louis XIV. Not only did La Fosse's Apollo preside majestically over the programme unfolding around him, but in *Painting* (fig. 244), for instance, the artist was shown working on an allegory in which a garden bloomed in the heat of a benevolent sun while the legend announced 'I make all things prosper'.[67] The reference to king and kingdom would have been impossible to miss. By contrast, Crozat selected as his household deity not Apollo but Minerva. Though the visual and documentary evidence is sadly insufficient to reconstruct with exactitude the appearance of the entire ceil-

ing (destroyed along with the building at the end of the eighteenth century) it seems likely that it consisted of a number of curved *quadri riportati* illustrating Minerva's succour of the wide province of human knowledge – from the painstaking architectural education she handed down to Daedalus (fig. 247) to her personal encouragement of the Muses – arranged around a central *percée* (fig. 245) depicting the goddess's birth. Lastly, further drawings in Stockholm suggest that at least two of the doors leading out of the gallery were crowned by putti brandishing attributes of the arts and sciences (figs 246, 248) painted, perhaps, in *trompe l'œil*.

Minerva, as presented by Perrault among others, was probably the ideal composite personification of the arts.[68] Where Apollo merely invoked inspiration and Mercury simply connoted labour, Minerva combined the capacities of both and assisted in encouraging the idea that fine art resided in the perfect co-ordination of hand and mind such that the former

219

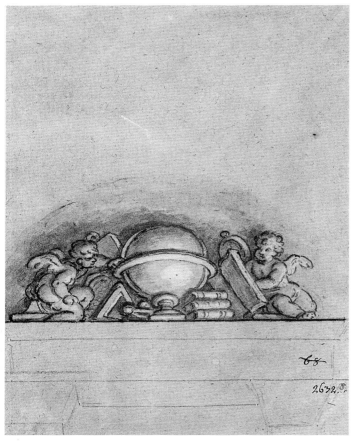

246 and 248 (above left and right) Charles de La Fosse, *Cupids with the Attributes of the Sciences* and *Cupids with the Attributes of the Arts*, designs for overdoors for the gallery at the hôtel Crozat, *c*.1704–7. Black and red chalk heightened with white on brown paper, 20.4 × 15.5 cm (fig. 247) and black chalk, pen and brown ink, brown wash on brown paper, 22.4 × 15.6 cm (fig. 248). Nationalmuseum, Stockholm.

247 (left) Charles de la Fosse, *Minerva Teaching Daedalus the Art of Architecture*, design for the ceiling of the gallery at the hôtel Crozat, *c*.1704–7. Black and red chalk, pen and brown ink, brown wash, heightened with white on brown paper; squared with red chalk, 22.2 × 17.2 cm. Nationalmuseum, Stockholm.

was always guided by the latter. For reasons of gender alone, patrons such as Crozat could scarcely hope to identify themselves with the daughter of Jupiter in the manner that princes had habitually likened themselves to Apollo. However, since Minerva was equipped better than most to personify the theoretical superiority of the fine over the mechanical arts, patrons who, in enlightened self-interest, showed her allegiance promoted at least indirectly their own social and cultural advancement. Further down the rue de Richelieu a likeminded Michel-Ollivier de Senozan, treasurer to the French clergy, therefore included as part of the refurbishment of the hôtel de Jars after 1715,[69] the creation of a Cabinet des Muses,

249 Nicolas Coypel, *Music*, *c*.1715. Pen, ink and wash on paper. Cabinet d'Estampes, Bibliothèque Nationale, Paris.

into the panelling of which were fitted six decorative paintings depicting 'Minerva and the Arts', a trace of which is possibly to be found in two drawings by Noël-Nicolas Coypel in the Bibliothèque Nationale, one representing *Music* (fig. 249) and the other *Medicine*.[70] Meanwhile, towards the end of the same decade François-Christophe de La Live commissioned thirty-five paintings from Jean-François De Troy to decorate his house in the rue du Luxembourg, of which an indeterminate number depicted the various skills of the Muses and which Jean-Luc Bordeaux has provisionally associated with an *Allegory of Poetry* (fig. 250) and an *Allegory of Painting* (fig. 251).[71]

Like Perrault, Senozan and La Live confined Minerva's empire to the *cabinet*, a comparatively modest social space traditionally reserved for business or the reception of friends and acquaintances. Crozat, on the other hand, had opted for a much more ample and public expression of cultural purpose in a gallery. Moreover, attention to the orientation and possible function of the gallery suggest artistic ambitions that extended well beyond the timid imitation of a noble way of life. Unlike the hôtels de Toulouse and de Villars, for instance, where the gallery projected into the garden at right angles to the *corps-de-logis*, Cartaud chose to position Crozat's gallery along the full width of the garden façade (fig. 252) in a manner conspicuously similar to the distribution of the Grande Galerie at Versailles. It was there too that Crozat came to hang some of the most distinguished works in his possession, masterpieces primarily from the Italian and Flemish schools such as a Veronese *Adoration of the Magi* (The Hermitage, St Petersburg) and Rubens's *Portrait of Isabella Brandt* (National

Gallery, Washington, D.C.) – pictures to compare favourably with the best of the royal and Orléans collections similarly displayed under painted skies in the *grands appartements* at Versailles and the Palais Royal.[72] If Crozat hoped parallels would be made, he intended they should be with princely and not merely noble collections, as was further demonstrated by the selection of sixty-five of his own works to be engraved alongside those of the king and the duc d'Orléans in the first volume of the *Receuil d'estampes d'après les plus beaux tableaux et d'après les plus belles desseins qui sont en France* (1729).[73]

Moreover, that Crozat envisaged his interventions in the contemporary art scene as amounting to more than the obliging actions of a social newcomer is suggested by the learned social intercourse roundly encouraged at the Maison Crozat. In 1708, shortly after the gallery was completed, Crozat extended protection and financial support to the art theorist Roger de Piles, thus inaugurating an aesthetic dialogue that later, during the Regency and early minority of Louis XV, evolved into the wider and more formal weekly gathering that brought together artists such as Watteau, Nicolas Vleughels and Pierre Legros, and amateurs and connoisseurs like Jean-Pierre Mariette, Jean de Jullienne, the comte de Caylus and Louis Petit de Bachaumont. Mariette's description of these occasions, at which the judgement and taste of those participating was refined by critical discussion of selected items in Crozat's collection, strongly and self-consciously evokes the *conférences* of the seventeenth-century Académie Royale at which 'the works of the great masters'

250 Jean-François De Troy, *Allegory of Poetry*, 1733. Oil on canvas, 100 × 93 cm. Location unknown.

221

251   Jean-François De Troy, *Allegory of Painting*, 1733. Oil on canvas, 88 × 109 cm. Location unknown.

had similarly stood as the focus for aesthetic debate by a society of '*nobles gens*', that is men noble not by birth (*gens nobles*), but by their vocation to and taste for the arts.[74] Crozat's mansion, therefore, did more than house a remarkable collection in magnificent rooms, it also offered itself as an academy, as a place of artistic formation at a time when the state was politically and financially least able to do its cultural duty. By implication, the Maison Crozat became the locus of the arts in exile, and it was a country only relinquished to the Louvre in the 1730s sometime after the peaceful succession of new regime.[75] Pierre Crozat, it seems, readily accepted the value the nobility had long attributed to high culture, but where for nobles it tended to be a value only implicitly realised in practice, art was transformed by Crozat, via the decoration of his house, his collections, his *réunions* and the text of the *Receuil*[76] into a discourse rationally and explicitly formulated and then promulgated abroad.

The inarticulate mystique of noble cultural distinction was thereby seriously threatened by an apparently bourgeois enlightenment.

LUXURY AND LAW'S SYSTEM

How did those of rank and title perceive and respond to this emulation of their taste by those whom they continued to regard as *roturiers* even after ennoblement? The answer is not entirely straightforward. For although the nobility might have responded to mimicry as to a challenge to their social superiority, they might equally have interpreted it (as in fact contemporary etiquette books suggested they should) as a sign of respect – as an expression of the willingness of inferiors to bridle their personal desires and preferences and submit to the wisdom of acknowledged superiors.[77] Indeed, since the begin-

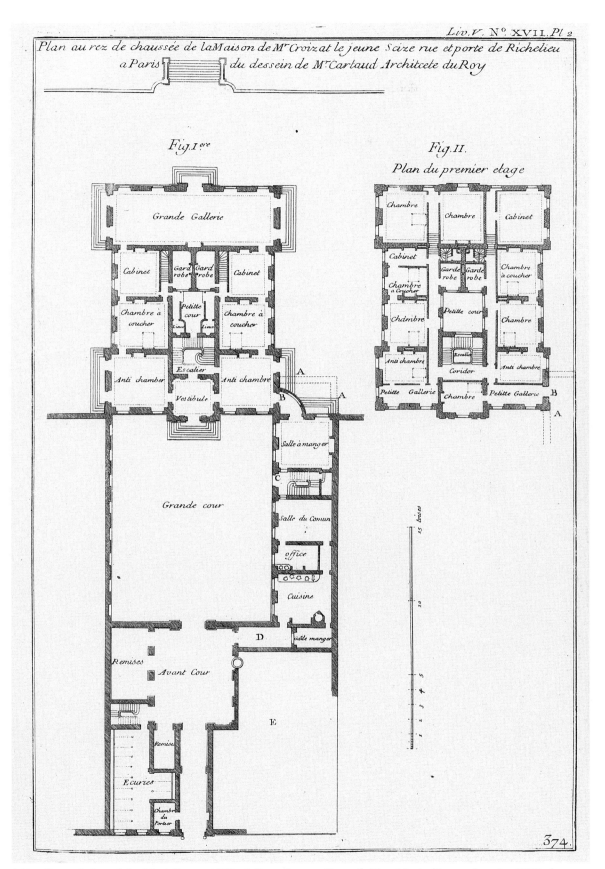

Plan au rez de chaussée de la Maison de Mr Croizat le jeune Scize rue et porte de Richelieu a Paris du dessein de Mr Cartaud Architcete du Roy

Fig.Iere

Grande Gallerie

Cabinet — Gard robe — Gard robe — Cabinet

Chambre à coucher — Petitte cour — chambre à coucher — Lieu — Lieu

Anti chambre — Escalier — Anti chambré

Vestibule

A
B
A

Salle à manger

C

Salle du Comun

office

Cuisine

Grande cour

salle manger

D

Remises

Avant Cour

E

Remises

Escuries

Chambre du Portier

Fig.II.
Plan du premier etage

Chambre — Chambre — Cabinet

Cabinet — Garde robe — Garde robe — Chambre à coucher

Chambre à coucher — Petitte cour — Chambre

Chambre — Escalier

Anti chambre — Coridor — Anti chambre

Petitte Gallerie — Chambre — Petitte Gallerie

B
A

374

252   Ground-plan of the hôtel Crozat, 1752–6. From Jacques-François Blondel, *Architecture françoise*, 1752–6.

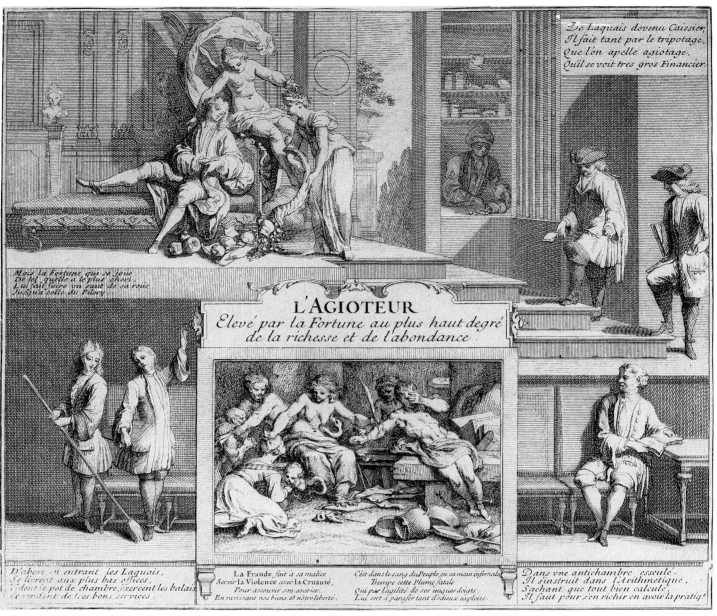

253 Claude Gillot, *The Speculator Raised by Fortune to the Greatest Heights of Wealth and Prosperity*, c.1720. Etching.

ning of the seventeenth century *précieux* circles had frequently operated as centres of acculturation for commoners and *annoblis* without apparently producing excessive unease amongst the nobility.[78] On the other hand, since criticism of upward social mobility invariably implied criticism of the *régime* that sanctioned or encouraged it, contemporary response to luxury – or the illegitimate acquisition of the signs and symbols of superior rank – would of necessity have been circumspect. Thus, as the eighteenth century dawned, the phenomenon of a rising third estate was still primarily acknowledged and articulated in terms of seemingly anomalous individual careers. In *The Speculator Raised by Fortune to the Greatest Heights of Wealth and Prosperity* (fig. 254), for

instance, Gillot described the long familiar trajectory of the *laquais-financier* who, with the help of Fraud, Violence and Cruelty plus a few basic rules of arithmetic, had made his way up from the hurly-burly of the antechamber to the deep ease of the *salon*.[79]

However, though fictional characters such as Messieurs Jourdan and Turcaret persisted as objects of fashionable derision,[80] from the 1690s there issued from the circle of the duc de Bourgogne a wider and more incisive response to the question of luxury than the conventions of personal satire had previously allowed. According to Fénelon, Beauvilliers and Chevreuse and later Saint-Simon and Boulainvilliers, *parvenus* were not isolated social aberrations but the necessary by-

224

254 Gillot, detail of fig. 253.

product of financial practices in which the king and bourgeoisie had colluded in order that the first might concentrate his power and finance the national debt and the second purchase privileges from which it was judicially debarred.[81] From such a perspective, luxury amounted to a deliberate assault on the social and political prerogatives of the nobility, and its critique was thus firmly anchored in the motives and interests of an increasingly radicalised second estate. It is therefore no surprise to discover among the reforms outlined by Fénelon and Chevreuse for implementation by a de Bourgogne government in the *Tables de Chaulnes* (1711), measures designed not only to maintain the semblance of an immaculate estates hierarchy (for example a proscription of misalliances, a prohibition on *roturiers* in possession of noble land from enjoying its titles and, of course, the implementation of the sumptuary laws to the very letter), but others (such as the abolition of venality and the positive reservation of offices in the king's household and armed services for gentlemen) that aimed at structurally sealing off the élite from all common adventurers.[82] In effect, noble ideology took up residence in the denunciation of luxury, refashioning the terms of moral indictment that had traditionally served the ancients and the church in order to articulate its own specific resistance to the gathering authority of market economics.[83] That luxury offered a lasting linguistic context within which a discontented nobility might make sense of its own predicament and imagine political solutions to its declining status, is attested by the aristocratic initiatives formulated at the *salon* of the duc de Noailles after de Bourgogne's death, most notably by Saint-Simon and Boullainvilliers and later still by the marquis d'Argenson and others at the Club de l'Entresol and the *salon* of Mme Fontaine-Martel.[84]

In view of the wide currency of the conspiracy theory that held king and financiers jointly responsible for luxury, the convocation within the first year of the Regency of a Chambre de Justice to search out the sources of 'fraud and abuse . . . illicit profiteering and usury', and force public restitutions by the meeting out of 'capital, corporal and pecuniary penalties' to the guilty, aroused much public interest.[85] During the year the chamber was in session it investigated the personal fortunes and business transactions of no less than 8,000 financiers, 4,410 of whom were subsequently fined a total of 219,500,000 *livres*.[86] Prominent among the impeached were Antoine Crozat and Paul Poisson de Bourvallais, one if not both of whom were the focus of satirical *libelles* published in the same year.[87] Indeed, the author of a Bourvallais satire discovered in his subject's imaginary *cabinet* a picture that perfectly foretold the moment which had come to pass. The apocryphal story of *Tobias and the Angel* painted by one 'Nicolas Poussin'[88] was in reality, it seems, a *roman-à-clef* in which the part of the young Tobias, walking the commercial road to Media, was played by the boy Louis XV, the part of Raphael the healer by the regent and, of course, the role of the 'poisson' by none other than its namesake. Thus, the arch-

angel's advice to his young charge to burn the fish's entrails and so smoke out the evil-doers and recidivists signified the regent's sage counsel to expose Bourvallais's heart to the heat of the court-room that its secrets might dissipate at last his pernicious influence and that of his kind.[89]

By and large, however, the humour of these libellous sketches was generated by the symbiotic relationship described as typically existing between the *nouveau riche* and his spoils. Bourvallais's other alleged paintings, for instance, contained the secrets of his past (*Hagar and the Ishmael* or a mother's premonition of her Bourvallais's fame; *Susannah and the Elders*, or Suzanne Guihou with protectors de Sourches and de Pontchartrain meeting Bourvallais at the baths of Bourbon), and a catechism of the financier's moral doctrine (*The Betrayal of Christ*, or the partisan's duplicity; *The Expulsion*, or an allegory of the financier's prideful attempts to equal the status and culture of princes).[90] Similarly, in Limognon de Saint-Didier's *Le Voyage du Parnasse* (1716), the anti-hero Nasidiene, very likely a synthesised portrait of the brothers Crozat,[91] less ambiguously decorated his gallery with eight pictures painted by 'different Modern Masters' and illustrating his history in a manner clearly derived from Rubens's Medici cycle.[92] Protected from birth by Mercury (a god of theft, cunning and enterprise in this imaginary sphere and not the personification of polite commerce familiar from actual *cabinets* and galleries) Nasidiene visibly prospered, to such a point that by the fifth canvas he was shown stationed between Ceres and Abundance, reaping the benefit of army contracts, and encircled by rough and vulgar putti gorging a *déjeuner de jambon* washed down with wine from their helmets.[93] After further commercial successes on the high seas aided by Thetis and Neptune, a triumphant Nasidiene was depicted riding at last into the capital on a chariot drawn by harpies and driven by a misguided Minerva only, in the last picture, to eke out a sybaritic and would-be noble existence as a latter-day Paris in the narrow confines of his superb mansion.[94] It was precisely because financiers were allegedly individualistic rather than corporatist in their cultural ventures that they were so vulnerable to this kind of attack. They had, apparently, little or no group culture behind which to shelter.[95] Moreover, from the extraordinary detail in which these fantasies were elaborated it is possible to sense something of the intense satisfaction apparently experienced by many as the Crozats and Bourvallais were publicly and summarily stripped of the glittering symbols of ill-gotten status. Indeed, according to the author of the first pamphlet, in the spring of 1716 the late and presumably repentent Louis XIV came once more to life in Girardon's statue, indicating with accusing finger to his councils in the Louvre which of the houses in the square still harboured the fortunes of force and fraud in order that their wealth might now be redistributed to alleviate the misery of a beggared *peuple*.[96]

However, those who hoped that the regent would forthwith bring commercial markets and financial services under stricter governmental control were shortly to be disappointed. The alienation of parts of the national debt and the fining of money-mongers went only so far in making good the Sun King's legacy of an accumulated deficit of some 4 billion *livres*, one proportionately greater than the shortfall that helped topple Louis XVI towards the end of the century.[97] Captivated by the audacious economic thinking of John Law, an ambitious regent was therefore soon casting his benevolent eye over the Scotsman's establishment, in the years 1716–17, of first a bank and then the Compagnie de l'Occident at the hôtel de Nevers.[98] From that moment onwards places of speculation broke out of the particular and intimate interiors of mansions to proliferate throughout the city. The rue Quincampoix, a narrow thoroughfare running parallel to and between the rues Saint-Denis and Saint-Martin in the popular *quartier* des Halles, became the capital's first stock- and money-exchange. The *Almanach de la fortune* (1720; fig. 255) depicts a place thronged with pedestrians, sedan-chairs and carriages whose occupants' hopeful prospects were distilled in the emblematic device at the foot of the scene, which combined a central meridian sun with a cockle-encrusted crown, lyres, trumpets and anchors, the whole supported on two cornucopias disgorging coin.[99] So fully indeed were those expectations initially met that, within a few years, the rue Quincampoix could no longer contain the joyous multitude of speculators and the exchange had to be moved. Appropriately, perhaps, it was first transferred to the place Vendôme only to relocate in July 1720 to the expansive gardens of the hôtel de Soissons off the rue des Deux-Ecus.[100] The recently arrived and heavily indebted prince de Carignan was only too eager to exploit by any means this unfashionable property and to that end trees were felled, terrain cleared and, as shown in Antoine Humblot's print (fig. 256) some 150 booths, known as *petites maisons*, were built around the periphery and leased to stock-jobbers for 500 *livres* per month.[101]

Emboldened no doubt by the illusion of his System's success and by the enthusiastic patronage of not only the regent but significant factions of the court nobility,[102] in November 1719 Law commissioned Giovanni Antonio Pellegrini to cover the ceiling of the Salles des Conseils at the now royal bank with an allegory of the virtues of trade and enterprise.[103] Conceived on a scale to equal the programmes of Versailles, and deploying the venerated language of allegory, the ceiling (now lost) depicted Religion and Hero (the duc d'Orléans) supporting a portrait of Louis XV whilst around them hatched symbols and personifications of prosperity.[104] One of the more important of the secondary groups portrayed Genius with the putto Invention at his feet, leading forth Commerce and followed by Wealth, Insurance and Credit. A sketch for the first three figures (fig. 257) has recently been identified by Claire Garas; ironically it had been masquerading under the spurious title, *Tobias and the Angel*.[105] Like the practices they symbolised, many of these allegorical figures were new, devoid of familiar iconographic origin, and they were inserted moreover into a universe that was itself subtly original. The expectation has always been that allegory enshrines a moral conundrum resolved only when the forces of good triumph over evil. What was remarkable, therefore, about Pelligrini's composition was the virtual absence of cardinal virtues and their replacement by social and political ones: to the regent's right, for instance, appeared Munificence, Magnanimity and Magnificence.[106] By implication, trade, commerce and the luxury to which they occasionally gave rise, had been withdrawn from a moral sphere and introduced into a no less celestial world of economy, but one where the principles of distributive justice that had traditionally governed attitudes to wealth were completely without purchase. Virtue was now only the vestigial product of a selfish pursuit of wealth, begotten merely of the *nouveau-riche*'s equally strong compulsion to purchase civility and honour (significantly, the area above the windows in the gallery was occupied by all the Arts and Sciences) and incidentally redistributing his gains thereby. Moreover, the association of commercial society with the progress of civilisation, which by juxtaposition this ceiling seemingly made good, lent its utopian discourse a positively urbane inflection. The pastoral paradise of Genesis, *L'Astrée* or *Télémaque* preferred by the likes of Beauvillier and Chevreuse because of its simplicity and very lack of polite pleasures[107] was here abandoned for the city without a backward glance. Thus, above the door by which the gallery was entered, Pellegrini depicted a portico symbolising the stock-exchange, in front of which were assembled people of all nationalities engrossed in financial transactions, while at the far end of the gallery appeared city gates opened on to quay-sides busy with dockers loading and unloading all manner of merchandise.[108] Though it was not long to survive Law's disgrace, the ceiling thus momentarily rehearsed (but without the usual cynicism) some of the most progressive and Mandevillian economic arguments of the day and anticipated the sustained disquisitions on luxury delivered by Jean-François Melon and Voltaire in the 1730s.[109]

Before then, however, Paris had experienced a dramatic economic set-back. In October 1720 Law's System crashed. The speculation mania of the previous years had been nourished by exaggerated accounts of the natural wealth of the Mississippi basin, and when the company's trade fell short of expectations the loss of confidence triggered a collapse in equity and the paper currency it was there to support.[110] From the moment the bubble burst Dutch and French caricatures flooded the market and, besides the predictable assaults on Law himself, many broached more abstract yet topical questions, such as the nature of the relationship between reality and delusion. In *Fancy, the Ruler of the Guild of Smoke-Sellers, Paints her Mississippi which Wastes the Treasures of France* (fig. 258), for instance, we immediately recognise a reworking of Claude II Audran's *Painting* (fig. 244), and it seems likely that for the educated reader/spectator much of the satire's wit depended on a conscious comparison between the two designs.[111] Perhaps the most conspicuous change lies in the

255 Bernard, *Almanach de la fortune*, 1720. Etching.

256 Antoine Humblot, *The Hôtel de Soissons*, 1720. Engraving and etching.

painting on the easel; instead of a garden-kingdom, Painting depicts a ship of state (she flies the royal enseign on her poop) sailing towards America. The accompanying verse adds that, 'Fancy paints her Mississippi apparently beautiful, but in colours that will soon fade', thereby reinterpreting the Ripan tradition according to which Painting is dressed in garments of changing hue to signify that her secret lies in a harmonious variety[112] in such a way as to suggest that a fickle nature produces only transitory illusions. Moreover, the mirror whose reflective surface had, in Perrault's *cabinet*, furnished an analogue to pictorial representation guaranteeing its veracity,[113] in the later context stands as a corrective to Painting, revealing that which she deliberately witholds. Thus, far from promising social redemption, art emerged during the Law crash as the gay deceiver whose charms had enticed the unwitting to perdition.

It must be said, however, that few satires of Law's System addressed the political consequences of self-deception in such overtly mimetic and aesthetic terms. Though details such as pictures, mirrors and peep-shows were constant reminders of the dangers of sophistry and illusion, in subject and composition lampoons such as *A Commemorative Arch to Deceased Speculators* (1720; fig. 259) owed conspicuously more to the engraved, topographical apologies for the System than to

known easel or decorative paintings.[114] Thus, in the *Commemorative Arch* and, for instance, the *Almanach de la fortune* (fig. 255) the figures occupying the space of the narrow street or surrounding the symbolically overwrought funerary monument seem as least as important as the accompanying devices and explanatory texts. The presence of these crowds suggests that a striking feature of the System had been the unprecedented contact it had effected between traditionally insulated orders of society. And indeed, according to one contemporary observer, 'clergy from the Roman purple to the curacy of the lowliest parishes, and laity from the *cordon bleu* to the meanest shoulder strap' were readily to be seen united in speculation.[115] However, where such identity of purpose was expressed in terms of harmony in the *Almanach* (the population, the nation even, seem to be moving in a common and progressive direction[116]) thereby promoting the view that prosperity was guaranteed in commercial societies by the providential balance between the vanity of the rich and the interests of the poor, in the satire, fighting has broken out beyond the gates and to the right men and women dance with unbuttoned enthusiasm to a maddening rhythm which has finally driven a man to his death from the window of a three-storey building. Accordingly, in this second instance, we are invited to understand that the pursuit of profit creates not concord but anarchy, and that it corrupts even the best. These same years had in fact witnessed the comte de Horn's murder of a stock-jobber in the rue Quincampoix out of a fit of desperate avarice and the duc de La Force's trial before the Parlement for succumbing too indiscreetly to the lure of the retail trade, specifically in chinoiserie and Far Eastern goods.[117] Only the interring of the System as a whole could apparently reinstate order of that exemplary kind enacted in the religious and civic processions of the *ancien régime* and shown already unfolding to the left of the composition.

If Mathieu Marais rejoiced when, on 29 October 1720, the gates did finally close behind the hôtel de Soissons and the surrounding streets became, in his words, 'liberated' from brigandage, his prediction that soon 'servants would return to their masters, artisans to their tasks [and] the peasant to his labour', each one finding once more his 'natural place' in society seems a trifle naïve.[118] Assuming for a moment that tales of dramatic reversals of fortune were sensationalised and that a return to order was logically possible, Marais nevertheless chose to overlook the fact that Law's System had profoundly altered society's perception and experience of upward social mobility. For instance, in his *Mémoire présenté à Monseigneur le duc d'Orléans* (1727), Boulainvilliers inveighed against the moral depredations of the new era, 'where personal interest is the general rule; [and] where speculation in influ-

257 Giovanni Pellegrini, *Genius, Invention and Commerce*, 1719. Pen, ink and wash on paper. Musée d'Art et Archéologie, Besançon.

258 *Fancy, the Ruler of the Guild of Smoke-Sellers*, *Paints her Mississippi which Wastes the Treasures of France*, 1720. Etching.

ence and favour has become as common as speculation in money',[119] thereby inferring that a corruption of the political order had followed the perversion of its economic base. Moreover, a second generation of political writers, such as the marquis de Mirabeau and the abbé Mably, was ultimately to attribute the origins of luxury and the decline of the nobility to the Law years.[120] The discursive and ideological importance so ascribed to the events of 1716–20 stemmed first and most importantly from the fact that by replacing the obscure irrationality of the state's former financial systems by the clear economy of a single fiscal discipline, directly responsible for the collection of state revenues and the provision of government loans, Law publicly, if briefly, exposed the causal relationship between government policy and the structuring of society.[121] Thus, critics of luxury were able to move beyond the inferential logic that had them arguing from effect (luxury) to cause (absolutism) towards a diagnostic analysis that ultimately revealed opulence as the source and not the consequence of the moneyed élite's increasing political influence. Second, Law's management of the Compagnie de l'Occident and other overseas trading enterprises drew attention to the imbrecation of commercial and fiscal interests and advertised the ever expanding scope of luxury. Last of all, thanks particularly to the representational strategies deployed by many Bubble caricaturists, critics became unusually alert to the dangers latent in the gap between *être* (being) and *paraître* (seeming) thus ironically heralding a revision of the aristocratic concept of the *honnête homme*.

By the time a benign economic climate once more encouraged a government official and, incidentally, a former secretary to John Law (Melon) in company with a man of letters (Voltaire) to reopen the luxury debate, it may have seemed as if *honnêteté* had been hijacked by commerce. In *Le Mondain* (1736), for example, Voltaire described as follows the polished existence of his 'luxury man':

> Entrez chez lui: la foule des Beaux-Arts
> Enfans du goût, se montre à vos regards . . .

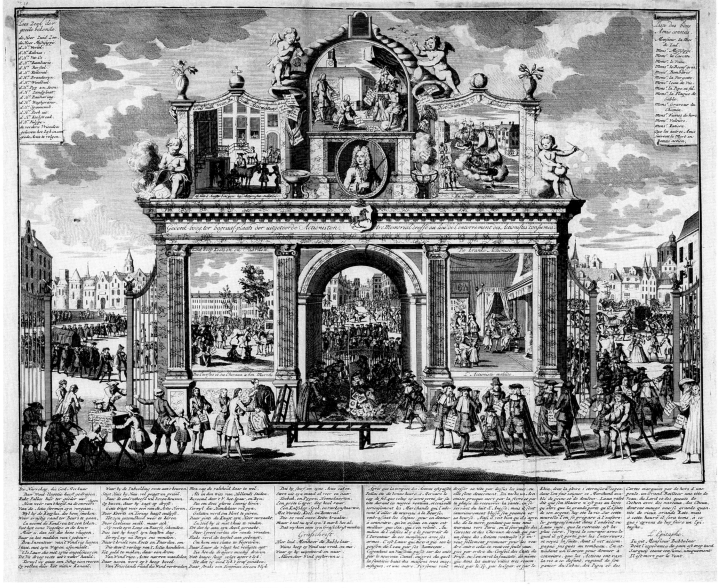

259 A *Commemorative Arch to Deceased Speculators*, 1720. Etching and engraving.

L'heureux Pinceau, le superbe Dessein
Du doux Corrège et du savant Poussin
Sont encadréz dans l'Or d'une bordure;
C'est Bouchardon qui fit cette figure,
Et cet Argent fut poli par Germain.
Des Gobelins l'aiguille et la teinture
Dans ces Tapis égalent la peinture.
Tous ces objets sont encor répétés,
Dans les Trumeaux tout brillans de clartés.[122]

Voltaire's feigned indifference to the social identity of his hero not only left it to the reader to attribute to the portrait the features of nobleman, financier or merchant, but suggested moreover, that the replication of the model was, in theory at least, universally attainable. It was merely a matter of acquiring a significant quantity of the right kind of things. Critics responded to this blithe commodification of culture by gleefully exposing the failure of newcomers to grasp the value of the symbols their transgressive purchasing power had apparently secured. For instance, Duclos in his *Confessions de M. le comte de**** (1733), remarked that the original function of a *petite maison* had been to provide a secret refuge for libertine affairs[123] but that, just as the wives of financiers 'regarded a lover like a piece of furniture'[124] – as a sign of status – so their husbands, having noted that such houses were favoured by 'those of superior rank', hastened to acquire ones of their own, 'where . . . they go and bore themselves in secret a little more than they would had they stayed quietly at home'.[125] In both cases Plutus was possessed of the outward sign of status but not its animating principle. Similarly, the financier apparently bought books by the yard,[126] harpsichords for show[127] and paintings 'like a foolish husband who takes a pretty wife in order to attract society to him'.[128] And predictably, 'his *salon* is filled with portraits, busts and statues, which depict him in all his manifold forms and dignity'.[129] However, the vehemence of the ridicule often seems in excess of its project. It was, indeed, precisely because the physical marks of culture so effectively conferred an aura of nobility and distinction that luxury aroused such hostility. The residual presupposition that the problem of luxury inhered primarily in its objects was thus ultimately dispelled and replaced by the growing certainty that what was at stake was not simply the appearance of status but the very tenancy of the language of social distinction. Since, as Mme de Genlis was not the first to acknowledge, luxury was a condition to which all might increasingly pretend,[130] passionate negation rapidly required bolstering by a re-invention of the mimetic preferences of non-nobles as a distinct form of wealthy bad taste if the nobility were to hold on to a measure of their previously hegemonic control over culture.

TASTE — GOOD AND BAD

Taste, its definition, acquisition, dynamics and judgement, was the topic of polite but committed discussion in many of the fashionable and literary *salons* of the early eighteenth century. The extent to which essays on the subject, such as that of the duchesse du Maine or Claude Buffier, were the distilled outcome of conversation and collective enquiry is suggested by the near identity of the views affirmed and by their similarity to those expressed in the *Réflexions sur le goût* by Mme Lambert, the *salonnière* whose circle they both frequented.[131] Since one of the more contentious issues of taste consisted in determining whether its judgements were personal and arbitrary or shared and absolute, it seems particularly fitting that so many of these dissertations should seemingly have been the product of a pitting of wits. Indeed Voltaire, appointed author of perhaps the most notorious contribution to the genre, the *Temple du goût* (1733), asserted in the preface to the Amsterdam edition that his prose-poem was no more than a witticism, a 'plaisanterie de société' to which members of Mme Fontaine-Martel's *salon* (at which Voltaire had been in regular attendance for several years) had each 'furnished their own ideas'.[132] Voltaire had reasons, no doubt, for partially disclaiming authorship, and it would be a mistake to assume that *salons* (Mme Lambert or Mme Fontaine-Martel's) occupied consistent and clearly defined intellectual positions, but by approaching the question of taste initially from the vantage point of *salons*, not writers, it may be possible to distinguish the constituencies whose interests the texts opined.

According to a particularly flattering epistle addressed to

Mme Lambert by one of her circle, Minerva had lately selected Paris for her daily realm and had elected, moreover, to mask her divine identity behind the marquise's charming but mortal features.[133] Such were the ambitious claims made on behalf of Lambert's court which from 1710 assembled twice weekly in an apartment she had leased for life on the first floor of the hôtel de Nevers, overlooking the rue de Richelieu.[134] Although Lambert was well over sixty by this date and had therefore lent the talent of her life largely to the *grand siècle*, she and her *salon* were nevertheless closely associated in contemporary minds not with the ancients but with the moderns. In a letter, Marais described her as one of Fontenelle's *caillettes* (ninnies), and in his diary he noted that she was a protector of the 'the new style's finest intellects',[135] among them scientists such as Dartous de Mairon, *belles-lettristes* such as La Motte, Jean Terrasson, Montesquieu and Marivaux (in addition to Fontenelle and Buffier already mentioned) and lastly musicians and painters such as Jean-Philippe Rameau, Hyacinthe Rigaud, Watteau and Marc Nattier.[136] At the same time one had only to connect, as many did, apologists for modernity and patrons of luxury for a broader ideological axis gradually to emerge.

To return, for a moment, to Bourvallais's imaginary *cabinet*, it seems that the pendant to Poussin's reforming *Tobias* was an equally apocryphal modern masterpiece, in which the spectator was asked to admire the money-mongers, financiers and plutocrats who richly grew in hell, depicted no doubt with all the daring colour and chiaroscuro that a Rubensian aesthetic could muster.[137] Likewise, the travelling companions to Limognon's Parnassus, Cliton and Crantor, were lured to Nasidiene's door by the promise that after dinner the poet 'Houdardus' (that is, Houdard de La Motte) would read passages from his new epic *Clovis*.[138] That the performance was to take place after the company had suffered through an Italian cantata of strangest novelty and in a space furnished not only with modern paintings but with mirrors, and encased in 'rich panelling almost suffocating in golden ornament', in a room decorated, furthermore, with modern bronze figures and busts and crowned by a grotesqued ceiling, only served to highlight the full bloom of Nasidiene's modernity.[139] Moreover, from the perspective of the Gallican Republic of Letters, as Marc Fumaroli[140] has succinctly dubbed the robe culture to which Mathieu Marais, for one, belonged, the commercial revolution of the Law period had merely acted to exalt the differences between the ancients and moderns and to make compact and palpable the ties between political, social, religious and aesthetic spheres. At one level the coincidental occupation of the hôtel de Nevers by both Law and his companies *and* Lambert and her *salon*, can only have eased the assimilation of concrete and ideological spaces. On an another, we find that among Lambert's *intimes* Houdard de La Motte had actually hailed Law without shame or caution,[141] and that the Jesuit Terrasson had indeed published a two-volume *Dissertation critique sur Homère* (1715), from which the classic bard emerged by no means unscathed, followed shortly by a collection of letters, nakedly supportive of the System.[142] Similarly, in the visual arts, those with eyes to see as this line of argument directed, might have noted that the signature on the picture of the *Family of Darius before Alexander* in the background of *Fancy Paints her Mississippi* (fig. 258) had been clumsily but appropriately changed from Le Brun to 'Rubbens'. Finally, by the 1730s and 1740s the elision of cultural and commercial modernity had become so common an ideological reflex that critics of the rococo or *goût moderne* could count on the connection automatically being made between new style and new wealth, a suggestion reinforced by the clustering of such value-laden terms as 'chaos', 'disorder', 'revolution' and 'licence' in their descriptions of the style's salient features.

Meanwhile, at no distance from the hôtel de Nevers, in a mansion overlooking the gardens of the Palais Royal, congregated the *salon* of Mme Fontaine-Martel.[143] She drew to her the same mixture of aristocratic high society and men of letters as Lambert, and initially, there seems little reason to expect marked differences in the cultural inclinations of the two groups, not least because Fontaine-Martel appears to have served an informed apprenticeship *chez* Lambert.[144] However, there stood at the centre of her *salon* a nucleus of noblemen and men of letters who, from the early 1730s at the latest, increasingly resisted the neo-*précieux* values of courtly culture, promoting in their place faith in the classical traditions of antiquity and the *grand siècle*. Prominent among these were cardinal Melchior de Polignac and Charles Alexandre d'Orléans, abbé de Rothelin. According to one contemporary, it was Polignac who chiefly sustained the nobility's classical interests.[145] In addition to contributing substantially to the waning tradition of modern Latin verse with his *Anti-Lucrèce*, the cardinal welcomed visitors at the hôtel de Mézières in the rue de Varenne where, displayed on the ground floor, was his outstanding collection of classical sculpture, including the famed Lycomedes group: antiquities all assiduously collected during his term as French ambassador in Rome.[146] Meanwhile, above on the first floor, the *cabinet de tableaux* enshrined a taste for the Roman and Bolognese schools of the seventeenth century, while not neglecting the most Italian of France's countrymen, Valentin and Poussin.[147] Moreover, Polignac's determination to establish a new Rome on French soil was underlined at a decorative level by the introduction throughout the hôtel of *devants-de-cheminée* depicting views of the eternal city and surrounding beauty-spots, executed no doubt in the manner of Giovanni Paolo Panini.[148] While affirming his patron Polignac's archaeological and antiquarian interests, the abbé Rothelin also brought the Fontaine-Martel coterie into contact with a further aspect of classical culture, thanks to his contacts with the capital's numismatists, among them intellectuals such as Beauvais, Gros De Boze and the abbé Legrand and noblemen of such lofty peerage as Victor-Marie duc d'Estrées.[149] D'Estrées was, like Polignac, a resident of the aristocratic faubourg Saint-Germain,[150] and possessed of an extensive medal and engraved gem collection, some notable examples of classical sculpture, including an important porphyry bust of Alexander the Great, and a not inconsequential body of pictures, well over one third of which were histories.[151] He was, moreover, a particularly significant figure because he combined this markedly elevated taste with the moral and political convictions of an ancient forever rooted in classical soil. Remembered particularly for his ardent endorsement of the sumptuary laws, he had apparently never lost an opportunity to preach the return to the 'beautiful order of the Romans' to anyone good enough to listen.[152]

D'Estrées's was by no means a lone voice. Within Fontaine-Martel's *salon* the marquis de Lassay wrote an essay on luxury in which he argued that the worlds of the counter and the coronet should remain absolutely distinct and that it was better by far to be noble and needy than *roturier* and rich.[153] Others, such as the marquis d'Argenson, while similarly recognising poverty as the inescapable fate of the less fortunate of his estate, instead of merely countenancing frugality with resignation, chose rather to protect it as a positive virtue. Nurtured in the Livian tradition according to which the greatness of ancient Rome was directly attributable to the rustic simplicity of her republican citizens, d'Argenson was heir also to the political thinking of the de Bourgogne *cabal*, which had earlier discovered in the example of the decline of Rome the metaphorical means of interpreting social change as corruption.[154]

Publicly at least, judging from the inventory of his hôtel in Paris, d'Argenson lived up to the Spartan ideals expressed repeatedly in his writings.[155] Other nobles, however, were less inclined to virtue by self denial. Marie-Charles d'Albert, duc de Chevreuse, descendent of the famous author of the *Tables de Chaulnes*, elected rather to contribute directly to the luxury debate in two overdoors depicting *Abdolonymus Working in his Garden* (fig. 260) and *Abdolonymus before Alexander* (fig. 261) commissioned in 1737 from Jean Restout to decorate Chevreuse's magnificent apartment at the hôtel de Luynes.[156] Recondite in the extreme, the subjects were taken from Quintus Curtius's *Life of Alexander the Great* and told the story of the search for and instatement of Abdolonymus as king of the Phoenicians.[157] The story went that Alexander, having conquered Sidon and deposed Straton (a champion of Darius) was urgently in need of a candidate to fill a now-vacant throne. Initially it seemed as if choice would settle on the most worthy, but the Phoenicians objected that heredity was essential to legitimate succession and so two brothers were entrusted with finding Abdolonymus, a patriarch distantly related to the royal house and one whose moral probity had reduced him to working as a day-labourer in gardens on the outskirts of the capital. The first picture shows the offer of crown and sceptre being made to this enlightened horticulturalist, singularly modest in both dress and bearing. The pendant depicted a later episode; the transformed hero's audience with Alexander during which the latter sought to test the

260   Jean Restout, *Abdolonymus Working in his Garden*, 1737. Oil on canvas, 93 × 151 cm. Musée des Beaux-Arts, Orléans.

quality of Abdolonymus's reputed virtue by asking him how he had borne his miserable plight. 'My hands provided for all my needs and for as long as I had nothing, I wanted for nothing', came the answer, and so impressed was Alexander by this simplicity of sentiment that he lost no time in recognising Abdolonymus as king and bestowing untold luxuries upon him.[158] Such a tale, which explicitly linked blood, virtue, honour and power, cannot but have appealed to a nobility anxious to deny the social and political impact of money's sordid charms. That it was told by a painter of unquestioned academic ancestry, in an idiom of such clarity and sobriety that it seemed directly to touch the classical tradition of the previous century, served further to endorse the equation of antiquity and birth.

By the following decade the conservative function attributed to antiquity in luxury discourse had invaded the language of art criticism. Saint-Yves, in a lengthy analysis of the respective virtues of ancient and modern forms which touched upon architecture, decoration and sartorial fashion, remarked that there was nothing to rival the beauty of female court-dress, a beauty no less actual for being conventional, because as he allowed, such dress 'seems majestic only because, being assumed by persons of eminent rank, one attributes to it a notion of grandeur'; a grandeur to which the use of court-dress in the performance of classical tragedy lent an 'aura of antiquity which further amplifies our illusion . . .'[159] The

availability of classical antiquity as a metaphor of the *ancienneté* of the second estate is conspicuously in evidence here; the aesthetic nobility of representation being so obviously derivative of the *de facto* nobility of its users. Indeed, Saint-Yves proceeded to draw out this inference, arguing that the palace of a monarch should always evoke 'la belle antiquité', because 'it exalts the soul and, led by imagination, propels the construction of the edifice right back to the birth of the monarchy, the genius of whose founders and whose original power our pride naturally exaggerates'. In the absence of such historicity, he claimed, 'the notion of the Prince's power disappears, to be recalled only by his physical presence'.[160] Saint-Yves thus rendered the origins of art and the origins of monarchy coterminal[161] and the values of antiquity and aristocracy coextensive.

Notwithstanding the multiple overlaps and continuities between the languages of luxury and taste, and despite the apparent consistency with which classicism was equated with aristocracy and modernity with plutocracy, it is clearly vital not to confuse questions raised by the polarisation of these cultural styles with questions of their assumed substance in action. Polignac may well have practised what Restout later preached, discovering in the cultivation of his garden the ideal opportunity for re-enacting antique virtues,[162] but he was also the very pink of courtesy at the duchesse du Maine's *précieux* gatherings at Sceaux.[163] Likewise, but to a less exaggerated

234

261   Jean Restout, *Abdolonymus before Alexander*, 1737–8. Oil on canvas, 100 × 163 cm. Musée des Beaux-Arts, Orléans.

degree, the marquis d'Argenson seems, from the early 1750s, frequently to have traded the austere temper of his life in town for the more luxurious conditions devised for his nephew at the château d'Asnières by Mansart de Sargonne and Nicolas Pineau.[164] Moreover, even the flaming morality of the Chevreuse Restouts, conspicuous at the Salons of 1737 and 1738, must surely have been stifled by the cheerful depictions of contemporary complacencies that permanently surrounded them in the rue Saint-Dominique.[165] The early eighteenth-century noble seems to have been an embodied paradox: practicing a courtly tradition of display yet stridently denouncing its ostentation, no more so than when it fell into the counterfeiting hands of non-nobles. Moreover, the chain of contradictions did not end there. Boulainvilliers pointed out that the republican authors whose views were so efficacious in sponsoring a patrician notion of virtue were the very same whose opinions also allowed the sons of grocers to imagine themselves the Scipios and Alexanders of the future.[166]

Boulainvilliers could have had Samuel Bernard particularly in mind, since, according to popular song, this son of a painter harboured martial pretensions[167] which were reflected in the decoration of the façade of his 'hôtel' in the rue Notre Dame-des-Victoires. Later, in 1723, the same aspirations resulted in a series of four large paintings depicting scenes from Roman history commissioned from Jean-François De Troy for the

decoration of the gallery.[168] On the surface, three at least of Bernard's canvases – the *Rape of the Sabine Women* (fig. 263), the *Continence of Scipio* (fig. 265) and *Coriolanus* (fig. 264) – would seem to lend weight to the expressed fear that the bourgeoisie was eager for its share of Roman virtue. Seemingly articulated here are the rude and sometimes savage mores habitually ascribed to the Romans by historians from Livy and Plutarch to Bossuet, Rollin and Vertot.[169] However, when prefaced by a fourth canvas depicting the *Birth of Romulus and Remus* (fig. 262), closer reflection suggests that the pictures were linked not so much chronologically or ethically as thematically. In particular, the juxtaposition of *Romulus and Remus* and the *Rape of the Sabine Women* functioned to reconstitute the gratuitous violence of the latter, presenting it rather as a necessary and legitimate step (the events are overseen, indeed put in motion by Romulus, seated above the throng) in the foundation of Rome, as she struggled to unstitch her history from the dull weave of a merely Italian past.[170] Moreover, while valour was invariably associated with the Roman race and therefore attached itself most particularly to the identity of its founding fathers, the story of the Sabine women acted as an important reminder that such an exclusively masculine virtue may not beget itself, and cannot therefore, alone sustain society. Only with the help of women and the civil virtues they represented was future prosperity to be secured. The theme's lesson of

262 Jean-François De Troy, *The Birth of Romulus and Remus*, 1728. Oil on canvas, 270 × 204 cm. Musée d'Art et d'Histoire, Neuchâtel.

263 Jean-François De Troy, *The Rape of the Sabine Women*, 1728. Oil on canvas, 270 × 204 cm. Musée d'Art et d'Histoire, Neuchâtel.

essential progress from origin to reproduction was made visually meaningful, moreover, by De Troy's choice largely to 'reproduce' the compositional arrangement of *Romulus and Remus*, with its dominant diagonal sweep from lower left to upper right, in the *Rape of the Sabine Women*, rather than compose them more conventionally as mirrored structures, that is as pendants.

Just as the narrative and design of the *Romulus and Remus* and the *Rape of the Sabine Women* seemingly bound them in closer conjunction with each other than with other works in the scheme, so *Coriolanus* and *The Continence of Scipio* were, I think, (though documentation has not survived to prove it) also arranged as a pair, opposite these first, but in such a manner that the heroes faced one another and this time offered the spectator a comparative lesson in classical 'virtu'. In *Coriolanus* the fate of Rome rests once again in a woman's touch. Volumnia, seconded by Virgilia, achieves the city's manumission from the Volscian threat by way of her literally winning graces. Indeed, in expressing the completeness of the mother's victory, De Troy portrays Coriolanus yielding to feeling in a manner – palms open, upper torso thrown back, head to one side, feet splayed –

which is decidedly effeminate. Thus, far from obstructing the hero's route to salvation (as Dido had in the story of Aeneas), woman here represents a civilised and refined order worthy of protection from barbarism. Meanwhile, the benignity and condescension so fatally lacking in Coriolanus[171] are precisely the qualities celebrated in Scipio. Not insensible to the passionate charms of the princess whose honour was his by right of conquest, Scipio nevertheless exercises a mannerly and exemplary restraint preferring to return her to the embrace of her fiancé, Allucius, whose identity is marked by his body's grateful stoop. Thus, despite the heroic scale of these antique actions, the restrained glister of their day and the gestural energy with which they seem individually capable of transmitting a lesson, together they added up to something less than the precedents needed to advertise the political principle of virtuous poverty which so transfixed the eighteenth-century nobility. On the contrary, what De Troy and Bernard discovered in these ancient moments was evidence of the origins and progress of *modern* civilisation. Understandably, therefore, its heroes were to be commended for the smoothness of their polish, rather than the strength of their virtue.

264 Jean-François De Troy, *Coriolanus*, 1728. Oil on canvas, 270 × 204 cm. Musée d'Art et d'Histoire, Neuchâtel.

265 Jean-François De Troy, *The Continence of Scipio*, 1728. Oil on canvas, 270 × 204 cm. Musée d'Art et d'Histoire, Neuchâtel.

It seems clear, in light of the rich variety of non-noble (or less-noble) patronage that the simplification of cultural currencies into ancient and modern, noble and common, was quite deliberate. By the 1730s and 1740s, critics such as Voltaire, increasingly used the vainly gibbering figure of the modern Croesus as a vehicle for attributing to the bourgeoisie a capacity for collective cultural action (suicide some would have it) which it did not actually possess. Thus, for instance, the *nouveaux riches* were held to be immoderately fond of things Italian. In political as well as literary terms Italy was to France as Carthage had been to Rome – source of its untimely corruption. Indeed, during the Fronde *italianisme* became so ringed about with treason, thanks principally to the activities of Mazarin,[172] that a century later patronage of the ultramontane still seemed to anounce sedition. Thus, when in 1728 Le Moyne published his own project for the decoration of Law's council chamber at the hôtel de Nevers (fig. 266), he suggested, indirectly at least, that had state and society remained faithful to home-grown talents and traditions, artistic (and financial) bankruptcy might well have been averted.[173] Moreover, the rhetorical coupling of corrupted financial practices with foreign cultural choices received further illustration

from another project of the 1720s. No sooner had the Piedmontese prince de Carignan recovered the gardens of the hôtel de Soissons, which he had so inadvisedly loaned to stock-jobbers during the System, than he conceived of further exploiting the site, this time by raising upon it a magnificently designed Opéra Lyrique to host performances from impresarios freshly imported from Italy.[174] At the time, the cause of Italian music was being most earnestly championed by Pierre Crozat, Mme de Prie and their club, Gli Academici Paganti, and it is perhaps to their influence that one should attribute the choice, in 1734, of Oppenord to design a 'théatre lyrique' or 'harmonique', most probably on the Soissons site.[175] The plans never left the page, but the survival of some eighteen large and detailed pen and ink drawings (fig. 267) testify to the commitment with which the project was initially pursued.

Just as Marais perceived the Crozat-de Prie concerts as an attack against 'the taste of the nation',[176] so Cochin accused Oppenord of leading taste away from the heroic idiom of Versailles towards a degenerate Italian baroque.[177] Both the score of the first and the drawings of the second were spurned for their easy artfulness and dash. Likewise, critics found fault

266 Nicolas-Charles Silvestre after François Le Moyne, project for a ceiling at the gallery of the Banque Royale, 1728. Etching.

with the *parvenus*' penchant for paintings that flattered the eye with 'brilliant colours',[178] and *fa presto* techniques, the hallmarks once again of an Italian genius. Brice, for instance, took Antoine Crozat's selection of Paolo Matteis in 1723 to decorate his gallery as a sign that 'bad taste still reigns in certain districts of Paris'.[179] It is almost as if Matteis's method of working 'with more speed and activity, than correctness and good taste'[180] was perceived to echo the financier's equally rushed and defective cultural efforts. Similar inferences may be drawn from Blondel's criticism of the treatment of the façades of the hôtel Peyrenc de Moras, in the rue de Varenne:

The complete construction of this building has been

267 Gilles-Marie Oppenord, project for an elevation of a Théâtre Lyrique, 1734. Pen, ink and wash on paper, 60 × 93 cm. Ecole des Beaux-Arts, Paris.

neglected, as has its appearance, executed with precious little care. This is the case with most buildings today which are erected too quickly because a prompt and immediate possession is preferred to the virtues of building for posterity.[181]

Again, facility of execution was contrasted with propriety and substance, just as in luxury lamentations, hasty and mysteriously gained financial fortunes were implicitly compared with the solid and legitimate wealth of landed and *rentier* interests.

Concurrently, those hostile to the *goût moderne* deplored the *vulgaire*'s preference for costly materials. According to Mirabeau, 'in the house of the *parvenu* . . . everything glitters azure and gold',[182] and Blondel complained that 'under the glare of gold' the poverty of modern design was 'applauded in a manner rightly reserved for judicious decoration'.[183] Caylus similarly found fault with the promiscuous gilding of rococo interiors,[184] and by the 1770s so excessive had the use of the metal apparently become that Blondel advised discerning gentlemen to renounce their former tastes and turn to the implicitly higher and purer values of panelling *à la capucine*.[185] Under the pressure of exchange, the pecuniary qualities of gold (its formlessness, its indiscriminacy) so effectively tarnished its reputation, that the natural properties of the metal (its brightness, colour and incorruptibility), which for so long had lent themselves to favourable cultural notice, were apparently robbed of their capacity to function symbolically.

Gold was not alone in losing its differential magic. Many

critics reflected upon the egregious proliferation of mirrors in interior decoration, attributing this also to the influence of an expanding consumer market. Brice, for instance, noted that in 1704 the gallery added to the hôtel Thévenin at a cost of two hundred thousand *livres*, was stuffed with 'everything singular and beautiful that the imagination could conjure up', notably 'mirrors of an extraordinary size', because these were 'the favourite ornaments of today's Financiers, for reasons', he added conspiratorially, 'it is impossible to divulge here'.[186] Despite Brice's ironic coyness, the reasons he had in mind seem clear enough: the plutocrat admired mirrors as he apparently favoured portraits – out of pomp and vanity.[187] Moreover, the scope of the mirror's reflection was such that it extended beyond the mere duplication of his person; it also amplified the number of his possessions, and here we touch a further strand of argument running through the critiques of luxury and modernity, namely that plutocratic values quicken a taste for lavishness for its own sake. Quality was thus sacrificed to number and beauty to richness. Accordingly, Blondel argued that the beauty of a room should consist 'less in the amassing of a prodigy of ornament, than in presenting *un simple beau*, and proportions pleasing to every eye'.[188] It goes without saying that the universal eye he had in mind was no less choice than the pleasure it was there to experience.

That art criticism borrowed and exploited some of the weapons forged by the luxury debate in order to condemn the *goût moderne* more soundly, implied, where it did not always state, that the rococo was in some measure the (mis)creation of a newly rich and culturally ambitious bourgeoisie (while I have been at some pains to establish that, on the contrary, it articulated certain noble ideals).[189] However, the exposure to ridicule of the bourgeois habit of gilding the lily also relied for its effectiveness on polarities operating within artistic discourse that set taste against fashion and, more broadly, the objective against the subjective order of things.[190] The bourgeois's response to the arts was deliberately construed as identical to his attitude to other consumer goods; a response governed by caprice.[191] This helps to explain the not infrequent use of sartorial analogies in so much rococo criticism. Frézier, for example, complained that architecture had become so disfigured by fashion that it was no more than 'a

canvas' upon which architects now 'embroider[ed] their ideas'.[192] Likewise, Laugier used the art of needlework to differentiate between good and bad ornament sculpture, decrying compositions that were so 'overcharged' and 'confused' that they had no other value than the 'labour' and 'expense' invested in them. 'On seeing a garment so designed', he concluded, 'one may say *there* is something which has cost a great deal; but beautiful it is not.'[193] By thus consigning bourgeois cultural practices to the realm of fashion and fancy, critics minimised the structual repercussions of the devaluation of cultural signs by market expansion.

Though the monotonous indictment of sparkle, technical brio, costliness and promiscuity might suggest otherwise, bad taste was not simply a matter of properties belonging to certain designated things; it was also a question of the orientation of those things. In so far as such would-be cultural symbols were exposed as providing the means and ends of the *nouveaux riches*'s particular purposes – a route to social advancement and a steady return on investment – they had the effect of privatising the spheres they occupied. The satirist with the self-appointed mission to gloat over the downfall of Poisson de Bourvallais made much, for instance, of the difficulty of gaining access to the private spaces behind the façades of the place Vendôme.[194] The social forces that had formerly acted to keep the nobleman's door permanently ajar, were the very same that now combined to enclose the world of self-interest, discovering in such a measure a method of domesticating the feral cultural confusions produced by the spread of commercial society. Instead of status distinctions being rehearsed within the household, and staged in the *appartements* of differentially decorated hôtels, they were increasingly being enacted across the threshold, that is, between worlds held physically apart. It is testimony to the place the *haute bourgeoisie* actually held in the unacknowledged class-structure of the *ancien régime* that the nobility, and those who spoke for them, were impelled into so decisive a subversion of the cultural system as constituted. By acknowledging the invasion of the hôtel (the last resort of aesthetic display and unforced sociability) by relations of exchange, they effectively argued themselves out of a feudal heritage in the hope, presumably, of keeping a grip on the ideology of culture, having lost the battle for a monopoly of its material signs.

268 Jacques Vigoureux-Duplessis, *Firescreen with Three Chinamen*, 1700. Oil on canvas, 87 × 122 cm. Walters Art Gallery, Baltimore.

10

The Rococo Exposed

In 1700 Jacques Vigoureux-Duplessis 'invented and painted' a firescreen (fig. 268) upon which three actors in Chinese costume juggle a picture of Danaë in the narrow, stage-like space between the firedogs of the hearth.[1] Superficially, the painter's devoted attention to the reflective surfaces of the gilded bronze andiron and the blue-edged golden curtain, to the extravagant attire of the figures and to the multiplied presence of artefacts within the frame merely suggests an unusually elaborate hymn in praise of luxury. However, the screen's function, its self-conscious illusionism and the metaphorical reference to the stage seem further promise-filled. The position of the screen in the grate necessarily lodges it with the creaturely comforts of the body. Moreover, its place in the realm of the passions seems doubly confirmed, first by seducer Jupiter's metamorphosis and secondly by the action of the 'sculpted' putto on the right who, lover-like, inscribes his initials in the bark of a tree for the sake of his fond companion. However, despite the immediacy and commitment of sensory life, its effects are visibly prone to trickery and illusion. The bas-relief deceives the eye. Danaë is ravished by that shower of fertile gold, and the carefully figured marble hearth readily turns into a miniature theatre where roguish feats of the utmost inconsequentiality are enacted with conspicuous drama. If this aesthetic and thematic performance conjures up questions already familiar to luxury discourse, questions about imitation, authenticity and intentionality, its narrative seems to promote a more substantive lesson. Since a history painting does not properly belong to the lower order of vision, we can only assume that it has landed in the fireplace either by neglect or by pernicious design. Accordingly, the Chinamen would seem to have caught a falling picture torn from the chimney-breast by biting Time or, more likely, cut down by the freebooting ambition of the pier-glass. In either case the rhetoric of Christian otherwordliness seems ready to accuse vanity of committing History and her lessons to the flames in order, presumably, to set fashionable flim-flams in her place. And yet by the eighteenth century the story of Danaë was able partially to deconstruct the opposition between wealth and virtue evoked by this demise of the physical body of the work. In verses attached to Louis Desplace's engraving of Louis de

Boullogne's version of the theme, Cupid jocularly advertised that, where formerly coin had had to catch a captive and shrinking Danaë by surprise, the day was imminent when others, less bashful, would gleefully advance to meet it.[2] Similarly, the humour of Vigoureux-Duplessis's screen seems to depend on the decorative vocation, this firescreen seems both to convey and to contribute to the disfigurement of a once immutable high culture. By juxtaposition, inversion and metaphor, the dislocated and seemingly incoherent syntax of the screen records the loosening of decorum's grip. Here, decoration is demonstrably unable to perform its traditional binding function: appropriately mapping disparate decorative motifs on to the hierarchized physical and social structures of the *ancien régime*. Instead, it appears to float free from its use-value, falling precipitously into exchange. Of course a decorative painting such as this could never truly become autonomous and circulate, because it was of very necessity bespoke. It was rather through the medium of print – pictorial and textual – that the rococo was transformed into both a product and a premonitory symptom of an apparently commercial society. Pattern, advertisment, commodity, riddle, critique; printed rococo played all these roles, often enough simultaneously. As such it opened up a new sphere of cultural enterprise, one which finally deprived the rococo decorative style of its original ideological purpose.

ROCOCO IN THE RUE SAINT-JACQUES

The rue Saint-Jacques, which etched a narrow but regular path across the city, from the Saint-Séverin fountain on the left bank, up and away past the Val-de-Grace to the south, had become home to the print trade towards the end of the sixteenth century.[3] At that time, the newly introduced technologies of engraving and etching on copper had impelled many printmakers and sellers to quit the local and artisanal world of the rue Montorgueuil for the wider intellectual and commercial horizons of the university and book-publishing quarter. A drawing by Jean-Michel Papillon that prominently features his shop opposite the pont Marie, conveys something of the

269 Jean I Bérain, *Grotesque*, c.1690. Etching.

atmosphere of the street's densely packed shops, each one with its owner's name and the nature of the business inscribed on the street-front or on signs hung low over the heads of passing shoppers.[4] Such close physical integration of the book- and print-publishing trades could scarcely have been more felicitous for the production of decorative prints, since it was booksellers who frequently initiated the execution of sets of engravings either for the illustration of architectural and other scientific texts or as pseudo-books (pattern-books) in their own right. Indeed, so interdependent were these two branches of the graphic and book-selling market that it is not uncommon to discover print-sellers markedly interested in ornament seeking and obtaining membership of the corporation of book-sellers and printers. At the turn of the eighteenth century, for example, Nicolas Langlois, himself a publisher of architectural manuals and a wide range of graphic design, most notably the work of Jean I Bérain (fig. 269),[5] presented his half-sibling,

Jean Mariette, on the occasion of the latter's reception as a brother *libraire*.[6]

Mariette's name, however, unlike those of the widow Chereau, Antoine Aveline or Gabriel Huquier, is not one that readily conjures up the image of an aggressively fashionable enterprise committed to the dissemination of the *goût moderne*, as contemporaries were apt to style the rococo. Rather, the Colonnes d'Hercule, the family business with its shop on the east side of the rue Saint-Jacques,[7] breathed out tradition and a stolid conservatism, which the venturesome publication of the *Architecture françoise* (1727–38) or *Collection of the plans, elevations, sections and outlines of the churches, palaces, hôtels and houses of Paris . . . newly built by the most talented architects*, did little to dispel. And yet, suprisingly, it was also Jean Mariette who issued prints after most, if not all, of Nicolas Pineau's graphic work. How can it have been that these engravings from so progressive a source should have passed then, as now, largely without effect or comment? The answer lies, I think, in the manner of their publication. The reproduction of Pineau's designs was conceived and realised, though not always mar-keted, as an integrated part of larger architectural publi-cations, specifically, the *Architecture françoise*, Mariette's 1738 edition of Charles-Augustin Daviler's *Cours d'architecture* and Jacques-François Blondel's *De la distribution des maisons de plaisance* (1737–8).

Traditionally, architectural treatises aimed at the establish-ment of aesthetic canons and universal codes of conduct, and they therefore constructed the world as a place of absolute values and conventional practice. Naturally enough, interior decoration, particularly that which eschewed the classical orders, was accorded only limited space, and was discussed as little more than an extension of planning, that is to say, as the visual endorsement of the hierarchical spatial arrangements determined upon for the building as a whole. Thus, for example, in Mariette's revised edition of Daviler's *Cours*, inte-rior decoration appears but twice: first, towards the end of part I, in that part consisting of an updated 'Vignola' devoted, essentially, to a consideration of the orders, and then again in the last chapter of part II, following Daviler's exhaustive exploration of the niceties of distribution, the intricacies of gardening and the complexities of construction.[8] Moreover, even in such architectural publications as Blondel's *Maisons de plaisance*, which substituted an apparently self-explanatory ar-rangement of the many aspects of the art of building for the contrived and overtly evaluative schedules of the Vitruvian tradition, the text, nevertheless, invariably conspires to con-tain and discipline the engraved decoration present. In the first volume of the *Maisons de plaisance*, the reader is led to approach the subject of architecture on foot, so to speak. That is to say, the book reads as a building occupying actual space through which the reader is invited to progress. A walk through the park and gardens is thus followed by an inspection of the layout of the house and an appraisal of its external features (courtyard side first, garden side next) and the tour ends with

270 Project for a vestibule and a *salon*, 1737–8. From Jacques-François Blondel, *De la distribution des maisons de plaisance*, 1737–8.

a circumspect exploration of significant rooms: the vestibule and *salon* (fig. 270), for instance.[9] Once again, therefore, decoration is accorded attention no more than proportionate to its social value. The same constraint is likewise felt in the first two volumes of Mariette's *Architecture françoise*, where, in the absence of text, the multiple plans and elevations of seventeenth- and eighteenth-century hôtels mount a tongueless vigil about the sections, which are allowed no more than to hint at the fashionable interiors to be found within. In short, so effectively do publications such as these seem to reproduce and explicate the social values inherent in the architectural forms of the *ancien régime* that it is almost possible to imagine away the printing press's legendary reputation for prizing objects from the world of tradition, privilege and ritual. Decoration caught between the expensive covers of a book seems scarcely closer to the competitive, bourgeois bustle of the street than decoration left safely corralled within the polished and precious walls of the hôtel.

These proud paper monuments were not free of all contradiction, however. In the case of the *Maisons de plaisance* for instance, it has often been noted that while Blondel's mind brought forth to press a text that, from the preface, admonished young architects to honour the ancients and hold fast to reason and hierarchy in the distribution and composition of decorative forms, his hand no less assiduously transcribed and

engraved accompanying plates of a decidedly fresher flavour.[10] Likewise, in the new, 1738 edition of Daviler, Mariette, on the one hand advertised substantial revision of both word and image, and, on the other, apologised repeatedly for the concessions thus made to the 'new style', insisting in his own defence, that far from promoting original designs, he was no more than reproducing such realised schemes as had already met with the general approbation of the public.[11] However, it was perhaps in the third volume of the *Architecture françoise*, published in 1738, that the tension between the orthodoxy of architectural discourse and the novelty of design often used to illustrate it, strained to such a point that the reproductive enterprise ended by working its own transformation. This volume consists chiefly of plates illustrating the multiple interior spaces of some of the buildings already described in volumes I and II.[12] In the absence of any regulating narrative, the enforced separation effected between interiors, on the one hand, and plans, elevations and sections, on the other, served largely to deprive the former of sense. While it is true, therefore, that in some instances (the hôtels de Toulouse and d'Evreux) the selection and arrangement of the illustrations were able to show the values of the *enfilade* to some degree, in most cases the hôtels were represented by so partial and partisan a choice of rooms that the spaces they isolated were emptied of their social distinctiveness. For example, the six

271   The Grand Cabinet at the hôtel de Rouillé, *c.*1735. From Jean Mariette, *Architecture françoise*, 1727.

272 The Grand Cabinet at the hôtel de Rouillé, *c*.1735. From Jean Mariette, *Architecture françoise*, 1727.

Through reproduction, it seems, interior decoration was rapidly preparing an escape from the ritualistic time and space of architecture. The escape was hastened above all, perhaps, by the determination of some publishers to lodge decoration on the side of fashion and sell art-books increasingly by their plates.[14] Thus, while the hôtel de Soubise might be known by its plan, elevations and section, some eleven plates were needed to establish in intimate detail the full compass of Louis Herpin's supposed decoration.[15] The axiom that in matters of decoration variety spoke louder than principle encouraged Mariette, in his 1738 Daviler, to multiply similarly the number of illustrations devoted to an examination of the new taste in panelling.[16] Moreover, hand in hand with the proliferation of engraved interiors travelled a fragmentation of decoration as an integrated design. Foremost among the elements to break away and carve out an autonomous existence in print was the fireplace. In the *Architecture françoise*, for instance, Pineau proposed a set of six chimney-piece designs (fig. 273), of which most are of unfixed location and all of which make but the barest reference to the scheme unfolding about them.[17]

273 Nicolas Pineau, design for a chimney-piece, *c*.1735–8. From Jean Mariette, *Architecture françoise*, 1727.

plates of the hôtel de Rouillé presented the interiors of just three out of the fifteen rooms that together made up the apartments of Antoine-Louis Rouillé and his wife on the first floor.[13] Indeed, Rouillé's apartment was represented by a solitary *cabinet* (figs 271, 272), in itself rarely a place of significance for the enactment of everyday social rituals. Moreover, shorn of the spaces – two antechambers, a bedchamber, a gallery-cum-library and a second *cabinet* – that surrounded and gave access to it, the *cabinet* necessarily admitted readers to its realm immediately and without ceremony. The respectful deference due to privilege and office traditionally exacted across actual thresholds was thus effectively negated. The plates extended entry to all, indiscriminately, and, unlike the places they purported to represent, functioned to lend the readership a common identity and a universal distinction.

Couronnem.t de Cheminée varié de deux façons, convenable pour une Chambre de parade

Traverse de la bordure de la glace qui pose sur la tablette du Chambranle.

274 Nicolas Pineau, design for a chimney-mantle, 1738. From Charles-Antoine Daviler, *Cours d'architecture*, 1738.

Ironically, then, it was the most symbolically freighted component of interior space that, by its very centrality perhaps, was most susceptible to the vagaries of fashion. The apparent shift in priority from the spiritually and physically nurturing values of the hearth to a merely fetishistic appetite for form was neatly, though unconsciously, illustrated by an analogous shift in focus from the place of the grate to the space above the mantle (fig. 274), a space in the eighteenth century eloquently occupied by the mirror.[18]

As a result of decisions by publishers such as Mariette to separate decoration from its architectural foundations, proliferate examples of its forms and dissolve the integrity of its schemes, interiors tended to present themselves in print, as scenes rather than spaces. In turn, the flatter reality of decorative prints allowed beholders to orientate themselves centrally before them. Thus, readers were not only given immediate access to all rooms, they were also introduced to those fictional places as hosts not visitors. Moreover, the right to dominion which the plates thereby implicitly extended, was itself susceptible to manipulation. In the *Architecture françoise*, for instance, the information given on many of the plates served to advertise the decorative products illustrated and the

skills of their authors. The names of architects and craftsmen are frequently cited. Moreover, in the case of the Rouillé *cabinet*, the key at the bottom of one of the plates (fig. 275) includes details about the materials used in the realisation of the actual scheme, thereby lending the engraving life and colour. By this process the reader was encouraged to move from the contemplation of the reproduction to contact with the original, at the same time translating the assertiveness of his or her gaze into an ambition to possess. In short, those who might have felt paralysed by the taste of their betters when stationed in the corner of a *chambre* or *cabinet* were emboldened to envy by its reproduction in print. Thus, within the constraints of the de luxe publication the display culture of the *ancien régime* was already making concessions to the marketplace, most importantly by seeming to construct its readership less as a society marked by rank and honour than as a market united by greed.

The decorative prints used to illustrate architectural publications were, however, exceptional in several respects. It was not only that they were lavishly bound into more-or-less permanent partnership with a narrative, and all that that entailed, but also that they were often great in number, large in scale and skilfully engraved. What this amounted to was an expensive product, and one comparatively inaccessible to those outside the charmed circle of good society. However, such plates demonstrate how and why decoration, merely by being reproduced, tended gradually to become alienated from the values of custom and decorum that ruled its existence in space. Of course, no simple progression had led decoration from the privileged interior of the hôtel out into the commercial world of the print-shop and from thence, finally, on to the street. On the contrary, since the sixteenth century, booksellers and print-sellers had habitually published and sold ornament prints in what were described as *cahiers* or *livrets*, that is to say, in unbound sets of four, six, eight or more plates. Some of these brochures or pamphlets contained material similar to the *Architecture françoise* – for instance, Nicolas-Jean-Baptiste de Poilly published a set of reproductive prints illustrating Mansart de Jouy's redecoration of the château de Brunoy (fig. 275) for Paris de Montmartel[19] – but most offered projected or original designs. The Colonnes d'Hercules issued its fair share of such pamphlets; Mariette's father had made a particular point of publishing the work of Daniel Marot and the Le Pautre,[20] while the son launched booklets as various as the collected designs for buffets, newly realised in the houses of Parisian *traitans*, Blondel's *Desseins pour cheminées et lambris* and, most notably perhaps, Oppenord's etched models for overdoors (fig. 276), one of the rare sets of Oppenord's designs to be published during the architect's lifetime.[21] Moreover, it is clear that Pineau's designs for altars and baldaquins, fireplaces, doorways and ceilings (fig. 277) that appeared in the *Architecture françoise* were also marketed as separate collections, since each set is individually numbered and the title-pages carry the publisher's name and address.[22]

246

Decoration du Lambris du côté du Sopha du Salon de Brunois.

Jean Mansart l'ainé. 　　　　　*Prix 1.lr 16.s* 　　　　*De Poilly, excudit.*

A Paris chez N.J.B. de Poilly rüe St. Jacques à l'Esperance. Et à present chez Daumont rüe St. Martin près St. Julien &c.

275   Jean-Baptiste Poilly, *salon* at the château de Brunoy, *c.*1710. Etching.

At the outset, the titles of these ornament pamphlets seemed to set them apart from the thick, square tomes compiled with greater care by established architects and their prosperous publishers. Readers were invited not so much to admire, preferably without desiring, the monuments of good taste raised before them, than to take hold of the patterns offered and put them to some immediate practical use. The designs that Pineau imagined for ceilings (fig. 277) were for *execution*. Either the painter's brush or the sculptor's mould would do. More generally, Toro, Cuvilliès, Lajoue and Huquier invented ornament for 'several', 'various' and 'different purposes', while Bellay and Oppenord addressed their wares to all those 'who love ornament' and 'are involved in the *Beaux-Arts*'.[23] Finally, not to be outdone by the simple limitations of medium and format, Huquier advertised in the foreword to his *Nouveau livre de principes d'ornemens* (fig. 278) that by taking a mirror and placing it at right-angles to the designs collected within, the artist could multiply to infinity the number of patterns from which to choose a model.

The price fetched by these allegedly didactic manuals would seem to confirm the implication of their titles, namely that they were intended for a market of artists and craftsmen, in other words, for those who fabricated ornament rather than sought after it. Unusually, the opening print (fig. 275) to Poilly's set of decorative plates carries precise details of its price. The booklet cost 1 *livre* and 16 *sols* or, to put it in context, just over 1 per cent of the price of a single volume of the *Architecture françoise*.[24] This was, in fact, still quite expensive. At the Image de Saint-Benoît, also in the rue Saint-Jacques, Poilly's uncle, François II de Poilly, sold ornament pamphlets for well under a *livre*. From the 1720s to the 1740s a book of cornices might go for 18 *sous*, a set of goldsmiths's designs for 12 *sous* and a book of fireplaces for 8 *sous*.[25] Clearly, these brochures made ornament accessible and available to an infinitely wider range of consumers than did decoration either in its original or reproductive varieties.

If price functioned to democratise decoration, it also liberated the city to it. Ornament prints were rarely sold in limited editions boasting the refined existence of subscription; rather, they were issued in large volume through a multiplicity of urban outlets.[26] The print of the *salon* interior at the château de Brunoy advises, for instance, that the set of prints to which it belongs was distributed in the rue Saint-Jacques by the editor at L'Espérance and by a second print-seller, Louis

247

276 Gilles-Marie Oppenord, design for an overdoor, *c*.1720–30. Etching. From *Desseins de couronemens et amortissemens convenables pour dessus de portes, voussures, croisées, niches, c*.1720–30, plate 6.

277 Nicolas Pineau, *New Designs for Ceilings, c*.1735–8. From Jean Mariette, *Architecture françoise*, 1727.

278 Gabriel Huquier after Claude Gillot, *Avis au Lecteur*, after 1759. Etching. From *Nouveau livre de principes d'ornemens, particulierement pour trouver un nombre infini de formes qui en dependent, c*.1760.

279 Detail of fig. 278.

Crépy, and that it was also available on the other side of the river, in the rue Saint-Martin, at the shop of the mercer, Jean-François Daumont. Prints endlessly changed hands, passing between several publishers and shopkeepers before reaching the final consumer. Moreover, shops, with their modest but often achingly genteel interiors, were only one of the places of sale for such 'facsimile' decoration.[27] Ornament prints were also sold by itinerant street-sellers across the bridges and along the breezy banks of the Seine.[28] Indeed, the entries in François II de Poilly's day-book suggest that in the thick of the commercial anarchy that often seemed to prevail in the streets of Paris, these *étaleurs* were surprisingly successful at moving considerable numbers of prints after designers as apparently *recherchés* as Meissonnier and Lajoue.[29] Liberated from the prescriptions of a lapidary noble culture, ornament circulated promiscuously.

It is possible that the perceived social and territorial emancipation of printed ornament helped, in part, to create the conditions for stylistic innovation. Certainly, Jacques-François Blondel drew a clear distinction between the designs he judged fit for the highbrow *De la distribution des maisons de*

280 Gabriel Huquier after Jacques de Lajoue, rococo design, *c*.1740. Etching. From *Second livre de tableaux et rocailles*, *c*.1740, plate 13.

plaisance, and therefore for realisation, and those, such as his designs for double cupboard doors, which he self-confessedly regarded as so *licentieux* that he abandoned them to the comparative anonymity of the pamphlet format.[30] It is almost as if artistic licence was smuggled into print on the premise that the unregulated use of etchings and engravings precluded the implementation of traditional rules of *convenance* and decorum. Moreover, the fluid nature of rococo syntax, which by dividing, dissolving and almost destroying form (fig. 280) argued the inherent adaptability of its models to any purpose, itself worked to subvert their stated usefulness. Ironically, by seeming fit for anything, rococo pattern became good for nothing. Cochin noted that contemporaries were so completely seduced by the flamboyant authority of Oppenord's designs that it was some time before they noticed that execution failed to bring similar effects to the round.[31] Likewise, Pierre-Jean Mariette roundly condemned Meissonnier for the fraudulent nature of his imaginings on paper.[32] In this, rococo prints perhaps resembled nothing so much as Law's paper money. For both, the promise of performance remained lustrous for as long as no attempt was made to redeem it. Accordingly, rococo ornament was truly a fantasy; a stylish currency that pledged elegance and distinction without liability. Moreover, as fiction thickened, the print medium gradually acquired all the density and detachment of the fibrous rag and viscous ink of which it was made. Paper lost its transparency; its lined surfaces became stubborn, refusing their place of mediation in the creative process. Instead, print offered up its ornamented tokens as autonomous, as objects in their own right.

Perhaps the most literal manifestation of this independence was to be found in the vogue for *découpures* that took hold in Paris in the 1720s and raged good-naturedly for several decades.[33] These were sheets of printed ornament which could be cut out, coloured and, according to size, used to decorate all manner of things from interiors to furniture, screens, fans, ladies's toilet-cases and gentlemen's snuffboxes. The earliest

examples of such cut-outs in France appear not to have been made especially for that purpose.[34] On the contrary, it is testimony to the entrepreneurial initiative of print-publishers that having uncovered the self-sufficiency of certain kinds of ornament prints they set about marketing them as fashion items. In 1727 and 1731, for instance, the dealer Gersaint launched new prints after Watteau, arabesques that he believed would lend themselves to the eager attentions of no doubt idle, silk-stockinged, nimble-fingered scissor-women.[35] Similarly, in 1738, the widow Chereau announced the publication of Pierre-Quentin Chedel's *Fantaisies nouvelles* (fig. 281), noting that they too might be dreamed into creative relief with the help of snippers and glue.[36] Moreover, in the same year Gabriel Huquier expanded the empire of such cut-outs by advertising not only ornament to be applied, but complete fans in the newest and most elegant Chinese manner (fig. 282), to be assembled by the ladies.[37] The transition from the habit of buying ornament prints such as these for some ulterior purpose to collecting them for their own sake may not seem an obvious one, but was seemingly accomplished without difficulty.[38] On the surface, fashion and curiosity, or the science of collecting, appear wholly antithetical, in as much as you do not collect fashions, you succumb to them; and you do not consume curiosities, but amass them. And yet in print they shared, momentarily at least, a common destiny.

Fashion, curiosity and the rococo perhaps first came together, typographically if not discursively, in the pages of the monthly society gazette, the *Mercure de France*. From its earliest issues the *Mercure* had shown a commitment to providing its readers with regular, detailed and sometimes illustrated articles about the latest Parisian fashions, and when editorship of the magazine passed to the amateur Antoine de La Roque in 1721, notices of the publication of new prints and details of forthcoming auctions and sales multiplied. Masquerading under the heading of public information,[39] these advertisments rapidly established a commercial space in the midst

281 Pierre-Quentin Chedel, cartouche, 1738. Etching. From *Second livres* [sic] *de fantaisies, cartouches, ornements et paysages*, 1738, plate 6.

of the *mondain* culture that the stories, letters, madrigals, sonnets, theatre-reviews, curious anecdotes and news from the provinces and abroad otherwise collectively articulated. What at once united fashions, prints and other curiosities, and differentiated them from the rest of the contents of the magazine, was that they represented a culture to be had, conspicuously for no more than money. The role of the *Mercure* was essentially to set the tepid traffic of possession to a smarter pace; the longest puffs invariably sought to launch an appetite for a shape, a colour, a cultural or natural artefact previously beyond the compass of polite desire, or to alert consumers to the expanding commercial competence of particular producers and entrepreneurs. Thus, in 1730 the ladies were informed at some length that contrast was the very essence of summer fashion;[40] in 1734 attention was drawn to the richly amiable assymetry of newly published designs after an artist, Meissonnier, until then more-or-less exclusively known as a silversmith;[41] and in 1735, by eloquent descriptions and skilled appeals to a prejudice for the rare and exotic, gentlemen were pressed to add shells to their shopping-lists.[42]

Implicitly or explicitly all these advertisements invoked a public of the polite. Indeed, in the case of prints, especially those after Watteau, earlier advertisements had carefully underlined the quality of their intended clientele. Notices began 'Collectors are advised that . . .', or they ended with the observation that the objects concerned were 'eagerly sought after by *Curieux*'.[43] Moreover, sometimes, as in the case of Meissonnier's *Livre d'ornemens* (fig. 283), it was felt that such an unadorned reference to the collector was alone inadequate and the exemplar was further defined by the epithetical phrase 'of the most refined taste'.[44] Later advertisements tended to substitute the general and less appetitive term 'public' for collector, but with no loss of the sense that its constituency was confined exactly to the genteel.[45] Unlike architectural discourse, commercial copy was structured, therefore, by a sense that what differentiated markets, and by extention society, was not birth or privilege but taste. Accordingly, advertisements addressed themselves across the narrow and parochial estate of nobility to a broad and anonymous class of potential consumers there and beyond, comprising all those who could convincingly lay claim to politeness, including the freshest recruits from the vulgar bourgeoisie. There is no denying, however, that since cultural prejudices were so well sown, a certain aristocratic exclusivity continued to cling to the newly reaped rococo commodity. Many of Lajoue's and Mondon's books of ornament, for instance, bore pompous dedications to princes and lords, thus invoking the snug conditions of patronage in which authors and patrons saw themselves as jointly implicated in the charms as well as the costs of the final product.[46] And yet there is no evidence to support the implication that the duc de Mortemart's 'suffrage' extended, for instance, to defraying a share of the expenses of publishing Lajoue's *Cartouches de guerre* (fig. 284). On the contrary, the dedication served rather as an alibi for the shift towards bel-

282 Gabriel Huquier, design for a Chinese fan, 1738. Etching. From *Livre de bordures d'écrans à la chinoise*, 1738, plate 4.

ligerent market conditions that had recently taken place. The ducal decoration was in reality then, no less an object of sale that the surrounding ornamental scrolls that it had seemingly co-authored.

In contrast to the remoteness of the public actually addressed by print advertisements, the language used to reach its number was remarkable for its propinquity. Persuasion to purchase invariably proceeded via the senses, and the rococo vision conjured up in words was thus densely packed with properties and things. Notices for the prints after Meissonnier, Mondon and Chedel read like invoices of agile goods, some natural (shells, dragons, Chinese birds, fruit, flowers), some artificial (architectural fragments, fountains, trophies, cartouches, scrolls)[47] – goods melded together into a single compositional embrace apparently by sole virtue of their fantastic shape. If the domiciliary power of listing thus put rococo ornament conceptually within reach of every civilised household, description of its attributes inserted the style, more securely yet, into the desires of potential consumers. The enlightened but dull rhetoric of rational necessity and material improvement used in the promotion of new inventions and remedies[48] was conspicuously shunned in favour of arousing displays of verbal superfluity, in which adjectives at full-

283 Laureolli after Juste-Aurèle Meissonnier, title-page, from *Livre d'ornemens*, 1734.

stretch of signification breathlessly stacked up one upon the next. The torpid appetites of the politely curious were seemingly to be booted into wakefulness by the swift vehicular movement of the text and by the promise of an extraordinary 'strangeness' and a novel 'piquancy' to be discovered in the prints themselves.[49] By thus articulating and mimicking the

284 Gabriel Huquier after Jacques de Lajoue, title-page, from *Livre de cartouches de guerre*, 1735.

excesses of rococo design, advertisment effectively raised acquisitiveness to the level of style. Moreover, descriptions in which adjectives such as 'various', 'ingenious', 'singular', 'choice' and 'picturesque' outperformed and even outnumbered the enumerated motifs they were there to particularise,[50] attracted notice to the faculties of discernment necessary to appropriation as well as to the qualities of the prints themselves. Thus, rococo prints and the literature used to advance them acted together to empower spectatorship, enfranchising consumers to discriminate by no more than their subjective and fleeting perceptions.

It has sometimes been argued that, in the absence of any contemporary theoretical exposition of the rococo,[51] it is to ornament that one must turn both for evidence of the propaganda by which the style was disseminated and for a means of accurately mapping the rococo's original cultural meanings.[52] However, the printing-press did more than simply replicate decoration; it transformed it in significant ways. It was not just that by reproduction decoration was brought out into spaces and situations beyond the scope of the schemes themselves, it was also that the rococo and the way of life it presupposed was thereby seemingly made widely accessible. In a set of prints depicting the Four Times of Day and entitled *The Activities of Polite Society*, Mondon combined extravagant cartouches with genre scenes, making explicit the connections between a style of ornamentation and the social existence it embellished and supported. *Midday* (fig. 285) depicts a luncheon party taking place within a highly fashionable interior. Along the lower edge, the cartouche, with the crest of the duc de Chatillon significantly superimposed upon it, functions as a barrier, distancing the party of pleasure from the vulgar, of whom the

285 Antoine Aveline after François-Thomas Mondon, *Midday*, 1738. Etching. From *Les Quatre Parties du Jour* or *Les Actions de la Vie Civil*, 1738, plate 2.

baker to the right may be taken as token. And yet as the scrolls curve round and unfold along the upper rim, they simultaneously reach back into the depths of the composition, fastening onto the buffet, chimney-breast and window, and wrenching the scene forwards for immediate consumption. The ambivalent proximity of rococo life was wholly illusionary, however, because the autonomy of ornament prints operated to bury the real problems posed by decoration – problems that lay not in the audacity of its design, but in the organisation and expense of its realisation in space. Like Barthes's photographs of food, rococo ornament prints offered possession by way of observation alone.[53]

The transformation of the rococo into a commodity was significant in other ways too. The separation of rococo decoration from the ritualistic context of noble architecture did more than redefine it as ornament, it also silenced the dialogic will at its centre. Removed from the confines of a notionally classical courtly culture, the rococo could no longer offer its playful and ironic critique of the coercive rationality of the state. Thus, print transformed the attributes of rococo design from relational and discursive qualities into essential and visible ones. Consequently, the objective or authentic meaning of the rococo was lost to the subjectively framed interpretations of spectator-consumers. In short, as will be seen, the rococo ultimately became hostage to the more-or-less arbitrary opinions that critics chose to inflict upon it.

ROCOCO AND THE CRITICS

On 25 August 1737, the feast-day of Saint-Louis, the doors opened on a square and capacious hall on the first floor of the Louvre, the walls of which had, over the preceding weeks, been worked into gorgeous scenes of painting and sculpture by members of the Académie Royale.[54] For those visitors resolutely blind to the majestic resonances of the time and place of this and subsequent exhibitions, the prefatory eulogies of the accompanying catalogues, or *livrets*, emphatically traced the passage of King Louis's allegedly protective hand across the destinies of *corps* and men. Recently, exclusive concern for this formal politics of the Salon has tended perhaps, to overdetermine accounts of its history. In an effort to trace the heroic campaigns of the opposition to liberate the Salon, a space engendered but never fully mastered by the forces of absolutism, it has too readily been assumed that the exhibits, if not exactly made for the exhibition, were nevertheless not entirely out of place there. Consequently, like the Salon critics before them, modern historians have attended, above all, to the exhibition-value of paintings and sculpture, to their assumed visuality, overlooking all the while the deracination and decontextualisation that this formalism (a formalism structuring both the display and responses to it) invariably performed. For, just as reproduction in print alienated the rococo from its original usefulness, removing it from its particular places and

putting it into a network of exchange, so exhibition ultimately functioned to waylay the rococo by diverting it from its intended decorative goals and putting it on display.

Though for most of the year the Salon ostensibly existed as no more than a *salon*, a particular room in a hierarchical sequence, indeed once a square room in an oblong apartment of a royal château,[55] during the month of September it emerged as a democratic space to which all of Paris had an equal invitation, a space thus rendered incapable of recreating the circuits of ritually and socially differentiated places that had insured the value and intelligibility of the rococo in its native habitat. Moreover, not only was the geography of the Salon inimical to decoration, but time, which in the domestic context exercised an integrative effect on the accumulation of social and cultural capital, acted through the exhibition to interrupt the flow of cultural experience, fragmenting it into those discrete and scheduled moments of pleasure that generally attend the consumption of commodities. Recognition of the essential differences between spaces of ritual and places of exhibition was, however, slow to crystallise. In the early years, both the Salon and the Salon *livret* tended to offer themselves as unproblematic, festive extentions of the hôtel. Spectators apparently remained insensible to the shock of seeing exposed the jagged edges of extravagantly contoured paintings abruptly separated from their enframing contexts. Indeed, Jean-André Portalis, the *tapissier* responsible for the hang of the 1738 Salon seemingly thought it appropriate to collect along the cornice overdoors by Trémolières, Carle Van Loo, Restout and Boucher destined for the *enfilades* at the hôtel de Soubise in what can only have been a parody of their authentic stately sequence.[56] If Servandoni's nine overdoors for the hôtel d'Auvergne were grouped together in the 1743 Salon, allegedly in recognition of the more rational principle of a common authorship, the *livret* description nevertheless moved to conjure up both the time and the place that had originally given them life. These modern views of ancient buildings mouldering into worth were, according to the catalogue, painted in no more than eight days in readiness for the reception which His Eminence, the cardinal d'Auvergne, generously gave on the occasion of the marriage of the princesse de Bouillon, later duchesse de Montbazon.[57] Hence, on one level the catalogue acknowledged, reinforced even, the fact that decorative painting was invariably destined to frame a spectacle more dazzling than its own illusionism. On another, it presumed a knowledge on behalf of exhibition-goers sufficient to transform them from merely passive spectators into people able and eager to imagine themselves in the place of those wedding guests invoked by the text or, more generally, in the role of *habitués* of a courtly society. Reference to the protocols of a noble existence thus helped to maintain about the pictures precisely those ritual performances that the exhibition worked to erase.

This hybrid situation, which filled the Salon with truant works temporarily separated from their duties but idling in the company of phantom uses, was not long to survive. By the 1740s and early 1750s the description of exhibits contained in the *livrets* suggests, if not the divorce of the spaces of the Salon and hôtel then at least some sort of decree *nisi*. The most vulgar and utilitarian decorative works, such as firescreens, examples of which had happily been shown by Lajoue in 1738 and Oudry in 1742, began to disappear.[58] At the same time, *livret* descriptions became less specific about the primary destination of decorative works; whether intended for *salons* dining-rooms or *cabinets*. Thus, in 1750, Servandoni exhibited two overdoors described simply as 'belonging to M. le comte de Choiseul', and in 1755 two of Van Loo's overdoors for Mme de Pompadour were referred to as having been 'drawn from the château de Bellevue'.[59] On other occasions, the term *dessus-de-porte*, or overdoor, was conspicuously avoided, such that paintings like Bachelier's *Four Continents*, exhibited in 1761, or Vernet's *Four Times of Day*, shown in 1763, were respectively described as having 'decorated' the *salon* at Choisy, and having been 'ordered' for the dauphin's library at Versailles.[60] Finally, statements in the *livret* about exhibited paintings made substantially less reference to the particularities of canvas shape. The adjective *chantourné*, which had habitually overrun descriptions of decorative paintings, slowly passed from use, and in 1753 Hallé was able to exhibit overdoors without the catalogue making the least reference to their form.[61]

By suppressing information about the use and context of decorative paintings the *livret* implicitly encouraged new patterns of discrimination to overtake those formerly honed by the ritual practices of élite sociability. The assumed rectangularity of exhibition pictures, the use of 'decorated' in the sense of adorned rather than attached to or part of, and the reference to works having been 'drawn' from other, implicitly enclosed and elevated places, were all qualifications more nearly associated with easel painting and the *loci* of connoisseurial scrutiny than with the life-world of *appartements* and *hôtels*. Increasingly, critics and spectators acknowledged the validity only of those aesthetic judgements made in the non-hierarchical and apparently a-social space of the exhibition.[62] The call for a vigorous commitment to history painting and for improved intellectual and artistic standards was thus made without reference to actual conditions of production and consumption. The patronage of the great was judged in the moment of exhibition – not in the context of patrimony – and according to a hierarchy of genres largely stripped of its social and behavioural functions.[63] The Salons thus enabled the public to encounter painting on new territory, on territory of their own discovery moreover, because exhibition served to transform pictures of a frequently narrow social and decorative function into 'homeless' images to be looked at and admired. The ostensibly enlightening and cleansing atmosphere of the Salon served ultimately, then, to mutilate decorative works not so much by exposing their fragmentary nature as by denying it, thus emptying the images of their maiden authority and offering them up as commodities for ideological manipulation. Ironically,

the apparent passivity of exhibition spectatorship (in contrast to the interactive viewing necessitated by decoration) was in reality highly exacting, because it involved quelling the original meanings of works of art and substituting alternative and invariably arbitrary significations.

* * *

Though there can be no doubt that the story of the rococo's transference to the Louvre was one of ultimate failure, it would be a mistake to assume that hostility to the phenomenon was born and resided at the Salon. Much the earliest instances of the 'rococo reaction', such as the stanzas from Voltaire's *Temple du goût* (1731) or letter XXXVI from the abbé Jean Bernard Leblanc's collected *Lettres d'un françois* (1745) belonged not to criticism as such but to the category of what has become known as *salon* literature. That is to say, that while such texts purported to voice the rational and consensual judgements of the public, albeit a self-consciously select *monde*, they looked askance at rococo choices from vantage-points often well outside the art world. Consequently, their judgements served extra-aesthetic causes. Voltaire, for instance, discovered in the inherent formal properties of the rococo a natural metaphor for the sins of Croesus and a handy weapon in the struggle for social esteem. Deluded into mistaking a mere ability to pay for the choicest discrimination, Voltaire's 'M. Jourdain' thinks to give good taste of himself by putting his cash flamboyantly to work:

> Certain maçon, en Vitruve érigé,
> Lui trace un plan d'ornements surchargé,
> Nul vestibule, encore moins de façade;
> Mais vous aurez une longue enfilade;
> Vos murs seront de deux doigts d'épaisseur,
> Grands cabinets, salons sans profondeur,
> Petit trumeaux, fenêtres à ma guise,
> Que l'on prendra pour des portes d'église;
> Le tout boisé, verni, blanchi, doré,
> Et des badauds à coup sûr admiré.[64]

However, precisely because the rococo served Voltaire as a kind of grotesque apparel by which to proclaim the pretence of his *bourgeois-gentilhomme*, its character and style were evoked less by the presence than by the absence of properties and principles: by the lack of a vestibule and a façade, by the lack of propriety and discrimination. Thus, the inversion of 'natural' hierarchies, which in social terms saw the low brought high, led, in cultural terms, to ornament taking precedence over structure, interior over exterior and appearance over essence. But beyond these generalities there is a sort of Lenten blindness to the sensual qualities of those interiors and ornaments, to those hundreds of traces by which they were made *rocaille*.

By contrast, Leblanc amply described the extravagances of the rococo. he recounted how *amorini* were forced to elope with dragons, how shells were pressed into service with bats' wings, how cornices, columns and bases came strangely to stop with cascades, bullrushes and rocks, and how the whole rococo universe was finally encircled by garlands of flowers.[65] If Leblanc's narration thus seems superficially more committed than Voltaire's to the imitation or replication of the objects of its own commentary and hence to an understanding of their meaning, closer reflection soon suggests that description actually operated not to emulate but to denigrate rococo charms. Paradoxically, the impetuous clash of motifs, which in commercial puffs promised so much pleasure, in Leblanc's description strove on the contrary to disgust. Moreover, the repetitiveness with which the excesses of the rococo – its 'extravagance', 'inventiveness', 'richness', 'superfluity' – were politely hashed up, worked to ensure that ubiquity would finally stale the style's consummate fecundity. Such ridicule restricted discussion to the aesthetic sphere. Where the rococo transgressed, it seems, was in ignoring the cardinal literary rule of verisimilitude. The chaos of fish and fowl, fact and fable alone condemned rococo diction. That, in defiance of logic and common sense, so copious a 'linguistic' feast should have taken flesh along asymmetrical lines and across disproportionate terrain merely compounded its trespasses.[66] Leblanc's intellectual vanity was no doubt soothed by so amusing a sleight of hand accomplished for the apparently more serious purpose of proving by exception the inherent cultural superiority of the French compared with the British. However, for him the rococo invited no searching cultural diagnosis beyond the conventional expression of regret for the 'natural inconstancy' of the Gallic temperament. Accordingly, he cast the rococo in the modest role of a bizarre curiosity.

* * *

In the *Reflexions sur quelques causes de l'état présent de la peinture en France*, a critical account of the Salon of 1746, its author, La Font de Saint-Yenne, declined to name or describe the rococo, or to use the style's native irreverence and frivolity as a means of deflating it. Instead his 'reflections' turned about and fixed on an object: a mirror.

> *Mirrors*, the description of whose effects we would liken to those of fairy-tale, to a wonder beyond belief, had not their presence become too familiar; *Mirrors*, which take on the guise of pictures of an imitation so perfect that it rivals nature . . . ; *Mirrors*, fairly rare during the last century and so plentiful in our own, have delt a mortal blow to this fine Art [of painting], and have been one of the principal causes for its decline in France, having banished the grandiose subjects of History which were its triumph from the places in their possession and having appropriated to themselves the decoration of *Salons* and Galleries. Piercing walls in order to enlarge apartments and join new ones to them; reflecting with usurious interest the rays of light which

strike them (those either of daylight or candlelight) how could man, the born enemy of darkness and everything which may occasion melancholy, how could he have denied himself the enjoyment of such specular decoration which cheers by illumnating him and which in tricking his eyes never tricked his heart of the very real pleasures which they afforded him? How could he have prefered the ideal and so often sombre beauties of painting, of which the satisfaction derives entirely from an illusion to which one must be party and which appeals neither to the vulgar nor to the ignorant?[67]

In this passage and much of what follows, La Font framed the mirror as a sign of the times and a symbol of corruption. He notes that technology had put mirrors into locations previously beyond their reach, and consequently that a new phase in decoration had been inaugurated, one in which the mechanical perfection of reflection came more-or-less abruptly to displace the ideal beauties of representation.[68] If technology had made such a transformation possible however, it was human nature that rendered it predictable. Mirrors, it seems, exercised a 'general appeal', pandering to the 'particular taste' of a nation markedly suseptible to the newness and sparkle of these high and widely polished surfaces. Here 'general' was to universal, as 'particular' was to public, such that the mirror was exposed as a commodity of the 'low', the sensual, of everyday and everyman. Furthermore, La Font portrayed mirrors as the children of interest, an interest operative in both the spheres of production and reception. It was a matter of common knowledge that the joint-stock company which was the Royal Manufactory of Saint-Gobain had (eventually) capitalised spectacularly on its investment in the development of plate-glass.[69] Moreover, the psychology of the profit-margin rendered aesthetically as well as commercially pleasing a commodity that, by its multiple reflections, yielded such exceptional 'gains'. To put it another way, it was the mirror's capacity (particularly where two were positioned opposite one another) to return tenfold the objects of its first 'imitation' that allegedly ensured its enthusiastic reception by a nascent market culture. However, for La Font at least, the psychology of the profit-margin was in fact a psychosis, and, paradoxically, the taste for mirrors no less than a distaste for, not to say a morbid fear of, enclosed spaces and unrelieved obscurity. The mirror thus functioned in La Font's text as immediate and material evidence of industrial growth and the corruption of taste that accompanies it, and as a metaphor for the specular values (of desire, gain, duplicity, emptiness, of something in nothing) that were essential to the projection of a commercial society and yet the cause of its numerous maledictions. However, as the critic proceeded to describe the role the painter might aspire to in such a society, the mirror metaphor fractured, running back on itself to become ensnared in its own reflexivity. According to La Font, the explanation for the notable exception made for portraiture by a society which otherwise found little use for the finer arts of painting was to be discovered in the agency of vanity:

> To Vanity, the power of whose dominion exceeds even that of fashion, belongs the *art* of putting before us, and particularly before the Ladies, mirrors (*miroirs*) which are the more enchanting for being less true, and as a result they are prefered by the majority to actual Looking-Glasses (*Glaces*) . . .[70]

whose reflections were now judged excessively sincere. Thus, when commercial society (the collectivity of La Font's wealthy but 'obscure beings of no character, name, rank or merit'[71]) set its face to fashioning its own self-image, it turned its back on the savagely exact repetitions of the looking-glass, and opted instead for the narcissistic idealisations afforded by the flattering turns of painting. Whether prized for its effortless 'productivity', its gratuitous exaggerations, or reviled for its unsparing honesty, the mirror invariably had something of the fallen about it, and as such it provided the perfect instrument to indict consumer society for its exclusive attachment to the things of this world.

Because the mirror is monopolised by its duty to reflect, it may, of itself, signify nothing. To a degree, La Font extended the mirror's inherent lack, its vast emptiness, to his characterisation of the rococo as a whole. He deliberately and repeatedly reduced the rococo to a combination of ingredients (glass, wood, varnish, gilt, stucco, cloth) and hence to an inclination for goods not ideas, or put another way, for economy not ideology. The mechanical perfection and tedious uniformity accomplished by manufacture and the material facility of handicraft were mocked and mercilessly contrasted with the variety, beauty and transcendence of the productions of the mind.[72] The wilderness of La Font's rococo interior exiled painting to the margins, allocating to it only a few concessionary places above doors, chimney-breasts and pier-glasses.

> There, beyond the reach of sight and confined by the lack of space to the representation of small, mean subjects, Painting is reduced . . . to cold, insipid and utterly uninteresting depictions: the four Elements, the Seasons, the Arts, the Muses, and other such formulations, the common triumphs of a plagiarising and labouring Painting, which require neither genius, nor invention and which have been turned and turned about in a hundred different ways over the past twenty years.[73]

La Font's account suggests that the repetitiveness and vacuity that so clearly defined the qualities of reflection, were rapidly invading and contaminating the adjacent realm of imitation. Mirror and painting, whose analogical relationship had long been central to the discourse on representation, were thus recast as adversaries. That this rejection of the specular analogy satisfied more than the particular rhetorical demands of the moment seems evident from the fact that repetition and vacancy reappeared as familiar tropes in La Font's discussion of

the work of François Boucher at the Salon of 1753. In that year Boucher had exhibited two of his most ambitious history paintings, the *Rising of the Sun* and the *Setting of the Sun* (figs 286, 289), works that had been executed for the king's mistress, Mme de Pompadour, most likely for the decoration of her château at Bellevue.[74] In general, La Font discovered monotony in the charming carriage of Boucher's heads; in particular, he accused the painter of the *Rising Sun* of an unwitting replication of figures for the sole purpose of filling space.[75] Moreover, however seductive their presence, these figures were prevented by their narrative irrelevancy and their shameless inattention to the central action from filling out the emptiness of Boucher's thought. The failure to compose (an organisational lack inherent to the reflective condition) was, according to La Font, even more marked in the case of the Sun's setting, a work he compared to a kind of 'music which is well executed but consists only in a collection of dissonances'.[76] Thus, like the mirror, and indeed the rococo interior as a whole, Boucher's art was appreciated for its facile technical sophistication and damned for its mindless incoherence. Carle Van Loo's four overdoors for Bellevue (figs 287, 288), exhibited in the same year, were likewise condemned by the critic for a conceptual triviality and a failure of invention, this time partly brought on by the rococo contraction of disposable space. La Font deplored the painter's choice of the bodies and hobbies of children for the personification of the Arts, because such a choice was 'more likely to bestow upon the fine arts an infantile character', than either the 'dignity' or 'respect' it was their right to expect.[77] Thus, the rococo not only restricted the sacred places of painting , it also seemingly foreclosed on its significations.

Inasmuch as La Font refused to argue the case against the rococo itself — its novelty, bizarreness and *pittoresque* asymmetry — and chose rather to despise the supports that bore its traces, he worked to elide the *rocaille* with the decorative, thereby reconfiguring the debate into a dispute over spaces not signs. It was a dispute in the thick of which the meanings of the *salon* and the Salon were increasingly produced in opposition to one another. Thus, the *salon*, and more generally the *hôtel* to which it belonged, was assigned to the realm of decoration, fashion and the corrupting influence of women. Van Loo's overdoors for Pompadour had, after all, elicited from La Font the general conclusion that 'It's is chiefly the Ladies one should blame if our productions so often descend to the level of trifles and trinkets'.[78] By contrast, the Salon was, at least ideally, the place of art and of such associated grand, masculine notions as history and virtue. The exemplary 'History Painter' of the *Réflexions* belonged to the public forum of the Salon like no other artists. To him fell the noble duty of fashioning modern heroes by the provision of inspiring images of the accomplishments of men of ancient fame in gigantic combinations of poetry and skill.[79] He was thus involved in the making as well as the recording of history (a discourse apparently unknown to the feminine gender). This process of polari-

sation resulted in denying the hôtel its place as the original and authentic scene for secular art; as the space where the duties and significations of painting daily and primarily occurred. On the contrary, the reality of the *salon* or *hôtel* was represented as the 'other scene', a place of fantasy and desire, a space for whatever was corrupted, bankrupt and forbidden. This was so both at the level of discourse, where the notion of decoration was so alienated from definitive example that the critic could and did make free with its meaning, projecting on to the word significations obedient to his polemical needs, and at the level of criticism, where about the idea of decoration was increasingly woven a narrative of gratification and *volupté*. In 1747, for instance, La Font warned of the dangers of painting decoration, though the dangers he specifically acknowledged were those loathesome but limited concessions made in the pursuit of profit to the tyranny of fashion.[80] However, because mirrors and allegorical and mythological paintings figured so strongly in framing the erotic narratives of eighteenth-century fiction, the 'rococo' as it was represented in criticism tended to incorporate something of the licentiousness ascribed to it in the literary context.[81] In 1754, La Font alleged that an *honnête* and reasonable modesty had prevented men of the cloth and impressionable young women from visiting the Salon the previous year for fear of coming nose to nose with the flauntingly naked sea-nymphs of Boucher's *Rising of the Sun* and *Setting of the Sun*.[82] By implication, the private places of the hôtel were revealed as the secret destination of a voluptuousness absol-

286   François Boucher, *The Rising of the Sun*, 1753. Oil on canvas, 318 × 261 cm. The Wallace Collection, London.

287   Carle Van Loo, *Painting*, 1753. Oil on canvas, 87.5 × 84 cm. The Fine Arts Museums of San Francisco, Mildred Anna Williams Collection.

288   Carle Van Loo, *Architecture*, 1753. Oil on canvas, 87.5 × 84 cm. The Fine Arts Museums of San Francisco, Mildred Anna Williams Collection.

289 François Boucher, *The Setting of the Sun*, 1753. Oil on canvas, 318 × 261 cm. The Wallace Collection, London.

utely opposed to public virtue and public space. The multiplicity of discourses put into action by actual interiors were thus silenced in criticism by the invasive and all-encompassing idea of the *boudoir*.[83]

* * *

In December 1754 and February 1755, Charles-Nicolas Cochin contributed to the mounting public condemnation of the rococo by publishing two lengthy articles in the *Mercure de France*, respectively entitled, 'A Petition to goldsmiths, chasers, panel-sculptors and others by a society of artists' and 'Letter to M. l'abbé R***, concerning a very poor pleasantry published in the *Mercure* December last, from a society of architects who may well pretend to the highest merit and the loftiest reputation but are not members of the Academy.'[84] The titles alone are richly suggestive. For a start, the reader is encouraged to anticipate an insider's revelations, perhaps even an 'outing' of secret *rocailleurs*. Voltaire and Leblanc had no more than distantly sneered at the rococo from across the Seine or the Channel, and La Font de Saint Yenne had evoked a rococo presence at the Louvre in order to distance it more securely from the hallowed artistic scene of the ideal Salon. By contrast, the present author promised to tackle the rococo at close quarters: in the workshop of taste. Second, Cochin's titles imply that instead of La Font's somewhat bloodless opposition of places of decoration and spaces of exhibition, we may hope for a more lively and immediate conflict between the partisans and opponents of the rococo and the institutions to which they respectively belonged: between 'artists' and 'architects', between academicians and non-academicians.

The closeness of focus in Cochin's texts is immediately felt. For although in the first of the two articles Cochin declined to name individual sinners, his proscription of modern taste so intimately followed the extraordinary contours of rococo things – the lid of a *pot-à-ouille*, a candlestick, a trophy, a pierglass, etc., – that they assume the concreteness and tangibility of those actually within a hand's reach. The critic thus brought forward for attention artefacts which, by the 1750s, were becoming temporally remote. The description of the rococo disruption of rules of proportion in metalwork, for instance, is sustained by reference to designs by Meissonnier, many of which were published in the *Livre de légumes* (fig. 290) some twenty years earlier. Moreover, the false sense of contiguity conjured up for the rococo by Cochin's vivid turn of phrase was reinforced by the critic's selection of material. For Cochin, unlike Voltaire or La Font de Saint Yenne, the rococo was not the bizarre and fantastic frame of an alien lifestyle. On the contrary, it was to be discovered in the most familiar things, in tableware (fig. 291), furniture and lighting (fig. 293); in short, in the supports of everyday life. Furthermore, when Cochin widened his focus to incorporate architecture his attention initially settled on those features – doors, windows – that are

common to all forms of accommodation and universally manage the experience of domestic space.[85] By so emphasising the installation of rococo design in household things and commonplaces, Cochin reached for that province of public opinion where resistance to innovation and novelty could most certainly be counted upon.[86] Suitability to function had, he implied, long since proscribed enduring and collectively imagined solutions to the design of candlestick-pans, door-frames and casements. Rococo invention was thus seen to intrude where it least belonged. Consequently, metal 'marvels', which encouraged candle-wax to flow unchecked across their burnished surfaces instead of discretely recouping it within concavities moulded for the purpose, were exposed as little more than absurdities. The humorous identification that Cochin thus implicitly accomplished between the much vaunted 'fantasy' of modern taste and good, old-fashioned folly resulted from a semantic slippage which the inherent instability of the rococo could not help but facilitate. Such identification, occurring as it apparently did in the most quotidian things, put the judgement of taste ostensibly within the reach

290   Laureolli after Juste-Aurèle Meissonnier, design for silverware, *c*.1732. Etching. From *Livre de Légumes*, *c*.1732.

291 Gabriel Huquier after Juste-Aurèle Meissonnier, *Different Designs for Saltsellers*, *c.*1742. Etching. From the *Oeuvres de Juste-Aurèle Meissonnier*, *c.*1738–51.

292 Laureolli after Juste-Aurèle Meissonnier, rococo design, *c.*1734. Etching. From the *Cinquieme livre d'ornemens*, *c.*1734, plate 2.

293 Gabriel Huquier after Juste-Aurèle Meissonnier, design for a candelabra, *c.*1738. Etching. From *Livre de chandeliers de sculpture en Argent*, *c.*1738, plate 1.

of all those with 'common sense'. Indeed, the compliance of Every-reader is so fully integrated into Cochin's text that it becomes impossible to respond other than with laughter at the ignorant antics of rococo pundits.

If one of Cochin's objectives in the 'Petition to goldsmiths . . .' was universally to lodge the rococo in the experience and within the judgement of readers, another was to set forth some of the themes to be developed more fully in the 'Letter to M. l'abbé R*** . . .' Most importantly, the rococo was to be understood as the creation of ignorance and vulgarity. The similarity uncovered between the extravagant 'S' scrolls of the sytle's ornamental syntax (fig. 292) and the flamboyant calligraphic flourishes of professional writing-masters[87] defined the rococo as a language of the illiterate, that is to say, as a scripture in which distinctiveness and singularity of form were consistently mistaken for significance of content. Moreover, by further describing this superabundant and senseless patterning as 'twisted merchandise' to be generously 'served-up' to provincials and foreigners, Cochin implied both that the impulse to rococo was driven by a quest for gain, and that the impulse for rococo was prompted by a desire for an almost saporous form of aesthetic pleasure.[88] In both manufacture and meaning the rococo was once again exposed as a product of the 'low'. There is therefore substance as well as wit to the repeated contrasts between the scrupulous politeness in the phrasing of the critic's requests, and the vigorous, almost physical descriptive lunge of the criticism itself. The smirking voice of the 'society of artists' 'prays', 'begs' and would be 'inexpressively obliged' by sundry 'small favours' and 'graces', while the smiths, chasers and carvers deafly continue to lay violent hands on the principles of classical culture, torturing and twisting its forms into a style to 'molest the eye' of the connoisseur.[89] Cochin suggested, however, that the very taste-lessness of the rococo also furnished a rare opportunity for a legitimate labouring, in fact, for an iconoclastic polishing – ironically, in view of the sharpness of the opposition, he was otherwise at pains to maintain between an impulsive, irrational *main d'œuvre*, driven by need, and a principled, ra-tional taste, grounded if not in leisure then in no more than intellectual and artistic effort. Thus, in those fortunate in-stances where rococo sculptors had been persuaded to lay straight the principal decorative moulding beneath *rocaille* obfuscation, 'the man of good taste' was invited cheerfully to roll up his sleeves, take up a chisel and hack off offending ornament until sanity reigned once more.[90]

The letter, published in February 1755, although addressed to a clergyman evidently more inclined to aesthetic than theo-logical speculation, ostensibly functioned as a vigorous rebut-tal of the 'Petition to goldsmiths . . .' It was allegedly written by a *corps* who named and claimed as their own that inveterate trio of rococo talent, Oppenord, Meissonnier and Pineau.[91] Much of the comedy and point-scoring is thus achieved by allowing rococo activists to condemn themselves out of their own mouths. Later, in the 1757 edition of his collected articles from the *Mercure*, Cochin denied that the mockery that so pervaded his writing laid him open to accusations of calumny because, he maintained, his sights had always been set at fashions and not at artists.[92] In this he aimed to distinguish himself from those critics – Salon critics by implication – who had and would continue to make fame and fortune out of the malicious critique of others. Thus, by a supreme act of ven-triloquism, that is to say by seeming to speak as the rococo, Cochin used a rule about politeness – that one should not speak ill of individuals, living or dead – in order to be indirectly but spectacularly rude about the creations that flowed from particular rococo hands. The letter reads, in fact, as a confession, scandalous for betraying throughout the kind of commercial and cultural cunning that apparently only at-tends determined intellectual incapacity.

As the analogy to confession anticipates, the rococo of the 'Letter to M. l'abbé R*** . . .' is an event; the result of an intention, the consequence of an action, the outcome of a plan. In that sense the representation it offers differs quite obtru-sively from a currently held view of the rococo as an organi-cally 'evolved' style,[93] and indeed from Cochin's earlier characterisation of it in the 'Petition to goldsmiths . . .' as an

accident of ignorance. The event the 'Letter . . .' narrates is the mock triumph of a thoughtful and shrewdly organised cam-paign, cynically mounted to further the interests of those styled 'architects' for lack of the academic training and creden-tials to proclaim themselves 'artists' and 'academicians'. By force of deductive reasoning, the reader was thus led to acknowledge that the authors of the 'Letter . . .' and of the rococo carnival described, had to be members of the Paris guild of painters and sculptors, the so-called Académie de Saint-Luc. These artisans tell of their awareness that classicism presented 'ordinary geniuses' with few opportunities to distin-guish themselves, and thence of their determination both to find 'a new style of architecture in which everyman may excel', and to force the public 'to take their pleasure' in these common but novel demonstrations of artistic skill.[94] However, in order successfully 'to overturn the ideas of beauty' long cherished by their 'enlightened nation', they needed to procede stealthily, mindful not to outrage 'ordinary prejudices' by suddenly introducing 'novelties too remote from the reigning taste'.[95] But all revolutions, however discreet, however disguised, must have their heroes, and the Académie de Saint-Luc was careful to rally some 'famous names', notably those of Oppenord and Meissonnier, to their cause.[96] These men obligingly set about altering the existing *grande manière* in such a way that a take-over of interior decoration by ornament sculptors became dis-tinctly possible. Together, Cochin alleged, they brought favourite rococo motifs into fashion and banished symmetry and geometry from interior design. But, since neither could completely forego his attachment to the antique and the grand manner, their usefulness was soon exhausted, and they were swiftly and carelessly discarded. Instead, Cochin has his 'society of architects' reserve its *Ecce homo* for Nicolas Pineau who, though unnamed, is so thoroughly present in the 'Letter' that the reader feels at last permitted to judge the genie behind the style. 'It is to him', willingly acknowledge our correspondents, 'that we are obliged for the superiority we have acquired and which we shall assuredly keep'; moreover, in writing his epitaph they enthusiastically attribute to 'his glory' the fact that 'everything which is far removed from Antique taste owes to him either its invention or its perfec-tion'.[97] To Pineau, apparently, also went the credit for a vic-tory of a more practical value, that of expanding sixfold the relative contribution made by ornament sculptors to smart decorative programmes. Specifically, he established 'the cus-tom of suppressing all [painted] ceilings by having carvers make pretty little bits of lacework in relief at competitive prices . . .'[98] Thus, instead of the compartmented ceilings of the seventeenth century, which had required a contribution from painters and figurative sculptors, 'he has imagined a charming rosette which can scarcely be perceived and which he sets in the middle of a ceiling in the place where the lustre is suspended'.[99] 'This', trumpeted the rococo lobby, with no less irony than satisfaction, 'is preferred and with reason, to the finest productions of Art.'[100]

Meissonnier, complete with extravagant title-pages, portraits and, in Oppenord's case, a eulogistic preface (figs 294, 295).[101] These massive volumes must have stood in sharp contrast to François-Bernard Lépicié's slight, octavo volumes containing the *Vies des premiers-peintres du roi, depuis M. Le Brun jusqu'à présent* (fig. 296), published more-or-less contemporaneously with Huquier's ventures. However, if names were used in the 'Letter . . .' simultaneously to expose and repress claims to artistic status, they had another, possibly unintended function. In singling out motifs and assigning them designers, Cochin deconstructed decoration, displaying it in discrete, saleable units. Decoration's relationship to commerce was thus doubly invoked, first by the denial of its aesthetic value and secondly by the commodification of its language.

Having charted the contribution by the founding fathers of the rococo, Cochin's protagonists proceeded to explain how, with a guile one can only admire, they made use of every argument at their disposal to discredit architects, sculptors and painters and thus improved their own claims to decoration. For instance, they contradicted the academicians'

294 Gabriel Huquier after Gilles-Marie Oppenord, title-page, from the *Oeuvres de Gilles-Marie Oppenord*, *c*.1738–50.

295 Gabriel Huquier after Juste-Aurèle Meissonnier, title-page, from the *Oeuvres de Juste-Aurèle Meissonnier*, *c*.1738–51.

Before proceeding further to examine the detail of Cochin's account of the rococo operation, it is perhaps briefly worth considering the effect of proper names in the 'Letter to M. l'abbé R*** . . .' The first-person slant of the narrative, one that ostensibly places the author, Cochin, on the side of the rococo, in fact does little to disguise the accusative function of 'Oppenord', 'Meissonnier' and 'Pineau'. It merely helps to veil the aggression in criticism's pointing finger by lending scorn an innocently comic face. Though much of the humour quite obviously derives from the actions, intentions and opinions attributed to particular individuals, it also arises in a more general sense out of the implied absurdity of assigning to a trophy, a tureen or a ceiling rosette, in short to ornament, an 'author', in the same way that the *Seven Sacraments* or *Alexander Before the Tent of Darius* was recognised as having an author. Cochin's desire to prick the pretentions of rococo *ornemanistes* was very likely provoked by Gabriel Huquier's recent, lavish, and folio publication of the collected works of Oppenord and

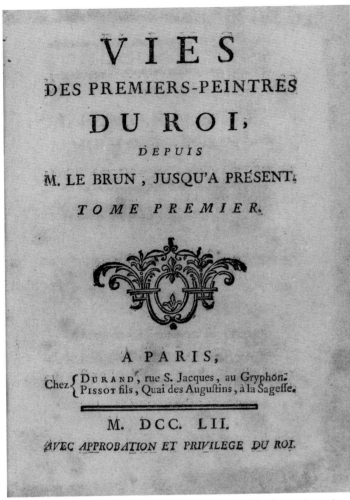

VIES

DES PREMIERS-PEINTRES

DU ROI,

DEPUIS

M. LE BRUN, JUSQU'A PRÉSENT,

TOME PREMIER.

A PARIS,

Chez { DURAND, rue S. Jacques, au Gryphon;
{ PISSOT fils, Quai des Augustins, à la Sagesse.

M. DCC. LII.

AVEC APPROBATION ET PRIVILEGE DU ROI.

296   Title-page, from François-Bernard Lépicié, *Vies des premiers-peintres du roi depuis M. Le Brun, jusqu'à présent*, 1752.

assertion that 'good taste in decoration' was the essence of architecture, finding it more convenient to reduce architecture to the art of distribution – thereby leaving decoration open to competitive tendering.[102] Moreover, they explained to clients that classical ornament was not only exorbitantly expensive but quite inappropriate to their needs, since decorum demanded that the orders be reserved for 'the temples of God and the palaces of Kings'.[103] Then, they announced and advertised the fashion for *petits appartements*, whose diminutive proportions made classical articulation impossible. Finally they convinced clients that their interiors should be as brightly lit as possible. Thus, they encouraged a taste for multiple fenestration and gloated over the piquant sight of 'a poor architect just returned from Italy', faced with the improbable task of matching 'those cherished principles which he has given himself so much trouble to learn' to the requirement of a glass-house.[104] In the unlikely event of his success they were quick to point out the dreariness and dullness of such work. The same accusation was used to banish painting and figurative sculpture from interiors: 'we have found means to persuade all those persons with whom we enjoy some credit that painted ceilings darken rooms and make them gloomy.'[105]

In this passage Cochin so successfully conjured up a picture of noisy, boastful and vituperative verbal exchange, of struggle for prevailing opinion and thus for work, that his text comes closer to imitating the texture of the residually oral culture of the market-place, than the politely literary world of the academies and *salons*. Not only is the narrative flow predicated on utterance, it contains at least one section of reported speech: 'You will not be able to see clearly in your house, we said . . . you will not be able to breathe, you will hardly see the sun on fine days . . .'[106] Moreover, the text's dialogic structure operates not for an exchange of opinion *en route* to consensus, but as a means of setting interlocutors to best one another's rhetorical performances in a knock-out contest for supremacy. In the thick of it, academicians were exposed as the 'criers', 'barkers' or 'shouters' of the dispute, rather than the 'writers' they knew themselves to be. And their conception of 'art' in the abstract, categorical terms of the 'beautiful' was routed by an artisanal definition, that saw 'art' in the operational terms of the technically and commercialy viable. Thus, while bold, silver-tongued craftsmen prospered on rococo nonsense, the noble academician apparently starved for want of impertinence.

Perhaps what is most remarkable about the 'Letter to M. l'abbé R*** . . .' is the way the rococo-as-event picked up, in Cochin's narrative, precisely those characteristics routinely attributed to the style itself. Thus, there was something 'fantastic' and extraordinary not only about the duke of Kingston's silver (Cleveland Museum of Fine Arts) or the Cabinet Bielenski, but also in the tale of modest, uneducated artisans seizing the cultural initiative from artists of academic standing. Likewise, there was something 'singular' and 'bizarre' not only in the elaborate and infinitely varied design of rococo frames but in the situation they created for painters, 'at a loss to compose their subjects among the incursions that our ornaments make on to their canvases'.[107] Lastly, there was, perhaps, something 'picturesque' in the transformation of the interior from its traditional representation as a place of established order, into a space animated by the incoherent, competitive, asymmetrical relationships particular to the market-place. In short, the occasion of the rococo seems to have been projected to cause almost as much astonishment as the visual evidence of the things themselves. Objects were found *rocaille* in Cochin's text by virtue of their 'history' as well as their aesthetic.

* * *

Attended to individually, these texts appear to offer a sequence of satisfyingly clear, coherent and unequivocal condemnations of the rococo; but attended to collectively, the impression of focus loses direction and we are left with a definition of the style that is appositely irregular about the edges. For some, the rococo was exclusively a problem for the decorative or mechanical arts; for others, it also involved painting and sculpture. For some, the causes were providential, discernible in the long-term cycles of time and fortune;[108] for others, the causes were social and political, attributable to the commercial and financial policies of the modern state or to the working practices of its corporate bodies. Packed up into the same concept went, often contradictory, accusations of luxury, philistinism, transgression, indolence, emptiness, ignorance, sharp-practice, industry and disparate notions of time, place and event. Within this variety it is, of course, possible to identify certain distinct critical genealogies; first, one informed and shaped by the discourse on luxury, and second, one moulded by academic and aesthetic theory. But if this insight allows us provisionally to group the texts of Voltaire and La Font and those of Leblanc and Cochin, it does not follow that an act of adjudication will subsequently deliver up those words from which a reliable interpretation of the rococo's meanings may legitimately be derived. Criticism, like mechanical reproduction, tended, on the contrary, 'to wrench' the rococo from the concrete realm of custom and tradition and insert it into the more fluid and unstable domain of opinion.

In this context, the importance of the Salons cannot be underestimated. Rococo painting, like some strange anamorphic illusion, assumed full intelligibility only when looked at obliquely by a gaze sustained, coloured and distorted by noble interest. When viewed directly and intensively at the Salon, at alien distances and angles and by an ostensibly objective and distinterested eye, rococo decorative paintings tended to dissolve into allegedly formless and meaningless blots, ones whose loss of intrinsic sense was accompanied by an unusual receptiveness to the projection of other critical interpretations. Moreover, the form of public assembly brought into existence by the exhibitions radically and permanently transformed the patterns of aesthetic discourse, such that the conditions of exhibition were assumed to obtain even when exhibits were not actually the subject of discussion. In other words, artistic discourse increasingly recognised in the contingencies of the Salon, the ideal, and only real, conditions of art. Critics were rarely go-betweens leading viewers forward towards an understanding of actual objects. They were 'strategists', re-presenting images for a public refashioned by the exigencies of the keenest contention. Hence, if we are unlikely to learn much about the rococo as such from these texts, we may perhaps hope for a better understanding of the impulses to discredit it.

Before trying to account for the variety of the critical responses to the rococo it is, I think, worth noting that the rococo defined by criticism consistently differed from the 'authentic' thing in one important respect. It presented the style's properties (of disproportion, exaggeration, imagination, instability, etc.) as essential not relational. Rococo decoration had variously articulated the early eighteenth-century nobility's sense of distinction, and its determination to overturn, or at least to limit, the scope of absolutism by contesting the comprehensiveness of the state's rationalist and classicising

vision. The rococo thus invoked classicism expressly to demonstrate a refusal to receive it passively. Instead, the rococo parodied, criticised and reworked classical precepts and formuli, relying on an assumed and implicit knowledge of tradition to accomplish a novel and astonishing contrast. However, if originally the rococo had worked above all to relativise and subjectivise standards of taste, at the hands of mid-century critics it became not an alternative to but the antithesis of classical, or good, taste. The symbiotic relationship between the cultural categories of classicism and rococo or ancient and modern, upon which so much of rococo pleasure and enlightenment depended, was thus effectively broken. Instead, the rococo was re-presented as an absence – an absence of proportion, harmony, symmetry, balance, sense, judgement, taste – and thus the liberation that it had offered by its aggressive meddling in canonical cultural matters was reinterpreted as a licence, a weakness, which undermined by impotence the bases of French civilisation. Whatever their other differences, Voltaire, Leblanc, La Font and Cochin were thus as one in their blindness to the original challenge of rococo. This is not to say that they were insensible to its threat; however, for them the danger lay not in the rococo's meanings, because they denied the capacity of its forms to generate sense, but in its popularity, in its mysterious ability to capture the collective imagination and dominate the market. Thus, the rococo was acknowleged to be primarily of economic concern. When, for instance, Cochin's rococo activists allegedly spoke of their desire to revolutionise the laws of decorum so that in future 'the greater the dignity of the person, the smaller will be his suite of rooms',[109] their ambition was framed not in terms of political radicalism and class-struggle but in the less subversive terms of commercial strategy: in the finite market, those able 'to lay out money lavishly will lay out only on small-scale work and will apply to us', leaving to painters in the grand manner, discerning would-be patrons, but ones 'without means to undertake anything'.[110] Succinctly put, small was beautiful because it put enterprises of historic proportion promptly out of commission. Thus, by the discreet interposition of not wholly applicable terms of reference, or to put it less strongly, by a subtle shift in the lines of interpretation, the rococo was alienated from its former self and became hostage to later anxieties.

If what united anti-rococo texts was their verdicts, their interpretative structures and their goals, what divided them was above all their orientation. The uniqueness of La Font's *Reflections* resided less, therefore, in his diagnosis of *arriviste* corruption, a view largely inherited from Voltaire,[111] than in the challenge levelled at the state. The luxury personified by the fictional Croesus in the 1730s and laughingly dismissed by a *monde* confident of its capacity for self-reform had, by the mid-1740s, been replaced in the minds of many by a *luxuria* with the undeniably seductive but emphatically bourgeois features of Jeanne-Antoinette Poisson, later the marquise de Pompadour.[112] By taking this daughter of Finance as his official favourite, the king had, to all appearances, exchanged the monarchy's longstanding policy of fiscal toleration, necessitated by economic realities, for one of active promotion, as a result of which the financier class was well on its way to becoming socially and politically, as well as economically established. Moreover, the appointment in 1746 of Pompadour's uncle, Le Normand de Tournehem, a former tax-farmer, to the post of Directeur Général des Bâtiments du Roi, a post to which her brother Marigny would later succeed, notionally confused the particular tastes of financiers with the public taste of the prince, and brought the apportioning of blame for the decline of the French school to within a few feet of the throne. This identification was facilitated, unwittingly no doubt, by the Salon *livrets*. Royal commissions were always identified as a matter of honour and prestige; the naming of other patrons, however, seems to have occurred on request. Since, generally speaking, the wealthy seem to have been so much more willing to appear than the noble, the *livrets* conveyed the impression that modern art was jointly and only sustained by the crown and its financiers.[113] From the early 1750s, moreover, the Pompadour clan, in particular, advertised its interventions in the arts; works for the marquise and the comte de Choiseul were acknowledged in the *livret* of 1750, and paintings for Bellevue, for Marigny and for La Live de Jully were identified in the 1753 catalogue.[114] Thus, when La Font denounced in the *Sentiments* the 'inhumanity of opulence' and the 'omnipotence of credit', he could have relied upon his readers to imagine particular physiognomies for the vices he had named.[115] In publicly contesting the achievements of the Academy and its patrons, La Font took up a position not only outside but against the establishment, a position whose moral authority and critical conviction no longer derived from privileged access to the *secret du roi*, but from an apparently cruder force of number, from its sympathy with 'public opinion'.

In matters of taste neither dissent nor appeals to public consensus were particularly new, but in the late 1740s and 1750s, in a climate of growing political crisis they gained in force and urgency. It seems likely that La Font's artistic views were widely recognised as consistent with *parlementaire* ideology and that his reviews therefore appeared to extend the judiciary's militant resistance to the crown's fiscal and religious initiatives to the cultural sphere. The Parlement de Paris had alone emerged from the speculation mania of the Regency with its credibility intact. Its refusal to endorse Law's programme had eventually earned it a period of exile in Pontoise from which, after the crash, it returned in triumph to be popularly associated with a wisdom, modesty and steadfastness it was far from actually possessing, but which nevertheless lingered long in society's collective memory.[116] Though many *robins* were not above frequenting financier circles, as a body the Parlement remained an unyielding opponent of financier interests.[117] Moreover, the magistrates' early association with a certain material restraint and moral discipline was consolidated in the 1750s during their last stand against ratification of the bull *Unigenitus*, the papal decree by which Louis XV sought finally to suppress the Jansenist cause.[118] Exposed to such public discourse, rococo taste no longer invited polite controversy but hard, political opinion, becoming a new and more punishing stick with which to beat the government. Where the rococo had originally served the nobility to resist and mock absolutism, it now abetted the Parlement's opposition by providing an extravagant charge to level at the monarchy. Thus, where it had formerly worked to distinguish nobles, it now operated to condemn kings. This modernisation of the rococo's function followed the shift in the places and spaces of dissent, from nobility to Parlement and from hôtel to Salon.

In so far as La Font alleged the complicity of certain painters in the elaboration of the rococo, he seemingly exposed the venality of the Académie Royale and the readiness of some of its most distinguished names to coin the honour of their talent into gold. Not surprisingly, in the arrogant breasts of the targeted, fury followed swiftly upon astonishment, and within weeks of the *Réflexions'* publication, all manner of rebuttals were in feverish preparation.[119] Separated from La Font's first review by some seven and eight years, Cochin's articles for the *Mercure* do not immediately suggest themselves as rejoinders of this kind, not least because they referred neither to the Salon nor to La Font. And yet, more successfully than the replies of those such as Coypel or Leblanc,[120] and perhaps precisely because they were published in the fallow period between exhibitions, Cochin's writings dealt with La Font's diagnosis of decline and corruption while managing to absolve 'artists', the Academy and the Bâtiments of all responsibility. He was able to do so chiefly by refusing to consider the possible existence of a rococo painting of a piece with the ornament that surrounded it. He insisted that the rococo belonged to a different season and a different country. 'We have been totally excluded from the royal buildings', complained Rococo and Co. in the 'Letter to M. l'abbé R*** . . .' and, as for the Academy, 'it seems', they continued, 'as if it wants only to award prizes to those who approach the Antique taste most nearly.'[121] Moreover, Cochin sharpened the sense of the rococo's 'otherness' by not only ascribing its origin to a single, institutional source – the Académie de Saint-Luc – but by designating as its natural constituency the world of corporation procurators, church wardens and successful businessmen,[122] implying thereby, that it belonged not to royal but to local authorities, and not to public but to private interests.

Cochin wrote these articles not simply as a committed academician but as a loyal governement agent. The year the 'Letter to M. l'abbé R*** . . .' was published was also the year he was officially charged with the Détail des Arts, a consultative and administrative position he had in fact largely been fulfilling since the death in 1752 of the Premier Peintre, Charles-Antoine Coypel.[123] He owed this dizzying and unexpected promotion (he was after all only a draughtsman and engraver in the king's household, not a history painter) almost entirely to the protection of the Pompadour family whose reputation he doubtless, in return, felt it his duty to protect. And it is in the 'Petition to goldsmiths . . .' and the 'Letter . . .', rather than Cochin's formal reply to La Font and others in 1753, or his more general, theoretical writings, that we see the first effective steps being taken by those in power to meet the accusations of their critics.[124] Repudiation alone was evidently insufficient, however subtly phrased. Success for La Font depended on his ability – ideally if not actually – to rob his audience of their settled responses and so remould their ideas that an inchoate mass of opinionated readers and spectators was converted into a public of fellow-travellers. Cochin's task was easier. From his established position, he needed only to activate convention, in the form of *vraissemblance* (or 'that which conforms to public opinion'[125]), to assure universal legitimacy for the Academy's cause, while also lending its rhetoric a confidently comic style. According to Cochin, everything about the rococo was *invraissemblable*: the authors' intentions – always pretensions; the patrons' aspirations – usually affectations;[126] and the product of their conjuction – fantastic obsessions, either scorned for their vulgarity, or ironically applauded for their excesses. Such a pitiless and comprehensive exposé of the rococo's contrariness ensured that, almost by the simple act of description, the rococo of Cochin's text was cajoled into carrying out its own deposition. Furthermore, the likelihood of such rococo ever having found sustenance at the Académie Royale now seemed absurd. Thus, paradoxically perhaps, the most extended verbal investigation of the rococo served to alienate it most thoroughly from the context that originally gave it meaning. Moreover, by so choosing not to answer La Font's insinuations point by point, but by publishing instead their own version of the rococo, the Academy and, by extension, the state were at last able to confiscate the style which had so provoked them in the past, and claim for themselves the very last laugh.

Years later, when Cochin came to commit his memories to paper, he alleged that criticism, his articles in particular, had indeed been most efficacious in bringing about the desired change in taste.[127] And yet the 'Letter to M. l'abbé R*** . . .' had been written after (in some cases years after) the deaths of Cochin's chief culprits, Oppenord, Meissonnier and Pineau.[128] Moreover, the 1740s had been a lean decade for Meissonnier,[129] and for Pineau, modest, some would say lacklustre commissions for the wealthy had largely supplanted the ambitious and radically rococo schemes for the nobility of the 1730s.[130] Meanwhile, the vibrancy and daring of the decorative works by Le Moyne, Boucher, Lajoue, Natoire and De Troy in the 1730s and early 1740s was arguably rarely bettered thereafter. The social and political conditions that had originally given life and vigour to the rococo had, with the competition of new wealth, the ministry of cardinal Fleury, the birth of the dauphin, not to mention the interventions of print, gradually withered away. The rococo was already in retreat, if not at the date of Voltaire's and Leblanc's critiques then certainly by the time that La Font de Saint Yenne came to review the Salons of 1746 and 1753 and Cochin to submit his petitions and letters to the *Mercure de France*. No, criticism did not defeat the rococo; on the contrary it resurrected it, cutting it loose from its moorings in decoration and setting it free to prosper as a richly derogatory sign in a multitude of other discourses.

Notes

NOTE: Works are cited in abbreviated form by author (or equivalent) plus date. The key to these abbreviations is provided by the Bibliography. Manuscript references are cited in full in the notes although the location of the document is once again abbreviated in the form of initials. Keys are provided by the Bibliography.

INTRODUCTION

1 Luynes 1860–65, i; 82–3.

2 Contract of sale between François de Mailly, duchesse de Mazarin and Jean Hector Dufay, marquis de Latour Maubourg, passed before Camuset, 15/vi/ 1736 (A.N.M.C. XXVI/382). The property was in fact bought for 226,000 livres of which 8,000 was paid on signing the contract and the balance on 18/ix/1737 (ibid.). For a history of the hôtel Mazarin, see Paris 1981, 42–7.

3 Blondel 1754, 66; Paris 1981, 44.

4 The architect employed by Mazarin was a certain duc de Fornari, apparently also responsible for the hôtel d'Etampes, 63 rue de Varenne. See Paris 1981, 42, 49.

5 See ibid., 45.

6 Mariette 1727, 454; Hautecœur 1943–52, iii, 168.

7 This evidence was brought together by the painstaking and meticulous research of Bruno Pons for an exhibition about the rue de Varenne held at the Musée Rodin in 1981. See Paris 1981, 42–7.

8 This drawing is reproduced in Pons 1985, fig. 21. For an assessment of Leroux's talents, see Hautecœur 1943–1952, iii, 168–70.

9 The following description is largely based on the information gleaned from the probate inventory of Françoise de Mailly, duchesse de Mazarin, 18/ix/1742, A.N. T*584[40]. All the items listed were given numbers and references to them below cite these numbers.

10 Ibid., 86.

11 Ibid., 97.

12 Paris 1981, 43.

13 The vestibule/antechamber was furnished with 11 items; the 'salon peint en blanc' with 18 (including the mirrors); and the bedchamber with 35 (including mirrors). I have not included the light-fittings in the figures, although there too, it is significant that the number and size of the chandeliers, candelabra and wall lights similarly increased from one of these rooms to the next.

14 The etiquette of planning will be discussed at greater length in chapters 4 and 5.

15 The inscriptions on the drawing read as follows: (Centre) 'Pour la chambre a/ coucher de M^e la/duchesse de Mazarin'; (clockwise from the top) 'L'ôuye/par une femme/quy joue de/la lir/et un/lievre'; 'La veue/par une/femme tenen/une Lunette/un Loup/Cervier, et un/Epervier'; 'Le gout/par une femme/tenant une pome d'apis/une Corbeille/de fruit, et un/ortalent'; 'L'od-orat/par une femme/un Bouquet de/Rozes un chien/et un vasse/pour les odeur/quon tirent par la distilation.' For the contract between Pineau and the duchesse de Mazarin, see A.N.M.C. XXVI/384 (26/x/ 1736). For the plaster and wood sculpture for the *salon* and *chambre à coucher* Pineau was to receive 3,600 *livres* paid in three equal instalments, during, after, and three months after the job.

16 A.N. T*584[40], 138: 'deux dessus de portes qui sont portraits de Dames dans leurs bordures de bois sculpté doré . . .'

17 The *cabinet de toilette* was decorated with three paintings, two of which were overdoors depicting 'traits de fable' and the third, which topped a pier-glass, portrayed 'des amours'. Ibid., 148.

18 The *cabinet* was apparently dubbed 'La Cage' because in addition to the ubiquitous *trumeaux*, the room's doors and the doors of the built-in cupboards were also faced with mirrors and amplified the reflection of the bronze and porcelain birds displayed in the room, thus presumably creating the impression of the inside of an aviary. For the furnishings of La Cage, see ibid., 151–62.

19 Ibid., 126.

20 Ibid., 198. On taste for the *Spinario* in the eighteenth century, see Haskell-Penny 1981, 308–9.

21 On the commission and surviving drawings, see Brunel 1986, 98–9. Bruno Pons has tentitively identified the composition, *L'Education de l'Amour* with a painting dated 1738 in the Los Angeles County Museum of Art. See New York 1986, 20 (1738, 18 Aug.–10 Sept.).

22 A.N. T*584[40], 227.

23 The two rooms are in fact qualified as 'doré' in the inventory.

24 The corridor was described as mounted with 'six panneaux de papier peint façon de la Chine dans leurs moulures peints . . .' Ibid., 236. Meanwhile, the chapel contained an altarpiece representing 'la Vierge et l'enfant Jesus dans sa bordure de Bois doré'. Ibid., 240.

25 Paris 1981, 44.

26 Pardailhé-Galabrun 1988, 26. For examples of recent histories which put probate inventories to such use, see Roche 1981, esp. chaps. 5 and 8; Bonfait, 1986, 28–42; Bonfait 1986[2], 125–51; Pardailhé-Galabrun 1988, 366–401.

27 The phrase is taken from the preface to Simon Schama's *Citizens*, a preface in which the author argues strongly for a narrative history which necessarily privileges the use of description. Schama 1989, xvi.

28 Darnton 1985, 12.

29 More accurately the 'Bon' is located centre-right. This is possibly because the drawing seems to offer alternative versions left and right and because the patron has therefore opted for the right-hand variant.

30 'Pour le petit Cabinet–Mme de Mazarin/Et pour la cheminée à Paris coupé de Mr le comte de Municz envoyé en fevrier 1740/ Bon.'

31 I am aware that this begs the question of the value ascribed to originality in the artisanal culture of the *ancien régime*. Quali-

fied support for the case for novelty is offered below.

32 Mercier 1782–8, i, 166.

33 *Dictionnaire de l'académie françoise* 1762, ad. voc. 'Décoration'.

34 Gerdil 1768, 11.

35 For a much fuller argument for 'appropriation' in this sense, and one to which I am greatly indebted, see Sahlins 1976, 166–204.

36 Paris 1981, 42.

37 Blondel 1774, i, 53.

38 Ibid., 89–90.

39 Saleran singles out Vouet as a particularly outstanding decorator. He contrasts a 'modern' *salon* with a seventeenth-century gallery, ostensibly coexistant in the same building. The hôtel de Mazarin had no gallery (still less one painted by Vouet) but it is conceivable that Blondel was in fact comparing the gallery of the palais Mazarin with the *salon* of the hôtel de Mazarin. In support of this case it is worth noting that the duchess lived in the palais before crossing to her new hôtel after her husband's death. On the other hand, the gallery ceiling was not, of course, the work of Vouet.

40 See Lougee 1976, *passim*.

1 THE PRODUCTION OF MATERIALS

1 Mercier 1782–8, i, 166.

2 For the history of the hôtel de Soubise, see Langlois 1922; Babelon 1969, esp. 24–48.

3 See Potain 1749, 193; Jombert 1752, iii, 126–32; Pons 1985, 50–51.

4 This suggestion has recently been made by Bruno Pons. See Paris 1986, 223.

5 See Pons 1985, 19.

6 Although traditionally attributed to Nicolas-Sébastien Adam, Pons has recently suggested that the elaborate cornice of the room was the work of Michel Lange (see Paris 1986, 224–5), an attribution made more plausible by the knowledge that Boffrand and Lange teamed up on other occasions, most notably at the Arsenal. Indeed, at the time of Lange's death in 1741, the architect owed him 2,000 *livres* for sculptural works. See A.N.M.C. XXXVIII/320 (IAD 29/viii/1741). Clients were often held responsible for the cost of the scaffolding necessary for installing such cornices. See, for instance, the contract passed between the comte de Matignon and the sculptors Henri de Lambillot and Michel Lange, 22/xii/1723, A.N. 201, M1 1–2, C³ 19/8.

7 The other overdoor in the room was François Boucher's *The Three Graces Ensnaring Cupid*, 1738, Archives Nationales, Paris.

8 The hangings are not original but merely appropriate to the room.

9 This figure is just one instance of a whole range of quantitative data which Lavoisier compiled in order to estimate consumer spending and collective wealth in late eighteenth-century Paris. See Sonenscher 1989, 1.

10 According to Kaplow there were no fewer than twenty ports or yards established along the banks of the Seine, each one specialising in a particular commodity. For the building trades, in addition to the port de la Grève, the port de la Conférence was important because it was here that stone arrived from nearby quarries. See Kaplow 1972, 15.

11 Blondel 1771–7, v, 7.

12 See Jaubert 1773, ii, 127. The abbé Cordemoy advised that in order to prevent rot, the *lambris* should either be given air holes, or a gap should be left between the supporting wall and the panelling. See Cordemoy 1714, 245.

13 Roubo 1772, 2.

14 Blondel 1771–7, v, 7.

15 See ibid., vi, 360; Roubo 1772, 22–3.

16 Ibid.; Potain 1749, 2.

17 Roubo 1772, 23.

18 Blondel 1771–7, vi, 360.

19 See Pons 1985, 51.

20 Blondel 1771–7, vi, 380. See also Pons 1985, 51.

21 Rambaud 1964–71, ii, 648.

22 See also the inventions of *carton moulé* submitted to the Académie Royale d'Architecture for approval by Morand in 1777 (P.-V.A. 1911–29, viii, 307) and Gardeur in 1778 (ibid., viii, 338, 351, 352, 363). For stucco decoration in the first half of the eighteenth-century, see Pons 1985, 7; and for the stucco samples submitted to the Academy by Clérici in 1759, see ibid., vii, 20–1, 27, and by Grisel in 1774, see ibid., viii, 200.

23 See Gallet 1976–7, 80–83. For sculptors such as François-Joseph Duret who produced applied plaster ornament, see Pons 1987², 137–78. Another important, late eighteenth-century stuccador, Nicolas-François-Daniel Lhuillier, like Duret, worked for Boullé and Chalgrin although his most important work was carried out under François-Joseph Bélanger. His probate inventory gives a full description of the contents of such an artist's studio, including itemised lists of his ornament moulds. The inventory of his papers lists amongst his clients the comte d'Artois, Baudard de Saint-James, the duc de Montmorency-Laval and the marquis de Mirabeau. See A.N.M.C. XXII/95 (IAD 19/vi/1793).

24 Blondel 1771–7, vi, 380.

25 On the hôtel Feuquières, see Paris 1981, 37–40.

26 Musée des Arts Décoratifs, Inv. CD 1651. The inscriptions on the drawing reads, 'Pour le Sallon de Mᵉ la marquisse de feuquiere' and then clockwise: 'bordure de glace/glace/parquet/Comme nous avons bessoins davoir deslargeurs, pour trasser nostre ouvrage, jay fait les esquisses de profils que vous aures la bonté de faire voir a Monsieur Boscrit, a fin quil les corigent s'y il le juge a propos, ou quil en fassent dautre, vous luy porteres aussy sil vous plaits les desseins, afin quil jugent mieux des profils jay fait deux profils de chambranlles, car jay dans l'ydé que vous mavé dit que les portes doivent ouvrir du costé du Sallon que nous allons faire, – vous aures la bonté de prendre aussy la sailly du porte tapilerie [?] de nostre corniche ou plafond de larchitrave/chambranlle pour etre seré du costé du Sallon/B. Chambranlle porte/Simaise du lambris d'apuis parraport a la sailly B du chambranlle/A. demie pilastres de la cheminé/cadre des grand paneaux'. (The transcription is faithful to the original authography.)

27 See A.N. 201, M1 1–2, C³.

28 A.A.P. MS. Carton 48/doss. II.

29 See A.N. 201, M1 1–2, C³ 19/31.

30 For the hôtel de Matignon, see A.N. 201, M1 1–2, C³ 19/29, 31, 32, 42; for the decoration of the hôtel de la Force, overseen by the architect Le Maître, see A.A.P. MS. Carton 48/doss. II; and for the *mémoires* subsequently submitted by the house-painter, La Martinière, see B.H.V.P. MS. CP 3317, f°339, 366.

31 For his work at the hôtel de Roquelaure, for instance, see Rambaud 1964–71, i, 453; Paris 1984, 165.

32 For this practice at the Bâtiments du Roi, see Engerand 1900, xv–vi.

33 See Agnew 1986, 17–56, esp. 36–8. Sonenscher was the first to note and expand upon the analogies between the bazaar economies of Morocco and Java, described by Clifford Geertz (see Geertz 1963; Geertz 1979), and aspects of the artisanal economy of eighteenth-century Paris. See Sonenscher 1989, *passim* and in the present context esp. 134–6.

34 See Paris 1984, 151, 191.

35 A.N. O¹ 1672/34. The suggestion was originally made by Bruno Pons. See, Pons 1985, 27.

36 Rambaud 1964–71, ii, 456–7. Similar arrangements were also entered into by painters. For example, in 1987 the painters Jean-Baptiste Bolignon and Jean Coste became partners in order to undertake the decoration of the *salle de spectacle* at Nantes. See A.N.M.C. XCI/1241 (30/iv/1787).

37 Ibid.

38 André Le Goupil was followed by his son

Mathieu who married the daughter of Marin Bellan, Marie-Jeanne. Meanwhile Jacques Verberckt took Marie-Madeleine Le Goupil, daughter of André, as his second wife and in the next generation Jean-Baptiste Taupin (son of Pierre) married Julie Degoullons (daughter of Jules). See the genealogical charts at the back of Pons 1985. See also the contracts of marriage and separation between Mathieu Le Goupil and Marie-Jeanne Bellan in ibid., 294, 308.

39 For the complex financial structure of the partnership, see Pons 1985, 55–83.

40 For the partnership documents, see ibid., 280–82, 292–4.

41 Ibid., 87.

42 Antoine-Nicolas Rivet was the son of Antoine Rivet, a master-joiner who worked consistently for the Bâtiments from 1678 until his death in 1702. In the partnership document between Pineau and Rivet son, the latter styled himself 'sculpteur' but there is no trace of him in either the lists of the Académie de Saint-Luc or in Guiffrey 1915. In an earlier partnership with the master-sculptor Louis Thibault, however, he was identified as a master-joiner (see A.N.M.C. xxx/170 26/v/1704). Whatever the legality of the case, Rivet seems to have been a craftsman who moved easily between two ostensibly autonomous trades. On 11 August 1728 Rivet and Pineau entered into an equal partnership, 'for all work of sculpture . . . whether in Paris or in the countryside, for the King or for others, whether in wood, stone, marble, lead or other materials', for six years in the first instance (see A.N.M.C. xxxvii/244 11/viii/1728). This document is important not just for what it reveals about Pineau's working practice but also because it puts back the date at which Pineau is thought to have returned from Russia by several years. This and other documentary material on Pineau will form the subject of a forthcoming article in the *Burlington Magazine*.

43 On the question of the economy of the luxury trades, see Sonenscher 1989, 210–43.

44 See Forster 1971, 130. According to Forster, in the 1770s explicit interest on outstanding obligations was not unknown and by the 1780s interest at 5–8% had become the rule.

45 See B.H.V.P. MS. cp 4606. Likewise, in 1741, the duc de Saint-Aignan still owed 3,141 *livres* to the ornament sculptor Charles-Louis Maurisan for work executed in 1729, and in 1745 he had an outstanding debt to Domenchin de Chavanne for a painting executed in 1722. (See Rambaud 1964–71, ii, 494, 928.) In the same year

Lambert-Sigisbert Adam featured amongst the cardinal de Polignac's creditors: owed 7,000 *livres*. (See ibid., i, 235–6, 709–10.) When the duc de Montmorency died in 1761 he left not inconsiderable sums owing to the upholsterer La Batte (8,000 *livres*), the joiners Cresson, Bastier and Fesse (1,815 *livres*, 15 *sous*) and the painters Peters, Lasnier, Berthe and Martin (3,385 *livres*, 12 *sous*), debts that were only settled two years later. See *Etat des dettes de M. le duc de Montmorency, acquitées en argent ou en contracts de constitutions* (1763), A.N. T 144⁴⁴⁻⁵. At the other end of the century, Joseph-Nicolas Guichard wrote a series of distressed letters to his client and then to the architect Lebrun in order to secure payment for ornament sculpture executed in 1772 (A.A.P. MS. Carton 39, sculpteur) and in the same year, Pierre-Joseph-Désiré Gouthière had to borrow 1,800 *livres* from the receiver-general, Simon Charles Boutin to pay the seigneurial dues on a property he had bought in the faubourg Saint-Martin, because the banker, Nicolas Beaujon had still not settled his account (A.A.P. MS. Carton 29, artisan).

46 Perard, the master-mason was owed 1,734 *livres*, 3 *sous* for work carried out on the quai Malaquai between 1737–40; Girardin, the carpenter 112 *livres*; Tramblin, the painter just 24 *sous*; L'Empereur, the jeweller, the more substantial sum of 6,840 *livres* for diamonds; and the painter Dumonchel 620 *livres*, of which 70 *livres* for a copy he had made of the portrait of 'S.A.S. dans le Bain' (Jean-Marc Nattier's *Mlle de Clermont en Sultane*, perhaps?). The amounts were settled on 4/x/1742. See B.H.V.P. cp 4606, fol. 16v, 32r, 44v.

47 See Crozat-Boulle (1700). It is interesting to note that Boulle agreed to execute the mouldings of the bas-reliefs on the pedestals, '*sur les modeles que le Sieur Crozat luy en donna* avec mesures, afin que ces ouvrages pussent estre placez dans le cabinet du Sieur Crozat' (ibid., 1).

48 Ibid., 3–4.

49 See Janneau 1975, 11–12.

50 See Sonenscher 1989, 133–4.

51 See Germain 1766, passim.

52 Defamatory articles were apparently published in the *Courier d'Avignon*, no. 54, 27/vi/1765; ibid., no. 70, 22/viii/1765, and in the supplement to the *Gazette d'Utrecht*, no. 70, 23/viii/1765.

53 After Rivet, Pineau is mentioned as having worked in 1731 in association with Charles Bernard. (See Rambaud 1964–71, i, 397). The documentation about this partnership has yet to come to light but it does seen to have been comparatively short-lived. From the inventory of Marie Humbline Regnault, Charles Bernard's widow, it is

known that the partnership was wound up on 17 June 1733, soon after Bernard's death. (See A.N.M.C. xxxviii/286, 28/iii/1736.) Indeed, at the time of Pineau's wife's death in 1735, Pineau still owed the window Bernard 1,760 *livres* to settle the affairs of the partnership. (See A.N.M.C. xxxviii/280, 26/i/1735.) These and other documents relating to Nicolas Pineau are the subject of a forthcoming article in the *Burlington Magazine*. For the remainder of his career Pineau appears to have operated alone.

54 B.N. Est. Rés. b6c; Cited in Kimball 1980, 13.

55 See Daviler 1760, 189.

56 See Blondel 1737–8, i, 25.

57 See Biver 1923, 152.

58 See Roubo 1772, 43.

59 Watin 1773, 2–3. On Watin, see Eriksen 1974, esp. 128, 139, 402–3. For an example of Watin's own activities as a house-painter, see Paris 1984, 122.

60 *Girard, Peintre, rue du faubourg, Mémoire concernant l'etablissement d'un peintre décorateur attaché et fixé au Département des châteaux du Roi*, 1785 (A.N. o¹ 1985/39). There are at least three Girards who could have been responsible for this *mémoire*, but the most likely is Jean-Baptiste, admitted as a master to the Académie de Saint-Luc in 1771 and whose address was given at that time as, 'au faubourg Saint Martin, près la foire'. See Guiffrey 1915, 20–21. A similar request had been put to Philibert Orry by Pierre-Nicolas Huilliot earlier in the century. See Engerand 1900, 235–6, n. 4. Both requests were turned down.

61 See *Journal Œconomique* Sept. 1752, 120; Blondel 1771–7, vi, 438. The taste for white and gold schemes seems to date from the 1690s. See Thornton 1981, 74.

62 According to *La Feuille Nécessaire* in 1757, 'La menuiserie sculptée, qui fait la principale décoration de nos appartemens, a repris de nos jours une très-grande faveur à cause des couleurs gayes & de l'éclat du vernis dont on la couvre'. (Ibid., 1757, 221). See also Daviler 1760, 189; Blondel 1771–7, 442–5.

63 For the decoration of these rooms, see Paris 1982, 157–9. On the Maurisan, see Pons 1983, 74. For one of Oudry's overdoors, see Paris 1982², 232, fig. 128b.

64 See the 'Etat des effets, marchandises et ustenciles' in Tramblin's studio, drawn up at the time he entered into a partnership with Louis Mautemps, A.N.M.C. lxvi/495 (12/x/1752).

65 On the changes in the colour preferences of the seventeenth and eighteenth centuries, see Pardailhé-Galabrun 1988, 398–401, and appendix 11, 480–81.

66 See Rambaud 1964–71, ii, 649.

67 Ibid., 649–50.

68 See Engerand 1900, 281–2; Bordeaux 1984, 47.

69 Blondel 1774, ii, 80. However, it should be noted that in the 1750s Blondel was of a different opinion. See, for instance, his remarks on the hôtel Castanier in Blondel 1752–6, ii, 114–15.

70 See Jaubert 1773, iii, 422.

71 *Mémoire des marchandises de peintures fournis par Monsieur Le Clef marchand de couleurs, rue des princes à Paris*, March 1756–Feb. 1757 (A.N. T 464). The Cayeux in question was probably Claude-Philibert Cayeux, admitted as a master to the Académie de Saint-Luc in 1755 and resident in the rue des Cordeliers. Certainly the contents of this Cayeux's workshop suggests a house-painter: large numbers of buckets, bottles and paint-pots, 36 brushes, 5 ladders, 30 pounds of charcoal black, etc. He also owned 3 stones for grinding colours, which indicates that he did not always buy ready-ground pigments. The inventory also itemises 30 lots of paintings ranging in value from 1 *livre*, 10 *sous*, to 8 *livres* (by Francisque Millet, after Watteau and Wouwermans, etc.) which suggests that Cayeux may have been a fine painter and/or a dealer as well. See A.N.M.C. LXV/353 (8/xi/1766); Guiffrey 1884–6, (i), 394–5; ibid., 1915, 214.

72 Ibid. In 1776, the *Almanach dauphin* gives his address as rue Meslay.

73 By contrast, in Britain ready-mixed paints were already available by the eighteenth century. See Bristow 1977, 246–8.

74 *Journal Œconomique*, Sept. 1752, 122. See also Blondel 1771–7, vi, 442.

75 According to the colour merchant Mauclerc, 'Quelquefois l'on peint les appartemens à cause des ameublemens; alors il faut que la couleur dominante de l'appartement soit la couleur dominante de l'ammeublement et la couleur du rechampissage, la couleur répandue dans la dominante de l'ammeublement . . . Si l'ammeublement est d'une seule couleur, la peinture de l'appartement ne peut souffrir qu'un encadrement doré ou couleur d'or.' See Mauclerc 1773, 108. Moreover, Bastide particularly praised the co-ordinated schemes of his *petite maison*. See Bastide 1879, 8–9.

76 See Gallet 1976–7, 76. On the method of executing 'peinture en chipolin', see Blondel 1771–7, vi, 439–40.

77 The name *chipolin* apparently derives from the onion used in the mixture of some varnishes. *Mercure de France*, 1 June 1757, 169. See also another notice in *La Feuille Nécessaire*, 1757, 12. Guiffrey mentions a single Dandrillon, Pierre-Bertrand, received into the Académie de Saint-Luc 24/

xii/1751 (Guiffrey 1915, 242), but the documents published by Wildenstein reveal that in the first half of the eighteenth century there were at least three Dandrillons active in Paris as master-painters: Claude, Bernard and Pierre. (Wildenstein 1956, 36.) Any one of these could correspond to the one cited.

78 P.-V.A. 1911–29, iv, 280, 291, 295.

79 Ibid., 295. See also *Mercure de France*, 2 June 1757, 143. To reinforce the credibility of his product, Odiot informed the public that he was currently working for the king at Choisy. On Odiot see Guiffrey 1915, 407. In the same year a third and a fourth painter, Lefevre and Michel, also announced odourless varnishes in the press. See respectively *Mercure de France*, Aug. 1757, 167; P.-V.A. 1911–29, vi, 302, and *La Feuille Nécessaire*, 1757, 221.

80 *Annonces, affiches et avis divers*, Thursday 15 July 1751, 146. For attitudes to smell in the domestic environment in the eighteenth century, see Corbin 1982, 189–205.

81 See Hahn 1971, 23, 65–71.

82 Bastide 1879, 10.

83 P.-V.A. 1911–29, vi, 311–12, 314–15. For other items submitted to the Academies of Painting and Sculpture and Architecture for inspection, see P.-V.A. 1911–29, vii, 42–3, 50–52; ix, 173–4, 179, 184 (pigments); P.-V. 1875–92, viii, 46, 82; ix, 80–81, 114–16, 299, 308; x, 110, 112–14 (pigments). P.-V.A. 1911–29, ix, 52, 53 (varnishes); P.-V. 1875–92, vi, 172–3, 200 (varnishes). P.-V.A. 1911–29, vii, 31; viii, 232; ix, 53–4 (gilding). See also the products submitted to the Bâtiments for scrutiny, A.N. O¹ 1294/231 (Huchot – paint cleaner); O¹ 1294/230, 341 (Gosse and Samousseau – varnish). And those submitted to the Bureau de Commerce, A.N. F¹² 2237 (Boichard – stucco; Cosseron – 'couleurs et papiers Lucidoriques').

84 On the economic value of privileges, see Sonenscher 1989, esp. 216–17. On the granting of privileges by the Bureau de Commerce, see Parker 1979, 47–69; Deyon-Guignet 1980, 611–32.

85 See Geertz 1963, 35.

86 The information is to be found jotted on the back of a drawing. See Musée des Arts Décoratifs, Paris, Inv. 1491B recto.

87 See Geertz 1963, 32–6; Agnew 1986, 37–9.

88 Quoted from Paris 1950, xxix.

89 For definitions of these terms, see Marsy 1746, i, 23, 293–4; Lacombe 1755, 320, 456; Watelet-Levesque 1792, i, 90–96.

90 Quoted from Paris 1950, xxix. For Bérain and Audran, see Weigert 1937; Paris 1950; Weigert 1955; La Gorce 1986.

91 See Babeau 1886, 83–5.

92 Paris 1950, xxix.

93 See ibid., 59–68 and the list of papers from his probate inventory which often cite the sums Audran was paid for such commissions, A.N.M.C. XLIX, 553 (1/vi/1734).

94 For all these figures see Paris 1950, 59–60. For the *Portières des Dieux*, see also Fénaille 1903–12, iii, 25.

95 Quoted from Paris 1950, xxix.

96 Ibid., xxix–xxx. It is perhaps worth noting in passing that Audran owned two Watteaus which he displayed in an upstairs room of his house overlooking the riding school of the Luxembourg Palace, along with other works, including unlikely 'pendents' by Le Brun and Lancret depicting children at play, a Virgin with the infant Christ by one of the Parrocel, and a Stella. See A.N.M.C. XLIX/553 (IAD 1/vi/1734).

97 Lacombe 1755, 214–15.

98 See La Gorce 1981, 71–80.

99 See Desportes's obituary in the *Mercure de France*, 1 June 1743, 1187. A printed fan in the Bibliothèque Nationale, published in July 1733 and depicting scenes from *Don Quixote* and the Comédie Italienne is accompanied by a note which alleges that one of these latter, *La Veuve Coquette* (performed by the Italians in October 1721), 'est de M. Desportes fils, Peintre de l'académie', which suggests that the painter not only designed but wrote for the theatre. See B.N. Cabinet des Estampes, Lc¹² in fol.

100 See Guiffrey 1887, 119–29. For Boucher's relationship with the theatre, see Landau 1983.

101 Pernety 1757, 123–4.

102 See the accounts in the *Mercure de France*, 1 Dec. 1737, 2653; ibid., 2 Dec. 1737, 2877–8; ibid., Feb. 1738, 319–20. On Servandoni, see Bouche 1910, 121–46; Bataille 1930, 379–92.

103 The drawings are attached to the masonry contract, see A.N.M.C. CXVII/421 (22/vii/1738); CXVII/423 (17/xii/1738). From the cardinal's probate inventory (A.N.M.C. CXVII/770 (IAO 2/v/1747) we learn that a number of the rooms in the hôtel were decorated with overdoors by Servandoni: 4 in the *salon*, 2 in the *chambre de parade* and 2 representing landscapes and architectural ruins in the *cabinet*. See Paris 1987², 97–9. Nine overdoors were exhibited at the Salon of 1743, 'représentans plusieurs sujets d'Architecture & Bâtimens antiques, Païsages & divers Vûes, lesquels ont été faits en huit jours, à l'occasion de la fête que Son Eminence M. le Cardinal d'Auvergne a donné dans son Hôtel, pour le marriage de la princess de Boüillon, aujourd'huy Duchesse de Montbazon'. See

104 For Brunetti, see Guiffrey 1887, 119–29. In 1757 Brunetti provided designs for the production of *Sémiramis*, see *La Feuille Nécessaire* 1757, 435. Moreover, the inventory drawn up after Brunetti's death styled him 'peintre décorateur de la Comédie Française'. Regrettably, the inventory of papers has nothing to say about his business; that it must have been reasonably successful may, however, be judged by his collection of books and prints. Most unusually for a painter, Brunetti had a library of some 730 volumes (valued collectively at 376 *livres*), which ranged from ancient history and literature (Charles Rollin, *Histoire ancienne* (1731–8); Virgil), to antiquities (Bernard de Montfaucon's *Antiquités Expliquées en figures* (1716), to travel literature (Jean Chardin, *Voyages en Perse* (1711), Le Brun, *Voyages*), to modern novels (Lesage, *Gil Blas de Santillane* (1715–35)); Hamilton, *Mémoires du comte de Gramont* (1713)), to plays, poetry (the works of Pierre Corneille), and the Bible. His prints included Mariette's *Architecture françoise* (1727), the complete works of Piranese and the Bibiena; prints after the Farnese ceiling, the chapel of the Enfants Trouvés, Vernet and Watteau. Finally, he also had Academy drawings and 'une petite optique', this last apparently of his father's devising. See A.N.M.C. IX/789 (IAD 23/x/1783).

105 See Langlois 1922, 181–2. Brunetti subsequently painted the dining-room of the hôtel de Rohan situated around the corner from Soubise. See ibid., 219.

106 See Paris 1984, 57. The photographs are held at the Bibliothèque Historique de la Ville de Paris. At the hôtel de Richelieu, Brunetti designed a stairwell which included, on the ceiling, a figure of Fame *di sotto in su*. See Piganiol de La Force 1765, iii, 132–3; Chevalier 1970–71, 109–22.

107 Thiery 1786, ii, 527–31.

108 These two worked with him on the stairwell at the hôtel de Richelieu, see *La Feuille Nécessaire*, 1757, 22. Examples of Soldini's decorative work, such as four overdoors depicting children at play, are to be found at the Musée des Beaux-Arts at Dijon.

109 See Guiffrey 1887, 125. Gaetano Brunetti worked in England from the early 1730s until 1739 when he rejoined his son in Paris. For Gaetano's work in Britain, see Beard 1981, pls. 99, 130.

110 See Paris 1984, 57.

111 Biver 1933, 49.

112 See Paris 1986, 267.

113 For other examples by native artists see Michel Boyer's perspective at the hôtel de Longueville executed in 1709 (Brice 1725, i, 127); Jacques Rousseau's for the hôtel Titon du Tillet (Brice 1752, ii, 261); Claude Leveilly's decoration of the concert chamber at the Tuileries (*Mercure de France*, 2 Dec. 1727, 2942–3); Pierre Le Maire's exterior perspective for an hôtel, rue d'Anjou (ibid., 1 Dec. 1734, 2684–6); Bonnart's perspective at the ménagerie of the château de Clagny (ibid., 1 June 1737, 1177), Jacques de Lajoue's for the library of St. Geneviève (Roland Michel 1984, 102–3) and Alexis Peyrotte's illusionistic garden-scape, with flowers and birds, painted around the walls of the hôtel de Conti, 1765–6. See A.N. O¹ 3618 (copy A.A.P. MS. 1076/42).

114 For a brief discussion of Louis-Denis de La Live de Bellegarde and his taste, see Bailey 1988, ix–xi; Fort Worth 1992, 348–53, no. 39.

115 See Lastic 1955, 26–31.

116 See Rambaud 1964–71, ii, 934–5.

117 See Engerand 1900, 309–10. The paintings were not mentioned in d'Antin's inventory because they were paid for by the exchequer and therefore reverted to the crown at the duke's death. See A.N.M.C. LVI/65 (IAD 7/xi/1736). For the paintings, see Zafran 1984, 128–9; New York 1986, 134–7. The story of Jacob and Laban seems to have been fairly popular in the 1730s and 1740s: a version by Jean Restout featured in the *cabinet* of the duc de Chevreuse at the hôtel de Luynes (see Paris 1984, 57) and another by an unknown painter decorated the *salon de compagnie* at the hôtel de Souvré (see Paris 1990, 66).

118 See Dézallier d'Argenville 1779, 193–6. No mention is made of these pictures in Noailles's probate inventory: A.N.M.C. XXIII/682 (30/vi/1766).

119 See Langlois 1922, 152–3. They were paid 100 *livres* for each portrait.

120 See Piganiol de La Force 1765, iii, 257–8. We learn from the duchesse de Penthièvre's inventory that all these paintings were 'encastrés dans la boiserie sous des bordures dorées'. They were not, therefore, valued separately, 'attendu que tous ces tableaux sont ajustés de manière qu'ils sont inhérens au fonds de l'hotel dont on ne pouroit les enlever sans dégradation' (A.N.M.C. XXXV/686 (30/iii/1756, no. 184)). According to Dézallier d'Argenville (1752, 122) the panelling of this room and the adjacent 'salle des rois', was the work of Vassé. However, by the time an inventory of the pictures of the hôtel was taken by Lebrun in An II, the schemes had disappeared. See A.N. F¹⁷ 1267/7.

121 See Paris 1989², no. 32.

122 See Schnapper 1967, 13.

123 See Wildenstein 1921, 37–9.

124 Ibid., 43–4.

125 See Rambaud 1964–71, ii, 395–6.

126 See Chastelus 1974, 129–38.

127 See Engerand 1900, 76, 98, 127, 136, 189, 203–4, 279, 293–4, 298, 355, 421, 459–60. For the commission, see Bordeaux 1984, 113–26.

128 See Rambaud 1964–71, ii, 396.

129 For Louvier's commission, see A.N. 201, M1 1–2, C³ 20/33, 34. Louvier was provided with stretchers and canvas at the duc de Valentinois's expense. Guillaume Louvier or Louvrier was admitted to the Académie de Saint-Luc in 1729 and appointed an officer in 1764. See Guiffrey 1915, 375. For Delaistre's commission for the hôtel Vatart, rue Poissonnière, which included 4 wall paintings and 11 overdoors, see Wildenstein 1921, 28–30.

130 In 1739, François Desportes was paid 5,000 *livres* for 5 overdoors for the *salle des jeux* at Compiègne (see Engerand 1900, 158–9) and Jean-Baptiste Oudry was payed 5,100 *livres* for 4 paintings executed in 1742 for Choisy, 2 of which were overdoors (ibid., 368).

131 See Engerand 1900, 495; Biver 1933, 40; Nice 1977, 76, nos. 148–50.

132 See Wildenstein 1921, 63–5.

133 It should be remembered that the Bâtiments paid painters on a fixed tariff, independent of merit. See below, n. 159.

134 The figure is taken from Crow 1985, 11. On the basis of the deed of settlement between Mme Boucher and her children, George Brunel has more recently revealed that the artist's estate was worth 152,618 *livres* at the time of his death in 1770, a figure that does not easily confirm the extravagance of the claims made about his yearly income. See Brunel 1986, 35.

135 For instance, in 1762 Noël Hallé confided to Cochin that he found himself 'sans ouvrages' and much bothered by 'la position de travailler sans but et de faire des tableaux sans destination'. On Charles-Nicolas Cochin's suggestion he was employed at the Gobelins, but not all were so lucky. See Furcy-Raynaud 1903, 240.

136 See Lastic 1955, 26.

137 Goldsmiths, engravers, paper-merchants and wallpaper manufacturers are among those who seem to have made particular use of elaborate tradecards. For the tradecard of the engraver and wallpaper manufacturer Langlois, see B.N. Est Li 4ga. An example of Réveillon's tradecard reads as follows: 'Aux Armes de son A.S. Madame la Princesse de Conty. Ruë de l'Arbre-Sec près la Ruë des Fossés. Reveillon, Mᵈ. Vend de trés beau Papier Battu, Lavé, Verny, d'Oré, Glacé, d'Hollande et de touttes qualités pour l'Ecriture et le dessin, Livres et Papier Reglés pour la Musique, *touttes sortes de Papiers à Fleurs*

Indienne, Damassés et autres qu'il employe pour les Tapisseries, Ecrans, et Paravants, Registres de touttes grandeurs Reglés pour les Comptes Etrangers Parties doubles, et Journaux, Boestes pour les Bureaux, Ecritoires de poches et de tables, Portefeuilles et Tablettes de Maroquin ferment à Clef, garnis d'Or et d'Argent. Plumes d'Hollande, Cire d'Espagnes, Canif, Gratoire Veritable Encre double et luisante, et touttes sortes de marchandises à l'usage des Bureaux' and is to be found at the Musée Carnavalet, Paris. The emphasis is mine and made necessary because the tradecard suggests that wallpapers were just one of Réveillon's multiple concerns and by no means conspicuously the most important. On tradecards, see Maillard 1898.

138 For an exception, see McAllister-Johnson 1983, 123–4. McAllister-Johnson draws attention to the role of engravings in art advertisement and it is worth noting that in 1768 the engravers Beauvarlet and Danzel asked permission to reproduce Boucher, Pierre, Van Loo and Vien's compositions for the Gobelins's series, *The Loves of the Gods*, a request that was granted because it was judged that the prints 'feront honneur aux meilleurs peintres de notre école' and, moreover, 'feront connaître aux étrangers ce que la manufacture peut leur offrir de plus agréable'. See Furcy-Raynaud 1903, 135–6. For a recent and general discussion of advertising in eighteenth-century Paris, see Todd 1989, 513–47.

139 *Journal Œconomique*, August 1751, 91–8.

140 La Font de Saint Yenne 1754, 126. On Le Lorrain, see Rosenberg 1978, 173–202.

141 See Guillerne 1983, 47–50.

142 Pernety 1757, 465–8.

143 See *Mercure de France*, 1 April 1767, 160–61.

144 For both positive and negative comments on the use of mirrors in interior decoration, see Daviler 1738, 189; Blondel 1774, i, 49.

145 Scoville 1950, 120. See also Roche 1957, 13–25.

146 On early seventeenth-century mirror rooms, see Thornton 1981, 75–8; Mérot 1990, 79–85.

147 See Scoville 1950, 120.

148 See Adrien Maurice, duc de Noailles's probate inventory, A.N.M.C. XXIII/682 (30/vi/1766). The furniture included 10 *fauteuils*, 2 *canapés*, 4 *tabourets*, all with gilded wooden frames and with loose scarlet and gold upholstery. The curtains were of matching material. The Chinese element was provided by 3 six-leaf screens, one faced with lacquer and the others decorated with Chinese papers, a lacquered box, a Chinese tray, 9 Chinese and Japanese urns

and 2 blue and white Far-Eastern pots-pourri.

149 Daumard-Furet 1961, 4.

150 See Kimball 1936, 259–80; Kimball 1980, 52; Thornton 1981, 66–7; Pons 1985, 87.

151 See Pris 1977, 5–23; Thornton 1981, 87–9; Pons 1985, 87.

152 See Pris 1977, 5–23.

153 The finishing plant in the faubourg Saint-Antoine where glass was polished, employed a labour-force of 500 in 1698, but only 400 in 1700; and the situation deteriorated before getting better. Demand fell off so dramatically during the war of the Spanish Succession that the Plastrier company running Saint-Gobain went bankrupt. It was only with the formation of the so-called Société Dagincourt under the directorship of the two bankers Etienne Demeuves and Jacques Brisson that matters began to improve. Although slumps continued to occur in response to the European military conflicts (1733, 1740s, 1756–63, 1773) they were henceforth only relative downturns in the context of overall growth. See Pris 1975.

154 See, for example, the Galerie des Glaces and the Chambre du Roi at Versailles (Thornton 1981, pl. 82).

155 When they were cast in two pieces they were to be hung, according to Bimont, 'à porté de la vue, & on doit prendre garde qu'elle ne soit point coupée par la jonction de deux glaces' (Bimont 1774, 93). *Miroitiers* installed these large mirrors and were paid 5% of their value for doing so – 'pour la raison que si les miroitiers cassent les grandes glasses soit en les deposant ou en les reposant, il est obliger d'en fournir des parailles a ces frais avec teint, comme il les à trouvées' – unless they, not the client, provided the mirrors. In that case, no installation charge was made because the miroitier earned his cut from the 10–20% margin between the wholesale price at which he bought them at Saint-Gobain and the retail price he was paid by the client. See Pietre, *Détails des bâtiments propre à un architecte fait en 1778* (A.A.P. MS. 51, f° 178).

156 Roche 1981, 153.

157 See Fénaille 1903–12, iii, 41.

158 See Daumard-Furet 1961, 29.

159 See Furcy-Raynaud 1903, 109. The smaller the scale of the figures, the higher the rate of pay. At half life-size, history painting was paid 50 *livres* the square *pied*; at a quarter life size, 100 *livres* and at under quarter life size, 200 *livres* the square *pied*.

160 See Fénaille 1903–12, iii, 190–91. For the most recent discussion of this series, see Standen 1988, 149–91.

161 See Pris 1975, 33, 64, 722.

162 B.H.V.P. MS. CP 4872.

163 See Pris 1977, 13.

164 For a discussion of the manufacturing value of privilege closely followed here, see Sonenscher 1989, esp. 136–8.

165 See Scoville 1950, 143–55. The complaints of critics like La Font de Saint Yenne (1747, 13–16) about the excessive use and deleterious effects of mirrors did nothing to curtail demand.

166 On the upholsterer's share in the seventeenth century, see Thornton 1981, 107–243, esp. 97–106, 130–35. On the *marchands-tapissiers* in the eighteenth century, see Jaubert 1773, iv, 202–8. Probate inventories drawn up before 1750 testify to the nobility's continued attachment to tapestries, though they found a place more frequently in country houses than urban residences. See Rambaud 1964–71, i, 713–48, ii, 1055–98.

167 A.N. F¹² 1456ᴮ/177.

168 A.N. F¹² 639ᴬ/209. For biographical information about these weavers, see Lacordaire 1897, 18–19, 22–7, 51–2. For a statement of the financial regime operative at the Gobelins during the first half of the eighteenth century, see Marcel 1906, 63–4.

169 A.N. F¹² 639ᴬ/209.

170 Ibid.

171 Ibid.

172 Work on ornamental borders was consistently well paid throughout the eighteenth century. In 1714 Blin de Fontenay was paid 1,100 *livres* for the borders of the *Don Quixote* series, while Charles-Antoine Coypel only received 400 *livres* for each of the canvases. And in 1717 when Coypel surrendered two larger works for the series, he was paid just 550 *livres* for each, while Audran received 900 *livres* for the borders. The latter had in fact asked for 1,450 *livres* for the work. See Fénaille 1903–12, ii, 158, 172. On Maurice Jacques, see ibid., iii, 228–30, 246–62, 301–4; Eriksen 1974, 192.

173 See Havard-Vachon 1889, 125–222; Deyon-Guignet 1980, 611–32. During the *ancien régime*, aside from their use in the royal palaces, Gobelins tapestries were presented by the crown as gifts to foreign heads of state. For those presented to Russian monarchs in the eighteenth century, see Birykova 1975, 458–65.

174 On Beauvais, see Badin 1909; Coural 1977, 66–84.

175 See Wilson 1983, 86–8.

176 B.M. MS. 3723 (2609), f° 203. Alterations to tapestries were made either at the Gobelins or by *marchands-tapissiers*. Dézallier d'Argenville admired a tapestry after Lucas van Leyden at the hôtel Tallard, 'qui a été ralongée aux Gobelins avec tant d'art qu'on ne le voit point . . .' (Dézallier

d'Argenville 1752, 215). For the more difficult task of reducing tapestries without destroying the intended effect, see Bimont 1774, 90–92.

177 Drawing schools for the training of apprentices were a central concern to all three manufactories. A school had been founded at the Gobelins in 1667 but by the eighteenth century it had lapsed. It was legally reinstituted under Philibert Orry by Arrest de Conseil (10/iv/1737); new regulations were discussed in 1751 (see B.M. MS. 3723 (2609), f° 279–307) and the implementation of the *Arrêt* was carried out in 1759 (see Mondain-Monval 1918, 15). On 4/vii/1720, the Conseil de Commerce moved to appoint Vigoureux-Duplessis as the head of a newly founded school at Beauvais (A.N. F^{12} 1456^A/4) and on 18/i/1742 an *Ordonnance de monseigneur l'intendant de la généralité de Moulins* founded two schools under the supervision of Jean-Joseph Dumons at Aubusson (A.N. F^{12} 1458^A/doss. vi). Finally, in 1774, a certain Béllanger applied for the post of painter to the Savonnerie and director of its (proposed) school (A.N. F^{12} 639^A/88). Meanwhile, attempts were also made to establish a drawing school for the Lyon silk industry in 1751. See Pérez 1980, 108–13.

178 The weekly salaries of these weavers (*c*.1750) were as follows:

Les officiers de la tête	12–18 *livres*
Les bons drapistes et paysagistes	9–12 *livres*
Les drapistes et paysagistes ordinaires	6–9 *livres*
Les fleuristes	4–6 *livres*
Les apprentifs à la fin de leurs tems	2–3 *livres*
Les commançans depuis 3 ans	1–1 *livres* 10 *sous*

(A.N. F^{12} 1456^B). According to Fenaille, weavers at the Gobelins earned between 7–15 *livres* p.w. in 1749 (Fenaille 1903–12, iii, 206). Such specialisation was deemed essential by all the manufactories. In a report written in 1751 on Le Blond's workshop at the Gobelins, De L'Isle explained that this *atelier* was, 'fort médiocre' because, 'il n'estoit composé que de huit ouvriers ce qui ne suffit pas pour en former en chaque genre, et que cela entraisne le deffaut de donner une piece en entier a un ouvrier, qui fait tous les differents ouvrages comme testes, carnation, Paysages, et par conséquent ne les fait pas bien' (A.N. F^{12} 639^A/50). Likewise, in a report on Aubusson written in 1754, it was noted that, 'Les ouvriers d'aubusson travaillent indifferement aux fleurs, aux plantes, aux drapperies, aux animalles c'est ce qui les rends mediocres dans tous les genres. a

Beauvais ils sont classés, et toujours occupés des mêmes sortes d'ouvrages ce qui contribuë beaucoup a perfectionner leurs talent' (A.N. F^{12} 1458^A/doss. v).

179 See Oppermann 1977, 93–8. Tapestries executed after Le Brun's designs in the 1680s used approximately 79 colour tones; by the 1730s the number used in new designs had increased to 364 and by 1780 topped 587. See Verlet 1965, 99. On the new dyes allowed in the manufacture of tapestry from the time of the 1737 regulation drawn up with the help of the chemist Dufay, see Pardailhé-Galabrun 1988, 398. Dyers were amongst the most prosperous entrepreneurs in the tapestry industry as a consequence of this growing sophistication. See, for example, the inventory of Charles Meriel (A.N. M.C. XC/369, (IAD 26/viii/1751)).

180 See *Des moïens d'accréditer les ouvrages de la manufacture d'Aubusson, par les secours de l'art dont ils sont susceptibles*, 20/ii/1750 (A.N. F^{12} 1458^A/doss. v).

181 Ibid.

182 According to ibid., 'Un assortissement de Desseins dans le goût Chinois paroit etre désiré a Paris, et conviendra toujours dans ces Cabinets dont la parure dominante roule sur les Porcelaines. Il ne seroit pas dificile de renchérir sur celui qui subsiste . . . Personne n'a peut-être porté plus loin ce goût là que le Sr Boucher. L'on pourroit tirer de lui des idées aussi neuves que charmantes, dont il se feroit un plaisir d'aider le S^r Du Mons qu'il aime, et des quelles il s'empresseroit de faire la cour. L'on est en etat de rendre temoignage à ses dispositions où il se trouve et dont on pourra profiter a peu de frais'. The Du Mons in question was Jean-Joseph Dumons (1687–1779), 'peintre et déssinateur pour la manufacture d'Aubusson' between 1731 and 1755, when he was replaced by one of Boucher's students, Nicolas-Jacques Juliard (see Arrêt de Conseil du Roy, 20/iii/1731, A.N. F^{12} 1458^A; *Disposition à faire pour l'avancement des manufactures d'Aubusson et de Feuilletin* 1756, A.N. F^{12} 1458^B/doss. xix). This was presumably the same Dumons responsible for, '6 Tableaux dont un se partage en deux representant des desseins chinois par le S. Dumont sur les esquisses du S. Boucher et retouché par M. Oudry', i.e. the cartoons for the *Tenture Chinoise* (Chinese hanging) (A.N. F^{12} 1456^B). It seems that Jean-Joseph retired from Aubusson in order to take up a permanent position at Beauvais as keeper of the manufactory's pictures and cartoons and director of the school (Arrêt de Conseil, 8/viii/1756). In a document amongst the Beauvais papers concerning Dumons's successor, Pierre Camousse, the

former's role at Aubusson is specifically mentioned and so too is the annual pension of 400 *livres* that he continued to receive from Aubusson. (See A.N. F^{12} 1456^B/186.) Dumons's connections with the two firms lead him to make copies of certain Beauvais tapestries by Oudry and Boucher, particularly the *Tenture Chinoise*, which were used at Aubusson. (See A.N. F^{12} 1458^A/doss. vi). For an example of Aubusson versions of the *Tenture Chinoise*, see Sotheby's Monaco 25–6/6/1983, 233, no. 516. For the Beauvais series, see Standen 1976, 103–17; New York 1986, 202–7, 339–41.

183 Anon. letter dated 19/ii/1752 (A.N. F^{12} 1458^A/doss. vi).

184 The administrative reports on Aubusson and Feuilletin reveal a much more consistent concern with costs, prices and outlets than those of either Beauvais or the Gobelins. See A.N. F^{12} 1458^A–1458^B.

185 Gobelins, Beauvais and Aubusson all introduced new lines in upholstered furniture in the eighteenth century and in 1751 Aubusson also appointed Roby to provide the first designs for and supervise the production of carpets at the manufactory. These carpets were probably the highest quality goods produced at Aubusson since in 1753 orders were filed by the financiers de Boullogne and Grimod de La Reynière, and in 1755, further orders were placed by the abbé de Breteuil, président Hénault, Bertin, Voyer de Paulmy and Mme Crozat du Châtel. See A.N. F^{12} 1458^A/doss. iii, xv; and A.N. F^{12} 1458^B/doss. xiv – for groundplans of the salons de Boullogne and de La Reynière for which the carpets were destined.

186 François Boucher, for example, provided forty-five designs for Beauvais alone in the years 1736–53. See Los Angeles 1983, 133. For a brief discussion of the designs provided for the Gobelins and Beauvais, see Jarry 1969, 111–18.

187 For a discussion of artisanal and industrial models of production to which I am much indebted, see Sabel-Zeitlin 1985, 133–76.

188 At the Gobelins, for instance, regular accounts were kept of expenditure on raw materials, such as the dyed silk and woollen skeins used in Gobelins weaves (see, for example, A.N. F^{12} 639^A, *Recette et dépense faites par Cozette . . . de touttes les étoffes à faire la tapisserie pendant les années de 1707, 1708*). Based on these costs, the finished works were usually discounted at a fixed tariff (see, for example, A.N. F^{12} 639^A, for a table of these tariffs during the successive administrations of Colbert, Louvois, and Villarcerf). By the end of Marigny's term of office the Gobelins workshops were in such financial difficulty that the entrepreneurs appealed to the *directeur* for an in-

crease in the tariff in order that they might recoup their losses from future sales (see A.N. F[12] 639[A], *Mémoire & Prix des Ouvrages*, 12/i/1773). At the other end of the spectrum, Aubusson weavers operated three different tariffs according to the different qualities and designs of the tapestries they manufactured (see A.N. F[12] 1458[A], *Etat des manufactures de tapisserie d'Aubusson, de Bourg la Cour, et de Feuilletin en 1751*).

189 According to Jacques Savary, perfect (and successful) tradesmen must know how to be 'agréables à l'achat, à la vente' and 'subtils et prompts à répondre par des argumens naturels' when fault was found with their wares. Moreover, so far as physical appearance was concerned, tradesmen should preferably have '... bonne mine; parce qu'elle convient fort bien à un Marchant, et la pluspart du monde aime mieux avoir affaire, et traiter avec un homme bienfait; parce qu'il se rend toujours plus agréable, qu'avec un autre qui n'a pas le mesme avantage exterieur'. See Savary 1675, 39.

In the case of Gobelins and Beauvais tapestries, these were mostly commissioned directly from the manufactory. Only an 'accidental' surplus of items in the Gobelins warehouses might occasionally prompt a sale. Aubusson and Feuilletin, on the other hand, relied much more heavily on retailers with outlets in Paris and elsewhere. According to the *Voyageur Fidèle*, 'elles se vendent en détail en différentes boutiques et magasins proche de la porte de Paris'. (Quoted from Pardailhé-Galabrun 1988, 369.) Tapestries of all kinds represented a considerable outlay for a *marchand-tapissier* or carpet-seller and it was not that unusual therefore for a number of them to buy more expensive items as a joint venture. For instance, the probate inventory of the *tapissier* Louis Credde makes mention of a tapestry in 6 pieces, 'fabrique d'Angleterre', depicting the *Story of David* in which Credde and fellow-merchant François Cellier each purchased a half share in May 1720. Such shares were not necessarily of equal value and on another occasion Credde took only a quarter share in a tapestry consisting of 11 pieces representing *The Passion*, leaving the other three quarters to Jullien Barure, yet another *tapissier*. See A.N.M.C. XIII/230 (IAD 21/i/1727).

190 The notion of a 'market principle' is borrowed (with attention to the full significance given to it by the author) from Kaplan 1986, esp. 221. Kaplan draws a distinction between the older, medieval marketplace and the market principle which destroyed and ultimately replaced it. 'More than a physical site, the market-place was an *idée force* of regulatory ideology. Marketplace meant surveillance and control for the sake of public order ... marketplace implied the domestication and moralization of commerce.' By contrast market principle, 'meant freedom from control and surveillance ... It vaunted self-interest as its calculus, without regard to moral or political factors ... Defined as a principle, the market was elusive, everywhere and nowhere at once, unclassifiable and mobile'. For a not unrelated discussion of market culture see Reddy 1984, *passim*, esp. 1–18.

191 See *Première idée de la curiosité, ou l'on trouve l'arrangement, la composition d'un cabinet, les noms de tous les meilleurs Peintres Flammands et leur genre de travail. Par Mr Blondel d'Azincourt*, n.d., A.A.P. MS. 34, f° 6; Bailey 1987, 431–47.

192 See Coural-Gastanier-Coural 1983, 49–64. For a particularly full biography and career outline of Marcelin Charlier, see ibid. n. 8, 58–60. Bérain provided Charlier with designs for brocades at the turn of the century. See La Gorce 1986, 46.

193 Quoted from Coural-Gastanier-Coural 1983, 52.

194 B.N. Est. HD 64 rés. f° 10; ibid., 53, 56.

195 See B.N. MS. f.f. 11855. J. Coural and C. Gastanier-Coural first drew attention to this unusually full and detailed memorandum (see ibid., 50). In it the merchants explained the effects of such political events as the Lit de Justice of 1716, the System and its demise, and public mourning on their industry and trade. They also analysed the structure of the domestic market and the character of market forces, emphasising above all the role played by the court.

196 See Thornton 1965, 81–3, 135–46; Los Angeles 1983, 73–4.

197 *Mercure de France*, April 1735, 760.

198 Ibid., 761.

199 Nemeitz 1727, 379–80; Paris 1950, 31. Two of the bedrooms on the first floor of Audran's house were decorated with flocked papers, presumably of his own making, and in his studio in the Luxembourg gallery were to be found a number of boxes containing various quantities of different coloured flock. See A.N.M.C. XLIX/553 (IAD 1/vi/1734).

200 Papillon designed an arabesque paper for the château de Bercy which must have been executed before 1723, the date at which Papillon sold his business to the widow Langlois, see Clouzot-Folio 1935, 16; Teynac-Nolot-Vivien 1982, 27, 36, pl. opposite p. 22; Préaud-Casselle-Grivel-Le Bitouzé 1987, 193–4. For the later development of this kind of paper with ultimately tragic consequences by Jean-Baptiste Réveillon, see Clouzot-Foliot 1935, 37–100; Paris 1967, 25–8, nos. 51–6; Teynac-Nolot-Vivien 1982, 86–94.

201 *Sommaire des volumes de gravures en bois des œuvres des Papillon qui sont au Cabinet des Estampes à la Bibliothèque du Roi*, B.N. Est. Yb[3], 381, i, 76: 'Deux grandes Planches a raports gravées en 1746 pour M. Martin l'aîné, vernisseur du Roi, pour servir à imiter le velour ciselé.' For a second paper 'de mosaïque à cartouche avec fleurs et Papillon', also engraved in 1746 for Martin, see ibid., 80.

202 See Peuchet 1799–1800, ii, 248.

203 *Journal Œconomique* 1755, 85–8. See also Jaubert 1773, iii, 351–2; *La Feuille Nécessaire*, 1757, 250–51, 285–6. According to this last article, proof of Aubert's fine workmanship was to be found in his use of copper-plates (rather than woodblocks) to print his designs.

204 Roland de La Platière 1776, iii, 146–7. Aubert's prices seem to have ranged from 35 *sous* to 3 *livres* the *aulne*. Jacques Cottin's papers, manufactured and discounted at the Arsenal, were priced between 45 *sous* and 12 *livres* the *aulne* (*La Feuille Nécessaire*, 1757, 438–40), and a manufactory above the foundling hospital in the rue de Charenton, produced 'tapisseries peintes', suitable for dining-rooms, *cabinets de toilette*, closets and *salons* at 10 to 12 *livres* the *aulne* (ibid., 441).

205 For example, Mme de Pompadour, for whom the Gobelins wove François Boucher's *The Rising of the Sun* and *The Setting of the Sun* in 1753 (see Fénaille 1903–12, iv, 173–87), in the same decade also bought Chinese and English wallpapers from Lazare Duvaux. See Duvaux 1873, entries: 1778, 1855, 2804, 3016, 3051, 3164, 3177.

206 See Honour 1961, 53–68; Jarry 1981, 9–14 and *passim*.

207 See Paris 1981, 42.

208 See Brice 1706, 267. Two other drawings of such interiors for the palace at Bonn are to be found among the de Cotte papers at the Bibliothèque Nationale along with the accompanying correspondence; see Marcel 1906, 166–95.

209 See Paris 1950, 24–5. An even earlier enterprise may have been run by Jacques Bailly. The *Confirmation des privilèges accordez aux ouvriers qui demeures dans la Galerie du Louvre*, March 1671, lists amongst the resident artists, 'Jacques Bailly, Peintre en Miniature & faiseur d'ouvrages façon de la Chine'. Moreover, according to Hautecœur, in 1730, the duc de Bourbon, 'fabriquait des toiles façon des Indes' and 'des vernis à la mode de la Chine' at Chantilly. See Hautecœur 1943–52, iii, 19.

210 Quoted from Paris 1950, 24. See also Sonenscher 1989, 221–2. At the mid-century de Neufmaison's varnish was still sufficently well remembered to warrant a mention in Blondel's *Architecture françoise*, 1752–6, ii, 98.

211 Dubois de Saint-Gelais 1885, 149. Audran appears to have had some interest in the genuinely Chinese, since he owned a 'cabinet de Chine à deux battants & deux tirroirs', valued at 40 *livres* and in his workshop were stacked at the time of his death, twelve 'feuilles de paravants de bois de la Chine', valued at 60 *livres*. See A.N.M.C. XLIX/553 (IAD 1/vi/1734).

212 See A.N.M.C. LXVI/495 (IAD 12/x/1752, art. xii).

213 The Fondation Doucet holds a manuscript family-tree for the Martin *vernisseurs* (A.A.P. MS. 1076/37), all of whom were descended from Etienne Martin 'tailleur d'habits'. Of his children, Guillaume I (d. 1749), Etienne-Simon (d. 1770), Julien (d. 1752) and Robert (1706–65) were all *vernisseurs* together with his grandchildren Etienne-François (d. 1771), Jean-Alexandre (b. 1738) and Antoine-Nicolas (b. 1742). On the Martins, see Sonenscher 1989, 210–43.

214 See Wilhelm 1967, 2–15.

215 Ibid. So far no documentory evidence has come to light to confirm Martin's involvment in the scheme. The overdoor frames were the work of François Roumier, see Pons 1985, 171–2. For descriptions of the Chinese cabinets at the hôtels du Maine and de Richelieu, see Antonini 1732, 78, 79. When Richelieu moved to the hôtel de Travers in 1756 he had a new *cabinet chinois* installed on the first floor. It was described in his inventory as a 'Salon de compagnie orné de huit portières de velours cramoisi à figures chinoises' accompanied by 'quatre dessus-de-porte de forme ovale à sujets de fable et panneau de laque'. (A.N.M.C. II/741 (IAD 19/viii/1788)). Cited in Chevalier 1970–71, 114. For a lacquer cabinet seized from the château de Saint-Maur-des-Fossées after the Revolution, see A.N. F17 1265/58.

216 See Sonenscher 1989, 210–43, esp. 230. Sonenscher is currently preparing a detailed study of the activities of Jean-Baptiste Réveillon.

217 Ibid.

218 See Pons 1987, 137–78.

219 Even the Salon did not totally exclude the decorative arts. In 1773 the duc d'Aumont requested that Gouthière be allowed to exhibit 'deux Tables de Porphyre, qu'il a montée d'une manière qui doit faire honneur à son talent' and, on the advice of Cochin, Gouthière was instructed to exhibit them on the ground-floor of the Louvre during the Salon. (See A.N. O¹ 1927/1774).

220 See *Mercure de France*, July 1736, 1691–4.

221 For reports of these exhibitions in the newspapers see, for example, *Mercure de France*, 2 June 1735, 1388–90; ibid., 2 June 1736, 1427–9; ibid., Jan. 1737, 126; *Journal Œconomique*, Jan. 1756, 111–16.

222 See *Mercure de France*, April 1733, 773–6. The *Mercure* noted quite precisely that Garnier had attracted to his workshop, 'un très grand concours de Curieux et de gens de la Cour et de la Ville, ainsi que les Entrepreneurs et Architectes des Bâtimens de S.M. . . .' Some artists in the Gobelins also opened their studios to the public. In July 1731 the *Mercure de France* noted that 'Quantité de personnes vont voir aux Gobelins . . .' Charles Parrocel's *Entrance of the Persian Ambassadors* (ibid., July 1731, 1777–8), a picture which was later exhibited for four days in the Salle de Diane at Versailles (ibid., Dec. 1731, 3092).

223 See Coural-Gastanier-Coural 1983, 53.

224 See *Des moïens d'accréditer les ouvrages de la manufacture d'Aubusson par les secours de l'Art dont ils sont susceptibles* 20/ii/1750 (A.N. F12 1458A/doss. xii). Aubusson also made use of gazettes to advertise their wares (see *Mercure de France*, 1 June 1738, 1172–3) and newspaper announcements were one of the measures suggested in 1758 as likely to renew confidence in the products of Feuilletin. See *Observation sur la manufacture de Feuilletin*, 6/xii/1758 (A.N. F12 1458B/doss. viii).

225 For a discussion of the constraints of location on decorative painting see, *Mercure de France*, 2 Jan. 1762, 159–65.

2   THE ORGANISATION OF PRACTICE

1 Regretably there has been comparatively little study of eighteenth-century French imagery of work, with the notable exceptions of Margarite Pitsch's alphabetical compendium of images and texts describing popular life in eighteenth-century Paris and Pinault and Sewell's studies which focus on the illustrations for the *Encyclopédie*. See Pitsch 1949 passim; Pinault 1984, 17–38; Sewell 1986, 258–86.

2 For a discussion of the significance of the language of kinship when exported to the public sphere, see Harris 1982, 143–52.

3 For a good summary of the technologies of the weavers, see Los Angeles 1983, 129–33.

4 See Sewell 1986, 268–79.

5 See Estournet 1905, 149–50, no. 108; Paris 1984–5, 272–4, no. 77.

6 Indeed in many trades it seems to have been considerably less than 50%. See Sonenscher 1989, 107–8.

7 See Lacordaire 1897, 35–7; Paris 1966, 31.

8 Lacordaire 1897, 19.

9 On the culture of the Gobelins, see Souchal 1967, 38–42.

10 Ménétra 1982, 137–8. For Daniel Roche's analysis of the relationship between Ménétra *père et fils* and of that relationship as typical of those pertaining between fathers and sons in the artisinal culture of the *ancien régime*, see ibid., 303–4.

11 Ibid., 191.

12 The Salon of 1767 included two paintings, *The Joiner's Workshop* and *The Gilder's Workshop* by Amand, the first of which was engraved in 1770 and published with accompanying verses which put the virtues of the *atelier* – specifically industry but also, by implication, community, harmony and fraternity – above those even of the church. Ten years after Hallé, Bernard Lépicié exhibited his *Joiner's Workshop* which likewise upheld the idea of *artisanat* as biological entity and a moral community. All these works were inspired, in varying degrees by Jean-Jacques Rousseau's *Emile* (1762) in book III of which Rousseau extols the virtues of apprenticeship as a moral education. See Rousseau 1946, 211–71, esp. 261–2.

13 On the guilds, see Lespinasse 1879–97; Olivier Martin 1938; Coornaert 1968; Sewell 1980, 16–39; Black 1984, 123–56; Bourgeon 1985, 241–53.

14 See Savary des Bruslons 1744, ii, 218–21.

15 See Olivier Martin 1938, 95–103; Mousnier 1979, 463–73.

16 On the guilds during Colbert's ministry, see Cole 1939, ii, 363–415; Coornaert 1968, 138–43. For a different picture, see Bourgeon 1985, 241–2. This author argues for a characterisation of Paris as 'le paradis du travail libre'.

17 On the financial role of the corporations, see Anon. 1761, 38–67; Coornaert 1968, 153–4, 216–17.

18 On the consequences for the guilds of the devolution of public finance away from corporative support in the late eighteenth century, see Sonenscher 1987, 102.

19 See Sewell 1980, 25–32.

20 On the corporations as moral communities, see Kaplow 1972, 34–41; Sewell 1980, 32–7.

21 Expilly 1762–8, v, 403. See also Sonenscher 1983, 151.

22 This is a conservative estimate. Scholars such as Bourgeon have applied a more generous ratio of 1:3 in their guesstimates. See Bourgeon 1985, 242. On the terms of employment of apprentices and journeymen by master-painters and sculptors, see Rambaud 1964–71, ii, xxxvi–xliv.

23 For estimates of the population of Paris in the eighteenth century, see Kaplow 1972, 19–22; Roche 1981, 21.

24 For a table drawn up from information in Savary des Bruslons's dictionary and which amply demonstrates both the range of Parisian trades and the working populations attached to each, see Sonenscher 1989, 8.

25 See Guiffrey 1915, 16–20; Sonenscher 1989, 212, esp. n. 7. For the annual admission of candidates between 1735 and 1754, see Pons 1985, 18. And for the ratio of painters to sculptors admitted in 1734 and 1744, see ibid., 17.

26 A handful of lists survives, held in a subsection of the Minutier Central at the Archives Nationales: 6c *Agriculture, Commerce, Industrie*. The earliest dates from 1725 (6c, 1) and the latest from 1759 (6c, 11). I thank Carolyn Sargentson for locating and photographing these lists for me.

27 See Piganiol de La Force 1765, i, 434–5; Guiffrey 1915, 31–2.

28 According to Le Sage, 3,000 families made up the Corps des Marchands-Merciers in 1769 (Anon. 1769, 280). For these *marchands*, see also Savary des Bruslons 1744, iii, 358–60; Lespinasse 1879–97, ii, 232–85; Coornaert 1968, 139; Verlet 1958, 10–29.

29 On the prestige of heritage and its expression in civic ceremonies, see Olivier Martin 1938, 121. The corporation's coat of arms consisted of three silver escutcheons and a golden fleur-de-lis on a blue field. A contemporary account explained the device as follows: 'Ces Trois Ecussons marquent l'Heureux accord qui se trouve entre la peinture et les armoires, qui font l'objet du Travail de laditte Communauté. Ils servent l'un et l'autre a publier les grandes actions, dont elles font passer le souvenir à la posterité, et cette fleur de lys est une marque d'honneur qui est dëue à cette communauté, soit par Raison de son Etablissement qui est royal soit à cause de la possession que la Communauté a de cette piece d'honneur depuis plusieurs siècles.' (B.N. MS. Joly de Fleury 1732, f° 51–2).

30 See Kaplan 1982, 283–8.

31 See ibid., 262–9.

32 See Coornaert 1968, 156–9. On the final demise of the guild system, see Kaplan 1986, 176–228.

33 The statutory period of training for painters and sculptors was 5 years but of the apprenticeship contracts published by Rambaud only 50% respected this regulation. See Rambaud 1964–71, ii, xli, xlii–iii.

34 On the *chef-d'œuvre*, see Savary des Bruslons 1744, i, 713–15.

35 Jacques-Louis Ménétra bought his mastership in this way, although he had served both an apprenticeship and a journeymanship. See Ménétra 1982, 335.

36 A.S.L. 1729, 2.

37 Guiffrey 1915, 24–5; Pons 1985, 19–20.

38 A.S.L. Statutes 1730, arts. xxxix, lxiv.

39 See A.S.L. 1730, 4.

40 Ibid., 4–5.

41 Ibid., 5.

42 Ibid., 4.

43 Ibid.

44 See Pons 1985, 20.

45 A.S.L. 1730, 2; A.S.L. 1736, *passim*; A.S.L. 1738, art. xxxix.

46 A.S.L. 1730, 2–3, 5–7. However in order to be legitimate, frames decorated with *argent vernis* had to be inscribed on the back with the words 'argent vernis sans or' and with the maker's name and stamped 'd'un fer chaud' by the corporation. See B.N. MS. Joly de Fleury 1728, f° 272 v. We can assume that the measure to prohibit the use of false gold was defeated because it threatened few invested interests within the corporation. The consequences of the relaxation of the regulation on gilding was in fact more likely adversely to affect the neighbouring trade of the *doreurs* than the painters themselves.

47 See Kaplan 1982, 262–9.

48 See Sonenscher 1989, 174–209, esp. 191.

49 See Parker 1979, 18. For silks see Ciriacono 1981, 176–7. For an example of the way that drapers used guild regulations to defeat commercial competition from independent brokers, see Bossenga 1988, 693–703.

50 See Delamare 1705–38, iii, 109–13.

51 See Kaplan 1982, 262–9.

52 See Honour 1961, 82–3; Jarry 1981, 50–54.

53 *Mémoire sur les communautés d'arts & métiers*, B.N. MS. Joly de Fleury 1729 (f° 121–42), f°123.

54 For a full discussion of the character and implications of strife within the guilds, see Kaplan 1985–6, 631–47.

55 See Pons 1985, 20.

56 On the constituency of the corporation's assemblies, see Kaplan 1985–6, 633–8, and esp. 634, 635, for the painters and sculptors. The ruling oligarchy that governed the corporation and Académie de Saint-Luc was much less narrowly selected than in other trades. To their business assemblies they called not only elders but 20 *modernes* and *jeunes*; to their electoral assemblies they admitted a delegation of 40 junior members.

57 Of the 22 members of this faction whose speciality is known 14 were painters and only 2 sculptors. For Simon Besançon, see Guiffrey 1883–6, iv, 318–21, and for André Tramblin see Pons 1987, 41–50.

58 See Pons 1987, 41–50.

59 A.S.L.-Tabletiers 1748, 3.

60 See Papillon n.d., 81 no. 2. A year earlier Papillon had designed for Martin, 'deux grandes Planches de raports . . . pour servir à imiter le Velours ciselé' and 'une planche de Mosaïque à cartouches avec fleurs et Papillions' (ibid., 76, 80, no. ˙1). For Martin's use of other designers, see Sonenscher 1989, 220.

61 In a dispute with the gilders on leather in the early eighteenth century the master-painters tried to insist on an exclusive right to use the paint-brush. However, they were smartly rebuked by the gilders who pointed out that the instruments and supports used by painters were in fact familiar to the workshops of all the luxury traders. What in their view singled out the painter was not his tools but the intention to make a 'tableau'. See Doreurs-A.S.L. n.d., 1–4.

62 For a number of *arrêts* registered by the Paris Parlement concerning the painters and grocers in the eighteenth century, see A.N. AD XI, 25. See also A.N. O¹ 1910/186, 188; Epiciers-A.S.L. 1737; A.S.L.-Epiciers 1762.

63 *Mercure de France*, Sept. 1754, 174–7.

64 La Font de Saint Yenne 1747, 98–100.

65 Ibid., 99; Rey 1819, 9.

66 See the Académie de Saint-Luc's appeal for support to the marquis de Marigny, 23/xii/1762 (A.N. O¹ 1910/186) and A.S.L.-Epiciers 1762. According to this last, in the late 1750s the grocer Baduleau, trading in the rue St-Jacques-de-la-Boucherie, was responsible for some near fatal accidents as a consequence of indiscriminately preparing and selling food and pigments on the same premises. Ibid., 18.

67 This information was provided in support of the painter Chevalier's request to d'Angivilliers for a financial reward for having invented a 'moulin à broyer les couleurs'. In addition to his costs he requested 3,600 *livres* for the invention, 'qui conserve la vie a un très grand nombre de sujets, et qui épargne à l'Etat au moins un million par an . . .' (A.N. O¹ 1294/303, 23/x/1775). The Chevalier in question was probably Jean-François Chevalier, director of the Académie de Saint-Luc from 1771 and whose address is given in the 1775 list of corporation's members and in this petition as rue Bailleut (see Guiffrey 1915, 233). The mill was sent to Trudaine de Montigny for inspection. Although Trudaine maintained that there was nothing novel about the mill except its adaptation to a purpose previously not envisaged, he clearly believed it to be an important development for painting and suggested that such mills should completely take over the task of grinding

colours. In the first instance because it was labour-saving and secondly because it would save life. 'On sait', wrote Trudaine, 'que les preparations de plomb causent les dangereuses coliques que l'on nomme coliques de peintre ou de poitou, que les préparations mercurielles occasionnent des tremblements, des salivations, des coliques, des Paralisières. Mais il semble qu'on ignore, ou qu'on semble ignorer que les peintres et les Marchands de couleurs fournissent chaque année tant à l'hôtel Dieu, qu'a l'hopital de la Charité, un grand nombre de malades affligés de ces coliques redoutables, et d'autres accidents extra-ordinaires; c'est cependant un objet très digne de l'attention des Magistrats. Il seroit facile de prevenir ces accidents et de conserver ces Malheures [sic] victimes du Luxe, en ordonnant que toutes les couleurs Métalliques, ne pourront être Broyées desormais que dans des Moulins Encaissés comme le pratique le S. Chevalier de façon que ceux qui dirigent cette opération ne puissent point être exposés a respirer les poudres subtiles qui s'en détachent; rien de plus aisé que de faire mouvoir à la fois plusieurs de ces petits Moulins, soit par un courant d'eau, soit par des chevaux ou par des anes; un grand Etablissement de cette Espèce Meriteroit d'Etre encouragé et provoqué pour le bien de l'Humanité' (A.N. O¹ 1294/305). I have so far, been unable to discover if Montigny's ideas were ever followed through and Chevalier rewarded for his ingenuity.

68 See Kaplan 1982, 273–81. For an account of the trades necessarily involved in the production of furniture, see London 1956, lvi–xi; for carriages, see Sonenscher 1983, 155.
69 On the guilds and their use of the law, see Sonenscher 1987, 77–109.
70 A.S.L.-Tabletiers 1748, 3.
71 Ibid., 4.
72 See Sonenscher 1989, 226.
73 Miroitiers-Tapissiers 1739, 4.
74 Ibid., 3.
75 For the disputes with fan-painters, see P.-V. 1875–92, vii, 127, 129–33, 254–5, 257, 287-90. For disputes with en-gravers and illuminators, see the Académie de Saint-Luc's confiscations of coloured engravings and wallpapers from Ribancourt and Lesneur, A.N. Y 15772 (26/xii/1738). For the disputes with bronze founders, see A.S.L.-Fondeurs 1702; P.V. 1875–98, iii, 384-7. Finally arts. viii–xi of the corporation's statutes (1738) were written expressly to prevent competi-tion from other corporations. See A.S.L. 1738.
76 See Kaplan 1979, 17–77.
77 For the Vincenot case, see A.N. Y 15776 (15/iii/1741) (copy A.A.P. MS. 1060ˣᵛ).

Vincenot's workshop was situated in the rue du Four, in a building whose main tenant was a certain Suet, *maître peintre*. For Bocquet, see A.N. Y 15776 (15/iii/1741) (copy A.A.P. MS. 1060ˣᵛ). Bocquet lived in the rue Saint Germain-l'Auxerrois. For Guéret, see A.N. Y 15776 (15/iii/1741) (copy A.A.P. MS. 1060ˣᵛ). Jean Guéret's overdoors are described as 'representant jeux champêtres, plaisirs champêtres'; Delagery's 'representant une danse d'enfans'.
78 A.N. Y 15779 (29/x/1743) (copy A.A.P. MS. 1060ˣᵛ). Michel Janson's workshop was situated on the first and attic floors of a building, rue des Moineaux. The *jurés* seized no less than 22 overdoors of various sizes from Janson's studio.
79 The first Letters Patent that legalised the privileges of the *artisans suivant la cour* were registered 19/iii/1543 (A.N. AD XI, 10). On these *artisans*, see Anon. 1737, ii, 325–8; Olivier Martin 1938, 252. In Paris they formed a confraternity which celebrated mass every Sunday at the church des Filles Pénitentes. Their chaplain held the title of Chapelain de Sainte Barbe. See Anon. 1737, ii, 325–8.
80 See B.N. rés. ms. Thoisy 72, f° 331–79.
81 The suggestion must remain tentative however, because, when in 1692, the mas-ter-painters initiated proceedings against Rigaud he was found to be working with just two assistants, in other words, well within both guild and Académie Royale regulations. See ibid., f° 346.
82 Court Artisans 1725, 2.
83 Much of what we know about the commer-cial importance of shop-signs in the eigh-teenth century arises from the resistance of retailers to the *Ordonnance du bureau des finances de Paris* of 25 May 1761 which sought to restrict the size and projection of signs. (See Enseignes-Ordonnance 1761). The appelants against the new regulations claimed that they were unfair to new traders because for them, 'il s'agit de former un établissement, de prendre aux yeux du Public, de le séduire par des apparences; de-là le faste extérieur qu'ils affectent: ils sacrifient tout à la nécessité de s'annoncer: souvent ils employent leur avoir à la construction de leurs Enseignes & Etalages: il en est qui ont dépensé plus de mille écus pour cet objet'. And all this precisely because, 'L'Enseigne d'un Marchand décide souvent de la valeur de sa Boutique' (see Enseignes-Mémoire B 1761). In another memorandum the appelants explained that the need 'to ap-pear' had resulted from the recent and rapid growth of the capital and the attendent claims of luxury. Thenceforth, 'le mérite personnel du Marchand ne fut plus un titre suffisant pour se concilier les

suffrages du Public'. Signs/advertisments had become a necessity (see Enseignes-Mémoire A 1761).
84 Court Artisans 1725, 6–8.
85 See Nemeitz 1727, 379–80; Paris 1950, 31.
86 See Boissonade 1932, 70.
87 See ibid., 69, and specifically for the case of Boulle, Montaiglon 1855–6, 332–3. In 1715 Charles André's debts ran at 26,339 *livres*, and even at his death totalled 20,000 *livres*. See Somoyault 1979, 7. Likewise, J.F. Oeben left comparable debts at the time of his death in 1764. See Stürmer 1979, 505, n. 11. For a brief biography and an account of Oeben's workshops at the Arsenal, see Eriksen 1974, 207–9.
88 For a discussion of the 'entrepreneurial potential' of privilege but one which offers different conclusions to those drawn here, see Stürmer 1979, 496–528. Recently, Gail Bossenga has argued that the cor-porate system, far from placing the economy in a straight-jacket offered a means by which enterprising merchants might ensure production quality and ob-tain better control of the sale of products. See Bossenga 1988, 693–703.
89 See Stürmer 1979, 517–23.
90 On the Martins, see Sonenscher 1989, 210–43. On the wallpaper manufacturers, see Clouzot-Foliot 1935, 1–120; Paris 1967, 11–14, 16; Teynac-Nolot-Vivien 1982, 21–38, 101–2.
91 For an, as yet, unchallenged assessment of Pineau's role, see Kimball 1980, esp. 162–70.
92 See Boissonade 1932, 61.
93 See Pons 1985, 21.
94 See Guiffrey 1883–5, vi, 25–33.
95 See Rambaud 1964–71, ii, 139–40.
96 See Ibid., i, 279.
97 See R.A.-A.S.L. 1761. On the Pourvoyeur case, see also Guiffrey 1873, 12; Furcy-Raynaud 1903, 203, 221, 276–7. The Artistes des Galleries du Louvre won their case and an *arrêt du Parlement*, 20/viii/1763 ordered the Académie de Saint-Luc to pay Pourvoyeur 300 *livres* in damages. See R.A. 1763, 11.
98 R.A.-A.S.L. 1762, 12.
99 Ibid., 15, 14.
100 Ibid., 13.
101 Ibid., 15.
102 I.F.F. XVIIIᵉ siècle, vi, 375–6, no. 125. A related drawing was sold at Sotheby's London, 9/iv/1970, no. 149. Demarteau subsequently engraved the pair to this work, Cochin's *The Pen is taken up with the help of Justice, and Reason dictates*. See ibid., 397, no. 194. See also Paris 1984–5, 501–2, no. 151.
103 To Audran's principal activities as a painter should be added his involvement in the lacquer and wallpaper businesses.

Charles-André Tramblain, erstwhile Académie Royale student (P.-V. 1875–92, iii, 398), acted as a painter, house-painter, scene-painter (Guiffrey 1887, 121–22, 126), coach-painter, as a partner (after Audran) in the De Neufmaison chinoiserie company (Sonenscher 1989, 222–3), as a firework display designer for the city of Paris (A.N. κ. 1008, 1009) and with his father André, operated as a dealer in pictures and frames on the pont Notre-Dame (Pons 1987, 42). On Roumier's activities as a sculptor, see Pons 1985, 153–76 and for his wallpaper design, 'd'ornemens, et fleurs avec plusieurs mosaïques' engraved in pear-wood, see Papillon n.d., 77.

104 In 1773 the heads of the Gobelins workshops (Michel Audran, Pierre-François Cozette and Jacques Nielson) pleaded with Marigny to increase the prices of the Gobelins tapestries in order to allow them to honour their debts. See A.N. F^{12} 639^A. On the financial difficulties at the Gobelins, which became endemic in the second half of the eighteenth century, see Mondain-Monval 1918, 89, 91, 102, 104, 106, 120, 121, 130, 144–6, 157–60, etc.

105 A.N. F^{12} 1660 [my emphasis].

106 Bossuet 1709, ii, 224. Cited in Boissonnade 1932, 5.

107 Aubusson produced three different qualities of tapestry: 'fils-simple' (10 *livres* 10 *sous* the square *aulne*), 'fils-double' (15–22 *livres* the square *aulne*) and 'étan' (36–62 *livres* the square *aulne*), each of which was targeted at different income groups. The first was thought suitable for 'bons artisans, chambres garnies and hotelleries de Paris'; the second for 'les petits particuliers et meme la bonne bourgeoisie', and the last for the wealthier bourgeoisie. For these prices, see *Etat des manufactures de tapisseries d'Aubusson . . . et de Feuilletin* 26/ii/1751 (A.N. F^{12} 1458^A/doss. xiii), and for the markets see *Mémoire concernant les manufactures de tapisseries d'Aubusson . . . et de Feuilletin*, 26/ii/1751 (A.N. F^{12} 1458^A/doss. x). According to Roche, between 1695–1715, all of the salaried workers whose inventories he studied, owned tapestries, although by the end of the century only 73 per cent still used them as their principal form of decoration. See Roche 1981, 140, 153 (table 24).

108 See anonymous letter dated 19/i/1751, A.N. F^{12} 1458^A/doss. vi.

109 Ibid.

110 See Los Angeles 1983, 133–4.

111 Sonenscher 1989, 226–7, 230.

112 See Aubusson-Tapissiers 1720.

113 See Paris-Privilèges 1716. For the list of respondents, see A.N. F^{12} 781^c/doss. xv. See also C.A. 1847–61, i, 922–3; ii, 405–8; Kaplan 1988, 353–78.

114 A memorandum of the 'locataires qui professent les arts et métiers' at the Quinze-Vings listed amongst others, Marion *peintre*, the gilders Hochet and Eloy, the sculptors Desjardin and Vinache, the *ébéniste* Jollin, a goldsmith Cotin, two upholsterers, three clockmarkers, three toymakers, two *compagnons maçons* and a carpenter (see A.N. F^{12} 781^c/doss. xv). A list of the *scellés* attached to and inventories taken of private property at the Temple between 1756–8 included those on behalf of a *tapissier*, a journeyman mason, an *argenteur sur métaux*, the wife of a gilder (Jean Pecault), and the wife of a painter (Jean-Michel Lingenfelder) (see A.N. z^2 3804). I am grateful to David Maskill for drawing my attention to these documents.

115 This was certainly the case with rights associated with religious orders.

116 See Foiret 1921, 93–100.

117 Saint-Germain 1718, art. i (prohibited blasphemy); iv (forbade innkeepers and wine merchants to play games of chance); v (imposed respect for feast days); xii (insisted that behaviour and dress be appropriate to the place); xix (prohibited the selling of illegal goods); xxii and xxxiv (forbade the throwing of rubbish and excrement from windows); xxiii (required that communal spaces such as landings, stairwells and courtyards be cleaned every Monday, Wednesday and Saturday), &c.

118 See ibid., arts. vii and xx (the gates were open from 6.00 a.m. to 9.00 p.m. between All Saints and Easter and from 5.00 a.m. to 10.00 p.m. between Easter and All Saints); ix (work was expressly prohibited on Sundays, and diocesan feast days, including the feast days of Sts Vincent, Germain, Symphorian and Sulpice).

119 The register of *scellés* and probate inventories for Saint-Germain-des-Prés records the presence of a picture dealer (Jean Girard Le Comte), five *marchands-merciers*, a *lapidaire* and a *tapissier* during the years 1745–55. See A.N. z^2 3625. Curiously the *enclos* was also home to some of the comte de Clermont's personnel. Otherwise, most prominent among the trades established there were clockmakers and makers of scientific instruments (6), victuallers (8 – mostly at the luxury end: biscuit and chocolate makers), those in the clothes industry (10) and horse-traders (6). A *Sentence du Baillage de S. Germain-des-Prez* 8/viii/1719 fixed the number of wig-makers and horse-traders to 12 indicating particular pressure from these quarters. I am grateful to David Maskill for drawing my attention to these documents.

120 See Derel 1956, 151–65; Rambaud 1964–71, i, 457–63, pls. I–IV; ibid., ii, 674–7, 690–92.

121 See Six-Corps 1716, 4. On the seventeenth-century *maîtrise de Saint-Germain-des-Prés*, see Guiffrey 1876, 93–123. On the violence that broke out as the guilds sought to exercise their right to inspect, see Farge 1979, 133; Farge 1986, 118.

122 See Maillard 1898, 19, 25.

123 Ibid., 46.

124 On the faubourg Saint-Antoine, see Monnier 1981, *passim.*.

125 *La Feuille Nécessaire*, 1757, 269. The example cited of such industry was a manufactory newly established in the rue de Charenton, near the rue Saint-Nicolas which produced, 'Velours & Laines Damassés', of all colours designed according to 'les Desseins les plus nouveaux'.

126 See Monnier 1980, 113.

127 See Kaplan 1988, 367.

128 See ibid., 353–78, esp. 370–73.

129 For studies of the Grande rue du Faubourg, see Hillairet 1970, *passim*, and Janneau 1975.

130 See Kaplow 1972, 3–26; Roche 1981, 11–19.

131 For the urban history of Paris, see Poète 1910.

132 See Bourdon-Chastel-Couzy-Hamon 1977, 75–151.

133 See the membership lists of the Académie de Saint-Luc, A.N.M.C. 6c.

134 On the importance of parish, see Daumard-Furet 1961, 50–4, esp. 51.

135 For the geographical distribution of trades in Paris, see Anon. 1769.

136 See ibid., 125; Kaplow 1972, 6.

137 See Duvaux 1873, 1xviii–cxlv.

138 See Anon. 1769, 70; Piganiol de La Force 1765, ii, 61; Kaplow 1972, 6.

139 On rough calculations made on the basis of the addresses given with Guiffrey's list of the guild membership (Guiffrey 1915, 161–484) I estimate that approximately – half to two-thirds of eighteenth-century painters and sculptors belonging to the Académie de Saint-Luc lived in this district of Paris.

140 On the subjective definition of neighbourhood, see Rapoport 1977, 157–69. For a particularly thorough architectural survey of one district in Paris – Les Halles – see Bourdon-Chastel-Couzy-Hamon 1977, *passim*.

141 This is clear from the most cursory reading of Ménétra's journal. For a specific example see the encounter between Ménétra and Elophe (Ménétra 1982, 138) for whom he was working (see below, chapter 3).

142 Janneau 1975, 29–53.

143 See Farr 1988, 14. On the importance of visibility in market-place culture, see Agnew 1986, esp. 39–40.

144 On the *privilégiés* in the Louvre, see Guiffrey 1873, 1–221; Merson 1881, 264–70, 276–88. For Robert's drawing, see Valence 1989, 142, no. 45.

145 On the artistic community of the Gobelins

at the beginning of the eighteenth century, see Souchal 1967, 37–42. During the last decades of the eighteenth century – when the number and intensity of labour disputes rose sharply throughout the capital and particularly in the faubourg Saint-Marcel – the royal administration made additional efforts to isolate privileged artisans from radical elements within the working class. See, in the case of the Gobelins, Burstin 1978, 765. On the buildings of Saint-Gobain, an analogously enclosed manufactory, see Hamon 1977, 37–9.

146 See Blondel 1752–6, ii, 96–8. For another comparison between the cultures of the Louvre and the Gobelins, see Souchal 1967, 39–42, and esp. 49.

147 See Mondain-Monval 1918, 13. However, during Marigny's *surintendance* the garden seems to have been handed over as an exclusive privilege to management and the workers thus lost the right to these extra-monetary benefits. See ibid., 151–2.

148 Ibid., 14.

149 In 1767, in order to maintain discipline at the manufactory, Soufflot supported a motion to station two resident guards on the premises, 'Car il y a des moments ou l'on a de la peine a mettre les ouvriers a la raison et ils auront plus d'egards pour les entrepreneurs lorsqu'ils craindrons d'être arrestés tout de suite quand ils seront mis dans le cas de le mériter' (Soufflot to ?, 19/vii/1769, A.N. F¹² 639ᴬ). However this precaution seems not to have secured the desired effect, and fears of insurrection at the Gobelins mounted in the following decades. Finally, in 1782–3, d'Angiviller was faced with repeated and persistent 'révolte' at the manufactory over the rates and frequency of salary payments (see Burstin 1978, 768–9).

150 A royal *ordonnance*, reaffirmed in 1748, prohibited Gobelins employees from leaving the manufactory without written permission on pain of imprisonment and a fine of 100 *livres*. In 1754, two weavers from the Gobelins, Richard and Bussière, were imprisonned at Moulins having fallen foul of this regulation. It appears that both weavers were natives of Aubusson and having entered the Gobelins to improve their skills had then returned, without notice, to their place of origin. Indeed, one of the *marchands-tapissier* at Aubusson, Dessarteaux, seems to have encouraged Richard's return from the capital by making him cash advances and promises of work. There was evidently intense competition for talented weavers within France and the Gobelins' system of *billets de congé* sought to ensure that it secured the best. However, for the most part, the Gobelins

was concerned less with the mobility of weavers at home than with the possibility that their workforce might be seduced abroad, to work for foreign companies and in so doing threaten exports. On the case of Richard and Bussière, see A.N. F¹² 639ᴬ. On concern over the mobility of the workforce, see Mondain-Monval 1918, 31, 33–4, 114–15, 214–15, 240–41.

151 See Darnton 1985, 79–104.

152 Darnton's essay on the Parisian printers' 'Great Cat Massacre' has provoked a great deal of discussion about the values of anthropological models for history to which Darnton responded in Darnton 1986. Most recently Michael Sonenscher has put forward an explanation of the massacre based on a much more precise understanding of the social and economic structure of the printer's workshop and it is on this study that I draw here. See Sonenscher 1989, 10–22.

153 On the mounting insubordination and riotous behaviour of the weavers at the Gobelins, see Burstin 1978, 766–75.

3 THE CO-ORDINATION OF WORK

1 Jaubert 1773, i, 126–7.

2 See Minvielle 1921.

3 See Kaplan 1979, 17–77; Sonenscher 1983, 147–72; Farge 1986, 125–94.

4 See Black 1984, 129–31.

5 See Coornaert 1968, 193–200.

6 See Farge 1986, 124–5.

7 See Hufton 1974, 107–27 from whom the phrase 'an economy of makeshifts' has been adapted.

8 On the mobility of journeymen in Paris, see Farge 1986, 127–9; in Dijon, see Shepherd 1986, 97–130. For a glazier's use of urban space, see Ménétra 1982, 355–77. Not only was there a high degree of labour turnover in eighteenth-century workshops (in Rouen, for example, journeymen wigmakers spent on average only four months in any one shop – see Sonenscher 1989, 154) but additionally, less than one-fifth of journeymen employed in the building and furnishing trades were even natives of the towns in which they worked (ibid., 295). The majority of journeymen were migrants opperating in trades that were rarely locally contained but were caught in wider urban networks stretching out into the surrounding countryside (ibid., 118–23).

9 On construction workers' strikes in the eighteenth century, see Kaplow 1972, 38–40.

10 Ordonnance de Police, 21/v/1667 (quoted from Delamare 1705–38, iv, 121).

11 See, for instance, Pierre-Jacques Brillon to

Marchais 28/i/1730, I.F., MS. P.J. Brillon, *Journal de Sceaux*, i, 50.

12 Ordonnance de Police, 5/x/1683 (A.N. O¹ 1045, f° 37). Cited in Stoloff 1978, 5.

13 A.S.L.-Compagnons 1748, 2.

14 A.S.L.-Compagnons 1748², 1–2, 10.

15 A.S.L.-Compagnons 1748, arts. i–ix.

16 See Sonenscher 1989, 202–3.

17 See Arrest 1765, arts. xii, xiii. *Broyeurs de couleurs* were to be payed 30 *sous* per day; *Apprêteurs*, 35 *sous*; house-painters, 35 *sous*, and *doreurs* and *embellisseurs*, 40 *sous*.

18 For masons' salaries, see Durand 1966, 468–80, esp. 473–5; for roofers' salaries, see Farge 1986, 142.

19 Martin 1786, 61.

20 See Sonenscher 1989, 235.

21 On other conflicts involving the length of the working day, see Sonenscher 1983, 167–8.

22 For a discussion of the quality of task-orientated time, see Thompson 1967, 56–97.

23 Sonenscher 1983, 147–72; Sonenscher 1989, 174–209.

24 Ibid., 161–2.

25 Potain 1749, 8.

26 See Arrest 1765, art. xv. For the violent protests that this provoked among journeymen, see Sonenscher 1989, 236–7.

27 Sonenscher 1989, 256–64, esp. 259.

28 Ibid., 186.

29 See Sonenscher 1983, 158–9.

30 See Kaplan 1979, 17–77. Sonenscher questions these assumptions in Sonenscher 1989, 275–6.

31 See Gallet 1972, xiv.

32 See Cobban 1972, 60–61.

33 See A.S.L.-Compagnons 1748, 3.

34 Quoted from Tadgell 1978, 99–100. See also Nolhac 1898, 104–14; Paris 1982, 157–9.

35 See Engerand 1900, 327–31.

36 For the new settlement made for the prices paid for tapestry models and cartoons, see ibid., xviii.

37 Ibid., 45.

38 Ibid., 47–8. Though ordered for the dauphin's apartment at Versailles, the paintings were in fact installed in the king's apartment at Marly. See Fack 1977, 829–33.

39 For a discussion of the value of time in labour to which I owe a considerable debt, see Thompson 1967, 56–97.

40 Engerand 1900, xvii, n. 1.

41 On the *livret*, see Kaplan 1979, 48–54, 56–7; Sonenscher 1983, 168–71. In 1787 fourteen master-painters and sculptors were each fined 10 *livres* for employing, 'en qualité d'Apprentifs des jeunes gens non-registrés au Bureau [de la Communauté]' and 'des Ouvriers sans livrets' (A.N. AD XI, 25).

42 In 1724 the journeymen silk-weavers (*bonnetiers*) resisted a diminution of their daily wage-rate by forming a counter-corporation in the Temple. See B.A. MS. Bastille 10846, f° 90–175. For the confraternity of the journeymen-painters, see B.A. MS. Bastille 12369, f° 2, 4, 12–46; Kaplan 1979, 46, 64–5. On confraternities in eighteenth-century Paris, see Garrioch-Sonenscher 1986, 24–45. On painters' confraternities in the seventeenth and eighteenth centuries, see Lombard-Jourdan 1981, 87–103.

43 See B.A. MS. Bastille 12369, f° 14v–15r.

44 Ibid., f° 12. Cited in Kaplan 1979, 46.

45 Ibid., f° 2. Their confraternity held its services in a chapel of the church of Sainte-Marie-du-Temple. For the complaints by the Académie de Saint-Luc which gave rise to the *arrests*, see ibid., f° 21.

46 Ibid., f° 45–6. Art. lxxi of the 1738 statutes prohibited journeymen 'de s'attrouper les dimanches & fêtes & autres jours près de la chapelle de Saint-Luc, dans les lieux privilegiés ou ailleurs, de cabaler entre eux pour fixer le prix de leurs journées, d'avoir aucune chapelle particuliere d'y tenir confrairie & d'y rendre le Pain à bénir, à peine d'être privé de travailler chez aucuns Maîtres, d'exclusion de la Maîtrise . . .' See A.S.L. 1738.

47 See Kaplan 1986, 176–228.

48 On the upholsterer's share, see Thornton 1981, 97–106, 130–48.

49 See Gallet 1964, 23.

50 See Gallet 1972, 21–2.

51 See *Masarinade ou portraict de l'architecte partisan*, reprinted in Braham-Smith 1973, 159. François Mansart left a fortune worth 300,000 *livres* to his two nephews, of which Jules Hardouin Mansart was one. The latter apparently demonstrated similar business acumen. In a popular song of 1706 which called for all *partisans* forcibly to surrender their ill-gotten gains, Hardouin Mansart was treated with particular bitterness and judged fit only for the hangman's noose. See Boislisle 1888, 7. See also Saint-Simon 1888, xvi, 43.

52 For the hôtel d'Aucezune, see Paris 1983, 68–70.

53 For the entrepreneurial and intellectual dimensions of the architect's profession from the beginning of the seventeenth to the end of the eighteenth centuries, see Stoloff 1978, 48–103.

54 The prohibition of entrepreneurial activities for class I members was introduced by statutory reform under Jules Hardouin Mansart (12/ii/1699). See art. iv of the 1717 statutes (Aucoc 1889, clxix).

55 See Gallet 1972, 22.

56 See Wildenstein 1921, 28–30.

57 See Stoloff 1978, 48–103.

58 See the statuary reform brought into effect by Hardouin Mansart, 12/ii/1699, P.-V.A. 1911–29, i: xii; Stoloff 1978, 83–100.

59 Jaubert 1773, i, 128.

60 Quoted from Savignat 1983, 114.

61 Sonenscher 1989, 322–3.

62 Ménétra 1982, 138. I have used the translation from the recent Columbia University Press edition, trans: by Arthur Goldhammer, 1986, 111.

63 See Deshairs n.d. *passim*; Rambaud 1964–71, i, 312–13, 580–83.

64 According to Pons, Hardouin Mansart was responsible for introducing the architecural office, in the modern sense. See Pons 1985, 29–30.

65 In Blondel's own words, 'Le dessein en général est nécessaire (to the architecte) pour *communiquer* ses pensées, pour *désigner* au sculpteur, au peintre, au ciseleur, la forme et le relief des différentes parties de la décoration, décidées par le Propriétaire sur ses projets, et qu'il se trouve ensuite obligé de confier à leur soins' (Blondel 1754, 52–3 – my emphasis).

66 On the *devis*, see Gallet 1972, 13–14.

67 Catheu 1957, 279.

68 See Rambaud 1964–71, ii, 649.

69 See also Savignat 1983, 135–43; Pons 1985, 49.

70 Quoted from Thiry-Druesne 1979, 57. See also the *devis* for the panelling of the hôtel Lassay, Pons 1985, 136.

71 Drawings or cartoons of this kind have survived rather better in the field of coach-painting than interior decoration. See, for example, Gilles-Marie Oppenord's design for the decoration of a coach panel with Diana in Fuhring 1989, i, 78, no. 56; and Alastair Laing's discussion of a group of three cartouche designs by François Boucher in ibid., 116–21, no. 65.

72 Photographic records of these drawings are be found in the archives of the Caisse Nationale des Monuments Historiques and reproduced in Gallet 1968, 80–85; Paris 1986, 232–3; Baulez 1976, 184–8. Pineau's contract for sculpture at the hôtel de Mazarin required that, 'led. S. Pineau a marqué en grand sur les murailles' all the sculpture for the panelling and plasterwork of the bedroom and *salon*. See A.N.M.C. XXVI/384 26/x/1736.

73 See Pons 1985, 165.

74 Ibid., 41–2, 260–62.

75 Ibid., 42, 167.

76 Ibid., 166.

77 Jacobins-Mémoire 1731, 3. The passage continues, 'Delà Roumier passa au maître Autel; & delà aux Pilastres, & à quelques Chapelles de la Nef; & jusques aux Confessionnaux, rien ne peut échapper à son ciseaux affectionné'. In desperation the Dominican Fathers tried in September

1731 to insist on a further *expertise*, this time by Germain Boffrand, who they hoped would find in their favour (see B.N. MS. Joly de Fleury, f° 148–9).

78 See Frémin 1702, 13–21, esp. 17, where he remarks that, 'un Bâtimet debout & élévé sur terre est bien autrement vue, qu'un Bâtiment couché sur un Carton; du papier déployé sur une table dérobe à la veuë des défauts que le grand jour découvrre'; and again p. 19, 'Je suis toûjours irrité contre les laveurs de desseins où il n'y a pas un rapport exact de l'idée avec l'effet'. Over a century later Rondelet, in the introduction to his *Traité théorique et pratique de l'art de bâtir* (1830), contrasted the 'études abstraites' of the science of construction with 'les charmes entraînant des arts du dessin' (i, p. xxiv). Owing to the latter, ornament sculpture had always escaped precise valuations and entrepreneurs had apparently been able to impose arbitrary and exaggerated invoices on consumers. Seemingly, only when journeymen-sculptors took over from their masters the contracts for the ornament for the church of Sainte-Geneviève in 1789 were any attemps made to draw up rational tariffs based on sound quantity surveying. See Rondelet 1830, iii, 246–7. For the tariffs for house-painting, see ibid., 248–59.

79 For a wide-ranging discussion of architectural drawing in relation to construction from the Middle Ages to the modern period, see Savignat 1983 *passim*.

80 Pierre Bullet and Amédée-François Frézier may be counted among those late seventeenth- and early eighteenth-century architects most concerned with the technical and constructional aspects of architecture. See Bullet 1691; Frézier 1738.

81 See Pérez-Gómez 1983, 88–127. On the aesthetic value and symbolic meaning of geometry in sixteenth-century construction, see Pérouse de Montclos 1982, 80–178; Sanabria 1989, 266–99, esp. 295–9.

82 Palissy 1880, 118–19. See also Pérez-Gómez 1983, 221.

83 Palissy 1880, 118. The ruler disputed the compass's claim to precedence on the grounds that he could only make circles while she conducted all things directly, 'et de long et de travers, et en quelque sorte que ce soit, je fay tout marcher droit devant moy', moreover, 'quand un homme est mal vivant, on dit qu'il vit desreiglement qui est autant à dire que sans moy, il ne peut vivre droitement' (ibid.).

84 See Bullet 1691, 1–47 and *passim*; Pérez-Gómez 1983, 204–35.

85 Bullet 1691, introduction. See also Langenskiöld 1959, 7–29.

86 The comparative importance of 'knacks' and draughtsmanship in the distribution of

knowledge and power across an enterprise or industry and the different roles played by word and image in the transfer and communication of technologies have been the subjects of a number of outstanding essays by John Harris set in the context of the British and French coal and metallurgical industries. See Harris 1976, 167–82, esp. 173; Harris 1986, 7–57; Harris 1988, 22–44. For a much wider perspective on the issue, see Styles 1988, 10–16. I should like to thank John Styles for the useful suggestions he put to me on this matter.

87   André Félibien claimed in the preface to his *Des Principes de l'architecture* (1676) that nothing was so important as the command of shared artisanal language: 'Car ce qui fait que les Ouvriers n'executent pas toujoûrs les choses comme on les est imaginées, & qu'ils font le contraire de ce que l'on souhaite, c'est qu'ils parlent un language que l'on n'entend pas bien, & que faute de leur exprimer dans ce mesme language ce que l'on desire, ils ne conçoivent qu'imparfaitement l'intention de ceux qui les employent . . .' (Félibien 1699, preface). This situation was recognised by a French inspector of industry as still pertaining to all manner of manufactures at the beginning of the nineteenth century (see Harris 1976, 179–80). For the problem of language as a vehicle of knowledge in the context of the enlightenment project, see Healey 1963, 837–59.

88   This was so not only of professional architectural discourse but also of amateur views. For instance, in the *Essai de la Peinture* (1765), Diderot advised his readers to beware of 'du talent d'un architecte qui n'est pas un grand dessinateur' (see Diderot 1875–7, x, 510–12).

89   See Braham-Smith 1973, 159.

90   See Pons 1985, 1.

91   Mariette 1851–60, ii, 276. Cited in Pons 1985, 34.

92   See Roubo 1772, 45.

93   Roland de Virloys 1770–71, i, 91.

94   On the identification of artisans with their trades as expressed through visual imagery, see Sewell 1986, 258–86. It may be significant in this context that artisans did not slander one another's professional competence. As David Garrioch has shown, instead they insulted one another by alleging fraud and bad faith, never lack of skill (see Garrioch 1987, 104–19, esp. 109).

95   See Pons 1985, 41.

96   See Hautecœur 1943–52, iii. 262.

97   See Blondel 1752–6, iii, 61; Hautecœur 1943–52, iii, 260.

98   The full title of the print reads as follows: 'Qui bastit ment. Il n'a pas bien pris ses mesures. Il a pris un point trop haut, il n'y trouvera pas son conte.' On the *Collection*

des Plus Illustres Proverbes (*c*.1657) to which this belongs, see Weigert 1967, 177–84; I.F.F. XVIIᵉ siècle, vi, 57–162, esp. 69. Of course compasses were used by a large number of artisans, but the latter's tools were firmly anchored to the ground, to practice. At the Musée Le Secq des Tournelles in Rouen, for instance, is to be found a *compas d'appareilleur* used for stone and timber cutting and on which is inscribed the following: 'Je plus de science dans ma tette que dans celle de mon maitre. Ci celle de mon maitre me conduit pas, la mienne ne luy sert de rien. Neyron Fecit 1751.' And on the reverse side: 'Laisse moy bon larron, j'apartien a maitre pierre pelegrin que peut etre tu ten serviras pas si bien. 1751.' (My transcription is faithful to the original authography.) Not unlike Lagniet's proverb, the compass insists that to possess the tool is nothing, it is possessing the skill to use it that counts.

99   The header and marginalia read as follows: 'Il n'est pas au bout de ses desseins. tous les esprits ne sont pas dans une teste. Il ne faut pas bastir sur l'heritage d'autrui.' 'Il fait des chasteaux en Espagne.' 'Cela va par compas et par mesure.' 'Le papier souffre tout.' 'Il se trompe a son calcul.'

100   The inscription reads, 'Il vit de règle', which also implies that he works routinely, though in this context I do not think that any pejorative significance should be attached to that statement. From the top, the rest of the inscriptions read as follows: 'Il alonge un col de granie.' 'Sujets a un coup de marteau.' 'Il met toute pierre en euvre [sic].' Collectively these texts help to reinforce the air of modesty, propriety and industry which characterises the dress and activities of the masons, in marked contrast to the architect's leisurely vanity.

101   See Kaplow 1972, 40.

102   The print depicts an artisan attended by three secondary figures: Minerva or 'la science' seated upon his head, Industry with a beehive and a spider's web upon his hand, and the Devil which he pulls by the tail. The artisan exclaims: 'O ciel qui scait comme je tire. faits que les deux un peut jattire.' The two in question are honour and profit (symbolised by the incense-burner and money-bag held by the Devil), the 'But de l'artisan'. Below reads the following inscription: 'L'artisan tire le diable par la queue. Tirez le diable par la queue/ Artisans par vostre industrie/Veillez cherchez la magie bleue/Pour bien profiter de la vie/Et si vous ramassez du bien/C'est que les arts ny valent rien.' In another version of the same print the sinfulness of greed is brought out more strongly by a different accompanying legend, one which draws a comparison between artisans and

'partisans', that is to say the money-mongers and financiers who prospered in the last decades of Louis XIV's reign. See I.F.F., XVIIᵉ siècle, v, 89–116. For a fuller interpretation of this image, see Sonenscher 1989, 42–4.

103   See Huard 1928, 317. For eighteenth-century responses to Oppenord's engineering abilities, see Buvat 1865, ii, 295.

104   On the political value of natural law in constitutional debate in the early modern period, see Skinner 1980, ii, 318–48. On natural rights theories, see Tuck 1979, esp. 119–73. I am grateful to Michael Sonenscher for drawing my attention to the importance of natural rights theories in discussions of the arts in the eighteenth century. For his analysis of the relationship between natural law and theories of labour, see Sonenscher 1987², 1–10.

105   See Auffray 1762, 15–9; Béliard 1771, 107–10.

106   A.S.L.-Compagnons 1748², 5.

107   Ibid.

108   See Sonenscher 1989, 236–9.

109   See Cœuffeurs-Perruquiers 1769; Goncourt 1982, 280–81.

110   See Cœuffeurs-Perruquiers 1769, 3–4; Anon. 1771, 294–300.

111   See Goncourt 1982, 281.

112   This work formed part of the series *Fragments de l'Opera* (1733–41) for which, see Fénaille 1903–12, ii, 321–43.

113   Eight (mostly undated) letters, addressed possibly to Philibert Orry, give detailed reports of these visits. The most pressing problem seems to have been the weavers' antagonism to working with the subtler colours needed for Coypel's designs. See A.N. 639ᴬ.

114   See Havard-Vachon 1889, 181–8; Opperman 1968–9, 49–71; Opperman 1973, 57–65.

115   See Roland Michel 1984, 71.

116   See Thiry-Druesne 1979, 53, 60, 61.

117   Quoted from Pons 1985, 49.

118   See Roland Michel 1984, 151, 172.

119   The drawing is with the Musée des Arts Décoratifs, Paris, Inv. 29 130.

120   According to Potain, 'Les chassis ronds ou ovales & toutes les traverses ou battons ceintrés ou chantournés' were paid at twice the rate of regular strechers. Is it possible that panel-sculptors and joiners had a direct interest in promoting the taste for extravagant overdoor frames? For the prices of stretchers, see Potain 1749, 63–6. For the prices for pre-stretched canvases in the 1750s, see Pernety 1757, 535.

121   See below, chapter 10.

122   See, for example, Verlet 1982, 28–30.

123   On the importance of designers to the Lyon silk industry, see Thornton 1965, 24–8. More recently, in a paper circulated at the

Victoria and Albert Museum workshop, *Design, commerce and the luxury trade in the eighteenth century* (23 October 1987), L.E. Miller offered conclusive documentary evidence to the effect that designers enjoyed similar status and commanded comparable incomes to their employers. See Miller 1987. Likewise, although Réveillon, in his *Exposé justificatif* (1789) undoubtedly inflated the rates of pay he claimed to have offered his employees in order to improve his case for compensation, there is no reason to doubt the stated hierarchy of rates of pay for different skills, a scale that categorically placed designers at the top. See Réveillon 1789.

124 See Braham-Smith 1973, 158. For similar complaints about Louis Le Vau, see Sauval 1724, iii, 22.

4 THE LANGUAGES OF ESTATES

1 For approaches to the issue of consumption to which I am particularly indebted, see Sahlins 1976, 166–204; Douglas-Isherwood 1980; Baudrillard 1981; Bourdieu 1984.

2 Delamare 1705–38, i, 379–81.

3 Ibid., 381.

4 Ibid. Similarly, Furetière defined 'magnificence' as a virtue 'qui enseigne à depenser son bien avec honneur & avec éclat . . . La magnificence est d'une bienséance necessaire aux Rois, & aux Potentas. Elle n'appartient pas aux simples particuliers . . .' (Furetière 1701, ii, *ad. voc.* 'Magnificence'). See also La Roque 1734, 234.

5 Scudéry 1698, i, 1–118, esp. 48.

6 Delamare 1705–38, i, 381.

7 Ibid.

8 According to Daumart-Furet, in 1751 the Parisian nobility were, by and large, better off than other groups in society. See Daumart-Furet 1961, 38. See also Chaussinand-Nogaret 1985, 43–64. In 1705 the marquis de Sourches judged 'poor' a noble family with an income of 6,000 *livres* p.a. (Sourches 1882–93, ix, 246), and by the 1730s this threshold had risen to 10,000 *livres*, according to the comte de Preux (see Carré 1920, 109–10).

9 An exception might be Coyer's *La noblesse commerçante* (1756) which povoked debate on the matter.

10 On the sumptuary laws at the beginning of the seventeenth century, see Mousnier-Labatut-Durand 1965, 166–7 n. 42.

11 François de Callière drew attention to the seemingly paradoxical nature of decorum, at once oral and informal, and unyielding and despotic. See Callière 1716, 89. On *bienséance*, see Dens 1981, esp. 112–19; and

with specific reference to architecture, Szambien 1986, 92–8. For a discussion of the differences between orality and textuality to which I am particularly indebted, see Ong 1982 *passim*.

12 Laugier 1755, 155.

13 Cordemoy 1714, 85.

14 Blondel 1774, ii, 46.

15 Laugier 1755, 172.

16 See Szambien 1986, esp. 92–8.

17 Anon. 1776, pl. I. The text reads as follows: 'Le Seigneur et la Dame de Cour. On qualifie du nom de Seigneur, les personnes de haute noblesse, ou celles qui sont retenus des hautes dignités de l'etat; pour l'ordinaire ils sont décorés de l'Ordre de leur Souverain; il n'appartient qu'à eux d'etre très recherchés dans leurs ajustemens; les talons rouges qu'ils portent sont la marque de leur noblesse et annoncent qu'ils sont toujours prets à fouler aux pieds les ennemis de l'Etat. Il faut distinguer du Seigneur l'homme riche et fat qui par des dehors trompeurs cherche à surprendre le peuple toujours eblouï par l'éclat d'un habit magnifique. sans cesse on le voit ramper auprès des gens en place pour en obtenir quelque marque de distinction; il n'est point de souplesse et d'intrigues qu'il ne se suggere pour venir à ses fins, et sçait bien se vanger sur ses Vassaux des mortifications qu'il reçoit. On entend par Dame de cour, une Femme de haute consideration, attaché à la Reine ou à quelque Princesse; elle est toujours obligée de paroitre dans l'eclat le plus brillant. les etoffes les plus riches, l'Or, les pierreries, les Equipages les plus elegants sont de son appanage. on la distingue aisément à son air, de ses Coquettes qui la copient et même la surpassent quelquefois, la Coefure de ces dernieres varie a l'exes, tantôt elle est haute, tantôt basse; aujourdhui en avant, demain en arriere; on voit construit sur leur têtes des compartimens de jardin à fleurs et à fruits; les plumes simbole de la legereté, n'y sont pas epargnées surtout dans ses derniers tems, elles ne pouvoient faire un meilleur choix pour exprimer leur vrai caractere; enfin leur toilette est une vraie etude, on pourroit faire un assés gros Dictionnaire des mots employés pour designer chaque chose qui sert à leurs parures.' It seems appropriate in the present context that the text should spend more time discussing the non-represented usurpers of status than describing the character of the 'Seigneur' and 'Dame de cour' depicted. On Charles Le Père and Pierre-Michel Avaulez, see Préaud-Casselle-Grivel-Le Bitouzé 1987, 216–17.

18 For a recent discussion of the relationship between rhetoric and architecture, see Coulet 1977, 291–306; Guilheux-

Rouillard 1985, 18–27.

19 Rykwert 1988, 31–48, esp. 46.

20 Lassay 1756, ii, 305.

21 See Paris 1979, 38.

22 Blondel, for one, acknowledged that in order to gain knowledge of appropriate form, 'il faut avoir beaucoup vêcu avec les differents Ordres de l'Etat qui composent la société civile'; in practice an almost impossible task. See Blondel 1771–7, v, 2. According to Rapoport the emergence of an architectural profession occurs at the very time when a universally accepted value-system of significant form breaks down, so that the architect may be seen as both the symptom and the cause of strain in architectural symbolism. The statements made by professionally designed buildings are therefore, at the very least, self-conscious. See Rapoport 1969, 6. By the second half of the eighteenth century there is evidence that the significance of architectural structure and decoration was gradually becoming obscured and unintelligable. See Patte 1754, 135–43.

23 See Ross 1976, *passim*.

24 In 1665 Colbert instituted the 'grande recherche' to detect usurpers of noble status and although the state's interest in the enquiry was primarily fiscal it did serve to pacify those *bona fide* noblemen outraged at the infiltration of their order by *parvenus*. The enquiry was suspended between 1674–96 and then resumed its task until it was officially declared at an end in 1727. See Ford 1953, 13.

25 [Courtin] 1719, 47.

26 Morvan de Bellegarde 1709, 155.

27 Ibid.

28 Ibid., 155–6.

29 Ibid., 156–7.

30 See Sabatier-Vignaud-Culand 1983, 18.

31 See Jouanna 1989, 22.

32 See Genlis 1818, ii, 259.

33 For splendour on the street, see La Bruyère 1965, 190, §1. According to Muralt and Mercier, nobles, in their search for visual distinction, had transformed themselves into little more than pure signifiers. At the court, Mercier remarked that 'One sees nothing . . . but surfaces . . . characters that seem little more than tapestry motifs.' (Mercier 1782–8, ix, 8) Meanwhile, for Muralt, the national trait of the French nobleman was his resemblance to '[le] cerf de la fable, qui estime beaucoup son bois *apparent*, ornement qui peut lui être funeste, tandis qu'il a honte de ses pieds menus, qui lui rendent un très bon *service*' (Muralt 1725, 105 – my emphasis). For royal ceremonies, Apostolidès 1981, 41–6; Elias 1983, 82–90. For civic and religious ceremonies, see Kaplan 1979–80, esp. 152–3; Darnton 1985, 105–40. See also

Sennett 1974, 65–72; Douglas-Isherwood 1980, 64–5.

34 It should be noted that the seventeenth- and eighteenth-century myths devised to explain the origins of architecture, notably the abbé Laugier's, invariably invoke man's need for protection from the elements rather than any need for privacy or intimacy as the motive force behind the first act of construction. See Rykwert 1981, 43–4.

35 See Ariès 1962, 391–3; Sennett 1974, 89–106. For a society in which 'public man' – or the man who grasps his sense of personal identity through the opinions of those who judge him – was not without a home or a protected and private realm, see Bourdieu 1965, 191–241, esp. 221–4.

36 For a discussion of the transformative effect of reproduction to which I am particularly indebted, see Benjamin 1973, 219–53.

37 The hôtel Desmarets in the rue Saint-Marc was built by Pierre Cailleteau called Lassurance for Thomas Rivié in 1704. It was bought by François Desmarets, the *controlleur général des finances* on 16 October 1710. From the contract of sale that included the permanent furnishings, we learn that in March 1709 Rivié had paid 10,000 *livres* for the mirrors decorating the various apartmemts. The hôtel was sold by Desmarets's heirs to the duc de Montmorency-Luxembourg (14 April 1723) for 500,000 *livres*. See A. N. T 144¹/163. See also Blondel 1752–6, iii, 95; Hautecœur 1943–52, iii, 44 n. 3, 116.

38 Furetière 1701, i, *ad. voc.* 'Lieu'; Marin 1991, 167–82, esp. 69–72.

39 Furetière 1701, i, *ad. voc.* 'conversation'. That the commingling of the spatial and the social was reciprocal may be judged by the definitions of places. For example in the entry 'Cabinet' Furetière notes that, 'On dit . . . qu'un homme tient *cabinet*, pour dire, qu'il reçoit chez luy les honnestes gens qui s'y veulent assembler pour faire une conversation sçavate & agreable.'

40 *Dictionnaire de l'Académie Françoise* 1762, ii, 11 [my emphasis].

41 Muralt 1725, 95.

42 Ibid., 109.

43 Indeed, according to Muralt the purpose of these calls was rarely conversation and almost always show: 'dès qu'ils [visitors] on été vus . . . ils disparaissent', scarcely bothering to say a word (Muralt 1725, 110).

44 On the hôtel d'Humières in the rue de Bourbon (de Lille) built by Armand-Claude Mollet for Louis d'Aumont, duc d'Humières in 1716–17, see Blondel 1752–6, i, 273–4; Hautecœur 1943–52, iii, 150; Paris 1983, 64–5. Visits to hôtels were also made by those unknown to the proprietors and who merely wished to see

the material symbols of station. Indeed, Blondel maintained that *appartements de parade* should be lavishly decorated not just because *noblesse oblige* but also in order to attract 'de dehors les étrangers qui plaisent à visiter la demeure des Grands Seigneurs'. (Blondel 1752–6, i, 27). 'Etranger' meant stranger, in other words a person unknown to the resident. It was not necessarily synonymous with foreigner, although many hôtel visitors may indeed have been tourists from abroad. Guidebook writers often refer to the accessibility of hôtels and encourage those interested to take a first-hand look rather than relying on written description (see, for example, Brice 1706, 210). That the nobility was not above exploiting its distinction is suggested by the entry tickets sold, for example, for access to the hôtel de Lassay. See Antonini 1732, 183; Paris 1984, 27. See also Oberkirch 1970, 179, for access to the Palais Royal.

45 See Neuschel 1988, 600.

46 See Jouanna 1989, 15.

47 Quoted from Duby 1980, 3–4. For *ancien-régime* perceptions of the French constitution, see Mousnier 1979, 3–47; Duby 1980, 1–119. On the meaning of 'état' and 'ordre', see Sewell 1974, 49–68.

48 For the substitution of pedigree for valour in the definition of nobility, as it evolved from the sixteenth to the seventeenth centuries, see Devyver 1973. See Billacois 1976, 258–77, esp. 277.

49 See Schalk 1986.

50 La Roque 1734, 251.

51 On theories of blood in the late seventeenth and early eighteenth centuries, see Devyver 1973, 243–437.

52 See Goubert 1973, 159. On the genealogical and historical consciousness of the French nobility, see Ellis 1986, 414–51.

53 It goes without saying that this was an image of negativity, of lack, constructed by the nobility for the *peuple*. On perceptions of time and on the value of history among non-nobles, see Davis 1977, 87–114.

54 Tocqueville 1961, 96–8.

55 On the attempts of the nobility to achieve and maintain a distinctive form of dress in the seventeenth century, see Godard de Donville 1978, *passim*.

56 Sièyes 1888, 9.

57 La Bruyère 1965, 191, §4.

58 Bernis 1903, i, 101. Cited in Forster 1971, 1.

59 See Forster 1971, 1–54.

60 Thrale 1932, 74.

61 Young 1769, 146.

62 Tessé 1888, 337 (25/xi/1710).

63 See Forster 1971.

64 At the beginning of the seventeenth cen-

tury the image of the nobleman shifted from fief-holder to country gentleman but the dignity of the *gentilhomme campagnard* proved fragile, and by the eighteenth century the nobility were primarily identified with court and capital. See Schalk 1986, 155–6.

65 Sièyes 1888, ii, var. 3.

66 For the Paris residences of the *ducs et pairs* in the seventeenth century, see Labatut 1972, 255–7. For the distribution of aristocratic residences in the capital in the eighteenth century, see Durand 1965, 21–5.

67 Furetière 1701, ii, *ad. voc.* 'Village'. Morvan de Bellegarde also noted that 'les personnes qui ont été élevées dans les Villes, ont un air honnête qui se trouve opposé à ce que l'on nomme *Rusticité* aux gens de Campagne' (Morvan de Bellegarde 1743, 18).

68 Labourdette 1978, 19–26. The nobility also spent more on the decoration of their town houses. For example, in 1712, Charles-Honoré d'Albert, duc de Chevreuse possessed 69,843 *livres* in goods and furnishings at his hôtel in the rue Saint-Dominique compared with 5,324 *livres* of the same in his apartment at Versailles; 2,274 *livres* at the hôtel de Chevreuse in Versailles and 27,689 *livres* at the château de Dampierre. See Labatut 1972, 301.

69 See for example Marais 1863–8, ii, 345. According to Marais the comtesse d'Evreux was knicknamed 'le petit Lingot' by the Bouillon family. See also Leroux-Cesbron 1924, 269. On the hôtel d'Evreux built in 1718 by Mollet, see Hautecœur 1943–52, iii, 150–4.

70 For a discussion of the difference between economic and symbolic value in matters of property, see Bourdieu 1977, 171–83.

71 See Matignon-Pons 1723, esp. 5. See also Paris 1987², 28–9.

72 On the difference between lineage property and *acquêts*, see Giesey 1977, 271–89.

73 A.N.M.C. CXVII/325 (20 April–28 Oct. 1722) marriage contract between the duc d'Epernon and Gillette-Françoise de Montmorency-Luxembourg.

74 Pardaillan II de Gondrin 1728, esp. 4. The memorandum submitted to the court by the duc d'Antin's creditors in 1734 estimated the value of the hôtel d'Antin at 400,000 *livres* and its contents at 200,000 *livres*, that is, approximately one-third of the total value of the duke's assets.

75 For the different definitions of 'palace', 'hôtel' and 'maison', see Blondel 1771–7, ii, 233–43; and see the definition of 'maison' given in Richelet 1769, ii, 11. On the hôtel d'Orrouer in the rue de Grenelle, see Catheu 1957, 20–35; Gallet 1968, 80–

85; Paris 1979, 39–40.

76 On the 'Grand Marot', see Mauban 1944, 77–98.

77 A.N.M.C. CXIII/303, *Substitution* (1/ii/ 1724) which states that: 'que le dit hostel appellé l'hostel de Matignon suivant l'inscription qui sera mise sur la porte d'entrée d'iceluy et que les armoires dudit seigneur comte de Matignon actuellement mises & placées au frontispiece du principal corps de logis dudit hôtel sur la grand-court et au fronton du meme corps de logis du costé du jardin de meme que celles qui seront mises sur la dite porte d'Entrées y demeuront et seront conservée et entrenües sans pouvoir y aporter aucun changement.' On the hôtel de Matignon, see Paris 1981, 27–37.

78 C.A. 1847–61, ii, 837.

79 See Gallet 1972, 69.

80 On street numbering, see Pronteau 1966.

81 From 1667 building regulations in Paris restricted the heights of buildings to 52 feet. Expansion outwards may therefore have been, in part, a virtue made of necessity. For eighteenth-century building regulations, see Harouel 1977, 135–49; Harouel 1983, 83–92.

82 Petity 1767, 449.

83 See Blondel 1752–6, i, 278.

84 On the *pavillon à l'italienne*, see Hautecœur 1943–52, iii, 204–6. On the palais Bourbon, see Paris 1987³, 18–23.

85 See Hamon 1978, 5–17, esp. 12. On the hôtel de Torcy and château de Sablé, see Strandberg 1982, 131–46; Paris 1986, 53–7, 211–12.

86 During the reign of Louis XIII, Richelieu ordered the destruction of all fortified châteaux in a bid to curtail the independence of the nobility's military strongholds. See Hamon 1978, 7. Likewise, after the Fronde, 'le Roy même que les Ordonnances deffendent aux particuliers de fortifier leurs maisons' (Savot-Blondel, 1685, 45). It is also worth noting that the models devised by architects were often deliberately ambivalent as to the urban or rural destiny of their designs. See, for example, Le Pautre 1652, 12, esp. the plate reproducing the garden façade.

87 Sites in the still rural districts of Paris and along the banks of the Seine were much sought after because they offered such views. Indeed the view from the hôtel de Bretonvillier appears to have provoked a more enthusiastic response from Bernini than Bourdon's paintings in the gallery; see Fréart de Chanteloup 1985, 14. See also Germain Brice's remarks about the views from the hôtel de Menars (Brice 1698, i, 155) and from the hôtel Du Bois (Brice 1706, i, 152).

88 On the duchesse du Maine's pavilion from which the view in fig. 96 was sketched, see Paris 1986, 43. According to the *Mercure de France* Milcent's print was issued in 1735. See *Mercure de France*, March 1736, 530.

89 According to Laugier an hôtel without a garden was deprived of a 'grande commodité' because 'un jardin dans une ville est d'une grande ressource; ne fût-ce que pour donner de l'air, & un peu de verdure & ce qui est encore plus gracieux, pour avoir chez soi une promenade qu'il ne faut point aller chercher, où l'on peut être à toute heure & en déshabillé, où l'on ne rencontre point d'importuns, où l'on ne voit que ceux que l'on veut voir' (Laugier 1755, 144).

90 Boileau-Despréaux, *Satires*. Quoted from Muralt 1725, 212. The poet then proceeded to versify on the need to avoid the congestion, noise and smells of the city. In like manner commentators on architecture encouraged clients to avoid commercial neighbourhoods. See Savot-Blondel 1685, 13–15; Petity 1767, 443.

91 Anon. 1788, i, 42–3.

92 The idealist nature of seventeenth- and eighteenth-century architectural treatises accounts for their comparative lack of practical guidelines on issues of site and building practice. Most authors added little to the general remarks make by Vitruvius in Book I, ch. iv of the *Ten Books on Architecture*. The priority given to abstract design over practical training was also a feature of academic education and it should be noted that it was not until the twentieth century that the Prix de Rome projects consistently imposed site specifications. See Egbert 1980, 11–35, 154–5.

93 Saint-Honoré 1733.

94 On the planning of the new city limits which gave rise to the *mémoire* cited in the note above, see Pronteau 1978, 707–45.

95 *Déclaration du Roy* 18/vii/1724, art. vii. See Saint-Honoré 1733, 2–3.

96 According to the same memorandum, 'Il n'y a pas long-tems que le Faubourg Saint Honoré n'étoit habité que par des Jardiniers, des Maraîchers, & du menu Peuple. Ce n'est que depuis la construction des Maisons de Messieurs Chevalier & le Gendre, que l'on a commencé à regarder ce Quartier comme un lieu propre à bâtir de grandes maisons.' (Saint-Honoré 1733, 1).

97 Ibid., 4.

98 For a theoretical discussion of the desirability of such isolation, see Savot-Blondel 1685, 15. For a discussion of the determining influence of urban tissue on architectural form, see Boudon-Chastel-Couzy-Hamon 1977, 37–53. The pattern-books of Le Muet (1647), Briseux (1728) and Neufforge (1757–72) confirm the conclusion of Boudon et al. that the smaller the surface area of a site the greater its determining influence on architectural form. Only beyond a certain surface area did architecture become completely liberated from the constraints represented by the plot outline.

99 Blondel praised the architect Jean Richer for his exceptional ingenuity in masking the irregularity of the plot on which he raised the hôtel d'Estrades in the rue de Clery (Blondel 1752–6, iii, 18–19). Moreover, in the case of the hôtel d'Antin, Blondel advises the reader that he has decided not to illustrate the ground-plan because of its grotesque irregularity (Ibid., 93).

100 For the *immeubles* built in the central districts of Paris in the second half of the eighteenth century, see Gallet 1964, 79–82.

101 A.N.M.C. XCI/745 *devis et marché* 12, 19/vi/ 1734; Rambaud 1964–71, i, 455.

102 On the aristocratic household, see Ariès 1962, 391–8; Maza 1983, 205. As a particularly immodest example of the entourage of certain houses, see Marais 1963–8, ii, 219. Marais records the prince de Conti's departure on a five to six-day excursion to his château at Ile-Adam, 'avec soixante seigneurs de la cour'.

103 See Blondel 1752–6, i, 238–40; Paris 1984, 198–9.

104 A.N.M.C. VIII/1020 *devis et marché* (17/vi/ 1737). On working-class housing, see Roche 1981, 100–30.

105 See Boudon 1975, 773–818.

106 Brice 1698, 226.

107 Mercier 1782–8, i, 157.

108 Cantillon 1952, 8.

109 Expilly's figures were based on the tax rolls for the *capitation* for 1765. See Expilly 1762–8, v, 401–2; Goery 1965, 25–60.

110 See Buhot, *Description du Quartier St Germain des Près* [1762], f° 22–3, 26 (A.A.P. MS. 53). Buhot was an Inspecteur de Police with responsibility for the district of Saint-Germain from 1752. On the Cour des Dragons, see Gallet 1972, 46; Gallet 1973, 268–74.

111 Paris 1987², 176–81.

112 Blondel 1752–6, i, 22, n. a.

113 On the interrelation of social and aesthetic conventions, see Dens 1981, 110–38.

114 For Blondel, as for all his contemporaries, symmetry was one of the fundamental principles of architecture. See Blondel 1752–6, i, 23.

115 Perrault 1684, 11, n. 9.

116 Ibid.

117 Savot-Blondel 1685, 221.

118 Ibid., 222.

119 See I.F.F. XVII⁰ siècle, v, 89–116.

120 Coyer 1755, 47.

121 See Sewell 1980, 19–25.

122 Coyer 1755, 48–9.

123 Laugier remarked that concern for symmetry and proportion were inappropriate in the case of 'petites maisons bourgeoises' for there 'l'on fait ce qu'on peut', given that 'l'économie bannit la règle' (Laugier 1765, 39). See also Rapoport 1969, 6.

124 Blondel 1771–7, ii, 238–9. As fine examples of, 'bâtiments à l'usage des riches particuliers', suitably designed without orders, Blondel cited the 'maisons' of MM. Janvry and Peyrenc de Moras in the rue de Varenne and M. d'Argenson in the rue des Bons Enfans.

125 See Thompson 1986, 1103–28, esp. 1106–11. The seventeenth-century genealogist and historian, André Duchesne, regularly referred to the scions of his 'houses' as columns of noble virtue. See, for instance, Duchesne 1621, dedication (unpag.).

126 On the tension between organic and artificial (or architectural) metaphors in political thought, see also Höpfl-Thompson 1979, 919–44.

127 On the debate over architectural proportion at the turn of the century, see Rykwert 1980, 23–53; Pérez-Gómez 1983, 18–83.

128 The unity offered by the hôtel was, however, more often apparent than real because, if the front and back façades were two-dimensionally symmetrical, they were not necessarily aligned in such a way as to create a three-dimensional harmony. In this sense, houses were designed to be seen as surfaces and the spectator was neither expected nor encouraged to explore the buildings as spatial – or by implication, social – structures. See Savot-Blondel 1685, 59–60. For a particularly exaggerated example of axial dislocation between the court and garden façades, see the hôtel de Pompadour in the rue de Grenelle, built by Pierre–Alexis Delamair: Blondel 1752–6, i, 236–7; Paris 1979, 24–7.

129 Audiger 1700, 21–2. See also Mignot 1989, 17–35.

130 The frontispiece of the first edition depicts the gigantic image of a monarch, majestically wielding sword and sceptre above a landscape. His body is entirely made up of the many miniature and overlapping citizens of the body politic. The frontispiece was designed during the time Hobbes was writing the *Leviathan* in Paris.

131 Vitruvius, quoted from Szambien 1986, 62.

132 Laugier 1765, 198. See also Paris 1983, 60.

133 Ibid.

134 See Castan 1974, 284; Maza 1983; 199–243.

135 Luynes 1860–63, i, 176.

136 See Maza 1983, 157–98.

137 See Ariès 1962, 366–7.

138 See Sewell 1980, 19–25.

139 See Savot-Blondel 1685, 46.

140 See Marais 1863–8, ii, 69 (6/ii/1721).

141 Mathieu Marais confided in his diary that on a particular evening at the hôtel de Nesle a group of gentlemen got a certain Mme Gracé drunk. Having had her dance for them in the most provocative manner, 'ils la livrèrent dans une antichambre à des valets qui en firent à leurs plaisirs'. Ibid., i, 215 (16/vii/1717).

142 Buvat 1865, i, 106–7.

143 Marais 1863–8, ii, 361.

144 See Savot-Blondel 1685, 65; Gallet 1972.

145 Dangeau 1854–60, xvi, 374 (4/v/1716).

146 Ibid., xvii, 84 (12/v/1717). For Coypel's decoration of the Noailles chapel, see the probate inventory of Adrien-Maurice, duc de Noailles, A.N.M.C. XXIII/682 (IAD 24/vi/1766). According to the inventory the chapel was decorated with five paintings by Coypel representing: the *Nativity*, *Faith*, *Hope*, *Charity* and *Religion*. However, according to Blondel the chapel had an altarpiece by Philippe de Champaigne and a ceiling decorated by Brunetti in 1740 to which Parrocel contributed grisaille figures. (See Blondel 1752–6, iii, 132.) Nicole Garnier's catalogue raisonné makes no reference to Noailles as a patron of Coypel.

147 Briseux 1743, i, 25.

148 In the seventeenth century, Savot maintained that women's apartments should be placed neither above nor below the chapel thus implying that menstruation rendered women impure and therefore unworthy of physical proximity to the sacred (see Savot-Blondel 1685, 35). By the eighteenth century, however, architects showed greater concern with segregating eating from worship. See, for example, Blondel's criticism of the distribution in the hôtel du Maine (Blondel 1752–6, i, 277).

149 Le Roy Ladurie 1983, 26–8.

150 See Ranum 1980², 426–51.

151 See Bloch 1924, 344–60, 397–405; Mousnier 1979, 653–8, 670–77.

152 Le Roy Ladurie 1983, 26–7.

153 See Thornton 1981, 52–96; Neuschel 1988, 595–622.

154 See Roche 1981, 100–30.

155 At the beginning of the seventeenth century Savot identified two kinds of *salles*, those where a gentleman entertained his equals and those where he received his inferiors (Savot-Blondel 1685, 82–3) but by the eighteenth century 'salle' was usually qualified by a function: 'd'audience', 'de dais', 'de billard', etc. For the full range of such rooms, see Blondel 1752–6, i, 31–2.

156 Laugier 1755, 150.

157 Ibid., 151.

158 See Newman 1980, 128–44.

159 Patte 1765, 6.

160 Delamare 1705–38, i, 388.

161 Genlis 1818, ii, 341.

162 The king's Grand Appartement at Versailles was hung with red damask and the same colour was retained for the hangings of the first public museum opened at the Luxembourg Palace in 1751.

163 Delamare 1705–38, i, 395.

164 Ibid., 387.

165 Ibid., 398. See also the edicts of July 1601, Nov. 1606 and March 1613 in ibid., 394–5.

166 Ibid., 401–2.

167 On this print, see I.F.F. XVIIᵉ siècle, vi, 49–126.

168 C.A. 1847–61, ii, 80. For the gilding of carriages, see ibid., 829.

169 For examples of aristocratic hôtels with gilded interiors, see Catheu 1957, 271–84.

170 See Pitt-Rivers 1965, 21–77, esp. 31.

171 Delamare 1705–38, i, 384.

172 Ibid., 392.

173 *Mémoire instructif concernant les privilèges et franchises des manufactures des Gobelins, de la Savonnerie et des Galleries du Louvre* n.d. (A.N. F¹² 781ᴰ/doss. xxx).

174 See Guiffrey 1873³.

175 The first copyright acts to give legal protection to artists generally, that is by virtue of being academicians, was passed by *arrêt du Conseil* on 21 June 1676. See Brillon 1711, iii, *ad. voc.* 'sculpteurs'. In 1714 these privileges, initially granted exclusively to sculptors, were extended to academicians working in two dimensions. See Saugrain 1744, 462–4.

5 A WORLD OF DISTINCTIONS

1 Sieyès 1888, 12.

2 Goubert 1973, 167.

3 Brice 1698, 215.

4 For a contemporary description of the hôtel, see Sauval 1724, ii, 194–7. See also Crelly 1962, 112–15; Paris 1990–91, 269–85 (nos. 36–9).

5 See Ellis 1986, 414–51, esp. 423.

6 In his genealogical history of the Montmorency family, André Duchesne claimed to have admitted nothing but the 'good' and 'reliable' testimony of original documentation. Indeed, he published his sources, which dated back to the tenth century, in a supplementary volume entitled *Preuves de l'Histoire de la Maison de Montmorency tirées des Chartes de divers Eglises, des Registres de la Chancellerie, du Parlement, & de la Chambre des Comtes, & de plusieurs Tiltres et Historiens* which ran to some 420 pages. Unhappy with Duchesne's brief and comparatively lacklustre

account, a later and more intrepid 'historian' published a 'Discours nouveau sur l'Origine, la Genealogie, & la Maison de Montmorency' in the *Mercure de France*, where he suggested that the family had originated either with Grand Baron François, known as Lisoie and baptised by Clovis in 499, or, with Lisibus, the first French Christian converted by St Denis. First baron or first Christian of the realm were the only plausible 'births' for so illustrious a household. See Duchesne 1624; *Mercure de France* 1712, 18–34, esp. 20, 29.

7 See Sieyès 1888, 11 (b).

8 See Labatut 1972, 57–67, 380–406; Ellis 1988, 39–51.

9 See Elias 1983, 41–2.

10 For a discussion of 'falling status patterns' comparable to those of the *ancien-régime* monarchy, see Geertz 1980, 30–33.

11 For a ritual illustration of this equation, see Elias 1983, 82–5.

12 For a discussion of this effect on one particular family, the Saulx-Tavanes, see Forster 1971, 1–54.

13 On the city as an extension of the palace, see Savot-Blondel 1685, 22; Mumford 1938, 108–13, 129–35; Perrot 1975, i, 15–27; Lepetit 1978, 604–18.

14 On the link between the absolute ruler and the ruled, see Apostolidès 1981, 46–50.

15 Modern historians, most notably Roland Mousnier, have tended to represent the *ancien régime* as a society in which, on the contrary, the vertical bonds of fidelity and clientage were far more important than the corporative links which ostensibly connected members of an order. See Mousnier 1979.

16 Anon. 1784, 5. When plans for a royal square were invited for submission by Le Normand de Tournehem in 1747 many of those submitted by architects and laymen proposed a central location to counteract the degradation of the inner city. For instance, the anonymous author of a report, entitled *Embellissement de Paris*, noted that 'les habitations de ce centre ne sont que des cachots ou les bourgeois respire a peine, et ou ses enfans, quelque soin qu'ils aient de leur éducation demeurent tout contrefait' (A.N. κ 1025/5).

17 Saint-Honoré 1733, 7.

18 Ibid.

19 For a history that stresses the continuities between Paris and the provinces, see Roche 1978.

20 See Forster 1960, esp. 152–77; Meyer 1966; Dewald 1987.

21 See Mirabeau 1883, 85; Forster 1960, 152–5; Forster 1971.

22 Most sixteenth- and seventeenth-century nobles were, as James Woods's study of the nobility of the election of Bayeux amply

demonstrates (Princeton 1980), country gentlemen rather than courtiers. For criticism of their country houses as places of vice and decay, see Dewald 1993, 20.

23 See Sewell 1974, 49–68.

24 See Himelfarb 1986, 235–92.

25 See Lemoine 1984, 17–35.

26 See Bluche-Solnon 1983, *passim*.

27 See Bluche 1960, 175–8.

28 See Roche 1962, 541–78.

29 Brice 1698, i, 226.

30 Revisionist historians, by questioning and finally rejecting the old orthodox interpretation of 1789 as a 'bourgeois' revolution, have been led to the view that by the end of the *ancien régime* little importance attached to the distinctions between *épée* and *robe* or between noblemen and wealthy commoner. Many have argued instead, that France was dominated by a homogeneous élite to which the nobility contributed only some of the members. See Doyle 1980, 7–40. For one who continues to argue (in my view persuasively) that, on the contrary, many of these status distinctions remained socially vital, see Vovelle 1974, 49–72.

31 Blondel 1771–7, ii, 236.

32 Ibid., 237.

33 Ibid.

34 See Blondel 1752–6, i, 268. For a modern discussion of the sculpture, see Souchal 1980, 147–8.

35 Blondel 1771–7, ii, 237.

36 Blondel 1752–6, i, 274–5.

37 Blondel 1771–7, ii, 237.

38 Ibid.

39 See Hillier-Leaman-Stansall-Bedford 1976, 147–85.

40 Germain Boffrand, for instance, compared architecture to theatre and maintained that it too had its pastoral and tragic modes, inspired no doubt by Sebastiano Serlio's designs for tragic, comic and satiric scenes (*c*.1537). See Boffrand 1745, 16. On the notion of character in architecture in the eighteenth century, see Szambien 1986, 175–99.

41 For a discussion of this silence, see Himelfarb 1989, 85–100.

42 See Lassay 1756, i, 259–60.

43 See, for instance, the greater attention paid by the comte de Tessé to the means of keeping warm in Milanese palaces rather than to the aesthetic virtues of their construction and decoration. Tessé 1888, 8–10.

44 For a collection of essays on the ritual functions of architecture, see Bourke 1983.

45 Blondel 1752–6, ii, 26.

46 Genlis 1818, 39–40.

47 Ibid., 38–9.

48 Scudéry 1698, 1–37.

49 The print, one of six 'Appartemens' pub-

lished between 1694 and 1698, represents members of the royal family. On Antoine Trouvain, see Préaud-Casselle-Grivel-Le Bitouzé 1987, 293–8.

50 Blondel 1752–6, i, 27.

51 See Etlin 1978, 127–47.

52 Blondel 1752–6, i, 31.

53 Ibid., 33.

54 The set was entitled, *Differens desseins d'alcoves* and was published in one edition by Le Blond in 1667. The other plates staged the bedroom deaths of Alexander, Cleopatra, Agripina, Lucius Septimus Geta, and Varius Avitus Elagabalus. The frontispiece illustrated a generic version of these events.

55 See Etlin 1978, 127–47.

56 On the genesis of the dining-room, see Mignot 1989, 17–35.

57 See Marais 1863–8, ii, 299 (14/vi/1722).

58 Blondel 1752–6, i, 26. Blondel particularly admired the sequence of ten consecutive rooms at the hôtel de Maisons, in the rue de l'Université, 'qui forment un coup d'œil très considérable, & dont la magnificence de la décoration & l'élegance des meubles rendent . . . un des plus beaux Hôtels qui soit à Paris' (Ibid., 259).

59 See ibid., 241–2; Paris 1984, 73–5.

60 See ibid., 242–4; and also Boffrand 1745, 59; Paris 1984, 78–81; Paris 1986, 49–51.

61 Blondel 1698, 687. For a modern discussion about the influence of Italian architecture on the formation of the French hôtel, see Babelon 1977, 777–90, esp. 778–9; Babelon 1978, 83–108.

62 Tessé 1888, 7–10 (Tessé to the duchesse de Bourgogne 5/i/1701).

63 Ibid., 75–8 (Tessé to the duchesse de Bourgogne 27/xi/1701).

64 See Blondel 1698, 687–9.

65 Blondel 1752–6, i, 241–2.

66 Murray Baillie 1967, 169–99.

67 Ibid. See also Elias 1983, 83–5, 87–90.

68 Anon. 1767, 231.

69 Ibid., 232. Blondel, when discussing the distribution of the hôtel de Roquelaure, remarked that hôtels must have sufficient antechambers, *salles d'assemblées*, and *cabinets* to accommodate 'les personnes du dehors qui doivent être reçues ou attendre l'audience du maître séparément dans des lieux proportionnées à leur distinction, toutes celles qui sont amenées à la maison d'un grand Seigneur ne parvenant pas toujours à son cabinet, ni même à son appartement de parade ou de société' (Blondel 1752–6, i, 246).

70 See, for instance, Marais's account of a duel between the marquis de Courtanvaux and de la Baume (Marais 1863–8, ii, 361). It is perhaps also worth noting that when, in 1722, the marquis de La Fare was charged with arresting the maréchal de Villeroy,

the king's governor, he conducted the latter into an antechamber where musketeers could be and were in attendance before showing him the order of arrest (ibid., 324–25). Thus, if the antechamber was a potentially wayward place by virtue of its personnel, it was also by the same token a space that could be made secure.

71 See Simmel 1950, 51–3.

72 Marivaux was apparently using the fictional character of Mme Dorcin and her society as a cypher for describing the actual social intercourse facilitated by Mme Tencin. For a discussion of Mme Tencin and her portrayal in Marivaux's novel *Marianne*, see Sareil 1969, 229–42.

73 Blondel 1737, i, 30; Blondel 1752–6, i, 30.

74 Blondel 1752–6, i, 32.

75 Louis XIV's reception of his most important guests at the top of the Escalier des Ambassadeurs at Versailles was a custom sufficient to secure the symbolic importance of the staircase in aristocratic households. See Blondel's commendation of the cardinal d'Auvergne's decision not only to aggrandise the first floor of his hôtel in the rue de l'Université, but to make over the staircase. Auvergne engaged Servandoni for the purpose, who erected, 'dans un endroit très-resséré un des plus magnifiques escaliers qui se voyent à Paris . . .' (Blondel 1752–6, i, 261).

76 See Brooks 1969, 18.

77 The significance of 'superior' and 'right' was made clear by Morvan de Bellegarde when discussing, for instance, behaviour in the street: it was polite to cede 'la droite & le haut du pavé à des personnes de considération . . .' (Morvan de Bellegarde 1743, 21).

78 See Etlin 1978, 137–47.

79 Blondel 1752–6, i, 26.

80 See Blondel 1771–7, v, 5; Etlin 1978, 137–47.

81 For Blondel's criticism of schemes which seemed to announce the number of hands involved in their execution, see Blondel 1774, i, 226. Co-ordinated schemes not only proclaimed the architect's mastery of reigning conventions in design but testified to his mastery of the labour-force. See ibid., ii, 110–11.

82 See Blondel 1737–8, i, 66.

83 See Etlin 1978, 137–47.

84 Blondel 1752–6, i, 29.

85 Ibid., 33.

86 Chandeliers were reserved for the most prestigious rooms in an hôtel and the light they shed was amplified by mirrors; the latter were also denied a place in minor rooms like antechambers. See Blondel 1752–6, i, 29–30. Moreover, gloss ideally succeeded matt finished panelling in the

progression from minor to major rooms in an *enfilade* thus contributing to the sensation of moving towards light. See Blondel 1774, ii, 79.

87 On the *salons* at the Palais Royal, see Kimball 1980, 118–19; and at the hôtel d'Argenton, see Paris 1986, 190–93.

88 See Blondel 1771–7, v, 5; Blondel 1774, i, 45–6.

89 Blondel 1752–6, i, 33.

90 Ibid.

91 Cordemoy 1714, 263.

92 Brocher 1934, 28; Le Roy Ladurie 1987, 61–87, esp. 64–5.

93 See Daviler 1738, 193.

94 Even in the eighteenth century, many of the furnishings of the Chambre du Roi – including a 'double tenture de tapisserie' – were still habitually moved as the king made a tour of his palaces throughout the year. See Anon. 1737, i, 407.

95 For the taste for tapestries in the seventeenth century, see Apostolidès 1985, 363–73; for the eighteenth century, see Rambaud 1964–71, i, 713–48; ii, 1055–98.

96 See Maza 1983, 209.

97 See the drawings in the de Cotte collection at the cabinet des Estampes of the Bibliothèque Nationale. See Marcel 1906, 73. The tapestries are all listed in the Jerôme de Phelypeaux de Ponchartrain's inventory (A.N.M.C. XCVI/366 (IAD 14/ii/1747)) and include those especially woven by the Gobelins for Ponchartrain as chancellor and which bore the royal coat of arms.

98 On the nobility's attitude to portraiture, see Sieyès 1888, 10–11, var. 3.

99 A.N.M.C. XXIII/682 (IAD 24/vi/1766): 'Tableaux, lustres et marbres' of Adrien Maurice, duc de Noailles, valued by Antoine Le Gras. In the guard-room the portraits of Louis XIV, the Grand Dauphin, the duc de Bourgogne, the duc de Berry and the duc d'Anjou are all attributed to Hyacinthe Rigaud and the portrait of the Regent, Philippe d'Orléans, to Santerre; the family portraits in the antechamber, however, are all given anonymously.

100 The fact that religious devotion and Christian faith served a decidedly profane end in noble culture was also highlighted by Duchesne, in his history of the Montmorency family, where he discussed the symbiotic relationship between church and nobility: the latter extended generous financial benefices to the former in exchange for the former's care in recording and preserving proofs (by way of parish records and funerary monuments) of the latter's birth and status. See Duchesne 1624, 4.

101 See Paris 1981, 31. Pierre Gobert's portrait of the duc de Valentinois and his family in 1734 was later exhibited at the Salon of 1737.

102 In this sense the strategies and realities of noble portraiture were closely analogous to those of genealogical history. See, for example, the way the Grande Mademoiselle used portraiture in the decoration of her château de Choisy, Cholakian 1986, 3–20, esp. 14–15. See also Harth 1983, 68–128; Ellis 1986, 414–51.

103 Savot-Blondel 1685, 102.

104 See Apostolidès 1985, 363–73.

105 Le Paon was responsible for two large canvases – the *Battle of Norlingen* and the *Battle of Rocroi* – and four overdoors depicting the sieges of *Thionville*, *Philippsbourg*, *Dunkerque* and *Ypres*, while Casanova was responsible for two further wall paintings – the *Battle of Lens* and the *Battle of Fribourg*. All the paintings were commissioned in 1769. See Paris 1987³, 35, 38–9.

106 For the gallery at the hôtel Dupille, see Jacques-André Dupille's probate inventory (A.N.M.C. LXXXVIII/569bis (IAD 30/v/1740)). Among the French paintings hung in the gallery the inventory lists works by Parrocel the elder (no. 1), six by Fouquière (nos. 2, 4), an overdoor by Bon de Boullogne (no. 18), two by Jean Miel (no. 29), a *Leda* by Boullogne (no. 36), a *Hippomenes and Atalanta* by Bon de Boullogne (no. 44), a Bourdon (no. 48), a *Venus and Adonis* by Nicolas Poussin (no. 49), a *Woman Washing by a Fountain* by François Le Moyne (no. 50), two landscape pendants by Corneille (no. 61), and two works by Patel (no. 62). Overdoors by Charles de La Fosse and Pierre-Jacques Cazes decorated other rooms in the house. The paintings were all hung against a background of crimson brocatelle. For the gallery at the hôtel de Lassay, see Paris 1987³, 25–8.

107 The others represented *The End of the Hunt*, *Bathers* and a *Music Party*. On the pictures, see San Francisco 1987, 204–8.

108 For the decoration of the hôtel de Montbazon, see the *procès verbal* drawn up on 15/vii/1751 (A.N.M.C. CXVII/785) according to which a painting representing 'jeux d'enfants' was inset above a pier-glass in the *salon;* the three overdoors, meanwhile, represented 'sujets de l'histoire sacrée et profane'. For the decoration of the hôtel de Richelieu, see the probate inventory of François Armand de Vignerot du Plessis, duc de Richelieu (A.N.M.C. II/741 (IAD 19/viii/1788)), according to which the salon sported two overdoors 'representans des enfants peints par f. Boucher . . .' (no. 892). Amongst the other paintings in the hôtel were the following by French artists:

two further overdoors by François Boucher in the *salle de gardes* (no. 882), a Grimou representing the half-length figure of a man holding a bottle and a glass (no. 885), two gouaches, in the *cabinet du nord*, representing allegorical portraits of the royal family by Charlier (no. 895), two miniatures by Rosalba Carriera in the *cabinet jaune* (no. 948), the following in the *salle du dais* – *Still-life with Flowers* by Jean-Baptiste Oudry, two female portraits by Nicolas de Largillière, a *Portrait of Louis XIII* by Philippe de Champaigne and a *Portrait of Louis XIV* by Martin (nos. 1116–19), and finally, there were two battle paintings by Martin in the gallery (no. 1140).

109 On the hôtel Gontaud de Saint-Blancart, see Kimball 1980, 166–7.

110 On the hôtel de Feuquières, see Paris 1981, 37–40.

111 It was when ornament overflowed into the symbolic spaces of the houses that it became inappropriate. Such an occurrence in the case of the rococo was certainly one of the reasons for the antagonism the style provoked. See Blondel 1752–6, i, 116.

112 On the decoration of bedchambers, see Thornton 1981, 149–79, 293–6.

113 I have used the 1719 edition. See Anon. 1719, 75, and also 157.

114 Anon. 1737, i, 385.

115 See [Courtin] 1719, 50.

116 The symbolic importance of the Grand Appartement at Versailles ensured that its decoration barely changed during the eighteenth century (see Constans 1976, 157–64), and if greater freedom was taken with the decoration of the queen's apartment it was by no means greeted with universal approval. See for instance Saint Yves's response to the 1735 redecoration of Maria Leczinska's bedchamber (Saint-Yves 1748, 137).

117 [Courtin] 1719, 68.

118 Ibid., 66–7.

119 For a contemporary account of the one-upmanship in the realm of fashion, see Muralt 1725, 111.

120 See Baudrillard 1981, *passim*.

121 This is born out by the statistical analyses of patterns of taste carried out by Bonfait and Pardailhé-Galabrun. See Bonfait 1986, 28–42; Bonfait 1986², 125–50; Pardailhé-Galabrun 1988.

6 VERSAILLES AND ITS SATELLITES

1 See Saint-Simon 1974, i, 454–7. I am much indebted to Le Roy Ladurie's essay, 'Versailles Observed: The Court of Louis XIV in 1709', for this discussion of court schisms in the early eighteenth century.

See Le Roy Ladurie 1981, 149–73.

2 Lister 1699, 200.

3 See Biver 1923, 125–31.

4 Quoted from ibid., 218.

5 On the various works at Meudon see, in addition to Biver, Pons 1991², 59–76.

6 See Kimball 1980, 33–111; Marcel 1906, 5–8 and *passim*.

7 See Schnapper 1974, 13–9. Schnapper, in a later article, suggests that Bon de Boullongne's pastiches reflect not only a particular instance of artistic directionlessness but are further symptomatic of a whole generation's in search for a style. See Schnapper 1978, 123.

8 See Marcel 1906, 199; Schnapper 1968, 57–64.

9 See Magendie 1925, 120–24.

10 See Elias 1983, 103.

11 See Colbert 1861–83, v, 268–70; Lux 1982, 85–95.

12 On the Bâtiments, see Guillemet 1912; Marion 1923, 41. On the Menus Plaisirs, see Papillon de La Ferté 1887; Stern 1930, i, 1–15; Weigert 1937, i, 31–49; Souchal 1967, 363–7; La Gorce 1986, 17–18.

13 On the notions of 'inland' and 'outland' as a way of defining social or class difference, see Barthes 1964, 221–37, esp. 227–30.

14 In 1699, Berain dedicated his *Desseins de Cheminée* to Mansart in the hope of gaining favour. See Weigert 1937, i, 130, ii, 198–216; Kimball 1980, 62; Pons 1985, 31.

15 See Cochin 1880, 116; Souchal 1967, 366.

16 See Guillemet 1912, 32.

17 However, on Colbert's death the king compulsorily repurchased the office and awarded it to Louvois. See Tellier 1987, 333, 697.

18 The *survivance* of the office of Directeur des Bâtiments du Roi had been given to Louis de Pardaillan, marquis de Gondrin as part of his marriage settlement to Marie-Victoire-Sophie de Noailles 24/i/1707. Regrettably the contract does not survive. However, the bequest and the income of 18,000 *livres* which accompanied it were then passed to his son, Louis de Pardaillan-Gondrin, duc d'Antin, and later duc d'Epernon, and are mentioned in the latter's marriage contract, 20–28/x/1722 (A.N.M.C. CXVII/325). See also Luynes 1860–63, i, 115. That it was widely known that Epernon would inherit the post is suggested by Louis Fordrin's dedication of his *Nouveau livre de serrurerie* (1723) to him: 'Monseigneur, vous voyez pour la premiere fois vôtre nom à la teste d'un Ouvrage. Personne ne vous avoit encore rendu cette espece d'honneur public. J'ay osé en donner l'example, et vous consacrer le fruit de mon travail. Il faut, que ceux qui cherchent à se distinguer dans leur art, commencent à reconnoître en vous

celui qui doit un jour favoriser leurs efforts et recompenser leurs succés. Vous avez un droit acquis sur tout ce qui sort de leurs mains; mais aussi (permettez moi de vous le dire) ils pretendent avec un droit egal à l'honneur de vôtre protection, et vous la devez. La charge de Surintendant des Bâtiments du Roy, dont vous avez la Survivance, vous impose cette obligation. Quel avantage pour le public et pour vous même que cette Survivance vous apprenne de bonne heure à vous préparer aux fonctions qui vous attendent. Puissiez-vous Monseigneur en suivant le parfait modèle que vous avez devant les yeux justifier pleinement le choix du Prince et l'attente du public.'

19 The first gentlemen of the bedchamber included: from 1725, the duc d'Aumont; from 1741, the duc de Fleury; from 1744, the maréchal de Richelieu; from 1757, the duc de Duras; from 1759, the duc de Fronsac (Richelieu's son) and from 1762, the duc de Villequier (Aumont's son). The only Surintendant des Bâtiments with comparable pedigree was the duc d'Antin, followed much later in the century by the more modest comte d'Angivilliers. The other eighteenth-century *surintendants* – Orry, Tournehem, Marigny and Terray – all issued from finance dynasties. On the Menus Plaisirs and its officers, see Papillon de La Ferté 1887, esp. 4–10; Weigert 1937, i, 31–2, n. 3, 143, n. 3. On their precedence at the *lever* and *coucher du roi*, see Marion 1923, 348–9; Elias 1983, 82–3.

20 Luynes 1860–6, i, 115.

21 La Bruyère 1965, 190–240.

22 It is from La Bruyère that we have inherited the image of Paris: 'le singe de la cour' (La Bruyère 1965, 196, §15). Yet, according to other late seventeenth-century writers, such as Méré, 'il faut considerer la cour et le grand mode séparément, et ne pas ignorer que la cour, ou par coutume, ou par caprice, approuve quelquefois des choses que le grand monde ne souffrirait pas' (Méré 1930, ii, 111). Likewise, Tralage noted that, 'Les gens de Cour, et surtout les dames, affectent de mépriser ce que les Bourgeois ont estimé.' (Quoted from Moore 1957, 175). The court, it would appear from this evidence, tried to maintain a certain distinctiveness from *la ville*.

23 See Méré 1930, ii, 74.

24 See Saint-Simon 1879–1930, iv, 133. See also Biver 1923, 158.

25 See Garnier 1989, 25.

26 The secondary literature on the relationship between Paris and the court and their respective roles as disseminators of taste is extensive and varied. In the 1950s Pierre Francastel argued, in a series of articles for *Annales*, that the 'esprit classique' was not

to be found at court at all but originated in the 'bourgeois' intellectual circles of the capital (see Francastel 1955, 465–79; Francastel 1957, 207–22; Francastel 1959, 142–51). This thesis received qualified support from Pierre Jeannin in a pioneering paper on cultural attitudes and social stratification (Jeannin 1967, esp. 89–90), but this writer also pointed to the danger of Francastel's overly stark separation of court and capital, that of obscuring the degree of interdependence between the two spheres. Others, notably Eric Auerbach have argued that the interpenetration of actors and attitudes in Parisian and Versaillais society was such that, by the end of the seventeenth century, no essential difference existed between them. See Auerbach 1973, 133–79.

27 Knowledge of the ornament traditions of the sixteenth and seventeenth centuries was kept alive by print and architectural publishers in the following century. For example, Jean Mariette republished one of the many eighteenth-century editions of Androuet du Cerceau's *Cartouches*. He also owned the plates of du Cerceau's first *Livre de grotesques* (1550) which he reissued a number of times before ceding the plates to Jombert who inserted a copy of the set into his *Repertoire des artistes* (1752). See Destailleur 1863, 11–12, 14. In 1751 Jombert also republished Jean Le Pautre's ornament designs in three volumes and warmly commended the designer's early works to modern artists (Le Pautre 1751, i, 'avertissement'). These examples would seem to confirm Weigert's assertion that mannerism survived in pockets, often outside the domain of the Bâtiments, well into the eighteenth century (see Weigert 1937, i, 21). By contrast, Kimball emphasises the importance of Le Brun's classical arabesque for the development of this genre in the eighteenth century (Kimball 1980, 28–33, 54–7, 68–9). On the evolution of the grotesque and arabesque, see also Ward-Jackson 1972, 2–30; Chastel 1988. The chief exponents of painted grotesque decoration in the late seventeenth and early eighteenth centuries were Jean I Bérain and Claude III Audran. On these two artists, see Weigert 1937; Weigert 1950, 85–93; Weigert 1955, 100–6; Weigert 1960, 17–32; La Gorce 1986.

28 These drawings have traditionally been attributed to Jean I Bérain. For their proposed reattribution to Germain Gissey, see La Gorce 1986, 112.

29 See Moriarty 1988, 79.

30 See Lépicié 1752, ii, 4. For the commission, see Garnier 1989, 14–15, 101–2.

31 See Caylus's 'La vie d'Antoine Watteau peintre de figures et de paysages, sujets galants et modernes' (1748), reprinted in Rosenberg 1984, 60–61.

32 Lépicié 1752, ii, 20. See also Garnier 1989, 151–2.

33 In 1761 Maria Leczinska helped in the realisation of her *cabinet chinois* at Versailles and indeed, so proud was she of her work that she left the *cabinet* in her will to one of her ladies-in-waiting, the comtesse de Noailles. In a letter to Marigny (17/vii/1768) the comte de Noailles estimated that the honour would cost him some 10,000 *livres* in re-installation costs and that the paintings had no other virtue than 'd'avoir été peints par la Reine'. The symbolic value of such works more-or-less obscured their exchange value. On the *cabinet*, see Jallut 1969, 305–22.

34 Daniel Cronstöm to Nicodemus Tessin the younger 8/i/1700. See Weigert-Hernmarck 1964, 258.

35 *Mercure Galant*, March 1683, 313–14. Quoted from Weigert 1937, i, 81.

36 Of the grotesque ceiling decoration of the Appartement de Monseigneur at Meudon, Dézallier d'Argenville, for example, remarked simply that they were 'peints par Audran' (Dézallier d'Argenville 1752, 22), and of the chinoiserie decorations by Huet at Champs that 'il y a des ornemens légers entre-mêlés d'oiseaux & d'insectes' (ibid., 267).

37 See Paris 1950, 2, no. 3.

38 See ibid., 1–2.

39 See Kimball 1980, 28–33. On the evolution of the compositional domain of the grotesque, see Gombrich 1979, 279–81; Chastel 1988.

40 *Encyclopédie* 1751–65, viii, 967.

41 See Weigert 1931, 167–74; La Gorce 1986, 38. The *boiseries* of the *salon doré* and *chambre du lit* were replaced by copies before the First World War. The originals are at the château de La Borde at Vernon-en-Sologne.

42 See Pons 1991, 55–90.

43 Perrault 1684 (Bk VII, ch. 5), 242.

44 The 1717 Letters Patent of the Académie Royale d'Architecture explicitly asserted the pre-eminence of architecture over the other visual arts. See Aucoc 1889, clxvii. Significantly, such claims were dropped in the revised statutes drawn up in 1776; see ibid., clxxxi–cxv.

45 On the grotesque in antiquity see Ward-Perkins 1956, 209–19.

46 See Chastel 1988, 9.

47 Weigert first drew attention to the fact that Bérain's designs for tapestry were always loosely interpreted by the designers who acted as intermediaries between him and the Beauvais manufactory. See Weigert 1937, i, 105. On the series, see Badin 1909, 11–13.

48 See Paris 1950, 1, 59.

49 For a discussion of the literary representations of Sorel, Dancourt and Nemeitz, see Crow 1985, 46–7. On the *foire* Saint-Germain, see Isherwood 1986, 22–59.

50 Crow 1985, 53.

51 See Weigert 1937, i, 77.

52 *Mercure Galant*, March 1685, 226–7; Weigert 1937, i, 77; La Gorce 1986, 112.

53 Levi-Strauss 1966, 16–36.

54 'Your contours, a thousand time erased/ without defining a single form/leaves the paper under my hand/more changeable than Proteus's.' The poem is anonymous and circulated in manuscript at the duchesse du Maine's court. Her copy, bound in leather with the arms of the 'mouche à miel', and accompanied by the *mémoires* of the various artists who worked on the scheme is to be found in the Condé archive at Chantilly (MS. 550). The poem was published by A. Panthier in the *Bulletin des Amis de Sceaux* in 1930. See Panthier 1930, 72.

55 See Chastel 1988, 19–35.

56 Audran's books were collectively valued at 505 *livres*. The inventory does not identify very many of the items but those mentioned included a Lyon Bible, a dictionary of the Bible, a volume entitled *Veritez de la Religion*, Delamare's *Traité de Police* (? 'de la Maire du commerce'), volumes of the works of Homer and Virgil, an ancient history (possibly Rollin's), a collection of 'fables héroïques', two lots of the works of Mézeray (presumably the *Histoire de France*), and works by Corneille, Louis Silvestre de Sacy, Guez de Balzac, Rabelais and, lastly, the *Curiosités de Paris* and (de Piles's) *Abrégé de la vie des peintres* (1699). See A.N.M.C. xlix/553 (iad 1/vi/1734).

57 Le Moyne's library was much smaller consisting of just 102 volumes, all of which concerned antiquity with the exception of the works of Dancourt. See Bordeaux 1984, 191–2.

58 See Chastel 1988, 9.

59 Grancian 1685, 69.

60 See Lassay 1756, ii, 27.

61 Galant games included 'jeu des compliments ou flatteries', 'jeu des soupirs', and 'jeu de la perte du cœur' (Sorel 1671, 58–62). There was also a 'jeu des histoires ou fables' which required the players to illustrate proverbs with stories from Aesop, Homer and Ovid (ibid., 98–101) and a 'jeux de la similitude & de la metamorphose', which involved comparing oneself or one's mistress to something else and explaining why (ibid., 144). In addition to the game of the arts and sciences there were others also concerning the fine arts such as a 'jeu du bastiment et du jardinage' (ibid., 66), a 'jeu des bastiments' (ibid., 123) and

a 'jeu de la peinture', although of this last Sorel commented that it was 'trop mal aisé pour apporter du divertissement' (ibid., 130).

62 See De Vesme 1971, i, 105–7, nos. 489–541.

63 See Gordon 1989, 302–28.

64 For the *ballet de cour*, see Yates 1947, 236–74; Apostolidès 1981, 62–4; Isherwood 1973, 48–52.

65 The story of Clytie had already been told by Nicolas Loir in the decoration of the antechamber to the king's apartments at the Tuileries to impress on courtiers the necessity of fidelity (see Brice 1706, 83). For a full discussion of the icongraphic programme of the Grand Trianon, see Schnapper 1967), 38–48. For the most recent discussion of La Fosse's *Clytie*, see Fort Worth 1992, no. 3, 116–21.

66 See Moore 1957, 172–82.

67 See Whitman 1969, 286–8.

68 See Panthier 1930, 70–85; Paris 1950, 2–3.

69 'Creator of new forms/Abundant source of the imaginative arts/Principle of visual pleasure,/Pencil, by your faithful strokes/Draw with both grace and liberty/Subjects whose novelty/Will both charm and suprise us./Let everything shine in the realm/Where the divine Louisa/Convenes her felicitous court' (Panthier 1930, 72).

70 See Dens 1981, 33–58; Puttfarken 1985, 106–24.

71 Bouhours 1920, 194–213. Méré drew a distinction between beauty and grace. The first appealed to sight alone, leaving feelings untouched. The second could only be sensed and was measured by the pleasure it gave. See Méré 1930, i, 72, 132. See also Dens 1981.

72 Ibid., 195–6. The argument for aesthetic negligence and the abandonment of classical rules of composition was advanced with particular vigour in the case of opera and music. See, for example, Caux de Cappeval 1754, 45.

73 See Morvan de Bellegarde 1743, 265.

74 Perrault 1684, 242, n. 8.

75 It seems likely that Perrault used his 'bonnes raisons' with ironic intent since according to Muralt, in polite conversation, 'bon' invarably meant the opposite of its dictionary definition: 'les noms de bon homme, bonne femme sont sujets à être pris en mauvais part . . . ce sont des espèces d'injures qui ne désignent pas moin qu'un idiot, un homme simple, avec qui, surtout, on ne veut point de ressemblance. C'est par l'esprit, qu'ils envisagent généralement comme opposé à la bonté, que les Français veulent être loués' (Muralt 1725, 105). Good reason, therefore, could be tantamount to bad taste.

76 There were of course *honnêtes femmes* although the discourse of *honnêteté* scarcely acknowledges them as such. On the gendering of *honnêteté*, see Moriarty 1988, 38–52.

77 See Fumaroli 1980, 430–32.

78 The story was told by Guez de Balzac in *Les Entretiens* (1657). See Moriarty 1988, 69.

79 Morvan de Bellegarde 1720, 152.

80 The noble hero of Duclos's *Confessions du comte de *** (1741) is demonstrably complacent about the inadequacies of his upbringing: 'Étant destiné par la naissance à vivre à la cour, j'ai été élevé comme mes pareils, c'est à dire fort mal. Dès mon enfance, on me donna un précepteur pour m'enseigner le latin, qu'il ne m'aprit pas; quelques années après, on me remit entre les mains d'un gouverneur pour m'instruire de l'usage du monde qu'il ignorait' (Duclos 1965, 200).

81 Moriarty 1988, 96.

82 Ibid.

83 See Stanton 1980, 80–81.

84 Méré described courtiers as 'de fâcheux négociateurs', trading for influence. See Méré 1930, 47.

85 See Méré 1930, ii, 111; iii, 154–5.

86 This is surely one of the inferences that may be drawn from the fact that Méré refused to identify the *honnête homme* with the warrior, or the amateur with the professional man. *Honnêteté* was an ideal founded on a celebration of leisure. See ibid., iii, 69–102. See also Dens 1981, 11–24, esp. 24.

87 Ibid., 78.

88 See Stanton 1980, 47.

89 Ibid., 98–105.

90 For the notion and reality of cabal in *ancien-régime* politics, see Le Roy Ladurie 1981, 149–73; Mettam 1988, 45–101.

91 Lassay 1756, ii, 16–18.

92 Tellier 1987, *passim*.

93 On the duc de Bourgogne's circle and its programme for reform, see Rothkrug 1965, 262–86; Keohane 1980, 332–8, 343–6; Ellis 1988, 57–91.

94 See Michaux 1964, 61–7.

95 Saint-Simon described Vaucresson as 'une petite maison de campagne que le duc avoit achetée à portée de Versailles et de Marly, où il se retiroit le plus souvent que ses emplois le lui pouvoient permettre' (Saint-Simon 1879–1930, xi, 5). Although he later amplified the statement and acknowledged that at Vaucresson the duc de Beauvillier 's'étoit ajusté la plus jolie retraite du monde' (ibid., xix, 139), for the most part the *Memoirs* implicitly but insistently contrast the wordliness of Versailles and the court and the cloistered piety of Vaucresson. See ibid., xiii, 293; xxi, 300–2.

96 See Paris 1984, 54–7.

97 Predictably it was the antechambers that were hung with tapestries. More were stored in the *garde meubles*. Torcy's bedchamber was decorated with pictures representing: the *Entombment*, the *Pilgrims at Emmaus*, *Christ and Mary Magdalene*, the *Annunciation*, *Christ before Pilate*, *Jesus Christ*, the *Virgin*, *Jacob*, *Christ with St Francis*, *St Francis*, *The Infant Christ*. The only non-religious works were a painting of an '*Etranger et un petit chien*', very possibly a pilgrim, and a large portrait of the archbishop of Montpellier, one of Torcy's relations. However, I should not like to over-emphasise the sober character of the hôtel. In the main apartment on the first floor, the rooms were decorated predominantly with history paintings, but ones in which the heroic played no more than an equal part to the gallant. The subjects included, the *Rape of Helen*, 2 episodes from the life of Alexander the Great, 4 episodes from the life of Noah, the *Marriage of Hannibal*, the *Four Ages of Man*, and a *Bacchanal*, *Bacchus and Ceres*, *Venus and Cupid*, *Putti Playing*, *Rinaldo and Armida*, and the *Rape of Europa*. See Jean-Baptiste Colbert, marquis de Torcy's probate inventory, A.N.M.C. CXIII/358 (IAD 10/ix/1746).

98 See A.N. T¹/163, 168. The duc de Montmorency bought the house from the widow Desmarets on 14/iv/1723 for 500,000 *livres*.

99 See Keohane 1980, 343–6.

100 See Teyssèdre 1965, 406.

101 Fénelon 1752, ii, 72.

102 Fénelon 1968, 279–82.

103 Quoted from Finch 1966, 39.

104 For example, in Fénelon's *Télémaque* (1699), Mentor explained to Idoméné, king of Salente, that 'Il faut . . . employer les sculpteurs et les peintres que pour conserver la mémoire des grands hommes et les grandes actions. C'est dans les bâtiments publics ou dans les tribunaux qu'on doit conserver des representations de tout ce qui a été fait avec une vertu extraordinaire pour le service de la patrie' (Fénelon 1968, 281).

105 See Saint-Simon 1974, i, 454–7; Le Roy Ladurie 1981, 149–73.

106 See Dinaux-Brunet 1867, ii, 236–7.

107 Saint-Simon 1879–1930, v, 442. Quoted in Biver 1923, 236.

108 According to Saint-Simon, d'Antin helped to instigate Chamillart's downfall in the hope of replacing him at the Ministry of Finance, but in the end he had to content himself with the post of Directeur Général des Bâtiments. On this appointment, see Stoloff 1978, 2–46.

109 See Carlier 1989, 45–54.

110 See Verlet 1981, 285–8.

111 See Biver 1923, 188–90; Pons 1991,

67–74.

112 On the hôtel de Vendôme see, Paris 1981, 42. On the pavilion at Clichy, see Paris 1950, 64; Weigert-Dupont 1960, 223–32; Mathienssent-Trouilleux 1982, 213–24; Paris 1986, 7.

113 See Paris 1950, 3, no. 7; Marie 1972, i, 249; Paris 1985, 78–9, C. 22.

114 See Paris 1950, 27, no. 112, 44, no. 181.

115 Ibid., 4, no. 8.

116 Two drawings for the closet exist in the Crondstedt collection (III, 134, 227) in Stockholm.

117 See *Mercure de France*, July 1735, 1600.

118 See Paris 1950, 11–12, nos. 43–4.

119 Ibid., 59; Mabille 1974, 5–36. For the tapestries or flock papers designed by Audran for the Ménagerie, see Paris 1950, 13, no. 50.

120 See La Gorce 1986, 38. La Gorce has also identified a magnificent drawing in Stockholm as preparatory to an elaborate grotesque scheme realised for Seignelay in the dining-room at Sceaux. See ibid., 20, 36–8.

121 See Kimball 1980, 56, 109; Weigert 1937², 17–18. For a set of tapestries inspired by Bérain though not designed for him and executed for the duc du Maine, See Standen 1976, 103–17.

122 See Le Roy Ladurie 1981, 165.

123 Sceaux had been bought by the duc du Maine from the Seignelay family in 1699 for 900,000 *livres*. See Hautecœur 1943–52, ii, 459–61. The duchesse du Maine inaugurated a literary salon there in 1702. See Poisson 1987, 40–54.

124 The poem juxtaposes the image of Louis XIV as Mars to be seen in the château (in the battle paintings by Van der Meulen) with the nymphaeum of the dauphin in the gardens. See Boutard 1703, esp. 5.

125 For some of the continuities between Marly and Meudon, see Schnapper 1968, 57–64.

126 See ibid., 58.

127 See Paris 1950, 19, nos. 78–9, 62.

128 See Himelfarb 1986, 241–3.

129 See Schnapper 1967, 39–44.

130 See Félibien 1689, 145–60. For a discussion of these tapestries to which I owe much, see Kapp 1986, 179–95.

131 See Schnapper 1967, 43.

132 Félibien 1689, 155.

133 Scudéry 1698, ii, 479–95, for the description of the marvels see esp. 489–92. For an interpretation of the conversation, which I have been happy to follow, see also Goldsmith 1986, 17–25.

134 Scudéry 1698, ii, 495.

135 On the Coypel series see Schnapper 1967, 91–3 (I 55–62). For the more aimiable treatment of Hercules see ibid., 42.

136 'The God of war lives in Louis's breast;/On his august brow Venus dwells;/When so much valor is joined to so much charm,/Mortals, we must yield either through force or through love' (Félibien 1689, 156. Cited in Kapp 1986, 186).

137 Kapp 1986, 187.

138 Schnapper has noted that the two series by Verdier and Houasse depicting the stories of Io and Minerva fell almost entirely outside the iconographic programme of the Trianon. See Schnapper 1967, 44.

139 For a full discussion of the painted decoration at Meudon, see Schnapper 1968, 57–64.

140 For a discussion of the easel paintings at Meudon, see Biver 1923, 147–51.

141 For the most recent discussion of these paintings, see Fort Worth 1992, no. 7, 136–9.

142 See Hautecœur 1943–52, ii, 627; Kimball 1980, 106–7.

143 For the other paintings in the room, see Biver 1923, 150. They included a *Nativity* by Carlo Marratta to contrast perhaps with Jouvenet's *Birth of Bacchus*, and a *Marriage at Cana* by Bassano in which the sacramental and miraculous nature of the wine may have been open to mockery from the profane wine-party enjoyed by Bacchus, Venus and Ceres above in Bon de Boullogne's overdoor.

144 For a discussion of Shakespeare's characterisation of Henry V which I have found particularly suggestive when looking at the dauphin's cultural choices, see Mullaney 1983, esp. 53–62.

145 See Saint-Simon 1879–1930, v, 440–42; Biver 1923, 212–14.

146 Félibien 1689, 174; Kapp 1986, 190.

147 'To be well born is a happy occasion/But all is lost if the fruit does not ripen/Manners and intellect require polish/That is the essential point, and something not owing/To one's birth' (Benserade 1672, 67).

7 EARTHLY PARADISE ON THE LEFT BANK

1 See Ranum 1969, 274.

2 On the urban development of Paris in the early eighteenth century, see Roche 1981, 11–19.

3 See Nagle 1992, 139–50, esp. 141–2.

4 On the faubourg Saint-Germain, see Christ 1956; Paris 1979; Paris 1981; Paris 1983; Paris 1984; Paris 1987²; Paris 1990.

5 Brice 1725, i, 25. The first edition of the *Description* was published in 1684. Reprintings and new editions came out in 1687, 1698, 1713, 1717, 1725, 1752. Brice expressed fear at the consequences of this rapid urban expansion. See ibid., 364–5.

6 Piganiol de La Force 1765, i, 25.

7 Law himself projected the following advantages to his System: 'La construction d'une infinité de bâtimens de toutes espèces tant dans la ville que dans la campagne. La réparation des anciens, dont une partie étoit presque à tomber' (Law 1934, iii, 401). And he noted that 'la construction de bâtiments à continué, malgré la chèreté des ouvriers et des matériaux' (ibid., 406). See also Marion 1914, i, 99–100. On the development of the place Louis-le-Grand, see Boislisle 1888, 1–272; Dumolin 1931, 1–52. On the influx of property onto the market during the Regency as a result of equity speculation, see Poëte 1910, 145–8. On speculative building during the Regency, see Hautecoeur 1943–52, ii, 47–8.

8 According to d'Antin, 'Les Arts et les sciences sont bien à plaindre dans une longue minorité' (C.D. 1887–1908, iv, 426), and Haillet de La Couronne confirmed that substantial commissions for painters had indeed been scarce during the Regency (Dussieux 1854, ii, 428–9). For the plight of the Bâtiments and the Academy during the Regency, see Marcel 1906, 11–40. Deprived of institutional support, artists relied instead on the protection of private patrons. To Crozat's protection of La Fosse, Oppenord and Watteau may be added Berger's association with Le Moyne; Bernard's offer of lodgings to de Troy at Passy; Caylus's promotion of Lamy, Vassé, Bouchardon, Trémolières, Le Bas and Wille; the hospitality to and employment of the Van Loos by the Carignan family both in Italy and France; the personal and official favours secured for Oudry by Fagon; Polignac's patronage of Robert, whom he brought back from Italy; Titon du Tillet's largesse to the Parrocels, the family's poor relations; an apparently special relationship between the comtesse de Verrue and the Boullogne, and the close friendships between Saint-Bonnet and Bertin, and the duc de Vendôme and Raoux.

9 For Oppenord, see Huard 1928, 311–29; Macmillan 1982, iii, 324–7. Oppenord also worked for other members of the Orléans family, namely two of the regent's illegitimate sons, the chevalier d'Orléans and Charles de Saint-Albin. See Huard 1928, 317.

10 See Schnapper 1968, 59–60; Garnier 1989, 25–43.

11 Matteis was represented in the dauphin's collection by a *Rape of Europa* (see Schnapper 1968, 57), and in the regent's collection by *Salmacis and Hermaphroditus*. On the regent as collector, see Paris 1988, 95–115.

12 See Brejon de Lavergnée 1983, 45–8.

13 See Brice 1752, iv, 142; Hautecoeur 1943–52, iii, 19–21; Gallet 1972, 28; Pons

14 In 1722 Vendôme presented the Regent with Raoux's *Telemachus Telling Calypso of his Adventures* (Louvre; Inv. 7362). See *Mercure de France*, July 1722, 120–3; ibid., 1734, 348.

15 The duchesse de Bourbon herself reserved an 'arrière cabinet' for grotesque decoration. See Hautecoeur 1943–52, iii, 246; Pons 1985, 135.

16 See Pons 1985, 126.

17 On the evidence from Mariette's life of Lancret, inserted in Quentin de Lorangère's sale catalogue (1744), which mentioned a cabinet decorated by Lancret and belonging to M. de Boullogne (see Guiffrey 1873, 34), it was assumed by Féral (1896, 12) and Wildenstein (1924, 119–20) that this decorative scheme was exclusively the work of this painter, undertaken for the client named. More recently, Thiry-Druesne (1979, 51–84) has shown that the scheme was in fact a collective undertaking, conceived and designed by Claude III Audran in collaboration with Lancret, for Abraham Peyrenc de Moras, the previous tenant of the hôtel, place Vendôme. For the sculpture executed by Degoullons and Le Goupil, see Pons 1985, 122–4, 218–20.

18 See Macon 1903, 65–77; Hautecoeur 1943–52, iii, 232, 281.

19 Pons 1985, 137.

20 For the will of Jeanne-Baptiste d'Albert, comtesse de Verrue, and her bequest to Lassay, see Rambaud 1964–71, ii, 888.

21 See *Mercure de France*, July 1735 1600.

22 Paris 1986, 212–14.

23 Ibid., 93–7.

24 For the interrelationships between these families, see Tellier 1987.

25 For the chapel at Versailles, see Garnier 1989, 163–4. For the *Nursery of the Apes*, see Paris 1950, 19, no. 79.

26 Painters such as Oudry and Lajoue both initially trained in the more liberal and commercially oriented traditions of the Académie de Saint-Luc. That the Académie Royale de Peinture et de Sculpture was not alone under pressure to broaden its outlook is suggested by Petit de Bachaumont's attempt to secure Meissonnier's election to the Académie Royale d'Architecture (see B.A. MS. 4041 (327 HF) f° 321).

27 For the château de Champs, see Dézallier d'Argenville 1752, 267–9; Strandberg 1963, 81–100; Taralon 1974, 49–65.

28 For Malgrange, see Paris 1986, 215–17.

29 See Pons 1985, 117–21, 125–9.

30 See Paris 1987³, 184–8.

31 See Roland Michel 1979, 20; Roland Michel 1984², 292–3; Washington 1984, 248–50.

32 Cailleux 1961, i–v.

33 See Bocquet 1977, 189–214.

34 For Peyrenc de Moras and the decoration of his *cabinet*, see Thiry-Druesne 1979, 51–84. For the decoration of the château de Bercy, see Pons 1985, 207–8.

35 On Watteau's patrons, see Posner 1984, 116–28.

36 It is perhaps worth noting that Watteau's decorative works seem to have been executed for his highest ranking patrons.

37 See Elias 1983, 214–67; Harth 1983, 34–67.

38 For a discussion of the symbolic and exchange values of landed property, see Bourdieu 1977, 159–97; Reddy 1987, 107–43, esp. 117–27.

39 La Bruyère 1965, 198, §21.

40 Ibid.

41 See Bloch 1961, 311.

42 On good-faith economies, see Bourdieu 1977, 173–4.

43 Montesquieu 1964, 42.

44 On the transformative effect of capitalism on social relationships, see Barbier 1979, 56–83, esp. 69–81.

45 On the connections between love, nature and virtue in eighteenth-century France, see Mauzi 1960, 472–84. On love and pastoralism, see Ehrard 1963, 271; Menant 1981, 117–19.

46 On the iconography of bird-catching, see Wildenstein 1924, 100–1, nos. 455–68; Bordeaux 1976, 75–101.

47 For example, François-Philippe Morel's probate inventory revealed that in 1731 one of the rooms in his house in the *cloître* Notre-Dame was decorated with '8 dessus de portes d'après Watteau' (Rambaud 1964–71, i, 569). Likewise a room in the hôtel de Bretagne, rue de la Chaise, sported in 1734 a *Concert* 'd'après Watteau, dessus de porte' and in 1747 the inventory taken after the death of Joseph de Thiard de Bissy listed two overdoors 'représentant sujets de Watteau' in his apartment in the rue de Vaugirard (ibid., ii, 877–88, 930). See also Roland Michel 1984², 297–9.

48 For a discussion of the iconography of swinging, see Posner 1982, 75–88.

49 For the hôtel de Bonnac, see Paris 1979, 30–31.

50 See Wildenstein 1924, 100–1. This composition was used a number of times by Lancret and one version was engraved by Larmessin and accompanied with the following verses:

Que cet heureux oiseau, que votre main caresse,
Est bien récompensé de sa captivité!
Le Berger qui vous sert avec tant de tendresse
Est bien moins libre et moins bien traité.

On the iconography of bird-catching, see note 46, above.

51 For a particularly incisive discussion of the seventeenth-century pastoral novel, see Harth 1983, 35–67. In an essay on poetry, Fontenelle defended the aristocratic heroes and heroines germane to the pastoral and eclogue on the grounds that since 'real' peasants were poetically uninteresting, 'il faut qu'Ariane soit princesse; tant nous somme destinés à être ébloui par les titres' (see Ehrard 1963, 271).

52 See Washington 1984, 493–501.

53 See Démoris 1971, 337–57; Crow 1985, 56–7.

54 An abriged edition of d'Urfé's novel was published in 1712 by the abbé de Choisy under the title *La nouvelle Astrée* and according to Bruant, Gravelot illustrated another eighteenth-century edition of the same work (see Bruant 1950, 35–44). For the continued popularity of the novel, see Démoris 1971, 341; Ménant 1981, 114–15. It is difficult to determine the extent to which *L'Astrée* continued to be used as a literary source for painting in the eighteenth century, not least because it was cited almost as a generic label for the description of pastorals (see Laing 1986, 53–64). The fashion for portraits in the guise of d'Urfé's heroes and heroines, launched in 1645 by Claude Deruet's portrait of *Julie d'Angennes* (see Blunt 1957, 326–8), was maintained in the eighteenth century by Rigaud and Largillière with portraits such as the former's *Gaspard de Gueidan* (1735; Musée Granet, Aix-en-Provence) and the latter's *Marquise de Dreux-Brézé* (c.1715; Montreal Museum of Fine Arts, Montreal). For these portraits, see Colomer 1973; Rosenfeld 1979, 202–7. To my knowledge, only one decorative scheme is explicitly described by a contemporary source as illustrating episodes from the story of *Astrée*. According to Dézallier d'Argenville, Charles-Michel-Ange Challe executed for the *salon* of the château de Champlatreux, Molé's country residence, six paintings 'qui représentent les agrémens de la vie pastorale, imités du roman d'Astrée': 1) *The High Druid Adamas Revealing her Future to Astraea*; 2) *Astraea Consults the Fountain about True Love*; 3) *Celadon Receiving a Wreath of Roses from Astraea*; 4) *The Marriage of Astraea and Celadon*; 5) *Celadon Finding the Sleeping Astraea*. 6) and 7), two overdoors, *The Peacefulness of Pastoral Life*. See Dézallier d'Argenville 1779, 401–3. The paintings were probably executed between 1751–7 at the time when Jean-Michel Chevotet was employed by Molé to remodel the château. See Chevallier 1970–71, 69–86.

55 Elias 1983, 248.

56 On the *cabinet vert* at the hôtel de Soubise, see Paris 1986, 223–4; for the Natoires at the hôtel de Roquelaure, see Troyes 1977, 60, no. 15; Paris 1984, 166.

57 See Wildenstein 1924, 271; Paris 1981, 35–6.

58 For the history of eighteenth-century French gardens, see Paris 1978; Wiebenson 1978.

59 For *La Perspective*, see Washington 1984, 300–4, no. 25.

60 See, for example, the paintings executed for the Trianon representing the surrounding park and gardens. Schnapper 1968, esp. figs. 70, 71.

61 See, for instance Washington 1984, 300–3, no. 25.

62 Quoted from Elias 1983, 227 (my emphasis).

63 For the château de Montmorency, see Hautecœur 1943–52, ii, 198–9; iii, 162–3.

64 On the importance and significance of perspective in theoretical writings of the late seventeenth and early eighteenth centuries, see Puttfarken 1985, 96–101.

65 The visual ambiguity of Oppenord's designs, engraved by Huquier, has been discussed by Roland Michel 1979, 7; Roland Michel 1984, 159–60.

66 See Collins 1965, 27–8.

67 Mirrors played an important role in Mélite's seduction, creating wonder and enjoyment and also providing opportunities for the indirect and coquettish glance. See Bastide 1879.

68 On Servandoni's stage designs, see Bjurström 1954, 150–59; Bjurström 1959, 222–4.

69 See Roland Michel 1984, 195–6, P45.

70 See Caylus's 'Vie de Watteau . . .' (3/iii/1748) reprinted in Rosenberg 1984, 80.

71 See [Le Clerc] 1669. The book's dedication to the marquis de Seignelay emphasises, as follows, the importance of geometry for statesmen and most particuarly the *noblesse d'épée*: '[La Geométrie] ne doit elle pas preparer aux grands Emplois qui vous attendent? Puis que soit en Paix, soit en Guerre, l'Architecture Civile & Militaire ne scauroit rien executer sans Elle; & que la Fortification des Places & la construction de tous ces Monumens publics qui rendent la mémoire des grands Princes si recommendable à la posterité, ne subsiste que par ses règles.' (Ibid., unpag.).

72 See Ellis 1988.

73 For a discussion of the Regency that is particularly sensitive to the lack of definition of its political culture, and to the opportunities thus created for those with political ambition, see Le Roy Ladurie 1984, 286–305. On the *Polysynodie*, see Antoine 1970, 77–100; Shennan 1979,

34–50.

74 See Ellis 1988, esp. 169–206.

75 See Saint-Simon 1879–1930, xxix, 201, xxxi, 195. Quoted from Lassaigne 1965, 141. I have been unable to determine the exact meaning of 'safraniers' but assume that it derives from 'safre' or orphrey, a rich, golden embroidery associated particularly with robes and vestments. Saint-Simon thus suggests that the *noblesse* of these upstarts was more apparent (and the result of appointments) than real.

76 For the hôtel de Rouillé, See Lorgues 1979, 37–49.

77 The 'petites maisons', or villas on the outskirts of Paris were reputedly the setting for discrete assignations and the bawdy parties of young *roués*. Bastide's *La Petite Maison*, possibly modelled on Bouret's pavilion at Croix-Fontaine, tells the story of a young girl seduced in (if not by) such a 'petite maison' by the conscienceless marquis de Trémicour. See Bastide 1879. The duc de Richelieu had a folly at the *barrière* Vaugirard where he held parties in the 1740s. According to the marquis d'Argenson: 'Tout y est en galanteries et en obscénités; les lambris surtout ont au milieu de chaque panneau des figures fort immodestes en bas relief' (Argenson 1859–67, iii, 234; Hautecoeur 1943–52, iii, 45). Although little is known about this pavilion, the regent at an earlier date possessed a hermitage at Bagnolet, decorated with an apparently indecent series of 'grisaille brune' paintings depicting the *Temptation of St Anthony* by Valade. See Hillairet 1963–72, i, 138.

78 Tessé 1888, 421–2.

79 On Boucher's pastorals, see Landau 1983, 360–78; but especially Laing 1986, 55–64; New York 1986, 56–72.

80 On the tapestry series *The Fêtes italiennes*, of which *The Charlatan and the Peep Show* is a component, see Standen 1977, 107–30; New York 1986, 334–9, nos. 86–9.

81 See Isherwood 1986, 103–9; Laing 1986, 55–64.

82 See Harth 1983, 35–48.

83 See Crow 1985, 55–74; Vidal 1992.

84 See Isherwood 1986, 106–7. In 1754, Boucher designed a frontispiece for this play which was only performed at the Opéra Comique in the following year. See Jean-Richard 1978, no. 1349.

85 The *mémoires* concerning pictorial subject-matter drawn up by Petit de Bachaumont seem to suggest that connoisseurs and patrons played an instrumental role in devising decorative schemes, although to what extent Bachaumont's role as an artistic counsel may be taken as exceptional is hard to determine. See B.A. MS. 4041 (327 HF) *Histoire d'Esther* (f° 345–50); *Suite de*

tableaux agréables à faire, novembre 1756 (f° 354–5); *Psyche* (f° 362–3).

86 According to Ingamells (London 1989, 61–3, 81–2, nos. P489, P489) these two pictures originally decorated the salon of the château de Montigny-Lencoup which belonged to one of the Trudaine, presumably Jean-Charles Trudaine de Montigny (1733–77); however, I have been unable to trace them in his inventory after death (A.N.M.C. CXII/789^A (IAD 12/viii/1777)) nor do they appear in the Trudaine inventory taken by Le Brun in An III (A.N. F^17 1267/109). On the other hand, according to a *Mémoire sur la manufacture de tapisseries de Beauvais* (1780), it was Trudaine who encouraged Beauvais to produce pastoral designs: 'Il pensa avec raison que des paysages avec des objets champêtres, des animaux et des figures d'une moyenne grandeur, seroient des objets non seulement plus analogues aux talens des ouvriers qui s'étoient formés dans le genre d'Oudry, mais encore d'un débit beaucoup plus facile. Il fit donc choix de M. Casanova pour peintre dont le genre se rapprochoit de celui qu'il paroissoit convenable de rétablir . . .' (A.N. F^12 1456^B/177).

87 Laing 1986, 55–64.

88 On Boucher's overdoor, see London 1989, 31–2, P385. On the popularity of the theme of Daphnis and Chloe in the eighteenth century, see Munro 1982, 117–36. Art historians have tended to stress the importance of Boucher's apprenticeship – engraving Watteau's arabesques (see Jean-Richard 1978, nos. 157–63) – for the development of his own pastoral idiom. Laing has shown that contemporaries were more sensitive than we are to Boucher's originality, and has argued, together with Posner, that the *fête galante* and the pastoral constitute two very different genres. See Posner 1984, 15–31; Laing 1986, 55–64.

89 See Menant 1981, 111–53.

90 The importance of parody and the burlesque for the development of literary realism has been studied in detail (see, for example, Von Stackelberg 1970, 208) and it is worth noting that in the visual arts, many of those recognised for their naturalistic images, such as Desportes and Oudry, began their careers in Claude III Audran's studio.

91 Quoted from Menant 1981, 148.

92 'Ce [pastoral] n'est . . . qu'une belle fable:/ N'envions rien à nos aieux;/En tout temps l'homme fut coupable,/En tout remps il fut malheureux.' See Finch-Joliat 1971, 175–9.

93 See Paris 1987², 33.

94 See Du Bos 1755, i, 133–49.

95 Lorangère 1744, 197–8. Cited in New York 1986, 83.

96 Tallard 1756, 88–9, lots 185–191.

97 See A.N.M.C CXVII/785, *Procès verbal d'estimation* 15/vii/1751.

98 See Paris 1981, 38.

99 For the landscapes, see Rosenberg-Babelon 1968, 211–16; Cholet 1973, 74–5, no. 25; New York 1986, 175. The panelling for the *cabinet vert* has been attributed to Jacques Verberckt by Bruno Pons; see Paris 1986, 223–4. The cartouches depicted episodes from Aesop's fables and included, in addition to those illustrated here, *Le Chat et le Renard, La Lice et sa Compagne, Le Chien Envieux, Le Loup et l'Agneau, Le Renard et les Raisins, Le Chien qui Lâche la Proie pour l'Ombre*. The designs are, as Kimball and Donnell (1928) have shown, directly inspired by Francis Barlow's illustrations to Robert Lestrange's edition of the fables (1666), French translations of which were well known in France. For the two illustrated here, see Aesop 1714, 174–5 (fable lxxxviii, *L'Ours et les Mouches à Miel*), and 180–1 (fable xci, *Les Deux Coqs et la Perdrix*).

100 On Boucher's landscape practice, see Washington 1973–4, 72–7, nos. 56–9.

101 Voltaire, quoted from Menant 1981, 150.

102 See Bray 1927, 330–31; and more generally Menant 1981, 111–53.

103 Hénault 1806, 273.

104 On the duc and duchesse de Maine's political fortunes, see Campbell 1985, 64–8.

105 In the preface to the popular *Spectacle de la nature* (1732–51), the abbé Pluche argued for the importance of natural history in the nobleman's education precisely because it combined instruction with pleasure. As the title suggested, the element of pleasure was primarily visual: 'Tout y est capable de plaire . . . parce que tout y est plein de desseins, de proportions, de précautions' (ibid., i, iv). Moreover, Pluche maintained that nature's 'decoration extérieur' was rendered 'si brillant que pour piquer notre curiosité' (ibid., i. xi–ii). For an excellent introduction to the sociology of science in the seventeenth century, see Harth 1983, 222–309.

106 Duclos noted, for instance, that although the 'savants qui s'occupent des sciences exactes' were esteemed by the *monde* and their utility acknowledged, 'leur nom est cependant plus à la mode que leur personne, à moins qu'ils n'ayent d'autres agrémens que le mérite qui fait leur célébrité.' (Duclos 1751, 134). On the gradual detachment of science from the 'polite' arts, see Harth 1983, 222–309.

107 On the hôtel du Lude, its decoration and Bonnier de La Mosson's collections, see Bourdier 1959, 52–9; Roland Michel 1976, 211–21; Paris 1984, 150–63; Roland Michel 1984, 41–45, 185–8 (P. 5).

108 See Roland Michel 1984, 184–5 (P. 3).

109 See Bonnier de la Mosson 1744, esp. lots 397–620 (*cabinet de mécanique et de physique*). Of this room, Gersaint remarked that it was 'le plus recreatif pour l'esprit et pour les yeux, puisque tout ce qui le compose instruit en même tems qu'il amuse' (ibid., 83).

110 On Courtonne's drawings, see Paris 1984, 158, no. 246.

111 See Watson 1939, 556–75.

112 See Harth 1983, 261–4.

113 For a discussion of the spaces of sciences in seventeenth-century England that I have found particularly useful, see Shapin 1988, 373–404.

114 For a comparable example of the interplay between technology and the aesthetic, see Cardy's discussion of Vaucauson's automata. Cardy 1986, 109–23.

115 The main contemporary treatise on turning was Plumier's *L'art de tourner* (1701). For a study of the taste and art of turning at the Danish court, see Gouk 1983, 411–36.

116 For examples of work in Bonnier's collection, see Paris 1984, 158–9. Other examples are now in the Swedish royal collection at Drottingholm.

117 On the *Société des Arts*, see See B.N. MS. n.a.f. 11225, f° 174–97; Hahn 1963, 829–36; Hahn 1981, 77–93; Paris 1984, 161–2. Roland Michel has persuasively discussed the significance of this academy for the development of the rococo. See Roland Michel 1984, 30–33.

118 A preparatory drawing thought by Roland Michel to be a study for this overdoor (Fine Arts Museum of San Francisco) locates the garden above the library so that nature seems to flow down the steps into the room. See San Francisco 1977, 108, no. 67. (Pons, however, thinks that it is a project for a commission from the duc de Chevreuse for overdoors for a *cabinet* in the hôtel de Luynes. See Paris 1984, 61). On Bonnier's globes, see ibid., 162, and, since the acquisition by the J. Paul Getty Museum (Malibu) of two globes thought to be the companion pieces to those in Bonnier's library, see Ronfort 1989, esp. 61–6.

119 On the policy of the Académie Royale des Sciences towards other scientific societies, see Hahn 1971.

120 For a full discussion of Sebastien Leclerc's scientific engravings to which I am greatly indebted, see Harth 1983, 258–78.

121 Perrault 1671–6, preface (unpag.). In the preface Perrault also distinguished between two kinds of history: *histoire générale*, '[où] l'on rapporte toutes les choses qui ont esté recueïllies en plusieurs temps, & qui appartiennent au sujet qu'elle traitte', and *commentaires* or *mémoires* which 'bien qu'elle ne contienne que les parties, &

Comme les élemens qui composent l'Histoire, & qu'elle n'ait pas la majesté qui se trouve dans celle qui est générale, a néanmoins cet avantage, que la *Certitude & la Verité, qui sont les qualités les plus recommendables* de l'Histoire, ne lui sçauroient manquer . . .' (ibid.). His plates were the pictorial equivalent of the latter.

122 For a study of the dimension of theatricality in natural philosophy, see Schaffer 1980, 55–91, esp. 80–83; Schaffer 1983, 1–43.

123 See Grollier de Servière 1733, 27–8.

124 Ibid., 28–9.

125 Paris 1984, 152.

126 Although the de-fictionalisation of natural history (hydras, dragons, unicorns, sphinxes and mermaids disappeared from serious scientific publications at the end of the seventeenth century; see Guyénot 1941, 39–77) stripped it of its most obviously pictorial features, Schaffer has shown that natural forces, such as electricity and earthquakes remained aesthetically and morally significant for the eighteenth century (Schaffer 1983, 1–43). And Minguet (1966, 244–5, 257–61) and Stafford (1981, 17–75) have traced the lines of coincidence between scientific and aesthetic interests in 'singularity'.

127 See Roland Michel 1984, 22, 45–7.

128 The cases from Bonnier's natural history cabinet were put up for sale along with the specimens in 1744, and were bought by Buffon to house the royal collection at the Jardin du Roi, now the Museum of Natural History. See Paris 1984, 159.

129 In 1565 there appeared anonymously in Paris *The Absurd Dreams of Pantagruel*, a series of engraved visualisations of the world of Rabelais and ones in which the grotesque and the monstrous underlined the fabulous origins of the hero. See Chastel 1988, 57–9. On the continued taste for Rabelais in high society during the Regency, see Marais 1863–8, i, 288–9.

130 *Mercure de France*, April 1727, 677 (my emphasis).

131 It is clear, I hope, that pastoralism and natural history, far from presenting conflicting responses to the natural world, were in fact united by a common system of knowledge. It was that which gave Fontenelle the freedom to pen both eclogues and the *Entretiens sur la pluralitée des deux mondes* (1686). See Yates 1947, 307–8. Moreover, natural philosophy promised a kind of knowledge analagous to that enjoyed by Adam in Eden and therefore offered the prospect of a return to the very prelapsarian golden age evoked in pastoral literature and painting. See Rykwert 1980, 132–3.

132 See Hautecœur 1943–52, iii, 298–301.

133 See, for example, Degoullons, Le Goupil and Verbeckt's panelling for the Chambre de la Reine at Versailles. Kimball 1980, 140–41.

134 For example, a triumphal arch raised to decorate Louis XIV's processional entry into Paris after his marriage to Anne of Austria, incorporated palm-trees twisted with laurel. See Anon. 1662, opp. 8; Isherwood 1973, 293.

135 See Ward-Jackson 1972, 31–44. The ground-floor of the Ménagerie contained a Salon Octagone decorated as a grotto. Realised by Pierre de Cussy and Jean de Launay in 1664, it was still warmly recommended to tourists by eighteenth-century guide books and was deemed worthy of substantial restoration in 1724. See Mabille 1974, 18.

136 See the definitions given of 'rocaille' in, Marsy 1746, ii, 165; Lacombe 1755, 586–7; Pernety 1757, 504.

137 On the expansion of the market for shells and natural curiosities, see Laissus 1964, 663–5; Dance 1966, 61, 66; Pomian 1976, 1677–1703; Laing 1983, 114–17. Artists (particularly painters) were, of course, already familiar with scallop shells because they were habitually used in the studio for mixing paints. Moreover, some painters, such as Boucher, were avid collectors of shells (see Boucher 1771, 203–49). Others may have been brought into contact with shells via engravings. Huquier, the most prolific publisher of rococo ornament prints, also sold natural history engravings. See *Mercure de France*, Jan. 1736, 134–5.

138 Seba described his project in publishing his collection as one of description ('Je laisse volontiers à d'autres le soin de digérer, d'amenager, de mettre en ordre les matériaux que je leur fournis en abondance . . .'), and his use of language is thus markedly pictorial. See Seba 1734–65, iii, 119. Of the plates that illustrate the arrangement of his shells in drawers he remarked: 'pour montrer aux Curieux comment je dispose *artistement* les plus petites coquillages, je donne exprès . . . la representation de six Tiroirs qui les renferment, persuadé que ma méthode ne déplaira pas' (ibid., iii, 110). The publication no less than the collection seems orientated towards an amateur audience of collectors rather than towards the world of professional science.

139 *Mercure de France*, Feb. 1736, 303 (extracts from Gersaint's *Catalogue raisonné de coquilles & autres curiosités naturelles*, Paris 30/i/1736).

140 *Mercure de France*, Nov. 1735, 2461. Beyond the visual attraction of individual specimens, shells seem to have appealed to eighteenth-century collectors as instances

of the 'non-finito'. In a poem entitled *Les Coquillages* (1733) for instance, Desforges-Maillard praised Thetis's grotto above the most lavish royal palace, because in this shell encrusted cavern 'notre œil . . . trouve . . . /Ce qu'il nous plaît d'imaginer' (Desforges-Maillard 1959, ii, 295). The poem was first published by the author in the *Mercure de France* (Feb. 1733) under the pseuodonym Mlle de Malcrais de la Vigne. See also Laing 1983, 114. Even in the abbé Pluche's seemingly scientific publication, *Le Spectacle de la nature* (1732–51) shells are described by similes. For example, du Breuil remarked of the nautilus shell: 'J'ai toujours été charmé de la figure de ce petit batteau naturel, dont la poupe a tant de grace, & qui réunit tout ensemble la solidité, la plus grande légèreté, & les couleurs les plus brillantes' (Pluche 1732–51, iii, 231).

141 *Mercure de France*, Feb. 1736, 305 (extracts from Gersaint's *Catalogue raisonné de coquilles & autres curiosités naturelles*, Paris 30/i/1736).

142 Lassay 1756, ii, 140–41.

143 See Baltimore 1985, 92–3, no. 20. A year earlier Boucher had provided a *rocaille* design, engraved by Duflos, for Gersaint's *Catalogue raisonné de coquilles & autres curiosités naturelles* (30/i/1736) and in 1742 he provided the frontispiece (engraved by Chedel) for Dézallier d'Argenville's *Histoire naturelle eclaircie dans deux principes, la lithologie et la conchyliologie*.

144 On the duc de Sully's *cabinets* see Paris 1984, 177–80.

145 Ibid., 178.

146 Lister 1699, 205–6.

147 For an exploration of the relationships between natural and cultural curiosities see Mullaney 1983, 40–65; Benedict 1990, 59–98.

148 On the question of mounted Chinese porcelain, see Watson 1965, 347–51; Jarry 1981, 204–14.

149 See Rykwert 1980, 54–75.

150 See New Orleans 1984–85, esp. 70–103.

151 Ibid., 164–7.

152 For a brief discussion of amateur science in the eighteenth century, see Fontenelle 1953, 9–10; Roger 1980, 258–63.

153 On the idea of the rehearsal of cultural differences, see Mullaney 1983, 40–65.

8 THE ECLIPSE OF THE HEROIC DECORATIVE MODE

1 On the humanist tradition of history in France, see Huppert 1970, 3–27; Kelley 1970, 19–50, esp. 21–8. On the various genres of historical writing current in France in the seventeenth and eighteenth

centuries, see Ranum 1980, 17–21; Furet 1984, 77–98. For an excellent account of the relationship between history and fable from the sixteenth to the end of the seventeenth centuries, see Harth 1983, 129–62.

2 Even though Lemoyne allowed, in chapter 8 of *The Art of Writing History* (English trans. 1695), that 'private actions' might rightfully take their place in history, it is clear that the actions he envisioned could only have been performed by a nobility, since they were actions that had to exhibit 'some strong and lively Character of Justice, Valour, Moderation or Continence Extraordinary'. Of the actions of 'Particuliers', such as gaming, hunting and dancing, Lemoyne claimed that, 'Twould be more seemly to see in a Temple or Palace, the signs of shops than admit them into the Temple of History (Lemoyne 1695, 104–5). In addition to being excluded from historical narrative, the commoner, according to Fleury, also had little use for history which, as the passage below reveals, in nobiliary societies was almost indistinguishable from patrimony. 'Un homme de condition médiocre', claimed Fleury, 'a besoin de fort peu d'histoire; celui qui peut avoir quelque part aux affaires publiques en doit savoir beaucoup plus, et un prince n'en peut trop savoir. *L'histoire de son pays lui fait voir ses affaires et comme les titres de sa maison*' (Fleury 1686, 226 – my emphasis). History was apparently only of interest to those entitled to behold their part in its making. See Faret 1925, 27, 29.

3 For a dicussion of the humanist tradition which construed the printed book as an object to be entered, see Fumaroli 1975, 19–34.

4 'In these frames remaining as yet empty of histories/Will be painted your victories, O Magnificent Clovis.' Desmarets de Saint-Sorlin 1657, 'Au Roy', 32. For a recent discussion of the poet and his work, see Hall 1990, esp. 286–309.

5 Lemoyne 1670, 45–6. See also Rapin 1725, ii, 231; Rollin 1730, iii, 3.

6 See Tyvaert 1974, 521–47, esp. 531–47.

7 See Ranum 1980, 157–68; Harth 1983, 153–62.

8 Chapelain 1880–83, ii, 275.

9 Chapelain's letter ends, 'Il y a bien, Monsieur, d'autres moyens louables de repandre et de maintenir la gloire de Sa Majesté, desquels mesures les anciens nous ont laissé d'illustres exemples qui arrestent encore avec respect les yeux des peuples, comme sont les pyramides, les colonnes, les statues colosses, les arcs de triomphes, les bustes de marbre et de bronze, les basses-tailles, tous les monumens historiques auxquels on pourroit ajouter nos riches

fabriques de tapisserie, nos peintures à fresques et nos estampes au burin...' (ibid., 277). See also Colbert 1861–83, v, 268–70. Moreover, Pierre Patte noted the benefit of the customary exclusivity enjoyed by the monarch in the sphere of commemorative monuments: 'Il n'est pas d'usage d'élever en France des monumens aux grands généraux ou aux grands hommes célèbres; les Rois seuls obtiennent cette distinction' (Patte 1765, 93). As a result of the Colbert-Chapelain discussions, from the following year (1663), the Académie des Inscriptions et Belles Lettres began to play an increasingly active role in the dissemination of royal propaganda; see Fabre 1890, 411–94.

10 Aucoc 1889, cxviii.

11 'Let your diligent hand always/Follow Louis's glorious actions/[And let] no other labour nor lesser works/Henceforth profane your illustrious brushes.' Perrault 1843, 308–9. This view of the duties of the Premier Peintre du Roi was also clearly expressed in the preamble to Charles Le Brun's letters of enoblement: '. . . ceux qui ont excellé dans la peinture ont toujours ésté, dans tous les temps, très favorablement traitez dans la cour des plus grands princes, où non seulement leurs ouvrages ont servi à l'embellissement de leurs palais, *mais encore de monuments à leur gloire, exprimant par un language muet leurs plus belles et plus héroiques actions*' (quoted from Guiffrey 1873, 4–6). For a discussion of the ennoblement of artists and changing attitudes towards their role in society as expressed in these preambles, see Chaussinand-Nogaret 1985, 38.

12 See Eliade 1957, 21–98.

13 The unifying principle of monarchy found plastic expression in court ceremonies such as the *carrousel* (see Apostolidès 1981, 41–6) and although the notion of the state incarnate took on its most concrete form in the person of Louis XIV, it was still defended as one of the fundamental laws of the kingdom by his heir. In a seance of the Paris Parlement in March 1766, the so-called 'Séance de Flagellation', Louis XV reminded the magistrates that 'Les droits et les intérêts de la nation . . . sont nécessairement unis avec les miens et ne reposent qu'en mes mains' (Flammermont 1888–98, ii, 558). For the significance of the notion of the king's two bodies on literary and historical writing in the eighteenth century, see Snyders 1965, 371–3; Démoris 1978, 9–30; Kelley 1970, 4.

14 See Jammes 1965, 1–12.

15 See Stephens 1978, 119–20, no. 1364. The plate discussed below was the twentieth out of a collection of forty.

16 Ibid., 119.

17 Ibid., 120.

18 'Not unequal among many' was thus changed to 'Now unequal among many'.

19 On caricature in France in the late seventeenth and eighteenth centuries, see Blum 1910.

20 For an introduction to the medals of Louis XIV, see Jones 1979.

21 For an enlightening contemporary discussion of the differences between medals and texts, see Limiers 1720, vi, 17–22.

22 See Jones 1982, 124–5.

23 As Mark Jones has pointed out, when the medal was struck in 1706, the legend 'he drowns in the Po' served equally to describe the fate of Louis at the hands of the duke of Savoy, as Phaeton's by the bolts of Jupiter. See Jones 1983, 204.

24 See, for example, Stephens 1978, 202–3, no. 1446.

25 See Jones 1979, 18, n. 2.

26 See Church 1975, 43–66, esp. 59. On the propaganda war which ensued, and Torcy's attempts to legitimise France's claims to the Spanish throne, see Klaits 1976, *passim*.

27 See Church 1975, 59–60. Even after the battle of Fontenoy (1745), possibly France's only moment of unquestioned military glory in the eighteenth century, some men of letters, such as the poet Fréron, continued to speak out against the absurdity of wars which resulted from no more than the bickering of kings:

Jusqu'à quand sera-tu [Flanders] le théatre des armes,
Le culte des alarmes,
Et le triste jouet des querelles des rois.

(*Mercure de France*, Aug. 1745, 127.)

28 For the circle around Mme de Maintenon, see Tellier 1987, 475–509.

29 See Keohane 1980, 327–31.

30 St Augustine had taught that the celebration of heroism was but a form of vanity (see Browne 1969, 109–110), a view developed in the seventeenth century by Pascal and La Rochefoucault, who both denounced 'gloire' as no more than pretentious pride (see Bénichou 1948, 155–80). For a continuation of this theme in the early eighteenth century, see Massillon 1865, i, 58–64. On Jansenism as an ideology of opposition during the seventeenth century, see Goldmann 1964, 103–41.

31 'Warriors, if you are off to defend your battlements/Go!, and if you must, shine in a hundred Battles/But, if you want only to travel as Conquerors/Take your fearful Plans no further/What do you want from the blood you will spill?/From our desolated Fields, and our burned-out Towns?/Heroes, Scourge of the universe, are you born/Only to create misery here on earth?' This print was one of a set of four entitled

The Passions of Mankind Expressed by Satyrs, all engraved by Jean Audran. See Populus 1930, 150–3, nos. 227–30.

32 See Crow 1985, 59. In 1727, Nemeitz selected as one of the chief attractions of the fairs, 'un singe . . . en mousquetaire', who performed all the appropriate military exercises and, waving a flag, rode upon a dog (Nemeitz 1727, 177–8). Since the monkey's manager allegedly earned 5,000 *livres* for staging these performances, it seems that Parisians were admirers of both animate and inanimate forms of *singerie*.

33 For a more detailed discussion of the subversive potential of the rococo cartouche, See Starobinski 1964, 22; Roland Michel 1984, 140–2.

34 See Paris 1983, 59–63, ill. p. 63. The panels are there attributed to Christophe Huet.

35 'Our son is dead in battle:/As for the rest of his misfortunes/Flayed skin and nakedness/Crushed kidneys and a filthy arse/A torn stomach and a loss of guts/These are the results of war . . .' Quoted from Gilot 1970, 198. In his *oraison funèbre* on the death of Louis XIV, Massillon claimed that the monuments erected by the deceased, ostensibly in celebration of his victories, in fact reminded the populace of the horrors of war (see Anon. 1802, 303–4). The same theme was explored on the occasion of the battle of Fontenoy, this time by Roy and the abbé Porte in the *Mercure de France* in 1745 (1 June, 14–17; ibid., ii, 61–5).

36 '. . . folly it is to consider great/These miserable killers of men.' Quoted fom Gilot 1970, 198. The same attitude towards the warrior is apparent in Piron's *Temple de la mémoire*. See Piron 1776, viii, 265–72. However, the poems, biographies and funeral orations written after the death of the maréchal de Saxe reveal that for the low-born and Protestant hero of the battle of Fontenoy fulsome praise was not withheld. See Lorentz 1751; Piron 1776, ix, 95–6; Neel 1770, i, iii–xii.

37 'Me, I would say that a surgeon/Is as important as these [so-called] heroes'. Quoted from Gilot 1970, 198. In the same year, Louis de Sacy published his treatise on glory, which warned against the error of believing that 'l'on est Héros dès que l'on est Conquérant; que traîner après soi le carnage & la terreur; qu'innonder de sang la surface de la terre; que faire gémir dans les fers cent peuples desolez, en soit le caractère' (Sacy 1715, 149). The hero he proposed was a person who promoted and protected the public good and to that end he argued that merchants and men of letters were as capable of *gloire* as men of valour (see ibid., 77–147). Likewise, Le Maître de Claville, in his *Traîté sur le vrai*

mérite de l'homme (reprinted twelve times between 1734–61), argued that men of virtue were not simply of the nobility – though he did acknowledge that for sociological reasons virtue and *gloire* originated most frequently in its midst; see Le Maître de Claville 1734, i, 69–158.

38 First published in 1677–8, the book was extremely popular during the Regency and went through no less than twenty editions and re-printings between 1730 and 1780. It is perhaps worth noting that this translation was dedicated to the Grand Dauphin by an editor who thought it appropriate to make the prince laugh. See Bardon 1931, 97–106. For Coypel's tapestries, see Fenaille 1903–12, iii, 157–282; Standen 1975, 97–106.

39 In popular broadsheets such as Romeyn de Hooge's *'t Gednonge Huwelyk van Don Quichot de la France* (1706) Louis XIV appears as a malevolent Quixote trying to impose his ephemeral claims to the Spanish throne. On prints such as this, see Hartau 1985, 234–8.

40 In the *Réflexions critiques sur la poésie & la peinture* (1719), Du Bos confirms that the humour of Cervantes's novel, like that of Charles Sorel's *Le Berger extravagant* (1649), resided for eighteenth-century readers in the hero's confusion of literary metaphor with commonplace actuality. See Du Bos 1755, i, 31. For a modern study of eighteenth-century interpretations of *Don Quixote*, see Close 1974, 365–78.

41 For the series for the duc d'Antin, see Fénaille 1903–12, ii, 190–94. The tapestries were recently auctioned at Christie's (St James's), 10 July 1993. For the hôtel de Charost, see Rambaud 1964–71, ii, 1089.

42 The first set of borders for this series featured grotesques and were designed by Claude III Audran.

43 I am much indebted here to Foucault's illuminating discussion of the novel. See Foucault 1982, 46–50.

44 Du Bos was among many to recognise the latent political power of images. He maintained that 'ceux qui ont gouverné les peuples dans tous les tems, ont toujours fait usage des peintures & des statues pour mieux inspirer les sentimens qu'ils vouloient leur donner, soit en religion, soit en politique' (Du Bos 1755, i, 34). Moreover, where preemptive methods failed censorship took over. Amongst its many victims was Nicolas Fréret, imprisoned in the Bastille in 1715 for questioning the official view of the origins of the Franks (see Church 1975, 62). The optimism of those who believed that the Regency would bring a relaxation of the laws governing political expression was rudely quashed when Lagrange de Chancel was

similarly imprisoned for his attacks on Orléans in *Les Philippiques* (*c*.1720); see Johnson 1978, 19–20.

45 On the relationship between subject and monarch under absolutism, see Apostolidès 1981, 46–50.

46 This is what Church has described as subject-centred patriotism. See Church 1975, 64.

47 See ibid., 61–2; Leffler 1985, 1–22. Particularly important seems to have been the Dutch periodical press. See Hatin 1865, 82–134; Yarendi 1973, 208–29; Klaits 1976, 19–21. Some contemporaries, such as the marquis de La Fare, even suggested that the French invasion of the Low Countries in 1672 was prompted by a desire to silence the scandal-mongering Dutch gazetteers. See Hatin 1865, 65–8.

48 Limiers 1718, 'préface de la première édition'; Bayle 1715, iii, 852 [F]. See also Cassirer 1951, 208–9.

49 See Leffler 1976, 230–3.

50 An important early advocate of the plain-speaking topos was Isaac de Larrey. In his *Histoire de France sous le règne de Louis XIV* he argued that the reign did not require 'L'art de l'Historien pour l'orner & pour l'embellir', because the king's conquests could and would stand on their own merits. Instead, 'Il suffit de les mettre en ordre, & de leur donner cet arrangement qui fait la netteté & la clarté de la narration' (Larrey 1722, i, 'preface' – unpag.). See also Bruzen de La Martinière's summation of the historian's task in which many of these themes are further developed. Bruzen de La Martinière 1740–2, ii, *avertissement* (unpag.).

51 Quoted from Leffler 1976, 233.

52 See Foucault 1982, esp. 17–77, 217–43.

53 See New Orleans 1984–5, 209, no. 51.

54 See Wicquefort 1673, pl. immediately before p. 55.

55 The corresponding textual description of events is to be found in ibid., 49–53.

56 In the 1680s and 1690s Courtilz de Sandras wrote a number of semi-pornographic novels about the king and his court, starting with his own version of Bussy Rabutin's *Histoire amoureuse des Gaules* (1684) and culminating with *Le Grand Alcandre frustré* (1696). For a discussion of these works, see Harth 1983, 190–206. Louis XIV's sexual incontinence was also parodied in popular song. See Raunié 1879, i, 8 for one entitled *La Vie de Louis XIV* (1715) in which sexual immorality was directly linked to political tyranny.

57 René Démoris has persuasively argued that attention to the common and passionate body to the king offered readers the opportunity to identify with the mysteries of the embodied state. See Démoris 1978, 9–30.

58 In 1739 the Jansenist abbé de Tamiers, Jacques-Joseph Duguet, launched a bitter denunciation of the analogical apparatus that sustained the king's glory: 'Je sais que les noms de Mars, de Neptune, de Jupiter sont des noms vides de sens; mais se sont des noms qui ont servi au démon pour tromper les hommes, et pour faire rendre par eux les hommes divins. C'est donc faire injure au prince que de le mettre à la place de cet usurpateur, et le prince se déshonore en consentant à cet impiété. Cependant les théâtres en retentissent; la musique s'exerce sur ces indignes fictions; les peuples s'infectent de cet espèce d'idolâtrie; les châtiments pleuvent en foule du Ciel sur une nation qui s'est fait un jeu d'un si grand mal' (Duguet 1739, 51). Several years later, the historian Bruzen de la Martinière advanced a more direct attack on the second volume of the *Médailles sur les principaux événements du règne de Louis le Grand, avec des explications historiques, par l'Académie Royale des Médailles et des Inscriptions* (Paris 1723). Bruzen more or less denounced the project as the misguided result of Colbert's passion 'de flatter son maître et de contribuer à sa gloire' (Bruzen de La Martinière 1740–42, iii, 92). Of the medal struck in 1663 to commemorate the foundation of the Petite Académie, and which bore the inscription *Rerum Gestarum Fides*, Bruzen remarked, 'Il est pourtant certain que les membres de cette Académie avoient grandes dispositions à la flatterie, & qu'ils remplirent parfaitement les vües de leur instituteur (Colbert)' (Ibid., 93). As examples of such flattery, which resulted in flagrant distortions of historical fact, Bruzen instanced, amongst others, the medal struck to celebrate the conquest of Charolais in 1693 (ibid., v, 18–19) and those that cloaked the invidious Netherlands campaigns of 1696 with the legend of *Mars in hostili sedens* (ibid., 107–8). See also Ferrier-Caverivière 1985, 52–3.

59 Banier 1715, i, 35.

60 For a general discussion of allegory, see Du Bos 1755, i, 175–204; for the Medici cycle, see ibid., 180–4. See also Saisselin 1979, 121–47.

61 Ibid., 201–4.

62 On the Palais Royal, see Champier-Sandoz 1990, esp. i, 215–21 for the gallery; Kimball 1936, 113–17; Kimball 1980, 112–17, 120–2; Paris 1988, 53–115.

63 See Paris 1988, 61, 66–8. The so-called *appartement des roués* was probably built by Jean-Sylvain Cartaud in 1715 but decorated later by Oppenord.

64 Ibid., 59, no. 33.

65 On the painted decoration of the gallery, see Schnapper 1969, 33–42; Paris 1988, 79–94; Garnier 1989, 26–7, 34, 151–5

(nos. 90–6), 170–5 (nos. 127–33).

66 Blondel chose to include the engraving in his *Cours d'architecture* thus testifying to the long-term renown of Oppenord's design. See Paris 1988, 71, no. 40.

67 On the Arsenal, see Batiffol 1931, 205–55; Babelon 1970, 267–310; Paris 1986, 41–2.

68 These drawings are in the Kunstbibliothek, Berlin; see Berlin 1970. They are fully discussed by Bruno Pons in Paris 1986, 207–11.

69 On the hôtel de Toulouse, see Ludmann-Pons 1979, 116–28; Kimball 1980, 117–19.

70 For the most recent and thorough discussion of the *affaire des princes*, see Ellis 1988, 169–206.

71 It is clear from surviving drawings that the doors of the *salon* and flanking vestibules at Marly were crowned with paired allegorical figures. Moreover, the exterior of the pavilion was decorated with paintings, after designs by Charles Lebrun, which once again invoked princely virtue by allusion to the divine Apollo. See the elevation and section preserved at the Nationalmuseum, Stockholm (CC 2206, THC 6690). New York 1988, 42–3, nos. 24–5.

72 Boffrand's design for the chimney-piece wall is preserved at the Hermitage, St Petersburg, and is illustrated in Paris 1986, 210. Since this room served as an antechamber to both the male and female apartments, Boffrand used the sexes of Bellona and Mars to signal the respective entrances to the duke and duchess's suites.

73 The suggested identification of the subject of the frieze was made by Pons in ibid., 209.

74 For what follows, see Ellis 1988, 170–2.

75 This suggestion seems entirely plausible in view of the duke's later choice of tapestries of the *Conquests of Louis XIV* for the decoration of his hôtel in the faubourg Saint-Germain. See Catheu 1945–6, 100–8; Paris 1983, 60.

76 See Ellis 1988, 173–5.

77 Although by the seventeenth century historians were willingly abandoning the search for a Trojan origin to the French monarchy, the popular belief that the kings of France were descendents of an heroic line stretching back to antiquity was slower to dissipate. See Tyvaert 1974, 523.

78 On the paintings of the Galerie Dorée, see Bertin 1901, 1–36; Vitzthum 1966, 24–32; Paris 1989, 29–46, 184–90 (nos. 53–5), 241–7 (nos. 84–6), 271–4 (no. 98), 305–7 (no. 116), 326–9 (no. 128). The widow Rouillé kept back for herself a painting of *Andromeda* after Carracci when she sold the hôtel to Toulouse. See Ludmann-Pons 1979, 122, 125, n. 42.

79 In exactly the same years de Cotte's office was however, elaborating very similar schemes for the Elector of Cologne, for the King of Spain at Buen Retiro and for the Prince of Hesse-Kassel. See Ludmann-Pons 1979, 120–1, figs. 7, 8 (fig. 8 is reproduced upside down).

80 Most notably in the gallery at the hôtel du Grand Maître at Versailles (*c.* 1727), and then later in Gabriel's decorations for the Salon de la Pendule (*c.*1738) and the Salon du Conseil (1755) at the château de Versailles. See ibid., fig. 9.

81 In addition to the *Andromeda* held back by Rouillé, Toulouse rejected a *Cephalus and Aurora* after Carracci's Farnese gallery and a *Sacrifice* by Cartouchio. For one outraged response to the remodelling of the gallery, see Maihows 1881, 233–4.

82 See Paris 1989, 39–46, esp. 41–3.

83 Illustrated in Paris 1989, 42–6, figs. 8–17.

84 Much later La Font de Saint Yenne was still arguing in favour of using explanatory cartouches for history paintings precisely to avoid such ambiguity or confusion. See La Font de Saint Yenne 1754, 110–15.

85 For the hôtel de Seignelay, see Paris 1983, 53–8.

86 For the hang of the Grand Appartement at Versailles, see Constans 1976, 157–64.

87 See Lamy-Lassale 1979, 142–8; Paris 1979, 10–12.

88 Some of the copies have been identified by Lamy-Lassale: a *Sybille* after Guido Reni; a *Danaë* after Correggio; a *Pomona* after Nicolas Fouché and a *Nymphe* after del Sarto. See Lamy-Lassale 1979, 144.

89 Villars reserved for the garden the most blatant expression of his martial endeavours. In 1719, he commissioned from Nicolas Coustou a full-length portrait of himself, described by Dézallier d'Argenville as follows: 'Il est vêtu à la Romaine, & on voit sur son front cette noble audace qui caractérise les Héros. La base de cette statue offre différens attributs qui sont autant de symboles de son goût pour les lettres & les arts, de l'abondance & de la paix qu'il a procurées à sa Patrie' (Dézallier d'Argenville 1752, 342). Though described as a hero, no mention is made of the battles in which he fought or the conquests he made; he is praised instead as a patron of the arts and the herald of peace. The hero is no longer the valiant soldier but the cultured diplomat, as the inscription in golden letters on the façade of the hôtel de Villars (*Mars restituor vendex pacifer/Et pacem et pacis perperit victoria fructus*) insisted, Villars's Roman armour notwithstanding. See Paris 1979, 10, 34.

90 See Paris 1979, 34–5.

91 See Parker 1969, 135; Paris 1984, 73–7.

92 There is an analogy to be made here between the nobility's visual and textual enjoyment of history. In the preface to his *Histoire du règne de Louis XIII, roi de France et de Navarre*, (1700–11), for instance, Michel Levassor remarked upon the similarity between a nobleman's demands of history and his requirements of travel – that they should both afford pleasure and diversion. 'On veut tuer le temps & se desennuer. Il suffit qu'un livre soit agréable & divertissant. On ne se met nullement en peine de profiter des examples de la vertu qui s'y rencontrent, ni de refléchir sur les fautes de ceux dont il est parlé' (Levassor 1700–11, i, preface – unpag.). There are of course exceptions to every generalization and some nobles apparently continued to favour battle paintings. Parrocel the elder, for instance, provided some such overdoors for the hôtel de Tallard (see Dézallier d'Argenville 1752, 211), and in the gallery of the hôtel de Richelieu hung two battle paintings by Martin, though they were not to compare in value with François Boucher's overdoors for the *salle des gardes* and the *salon* (see A.N.M.C. II/741 (IAD 19/viii/1788, items 882, 892 1140)).

93 See Gallet 1976–77, 84–5.

94 See Ellis 1988, 180.

95 For the duc de Bourbon's so-called 'regiment' or faction, see Arsenal MS. 3892, f° 68–70; Marais 1863–8, i, 293.

96 See Paris 1983, 71–4. For de Belle-Isle's taste in decorative painting, see Cholet 1973, 88.

97 For a detailed discussion of the political factionalism during the Regency, see Campbell 1985, 64–98.

98 The irony was particularly acute in the case of the duc du Maine, in whom a sympathetic reading of the memoirs of the Cardinal de Retz had apparently provoked a treasonable desire to play a latter-day duc de Beaufort. See Saint-Simon 1879–1930, xxix, 86–7.

99 The *Aeneid* was, in fact, just the opening poem of a translation of Virgil's complete works. See Marolles 1655.

100 Ibid., 'Au Roy'.

101 Segrais, 1700, 'Au Roy'.

102 See Du Plaisir 1683, 41. Meanwhile, Perrault argued in more general terms that, 'comme les poètes grecs et latins n'employerent point dans leurs ouvrages la mythology des Egyptiens, les poètes françois ne devoient point employer les fables des Romains et des Grecs' (Perrault 1688–97, iv, 316). For a discussion of Perrault as a *moderne*, see Picon 1989, 103–14.

103 Charles-Antoine Coypel recorded in his life of his father that the prettiest women at court vied with one another to model for a place in the *Assembly of the Gods*. See Lépicié

1752, ii, 20.

104 The vault was painted between 1703–5 and the wall paintings between 1714–18. For a discussion of the disruptive effect of the chronology of the commission on the sequence of Coypel's Virgilian narrative, see Schnapper 1969, 33–42, esp. 39.

105 Otherwise, Aeneas makes only one further appearance on the vault, in the *Assembly of the Gods* sheltered under an eagle's wing between Venus and Jupiter. His presence clarifies in visual terms Venus's purpose and announces a blessed future but it is not sanctioned by the Virgilian text.

106 Thus while Coypel elaborated the *Assembly of the Gods* (see n. 118) he also omitted episodes from books 5 and 10.

107 Le Rouge 1719, i, 144–5.

108 Brice 1725, i, 242–3.

109 It should be noted however, that Le Rouge himself made mistakes in the sequence he mapped out. See Le Rouge 1719, i, 144–8.

110 Ibid., 147. The brilliance of the colours was shortlived however, thanks to Coypel's ill-fated experiments in technique. See Lépicié 1752, ii, 35. The paintings were probably removed from the gallery in 1783 and were then sent to Saint-Cloud. According to the architect Henri Piètre, Jean-Baptiste-Marie Pierre was behind the removal of the paintings from the Palais Royal. Jealous of Coypel's reputation, Pierre, had he dared 'les auroient Brulés afin qu'il ne restat dans Paris que les tableaux de son tems ou de son Ecolle...' However, the painter apparently contented himself with persuading the abbé de Breteuil, Orléans's chancellor, and Liebaut, the concièrge of the Palais Royal, that the paintings should go. The day came for their removal; 'L'inexorable Pierre, et l'imbécile Liebaut vainrent dans cette gallerie, avec le grand secret, dans la crainte que je [Piètre] ne fïs des représentations a Mᵍʳ le duc d'Orleans, et ordonnerent (non pas que l'on deposa les dits tableaux avec leurs chassis, n'y que l'on en deposa les Bordures) qu'on ce servoit de couteaux et que l'on coupa les toilles au tour des bordures afin que cela soit plus tot fait, et dans la crainte qu'il ne vaint contre ordre, ces tableaux furent portés au chateau de St Cloux comme au magazin des tableaux de nule valeur de la maison d'Orleans, et dans Les Bordures restantes de ces grands tableaux de la gallerie du Palais Royal, Mʳ Pierre fit mettre Les tableaux les plus precieux du Palais Royal. Mais ces tableaux netoient point faits pour cette gallerie n'y la gallerie faite pour ces tableaux' (A.A.P. MS. 51, f° 250–52). Could this be the reason behind the delay of over a year between the removal of the pictures and the destruction of the gallery?

111 One dimension of the quarrel concerned the right of the translator to intervene in the original text, changing and rearranging those passages which seemed outmoded or even shocking to 'modern' minds. See La Motte 1714, cxxxviii–clxxii; Dacier 1715, 225–60.

112 See Bordeaux 1974, 309–10.

113 The accent on the regent's taste was made the clearer by the inclusion of certain choice paintings from the Orléans collection, hung in all likelihood between the windows (see Paris 1988, 63). Included among them was a *Portrait of Charles I and his Family* after van Dyck, currently at Goodwood House, W. Sussex, for which Michel Lange provided a particularly elaborate frame (see Pons 1987, 46, fig. 14).

114 Best known was perhaps Boileau's translation, published after his death in 1670. According to the publisher, Boileau had frequently been called upon to read it out loud 'en plusieurs réduits celebres', and it had been much admired by those of the highest quality (see Boileau 1670, 1–67). However, more than forty years later and soon after Coypel had completed his representation of the theme, Jean Bouhier embarked upon a new translation, needed, he felt, because in Boileau's 'on... trouve... une infinité d'expressions qui blesseroient sans doute la délicatesse des oreilles modernes' (Bouhier 1742, xxii).

115 One of Jean Lemaire's overdoors in the Salle des Amiraux at the hôtel de Toulouse, for instance, depicted Aeneas's departure with Dido's suicide in the background. See Piganiol de La Force 1765, iii, 258.

116 Segrais 1700, 52–6.

117 On the commission for the château de La Chapelle Godefroy, see Troyes 1977, 54–60, nos. 7–14. The pictures, along with 'six bustes de marbre blanc representant des empereurs romains sur leurs pilastres couverts de marbres gris et blanc', are listed in both Philibert Orry and Orry de Fulvy's inventories (A.N.M.C. XXIX/477 (IAD 11/xii/1747); A.N.M.C. XXIX/488 (IAD 26/v/1751)). The *Télémaque* series consisted of two overdoors, *Mentor and Telemachus* (1740, Musée de Troyes) and *Calypso and Cupid* (Musée de Troyes) and four wall paintings: *Telemachus and Calypso* (c.1739; Hermitage, St Petersburg); *Telemachus's Ship Set Ablaze by Nymphs* (Hermitage, St Petersburg); *Venus Gives Cupid to Calypso* (c.1739; Pushkin Museum, Moscow) and *Telemachus and Eucaris* (c.1739; lost).

118 Fénelon 1968, 129.

119 Other versions of the Telemachus theme include Jean Raoux's *Telemachus Tells Calypso his Adventures*, presented by the duc

de Vendôme to the regent in 1722 (Louvre, inv. 7362); some nine canvases by Henri de Favanne, exhibited variously at the Salons of 1737, 1746 and 1748; Louis Galloche's two works exhibited in 1743 and 1746 and Natoire's own later treatment of the text fot the dauphin's apartments at Versailles. It is difficult to know precisely how the paintings were hung in the gallery, whether along a single wall as at the Galerie d'Enée or as complementary tales facing one another across the room. The Orry inventories describe them merely as located between windows. See above n. 117.

121 The phrase is borrowed from Sennett 1974.

122 On the hôtel d'Argenton, see Lépicié 1752, i, 24–6; Paris 1986, 190–93; Garnier 1989, 161–2 (no. 110).

123 See Campbell 1985, 186–7.

124 Ibid., 200–2, 215.

125 See Antoine 1989, 270.

126 Cobban 1972, 37.

127 For a general discussion of the economic fortunes of the nobility during the eighteenth century, albeit the later eighteenth century, see Chaussinand-Nogaret 1985, 43–64.

128 Antoine 1989, 265.

129 See Campbell 1985, 205–7.

130 See Brooks 1969, 40.

131 For recent discussions of this picture and its pendant, *Aurora and Cephalus*, see New York 1986–7, 133–8, nos. 17–18; Fort Worth 1992, 380–89, nos. 43–4.

132 Méré 1930, i, 52. Cited in Stanton 1980, 64.

133 'It is easy to forget a love that frightens/In favour of one that flatters./Let the care of charming/Be your unique concern./Remember that the art of loving/Is only that of pleasing./Do you want in passion/To find lasting happiness? / Be less amorous./ Become more aimiable.' Rousseau 1753, i, 289.

134 See Fort Worth 1992, 262–7, no. 26.

135 Quoted from Furet 1984, 130.

136 See Bardon 1957, 401–16.

137 For these pictures by Nicolas Loir, see Hautecoeur 1927, 133.

138 See Brice 1706, i, 81–3.

139 One exception to this general trend may have been La Fosse's ceiling for Pierre Crozat's gallery at Montmorency (see Stuffmann 1964, 16–17) which depicted the *Fall of Phaeton* (1707–9). According to Panofsky the fate of Phaeton was a warning to every 'temerarius' whose ambition tempted him to seek to rise above his allotted station in life (Panofsky 1972, 219). It is difficult to understand why Crozat should have chosen such an apparently self-reproaching theme, but he was by no means alone. In 1716, Henri de Favanne

painted a version of the subject on the ceiling of the salon at Chanteloup for Jean d'Aubigny (see Dussieux 1854, i, 241–2) and Nicolas Bertin treated the same theme between 1710–20 for his patron M. de Saint-Bonnet (see Lefrançois 1981, 282–6).

140 See Levey 1964, 53–8; Washington 1984, 324–8, nos. 34–5; Roland Michel 1984, 39–40.

141 On this series see Bordeaux 1971; Bordeaux 1984, 116–17, nos. 80–83; Fort Worth 1992, 263–75, no. 27.

142 In May 1705 the *Journal de Trévoux* announced with approbation the publication of a new Italian translation of the *Métamorphoses*, 'purgées de toute obscénité', by the Jesuit father Joseph Jouvency (May 1705, 833–7). Meanwhile, in France, the possibly more worldly abbé de Bellegarde seemed to defend the eroticism of the fables on the grounds that it would teach readers that 'les désordres des passions . . . leur font en quelque manière ressembler aux bêtes'. But he too felt the need to censor the text of descriptions and expressions that would seem 'un peu trop libre' in the vernacular (Morvan de Bellegarde 1712, *avertissement*). Finally, the abbé Banier in his 1732 translation argued that the passions of the gods 'sont toujours exposez avec trop de licence', and added that 'les portraits que fait Ovid dans ses occasions sont trop vifs; la pudeur y est peu menagée' (Banier 1738, xiii–xiv). In order to ensure that such passages should not excite the reader to sexual indulgence, but rather teach him or her to avoid the pleasures of the flesh, Banier felt justifed in curtailing the supposed excesses of the text. See also the review in the *Journal de Trévoux*, April 1733, 649–58. Rarely did such concern arise in the re-edition of the Latin original since it was believed to be linguistically and culturally inaccessible to those most prone to corruption, namely, women and those of the lower social orders.

143 Jean-Baptiste Van Loo soon after returning from Italy in 1719 painted 'de grands tableaux' inspired by the *Metamorphoses* for Carignan's hôtel de Soissons (Papillon de la Ferté 1776, ii, 606); Charles Natoire painted four overdoors, 'sujets de fables', in *c*.1737 for the second *salon* at the hôtel de Mazarin (see Paris 1981, 46); the *salon d'assemblée* at the hôtel de Montbazon was, in 1751, decorated with overdoors depicting subjects both sacred and profane (A.N.M.C. CXVII/785, *Procès verbal d'estimation* 15/vii/1751); and the decoration of the comtesse de Verrue's hôtel in the rue Cherche-Midi included a large number of mythological paintings, some of which can probably be identified with decorative works executed for her by the

Boullogne (Rambaud 1964–71, ii, 891).

144 See Langlois 1922, 170–72. Although this cornice was attributed to Nicolas-Sébastein Adam by eighteenth-century guide-books, Pons convincingly argues that the ornament sculptors Lange, father and son, and Herpin were the more likely executants of this scheme. See Paris 1986, 224–5.

145 On the pictorial fortune of the story of Cupid and Psyche, see Gallet 1972, 135–6.

146 On this series, see Langlois 1922, 174; Paris 1986, 255–67.

147 Quoted from Paris 1986; 258–9.

148 See Brooks 1969, 11–43, esp. 22–3, 40.

149 Duclos 1965, 239–40: 'C'est l'usage parmi les amants de profession d'éviter de rompre totalement avec celles qu'on cesse d'aimer. On en prend de nouvelles, et on tache de conserver les anciennes, *mais on doit surtout songer à augmenter la liste*' (my emphasis).

150 For a different interpretation of the same episode treated by Boucher in his Beauvais *Psyche*, see Hussman 1977, 45–50.

151 As Violette notes, Natoire once again takes liberties with the texts of Apuleius and La Fontaine in the depiction of this scene (Paris 1986, 261). Natoire or Soubise seem to have favoured a less violent conclusion to the story.

152 See for example, the recently acquired *Pan and Syrinx* at the Cleveland Museum of Art. See Talbot 1974, 250–59.

153 On Le Moyne's picture, exhibited at the 1725 Salon, see Bordeaux 1984, 93–5, no. 47; and for a discussion of a second autograph version, see New York 1985, 77–80, no. 8. For Omphale's place within the pantheon of *précieuses* heroines or *femmes fortes*, see Maclean 1977, 217–18. In the seventeenth century the story of Hercules and Omphale offered an instance of role reversal where triumphant woman enslaved heroic man. Omphale claimed the lion's skin and Hercules's club while Hercules himself was turned into an object of mockery, dressed up in women's clothing and wielding no more than a distaff and spindle. The iconography and anti-heroic spirit of the thus constituted myth were certainly known to Le Moyne, as he owned a copy of Le Comte's *Mythologie* (1610) in which the tale was so told, and his picture was faithful to the source in so far as the costume and attributes of the figures were concerned. However, by the eighteenth century the meaning of the story had undergone a subtle change, a change signalled in the picture by the prominence of Cupid. In a poem published in the *Mercure de France* in celebration of Le Moyne's canvas, the poet – M. Moraine – allows Hercules to explain that this burlesque episode of transvestism did not literally occur and that the purpose of the

myth (or more accurately the fiction within the myth) was to demonstrate the salutary and democratic power of love:

> L'Amour seul donne un caractere
> De bonne-foi, d'humanité:
> Vainqueur de plus d'une chimere,
> Il introduit par tout l'heureuse égalité.

(*Mercure de France*, March 1725, 468–73.) This 'heureuse égalité' was expressed formally by Boucher when he placed his two protagonists on exactly the same footing. See Fort Worth 1992, 372–9, no. 42. The meaning of Hercules and Omphale for the eighteenth century was therefore closer to the lesson of Cupid and Psyche discussed above, but the ribaldry traditionally associated with Hercules's time in Lydia no doubt explains its comparatively minor success as a vehicle for polite values. By contrast, examples of the seventeenth-century theme of 'women on top' were still to be found in eighteenth-century broad-sheets. See, for instance, Burke 1978, pl. 18.

154 For a seventeenth-century challenge levelled at male ideology, see Harth's discussion and interpretation of Mme de Lafayette's *La Princesse de Clèves* (Harth 1983, 201–3). Stanton suggests, moreover, that much of the satirical criticism ranged against the *précieuses* in the late seventeenth century was a response provoked by the feminist challenge for cultural superiority (see Stanton 1980, 28).

155 It should be noted that the story of Cupid and Psyche was also a popular subject for the decoration of royal palaces. See, for instance, the overdoors executed in 1746 by Carle Van Loo for Marie-Thérèse d'Espagne (Nice 1977, nos. 92–3) and those executed by Jean Restout for the apartment of Marie-Joseph de Saxe at Versailles in 1748 (Rouen 1970, 61–2, nos. 33–4).

156 See Hirschman 1977, *passim*.

9 COUNTERFEIT CULTURE ON THE RIGHT BANK

1 See C.A. 1847–61, ii, 836; Ranum 1969, 271; Elias 1983, 117–45.

2 For this commerce in nobility, see Ford 1953, 12–14.

3 See Boislisle 1888, 116–17, 147–53.

4 Quoted from Hautecœur 1943–52, ii, 611. Variations in prose occur in the letters of Mme Dunoyer and the memoirs of Saint Simon. See Boislisle 1888, 84.

5 Scarron, *Adieu au Marais et à la Place Royale* (1643), quoted from Boislisle 1888, 85.

6 See ibid., 94–209, esp. 108–9.

7 Germain Brice was among many others

deeply to regret this change of function. See Brice 1706, i, 184–5.

8 See Langeskiöld 1959, 74–94; Strandberg 1965, 71–90.

9 The anonymous author of a *Traîté contre le luxe des hommes et des femmes* (1705) claimed that 'que les Particuliers se donnent la licence de *contrefaire* les grands Seigneurs . . . est un abus insupportable . . .' (Anon, 1705, 158). However, as we shall see, counterfeiting invariably results (consciously or otherwise) in the creation of something new.

10 Brice 1706, i, 187–8.

11 Ibid.,

12 Ibid., 225–6. Brice noted that the house had formerly been occupied by 'd'illustres Magistrats, fort distinguez par leur sagesse & leur desinteressement; ce qui leur avoit procuré l'estime & l'amour du Public, qui trouvoit chez eux des secours contre la violence & la vexation . . .' Its occupation by a financier, the implicit cause of violence and vexation, indicated how far things had changed for the worse.

13 See Brice 1717, i, 259; Strandberg 1962, esp. 216–19.

14 See Strandberg 1965, 171–90.

15 Anon. 1716, 28.

16 For a discussion of the bourgeoisie's capacity to innovate and tendency to emulate, see Zukin 1977, 333–58.

17 According to Germain Brice, Bourvallais's collection chiefly consisted of a body of works acquired at the death of the farmer general, Bauyn de Cormery, and included a *Magdalene* by Rubens, an *Annunciation* by Poussin and a Veronese (see Brice 1706, i, 226). Olivier Bonfait has since located in a private collection an inventory of Bourvallais's pictures drawn up in 1719 (see Bonfait 1986², 125–151). Regrettably, I have been unable to trace it.

18 Anon. 1716, 10–11. This account is clearly fictional.

19 See Kimball 1980, 103.

20 See Babelon 1963, 169–96; Durand 1971, 475; Kimball 1980, 122–3.

21 See Durand 1971, 493–4.

22 See Dézallier d'Argenville 1752, 143; Durand 1971, 475; Paris 1986, 267.

23 See Chaussinand-Nogaret 1970, 308; Wilhelm 1975, 127.

24 See New York 1986, 173–7, nos. 30–31.

25 See Tours 1962, nos. 6–7; New York 1986, 263–7, nos. 62–3; Brunel 1986, 284–6.

26 See New York 1986, 163–8, no. 27. According to the duc's probate inventory, at his death Richelieu possessed four overdoors by Boucher, two of unspecified subject-matter in the *salle des gardes* of his hôtel, and two 'representant des enfants', in the salon. See A.N.M.C. II/741 (IAD 19/

viii/1788).

27 See New York 1986, 21 (18/v/1740).

28 See Engerand 1900, 309–10.

29 See Paris 1981, 46, no. 162.

30 See Dézallier d'Argenville 1752, 143–4; Hebert 1766, i, 236–7.

31 See Durand 1971, 485.

32 See Boyer 1952, 107–17; Aix-en-Provence 1977, 11–18.

33 See A.N.M.C. LXXXVIII/574 (IAD 24/vi/ 1740); Papillon de La Ferté 1776, ii, 658.

34 See A.N.M.C. LXXXVIII/564 bis (IAD 27/i/ 1739). Rooms on the ground floor of Bernard's hôtel in the rue Notre-Dame-des-Victoires were variously decorated with four overdoors telling the *Story of Venus*, two others depicting *Apollo and Issé*, and one other *Deinara and Nessus*. The dining-room contained an overdoor portraying *Bacchus and Hebe* and Mme Bernard's antechamber sported a *Venus and Vulcan*.

35 See Bordeaux 1971, 5–76; Fort Worth 1992, 268–75.

36 See A.N.M.C. LXXXVIII/570 (IAD 20/vii/ 1740). Senozan's bedchamber was decorated with a tapestry in four parts depicting the *Triumph of Bacchus* and his wife's antechamber displayed two overdoors of *Zephyr and Flora* and *Bacchus and Erigone*. See also Dussieux 1854, ii, 275.

37 See Durand 1971, 487.

38 See A.N.M.C. LXXXVIII/723 (IAD 28/ii/ 1770). There were in Mme de Berighen's bedchamber, 'Trois tableaux dessus de porte peints par M. Boucher representant des pastorales prisée 900 *livres*'.

39 See Brice 1706, i, 267.

40 Bertin's collection was sold 1–4/ii/1815 (Lugt 8637). The Fondation Jacques Doucet holds a bound volume of 24 watercolours depicting 'Vases chinois envoyés par les missionnaires à Mr Bertin' (A.A.P. MS. 408) and also a dossier of documents entitled *Bertin et la mission de Chine, 1704–92* of which f° 91 concerns Bertin's cabinet chinois at Chatou (A.A.P. MS. 131ᶜ).

41 See Durand 1971, 485, n. 1.

42 See Mousnier 1979, 510.

43 See Genlis 1818, ii, 70.

44 Durand estimates that, in the eighteenth century, of the 233 farmers general only 55 did not own a *seigneurie*. For this figure and a discussion of the eagerness of financiers to join the company of fief-holders, see Durand 1971, 144–6. On the transformation of the feudal system of land holding by such initiatives, see Goubert 1973, 82–7; Robin 1971, 554–602; Reddy 1987, 119–21.

45 Yves Durand's thorough and exhaustive study of the world of the *fermiers-généraux* in the eighteenth century at no point suggests the remotest interest in hunting

on behalf of this group.

46 See A.N.M.C. LXXXVIII/564 bis (IAD 27/i/ 1739). The pavilion in the grounds of the château was decorated with 'un grand tableau représentant un cerf forcé . . . deux dessus de porte en carré représentans des fruits et gibiers, poissons et oiseaux' and 'dix tableaux ronds représentans divers animaux, le tout encastré dans la boiserie de laditte salle'.

47 In 1708 Desportes executed 'de grandes chasses & d'autres tableaux pour M. Hogguer, pour sa maison de campagne à Chatillon, proche de Paris.' (*Mercure de France*, 1 June 1743, 1191–2). On the paintings, see Lastic 1961, 56–65. There were five Hogguers, all bankers in Paris in the first three decades of the eighteenth century and I have been unable to determine which one was the proprietor of Châtillon. On the Hogguers, see Luthy 1970, i, esp. 169–87.

48 *Mercure de France*, 1 June 1743, 1191. The dining-room at the château de Plaisance, Pâris Duvernay's country estate, was decorated with three overdoors depicting 'l'un un pâté, l'autre un gibier & la troisième un chien en arrêts', also possibly by Desportes. See A.N.M.C. CVII/550 (IAD 26/vii/1770). On the Pâris family, see Luthy 1970, i, 280; Dubois-Corneau 1917, and for the château de Plaisance, ibid., 136, 344.

49 *Mercure de France*, 1 June 1743, 1191.

50 See Engerand 1900, 362–3; Paris 1982–3, 96–9, no. 40.

51 See A.N.M.C. LXXXVIII/723 (IAD 28/ii/ 1770), no. 195; Locquin 1908, 375; Roland Michel-Rambaud 1977, i–viii.

52 See A.N.M.C. LXXVI/299, IAD 13/v/1744; Dussieux 1854, ii, 372, 400; London 1979, no. 16.

53 See Lorgues 1979, 37–49.

54 See A.N.M.C. LXXXXVII/629 (IAD 13/vii/ 1753), no. 869; Paris 1982–3, 208–10, no. 113.

55 Depictions of hounds attacking game were plentiful enough in the work of Desportes and Oudry (inspired as much perhaps by the *combats d'animaux* staged at the fairs and at the *ménagerie*, Porte Saint-Martin, as by the works of Flemish game painters like Snyders (see Fournel 1887, 439–50; Isherwood 1986, 209–10); however, hunters seem only to occur in depictions of exotic hunts, such as those by Parrocel for the duc de Mortemart and the series for the Petite Galerie at Versailles. See Hazlehurst 1984, 224–36. The great exception was, of course, Oudry's tapestry series *Royal Hunts*. See Opperman 1970, 206–14; Lastic 1977, 290–99; Paris 1982–3, 135–43, nos. 60–62. For the moral virtue of the hunt, fit for a prince as a preparation for heroic action see, for example, the essay by the Jesuit

56 For a comparison with British sporting art, see Deuchar 1988.

57 On this *cabinet* see Reuterswärd 1964, 142–52; Schnapper 1968, 241–4; Mirimonde 1970, 77–85. The *cabinet* was located in the hôtel d'Hemery which Perrault shared with the intendent de Finances, Hotman. See Brice 1685, i, 86; Boislisle 1888, 46–8. Recently, in an article on Louis de Boullogne's depictions of Minerva, Hélène Guicharnaud has cast doubt on whether the scheme was actually installed in the hôtel d'Hemcry (see Guicharnaud 1995, 44). However, the review of the book of the gallery in the *Mercure Galant* states quite positively that, 'Il y a quelques années qu'il [Perrault] fit peindre dans le Plafond de son Cabinet ceux d'entre les beaux Arts qu'il aime le plus . . .', and again, when discussing the book's frontispiece, '[il] represent *au naturel* le Cabinet où les Tableaux ont esté peints . . .'

58 See Perrault 1690, *passim*. This work was reviewed in the *Mercure de France* in August 1691 (161–6). The reviewer commented, 'Il est difficile de pouvoir exprimer la satisfaction que donne ce livre. Les yeux & l'esprit y trouvent également ce qui les peut contenter, et si l'on est charmé de la beauté des Tailles-douces, la lecture des explications cause un extrême plaisir' (ibid., 165).

59 1) *Music* by Antoine Coypel; 2) *Eloquence* by Houasse; 3) *Poetry* by Ubeleski; 4) *Painting* by Claude II Audran; 5) *Architecture* by Bon Boullogne; 6) *Sculpture* by Friquet de Vaurose; 7) *Optics* by Corneille; 8) *Mechanics* by Jouvenet. Three drawings of the entire ceiling in the Nationalmuseum in Stockholm have been attributed to Claude II Audran, thus ascribing to him the overall organisation, if not conception, of the scheme. See Bjurström 1976, nos 93–5.

60 Perrault 1690, 4.

61 Ibid., 1–2. Perrault compares the passion which inspires him and those like him to decorate their *cabinets* with personifications of the arts with that of the lover who decorates his *cabinet* with the portraits of his mistresses.

62 Ibid. dedication (unpag.).

63 Ibid., 3.

64 See Stuffmann 1968, 15–16.

65 See Crow 1985, esp. 39–41.

66 See Stuffmann 1964, 31–4; Stuffmann 1968, 16.

67 Perrault 1690, 30.

68 Minerva in the *cabinet des beaux-arts* was indeed, 'particulierement regardée comme president à l'adresse de la main conduite par le jugement . . .' Perrault remarked that, 'En effet, rien n'est plus necessaire pour la perfection d'une infinité d'ouvrages, que la dexterité de la main: mais il faut que le jugement et le bons sens accompagnent et conduisent cette dexterité: autrement les meilleurs ouvriers pourroient se rendre semblables à la malheureuse Arachné, qui se confiant en la seule adresse de ses doigts, défia temerairement la sçavante fille de Jupiter; et ils ne mériteroient pas plus de louänges, qu'en merite l'araignée par son travail tres fin et tres subtil mais frivole et tres inutile' (ibid., 9–10).

69 On the hôtel de Jars, which Senozan bought from the duchesse de Sully in 1713, see A.N.M.C. xxxvi/340, act of sale, 17/ii/1713; Hillairet 1966, 59–60.

70 See A.N.M.C. lxxxviii/570 (iad 20/vii/1740): in the 'cabinet de deffunt sieur de Senozan . . . six tableaux peints sur toille representans Minerve et les arts . . . encastrés dans la muraille . . .' The decoration also included two large pier-glasses, one above a chimney-piece. On the drawings, see Lomax 1982, 29–48.

71 See Chennevières 1851–2, 161; London 1990, 66–7, no. 20. Colin Bailey, in Fort Worth 1992 (224), advances an alternative possibility, that the painting depicting two Muses at the New Orleans Museum of Art may have constituted an element of this scheme.

72 See Stuffmann 1968, 11–144. On the hang of Old Masters in the Grands Appartements at Versailles in the eighteenth century, see Constans 1976, 157–73.

73 For the most recent and thorough discussion of the *Recueil*, see Haskell 1987.

74 See Crow 1985, 39–41.

75 Interestingly enough, during the Regency Antoine Coypel was commissioned to paint *Minerva Overseeing the Education of the Young Louis XV* to hang in the Louvre in a room where gathered another academy, the Académie des Inscriptions et Belles-Lettres. See Garnier 1989, 179, no. 141.

76 The text, by Mariette, is concerned above all with identifying and describing the authors of the works and their manner of representation, in contrast to the more conventional preoccupation with subject-matter. It introduced to the catalogue of a collection the language of connoisseurship which was being evolved by dealers in the sphere of the market, most particularly the auction house. See Pomian 1979, 23–36.

77 See, for example, [Courtin] 1719, 116–23.

78 See Lougee 1976, 113–70, 210–11.

79 On the stereotype of the *laquais-financier*, see Dessert 1979, 21–36. For Gillot's print, see Populus 1930, 86–7, no. 13.

80 Verses from Le Sage's *Turcaret* (1709; v xviii) were appended to Gillot's *Speculator*.

81 For other examples of the vilification and mockery of individual *parvenus*, see Montesquieu 1964, 86; La Bruyère 1965, 173–4, §21; Raunié 1879, ii, 139–45; Durand 1971, 403. According to Brice, amongst the plays staged by the Commedia dell'Arte at the hôtel de Bourgogne 'l'on a été charmé de voir quelques-unes de leurs Pièces remplies d'une satire très fine contre les déreglemens du siècle, sur tout contre l'insolence des Financiers qui ne donnent que trop de matieres de parler par leur conduite arrogante & fastueuse' (Brice 1706, i, 294). On the profound hatred for financiers and *gens d'affaires* fostered by certain sectors of sociey, see Boscher 1970, 17–19; Durand 1971, 179–86, 196–203.

82 See Galliani 1984, 53–64. This conspiracy theory was also a feature of early eighteenth-century *libelles*. For example, the fictional financier, Deschiens (alias Bourvallais), remarked on his death-bed that 'je me suis bien persuadé que *travaillant pour mon Roi* en égorgeant ses peuples sans aucun quartier, je faisois plaisir à quelque Divinité souteraine . . .' (Anon. 1708, 5). However, later in the pamphlet, financiers are portrayed no longer as instruments of a demonic absolutism but as tyrants, the author thus once more taking refuge in the kind of scapegoating habitual to the *ancien régime*. See ibid., 196–8.

82 See Galliani 1989, 144.

83 Ibid., 140–84.

84 See below and ibid., 148, 172–4.

85 See Luthy 1959–61, i, 283.

86 Ibid.

87 See below. Bourvallais appears to have been the subject of more than one of these *libelles*. Mathieu Marais identified the anti-hero, Deschiens, of the pamphlet *Pluton Maltôtier* (1708) with Bourvallais, and the same financier also makes an appearance in Jean-François Dreux du Radier's *Recréations historiques*, 1767 (ii, 33–40). See Marais 1863–8, i, 224.

88 Poussin is not known ever to have painted a picture of this subject. Bourvallais is however, recorded as having owned an *Annunciation* by Poussin (Brice 1706, i, 225), probably a copy of the Chantilly painting. See Blunt 1966, 31, no. 38.

89 Anon. 1716, 19–21.

90 Ibid., 12–17. Financiers were not alone in having their characters sketched via possessions attributed to them. See, for example, the portrait of cardinal de Noailles drawn by analogy to a fictional library and collection in Marais 1863–8, i, 310–13.

91 François Moureau was the first to draw attention to this pamphlet and to identify Nasidiene with Pierre Crozat. See

Washington 1984, 502. However, the emphasis on the character's active participation in financial markets and the descriptions of the interiors of his hôtel as having been decorated with arabesques as well as with paintings would seem to suggest that the functions and tastes of the two brothers were distilled into a single embodiment of plutocratic excess.

92 Saint-Didier 1716, ii, 162. The gallery is described as lit from one side by eight windows separated one from another by pier-glasses. More mirrors were located opposite the windows and they, in turn, were interspaced with paintings. 'Tout cela est renfermé dans un riche lambris presque suffoqué de la sculpture doré, & le plafond peint en grotesque sur un fonds blanc.'

93 Ibid., 167–9. The 8 pictures were as follows: 1) *The Birth of Nasidiene*; 2) *The Educaion of Nasidiene*; 3) *Nasidiene and Hercules*; 4) *Nasidiene and his Patron*; 5) *Nasidiene between Ceres and Abundance*; 6) *Nasidiene and Thetis*; 7) *The Triumphal Entry of Nasidiene*; 8) *The Judgement of Nasidiene/Paris*.

94 Ibid., 170–71.

95 This was in marked contrast to the robe, for instance, which had traditionally sought to couch its claims to social promotion in high-minded cultural terms. For the eighteenth century, see Bonfait 1986, 28–42.

96 Anon. 1716, 31.

97 The point is made by Cobban 1972, 22. At the time of the king's death the government faced the prospect of declaring the state bankrupt for the third time in less than a century. For an anatomy of the national debt, see Luthy 1959–61, i, 279–80.

98 On fiscal policy during the Regency with particular attention to experiments to get the state out of difficulty, see Marion 1914, i, 63–135; Chaussinand-Nogaret 1970, 125–63; Faure 1977, *passim*; Shennan 1979, 97–125; Kaiser 1991, 1–28.

99 On this print, see Stephens 1978, 426.

100 The Exchange was transferred to the place Vendôme in March 1720. However, the chancellor who resided there (the chancellery having been installed in the former hôtel de Bourvallais) demanded its immediate removal. It was then that Carignan offered the grounds of his hôtel. See Marais 1863–8, i, 359. On the hôtel de Soissons, see Boudon 1973, 267–307, esp. 269.

101 On Humblot's print see Stephens 1978, 426–7. Marais described the grounds of the hôtel de Soissons in terms that contrast radically with Humblot's image of more-or-less genteel behaviour. According to Marais, the gardens thronged with 'une assemblée tumultueuse'. '. . . c'étoit un réceptacle de fripons, de voleurs, de femmes de mauvaise vie et de toutes sortes de canailles, que l'avidité du gain y rassembloit et qui y vendoient non-seulement du papier et de l'argent, mais toutes sortes de marchandises en fraudes, et de la chair humaine. On m'y a presenté une tabatière avec des figures infames.' (Marais 1863–8, i, 472).

102 See ibid., i, 269, 273, 293, 350; ii, 52, 167; also Barbier 1857, i, 102.

103 See Garas 1962, 75–93, esp. 77. On the hôtel de Nevers which Law had bought from the duc de Nevers in May 1719 for 400,000 *livres*, see Hillairet 1966, 149–51. Law also bought the contiguous hôtel de Varennes and palais Mazarin.

104 The ceiling measured 41.60 × 8.60 m. It is known thanks to a lengthy description published in Mariette's *Abecedario*. See Mariette 1851–60, iv, 85–98.

105 See Garas 1962, 78.

106 See Mariette 1851–60, iv, 96.

107 See Galliani 1984, 55–6; Galliani 1989, 150–51, 160–66.

108 See Mariette 1851–60, iv, 97.

109 For the luxury debate in the 1730s, see Labriolle-Rutherford 1963, 1025–36; Ross 1975; Ross 1976, 1879–1913.

110 On the Mississippi basin as a 'paradis terrestre', see Marais 1863–8, i, 321. On the crash of the System, see Faure 1977.

111 For this print see Stephens 1978, 502–3.

112 Ibid., 503.

113 A mirror is placed next to the figure of Painting to signify 'le talent qu'il [Art] a de représenter avec justesse et avec promptitude tous les objets qui lui sont représentés.' See Perrault 1690, 30.

114 For this print see Stephens 1978, 526–30.

115 Quoted from Faure 1977, 247.

116 Indeed, so compelling is the effect of synchrony that Stephens claims that the pedestrians are actually 'moving in one direction'. See Stephens 1978, 426.

117 See Marais 1863–8, i, 453–4. Earlier, Marais had remarked that 'La noblesse de France n'a jamais été moins noble qu'en ce temps-ci' (ibid., 281). See also ibid., ii, 104).

118 Ibid., i, 473.

119 Boulainvilliers 1727, 7.

120 See Mirabeau 1883, 280; Mably 1794–5, iii, 298–9. See also Senac de Meilhan 1787, 152–3; Mercier 1782–8, i, 49; Cröy 1906, iii, 111; Montesquieu 1964, 219–20.

121 It is interesting to note, however, that a recurrent theme in the criticism of Law's System was that his measures obscured public understanding of the economy. See Kaiser 1991, esp. 19–28.

122 'Enter his house: a host of Arts/The offspring of taste, offer themselves to your attention . . . /the felicitous Brush, the superb Design/Of the gentle Correggio and the learned Poussin/Are edged by gilded frames;/Bouchardon made this figure,/And this silverware was polished by Germain./From the Gobelins, the needlework and dye/Of these carpets rivals [the effects of] painting./All these things are further multiplied by the brilliant sharpness of the mirrors' (Morize 1909, 136).

123 Duclos 1965, 233–4.

124 Ibid., 255.

125 Ibid., 234.

126 See Le Ferre 1759, 169; Anon. 1788, i, 36–7.

127 See Bridard de la Garde 1740–42, i, 12.

128 Anon. 1788, i, 166–8. See also Watelet-Levesque 1792, 57, 61.

129 Anon. 1788, i, 166–8. See also La Font de Saint Yenne 1747, 62–3.

130 See Genlis 1818, i, 334.

131 See Buffier 1732, 1497–1507; Lambert 1748.

132 Voltaire 1733, iv–v.

133 See Lambert 1748, i, xxiv.

134 On Mme Lambert's *salon* see Glotz and Maire 1949, 71–88.

135 Marais 1863–8, iii, 460, 114. Marais refered to Lambert's *salon* as an 'académie' and thereby lent it a pretentiousness, pedantry and purposefulness which the author of her obituary was anxious to contradict: 'Mme Lambert elle-même, très-délicate sur les discours et sur l'opinion du Public, craignoit quelquefois de donner trop à son goût; elle avoit le soin de rassurer, en faisant réflexion, que dans cette même Maison, si accusée d'esprit, elle y faisoit une dépense très-noble et y receveit beaucoup plus de gens du Monde et de condition que de gens illustres dans les Lettres' (*Mercure de France* Aug. 1733, 1846).

136 Hillairet 1966, 160–61.

137 Anon. 1716, 21–2.

138 Saint-Didier 1716, ii, 152, 178–95.

139 Ibid., 162–3.

140 Fumaroli 1980.

141 See Kortum 1967, 772.

142 See Terrasson 1720.

143 See Taylor 1982, 7–81.

144 Ibid., 13.

145 See Brossette 1910, i, 19; Taylor 1982, 21.

146 See Paris 1981, 50–53. The *Lycomedes* is now in the Staatliche Museen, Berlin.

147 On Polignac's collection, which was sold in December 1742 (Lugt 567), see Guiffrey 1899, 252–97; Rambaud 1964–71, i, 603; Blunt 1966, 123–4, 174; Paris 1981, 49–53.

148 Polignac was a great enthusiast of modern Italian painting, and apart from Pannini, owned works by Matteis, Conca, Gaulli, Franceschini, Brandi and Rosalba Carriera. See Brejon de Lavergnée 1990, 76.

149 For Rothelin's collecion of pictures, see Rambaud 1964–71, i, 612–13; for his collection of medals, which included those formerly belonging to the président de Maison, see *Mercure de France*, Dec. 1731, 3092. For Beauvais, see Taylor 1982, 19. For Legrand, an important figure in Torcy's Académie Politique, see Klaits 1971, 579–81. Legrand was employed for many years as the d'Estrée's family tutor. For d'Estrée's collection of medals, sold in December 1740, see Lugt 531. For the taste for medals among the eighteenth-century French nobility, see Pomian 1976, 1677–1703.

150 On the hôtel occupied by the maréchal d'Estrée in the rue de l'Université, see Paris 1987, 123.

151 See d'Estrée's inventory, A.N.M.C. LXXXVIII/558 (IAD 13/i/1738). D'Estrée had a collection of some 180 paintings, not counting decorative works. For the most part they are identified by subject alone. They included 47 religious works, 23 secular histories, 50 portraits, 20 landscapes and 40 still lifes and genre paintings.

152 See Galliani 1989, 199.

153 The marquis de Lassay's essay was published posthumously in the *Mercure de France*, Dec. 1754.

154 See Galliani 1989, 153–8.

155 See A.N.M.C. CXV/616 (IAD 4/ii/1757).

156 On the hôtel de Luynes, see Paris 1984, 56–67.

157 See Rouen 1970, 53, nos. 20–21.

158 See Curtius Rufus 1727, i, 417.

159 Saint-Yves 1748, 133.

160 Ibid., 135.

161 Saint Yves's analogical unity of the origins of monarchy and antiquity perhaps pays tribute to the myth of the Trojan founders of the French kingdom. On this issue, see Asher 1969, 409–19; Huppert 1970, 72–87; Duraton 1978, 205–6; Tyvaert 1974, 523–6.

162 According to the academician Mairan, Polignac *'avait une inclination marquée pour l'agriculture, cet art utile, si propre à nous rappeler le souvenir des mœurs antiques, et il l'entendoit, comme il paroit par plus d'un endroit de son poème. Il s'étoit procuré depuis quelques années dans Paris, et tout joignant son palais, un vate enclos, où il alloit tous les jours de la belle saison, et où il cultivoit d'excellens fruits et des plantes rares: c'est là aussi qu'il se plaisoit à philosopher avec ses amis'* (*Eloge de Mr le Cardinal de Polignac*, 3/vi/1742, quoted from Paris 1981, 50).

163 See Poisson 1987, 40–54.

164 For the château d'Asnières, see Kimball 1980, 191; Cachau 1994, 96–9.

165 At some point the Restouts were transformed from overdoors into easel paintings, and at the time of Chevreuse's death in 1748 they hung in the *cabinet des tableaux* alongside a Watteau, *Conversation in a Grove*; two Jeurats, *Angelica and Medor* and *Rinaldo and Armida* and a Lemoyne *Rape of Europa*. Meanwhile two of the overdoors represented *The Passions of Wine* and *The Passions of the Chase*, both again by Jeurat. See Paris 1984, 57.

166 See Boulainvilliers 1732, 290–91.

167 'Que de festons, d'emblèmes délicats/ Consacrés aux faits héroiques,/Villars tapisse ses portiques,/Cela ne me surprend pas./Mais que Bernard, qu'aucun exploit couronne,/Dont jamais il ne fut mentions/ Me présente ses actions,/Et qu'il use d'inscription,/Voilà ce qui m'étonne' *Le Faste de Samuel Bernard*, see Raunié 1879, iv, 62–3.

168 From the list of papers in Samuel Bernard's inventory we learn that by two contracts passed before Nicolas Charles De Beauvais, Samuel Bernard bought from Louis Denis Seguin two houses in the rue Notre-Dame-des-Victoires on 16 June 1714 for 212,000 *livres*, and 'tous les lambris, trumeaux, glaces, tableaux encadrés, chambranles de bois et de marbre, foyers, crochets de cheminées et autres ornemens etant dans [les] deux maisons . . .', on 15 June 1714 for a further 42,000 *livres*. Unfortunately these documents have not survived. See A.N.M.C. LXXXVIII/564bis (IAD 27/i/ 1739), *Papiers* no. 198. On De Troy's paintings see Dussieux 1854, ii, 275; Brière 1930, i, 12; London 1968, 122, nos. 672–4; Conisbee 1981, 86–7.

169 For a particularly influential discussion of the character of the Romans, see Bossuet 1681, 499–561. He noted in particular that the manners of the Romans had something rough, rigid, wild and savage about them (p. 503). Moreover, he compared ancient Romans and French nobles, noting that both were raised in the belief that humiliation would follow failure to be valiant in battle (ibid., 520). See also Rollin 1738–41 and Vertot 1720. This particular edition of Vertot was dedicated to Adrien Maurice, duc de Noailles, and the dedication takes the form of a comparison between Noailles and Scipio. De Troy may have used Mme Dacier's translation of Plutarch as his literary source. See Plutarch 1721, i, 87–9, 103–4, 118–24, ii, 535–57.

170 Here I follow closely Bryson's discussion of the theme of the rape of the Sabine women. See Bryson 1986, 155–60.

171 Rollin, for instance, warned 'Que les jeunes Seigneurs apprennent de cet exemple combien il est important de vaincre & de domter ce qu'on appelle l'humeur: car ce fut là ce vice dominant de Coriolan'. See Rollin 1738–41, i, 548.

172 See Carrier 1985, 247–61; Vicherd 1986, 55–62.

173 On Le Moyne's project for the ceiling, see Bordeaux 1984, 30–31, 146 (D23). The print was advertised in the *Mercure de France* in April 1728 (p. 784) for the price of 2 *livres*, 10 *sols*.

174 On the site, see Boudon 1973, 267–307.

175 On Oppenord's designs, see Rabreau 1983, 165–214.

176 Marais 1863–8, ii, 369. Cited in Taylor 1982, 57.

177 Cochin 1880, 140. On the similarities identified by critics between the works of rococo artists and Borromini, see Roland Michel 1984, 124–6.

178 Butini 1774, 133–4.

179 Brice 1706, i, 187–8.

180 Ibid., 273. It should be noted however, that this comment was made about de Matteis's ceiling for the library of the Couvent des Petits-Pères.

181 Blondel 1752–6, i, 207.

182 Mirabeau 1883, 227.

183 Blondel 1737–8, ii, 67.

184 Dussieux 1854, i, 457.

185 Blondel 1771–7, v, 39.

186 Brice 1706, i, 266–7. For a similar remark about the hôtel de Renouard de Touanne, see Brice 1698, i, 156–7.

187 See La Font de Saint Yenne 1747, 15, 24.

188 Blondel 1774, i, 133–4.

189 Saint-Yves, for instance, maintained that nobles were both financially deficient and intellectually indifferent patrons: 'Toujours épuisé par les dépenses attachées à leur état, les Grands, ces riches oberés, qui de l'abondance n'ont que les soins qui l'accompagnent, sans goût pour les talents, traînent leurs jours dans un éternelle indigence. Quant au petit nombre de ceux de leur ordre, dont la fortune est arrangée, ils ont d'autres penchans' (Saint-Yves 1748, 15). For his discussion of the patronage of the rich, see ibid., 16.

190 See Scott 1989, 320–28.

191 See for instance Coypel 1721, 11; Voltaire 1816, ix, 47,

192 Frézier 1738, 7.

193 Laugier 1755, 69.

194 Anon. 1716, 31.

10 THE ROCOCO EXPOSED

1 On Vigoureux-Duplessis, see Eidelberg 1977, 63–76; La Gorce 1981, 71–80.

2 The verse was as follows: 'L'or qui tombe à grands flots et penetre une Tour,/Dans le premier moment étonne cette Belle;/ L'Amour dit en riant, bien d'autres quelque jour,/Loin de fuir cette pluie, iront au devant d'elle.' The print was advertised

3 See Grivel 1986, 57–64. For the spatial distribution of the print trade in Paris, see Le Bitouzé 1986, 141–50.

4 Papillon executed a series of pen and ink drawings illustrating the spaces and processes of the wallpaper trade in Paris for Diderot and d'Alembert's *Encyclopédie*, of which this was one. In the event, they were not published. See Teynac-Nolot-Vivien 1982, 28–34.

5 See Weigert 1937, i, 48–51, 206, 264; Grivel 1986, 152; Préaud-Casselle-Grivel-Le Bitouzé 1987, 194–6.

6 See Préaud-Casselle-Grivel-Le Bitouzé 1987, 229–30.

7 On the Mariettes see Paris 1967²; Grivel 1986, especially as set in the context of a socio-economic study of the Paris print-sellers, pp. 69–82; Préaud-Casselle-Grivel-Le Bitouzé 1987, 229–34. Recent research by Anthony Griffiths and Craig Hartley has shown that if the house of Mariette did not always publish the most adventurous designs, they were responsible for supplying and arranging collections of prints, for instance that belonging to the duc de Mortemart, that included a significant number of the most radical rococo ornament prints. See Griffiths-Hartley 1994, 107–16. For Huquier, see Bruant 1950, 99–114, and esp. Roland Michel 1984, 148–50.

8 See Daviler 1738.

9 Blondel 1737–8, i, 12–70.

10 See Mandroux-França 1983, 85–108; Laing 1986.

11 Daviler 1738, viii and 188.

12 The plates of the *Architecture française* are not numbered and there seems not to have been an intended arrangement. However, the separation of the plates reproducing decoration from those of plans and sections is strongly supported not only by the example of extant volumes, but also by the fact that most of the schemes concerned post-date 1727, the publication date of the first if not the second volume. I have used the 1927 facsimile edition of the *Architecture française* edited by Louis Hautecœur. On the book, see Mauban 1945.

13 See Mariette 1927, iii, pls. 469–74.

14 Mariette, for instance, spoke of the need to increase the number of plates illustrating options in panelling in a way that suggested an awareness of his readers' wish to *see* alternatives. See Daviler 1738, 379. The increasing preoccupation with plates in architectural publications seems to indicate that they were no longer aimed exclusively or even primarily at the profession, but also addressed to a general readership.

15 On the status of Herpin's designs for Soubise, see Pons in Paris 1986, 221–2.

16 See Daviler 1738, 379.

17 See Mariette 1927, iii, pls. 508–17.

18 Sets of designs for chimney-mantles were of course published during the period but the fragmentation of the chimney into mantle and overmantle tended invariably to deflect attention from its function. Mariette was one of the few eighteenth-century commentators to note the social value of mirrors. He remarked that they not only allowed you to check on your own appearance but also enabled you to keep an eye on the entries and exits of others to and from the apartment. See Daviler 1738, 189.

19 On the château de Brunoy, see Hautecœur 1943–52, iii, 59.

20 Pierre II Mariette published the *Frises, Feuillages et autres Ornemens à l'Italienne*, the *Frises et Ornements à la moderne*, the *Vases à l'antique* (1661) and the *Vases, grottes et fantaisies de jardin à l'italienne* by Jean Le Pautre, and Pierre Le Pautre's *Dessins de Cheminées à la moderne*. Of Jean Marot's printed *œuvre* Mariette published the following sets, among others, *Plusieurs sortes de manieres de vases faicts et revestus de plusieurs ornemens a la methode antique*, and *Vazes de Jean Marot*, both *c*.1680.

21 The set of six plates which made up the *Livre de buffets* was first published by Nicolas Langlois and later reissued by Jean Mariette with his own inprint. It included the buffets of Le Normant (pl. 1), Thévenin (pl. 3) and Begon (pl. 6). For Oppenord's *Dessins de couronnemens & amortissemens convenables pour dessus de porte, voussures, croisées, niches &c.*, see Huard 1928, 327. Jean Mariette also issued a second edition of the *Petit Marot* in 1738.

22 See Mariette 1927, iii, pls. 428–33, 508–17, 534–9.

23 Toro, *Desseins et arabesques à plusieurs usages*; Cuvilliers, *Livre de cartouches et de morceaux de fantaisie propres à divers usages*; Lajoue, *Morceaux de fantaisie utiles à divers usages*; Huquier, *Livre propre à ceux qui veulent apprendre à dessiner l'ornement chinois et à differens usages comme pour feuilles de paravans, panneaux etc.*; Bellay, *Livre de panneaux et fantaisies propre à ceux qui aiment les ornemens*; Oppenord, *Premier livre de différens morceaux à l'usage de tous ceux qui s'appliquent aux beaux-arts*. See Roland Michel 1982, 70.

24 According to an undated book-order made by Jacques-François Blondel for the library of the Académie Royale d'Architecture, the *Architecture française* cost 100 *livres* per volume. See A.N. o¹ *livres* 1073/159.

25 See Le Bitouzé 1986, 268. The prices are taken from de Poilly's day-book soon to be published by J. Lothe. According to the *Mercure de France*, rococo ornament prints

could range in price from the expensive (a set of 12 Lajoue prints was advertised at 6 *livres*, see May 1736, 961–2), to average (Cuvilliès's *Livre de plafonds à l'usage des intérieurs des appartemens*, a set of seven plates was to cost 1 *livres* 16 *soldes*, see ibid., 1 Jan. 1756, 170), to the very modest (Mondon's third *Livre de formes singulieres* was offered for just 18 *soldes*, see ibid., April 1736, 962).

26 For one exception, see the terms of the subscription for Pierre Germain's *Elements d'orfevrerie divisés en deux parties* (1748), etched by J.J. Pasquier, in *Mercure de France*, Nov. 1747, 121.

27 In addition to the counter and upholstered chairs or stools that habitually furnished print shops, many were decorated with framed prints. The Deux Piliers d'Or was hung with portraits of Louis XV and *fêtes galantes* (including Watteau's *Fêtes Venitiennes*) when under the management of the *veuve* Chereau. See A.N.M.C. c/621 (IAD 23/iv/1755). The one with decoration that most completely masked the commercial function of the space by imitating a domestic interior was Gilles Demarteau's shop on the rue de la Pelleterie decorated in the late 1760s by members of Boucher's studio – Jean-Baptiste Huet and the young Fragonard. See Wilhelm 1975, 4–20.

28 See Grivel 1986, 63–4; Le Bitouzé 1986, 147–8. The view of the rococo as an unlicensed style can only have been reinforced by the company it kept on the *étalages* by the Seine. The *quais* were home above all to pornography and political satire.

29 On the Poilly family businesses and for a study of François II de Poilly's day book (Arch. de Paris, D.4B⁶, Registre 2766), see Lothe 1977. On the regulation of street-sellers see Le Bitouzé 1986, 349.

30 Blondel 1737–8, ii, 76–7; Laing 1986.

31 See *Mercure de France*, Feb. 1755, 153.

32 See Roland Michel 1982, 68.

33 In December 1727 the *Mercure de France* thought it worth mentioning that the ladies had abandoned needlework for the pleasure of *découpures* (see Laing 1983, 115). The fashion was sufficiently long-lasting that twenty years later Peyrotte's *découpures* were still thought worthy of pirating. See Fuhring 1985, 191–2.

34 See, for instance, those imported from Germany for the purpose by Louis Surugue and advertised in the *Mercure de France* in July 1731.

35 Ibid., Nov. 1727, 2492; ibid., June 1731, 1564–5.

36 Ibid., Feb. 1738, 320–21. I have chosen to illustrate a plate from the second book of *Fantaisies Nouvelles*, having been unable to locate a copy of the first book in a public collection. That the purpose of the series

was consistent is suggested by the comment concluding the February 1738 advertisement: 'L'Auteur compte donner plusieurs suites en ce genre.'

37 Ibid., Jan. 1738, 127–8. See also Jervis 1986, 113–20, for evidence of Huquier's larger cut-outs for screens, and for a discussion of their use and influence in England.

38 Laing 1983, 115–17.

39 On the advertising in the *Mercure de France*, see Todd 1989, 513–47.

40 *Mercure de France*, Oct. 1730, 2313.

41 Ibid., March 1734, 558–9.

42 Ibid., Nov. 1735, 2460–61.

43 Ibid., April 1731, 747; ibid., March 1730, 552.

44 Ibid., March 1734, 558.

45 See for example, ibid., March 1732, 549–50; ibid., June 1733, 1198; ibid., Feb. 1735, 141; ibid., April 1736, 768; ibid., 2 June 1736, 1427, etc.

46 Lajoue's sets of prints were dedicated to the duc d'Antin, the duc de Mortemart and Bonnier de la Mosson; Mondon's to the prince de Carignan, and the duc de Chatillon.

47 *Mercure de France* March 1734, 558–9; ibid., April 1736, 768; ibid., 1736, 962; ibid., 2 June 1736, 1427; ibid., Feb. 1738, 320–21; ibid., April 1738, 739–40.

48 See Todd 1989, 513–47.

49 See, for example, *Mercure de France*, March 1734, 558–9: 'Il paroît une suite d'Estampes en large, dans le goût *d'Etienne la Belle*, qui doivent piquer la curiosité du Public et des Curieux du meilleur goût. Ce sont des Fontaines, des Cascades, des Ruines, des Rocailles, et Coquillages, des morceaux d'Architecture, qui font des effects bizarres, singuliers et pittoresques, par leurs formes piquantes et extraordinaires, dont souvent aucune partie ne répond à l'autre, sans que le sujet ne paroisse moins riche et moins agréable. Il y a aussi des especes de plafonds avec figures et animaux, groupez avec intelligence, dons les bordures sont extrémement ingénieuses et variés.'

50 For example, ibid., April 1736, 768, 961–2.

51 Meissonnier certainly planned to publish a treatise on architecture which would presumably have promoted the rococo (see Nyberg 1969, 9–14), but in the end, the architect de Vigny, was alone in mounting any kind of defence in writing of the style. See *Journal OEconomique*, March 1752, 68–107.

52 See Laing 1983, 117; Roland Michel 1982.

53 See Barthes 1973, 78–80.

54 For still and by far the most persuasive history of the Salon, see Crow 1985.

55 Originally built as an element in a programme to join the Louvre with the Tuileries, the Salon Carré long served as an antechamber to the Grande Galerie. It was last used as a room in an 'appartement' when the Louvre was occupied by the Infanta (Louis XV's prospective bride) and her retinue between 1722 and 1725. See Aulanier 1950, 16–18.

56 Guiffrey 1869–71, i, *Salon* 1738, nos. 101–6.

57 Ibid., 1743, no. 60: 'Neuf Tableaux dessus de Porte désignez sous le même Numero représentans plusieurs sujets d'Architecture & de Bâtimens antiques, Païsages & divers vûës, *lesquels ont été faits en huit jours, à l'occasion de la fête que Son Eminence M. le Cardinal d'Auvergne a donné dans son Hôtel, pour le marriage de la Princesse de Bouillon, aujourd'huy Duchesse de Montbazon*' (my emphasis). For the hôtel d'Auvergne, see Paris 1987², 96–9.

58 Guiffrey 1738, no. 80; ibid., 1742, no. 4.

59 Ibid., 1750, no. 34.

60 Ibid., 1761, no. 61–3; ibid., 1763, no. 91.

61 Ibid., 1753, no. 50–52.

62 After 1750 reference to the decorative context for which exhibits were ultimately intented was invariably made derogatively. See La Font de Saint Yenne 1747, 20; *Journal de Paris*, 8 April 1777, 3; *Mémoires Secrets*, 1780, xiii, 35; *L'Ami des artistes au sallon*, Paris 1787, 16; Joullain 1786, 23.

63 For a discussion of the expectations of the nobility as patrons expressed by Salon critics, see Crow 1985, 104–10. 'A common mason, self-promoted as Vitruvius,/ Traces for him a plan overcharged with ornament,/No hall, even less frontage;/But you will have a long *enfilade*;/Your walls will have the thickness of two fingers,/ Large closets, *salons* without room./Small pier-glasses, windows as I please,/Which will be mistaken for church portals;/The whole *ensemble* panelled, varnished, whitewashed, gilded,/And by the curious assuredly admired.'

64 Voltaire 1733, 6–7.

65 Leblanc 1745, ii, 41–52, specifically 48.

66 Ibid., 46.

67 La Font de Saint Yenne 1747, 13–15.

68 Ibid., 15.

69 See above, chapter 1.

70 La Font de Saint Yenne 1747, 23–4.

71 Ibid., 22.

72 Ibid., 16.

73 Ibid., 16–17.

74 On these paintings, see London 1989, 68–78 (P485–P486).

75 La Font de Saint Yenne 1754, 35.

76 Ibid., 40.

77 Ibid., 33.

78 Ibid.

79 La Font de Saint Yenne 1747, 8–13, 76–107.

80 Ibid., 20–21.

81 See, for example, Rochette de la Morlière 1751, esp. 101, 127. However, the association of the rococo with an exaggerated *volupté* was perhaps achieved more effectively by the illustrations than by the texts of eighteenth-century novels. See Holloway 1969 and, more recently, Stewart 1992.

82 La Font de Saint Yenne 1754, 42–3.

83 See Cassid 1989, *passim*.

84 See *Mercure de France*, Dec. 1754, 178–87; ibid., Feb. 1755, 148–71.

85 Ibid., Dec. 1754, 181–2.

86 I am here particularly indebted to Norman Bryson's discussion of still life. See Bryson 1990.

87 *Mercure de France*, Dec. 1754, 181–2.

88 Ibid., 182.

89 Ibid., 182–3.

90 Ibid., 183.

91 Cochin selects for particular attention artists who could be made to represent a line of succession. Other critics targeted artists who could be made to exemplify the different arts of painting (Lajoue), sculpture (Pineau) and architecture (Meissonnier). See Roland Michel 1984, 154–8.

92 Cochin 1757, v–vi.

93 See Kimball 1980, *passim*, and more recntly Laing 1983.

94 *Mercure de France*, Feb. 1755, 153.

95 Ibid.

96 Ibid.

97 Ibid., 159.

98 Ibid., 158–9.

99 Ibid., 160.

100 Ibid., 160–61.

101 In the 'Avis aux Amateurs du Dessein' Huquier firmly promoted Oppenord as the Le Brun of architecture and added by way of justification that 'L'abondante varieté dont cet ouvrage est composé, fait connoitre un homme profond dans son Art, et qui a mis à proffit dans le plus haut degré de perfection, l'Etude qu'il à fait pendant environ 20. année en Italie d'apres les plus beaux monuments anciens et modernes'. Huquier was making these claims in the early 1750s just at the moment when La Font de Saint Yenne and Cochin were formulating their strongest critiques of the rococo. For the dating of Huquier's *Oppenord*, see Roland Michel 1984, 158. For the publication of Meissonnier's *Oeuvre*, see Nyberg 1969.

102 *Mercure de France*, Feb. 1755, 161.

103 Ibid., 164.

104 Ibid., 162–3.

105 Ibid.

106 Ibid., 163.

107 Ibid., 165.

108 For examples of this type of argument other than Leblanc 1745, see Herrmann 1985, 218–20.

109 *Mercure de France*, Feb. 1755, 165.

110 Ibid., 165–6.

111 See La Font de Saint Yenne 1747, 20, where he quotes favourably from Voltaire's *Le Mondain*.

112 See Crow 1985, 110–33.

113 The work of one particular painter fully illustrates the point. Jean-Baptiste Oudry frequently identified for whom his exhibited works were destined. The 1742 Salon included two paintings by Oudry for Jacques-Samuel Bernard, the son of the famous banker (nos 32–3), one – an overmantle – for Jombert (no. 33); another – a firescreen – for the connoisseur and Receveur-Général des Finances Watelet (no. 41), and two for the king (nos 37–38). At the 1746 Salon he exhibited works for Fermier-Général François Berger (no. 45 bis) and for Choisy (nos 41–2). At the 1748 Salon he showed only works commissioned by financiers, namely Trudaine (nos 22–5) and another Fermier-Général Savalette (no. 26), but colleagues Restout and Pierre exhibited works destined for the apartments of the dauphin and the dauphine at Versailles (nos 8–9, 41 bis).

114 Works by Oudry (no. 36) and Pierre (no. 60) for Bellevue, as well as two Servandonis for Choiseul appeared in the 1750 Salon. At the Salon of 1753 Carle Van Loo exhibited his four overdoors of the arts 'for Bellevue' (no. 180) and Mme de Pompadour was also mentioned in relation to a Lajoue (no. 92). La Live was identified as the patron of Oudry (no. 34) and Chardin (no. 59), and Vandière, who featured much more prominently in the 1755 and 1757 Salons, was nonetheless here identified with Chardin and Laurent Cars (p. 29). The influence of financiers, and the Pompadour 'clan' in particular, is increasingly apparent in the *livrets* of the 1755 and 1757 Salons.

115 La Font de Saint Yenne 1754, 138.

116 See Barbier 1857, i, 103; Marion 1914, i, 107.

117 According to the marquis d'Argenson, for instance, 'Il faut savoir que la finance et la robe ont, depuis longtemps grande antipathie ensemble, que se sont comme deux meutes qui chassent volontiers l'une apres l'autre . . .' See Egret 1970, 13. Malesherbe went further. He accused financiers of being in league with those bent on destroying the Parlement. See Durand 1971, 202–3.

118 At the beginning of the century chancellor d'Aguesseau, in his 5th *mercuriale* entitled *L'Amour de la simplicité* (1702) had already insisted that a certain asceticism was required of a magistrate, a view later reiterated in the 8th *mercuriale* – *L'Homme public, ou l'attachement du magistrat au service public* (1706) – in which he called upon magistrates to set an example because, he believed, 'le luxe est une maladie dont la guérison est réservée à l'example'. See Aguesseau 1816, i, 95–106, 129–34. On the Parlement and the *affaire Unigenitus*, see Van Kley 1975, and Van Kley 1984. On the relationship between Parlementaire politics and the arts around the mid-century, see Crow 1985, 118–33.

119 See Crow 1985, 7–11.

120 See, *Dialogue de M. Coypel, premier peintre du Roi, sur l'exposition des tableaux dans le Salon du Louvre en 1747* (Deloynes no. 28); Jean-Bernard Le Blanc, *Lettre sur l'exposition des ouvrages de peinture et sculpture de l'année 1747 et en général sur l'utilité de ces sortes d'expositions, à R.D.R.* (Deloynes no. 26).

121 *Mercure de France*, Feb. 1755, 168–9.

122 Ibid., 171.

123 See Rocheblave 1889, 131–47, and more recently Michel 1993, 485–37.

124 See *Lettre à un amateur en réponse aux critiques qui ont paru sur l'exposition des tableaux*, 1753 (Deloynes no. 61). See also Crow 1986, 11–14.

125 See Furetière 1701, iii, to *ad. voc.* 'Vraissemblance'.

126 In the foreword to the collected writings, Cochin noted with regret that 'Il n'est que trop rare que l'Artiste soit en liberté de traiter ses ouvrages dans le goût qu'il connoît être le meilleur. Tant de personnes se mêlent de le diriger, & tant de circonstances l'obligent à se soumettre à leur volonté, qu'il n'arrive presque jamais qu'on puisse s'en prendre à lui'. See Cochin 1757, vi.

127 Cochin 1880, 142.

128 It has even been suggested that Cochin was the author of Meissonnier's obituary, which appeared in the *Mercure de France* in October 1750, 138–41.

129 See Kimball 1980, 190–91.

130 See ibid., 191–3.

Bibliography

A.A.F.: Archives de l'Art Français

A.A.P.: Bibliothèque d'Art et d'Archéologie, Paris

Aesop 1714: *Les Fables d'Esope, et de plusieurs autres excellens mythologistes, accompagnées du sens moral et des reflexions de monsieur le chevalier Lestrange. Avec les figures dessinées et gravées par F. Barlouw {sic} d'une manière savante et pittoresque. Ouvrage très utile aux peintres, sculpteurs, graveurs, et autres artistes ou amateurs du dessin, qui y trouveront des animaux et des oiseaux dessinez d'un goût exquis et d'une touche savante*, Amsterdam 1714

Agnew 1986: J.-C. Agnew, *Worlds Apart: The Market and the Theatre in Anglo-American Thought, 1550–1750*, Cambridge 1986

Aguesseau 1816: H. d'Aguesseau, *Oeuvres*, 16 vols., Paris 1816

Aix-en-Provence 1977: *Don Quichotte vu par un peintre du XVIIIᵉ siècle: Natoire*, Musée des Tapisseries d'Aix-en-Provence, Aix-en-Provence 1977

Almanach dauphin, Paris 1776

Almanach des négociants, Paris 1776

Almanach Général des marchands, Paris 1778

A.N.: Archives Nationales, Paris

A.N.M.C.: Archives Nationales, Minutier Central, Paris

Annales E.S.C.: Annales: Economie, Société, Civilization

Annonces, Affiches & Avis Divers, Paris 1773–81

Anon. 1662: *L'Entrée triomphante de leurs Majestés Louis XIV, roi de France et de Navarre, et de Marie Thérèse d'Autriche, son épouse, dans la ville des rois, capitale de leur royaume*, Paris 1662

Anon. 1705: *Traité contre le luxe des hommes et des femmes*, Paris 1705

Anon. 1708: *Pluton Maltotier nouvelle galante en six parties*, Cologne 1708

Anon. 1716: *Médailles sur la Régence avec les tableaux symboliques du sieur Paul Poisson de Bourvalais, premier maltotier du Royaume, & le songe funestre de sa femme*, Sipar {Paris} 1716

Anon. 1719: *Nouvean Traité de la civilité qui se pratique en France parmi les honnêtes gens*, Paris 1719

Anon. 1737: *Etat de France*, 5 vols., Paris 1737

Anon. 1745: *Bibliothèque Poëtique, ou nouveau choix des plus belles pièces de vers de tout genre depuis Marot jusqu'aux poëtes de nos jours*, 4 vols., Paris 1745

Anon. 1752: *Histoire des singes et autres animaux curieux dont l'instinct et l'industrie excitent l'admiration des hommes*, Paris 1752

Anon. 1761: *Code municipal des règlements concernant les officiers municipaux*, Paris 1761

Anon. 1767: *Dictionnaire d'anecdotes, de traits-singuliers et caractéristiques, historiettes, bons-mots, naïvetés, saillies, repartis ingénieuses &c*, Paris 1767

Anon. 1769: *Le Géographe parisien, ou le conducteur chronologique et historique des rues de Paris*, 2 vols., Paris 1769

Anon. 1771: *Dictionnaire des gens du monde, historique, littéraire, critique, morale, physique, militaire, politique, caractèristique & sociale*, 3 vols., Paris 1771

Anon. 1776: *Les Costumes françois representans des differens états du royaume avec les habillemens propres à chaque état et accompagnés de réflexions critiques & morales*, Paris 1776

Anon. 178*: *Portefeuille d'un talon rouge concernant des anecdotes galantes & secrètes de la cour de France*, Paris 178*

Anon. 1784: *Paris en miniature d'après les dessins d'un nouvel Argus*, {Paris} 1784

Anon. 1788: *Petit dictionnaire de la cour et de la ville*, 2 vols., London 1788

Anon. 1802: *Oraisons funèbres choisies de Mascaron, Bourdaloue, La Rue et Massillon*, Paris 1802

Antoine 1970: M. Antoine, *Le Conseil du roi sous le règne de Louis XV*, Paris 1970

Antoine 1978: M. Antoine, *Le Gouvernement et l'administration sous Louis XV: Dictionnaire biographique*, Paris 1978

Antoine 1989: M. Antoine, *Louis XV*, Paris 1989

Antonini 1732: Abbé Antonini, *Mémorial de Paris et de ses environs à l'usage des voyageurs*, Paris 1732

Antonini 1749: Abbé Antonini, *Mémorial de Paris et de ses environs à l'usage des voyageurs*, 2 vols., Paris 1749

Apostolidès 1981: J.-M. Apostolidès, *Le Roi-machine. Spectacle et politique au temps de Louis XIV*, Paris 1981

Apostolidès 1985: J.-M. Apostolidès, 'Les différents types de mécénats et la tapisserie', in *L'Âge d'or du mécénat (1598–1661)*, eds. R. Mousnier and J. Mesnard, Paris 1985

Argenson 1784: R.L. de Voyer, marquis d'Argenson, *Considérations sur le gouvernement ancien et présent de la France*, Amsterdam 1784

Argenson 1857–8: R.L. de Voyer, marquis d'Argenson, *Mémoires et journal inédits*, ed. C.R. d'Argenson, 5 vols., Paris 1857–8

Argenson 1859–67: R.L. de Voyer, marquis d'Argenson, *Journal et mémoires*, ed. E.J.B. Rathery, 9 vols., Paris 1859–67

Ariès 1962: P. Ariès, *Centuries of Childhood*, trans. R. Baldick, London 1962

Arrest 1765: *Arrest de la Cour de Parlement, qui ordonne l'éxécution d'une sentence du Châtelet de Paris homologative d'une déliberation de l'Académie de Saint-Luc, & Communauté des Peintres & Sculpteurs, contenant réglement au sujet des compagnons peintres & doreurs . . .*,

13/xii/1765, Paris 1766 (B.A. MS. Bastille 12369)

Asher 1969: R.E. Asher, 'Myths, Legends and History in Renaissance France', *Studi Francesi*, 1969, pp. 409–19

A.S.L. 1729: *Arrêt du Conseil du Roy rendu en faveur de la communauté des arts de peinture et sculpture, sous titre de l'Académie de Saint-Luc*, 27/xii/1729, Paris 1729 (A.N. AD XI, 25)

A.S.L. 1730: *Mémoire pour les directeurs, corps et communauté de l'Académie de Saint-Luc des arts de peinture, sculpture, gravure, dorure, marbrerie, desseins lavez de coloris sur toutes sortes de papiers, etoffes, toiles, canevas, & autres choses sur lesquelles le pinceau peut & doit employer la couleur, soit en huile ou détrempe, dans l'étendue de la ville, fauxbourgs & banlieüe de Paris, demandeurs & défendeurs. Contre Simon, Besançon, André Tramblin & consors. Pierre Contat, Nicolas Contat & Antoine Portier. Et Gabriel-Jacques Cressé*, Paris c.1730 (A.N. AD VIII, 1)

A.S.L. 1736: *Arrêt du Parlement de Paris*, 20/vi/1736 (A.N. K1032)

A.S.L. 1738: *Lettres patentes du Roy qui approuvent & confirment les nouveaux statuts de la communauté des peintres & sculpteurs de l'Académie de Saint-Luc, de la ville de Paris*, Paris 1738 (B.N. F 22811)

A.S.L.-Compagnons 1748: *Arrest du Parlement, portant homologation d'une délibération de l'Académie de Saint-Luc pour la police qui doit être observée par les compagnons travaillants des arts de peinture et sculpture, au sujet de leur travail*, 4/v/1748, Paris 1749 (A.N. AD VIII, 1)

A.S.L.-Compagnons 1748[2]: *Mémoire surdélibéré par les directeurs en charge & communauté des peintres-sculpteurs de l'Académie de Saint-Luc. Contre les compagnons peintres-sculpteurs de la même Académie, & quelques maîtres d'icelle, intervenans & revenans contre leurs signatures*, Paris 1748 (B.N. 4° Fm 29083)

A.S.L.-Epiciers 1762: *Mémoire pour l'Académie de Saint-Luc contre le corps des épiciers*, Paris 1762 (B.N. 4° Fm 290820)

A.S.L.-Fondeurs 1702: *Mémoire pour les jurez, corps & communauté des maîtres fondeurs de Paris, intimez. Contre les jurez de la communauté des peintres & sculpteurs de la même ville, appelans d'une sentence rendue pour le sieur lieutenant de police le 12 juillet 1702*, Paris 1702 (B.N. Fm 12456)

A.S.L.-Graveurs 1731: *Arrest de la Cour du Parlement, rendu en faveur de la communauté des maîtres peintres & sculpteurs, & Académie de Saint-Luc de la ville de Paris. Contre la communauté des maîtres graveurs de la même ville*, 19/vi/1731 (A.N. AD XI, 25)

A.S.L. Statutes 1730: *Confirmation des statues de la Communauté et Académie de Saint-Luc*, March 1730 (A.N. K1032)

A.S.L.-Tabletiers 1748: *Sommaire signifié pour les directeurs en charge & communauté des peintres-sculpteurs de l'Académie de Saint-Luc, intimés & demandeurs. Contre la communauté des tabletiers, prenant le fait & causes de Pourquier, Grujon & Rondonot, appelans & défandeurs*, Paris 1748 (B.N. f° Fm 15116)

Aubusson-Tapissiers 1720: *Mémoire pour les manufactures royales des tapisseries d'Aubusson et Feletin*, Paris [1720] (A.N. F[12] 1458[A])

Aucoc 1889: L. Aucoc, *L'Institut de France. Lois, statuts et règlements concernant les anciens académies et l'Institut de 1635 à 1889*, Paris 1889

Audiger 1700: Audiger, *La Maison réglée, et l'art de diriger la maison*, Amsterdam 1700

Auerbach 1973: E. Auerbach, *Scenes from the Drama of European Literature*, Gloucester, Mass., 1973

Auffray 1762: J. Auffray, *Le Luxe considéré relativement à la population et à l'économie*, Lyon 1762

Aulanier 1950: C. Aulanier, *Histoire du palais et du musée du Louvre*, ii, *Le Salon carré*, Paris 1950

B.A.: Bibliothèque de l'Arsenal

Babeau 1886: A. Babeau, *Les Bourgeois d'autrefois*, Paris 1886

Babelon 1963: J.-P. Babelon, 'L'hôtel d'Assy, 58 bis rue des Francs-Bourgeois', *Paris et l'Ile-de-France. Mémoires publiés par le Fédération des Sociétés d'histoire et d'archéologie de Paris et de l'Ile-de-France*, vol. xiv, 1963, pp. 163–96.

Babelon 1969: J.-P. Babelon, *Les Archives Nationales. Histoire et description des bâtiments*, Paris 1969

Babelon 1970: J.-P. Babelon, 'Le palais de l'Arsenal à Paris: étude architecturale et essai de répertoire iconographique critique', *Bulletin Monumental*, vol. cxxviii, 1970, pp. 267–310

Babelon 1977–8: J.-P. Babelon, 'Histoire de l'architecture classique. La construction privée à Paris dans la seconde moitié du XVIIe siècle', *Annuaire de l'Ecole Pratique des Hautes Etudes*, IVe section, 1977–8, pp. 777–90

Babelon 1978: J.-P. Babelon, 'Du "Grand Ferrare" à Carnavalet. Naissance de l'hôtel classique', *Revue de l'Art*, nos. 40–41, 1978, pp. 83–108

Badin 1909: J. Badin, *La Manufacture de tapisseries de Beauvais depuis les origines jusqu'à nos jours*, Paris 1909

Bailey 1987: C.B. Bailey, 'Conventions of the Eighteenth-century Cabinet de Tableaux: Blondel d'Azincourt's *La première idée de la curiosité*', *Art Bulletin*, vol. lxix, no. 3, Sept. 1987, pp. 431–47

Bailey 1988: *Catalogue Historique du cabinet de peinture et sculpture fraçoise de M. de Lalive*, ed. and intro. by C.B. Bailey, New York 1988

Ballot 1930: M.J. Ballot, *Le Décor intérieur au XVIIIe siècle dans la région Parisienne*, Paris 1930

Baltimore 1985: *Regency to Empire. French Printmaking, 1715–1814*, Baltimore Museum of Art, Baltimore 1985

Banier 1715: A. Banier, *Explication Historique des fables*, 3 vols., Paris 1715

Banier 1738: A. Banier, *La Mythologie et les fables expliquées par l'histoire*, 3 vols., Paris 1738

Barbier 1857: E.-F.-J. Barbier, *Chronique de la Régence et du règne de Louis XV (1718–1763)*, 4 vols., Paris 1857

Barbier 1979: J.M. Barbier, 'Capitalisme, "vie quotidienne" et production de personnalités sociales au XVIIIe siècle', *Pensée*, vol. ccvii, Sept.–Oct. 1979, pp. 56–83

Bardon 1957: H. Bardon, 'Ovide et le grand roi', *Les Etudes Classiques*, Oct. 1957, pp. 401–16

Bardon 1931: M. Bardon, *Don Quichotte en France au XVIIe et au XVIIIe siècles (1605–1815)*, 2 vols., Paris 1931

Barthes 1964: R. Barthes, *Essais Critiques*, Paris 1964

Barthes 1973: R. Barthes, *Mythologies*, London 1973

Bastide 1879: J.F. Bastide, *La Petite Maison*, ed. Jacob, Paris 1879

Bataille 1930: M. Bataille, 'Servandoni (1695–1766)', in *Les Peintres du dix-huitième siècle*, ed. L. Dimier, 2 vols., Paris 1929–30, vol. ii, pp. 379–92

Battifol 1931: L. Battifol, 'La construction de l'Arsenal au XVIIIe siècle et Germain Boffrand', *R.A.A.M.*, vol. lix, 1931, pp. 205–55

Baudeau 1912: N. Baudeau, *Principes de la science morale et politique sur le luxe et les loix somptuaires*, ed. A. Dubois, Paris 1912

Baudrillard 1981: J. Baudrillard, *For a Critique of the Political Economy of the Sign*, trans. C. Levin, St Louis 1981

Baudrillart 1878–80: H. Baudrillart, *Histoire du luxe privé et public depuis l'antiquité jusqu'à nos jours*, 4 vols., Paris 1878–80

Baulez 1976: C. Baulez, 'Le grand cabinet et la chambre de la dauphine', *Revue du Louvre*, vol. xxvi, 1976, pp. 184–88

Bayle 1715: P. Bayle, *Dictionnaire historique et critique*, 3 vols., Rotterdam 1715

Beard 1981: G. Beard, *Craftsmen and Interior Decoration in England, 1660–1820*, Edinburgh 1981

Béliard 1771: F. Béliard, *Lettres Critiques sur le luxe et les moeurs de ce siècle à Madame ****, Amsterdam 1771

Benedict 1990: B. Benedict, 'The "Curious Attitude" in Eighteenth-Century Britain: Observing and Owning', *Eighteenth-Century Life*, vol. xiv, no. 3, 1990, pp. 59–98

Bénichou 1948: P. Bénichou, *Morales du grand siècle*, Paris 1948

Benjamin 1973: W. Benjamin, *Illuminations*, London 1973

Benserade 1672: I. de Benserade, *Les Métamorphoses en rondeaux*, Paris 1672

Berlin 1970: *Die Französischen Zeichnungen der Kunstbibliothek Berlin*, Kunstbibliothek, Staatliche Museen, Berlin 1970

Bernis 1903: F.J. de Pierres, Cardinal de Bernis, *Mémoires et lettres*, ed. F. Masson, Paris 1903

Bertin 1901: G.E. Bertin, 'Notice sur l'hôtel de La Vrillière et de Toulouse occupé depuis 1810 par la Banque de France', *M.S.H.P.*, vol. xxviii, 1901, pp. 1–36

Besterman 1974: T. Besterman, *Voltaire on the Arts: Unity and Paradox*, Zaharoff Lecture for 1973, Oxford 1974

Bertholot 1976: L. Bertholot, *L'Hôtel de Roquelaure et l'hôtel de Lesdiguière-Sully*, Paris 1976

B.H.V.P.: Bibliothèque Historique de la Ville de Paris, Paris

Bien 1974: D.D. Bien, 'La réaction aristocratique avant 1789: l'exemple de l'armée', *Annales E.S.C.*, vol. xxix, 1974, pp. 23–48, 505–34

Bien 1987: D.D. Bien, 'Offices, Corps, and a System of State Credit: The Uses of Privilege under the *ancien régime*', in *The French Revolution and the Creation of Modern Political Culture*, vol. i, *The Political Culture of the Ancien Régime*, Oxford 1987, pp. 89–114

Billacois 1976: F. Billacois, 'La crise de la noblesse européenne (1550–1650)', *R.H.M.C.*, vol. xxiii, 1976, pp. 258–67

Bimont 1774: Bimont, *Principes de l'art du tapissier. Ouvrage utile aux gens de profession & à ceux qui les emploient*, Paris 1774

Birykova 1975: N. Birykova, "Decoration and diplomacy: eighteenth-century French tapestries', *Apollo*, vol. ci, June 1975, pp. 458–65

Biver 1923: P. Biver, *Le Château de Meudon*, Paris 1923

Biver 1933: P. Biver, *Histoire du château de Bellevue*, Paris 1933

Bjurnström 1954: P. Bjurnström, 'Servandoni décorateur de théatre', *Revue de l'Histoire du Théâtre*, vol. vi, 1954, pp. 150–59

Bjurnström 1959: P. Bjurnström, 'Servandoni et la salle des machines du Palais des Tuileries', *Revue de l'Histoire du Théâtre*, vol. xi, 1959, pp. 222–4

Black 1984: A. Black, *Guilds and Civil Society in European Political Thought from the Twelfth Century to the Present*, London 1984

Bloch 1924: M. Bloch, *Les Rois thaumaturges*, Paris 1924

Bloch 1961: M. Bloch, *Feudal Society*, trans. L.A. Manyon, London 1961

Blondel 1698: F. Blondel, *Cours d'architecture enseigné dans l'Académie Royale d'Architecture*, Paris 1698

Blondel 1737–8: J.-F. Blondel, *De la Distribution des maisons de plaisance*, 2 vols., Paris 1737–8

Blondel 1747: J.-F. Blondel, *Discours sur la manière d'étudier l'architecture*, Paris 1747

Blondel 1752–6: J.-F. Blondel, *L'Architecture françoise*, 4 vols., Paris 1752–6

Blondel 1754: J.-F. Blondel, *Discours sur la nécessité de l'étude de l'architecture*, Paris 1754

Blondel 1771–7: J.-F. Blondel, *Cours d'architecture*, 9 vols., Paris 1771–7

Blondel 1774: J.-F. Blondel, *L'Homme du monde éclairé par les arts*, 2 vols., Paris 1774

Bluche 1960: F. Bluche, *Les Magistrats du Parlement de Paris au XVIIIᵉ siècle*, Paris 1960

Bluche-Solnon 1983: F. Bluche and J.-F. Solnon, *La Véritable hiérarchie sociale de l'ancienne France. Le tarif de la première capitation, 1695*, Geneva 1983

Blum 1910: A. Blum, 'L'estampe satirique et la caricature en France au XVIIIᵉ siècle', *G.B.A.*, 4ᵉ per., vol. iii, 1910, pp. 379–92

Blunt 1957: A. Blunt, 'The précieux and the arts', in *Fritz Saxl 1890–1948. A Volume of Memorial Essays from his Friends in England*, London 1957, pp. 326–38

Blunt 1966: A. Blunt, *The Paintings of Nicolas Poussin. A Critical Catalogue*, London 1966

Blunt 1977: A. Blunt, *Art and Architecture in France, 1500–1700*, Harmondsworth 1977

B.M.: Bibliothèque Mazarine, Paris

B.N.: Bibliothèque Nationale, Paris

Bocquet 1977: G. Bocquet, 'La Comédie italienne sous la Régence: Arlequin poli par Paris', *R.H.M.C.*, vol. xxiv, April–June 1977, pp. 187–214

Boffrand 1745: G. Boffrad, *Livre d'architecture*, Paris 1745

Boileau 1670: G. Boileau, *Les Oeuvres posthumes de defunt Monsieur B. de l'Académie françoise*, Paris 1670

Boislisle 1888: A. de Boislisle, 'Notices historiques sur la place des Victoires et la place Vendôme', *M.S.H.P.*, vol. xv (1888), 1889, pp. 1–272

Boissonnade 1932: P. Boissonnade, *Colbert. Le triomphe de l'étatisme. La fondation de la suprématie industrielle de la France. La dictature du travail, 1661–1683*, Paris 1932

Bonfait 1986: D. Bonfait, 'Les collections des parlementaires parisiens du XVIIIᵉ siècle', *Revue de l'Art*, no. 73, 1986, pp. 28–42

Bonfait 1986²: D. Bonfait, 'Les collections picturales des financiers à la fin du régne de Louis XIV', *XVIIᵉ Siècle*, April–June 1986, pp. 125–51

Bonneval 1743: R. Bonneval, *Les Eléméns de l'éducation*, Paris 1743

Bonnier de la Mosson 1744: *Catalogue Raisonné d'une collection considérable de diverses curiosités en tous genres, contenües dans les cabinets de feu M. Bonnier de la Mosson, bailly et captaine des chasses de la Varenne des Thuilleries, & ancien colonel du régiment dauphin*, Paris 1744

Bordeaux 1971: J.-L. Bordeaux, 'François Le Moyne et la décoration de l'hôtel de Peyrenc de Moras', *G.B.A.*, vol. lxxxiii, Feb. 1971, pp. 65–76

Bordeaux 1974: J.-L. Bordeaux, 'François Le Moyne's Painted Ceiling in the *Salon d'Hercule* at Versailles: A long overdue study', *G.B.A.*, vol. lxiii, May–June 1974, pp. 301–18

Bordeaux 1976: J.-L. Bordeaux, 'The Epitome of the Pastoral Genre in Boucher's Oeuvre: *The Fountain of Love* and *The Bird Catcher* from *The Noble Pastorale*', *J. Paul Getty Museum Journal*, vol. iii, 1976, pp. 75–101

Bordeaux 1977: J.-L. Bordeaux, 'The Tragic Loss of the Grand Salon from the Hôtel Cordier de Launay', *J. Paul Getty Museum Journal*, vol. iv, 1977, pp. 51–62

Bordeaux 1984: J.-L. Bordeaux, *François le Moyne (1688–1737) and his generation*, Geneva 1984

Bordeaux 1984²: J.-L. Bordeaux, 'La commande royale de 1724 pour l'hôtel du Grand-Maître à Versailles', *G.B.A.*, vol. clv, Oct. 1984, pp. 113–26

Boscher 1970: J.F. Boscher, *French Finances, 1770–1795: From Business to Bureaucracy*, Cambridge 1970

Bossenga 1988: G. Bossenga, 'Protecting Merchants: Guilds and Commercial Capitalism in Eighteenth-century France', *French Historical Studies*, vol. xv, no. 4, Fall 1988, pp. 693–703

Bossuet 1681: J.B. Bossuet, *Discours sur l'histoire universelle*, Paris 1681

Bossuet 1709: J.B. Bossuet, *Politique tirée des propres paroles de l'écriture-sainte*, 2 vols., Paris 1709

Bouche 1910: J. Bouche, 'Servandoni (1695–1766)', *G.B.A.*, 4ᵉ per., vol. iv, 1910, pp. 121–46

Boucher 1771: *Catalogue Raisonné des tableaux, desseins, estampes, bronzes, terres cuites, lacques, porcelaines de différentes sortes . . . coquilles et autres curiosités, qui composent de cabinet de feu M. Boucher, premier peintre du roi*, Paris 1771

Boudon 1973: F. Boudon, 'Urbanisme et spéculation à Paris au XVIIIᵉ siècle: le terrain de l'hôtel de Soissons', *Journal of the Society of Architectural Historians*, vol. xxxii, no. 4, 1973, pp. 267–307

Boudon 1975: F. Boudon, 'Tissu urbaine et architecture. L'analyse parcellaire comme base d'histoire de l'architecture', *Annales E.S.C.*, July–Aug. 1975, pp. 773–818

Boudon-Chastel-Couzy-Hamon 1977: F. Boudon, A. Chastel, H. Couzy and F. Hamon, *Système de l'architecture urbaine; le quartier des Halles à Paris*, Paris 1977

Bouhier 1742: J. Bouhier, *Les Amours d'Enée et de Didon, poème traduit de Virgile*, Paris 1742

Bouhours 1920: D. Bouhours, *Entrennes d'Ariste et d'Eugène*, ed. R. Radouant, Paris 1920

Boulainvilliers 1727: H. de Boulainvilliers, *Mémoires présentés à monseigneur le duc d'Orléans, régent de France, contenant les moyens de rendre ce royaume très puissant et d'augmenter considérablement le revenu du roi et du peuple*, The Hague 1727

Boulainvilliers 1732: H. de Boulainvilliers, *Essais sur la noblesse de France*, Amsterdam 1732

Bourdier 1959: F. Bourdier, 'L'extravagant cabinet de Bonnier', *Connaissance des Arts*, Aug. 1959, no. 90, pp. 52–9

Bourdieu 1965: P. Bourdieu, 'The Sentiment of Honour in Kabyle Society', in *Honour and Shame: The Values of Mediterranean Society*, ed. J.G. Peristiany, London 1965, pp. 191–241

Bourdieu 1977: P. Bourdieu, *Outline of a Theory of Critical Practice*, trans. R. Nice, Cambridge 1977

Bourdieu 1984: P. Bourdieu, *Distinction. A Social Critique of the Judgement of Taste*, trans. R. Nice, London 1984

Boureau-Deslandes 1745: A.F. Boureau-Deslandes, *Lettre sur le luxe*, Frankfurt 1745

Bourgeon 1985: J.-L. Bourgeon, 'Colbert et les corporations: l'exemple de Paris', *Un Nouveau Colbert*, Actes du Colloque pour le tricentenaire de la mort de Colbert, eds. J. Favier and R. Mousnier, Paris 1985, pp. 241–53

Bourke 1983: J. Bourke, 'Ritual', *Princeton Journal of Thematic Studies in Architecture*, ed. J. Bourke, vol. i, 1983

Boutard 1703: F. Boutard, *Description de la maison royale de Meudon, dediée à monseigneur le dauphin*, trans. abbé du Jany, n.p. 1703

Boyer 1952: F. Boyer, 'Les hôtels parisiens et les châteaux des Grimod d'Orsay au XVIIIᵉ siècle', *B.S.H.A.F.* (1951), 1952, pp. 107–17

Brady 1984: P. Brady, *Rococo Style Versus Enlightenment Novel*, Geneva 1984

Braham-Smith 1973: A. Braham and P. Smith, *François Mansart*, London 1973

Bray 1927: R. Bray, *La Formation de la doctrine classique*, Paris 1927

Brejon de Lavergnée 1983: A. Brejon de Lavergnée, 'Le regent, amateur de l'art moderne', *Revue de l'Art*, no. 62, 1983, pp. 45–8

Brejon de Lavergnée 1990: A. Brejon de Lavergnée, 'Plaidoyer pour un peintre de "pratique": le séjour de Paolo de Matteis en France (1702–1705)', *Revue de l'Art*, 1990, no. 88, pp. 70–79

Brice 1685: G. Brice *Description nouvelle de ce qu'il y a de plus remarquable dans la ville de Paris*, 2 vols., Paris 1685

Brice 1698: G. Brice, *Description de la ville de Paris*, 2 vols., Paris 1698

Brice 1706: G. Brice, *Description de la ville de Paris*, 2 vols., Paris 1706

Brice 1725: G. Brice, *Description de la ville de Paris*, 4 vols., Paris 1725

Brice 1752: G. Brice, *Description de la ville de Paris*, 4 vols., Paris 1752

Bridard de la Garde 1740–42: P. Bridard de la Garde, *Lettres de Thérèse ***, ou mémoires d'une jeune demoiselle de province, pendant son séjour à Paris*, 2 vols., Paris 1740–42

Brière 1930: G. Brière, 'Detroy (1679–1752)', in *Les Peintres français du XVIIIᵉ siècle*, ed. L. Dimier, 2 vols., Paris 1929–30, vol. i, pp. 1–48

Brillon 1711: P.-J Brillon, *Dictionnaire des arrêts*, 3 vols., Paris 1711

Briseux 1728: C.E. Briseux, L'*Architecture moderne ou l'art de bien bâtir pour toutes sortes de personnes*, Paris 1728

Briseux 1743: C.E. Briseux, L'*Art de bâtir des maisons de campagne, où l'on traite de leur distribution, de leur construction, & leur décoration*, 2 vols., Paris 1743

Bristow 1977: I. Bristow, 'Ready-mixed Paints in the Eighteenth Century', *Architectural Review*, vol. clxi, April 1977, pp. 246–8

Brocher 1934: H. Brocher, *A la Cour de Louis XIV: le rang et l'etiquette sous l'ancien régime*, Paris 1934

Brockett 1965: O.G. Brockett, 'The Fairs of Paris in the Eighteenth Century: The Undermining of the Classical Ideal', in *Classical Drama and its Influence. Essays Presented to H.D.F. Kitto*, ed. M.J. Anderson, London 1965, pp. 251–70

Brockliss 1987: L.W.B. Brockliss, *French Higher Education in the Seventeenth and Eighteenth Centuries: A Cultural History*, Oxford 1987

Brooks 1969: P. Brooks, *The Novel of Wordliness. Crébillon, Marivaux, Laclos, Stendhal*, Princeton 1969

Brossette 1910: C. Brossette, *Correspondance de J.B. Rousseau et de Brossette*, 2 vols., Paris 1910

Browne 1969: P. Browne, *Augustine of Hippo*, Berkeley, Ca., 1969

Bruant 1950: Y. Bruant, 'Un grand collectionneur, marchand et graveur du XVIIIᵉ siècle – Gabriel Huquier (1695–1772)', *G.B.A.*, 6ᵉ pér., vol. xxxvii, July–Sept. 1950, pp. 99–114

Brunel 1986: G. Brunel, *Boucher*, London 1986

Bruzen de La Martinière 1740–42: A.-A. Bruzen de la Martinière, *Histoire de la vie et du règne de Louis XIV*, 5 vols., The Hague 1740–42

Bryson 1981: N. Bryson, *Word and Image. French Painting of the Ancien Régime*, Cambridge 1981

Bryson 1986: N. Bryson, 'Two Narratives of Rape in the Visual Arts: Lucretia and the Sabine women', in *Rape*, ed. S. Tomasselli and R. Porter, Oxford 1986, pp. 152–73

Bryson 1990: N. Bryson, *Looking at the Overlooked. Four Essays on Still-life Painting*, London 1990

B.S.H.A.F.: *Bulletin de la Société d'Histoire de l'Art Français*

B.S.H.P.: *Bulletin de la Société de l'Histoire de Paris et de l'Ile de France*

Buffier 1732: C. le père Buffier, *Cours de science sur les principes nouveaux et simples*, Paris 1732

Bullet 1691: P. Bullet, *Pratique d'architecture*, Paris 1691

Burke 1978: P. Burke, *Popular Culture in Early Modern Europe*, London 1978

Burstin 1978: H. Burstin, 'Conflitti sul lavoro e protesta annonaria a Parigi alla fine dell' ancien-régime', *Studi Storici*, vol. xix, no. 4, 1978, pp. 735–75

Butel-Dumont 1771: G.M. Butel-Dumont, *Théorie du luxe*, Paris 1771

Butini 1774: J. F. Butini, *Traité du luxe*, Geneva 1774

Buvat 1865: J. Buvat, *Journal de la régence*, ed. E. Compardon, 2 vols., Paris 1865

C.A.. 1847–61: *Correspondance administrative sous le règne de Louis XIV*, ed. G.B. Depping, 4 vols., Paris 1847–61

Cachau 1994: P. Cachau, 'Jacques Hardouin Mansart de Sargonne ou l'art du dernier des Mansart', *B.S.H.A.F.* 1993 (1994), pp. 85–100

Cailleux 1961: J. Cailleux, 'Decorations by Antoine Watteau for the Hôtel Nointel', *Burlington Magazine*, vol. ciii (supplement) March 1961, pp. i–v

Callière 1716: F. de Callière, *De la science du monde*, Paris 1716

Campbell 1985: P.R. Campbell, 'The Conduct of Politics in France in the Time of Cardinal Fleury, 1723–1743', PhD thesis, Queen Many College, University of London 1985

Cantillon 1952: R. Cantillon, *Essai sur la nature du commerce en général. Texte de l'édition originale de 1755*, eds. A. Sanvy, A. Fanfain, J.J. Spengler and S. Salleron, Paris 1952

Cardy 1986: M. Cardy, 'Technology as Play: The Case of Vaucanson', *S.V.E.C.*, vol. ccxli, 1986, pp. 109–23

Carlier 1989: Y. Carlier, 'Les cabinets du Grand Dauphin au château de Versailles (1684–1711)', *B.S.H.A.F.*, 1987 (1989), pp. 45–54

Carré 1920: H. Carré, *La Noblesse de France et l'opinion publique au XVIIIᵉ siècle*, Paris 1920

Carrier 1985: H. Carrier, 'Mécénat et politique: l'action de Mazarin jugée par les pamphlétaires de la Fronde', in *L'Age d'or du mécénat (1598–1661)*, eds. R. Mousnier and J. Mesnard, Paris 1985, pp. 247–61

Carsix 1909: R. Carsix, 'Juste Aurèle Meissonnier', *Revue de l'art Ancien et Moderne*, vol. xxvi, 1909, pp. 393–401

Cassid 1989: J. Casid, 'Configurations of the Ideas of Woman, Commerce and Luxury: the Boudoir in Salon Criticism 1769–1787', MA report, Courtauld Institute of Art, London 1989

Cassirer 1951: E. Cassirer, *The Philosophy of the Enlightenment*, Princeton 1951

Castan 1974: Y. Castan, *Honnêté et relations sociales en Languedoc 1715–1780*, Paris 1974

Catheu 1945–6: F. de Catheu, 'La decoration des hôtels du Maine au faubourg Saint-Germain', *B.S.H.A.F.*, 1945–6, pp. 100–8

Catheu 1957: F. de Catheu, 'La décoration intérieure des hôtels parisiens au début du XVIIIᵉ siècle', *G.B.A.*, vol. 1, 1957, pp. 271–84

Caux de Cappeval 1754: N. de Caux de Cappeval, *Apologie du goût françois relativement à l'opéra*, Paris 1754

Caylus 1910: A.C.P. de Tubière de Grimoard de Pestels de Levis, comte de Caylus, *Vies d'artistes de XVIIIᵉ siècle, Discours sur la peinture et la sculpture, Salons de 1751 et de 1753, Lettre à Lagrenée*, ed. A. Fontaine, Paris 1910

C.D. 1887–1908: *Correspondance des directeurs de l'Académie de France à Rome avec les Surintendents des Bâtiments*, ed. A de Montaiglon, 17 vols., Paris 1887–1908

Champeaux 1898: A. de Champeaux, *L'Art décoratif dans le vieux Paris*, Paris 1898

Champier-Sandoz 1900: V. Champier and R. Sandoz, *Le Palais Royale d'après des documents inédits, 1624–1900*, 2 vols., Paris 1900

Chapelain 1880–83: J. Chapelain, *Lettres de Jean Chapelain*, ed. P. Tamizey de Larroque, 2 vols., Paris 1880–83

Chartier 1987: R. Chartier, *The cultural Uses of Print in Early Modern France*, trans. L.G. Cochrane, Princeton 1987

Chastel 1988: A. Chastel, *La Grotesque*, Paris 1988

Chastelus 1974: J. Chastelus, 'Thèmes picturaux dans les appartements des marchands et artisans parisiens du XVIIIᵉ siècle', *XVIIIᵉ siècle*, vol. vi, 1974, pp. 302–24

Chastelus 1988: J. Chastelus, 'Quelques réflexions sur les peintres et l'argent à Paris au XVIIIᵉ siècle', in *La France d'ancien régime. Etudes réunis en l'honneur de Pierre Goubert*, Paris 1988, pp. 107–32

Chaussinand-Nogaret 1970: G. Chaussinand-Nogaret, *Les Financiers de Languedoc au XVIIIᵉ siècle*, Paris 1970

Chaussinand-Nogaret 1985: G. Chaussinand-Nogaret, *The French Nobility in the Eighteenth Century. From Feudalism to Enlightenment*, trans. W. Doyle, Cambridge 1985

Chennevières 1851–2: P. de Chennevières, 'Jean-François de Troy', *A.A.F.*, 1851–2, p. 161

Chevalier 1970–71: B. Chevalier, 'Jean Michel Chevotet, 1698–1772', Mémoire de Maîtrise, Université de Paris 1970–71

Cholakian 1986: P.F. Cholakian, 'A House of Her Own: Marginality and Dissidence in the "Mémoirs" of La Grande Mademoiselle (1627–1693)', *Prose Studies*, no. 9, 1986, pp. 3–20

Cholet 1973: *Pierre-Charles Trémolières, 1703–1739*, Musée de Cholet 1973

Christ 1956: Y. Christ, J. de Sacy and P. Siguret, *Le Faubourg Saint-Germain*, Paris 1956

Church 1975: W.F. Church, 'France', in *National Consciousness, History and Political Culture in Early Modern Europe*, ed. O. Ranum, Baltimore 1975

Ciriacono 1981: S. Ciriacono, 'Silk Manufacturing in France and Italy in the XVIIth Century: Two models compared', *Journal of Economic History*, vol. x, no. 1, Spring 1981, pp. 167–99

Clark 1987: H.C. Clark, 'La Rochefoucault and the Social Bases of Aristoctatic Ethics', *History of European Ideas*, vol. viii, no. 1, 1987, pp. 61–76

Close 1974: A. Close, 'Don Quixote as a burlesque hero: A Reconstructed Eighteenth-century View', *Forum of Modern*

Language Studies, vol. x, 1974, pp. 365–78

Clouatre 1984: D.L. Clouatre, 'The Concept of Class in French Culture Prior to the Revolution', *J.H.I.*, vol. xlv, no. 2, April–June 1984, pp. 219–44

Clouzot-Foliot 1935: H. Clouzot and C. Foliot, *Histoire du papier peint en France*, Paris 1935

Cobban 1972: A. Cobban, *A History of Modern France*, vol. i, London 1972

Cochin 1757: C.N. Cochin, *Receuil de quelques pièces de M. Cochin*, Paris 1757

Cochin 1771: C.N. Cochin, *Oeuvres Diverses de M. Cochin*, Paris 1771

Cochin 1880: C.N. Cochin, *Mémoires Inédits*, Paris 1880

Colbert 1861–83: *Lettres et mémoires de Colbert*, ed. P. Clément, 10 vols., Paris 1861–83

Cœuffeurs-Perruquiers 1769: *Mémoire pour les coëffeurs de dames de Paris. Contre la communauté des maîtres barbiers-perruquiers, baigneurs, étuvistes*, Paris 1769 (B.N. 4° Fm 7199)

Cole 1939: C.W. Cole, *Colbert and a Century of French Mercantilism*, 2 vols., Columbia 1939

Collins 1965: P. Collins, *Changing Ideas in Modern Architecture, 1750–1950*, London 1965

Colomer 1973: C. Colomer, *Hyacinthe Rigaud, 1659–1743*, Perpignan 1973

Conisbee 1981: P. Conisbee, *Painting in Eighteenth-century France*, Oxford 1981

Constans 1976: C. Constans, 'Les tableaux du Grand Appartement du Roi', *Revue du Louvre*, vol. xxvi, 1976, pp. 157–64

Coornaert 1968: E. Coornaert, *Les Corporations en France avant 1789*, Paris 1968

Corbin 1982: A. Corbin, *Le Miasme de la jonquille. L'odorat et l'imaginaire social 18e–19e siècles*, Paris 1982

Cordemoy 1714: J.-L. de Cordemoy, *Nouveau Traité de toute l'architecture où l'art de bastir utile aux entrepreneurs et aux ouvriers*, Paris 1714

Correspondance Littéraire, ed. M. Tourneux, 16 vols., Paris 1877–82

Coulet 1977: H. Coulet, 'La métaphore de l'architecture dans la critique littéraire au XVIIe siècle', in *Critique et création littéraires en France au XVIIe siècle*, Paris 1977, pp. 291–306

Coural 1977: J. Coural, 'La manufacture royale de Beauvais', *Monuments Historiques de la France*, vol. vi, 1977, pp. 66–84

Coural-Gastanier-Coural 1983: J. Coural and C. Gastanier-Coural, 'La fabrique lyonnaise au XVIIIe siècle. La commande royale de 1730', *Revue de l'Art*, no. 62, 1983, pp. 49–64

Court Artisans 1725: *Lettres Patentes portant confirmation des marchands & artisans privilegiez suivant la cour, sous la charge du Prevôt de l'Hôtel & Grand Prevôt de France*, 29/x/1725 (A.N. F¹² 781ᶜ)

[Courtin] 1719: [A. de Courtin], *Nouveau Traité de la civilité qui se pratique en France parmi les honnêtes gens*, Paris 1719

Coyer 1749: G.F. Coyer, *Lettre à une dame nouvellement mariée*, Paris 1749

Coyer 1755: G.F. Coyer, *Dissertation pour être lues: la premiere sur le vieux mot de 'patrie': la seconde sur la nature du peuple*, The Hague 1755

Coyer 1756: G.F. Coyer, *La Noblesse commerçante*, Paris 1756

Coypel 1721: C.A. Coypel, *Discours Prononcez dans les conférences de l'académie*, Paris 1721

Crébillon 1965: C.P. Crébillon fils, *Les Egarement du cœur et de l'esprit* in *Romanciers du XVIIIe siècle*, vol. ii, Paris 1965, pp. 5–188

Crelly 1962: W.R. Crelly, *The Painting of Simon Vouet*, London 1962

Crow 1985: T.E. Crow, *Painters and Public Life in Eighteenth-century Paris*, New Haven and London 1985

Crow 1986: T.E. Crow, 'La critique des Lumières dans l'art du dix-huitième siècle', *Revue de l'Art*, no. 73, 1986, pp. 11–14

Cröy 1906: E. duc de Cröy, *Journal Inédit*, 4 vols., Paris 1906

Crozat 1729: P. Crozat, *Receuil d'estampes d'après les plus beaux tableaux et d'après les plus beaux desseins qui sont en France dans le cabinet du Roy, dans celui de Monseigneur le duc d'Orléans, & d'autres cabinets*, Paris 1729

Crozat-Boulle 1700: P. Crozat, *Mémoire pour Pierre Crozat, ecuyer, demandeur & défendeur contre Charles Boulle, ébeniste du Roy, défendeur & demandeur*, Paris n.d. [1700]

Crozat 1954: R. Crozet, *La Vie artistique en France au dix-septième siècle*, Paris 1954

Curtius Rufus 1727: Q. Curtius Rufus, *De la vie et des actions d'Alexandre le grand*, trans. C.F. de Vaugelas, 2 vols., 3rd ed., The Hague 1727

Dacier 1715: A.L. Dacier, *Des Causes de la corruption du goût*, Amsterdam 1715

Dacier-Vuaflart 1921–9: E. Dacier and A. Vuaflart, *Jean de Julienne et les graveurs de Watteau au XVIIIe siècle*, 4 vols., Paris 1921–9

Dance 1966: S.P. Dance, *Shell Collecting. An Illustrated History*, London 1966.

Dangeau 1854–60: P. de Courcillon, Marquis de Dangeau, *Journal du marquis de Dangeau avec des additions du duc de Saint-Simon*, ed. E. Soulié, 19 vols., Paris 1854–60

Darnton 1985: R. Darnton, *The Great Cat Massacre and Other Episodes in French Cultural History*, Harmondsworth 1985

Darnton 1986: R. Darnton, 'The Symbolic Element in History', *J.M.H.*, vol. lviii, 1986, pp. 218–34

Daumard-Furet 1961: A. Daumart and F. Furet, 'Structures et relations sociales à Paris au milieu du XVIIIe siècle', *Cahiers des Annales*, no. 18, 1961

Daviler 1738: A.-C. Daviler, *Cours d'architecture*, Paris 1738

Daviler 1760: A.-C. Daviler, *Cours d'architecture*, Paris 1760

Davis 1977: N.Z. Davis, 'Ghosts, Kin, and Progeny: Some Features of Family Life in Early Modern France', *Daedalus*, vol. cvi, 1977, pp. 87–114

Delamare 1705–38: N. Delamare, *Traité de police*, 4 vols., Paris 1705–38

Deloffre-Gilot 1988: *Journaux et œuvres diverses de Marivaux*, eds. F. Deloffre and Michel Gilot, Paris 1988

Démoris 1971: R. Démoris, 'Les fêtes galantes chez Watteau et dans le roman contemporain', *XVIIIe siècle*, 1971, pp. 337–57

Démoris 1978: R. Démoris 'Le corps royal et l'imaginaire au XVIIe siècle: *Le portrait du Roy* par Félibien', *Revue des Sciences Humaines*, vol. clxxii, Dec. 1978, pp. 9–30

Dens 1981: J.P. Dens, *L'Honnête homme et la critique du goût esthétique et de société au XVIIe siècle*, Lexington, Ky 1981

Derel 1956: M. Derel, 'Constructions civiles du début du XVIIIe siècle à Saint-Martin-des-Champs de Paris', *B.S.H.A.F.*, 1956, pp. 151–65

Desforges-Maillard 1759: P. Desforges-Maillard, *Oeuvres en vers et en prose*, 2 vols., Paris 1759

Deshairs n.d.: L. Deshairs, *Nicolas et Dominique Pineau*, Paris n.d.

Desmarets de Saint-Sorlin 1657: J. Desmarets de Saint-Sorlin, *Clovis, ou la France chrétienne* (1657), eds. R. Freudmann and H.G. Hall, Paris 1972

Dessert 1979: D. Dessert, 'Le "Lacquais-financier" au grand siècle:

mythe ou réalité?', *XVIIᵉ siècle*, vol. cxxii, Jan.–March 1979, pp. 21–36

Destailleur 1863: H. Destailleur, *Recueil d'estampes relatives à l'ornementation des appartements aux XVIᵉ, XVIIᵉ, et XVIIIᵉ siècle*, Paris 1863

Deuchar 1988: S.J. Deuchar, *Sporting Art in Eighteenth-century England: A Social and Political History*, London 1988

De Vesme 1971: A. De Vesme, *Stefano della Bella: Catalogue raisonné*, 2 vols., New York 1971

Devyver 1973: A. Devyver, *Le Sang épuré. Les préjugés de race chez les gentilhommes français de l'ancien-régime, 1560–1720*, Brussels 1973

Dewald 1987: J. Dewald, *Pont-Saint-Pierre, 1398–1789: Lordship, community, and Capitalism in Early Modern France*, Berkeley 1987

Dewald 1993: J. Dewald, *Aristocratic Experience and the Origins of Modern Culture*, Berkeley 1993

Deyon-Guignet 1980: P. Deyon and P. Guignet, 'The Royal Manufactories and Economic and Technical Progress in France Before the Industrial Revolution', *Journal of European Economic History*, vol. ix, no. 3, Winter 1980, pp. 611–32

Dézallier d'Argenville 1742: A.J. Dézallier d'Argenville, *Histoire Naturelle eclaircie dans deux principes, la lithologie et la conchyliologie*, Paris 1742

Dézallier d'Argenville 1762: A.J. Dézallier d'Argenville, *Abrégé de la vie des plus fameux peintres & sculpteurs*, 4 vols., Paris 1762

Dézallier d'Argenville 1752: A.N. Dézallier d'Argenville, *Voyage Pittoresque de Paris*, Paris 1752

Dézallier d'Argenville 1779: A.N. Dézallier d'Argenville, *Voyage Pittoresque des environs de Paris*, Paris 1779

Dictionnaire de l'Académie françoise, 2 vols., Paris 1694

Dictionnaire de l'Académie françoise, 2 vols., Paris 1762

Diderot 1875–7: D. Diderot, *Oeuvres Complètes de Denis Diderot*, eds. J. Assézat and M. Tourneux, 20 vols., Paris 1875–7

Diderot 1960: D. Diderot, *Diderot Salons*, eds. J. Seznec and J. Adhémar, vol. ii, Oxford 1960

Dimier 1928–30: L. Dimier, *Les Peintres français du XVIIIᵉ siècle: histoire des vies et catalogue des œuvres*, 2 vols., Paris 1928–30

Dinaux-Brunet 1867: A. Dinaux and G. Brunet, *Les Sociétés badines, bachiques, littéraires et chantantes; leurs histoires et leurs travaux*, Paris 1867

Donnell 1941: E. Donnell, 'Juste-Aurèle Meissonnier and the rococo style', *Metropolitan Museum of Art Bulletin*, vol. xxxvi, 1941, pp. 254–60

Doreurs-A.S.L.: *Factum pour les maistres jurez de la communauté des doreurs sur cuir de cette ville de Paris, garnisseurs, enjoliveurs, & faiseurs d'esventails, apelans & intimez; contre les jurez peintres & sculpteurs de la dite ville de Paris, ayant pris le fait & cause de quelques peintres & compagnons peintres de la mesme ville, intimez & apelans*, n.p., n.d. (B.N. Rés Thoisy 369, fº 225–6)

Douglas-Isherwood 1980: M. Douglas and B. Isherwood, *The World of Goods: Towards an Anthropology of Consumption*, London 1980

Doyle 1972: W. Doyle, 'Was There an Aristocratic Reaction in Pre-revolutionary France?', *Past and Present*, vol. lvii, Nov. 1972, pp. 97–122

Doyle 1980: W. Doyle, *Origins of the French Revolution*, Oxford 1980

Dubois-Corneau 1917: R. Dubois-Corneau, *Paris de Montmartel, banquier de la cour*, Paris 1917

Dubois de Saint-Gelais 1885: L.F. Dubois de Saint-Gelais, *Histoire Journalière de Paris, 1716–1717*, ed. M. Tournieux, Paris 1885

Du Bos 1755: J.B. Du Bos, *Réflexions Critiques sur la poésie et la peinture*, 3 vols., Paris 1755

Duby 1980: G. Duby, *The Three Orders: Feudal Society Imagined*, trans. A. Goldhammer, Chicago 1980

Duchesne 1621: A. Duchesne, *Histoire de la maison de Chastillon sur Marne*, Paris 1621

Duchesne 1624: A. Duchesne, *Histoire généalogique de la maison de Montmorency et de Laval justifiée par chartes, tiltres, arrests, & autres bonnes & certaines preuves*, Paris 1624

Duclos 1751: C. Pinot Duclos, *Considérations sur les moeurs de ce siècle*, Paris 1751

Duclos 1965: C. Pinot Duclos, *Conféssions du comte de ****, in *Romanciers du XVIIIᵉ siècle*, vol. ii, Paris 1965, pp. 195–301

Duguet 1739: J.-J. Duguet, *Instruction d'un prince ou traité des qualités, des vertus et des devoirs d'un souverain, soit par rapport au gouvernement temporel de ses états, ou comme chef d'une société chrétienne qui est nécessairement liée avec la religion*, London 1739

Dumolin 1924: M. Dumolin, 'Notes sur les vieux guides de Paris', *M.S.H.P.*, vol. xcvii, 1924, pp. 209–85

Dumolin 1931: M. Dumolin, 'La Place Vendôme', *Procès Verbaux de la Commission Municipale du Vieux Paris*, 1931, pp. 1–52

Du Plaisir 1683: Du Plaisir, *Sentiments sur les lettres et sur l'histoire avec scrupules sur le style* (1683), Geneva 1975

Durand 1965: Y. Durand, 'Répartition de la noblesse dans les quartiers de Paris', *Commission d'Histoire Economique et Sociale de la Révolution Française. Mémoires et Documents*, vol. xviii, 1965, pp. 21–5

Durand 1966: Y. Durand, 'Recherches sur les salaires des maçons à Paris au XVIIIᵉ siècle', *Revue d'Histoire Economique et Sociale*, vol. xliv, 1966, pp. 468–80

Durand 1971: Y. Durand, *Les Fermiers généraux au XVIIIᵉ siècle*, Paris 1971

Duraton 1978: H. Duraton, 'Le mythe de la continuité monarchique chez les historiens français du XVIIIᵉ siècle', in *Modèles et moyens de la réflexion politique au XVIIIᵉ siècle*, Actes du Colloque organisé par l'Université Lilloise des Lettres, Sciences Humaines et Arts, 16–19/x/1973, vol. iii, Lille 1978, pp. 203–22

Dussieux 1854: L. Dussieux, *Mémoires Inédits sur la vie et les ouvrages des membres de l'Académie royale de peinture et de sculpture*, 2 vols., Paris 1854

Duvaux 1873: *Livre-Journal de Lazare Duvaux, marchand-bijoutier ordinaire du roy, 1748–1758*, ed. L. Courajod, 2 vols., Paris 1873

Egbert 1980: D.D. Egbert, *The Beaux-arts Tradition in French Architecture Illustrated by the Grands Prix de Rome*, Princeton 1980

Egret 1970: J. Egret, *Louis XV et l'opposition parlementaire*, Paris 1970

Ehrard 1963: J. Ehrard, *L'Idée de la nature en France dans la première moitié du XVIIIᵉ siècle*, Paris 1963

Eidelberg 1968: M.P. Eidelberg, 'Watteau, Lancret and the Fountains of Oppenord', *Burlington Magazine*, vol. cx, Aug. 1968, pp. 444–56

Eidelberg 1977: M.P. Eidelberg, 'A Chinoiserie by Jacques Vigoureux Duplessis', *Journal of the Walters Art Gallery*, vol. xxvi, 1977, pp. 63–76

Eliade 1957: M. Eliade, *Le Sacré et le profane*, Paris 1957

Elias 1983: N. Elias, *The Court Society*, Oxford 1983

Elias 1983²: N. Elias, *The Civilizing Process. The History of Manners*, Oxford 1983

Ellis 1986: H.A. Ellis, 'Genealogy, History and Aristocratic Reaction in early Eighteenth-century France: The Case of Henri de Boullainvilliers', *J.M.H.*, vol. lviii, 1986, pp. 414–51

Ellis 1988: H.A. Ellis, *Boullainvilliers and the French Monarchy. Aristocratic Politics in Early Eighteenth-century France*, Ithaca 1988

Encyclopédie 1751–65: D. Diderot and J. Le Rond d'Alembert, *Encyclopédie ou dictionnaire raisonné des sciences, des arts et des métiers*, 17 vols., Paris 1751–65

Engerand 1900: F. Engerand, *Inventaire des tableaux commandés par la direction des Bâtiments du Roi (1709–1792)*, Paris 1900

Epiciers-A.S.L. 1737: *Factum Signifié pour les maîtres & gardes des marchands epiciers, grossiers, droguistes & apothicaires, épiciers de la Ville de Paris, intimés & défendeurs. Contre les jurez des maîtres peintres à Paris appelans*, Paris 1737 (B.N. f° Fm 12438)

Eriksen 1974: S. Eriksen, *Early Neo-classicism in France*, London 1974

Estournet 1905: O. Estournet, *La Famille des Hallé*, Paris 1905

Etlin 1978: R.A. Etlin, '"Les dedans", Jacques François Blondel and the system of the house *c.*1740', *G.B.A.*, vol. xci, April 1978, pp. 137–47

Evans Dee 1990: E. Evans Dee, 'Ornament Thoughts: Gilles-Marie Oppenord', *Master Drawings*, vol. xxviii, no. 3, 1990, pp. 332–7

Expilly 1762–8: J.J. Expilly, *Dictionnaire géographique, historique, et politique des Gaules et de la France*, 6 vols., Paris 1762–8

Fabre 1890: A.V.D.P. Fabre, *Etudes littéraires sur le XVIIe siècle. Chapelain et nos deux premières académies*, Paris 1890

Fack 1977: J. Fack, 'The Apotheosis of *Aeneas*: A Lost Royal Boucher Rediscovered', *Burlington Magazine*, vol. cxix, Dec. 1977, pp. 829–33

Faret 1925: N. Faret, *L'Honnête homme ou l'art de plaire à la cour*, ed. M. Magendie, Paris 1925

Farge 1979: A. Farge, *Vivre dans la rue de Paris au XVIIIe siècle*, Paris 1979

Farge 1986: A. Farge, *La Vie fragile. Violence, pouvoirs et solidarités à Paris au XVIIIe siècle*, Paris 1986

Farge-Zysberg 1979: A. Farge and A. Zysberg, 'Les théâtres de la violence à Paris au XVIIIe siècle', *Annales E.S.C.*, Sept.–Oct. 1979, pp. 984–1015

Farr 1988: J.R. Farr, *Hands of Honour. Artisans and Their World in Dijon, 1550–1650*, Ithaca 1988

Faure 1977: E. Faure, *La Banqueroute de Law (trente journées qui ont fait la France: 17 juillet 1720)*, Paris 1977

Félibien 1689: A. Félibien, *Recueil de description de peintures et d'autres ouvrages fait pour le roi*, Paris 1689

Félibien 1697: A. Félibien, *Principes d'architecture, de la sculpture, de la peinture*, 3rd ed., Paris 1697

Fénaille 1903–12: M. Fénaille, *Etat Générale des tapisseries de la manufacture des Gobelins*, 4 vols., Paris 1903–12

Fénelon 1752: F. de Salignac de la Mothe Fénelon, *Dialogues des morts*, 2 vols., Paris 1752

Fénelon 1968: F. de Salignac de la Mothe Fénelon, *Télémaque*, 2 vols., Paris 1968

Féral 1896: E. Féral, 'Notice sur un très beau salon décoré par N. Lancret dont la vente aura lieu à Paris', Galerie George Petit, Paris, 27 May 1896

Feray 1963: J. Feray, 'L'hôtel Tannevot et sa décoration attribuée à Nicolas Pineau', *B.S.H.A.F.*, 1963, pp. 69–84

Ferrier-Caverivière 1985: N. Ferrier-Caverivière, *Le Grand roi à l'aube des Lumières, 1715–1751*, Paris 1985

Finch 1966: R. Finch, *The Sixth Sense. Individualism in French Poetry, 1686–1760*, Toronto 1966

Finch 1979: R. Finch, '"Je suis dehors": Benserade's declaration of independence', *French Studies*, vol. xxxiii, 1979, pp. 137–54

Finch-Joliat 1971: R. Finch and E. Joliat, *French Individualist Poetry 1686–1760: An Anthology*, Toronto 1971

Fitz-Gerald 1964: D. Fitz-Gerald, 'An Unpublished "chinoiserie" by Jacques de La Joue (1686–1761) with some Thoughts on the Evolution of the "genre pittoresque" in Eighteenth-century France', *Connoisseur*, vol. clvii, 1964, pp. 109–13, 156–61

Flammermont 1888–98: J. Flammermont, *Les Remonstrances du parlement de Paris au XVIIIe siècle*, 3 vols., Paris 1888–98

Fleury 1686: C. Fleury, *Traité du choix et de la méthode des études*, Paris 1686

Foiret 1921: F. Foiret, 'Notes et documents – Le Cardinal de Bissy', *Bulletin de la Société Historique du VIe Arrondissement*, vol. xxii, 1921, pp. 93–100

Fondeurs-A.S.L. 1702: *Mémoire pour les jurez, corps & communauté des maîtres fondeurs de Paris, intimez. Contre les jurez de la communauté des peintres & sculpteurs de la même ville, appelans d'une sentence rendue par le lieutenant de police le 12 juillet 1702*, Paris 1702 (B.M. f° Fm 12456)

Fontenelle 1953: B. Le Bovier de Fontenelle, *Entretiens sur la pluralité des mondes*, ed. R. Shackleton, Oxford 1953

Ford 1953: F.L. Ford, *Robe and Sword. The Regrouping of the French Aristocracy after Louis XIV*, Boston, Mass., 1953

Forster 1960: R. Forster, *The Nobility of Toulouse in the Eighteenth Century*, London 1960

Forster 1971: R. Forster, *The House of Saulx-Tavanes. Versailles and Burgundy, 1700–1830*, London 1971

Fort Worth 1992: *The Loves of the Gods. Mythological Painting from Watteau to David*, Grand Palais, Paris: Philadelphia Museum of Art, Philadelphia: Kimbell Art Museum, Fort Worth: 1991–2

Foucault 1982: M. Foucault, *The Order of Things. An Archeology of the Human Sciences*, London 1982

Fournel 1887: V. Fournel, *Le Vieux Paris, fêtes, jeux, spectacles*, Tours 1887

Francastel 1955: P. Francastel, 'Versailles et l'architecture urbaine', *Annales E.S.C.*, 1955, pp. 465–79

Francastel 1957: P. Francastel, 'Baroque et classique', *Annales E.S.C.* 1957, pp. 207–22

Francastel 1959: P. Francastel, 'Baroque et classique', *Annales E.S.C.*, 1959, pp. 142–51

Fréart de Chantelou 1985: P. Fréart de Chantelou, *Diary of the Cavaliere Bernini's Visit to France*, eds. A Blunt and G.C. Bauer, Princeton 1985

Frémin 1702: M. de Frémin, *Mémoires Critiques sur l'architecture*, Paris 1702

Frézier 1738: A.-F. Frézier, *Dissertation sur les ordres d'architecture*, Strasbourg 1738

Fried 1980: M. Fried, *Absorption and Theatricality. Painting and the Beholder in the Age of Diderot*, London 1980

Fuhring 1985: P. Fuhring, 'The Print Privilege in Eighteenth-century France, I', *Print Quarterly*, vol. ii, no. 3, 1985, pp. 174–93

Fuhring 1986: P. Fuhring, 'The Print Privilege in Eighteenth-century France, II', *Print Quarterly*, vol. iii, no. 1, 1986, pp. 19–33

Fuhring 1989: P. Fuhring, *Design into Art. Drawings for Architecture and Ornament: The Lodewijk Houthakker Collection*, 2 vols., London 1989

Fumaroli 1975: M. Fumaroli, 'Réfléxions sur quelques frontispieces gravés d'ouvrages de rhétorique et d'éloquence (1594–1641)', *B.S.H.A.F.*, 1975, pp. 19–34

Fumaroli 1980: M. Fumaroli, *L'Age de l'eloquence: rhétorique et 'res literaria' de la renaissance au seuil de l'époque classique*, Geneva 1980

Furcy-Raynaud 1903: 'Correspondance de M. de Marigny avec Coypel, Lépicié et Cochin', ed. M. Furcy-Raynaud, *Nouvelles Archives de l'Art Français*, vol. xix, 1903

Furet 1984: F. Furet, *In the Workshop of History*, trans. J. Mandelbaum, Chicago 1984

Furetière 1701: A. Furetière, *Dictionnaire Universel*, 3 vols., The Hague 1701

Furetière 1727: A. Furetière, *Dictionnaire Universel*, 4 vols., Paris 1727

Gallet 1964: M. Gallet, *Demeures Parisiennes: l'époque Louis XVI*, Paris 1964

Gallet 1966: M. Gallet, 'Quelques étapes du rococo dans l'architecture parisienne', *G.B.A.*, vol. clvii, 1966, pp. 145–68

Gallet 1968: M. Gallet, 'The Hôtel Orrouer in Paris', *Apollo*, vol. lxxxviii, Feb. 1968, pp. 80–85

Gallet 1972: M. Gallet, *Paris: Domestic Architecture*, London 1972

Gallet 1973: M. Gallet, 'L'architecte Pierre de Vigny, 1690–1772. Ses constructions, ses esthetiques', *G.B.A.*, vol. lxxxii, 1973, pp. 263–86

Gallet 1976–77: M. Gallet, 'Trois décorateurs parisiens du XVIIIe siècle: Michel II Lange, J.B. Boistou, Joseph Metivier', *B.S.H.P.*, 1976–7, pp. 76–87

Galliani 1976: R. Galliani, 'Le débat du luxe en France: Voltaire ou Rousseau?', *S.V.E.C.*, vol. clxi, 1976, pp. 205–17

Galliani 1983: R. Galliani, 'L'idéologie de la noblesse dans le débat sur le luxe, 1699–1756', *S.V.E.C.*, vol. ccvi, 1983, pp. 173–4

Galliani 1984: R. Galliani, 'L'idéologie de la noblesse dans le débat sur le luxe (1699–1756)', in *Etudes sur le XVIIIe siècle*, xi, *Idéologies de la noblesse*, eds. R. Mousnier and H. Hasquin, Brussels 1984, pp. 52–64

Galliani 1989: R. Galliani, 'Rousseau, le luxe et l'idéologie nobiliaire: étude socio-historique', *S.V.E.C.*, vol. cclxviii, 1989, pp. 1–411

Garas 1962: C. Garas, 'Le plafond de la banque royale de Giovanni Antonio Pelligrini', *Bulletin du Musée Hongrois des Beaux-Arts*, vol. xxi, 1962, pp. 75–93

Garnier 1989: N. Garnier, *Antoine Coypel*, Paris 1989

Garrioch 1986: D. Garrioch, *Neighbourhood and Community in Paris, 1740–1790*, Cambridge 1986

Garrioch 1987: D. Garrioch, 'Verbal Insults in Eighteenth-century Paris', in *The Social History of Language*, eds. P. Burke and R. Porter, Cambridge 1987, pp. 104–19

Garrioch-Sonenscher 1986: D. Garrioch and M. Sonenscher, 'Compagnonage, confraternities and associations of journeymen in eighteenth-century Paris', *European History Quarterly*, vol. xvi, 1986, pp. 25–45

G.B.A.: *Gazette des Beaux-Arts*

Geertz 1963: C. Geertz, *Pedlars and Princes: Social Change and Economic Modernization in Two Indonesian Towns*, Chicago 1963

Geertz 1977: C. Geertz, 'Centers, Kings and Charisma: Reflections on the Symbolics of Power', in *Culture and its Creators. Essays in Honour of Edward Shils*, eds. J. Ben-David and T. Nichols Clark, London 1977, pp. 150–71

Geertz 1979: C. Geertz, 'Suq: The Bazaar Economy in Sefrou', in *Meaning and Order in Moroccan Society*, Cambridge 1979

Geertz 1980: C. Geertz, *Negara. The Theatre State in Nineteenth-century Bali*, Princeton 1980

Geertz 1983: C. Geertz, *Local Knowledge. Further Essays in Interpretive Anthropology*, New York 1983

Genest 1712: C.C. Genest, *Les Divertissements de Sceaux*, Paris 1712

Genlis 1818: S.F. Brulart de Genlis, *Dictionnaire critique et raisonné des étiquettes de la cour*, 2 vols., Paris 1818

Gerdil 1768: G.S. Gerdil, *Discours de la nature et des effects du luxe*, Turin 1768

Germain 1766: F.-T. Germain, *Mémoire à consulter et consultation pour le sieur François-Thomas Germain, écuyer, sculpteur, orfèvre du Roi*, Paris 1766 (B.N. 4 Fm 13601)

Gersaint 1736: E.F. Gersaint, *Catalogue raisonné des coquilles*, Paris 30/i/1736

Giesey 1977: R.E. Giesey, 'Rules of Inheritance and Strategies of Mobility in Prerevolutionary France', *American Historical Review*, vol. lxxxii, 1977, pp. 271–89

Gille 1962: B. Gille, 'Fonctions économiques de Paris', in *Paris: fonctions d'une capitale*, Colloques, Cahiers de Civilizations, ed. G. Michaud, Paris 1962, pp. 115–51

Gilot 1970: M. Gilot, 'Un étrange divertissement: "L'Iliade travesti" ', *La Régence*, Colloque, Centre Aixois d'Etudes et de Recherches sur le Dix-huitième Siècle, Paris 1970, pp. 186–205

Glotz and Maire 1949: M. Glotz and M. Maire, *Salons du XVIIIᵉ siècle*, Paris 1949

Godard de Donville 1978: L. Gondard de Donville, *Signification de mode sous Louis XIII*, Aix-en-Provence 1978

Goery 1965: J.C. Goery, 'Evolution démographique et sociale du faubourg Saint-Germain', *Commission d'Histoire Economique et Sociale de la Révolution Française. Mémoires et Documents*, vol. xviii, 1965, pp. 25–60

Goldmann 1964: L. Goldmann, *The Hidden God. A Study of the Tragic Vision in the 'Pensees' of Pascal and the Strategies of Racine*, London 1964

Goldsmith 1986: E.C. Goldsmith, ' "L'art de détourner les choses": Sociability as euphoria in Madeleine de Scudéry's *Entretiens*', *Papers on French Seventeenth-Century Literature*, vol. xiii, 1986, pp. 17–25

Gombrich 1979: E.H. Gombrich, *The Sense of Order. A Study in the Psychology of Decorative Art*, London 1979

Goncourt 1982: E. and J. de Goncourt, *La Femme au dix-huitieme siècle*, ed. E. Badinter, Paris 1982

Goodwin 1964–5: A. Goodwin, 'The Social Origins and Privileged Status of the French Eighteenth-century Nobility', *Bulletin of the John Rylands Library*, vol. xlvii, 1964–5, pp. 382–403

Gordon 1989: D. Gordon, ' "Public Opinion" and the Civilizing Process in France: The Example of Morellet', *E.C.S.*, vol. xxii, no. 3, Spring 1989, pp. 302–28

Goubert 1973: P. Goubert, *The Ancien Régime: French Society, 1600–1750*, trans. S. Cox, New York 1973

Gougenot 1748: L. Abbé Gougenot, *Lettre sur la peinture, la sculpture et l'architecture*, Amsterdam 1748

Gouk 1983: P. Gouk, 'The Union of the Arts and Sciences in the

Eighteenth Century: Lorenz Spengler (1720–1807): Artistic Turner and Natural Scientist', *Annals of Science*, vol. xl, 1983, pp. 411–36

Grancian 1685: B. Grancian, *L'Homme de cour*, trans. A. de Houssaye, Paris 1685

Grandmaison 1851: C. Grandmaison, 'Jean-François de Troy. Quittance à M. Delalive', *A.A.F.*, vol. i, 1851, p. 160

Griffiths-Hartley 1994: A. Griffiths and C. Hartley, 'The Print Collection of the Duc de Mortemart', *Print Quarterly*, vol. xi, no. 2, June 1994, pp. 107–16

Grivel 1986: M. Grivel, *Le Commerce de l'estampe à Paris au XVIIᵉ siècle*, Paris 1986

Grollier de Servière 1733: N. Grollier de Servière, *Receuil d'ouvrages curieux de la mathématique et de mécanique, ou description du cabinet de monsieur Grollier de Servière*, 2nd ed., Lyon 1733

Guicharnaud 1995: H. Guicharnaud, 'Les *Minerve* de Louis de Boullongue (1654–1733)', *Revue du Louvre*, vol. xlv, no. 2, 1995, pp. 44–50

Guiffrey 1869: J. Guiffrey, *Le Duc d'Antin et Louis XIV*, Paris 1869

Guiffrey 1883–6: J. Guiffrey, *Scéllés et inventaires d'artistes français, N.A.A.F.*, 4 vols., 1883–6

Guiffrey 1915: J. Guiffrey, 'La Communauté des maîtres peintres et sculpteurs dite Académie de Saint-Luc depuis son origine en 1391 jusqu'à la suppression des maîtrise et corporations en 1776', *N.A.A.F.*, vol. ix, 1915

Guiffrey 1869–71: J.J. Guiffrey, *Collections des livrets des anciennes expositions depuis 1673 jusqu'en 1800*, 4 vols, Paris 1869–71

Guiffrey 1873: J.J. Guiffrey, 'Logements d'artistes au Louvre', *N.A.A.F.*, 1873

Guiffrey 1873²: J.J. Guiffrey, *Nicolas Lancret, sa vie et son oeuvre 1690–1743*, Paris n.d. [1873]

Guiffrey 1873³: J.J. Guiffrey, *Lettres de noblesse et decoration de l'ordre de Saint-Michel conférées aux artistes au XVIIe et XVIIIe siècles*, Paris 1873

Guiffrey 1876: J.J. Guiffrey, 'La maîtrise des peintres de Saint-Germain-des-Près. Réceptions et visites 1548–1644', *N.A.A.F.*, vol. xxii, 1876, pp. 93–123

Guiffrey 1887: J.J. Guiffrey, 'Les Peintres décorateurs du XVIIIe siècle. Servandoni, Brunetti, Tramblin etc., Notes inédits de Favart', *Revue de l'Art Francais*, vol. iii, 1887, pp. 119–29

Guiffrey 1899: J.J. Guiffrey, 'Inventaire du mobilier et des collections du cardinal de Polignac', *N.A.A.F.*, vol. xv, 1899, pp. 252–97

Guilheux-Rouillard 1985: A. Guilheux and D. Rouillard, 'Echanges entre les mots et l'architecture dans la seconde moitié du XVIIe siècle à travers les traités de l'art de parler', *Les Cahiers de la Recherche Architecturale*, vol. xviii, 1985, pp. 18–27

Guillaume 1963: G. Guillaume, 'La collection d'estampes du duc de Mortemart (1681–1746) en son hôtel au 14, rue Saint-Guillaume', *B.S.H.A.F.*, 1963, pp. 285–92

Guillemet 1912: R. Guillemet, *Essai sur la surintendance des bâtiments du roi sous le règne personnel de Louis XIV (1662–1715)*, Paris 1912

Guillerne 1983: J. Guillerne, 'Caylus "technologue": notes sur les commencements problématiques d'une discipline', *Revue de l'Art*, no. 60, 1983, pp. 47–50

Guenot 1941: E. Guenot, *Les Sciences et la vie aux XVIIe et XVIIIe siècles*, Paris 1941

Hahn 1963: R. Hahn, 'The Application of Science to Society: The Society of Arts', *S.V.E.C.*, vol. xxv, 1963, pp. 829–36

Hahn 1971: R. Hahn, *The Anatomy of a Scientific Institution: The Paris Academy of Sciences, 1666–1893*, Los Angeles 1971

Hahn 1981: R. Hahn, 'Science and the Arts in France: The Limits of the Encyclopedic Ideology', *S.V.E.C.*, vol. x, 1981, pp. 77–93

Hall 1990: H.G. Hall, *Richelieu's Desmarets and the Century of Louis XIV*, Oxford 1990

Hamilton 1936: E.J. Hamilton, 'Prices and Wages at Paris under John Law's "Système"', *Quarterly Journal of Economics*, vol. li, 1936, pp. 42–70

Hamon 1978: F. Hamon, 'Le château dans le discours sur l'architecture, XVIe–XVIIIe siècles', *Arts de l'Ouest. Etudes et Documents*, vol. v, June 1978, pp. 5–17

Hamon 1977: M. Hamon, 'La manufacture royale de glaces de Saint-Gobain', *Monuments Historiques*, vol. xxiii, no. 3, 1977, pp. 33–9

Hannaway 1986: O. Hannaway, 'Laboratory Design and the Aims of Science: Andreas Libavius Versus Tycho Brahe', *Isis*, vol. lxxvii, 1986, pp. 585–610

Harouel 1977: J.-L. Harouel, 'Les fonctions de l'alignement dans l'organisme urbain', *XVIIIe Siècle*, vol. ix, 1977, pp. 135–49

Harouel 1983: J.-L. Harouel, 'Oriented on the common weal: Building regulations under the ancien regime', *Daidalos*, vol. vii, March 1983, pp. 83–92

Harris 1976: J.R. Harris, 'Skills, Coal and British Industry in the Eighteenth Century', *History*, vol. lxi, 1976, pp. 167–82

Harris 1986: J.R. Harris, 'Michael Alcock and the Transfer of Birmingham Technology to France Before the Revolution', *Journal of European Economic History*, vol. xv, 1986, pp. 7–57

Harris 1988: J.R. Harris, 'The Diffusion of English Metallurgical Methods to Eighteenth-century France', *French History*, vol. ii, 1988, pp. 22–44

Harris 1982: O. Harris, 'Households and their Boundaries', *History Workshop Journal*, vol. xiii, 1982, pp. 143–52

Hartau 1985: J. Hartau, 'Don Quixote in Broadsheets of the Seventeenth and Eighteenth centuries', *J.W.C.I.*, vol. xlviii, 1985, pp. 234–8

Harth 1983: E. Harth, *Ideology and Culture in Seventeenth-century France*, Ithaca 1983

Haskell 1980: F. Haskell, *Patrons and Painters in Baroque Italy*, New Haven and London 1980

Haskell 1987: F. Haskell, *The Painful Birth of the Art Book*, London 1987

Haskell-Penny 1981: F. Haskell and N. Penny, *Taste and the Antique. The Lure of Classical Sculpture, 1500–1900*, New Haven and London 1981

Hatin 1865: E. Hatin, *Les Gazettes de Hollande*, Paris 1865

Hautecoeur 1927: L. Hautecoeur, *Histoire des châteaux du Louvre et des Tuileries tels qu'ils furent nouvellement construits, amplifies, embellis, sous le règne de Louis XIV*, Paris 1927

Hautecoeur 1943–52: L. Hautecoeur, *Histoire de l'architecture classique*, 7 vols., Paris 1943–52

Havard-Vachon 1889: H. Havard and M. Vachon, *Les Manufactures nationales: les Gobelins, la Savonnerie, Sèvres, Beauvais*, Paris 1889

Hawley 1978: H.H. Hawley, 'Meissonnier's Silver for the duke of Kingston', *Cleveland Museum of Art Bulletin*, vol. lxv, no. 10, Dec. 1978, pp. 313–41

Hazlehurst 1984: F.H. Hazlehurst, 'La petite galerie de Louis XV à Versailles', *Art Bulletin*, vol. lxvi, no. 2, 1984, pp. 224–36

Healey 1963: F.G. Healey, 'The Enlightenment View of "homo faber"', *S.V.E.C.*, vol. xxv, 1963, pp. 837–59

Hebert 1766: Hebert, *Dictionnaire Pittoresque et historique*, 2 vols., Paris 1766

Henault 1806: C.J.F. Henault, *Oeuvres inédits du président Henault*, ed. A. Serieys, Paris 1806

Herrmann 1985: W. Herrmann, *Laugier and eighteenth-century French theory*, London 1985

Hill 1986: C.R. Hill, 'The cabinet of Bonnier de la Mosson (1702–1744)', *Annals of Science*, vol. xliii, 1986, pp. 147–74

Hillairet 1963–72: J. Hillairet, *Dictionnaire historique des rues de Paris*, 3 vols., Paris 1963–72

Hillairet 1966: J. Hillairet, *La Rue de Richelieu*, Paris 1966

Hillairet 1970: J. Hillairet, *La Rue Saint-Antoine*, Paris 1970

Hillier-Leaman-Stansall-Bedford 1976: B. Hillier, A. Leaman, P. Stansall and M. Bedford, 'Space Syntax', *Environment and Planning B*, vol. iii, no. 2, 1976, pp. 147–85

Himelfarb 1986: H. Himelfarb, 'Versailles: fonctions et légendes', in *Les Lieux de la memoire*, ii, *La Nation*, ed. P. Nora, Paris 1986, pp. 235–92

Himelfarb 1989: H. Himelfarb, 'Regards Versaillais sur l'hôtel parisien: le silence des chroniqueurs et épistoliers de la cour à la fin du règne de Louis XIV', *XVIIIe Siècle*, no. 162, Jan.–March 1989, pp. 85–100

Hirschman 1977: A.O. Hirschman, *The Passions and the Interests. Political Arguments for Capitalism before its Triumph*, Princeton 1977

Holloway 1969: O.E. Holloway, *French Rococo Book Illustration*, London 1969

Honour 1961: H. Honour, *Chinoiserie: The Vision of Cathay*, London 1961

Hopfl-Thompson 1979: H. Hopfl and M.P. Thompson, 'The historical Contract as a Motif in Political Thought', *The American Historical Review*, vol. lxxxiv, 1979, pp. 919–44

Huard 1928: G. Huard, 'Oppenord (1672–1754)', in *Les Peintres du dix-huitième siècle*, ed. L. Dimier, 2 vols., Paris 1928–30, vol. i, pp. 311–29

Huard 1928[2]: G. Huard, 'Pineau père (1684–1754)', in *Les Peintres du dix-huitième siècle*, ed. L. Dimier, 2 vols., Paris 1928–30, vol. i, pp. 331–50

Hufton 1974: O.H. Hufton, *The Poor of Eighteenth-century France, 1750–1789*, Oxford 1974

Huppert 1970: G. Huppert, *The Idea of Perfect History*, Urbana 1970

Huppert 1977: G. Huppert, *Les Bourgeois-gentilhommes*, Chicago 1977

Hussman 1977: G.C. Hussman, 'Boucher's *Psyche at the Basketmakers*: A closer look', *J. Paul Getty Museum Journal*, vol. iv, 1977, pp. 45–50

I.F.F. 17e siècle: *Inventaire du fonds français. Les graveurs du dix-septième siècle*, Paris 1930–

I.F.F. 18e siècle: *Inventaire du fonds français. Les graveurs du dix-huitième siècle*, Paris 1930–

Isherwood 1973: R.M. Isherwood, *Music in the Service of the King*, London 1973

Isherwood 1986: R.M. Isherwood, *Farce and Fantasy: Popular Entertainment in Eighteenth-century Paris*, Oxford 1986

Jacobins-Mémoire 1731: *Mémoire signifié pour les prieurs & religieux Dominiquains du faubourg Saint-Germain à Paris, appelans & demandeurs. Contre François Roumier, maître sculpteur à Paris, intimé & demandeur*, Paris 1731 (B.N. F Fm 12678)

Jallut 1969: M. Jallut, 'Marie Leczinska et la peinture', *G.B.A.*, vol. lxxiii, May–June 1969, pp. 305–22

Jammes 1965: A. Jammes, 'Louis XIV, sa bibliothèque et le cabinet du roi', *The Library*, vol. xx, March 1965, pp. 1–12

Janneau 1975: G. Janneau, *Les Ateliers d'ébénistes et de menuisiers au XVIIe et XVIIIe siècles*, Paris 1975

Jarry 1969: M. Jarry, 'Esquisses et maquettes de tapisseries du XVIIIe siècle pour les manufactures royales (Gobelins et Beauvais)', *G.B.A.*, vol. lxxiii, Feb. 1969, pp. 111–18

Jarry 1981: M. Jarry, *Chinoiserie: Chinese Influence on European Decorative Art. Seventeenth and Eighteenth Centuries*, London 1981

Jaubert 1773: P. Jaubert, *Dictionnaire Raisonné universel des arts et métiers*, 5 vols., Paris 1773

Jeannin 1967: P. Jeannin, 'Attitudes culturelles et stratifications sociales: réflexions sur le XVIIe siècle européen', in *Niveaux de culture et groupes sociaux*, ed. L. Bergeron, Paris 1967, pp. 67–137

Jean-Richard 1978: P. Jean-Richard, *L'Oeuvre gravé de François Boucher dans la collection d'Edmond de Rothschild*, Paris 1978

Jehasse 1981: J. Jehasse, 'De la fable aux fables. Benserade et La Fontaine', in *Mélanges Offerts à Georges Couton*, Lyon 1981, pp. 323–44

Jervis 1986: S. Jervis, 'Huquier's *Second Livre*', *J. Paul Getty Museum Journal*, vol. xiv, 1986, 113–20

Jèze 1760: Jèze, *Etat ou tableau de la ville de Paris considérée rélativement au necessaire, à l'utile, à l'agréable, & à l'administration*, Paris 1760

J.H.I.: *Journal of the History of Ideas*

J.M.H.: *Journal of Modern History*

Johnson 1978: N.R. Johnson, 'Louis XIV and the Enlightenment', *S.V.E.C.*, vol. clxxii, 1978, pp. 7–350

Jombert 1752: C.A. Jombert, *Répertoire des artistes*, Paris 1752

Jones 1979: M. Jones, *Medals of the Sun King*, London 1979

Jones 1982: M. Jones, 'The Medal as an Instrument of Propaganda in Late Seventeenth- and Early Eighteenth-century Europe – Part I', *Numismatic Chronicle*, vol. cxlii, 1982, pp. 117–26

Jones 1983: M. Jones, 'The Medal as an Instrument of Propaganda in Late Seventeenth- and Early Eighteenth-century Europe – Part II', *Numismatic Chronicle*, vol. cxliii, 1983, pp. 202–13

Jouanna 1989: A. Jouanna, *Le Devoir de revolte*, Paris 1989

Joullain 1786: C.F. Joullain, *Réfléxions sur la peinture et la gravure*, Paris 1786

Journal Œconomique, Paris 1751–

Journal de Trevoux, Paris 1701–

Jullien 1876: A. Jullien, *Les Grands nuits de Sceaux*, Paris 1876

J.W.C.I.: *Journal of the Warburg and Courtauld Institutes*

Kaiser 1991: T.E. Kaiser, 'Money, Despotism, and Public Opinion in Early Eighteenth-century France: John Law and the Debate on Royal Credit', *J.M.H.*, vol. lxiii, no. 1, March 1991, pp. 1–28

Kaplan 1976: S.L. Kaplan, *Bread, Politics and Political Economy in the Reign of Louis XV*, 2 vols., The Hague 1976

Kaplan 1979: S.L. Kaplan, 'Réflexions sur la police du monde de travail, 1700–1815', *Revue Historique*, vol. dxxix, Jan.–March 1979, pp. 17–77

Kaplan 1979–80: S.L. Kaplan, 'Religion, Subsistence and Social Control: The Uses of Saint-Geneviève', *Eighteenth-Century Studies*, vol. xiii, Winter 1979–80, pp. 142–68

Kaplan 1982: S.L. Kaplan, 'The Luxury Guilds in Paris in the

Eighteenth Century', *Francia*, vol. ix, 1982, pp. 257–98

Kaplan 1985–6: S.L. Kaplan, 'The Character and Implications of Strife Among Masters Inside the Guilds of Eighteenth-century Paris', *Journal of Social History*, vol. xix, 1985–6, pp. 631–47

Kaplan 1986: S.L. Kaplan, 'Social Classification and Represention in the Corporate World of Eighteenth-century France: Turgot's "Carnival"', in *Work in France. Representation, Meaning, Organisation and Practice*, ed. S.L. Kaplan and C.J. Koepp, London 1986, pp. 176–228

Kaplan 1988: S.L. Kaplan, 'Les corporations, les "faux ouvriers" et le faubourg Saint-Antoine au XVIIIe siècle', *Annales E.S.C.*, March–April 1988, pp. 353–78

Kaplow 1972: J. Kaplow, *The Name of Kings. The Parisian Poor in the Eighteenth century*, New York 1972

Kapp 1986: V. Kapp, 'Félibien interprète des *Quatre Saisons* de Le Brun', *Cahiers de Littérature du XVIIe Siècle*, no. 8, 1986, pp. 179–96

Kaufmann 1949: E. Kaufmann, 'The Contribution of Jacques-François Blondel to Mariette's *Architecure françoise*', *Art Bulletin*, vol. xxxi, no. 1. 1949, pp. 58–9

Kelley 1970: D.R. Kelley, *Foundations of Modern Historical Scholarship*, New York 1970

Keohane 1980: N. Keohane, *Philosophy and the State in France. The Renaissance to the Enlightenment*, Princeton 1980

Kimball 1936: F. Kimball, 'The Development of the cheminées à la royale', *Metropolitan Museum of Art Studies*, vol. v, 1936, pp. 259–80

Kimball 1936^2: F. Kimball, 'Oppenord au Palais Royal', *G.B.A.*, 5e pér., vol. xv, 1936, pp. 113–17

Kimball 1942: F. Kimball, 'J.-A. Meissonnier and the genre pittoresque', *G.B.A.*, vol. xxii, 1942, pp. 27–40

Kimball 1980: F. Kimball, *The Creation of the Rococo Decorative Style*, New York 1980

Kimball-Donnell 1928: F. Kimball and E. Donnell, 'Les boiseries du cabinet vert de l'hôtel de Soubise', *G.B.A.*, vol. xvii, March 1928, pp. 183–6

Klaits 1971: J. Klaits, 'Men of Letters and Political Reform in France at the End of the Reign of Louis XIV', *J.M.H.*, vol. xliii, 1971, pp. 577–97

Klaits 1976: J. Klaits, *Printed Propaganda under Louis XIV. Absolute Monarchy and Public Opinion*, Princeton 1976

Kortum 1967: H. Kortum, 'Frugalité et luxe à travers la querelle des anciens et des modernes', *S.V.E.C.*, vol. lvi, 1967, pp. 765–75

Labatut 1972: J.P. Labatut, *Les Ducs et pairs de France au XVIIe siècle. Etude sociale*, Paris 1972

Labourdette 1978: J.F. Labourdette, 'Etude comparative de quatre fortunes ducales françaises au XVIIIe siècle', *Travaux sur le XVIIIe siècle*, Angers, 1978, pp. 19–26

Labriolle-Rutherford 1963: M.R. Labriolle-Rutherford, 'L'Evolution de la notion du luxe depuis Mandeville jusqu'à la Revolution', *S.V.E.C.*, vol. xxvi, 1963, pp. 1025–36

La Bruyère 1965: J. La Bruyère, *Les Caractères*, Paris 1965

Lacombe 1755: J. Lacombe, *Dictionnaire Portatif des beaux-arts*, 2 vols., Paris 1755

Lacombe 1763: J. Lacombe, *Le Spectacle des beaux-arts*, Paris 1763

Lacordaire 1897: A.L. Lacordaire, 'Etat-civil des tapissiers des Gobelins au dix-septième et dix-huitième siècle', *N.A.A.F.*, vol. xiii, 1897, pp. 1–60

La Font de Saint Yenne 1747: La Font de Saint Yenne, *Réflexions sur quelques causes de l'état présent de la peinture en France*, The Hague 1747

La Font de Saint Yenne 1754: La Font de Saint Yenne, *Sentimens sur quelques ouvrages de la peinture, sculpture et gravure écrits à un particulier en province*, [Paris] 1754

La Gorce 1981: J. de La Gorce, 'Un peintre du XVIIIe siècle au service de l'Opéra de Paris: Jacques Vigoureux Duplessis', *B.S.H.A.F.*, 1981, pp. 71–80

La Gorce 1986: J. de La Gorce, *Bérain, dessinateur du Roi Soleil*, Paris 1986

Laing 1983: A. Laing, 'French Ornament Engravings and the Diffusion of the Rococo', *Le Stampe e la diffusione delle imagini e degli stili*, ed. H. Zerner, Atti di XXIV Congresso Internazionale di Storia dell'Arte 1979, vol. viii, Bologna 1983, pp. 109–27

Laing 1986: A. Laing, 'Boucher et la pastorale peinte', *Revue de l'Art*, no. 73, 1986, pp. 55–64

Laing 1986^2: A. Laing, 'Jacques-François Blondel', in *An Exhibition of ornament drawings 1520–1920*, Armin B. Allen Inc., New York 1986

Laissus 1964: Y. Laissus, 'Les cabinets d'histoire naturelle', in *Enseignement et diffusion des sciences en France au XVIIIe siècle*, ed. R. Taton, Paris 1964

La Live de Jully 1764: *Catalogue historique du cabinet de peinture et sculpture françoise de M. de La Live*, 1764, fasc. repr., New York 1988

Lambert 1748: A.T. de Marguenat de Courcelles, Marquise de Lambert, *Oeuvres de madame la marquise de Lambert avec un abrégé de sa vie*, 2 vols. Paris 1748

Lami 1910: S. Lami, *Dictionnaire des sculpteurs de l'école française au XVIIIe siècle*, 2 vols., Paris 1910–11

La Motte 1714: A. Houdard de La Motte, *L'Iliade, poëme avec un discours sur Homère*, Paris 1714

Lamy 1930: E. Lamy, *Les Cabinets d'histoire naturelle au XVIIIe siècle*, Paris [1930]

Lamy-Lassale 1979: C. Lamy-Lassale, 'La Galerie de l'hôtel de Villars. Essai de mise au point', *B.S.H.A.F.*, 1978 (1979), pp. 142–8.

Landau 1983: E.G. Landau, '"A Fairy-tale Circumstance": The Influence of Stage Design on the Work of François Boucher', *Cleveland Museum of Art Bulletin*, vol. lxx, Nov. 1983, pp. 360–78

Langenskiöld 1959: E. Langenskiöld, *Pierre Bullet*, Stockholm 1959

Langlois 1922: C.V. Langlois, *Les Hôtels de Clisson, de Guise et de Rohan-Soubise au Marais*, Paris 1922

La Rochefoucault 1977: F. de La Rochefoucault, *Maximes*, Paris 1977

La Roque 1734: G.A. La Roque, *Traité de noblesse*, Rouen 1734

Larrey 1722: I. de Larrey, *Histoire de France sous le règne de Louis XIV*, 3 vols., Rotterdam 1722

Lassaigne 1965: J.-D. Lassaigne, *Les Assemblées de la noblesse en France aux dix-septième et dix-huitième siècles*, Paris 1965

Lassay 1756: A.L. de Madaillan de Lesparre, Marquis de Lassay, *Receuil de différentes choses par M. le marquis de Lassay*, 2 vols., Lausanne 1756

Lastic 1955: G. de Lastic, 'Des découvertes à faire. Les devants de cheminée', *Connaissance des Arts*, no 39, May 1955, pp. 26–31

Lastic 1961: G. de Lastic, 'Desportes: j'ai réussi à regrouper ses tabeaux dispersés, à retrouver ses tableaux disparus', *Connaissance des Arts*, vol. cvii, Jan. 1961, pp. 56–65

Lastic 1977: G. de Lastic, 'Desportes et Oudry peintres des chasses royales', *Connoisseur*, vol. cxcvi, Dec. 1977, pp. 290–99

Laugier 1755: M.A. Abbé Laugier, *Essai sur l'architecture*, Paris 1755

Laugier 1765: M.A. Abbé Laugier, *Observations sur l'architecture*, Paris 1765

Law 1934: J. Law, *Oeuvres Complètes*, ed. P. Harsin, 3 vols., Paris 1934

Le Bitouzé 1986: C. Le Bitouzé, 'Le Commerce de l'estampe à Paris dans la première moitié du XVIIIᵉ siècle, Thèse de l'École Nationale des Chartes, 2 vols., 1986

Leblanc 1745: J.-B. Abbé Leblanc, *Lettres d'un François*, 2 vols., The Hague 1745

Leblanc 1747: J.-B. Abbé Leblanc, *Lettre sur l'exposition des ouvrages de peinture et sculpture de l'année 1747 et en général sur l'utilité de ces sortes d'expositions*, n.p. 1747

[Leblanc] 1753: J.-B. Abbé Leblanc, *Observations sur les ouvrages de MM. de l'Académie de peinture et de sculpture, exposé au Salon du Louvre en l'année 1753*, n.p. 1753

Le Camus de Mézière 1780: N. Le Camus de Mézière, *Le Génie de l'architecture*, Paris 1780

[Le Clerc] 1669: S. Le Clerc, *Pratique de la géométrie sur le papier et sur le terrain*, Paris 1669

Le Ferre 1759: A.-M. Le Ferre, *La Nouvelle Athenes. Paris, le séjour des Muses*, Paris 1759

Leffler 1976: P.K. Leffler, 'The *Histoire Raisonnée*, 1660–1720: A pre-Enlightenment Genre', *J.H.I.*, vol. xxxvii, no. 2, April–June 1976, pp. 219–40

Leffler 1985: P.K. Leffler, 'French Historians and the Challenge to Louis XIV's Absolutism', *French Historical Studies*, vol. xiv, no. 1, 1985, pp. 1–22

Lefrançois 1981: T. Lefrançois, 'Phaéton conduisant le char du soleil de Nicolas Bertin', *Revue du Louvre*, vol. xxxi, no. 4, 1981, pp. 282–6

Le Maître de Claville 1734: C.F.N. Le Maître de Claville, *Traité du vrai mérite de l'homme considéré dans tous les âges et dans tous les conditions*, 2 vols., Paris 1734

Le Moël-Rosenberg 1969: M. Le Moël and P. Rosenberg, 'La collection de tableaux du duc de Saint-Aignan et le catalogue de vente illustré par Gabriel de Saint-Aubin', *Revue de l'Art*, no. 6, 1969, pp. 51–67

Lemoine 1976: P. Lemoine, 'La chambre de la reine', *Revue du Louvre*, vol. xxvi, 1976, pp. 138–45

Lemoine 1984: P. Lemoine, 'Les logements de Saint-Simon au château de Versailles', *Cahiers Saint-Simon*, no. 12, 1984, pp. 17–35

Lemoine 1986: P. Lemoine, 'Nouveaux aménagements au château de Versailles', *Revue du Louvre*, vol. xxxvi, no. 2, 1986, pp. 89–94

Lemoyne 1670: P. Lemoyne, *De l'histoire*, Paris 1670

Lemoyne 1695: P. Lemonyne, *On the Art both of Writing and Judging History*, London 1695

Le Muet 1647: P. Le Muet, *Manière de bien bastir pour toutes sortes de personnes*, Paris 1647

Le Pautre 1652: A. Le Pautre, *Les Oeuvres d'architecture d'Antoine Le Pautre, architecte ordinaire du roy*, Paris 1652

Le Pautre 1751: J. Le Pautre, *Oeuvres d'architecture de Jean Le Pautre, architecte, dessinateur & graveur du roi*, 3 vols., Paris 1751

Lepetit 1978: B. Lepetit, 'Une création urbaine: Versailles de 1661 à 1722', *R.H.M.C.*, vol. xxv, Oct.–Dec. 1978, pp. 605–18

Lépicié 1752: F.-B. Lépicié, *Vies des premiers peintres du roi, depuis M. Le Brun, jusqu'à présent*, 2 vols., Paris 1752

[Le Rouge] 1719: Le Rouge, *Les Curiositez de Paris, de Versailles, de Marly, de Vincennes, de S. Cloud, et des environs*, Paris 1719

Leroux-Cesbron 1924: C. Leroux-Cesbron, 'Le Palais de l'Elysée', *Bulletin de la Société Historique et Archéologique du XVIIᵉ et XVIIIᵉ Arrondissements*, vol. iv, 1924, pp. 265–92

Le Roy Ladurie 1981: E. Le Roy Ladurie, *The Mind and Method of the Historian*, Brighton 1981

Le Roy Ladurie 1983: E. Le Roy Ladurie, 'Auprès du roi, la cour', *Annales E.S.C.*, Jan.–Feb. 1983, pp. 21–41

Le Roy Ladurie 1984: E. Le Roy Ladurie, 'Réflexions sur la Régence, 1715–1723', *French Studies*, vol. xxxviii, no. 3, July 1984, pp. 286–305

Le Roy Ladurie 1987: E. Le Roy Ladurie, 'Rangs et hierarchie dans la vie de cour', in *The French Revolution and the Creation of Modern Political Culture*, vol. i, *The Political Culture of the Old Régime*, ed. K.M. Baker, Oxford 1987, pp. 61–75

Lespinasse 1879–97: R. de Lespinasse, *Les Métiers et corporations de la ville de Paris*, 3 vols., Paris 1879–97

Levassor 1700–11: M. Levassor, *Histoire du règne de Louis XIII, roi de France et de Navarre*, 10 vols., Amsterdam 1700–11

Levey 1964: M. Levey, 'A Watteau Rediscovered: *Le Printemps* for Crozat', *Burlington Magazine*, vol. cvi, Feb. 1964, pp. 53–8

Levi-Strauss 1966: C. Levi-Strauss, *The Savage Mind*, Chicago 1966

Levy-Henry 1960: C. Levey and L. Henry, 'Ducs et pairs sous l'ancien régime, caractéristiques d'une caste', *Population*, vol. xv, 1960, pp. 807–30

Limiers 1718: H.P. de Limiers, *Histoire du règne de Louis XIV*, 10 vols., Amsterdam 1718

Limiers 1720: H.P. de Limiers, *Atlas Historique*, 7 vols., Amsterdam 1720

Lister 1699: M. Lister, *A Journey to Paris in the year 1689*, 2nd edn. London 1699

Locquin 1908: J. Locquin, 'Le paysage en France au début du XVIIIᵉ siècle et l'œuvre de J.-B. Oudry', *G.B.A.*, 4ᵉ pér., vol. xi, 1908, pp. 353–80

Locquin 1912: J. Locquin, *La Peinture d'histoire en France de 1747 à 1785*, Paris 1912

Lomax 1982: D. Lomax, 'Nöel-Nicolas Coypel', *Revue de l'Art*, no. 57, 1982, pp. 29–48

Lombard 1913: A. Lombard, *L'Abbé Du Bos. Un imitateur de la pensée moderne (1670–1742)*, Paris 1913

Lombard-Jourdan 1981: A. Lombard-Jourdan, 'Les confréries parisiennes des peintres', *B.S.H.P.*, 1980 (1981), pp. 87–103

London 1956: *Wallace Collection Catalogues: Furniture*, by F.J.B. Watson, London 1956

London 1968: *France in the Eighteenth Century*, Royal Academy of Arts, London 1968

London 1979: *Recent Acquisitions, French Paintings and Sculptures of the Seventeenth and Eighteenth Centuries*, Heim Gallery, London 1979

London 1981: *Art as Decoration*, Heim Gallery, London 1981

London 1989: *The Wallace Collection Catalogue of Pictures*, vol. iii, *French before 1815*, by J. Ingamells, London 1989

London 1990: *Three Eyes: The Old Master Painting from Different Viewpoints*, Heim Gallery, London 1990

Lorangère 1744: *Catalogue raisonné des divers curiositès du cabinet de feu M. Quentin de Lorangère, composé de tableaux originaux des meilleurs maîtres de Flandres; d'une très nombreuse collection de desseins & d'estampes de toutes écoles; de plusieurs atlas & suites de cartes; de quantité de morceaux de topographie, et d'un coquillier fait avec choix, par E.F. Gersaint*, Paris 1744

Lorentz 1751: J.M. Lorentz, *Oraison funèbre*, Strasbourg 1751

Lorgues 1979: C. Lorgues, 'L'hôtel Rouillé. Une résidence du XVIIIᵉ siècle détruite en 1766 pour le dégagement de la colonnade du Louvre', *B.S.H.P.*, 1979, pp. 37–49

Los Angeles 1983: *An Elegant Art. Fashion and Fantasy in the Eighteenth Century*, Los Angeles County Museum of Art, Los Angeles 1983

Lothe 1977: J. Lothe, *François de Poilly, graveur et marchand d'estampes (1623–1693)*, thèse de 3ᵉ cycle, Paris IV, 1977 (B.N. Cabinet des Estampes)

Lougee 1976: C.C. Lougee, *Le Paradis des femmes*, Princeton 1976

Lucas 1973: C. Lucas, 'Nobles, Bourgeois and the Origins of the French Revolution', *Past and Present*, vol. lx, Aug. 1973, pp. 84–126

Ludmann-Pons 1979: J.-D. Ludmann and B. Pons, 'Documents inédits sur la galerie de l'hôtel de Toulouse', *B.S.H.A.F.*, 1979, pp. 116–28

Lugt 1938: F. Lugt, *Répertoire des catalogues de ventes publiques, interessant l'art ou la curiosité, première période c.1600–1825*, The Hague 1938

Luthy 1970: H. Luthy, *La Banque protestante en France de la Révocation de l'Edit de Nantes à la Révolution*, 2 vols., Paris 1970

Lux 1982: D. Lux, 'Patronage in the Age of Absolutism: Royal Academies and State Building Policy in Seventeenth-century France', in *Proceedings of the 9th Annual Meeting of the Western Society of French History*, 22–4 October 1981, Greesley, Colo., 1982

Luynes 1860–65: C.-P. d'Albert, duc de Luynes, *Mémoires du duc de Luynes sur la cour de Lous XV, 1735–58*, ed. L. Dussieux and E. Soulié, 17 vols., Paris 1860–65

Mabille 1974: G. Mabille, 'La Ménagerie de Versailles', *G.B.A.*, vol. lxxxiii, 1974, pp. 5–36

Mabille 1975: G. Mabille, 'Les tableaux de la Ménagerie de Versailles', *B.S.H.A.F.*, 1974 (1975), pp. 89–101

Mably 1794–5: G. Bonnot, abbé de Mably, *Collection complète des œuvres de l'abbé Mably*, 15 vols., Paris 1794–5

Maclean 1977: I. Maclean, *Woman Triumphant*, Baltimore 1977

Macmillan 1982: *Macmillan Dictionary of Architects*, London 1982

Macon 1903: G. Macon, *Les Arts dans la maison Condé*, Paris 1903

Magendie 1925: M.M. Magendie, *La Politesse mondaine et les théories de l'honnêteté en France au XVIIᵉ siècle de 1600 à 1660*, Paris 1925

Maihows 1881: Maihows, *Paris Artistique et monumental en 1750. Lettres traduites de l'anglais par P.F. de Puisieux*, ed. H. Bonnardot, Paris 1881

Maillard 1898: L. Maillard, *Les Menus programmes illustrées, invitations, billets de faire part, cartes addresse, petits estampes du XVIIᵉ siècle jusqu'à nos jours*, Paris 1898

Mandeville 1740: B. Mandeville, *La Fable des abeilles ou les fripons devenus honnêtes gens*, 2 vols., [Amsterdam] 1740

Mandroux-França 1974: M.-T. Mandroux-França, 'Information artistique et "mass media" au XVIIIᵉ siècle: la diffusion de l'ornement gravé rococo au Portugal', *Bracara Augusta*, vol. xxvii, 1974, pp. 3–36

Mandroux-França 1983: M.-T. Mandroux-França, 'La Circulation de la gravure d'ornement en Portugal au XVIIIᵉ siècle', *Le Stampe e la diffusione delle imagini e degli stili*, in *Actes du XXIVᵉ Congrès du C.I.H.A.*, Bologna, vol. viii, 1983, pp. 85–108

Mantz 1851: P. Mantz, 'J.B. Le Paon', *A.A.F.*, vol. i, 1851, pp. 181–2.

Marais 1863–8: M. Marais, *Journal et mémoires de la régence et le règne de Louis XV (1715–1737)*, 4 vols., Paris 1863–8

Marcel 1906: P. Marcel, *Inventaire des papiers manuscrits du cabinet de Robert de Cotte, premier architecte du Roi (1656–1735), et de Jules-Robert de Cotte (1683–1767) conservés à la Bibliotheque Nationale*, Paris 1906

Marcel 1906²: P. Marcel, *La Peinture française au début du dix-huitième siècle, 1690–1721*, Paris 1906

Marie 1972: A. and J. Marie, *Mansart à Versailles*, 2 vols., Paris 1972

Marie 1984: A. Marie, *Versailles au temps de Louis XV*, Paris 1984

Mariette 1927: J. Mariette, *Architecture françoise, ou receuil de plans, elevations, coupes et profils*, 3 vols., Paris 1727, facs. edn. ed. L. Hautecœur, Paris 1927

Mariette 1851–60: P.-J. Mariette, *Abecedario*, ed. P. de Chennevières and A. de Montaiglon, 6 vols., Paris 1851–60

Marin 1991: L. Marin, 'Classical, Baroque: Versailles, or the Architecture of the Prince', *Yale French Studies*, no. 80, 1991, pp. 167–82

Marion 1914: M. Marion, *Histoire Financière de la France depuis 1715*, 3 vols., Paris 1914

Marion 1923: M. Marion, *Dictionnaire des institutions de la France au XVIIᵉ et XVIIIᵉ siècle*, Paris 1923

Marolles 1655: M. de Marolles, *Les Oeuvres de Virgile traduites en prose, et dédiées au roy*, Paris 1655

Marsy 1746: F.M. de Marsy, *Dictionnaire Abrégé de peinture et d'architecture*, 2 vols., Paris 1746

Martin 1786: *Mémoire pour le sieur Martin, peintre-vernisseur du roi, le sieur Charny, peintre, ancien professeur de l'académie & communauté de peinture, sous l'invocation de Saint-Luc, supprimée; le sieur Bunel, & les autres peintres de la même ancienne académie, dénommés dans l'arrêt du 23 novembre 1785, appelans & demandeurs, contre les sieurs Arnoult, Mentabene, Passinge, & Deblans, nouveaux maître peintre & sculpteurs, syndics & adjoins de la nouvelle commuauté créée en 1776, se disant faussement directeurs-gardes de l'académie de Saint-Luc, intimés & défendeurs*, Paris 1786

Mason 1978: H.T. Mason, 'Voltaire's Poems on luxury', in *Studies in the French Eighteenth Century Presented to John Lough by Colleagues, Pupils and Friends*, ed. D.J. Mossop, G.E. Rodmell and D.B. Wilson, Durham 1978, pp. 118–22

Massillon 1865: J.B. Massillon, *Oeuvres Complètes*, 2 vols., Paris 1865

Mathieussent-Trouilleux 1982: M. Mathieussent and R. Trouilleux, 'Le pavillon de Vendôme à Clichy-la-Garenne', *B.S.H.P.*, 1982, pp. 213–24

Matignon-Pons 1723: *Réflexions Sommaires pour monsieur le comte de Matignon, intimé contre monsieur le prince de Pons, appelant*, Paris 1723 (B.N. f° Fm 10886)

Mauban 1944: A. Mauban, *Jean Marot, architecte et graveur parisien*, Paris 1944

Mauban 1945: A. Mauban, *L'Architecture française de Jean Mariette*, Paris 1945

Mauclerc 1773: M. Mauclerc, *Traité des couleurs et vernis*, Paris 1773

Mauzi 1960: R. Mauzi, *L'Idée du bonheur dans la littérature du XVIIIᵉ siècle*, Paris 1960

Maza 1983: S. Maza, *Servants and their Masters in Eighteenth-century France. The Uses of Loyalty*, Princeton 1983

McAllister-Johnson 1983: W. McAllister-Johnson, 'Affiches, annonces et avis divers. The *estampe-publicité* in the Eighteenth Century', *G.B.A.*, vol. cii, Oct. 1983, pp. 121–8

Melon 1734: J.F. Melon, *Essai Politique sur le commerce*, Paris 1734

Mémoires Secrets pour Servir à l'Histoire de la République des Lettres en France, London 1780–

Menant 1981: S. Menant, *La Chute d'Icare. La crise de la poésie française (1700–1750)*, Geneva 1981

Ménétra 1982: *Journal de ma vie. Jacques-Louis Ménétra compagnon vitrier au 18ᵉ siècle*, ed. D. Roche, Paris 1982

Mercier 1782–8: L.S. Mercier, *Tableau de Paris*, 12 vols., Amsterdam 1782–8

Mercure de France, Paris 1678–

Méré 1930: A.G. Méré, *Oeuvres Complètes*, ed. C.H. Bouhours, 3 vols., Paris 1930

Merot 1990: A. Merot, *Retraites Mondaines. Aspects de la décoration interieure à Paris au XVIIe siècle*, Paris 1990

Merson 1881: O. Merson, 'Les logements d'artistes au Louvre de la fin du XVIIIᵉ siècle et au commencement du XIXᵉ siècle', *G.B.A.*, 2ᵉ pér., vol. xxiii, 1881, pp. 264–70; vol. xxiv, 1881, pp. 276–88

Mettam 1988: R. Mettam, *Power and Faction in Louis XIV's France*, Oxford 1988

Meyer 1966: D. Meyer, *La Noblesse bretonne au XVIIIᵉ siècle*, 2 vols., Paris 1966

Michaux 1964: M. Michaux, 'L'hôtel de Beauvillier et le cercle militaire de Versailles', *Revue Historique de l'Armée*, 1964, pp. 61–8

Michel 1993: C. Michel, *Charles-Nicolas Cochin et l'art des lumières*, Paris 1993

Mignot 1989: C. Mignot, 'De la cuisine à la salle à manger, ou de quelques détours de l'art de la distribution', *XVIIᵉ Siècle*, no. 162, 1989, pp. 17–35

Miller 1987: L.E. Miller, 'Design, Technique and the Division of Labour in the Lyon Silk Industry', paper circulated at the 'Design, Commerce and Luxury Trades in the Eighteenth Century' workshop, Victoria and Albert Museum 23 October 1987

Minguet 1966: P. Minguet, *Esthétique du rococo*, Paris 1966

Minvielle 1921: G. Minvielle, *Histoire des conditions juridiques de la profession d'architecture*, Bordeaux 1921

Mirabeau 1883: V. de Riquetti, Marquis de Mirabeau, *L'Ami des hommes ou traité de la population*, Paris 1883

Mirimonde 1970: A.P. de Mirimonde, 'La musique dans le "cabinet des beaux-arts" de Charles Perrault', *B.S.H.A.F.*, 1970, pp. 77–85

Miroitiers-Tapissiers 1739: *Mémoire Signifié pour les jurez en charge de la communauté des maîtres & marchands miroitiers de la ville & fauxbourgs de Paris appelans. Contre les syndics & jurez de la communauté des maîtres & marchands tapissiers de Paris, intimez. Et contre Jean-Baptiste Gervais; & Firmin Cognard, aussi maîtres tapissiers, intimez*, Paris 1739 (B.N. f° Fm 12567)

Mondain-Monval 1918: J. Mondain-Monval, *Correspondance de Soufflot avec les directeurs des bâtiments concernant la manufacture des Gobelins (1756–1780)*, Paris 1918

Monk 1944: S.H. Monk, '"A Grace Beyond the Reach of Art"', *J.H.I.*, vol. v, no. 2, April 1944, pp. 131–50

Monnier 1980: R. Monnier, 'Les structures de l'artisanat au faubourg Saint-Antoine sous la Révolution', *B.S.H.P.*, 1979 (1980), pp. 113–31

Monnier 1981: R. Monnier, *Le Faubourg Saint-Antoine (1789–1815)*, Paris 1981

Montesquieu 1964: C.-L. de Secondat de Montesquieu, *Lettres persanes*, Paris 1964

Montesquieu 1968: C.-L. de Secondat de Montesquieu, *Considérations sur les causes de la grandeur des romains et de leur décadence*, ed. J. Ehrard, Paris 1968

Montias 1987: J.M. Montias, 'Cost and Value in Seventeenth-century Dutch art', *Art History*, vol. x, no. 4, 1987, pp. 455–66

Moore 1957: W.G. Moore, 'Le Goût de la cour', *Cahiers de l'Association Internationale des Etudes Françaises*, vol. ix, June 1957, pp. 172–82

Moore 1969: W.G. Moore, *La Rochefoucault, His Art and Mind*, Oxford 1969

Moriarty 1988: M. Moriarty, *Taste and Ideology in Seventeenth-century France*, Cambridge 1988

Morize 1909: A. Morize, *L'Apologie du luxe au XVIIIᵉ siècle et 'Le Mondain' de Voltaire*, Paris 1909

Morvan de Bellegarde 1709: J.B. Morvan de Bellegarde, *L'Art de connoître les hommes*, Amsterdam 1709

Morvan de Bellegarde 1719: J.B. Morvan de Bellegarde, *Modèles de conversations pour les personnes polies*, Paris 1719

Morvan de Bellegarde 1720: J.B. Morvan de Bellegarde, *Lettres curieuses de littérature et de morale*, Paris 1720

Morvan de Bellegarde 1743: J.B. Morvan de Bellegarde, *L'Art de plaire dans la conversation*, The Hague 1743

Mousnier 1962: R. Mousnier, 'Paris, capitale politique au moyen age et dans les temps modernes (environ 1200 à 1789)', in *Paris: fonctions d'une capitale*, Colloques Cahiers de Civilization, dir. G. Michaud, Paris 1962, pp. 39–80

Mousnier 1976: R. Mousnier, *La Classification sociale à Paris au XVIIᵉ et XVIIIᵉ siècles*, Paris 1976

Mousnier 1979: R. Mousnier, *The Institutions of France under the absolute monarchy, 1598–1789. Society and the state*, trans. B. Pearce, Chicago 1979

Mousnier-Labatut-Durand 1965: R. Mousnier, J.-P. Labatut and Y. Durand, *Problèmes de stratification sociale, deux cahiers de la noblesse (1649–1651)*, Paris 1965

M.S.H.P.: *Mémoire de la Société de l'Histoire de Paris et de l'Ile de France*

Mullaney 1983: S. Mullaney, 'Strange Things, Gross Terms, Curious Customs: The Rehearsal of Cultures in the Late Renaissance', *Representations*, vol. iii, 1983, pp. 40–65

Mumford 1938: L. Mumford, *The Culture of Cities*, London 1938

Munro 1982: J. Munro, 'On the Frontiers of Myth: Daphnis and Chloe, the Romance Tradition, the *Théatre Italien* and Marivaux', in *Myth and Legend in French Literature. Essays in Honour of A.J. Steele*, ed. K. Aspley, London 1982, pp. 117–36

Muralt 1725: B.L. de Muralt, *Lettres sur les anglois et les françois (1725)*, repr. Lausanne 1972

Murray Baillie 1967: H. Murray Baillie, 'Etiquette and Planning of the State Apartments in Baroque Palaces', *Archaelogia*, vol. ci, 1967, pp. 169–99

N.A.A.F.: *Nouvelles Archives de l'Art Français*

Nagle 1992: J. Nagle, 'Le faubourg Saint-Germain, démarcation sociale ou intégration', *Cahiers du Centre de Recherche et d'Études sur Paris et l'Ile de France*, no. 38, *Les Quartiers de Paris du Moyen Age au début du XXᵉ Siècle*, March 1992, pp. 139–50

Neel 1770: L.B. Neel, *Histoire de Maurice, comte de Saxe*, 2 vols., Dresden 1770

Nemeitz 1727: J.C. Nemeitz, *Séjour de Paris*, Leyden 1727

Neufforge 1757–72: J.-F. Neufforge, *Recueil élémentaire d'architecture*, 9 vols., Paris 1757–72

Neuschel 1988: K.B. Neuschel, 'Noble Households in the Sixteenth

Century: Material Settings and Human Communities', *French Historical Studies*, vol. xv, no. 4, Fall 1988, pp. 595–622

Newman 1980: R. Newman, 'French Domestic Architecture of the Early Eighteenth Century: The Town Houses of Robert de Cotte', *Journal of the Society of Architectural Historians*, vol. xxxix, 1980, pp. 128–44

New Orleans 1984–5: *The Sun King: Louis XIV and the New World*, Louisiana State Museum, New Orleans 1984–5

New York 1985: *The First Painters of the King. French Royal Taste from Louis XIV to the Revolution*, Stair Sainty Matthiessen, New York 1985

New York 1986: *François Boucher, 1703–1770*, Metropolitan Museum of Art, New York; Detroit Institute of Fine Arts, Detroit; Grand Palais, Paris, 1986–7

New York 1988: *Versailles. The View from Sweden*, Cooper-Hewitt Museum of Art and Design, New York 1988

Nice 1977: *Carle Van Loo, 1705–1765*, Musée Cheret, Nice 1977

Nolhac 1898: A.M.P.G. de Nolhac, *Le Château de Versailles sous Louis XV*, Paris 1898

Nyberg 1969: D. Nyberg, *Oeuvre de Juste Aurèle Meissonnier*, New York 1969

Oberkirch 1970: H.L. Baronne d'Oberkirch, *Mémoires de la baronne d'Oberkirch sur la cour de Louis XVI et la société française avant 1789*, ed. S. Burkard, Paris 1970

Olivier Martin 1938: F. Olivier Martin, *L'Organisation corporative de la France d'ancien-régime*, Paris 1938

Ong 1982: W.J. Ong, *Orality and Literacy. The Technologizing of the Word*, London 1982

Opperman 1968–9: H. Opperman, 'Observations on the Tapestry Designs of J.B. Oudry for Beauvais', *Allen Memorial Art-Museum Bulletin*, vol. xxvi, 1968–9, pp. 49–71

Opperman 1970: H. Opperman, 'The Genesis of the *Chasses Royales*', *Burlington Magazine*, vol. cxii, 1970, pp. 216–27

Opperman 1973: H. Opperman, 'Oudry aux Gobelins', *Revue de l'Art*, no. 22, 1973, pp. 57–65

Opperman 1977: H. Opperman, *Jean-Baptiste Oudry (1686–1755)*, 2 vols. London 1977

Palissy 1880: B. Palissy, *Les Oeuvres de B. Palissy*, ed. A. France, Paris 1880

Panofsky 1972: E. Panofsky, *Studies in Iconology. Humanistic Themes in the Art of the Renaissance*, New York 1972

Panthier 1930: E. Panthier, 'L'appartment de la duchesse du Maine à Sceaux', *Bulletin des Amis de Sceaux*, 1930, pp. 70–85

Papillon n.d.: J.-B. Papillon, *Oeuvres*, 4 vols. n.p., n.d.

Papillon de La Ferté 1776: D.P.J. Papillon de la Ferté, *Extraits des différents ouvrages publiés sur la vie des peintres*, 2 vols., Paris 1776

Papillon de la Ferté 1887: D.P.J. Papillon de la Ferté, *L'Administration des Menus. Journal de Papillon de La Ferté, intendant et contrôleur de l'argenterie, Menus Plaisirs et affaires de la Chambre du Roi (1756–80)*, ed. E. Boysse, Paris 1887

Pappas 1979: J.N. Pappas, 'Voltaire et le luxe: une mise au point', in *Enlightenment studies in honour of Lester G. Crocker*, eds. A.J. Bingham and V.W. Topazio, Oxford 1979, pp. 221–30

Pardailhé-Galabrun 1988: A. Pardailhé-Galabrun, *La Naissance de l'intime. 3000 foyers parisiens, XVIIᵉ–XVIIIᵉ siècles*, Paris 1988

Pardaillan II de Gondrin 1728: *Consultation. Le conseil sousigné qui a vû le contract de marriage de M. le duc d'Epernon, depuis duc d'Antin, du 28 octobre 1722, contenant donation avec substitution par M. le duc d'Antin, ayeul à M. le duc d'Epernon, son petit-fils, de l'hôtel d'Antin,* *meubles y étant, & qui y trouveroient au décès, insinué seulement en 1728*, n.p., n.d. (B.N. f° Fm 317)

Paris 1728: *Declaration du roy concernant les limites de Paris*, Fontainbleau 28/ix/1728

Paris 1950: *Claude III Audran (1658–1734), dessins du Nationalmuseum de Stockholm*, Bibliothèque Nationale, Paris 1950

Paris 1966: *Les Gobelins. Trois siècles de tapisserie*, Mobilier National, Paris 1966

Paris 1967: *Trois siècles de papiers-peints*, Musée des Arts Décoratifs, Paris 1967

Paris 1967²: *J.-P. Mariette, le cabinet d'un grand amateur*, Musée du Louvre, Paris 1967

Paris 1977: *Collection de Louis XIV, dessins, albums, manuscrits*, Orangerie, Paris 1977

Paris 1978: *Jardins en France, 1760–1820*, Caisse Nationale des Monuments Historiques et des Sites, Paris 1978

Paris 1979: *La Rue de Grenelle*, Musée-galerie de la S.E.I.T.A., Paris 1979

Paris 1981: *La Rue de Varenne*, Musée Rodin, Paris 1981

Paris 1982: *Les Gabriels*, Hôtel de Rohan, Paris 1982

Paris 1982²: *Jean-Baptiste Oudry 1686–1755*, Grand Palais, Paris 1982–3

Paris 1982–3: *L'Atelier de Desportes à la manufacture de Sèvres*, Musée du Louvre, Paris 1982–3

Paris 1983: *La Rue de Lille*, Institut Néerlandais, Paris 1983

Paris 1984: *La Rue Saint-Dominique*, Musée Rodin, Paris 1984

Paris 1984²: *Jean-François de Troy: l'Histoire d'Esther*, Palais Tokyo, Paris 1984

Paris 1984–5: *Diderot et l'art de Boucher à David*, Hôtel de la Monnaie, Paris 1984–5

Paris 1985: *Versailles à Stockholm. Dessins du Nationalmuseum; peintures, meubles et arts décoratifs des collections Suédois et Danoises*, Hôtel de Marles, Paris 1985

Paris 1985–6: *Le Brun à Versailles*, Musée du Louvre, Paris 1985–6

Paris 1986: *Germain Boffrand, 1667–1754. L'aventure d'un architecte indépendant*, Musée Carnavalet, Paris 1986

Paris 1987: *Subleyras, 1699–1749*, Musée du Luxembourg, Paris 1987

Paris 1987²: *La Rue de l'Université*, Institut Néerlandais, Paris 1987

Paris 1987³: *Palais Bourbon, sa place*, Institut Néerlandais, Paris 1987

Paris 1987⁴: *Desseins Français du XVIIIᵉ siècle de Watteau à Lemoyne*, Musée du Louvre, Paris 1987

Paris 1988: *Le Palais royal*, Musée Carnavalet, Paris 1988

Paris 1989: *Le Peintre, le roi, le héros: l'Andromède de Pierre Mignard*, Dossiers du Departement des Peintures, no. 37, Musée du Louvre, Paris 1989

Paris 1989²: *Seicento: le siècle de Caravage et les collections françaises*, Grand Palais, Paris 1988–9

Paris 1990: *La Rue du Bac*, ed. B. Pons and A. Forray-Carlier, Paris 1990

Paris 1990–91: *Vouet*, Grand Palais, Paris 1990–91

Paris-Privilèges 1716: *Au Roy et à nosseigneurs les commissaires députez par l'Arrest du Conseil d'Etat*, 28/xi/1716 (B.N. f° Fm 1253)

Park-Daston 1981: K. Park and L.J. Daston, 'Unnatural Conceptions: The Study of Monsters in Sixteenth- and Seventeenth-century France and England', *Past and Present*, vol. xcii, 1981, pp. 20–54

Parker 1979: H.T. Parker, *The Bureau of Manufactures During the*

French Revolution and Under Napoleon. The Bureau of Commerce in 1781 and its Policies with Respect to French Industry, Durham, N.C., 1979

Parker 1969: J. Parker, 'The Hôtel de Varengeville Room and the Room from the Palais de Paar: A Magnificent Donation', *Metropolitan Museum of Art Bulletin*, vol. xxviii, no. 3, Nov. 1969, pp. 129–46

Patte 1754: P. Patte, *Discours sur l'architecture*, Paris 1754

Patte 1765: P. Patte, *Monuments érigés à la gloire de Louis XV*, Paris 1765

Patterson 1988: A. Patterson, *Pastoral and Ideology. Virgil to Valéry*, Oxford 1988

Payne 1979: H.C. Payne, 'Elite Versus Popular Mentality in the Eighteenth Century', *Studies in Eighteenth-Century Culture*, vol. viii, 1979, pp. 3–32

Pelpel 1980: L. Pelpel, *La Formation architectural au XVIIIᵉ siècle en France*, Paris 1980

Pérez 1980: M.F. Pérez, 'Soufflot et la création de l'école de dessin de Lyon 1751–80', in *Soufflot et l'architecture des lumières*, Paris 1980, pp. 108–13

Pérez-Gómez 1983: A. Pérez-Gómez, *Architecture and the Crisis of Modern Science*, Cambridge, Mass., 1983

Pernety 1757: A.-J. Pernety, *Dictionnaire portatif de la peinture, sculpture et gravure*, Paris 1757

Pérouse de Montclos 1982: J.-M. Pérouse de Montclos, *L'Architecture à la française, XVIᵉ, XVIIᵉ, XVIIIᵉ siècles*, Paris 1982

Perrault 1690: Ch. Perrault, *Le Cabinet des beaux-arts, ou receuil d'estampes gravées d'après les tableaux d'un plafond ou les arts sont représentés avec l'explication de ces mêmes tableaux*, Paris 1690

Perrault 1688–97: Ch. Perrault, *Parralèle des anciens et des modernes*, 4 vols., Paris 1688–97

Perrault 1843: Ch. Perrault, *Mémoires, Contes et autres œuvres*, ed. P.L. Jacob, Paris 1843

Perrault 1671: Cl. Perrault, *Mémoires pour servir à l'histoire des plantes*, Paris 1671

Perrault 1671–6: Cl. Perrault, *Mémoires pour servir à l'histoire naturelle des animaux*, Paris 1671–6

Perrault 1684: Cl. Perrault, *Les Dix livres d'architecture de Vitruve corrigé et traduits en 1684 par Claude Perrault* (1684) repr. Liège 1979

Perrot 1973: J.C. Perrot, 'Rapports sociaux et villes au XVIIIᵉ siècle', in *Ordres et classes*, ed. D. Roche, Colloque d'Histoire Sociale, Saint Cloud 24–5 May 1967, Paris 1973, pp. 141–66

Perrot 1975: J.C. Perrot, *Genèse d'une ville moderne. Caen au XVIIIᵉ siècle*, 2 vols., Paris 1975

Petity 1767: J.R. Abbé de Petity, *L'Encyclopédie élémentaire*, 2 vols., Paris 1767

Peuchet 1799–1800: J. Peuchet, *Dictionnaire universel de la géographie commerçante*, 5 vols., Paris 1799–1800

Pevsner 1940: N. Pevsner, *Academies Past and Present*, Cambridge 1940

Picon 1989: A. Picon, *Claude Perrault*, Paris 1989

Piganiol de La Force 1765: Piganiol de La Force, *Description de la ville de Paris et de ses environs*, 10 vols., Paris 1765

Piles 1699: R. de Piles, *Abrégé de la vie des peintres*, Paris 1699

Pinault 1984: M. Pinault, 'Diderot et les illustrateurs de l'Encyclopédie', *Revue de l'Art*, no. 66, 1984, pp. 17–38

Piron 1776: A. Piron, *Oeuvres complettes d'Alexis Piron*, 9 vols., Paris 1776

Pitsch 1949: M. Pitsch, *La Vie populaire à Paris au XVIIIᵉ siècle*, Paris 1949

Pitt-Rivers 1965: J. Pitt-Rivers, 'Honour and Social Status', in *Honour and Shame. The Values of Mediterranean Society*, ed. J.G. Peristiany, London 1965, pp. 19–77

Pluche 1732–51: N.A. Pluche, *Le Spectacle de la nature*, 8 vols., Paris 1732–51

Pluquet 1786: F.A. Pluquet, *Traité Philosophique et politque sur le luxe*, 2 vols., Paris 1786

Plutarch 1721: Plutarch, *Les Vies des hommes illustres de Plutarque*, trans. M. Dimier, 8 vols., Paris 1921

Poète 1910: M. Poète, *Formation et évolution de Paris*, Paris 1910

Poisson 1987: G. Poisson, 'La petite cour de Sceaux', *Historia*, no. 488, Aug. 1987, pp. 40–54

Poisson 1973: J.-P. Poisson, 'Introduction à une étude statistique de la situation socio-économique des artistes parisiens sous l'ancien-régime (peintres, desssinateurs et graveurs de la Iʳᵉ moitié du XVIIIᵉ siècle)', *B.S.H.A.F.* 1973, pp. 363–6

Poisson 1978: J.-P. Poisson, 'L'insertion des artistes parisiens dans la société globale d'après les actes notoriés (1700–1750)', *Journal de la Société de Statistiques de Paris*, vol. cxix, no. 4, 1978, pp. 387–9

Pomian 1976: K. Pomian, 'Médailles/coquilles = érudition/philisophie', Transactions of the IVth International Congress on the Enlightenment, vol. iv, *S.V.E.C.* 1976, pp. 1677–1703

Pomian 1979: K. Pomian, 'Marchands, connoisseurs, curieux à Paris au XVIIIᵉ siècle', *Revue de l'Art*, no. 43, 1979, pp. 23–36

Pons 1983: B. Pons, 'Les Boiseries de l'hôtel Cressart – 18 place Vendôme, au J. Paul Getty Museum', *J. Paul Getty Museum Journal*, vol. xi, 1983, pp. 67–86

Pons 1985: B. Pons, *De Paris à Versailles, 1699–1736. Les sculpteurs ornemanistes parisiens et l'art décoratif des Bâtiments du Roi*, Strasbourg [1985]

Pons 1987: B. Pons, 'Les cadres français du XVIIIᵉ siècle et leurs ornements', *Revue de l'Art*, no. 76, 1987, pp. 41–50

Pons 1987²: B. Pons, 'Un collaborateur de Chalgrin: François-Joseph Duret (1729–1816), sculpteur en ornement et sculpteur figuriste. Son livre-journal de 1767 à 1806', *B.S.H.A.F.*, 1985 (1987), pp. 137–78

Pons 1991: B. Pons, 'Le château du duc d'Antin, surintendant des bâtiments du roi, à Petit-Bourg', *B.S.H.A.F.*, 1987 (1991), pp. 55–90

Pons 1991²: B. Pons, 'Le décor de l'appartement du Grand Dauphin au château neuf de Meudon (1709)', *G.B.A.*, vol. cvii, February 1991, pp. 59–76

Pons 1992: B. Pons, 'Jacques Verberckt (1704–1771), sculpteur des bâtiments du roi', *G.B.A.*, vol. cxix, April 1992, pp. 173–88

Populus 1930: B. Populus, *Claude Gillot (1673–1722). Catalogue de l'œuvre gravée*, Paris 1930

Posner 1982: D. Posner, 'The Swinging Women of Watteau and Fragonard', *Art Bulletin*, vol. lxiv, no. 1, March 1982, pp. 75–88

Posner 1984: D. Posner, *Antoine Watteau*, London 1984

Potain 1749: Potain, *Détails des ouvrages de menuiserie pour les bâtimens*, Paris 1749

Préaud-Casselle-Grivel-Le Bitouzé 1987: M. Préaud, P. Casselle, M. Crivel and C. Le Bitouzé, *Dictionnaire des éditeurs d'estampes à Paris sous l'ancien régime*, Paris 1987

Pris 1975: C. Pris, *La Manufacture des glaces de Saint-Gobain, 1665–*

1830, 2 vols., Lille 1975

Pris 1977: C. Pris, 'La glace en France au XVIIe et XVIIIe siècles. Monopole et liberté d'entreprise dans une industrie de pointe sous l'ancien-régime', *Revue d'Histoire Economique et Sociale*, vol. lv, no. 1–2, 1977, pp. 5–23

Pronteau 1966: J. Pronteau, *Le Numérotage des rues de Paris*, Paris 1966

Pronteau 1978: T. Pronteau, 'Le travail des limites de la ville et faubourgs de Paris', *Annuaire de l'Ecole Pratique des Hautes Etudes*, IVe Section, 1978, pp. 707–45

Puttfarken 1985: T. Puttfarken, *Roger de Piles' Theory of Art*, New Haven and London 1985

P.-V. 1875–92: *Procès-Verbaux de l'Académie Royale de Peinture et de Sculpture, 1648–1792*, ed. A. de Montaiglon, 10 vols., Paris 1875–92

P.-V.A. 1911–29: *Procès-Verbaux de l'Académie Royale d'Architecture, 1671–1793*, ed. H. Lemmonier, 10 vols., Paris 1911–29

R.A. 1763: *Arrest de la cour du Parlement en faveur des artistes logés aux galeries du Louvre*, 20/viii/1763 (B.N. 8° z Le Senne 6592)

R.A.A.M.: *Revue de l'Art Ancien et Moderne*

R.A.-A.S.L. 1762: *Mémoire pour les artistes des galeries du Louvre intervenans. Contre les directeurs et gardes de la communauté des maîtres peintres & sculpteurs à Paris, intimés. En présence du sieur Pourvoieur, apprentif en l'art de peinture et l'un des artistes logés aux galeries du Louvre, appelant*, Paris [1762] (V&A 20. T)

Rabreau 1983: D. Rabreau, 'L'Opéra du mont olympe en 1734, à propos d'un projet de Gilles-Marie Oppenord', in *Rameau en Auvergne, receuil établi et présenté par Jean-Louis Jam*, Clermont-Ferrand 1983, pp. 165–91

Rambaud 1964–71: M. Rambaud, *Documents du Minutier Central concernant l'histoire de l'art (1700–1750)*, 2 vols., Paris 1964–71

Ranum 1969: O. Ranum, 'The Court and Capital of Louis XIV: Some Definitions and Reflections', in *Louis XIV and the Craft of kingship*, ed. J.C. Rule, Englewood Cliffs 1969, pp. 265–85

Ranum 1980: O. Ranum, *Artisans of Glory*, Chapel Hill 1980

Ranum 1980^2: O. Ranum, 'Courtesy, Absolutism and the Rise of the French State, 1630–1660', *J.M.H.*, vol. lii, 1980, pp. 426–51

Rapin 1725: R. Rapin, *Oeuvres*, 3 vols., Paris 1725

Rapoport 1969: A. Rapoport, *House, Form and Culture*, Englewood Cliffs 1969

Rapoport 1977: A. Rapoport, *Human Aspects of Urban Form*, Oxford 1977

Raunié 1879: M.A.A.E. Raunié, *Chausonnier Historique du XVIIIe siècle*, 10 vols., Paris 1879

Réau 1946: L. Réau, *Le Rayonnement de Paris au XVIIIe siècle*, Paris 1946

Reddy 1984: W.M. Reddy, *The Rise of Market Culture. The Textile Trade and French Society, 1750–1900*, Cambridge 1984

Reddy 1987: M. Reddy, *Money and Liberty in Modern Europe. A Critique of Historical Understanding*, Cambridge 1987

Rémond de Saint-Mard 1734: T. Rémond de Saint-Mard, *Réflexions sur la poésie*, Paris 1734

Reuterswärd 1964: P. Reuterswärd, 'Drawings by Claude II Audran', *Master Drawings*, vol. ii, no. 2, 1964, pp. 142–52

Réveillon 1789: J.B. Réveillon, *Exposé justificatif pour le sieur Réveillon, entrepreneur de la manufacture royale des papiers peints, faubourg Saint-Antoine*, Paris 1789

Revel 1987: J. Revel, 'Les Corps et communautés', in *The French Revolution and the Creation of Modern Political Culture*, vol. i, *The Political Culture of the Old Regime*, ed. K.M. Baker, Oxford 1987, pp. 225–42

Rey 1819: Rey, *Observations et recherches sur l'impression des fonds propres à recevoir la peinture*, Paris 1819

R.H.M.C.: *Revue d'Histoire Moderne et Contemporaine*

Richelet 1692: P. Richelet, *Dictionnaire françois*, Geneva 1692

Richelet 1769: P. Richelet, *Dictionnaire de la langue françoise*, 3 vols., Lyon 1769

Robin 1971: R. Robin, 'Fief et seigneurie dans le droit et l'ideologie juridique à la fin du XVIIIe siècle', *Annales Historiques de la Révolution Française*, vol. ccvi, Oct.–Dec. 1971, pp. 554–602

Robin 1975: R. Robin, *La Société française en 1789*, Paris 1975

Roche 1962: D. Roche, 'Recherches sur la noblesse parisienne au milieu du XVIIIe siècle: la noblesse du Marais', *Actes du 86e Congrès National des Sociétés Savantes*, 1962, pp. 541–78

Roche 1978: D. Roche, *Le Siècle des lumières en province: académies et académiciens provinciaux, 1680–1789*, Paris 1978

Roche 1981: D. Roche, *Le Peuple de Paris. Essai sur la culture populaire du XVIIIe siècle*, Paris 1981

Roche 1957: S. Roche, *Mirrors*, trans. C. Duckworth, London 1957

Rocheblave 1893: S. Rocheblave, *Les Cochin*, Paris 1893

Rocheblave 1889: S. Rocheblave, *Essai sur le comte de Caylus, l'homme, l'artiste, l'antiquaire*, Paris 1889

Rochester 1987: *La Grande manière. Historical and Religious Painting in France, 1700–1800*, Memorial Art Gallery of the University of Rochester, Rochester, N.J., 1987

Rochette de La Morlière 1751: C.J.L.A. Rochette de la Morlière, *Angola*, Paris 1751

Roger 1980: J. Roger, 'The Living World', in *The Ferment of Knowledge. Studies in the Historiography of Eighteenth-century Science*, eds. G.S. Rousseau and R. Porter, Cambridge 1980

Roland de La Platière 1776: J.M. Roland de La Platiere, *Dictionnaire de l'industrie ou collection raisonnée des procédées utiles dans les sciences & dans les arts*, 3 vols., Paris 1776

Roland de Virloys 1770–71: C.F. Roland de Virloys, *Dictionnaire d'architecture*, 3 vols., Paris 1770–71

Roland Michel 1976: M. Roland Michel, 'Le cabinet de Bonnier de La Mosson et la participation de Lajoue à son décor', *B.S.H.A.F.* 1975 (1976), pp. 211–21

Roland Michel 1976^2: M. Roland Michel, 'Représention de l'exotisme dans la peinture en France de la première moitié du XVIIIe siècle', *Transactions of the IVth International Congress on the Enlightenment*, vol. iv, *S.V.E.C.*, 1976, pp. 1437–59

Roland Michel 1979: M. Roland Michel, 'Eighteenth-century Decorative Painting: Some False Assumptions', *British Journal for Eighteenth-Century Studies*, vol. ii, no. 2, Spring 1979, pp. 1–36

Roland Michel 1981: M. Roland Michel, 'François-Thomas Mondon, artiste "rocaille" méconnu', *B.S.H.A.F.*, 1978 (1981), pp. 150–58

Roland Michel 1982: M. Roland Michel, 'L'ornement rocaille: quelques questions', *Revue de l'Art*, no. 55, 1982, pp. 66–75

Roland Michel 1984: M. Roland Michel, *Lajoue et l'art rocaille*, Geneva 1984

Roland Michel 1984^2: M. Roland Michel, *Watteau: An Artist of the Eighteenth Century*, New York 1984

Roland Michel-Rambaud 1977: M. Roland Michel and M. Rambaud, 'On the Subject of Some Works Exhibited by the

Galerie Cailleux at the Burlington International Fine Art Fair', *Burlington Magazine*, vol. cxix, Dec. 1977 (supplement), pp. i–viii

Rollin 1730: C. Rollin, *De la manière d'enseigner et d'étudier les belles lettres par rapport à l'esprit & au cœur*, 4 vols., Paris 1730

Rollin 1738–41: C. Rollin, *Histoire Romaine depuis la fondation de Rome jusqu'à la bataille d'Actium, c'est à dire, à la fin de la république*, 7 vols., Paris 1938–41

Roman 1982: C. Roman, 'Les pauvres à Paris', *Annales E.S.C.*, July–Aug. 1982, pp. 729–63

Rondelet 1830: J. Rondelet, *Traité Théorique et pratique de l'art de bâtir*, 3 vols., Paris 1830

Ronfort 1989: J.-R. Ronfort, 'Science and Luxury: Two Acquisitions by the J. Paul Getty Museum', *J. Paul Getty Museum Journal*, vol. xvii, 1989, 47–82

Rosenberg 1978: P. Rosenberg, 'Louis-Joseph Le Lorrain (1715–1759)', *Revue de l'Art*, nos. 40–41, 1978, pp. 178–202

Rosenberg 1984: P. Rosenberg, *Vies Anciennes de Watteau*, Paris 1984

Rosenberg-Babelon 1968: P. Rosenberg and J.P. Babelon, 'Les dessus de portes de l'hôtel de Soubise. A propos de deux retrouvés', *B.S.H.A.F.*, 1967 (1968), pp. 211–16

Rosenfeld 1979: M. Rosenfeld, 'Nicolas Largillière's portrait of the marquise de Dreux-Brézé', *Apollo*, vol. cix, 1979, pp. 202–7

Ross 1975: E. Ross, 'The Debate on Luxury in Eighteenth-century France: A Study in the Language of Opposition to Change', PhD University of Chicago 1975

Ross 1976: E. Ross, 'Mandeville, Melon and Voltaire: The Origins of the Luxury Controversy in France', *Transactions of the ivth International Congress on the Enlightenment*, vol. v, *S.V.E.C.*, 1976, pp. 1879–1913

Rothkrug 1965: L. Rothkrug, *Opposition to Louis XIV: the Political and Social Origins of the French Revolution*, Princeton 1965

Roubo 1772: A.J. Roubo, *L'Art du menuisier en meubles*, Paris 1772

Rouen 1970: *Jean Restout, 1692–1768*, Musée des Beaux-Arts, Rouen 1970

Rousseau 1753: J.J. Rousseau, *Narcisse, ou l'amant de lui même*, [Paris] 1753

Rousseau 1946: J.J. Rousseau, *Discours sur les sciences et les arts*, ed. G. Havens, New York 1946

Rykwert 1980: J. Rykwert, *The First Moderns. The Architects of the Eighteenth Century*, Cambridge, Mass., 1980

Rykwert 1981: J. Rykwert, *On Adam's House in Paradise. The Idea of the Primitive Hut in Architectural History*, London 1981

Rykwert 1988: J. Rykwert, 'On the Transmission of Architectural Theory', in *Les Traités d'architecture de la renaissance*, ed. J. Guillaume, Paris 1988, pp. 31–48

Sabatier-Vignaud-Culand 1983: F. Sabatier, B. du Vignaud and P. Culand, *Châteaux, abbayes et jardins historiques ouvert au public*, Paris 1983

Sabel-Zeitlin 1985: C. Sabel and J. Zeitlin, 'Historical Alternatives to Mass Production: Politics, Markets and Technology in Nineteenth-century Industrialization', *Past and Present*, vol. cviii, Aug. 1985, pp. 133–76

Sacy 1715: L. de Sacy, *Traité de la gloire*, The Hague 1715

Sahlins 1976: M. Sahlins, *Culture and Practical Reason*, Chicago 1976

Sahlins 1981: M. Sahlins, *Historical Metaphors and Mythical Realities*, Ann Arbor 1981

Sahlins 1985: M. Sahlins, *Islands of History*, London 1985

Saint-Didier 1716: I. Limognon de Saint-Didier, *Le Voyage au Parnasse*, 2 vols., Rotterdam 1716

Saint-Evremond 1739: C. Marguetel de Saint Denis de Saint-Evremond, *Oeuvres*, 5 vols., Paris 1739

Saint-Germain 1960: J. Saint-Germain, *Samuel Bernard. Le Banquier des rois*, Paris 1960

Saint-Honoré 1733: *Mémoire pour les habitans du faubourg Saint Honoré*, Paris 1733 (A.N. к 982/98)

Saint-Pierre 1733–41: C.I. Castel, Abbé de Saint-Pierre, *Ouvrajes de politiques*, 16 vols., Rotterdam 1733–41

Saint-Simon 1879–1930: L. de Rouvroy, Duc de Saint-Simon, *Mémoires de M. le duc de Saint-Simon*, eds. A. de Boislisle et al., 43 vols., Paris 1879–1930

Saint-Simon 1974: L. de Rouvroy, Duc de Saint-Simon, *Historical Memoirs of the Duc de Saint-Simon*, ed. L. Norton, 3 vols., London 1974

Saint-Yves 1748: Saint-Yves, *Observations sur les arts et sur quelques morceaux de peinture et de sculpture exposés au Louvre en 1748*, Leyden 1748

Saisselin 1979: R.G. Saisselin, 'Painting and Writing: From the Poetry of Painting to the Writing of the *Dessin Idéal*', *Eighteenth-Century Studies*, vol. xx, no. 2, Spring 1979, pp. 121–47

Saisselin 1981: R.G. Saisselin, 'Neo-classicism: Images of Public Virtue and Realities of Private Luxury', *Art History*, vol. iv, no. 1, March 1981, pp. 14–36

Sanabria 1989: S.L. Sanabria, 'From Gothic to Renaissance Stereotomy: The Design Methods of Philibert de l'Orme and Alonso de Vandelvira', *History of Technology*, 1989, pp. 266–99

San Francisco 1977: *Four Centuries of French Drawings in the Fine Arts Museum of San Francisco*, San Francisco 1977

San Francisco 1987: *French Paintings, 1500–1825. The Fine Arts Museum of San Francisco*, by P. Rosenberg and M.C. Stewart, San Francisco 1987

Sareil 1969: J. Sareil, *Les Tencins. Histoire d'une famille au dix-huitième siècle*, Geneva 1969

Saugrain 1744: C.M. Saugrain, *Code de la librairie et imprimerie de Paris*, Paris 1744

Sauval 1724: H. Sauval, *Histoire et recherches des antiquités de la ville de Paris*, 3 vols., Paris 1724

Savary 1675: J. Savary, *Le Parfait négociant*, Paris 1675

Savary des Bruslons 1744: J. Savary des Bruslons, *Dictionnaire universel du commerce*, 3 vols., Paris 1744

Savignat 1983: J.M. Savignat, *Dessin et architecture du moyen âge au XVIIIe siècle*, Paris 1983

Savot-Blondel 1685: L. Savot, *L'Architecture françoise des bastimens particuliers*, ed. F. Blondel, Paris 1685

Schaffer 1980: S. Schaffer, 'Natural philosophy', in *The Ferment of Knowledge. Studies in the Historiography of Eighteenth-century Science*, eds. G.S. Rousseau and R. Porter, Cambridge 1980

Schaffer 1983: S. Schaffer, 'Natural Philosophy and Public Spectacle', *History of Science*, vol. xxi, no. 51, March 1983, pp. 1–43

Schalk 1986: E. Schalk, *From Valor to Pedigree. Ideas of Nobility in France in the Sixteenth and Seventeenth centuries*, Princeton 1986

Schama 1989: S. Schama, *Citizens: A Chronicle of the French Revolution*, London 1989

Schnapper 1967: A. Schnapper, *Tableaux pour le Trianon de Marbre 1688–1714*, Paris 1967

Schnapper 1968[2]: A. Schnapper, 'Le Grand Dauphin et les tableaux de Meudon', *Revue de l'Art*, no. 1–2, 1968, pp. 57–64

Schnapper 1968: A. Schnapper, 'Musée des Beaux-Arts de Brest. À propos d'une récente acquisition. Houasse et le "cabinet des beaux-arts" de Perrault', *Revue du Louvre*, vol. xviii, 1968, pp. 241–4

Schnapper 1969: A. Schnapper, 'Antoine Coypel – la Galerie d'Enée au Palais Royal', *Revue de l'Art*, no. 5, 1969, pp. 33–42

Schnapper 1974: A. Schnapper, *Jean Jouvenet (1644–1717) et la peinture d'histoire à Paris*, Paris 1974

Schnapper 1978: A. Schnapper, 'Plaidoyer pour un absent: Bon Boullogne (1649–1717)', *Revue de l'Art*, no. 40–41, 1978, pp. 121–40

Scott 1973: B. Scott, 'Pierre Crozat: A Maecenas of the Régence', *Apollo*, vol. xcvii, Jan. 1973, pp. 11–19

Scott 1973: B. Scott, 'La Live de Jully: Pioneer of Neo-classicism', *Apollo*, vol. xcvii, Jan. 1973, pp. 72–77

Scott 1989: K. Scott, 'Hierarchy, Liberty and Order: languages of Art and Institutional Conflict in Paris (1766–1776)', *The Oxford Art Journal*, vol. xii, no. 2, 1989, pp. 59–70

Scoville 1950: W.C. Scoville, *Capitalism and French Glass-making, 1640–1789*, Los Angeles 1950

Scudéry 1698: M. de Scudéry, *Conversations nouvelles sur divers sujets dediées au roy*, 2 vols., Paris 1698

Seba 1734–65: A. Seba, *Locupletissimi rerum naturalium thesauri accurata descriptio, et iconibus artificiosissimis expresso, per universam physices historiam*, 4 vols., Amsterdam 1734–65

Segrais 1700: J.R. de Segrais, *Traduction de l'Eneïde de Virgile par M. de Segrais*, 2nd edn., Amsterdam 1700

Senac de Meilhan 1787: G. Senac de Meilhan, *Considérations sur les richesses et le luxe*, 2 vols., Amsterdam 1787

Sennett 1974: R. Sennett, *The Fall of Public Man*, Cambridge 1974

Sensier 1865: A. Sensier, *Journal de Rosalba Carriera pendant son séjour à Paris*, Paris 1865

Sewell 1974: W.H. Sewell, 'Etats, corps and ordre: Some Notes on the Social Vocabulary of the French Old Regime', in *Sozial Geschichte heute: Festschrift für Hans Rosenberg zum 70*, Göttingen 1974, pp. 49–68

Sewell 1980: W.H. Sewell, *Work and Revolution in France. The Language of Labor from the Old Regime to 1848*, Cambridge 1980

Sewell 1986: W.H. Sewell, 'Visions of Labor: Illustrations of the Mechanical Arts before, in, and after Diderot's *Encyclopédie*', in *Work in France. Representations, Meaning, Organisation and Practice*, eds. S.L. Kaplan and C.J. Koepp, London 1986, pp. 258–86

Shapin 1988: S. Shapin, 'The House of Experiment in Seventeenth-century England', *Isis*, vol. lxxix, 1988, pp. 373–404

Shennan 1979: J.H. Shennan, *Philippe, Duke of Orléans, Regent of France, 1715–1723*, London 1979

Shepherd 1986: E.J. Shepherd, 'Social and Geographical Mobility of the Eighteenth-century Artisan: An Analysis of the Guild Receptions in Dijon, 1700–1790', in *Work in France. Representation, Meaning, Organization and Practice*, eds. S.L. Kaplan and C.J. Koepp, London 1986, pp. 97–130

Sheriff 1986: M.D. Sheriff, 'For Love or Money? Rethinking Fragonard', *Eighteenth-Century Studies*, vol. xix, 1986, pp. 333–48

Sièyes 1888: E. Sièyes, *Qu'est-ce-que le Tiers Etat? Précédé de l'essai sur les privilèges*, ed. E. Champion, Paris 1888

Simmel 1950: G. Simmel, *The Sociology of Georg Simmel*, trans. K.H. Wolff, New York 1950

Six-Corps 1716: *Au Roy & à nosseigneurs les commissaires députez par l'Arrest de Conseil d'Etat du 28 novembre 1716*, Paris 1716 (B.N. f° FM 1253)

Skinner 1980: Q. Skinner, *The Foundations of Modern Political Thought*, 2 vols., Cambridge 1980

Snyders 1965: G. Snyders, *La Pédagogie en France au XVIIᵉ et XVIIIᵉ siècles*, Paris 1965

Soboul 1965: A. Soboul, 'Problèmes de l'apprentissage (seconde moitié du XVIIIᵉ siècle). Réalités sociales et nécéssités économiques', VIIIᵉ Colloque d'Histoire sur *L'Artisanat et l'apprentissage*, Aix-en-Provence 1965, pp. 7–23

Sombart 1967: W. Sombart, *Luxury and Capitalism*, Ann Arbor 1967

Somoyault 1979: J.P. Somoyault, *André-Charles Boulle et sa famille*, Geneva 1979

Sonenscher 1983: M. Sonenscher, 'Work and Wages in Paris in the Eighteenth Century', in *Manufacture in Town and Country Before the Factory*, eds. M. Berg, P. Hudson and M. Sonenscher, Cambridge 1983, pp. 147–72

Sonenscher 1987: M. Sonenscher, 'Journeymen, the Courts and the French Trades, 1781–1791', *Past and Present*, vol. cxiv, Feb. 1987, pp. 77–109

Sonenscher 1987²: M. Sonenscher, *The Hatters of Eighteenth-century France*, London 1987

Sonenscher 1989: M. Sonenscher, *Work and Wages. Natural Law, Politics and the Eighteenth-century Trades*, Cambridge 1989

Sorel 1671: C. Sorel, *Les Récréations galantes*, Paris 1671

Souchal 1967: F. Souchal, *Les Slodtz*, Paris 1967

Souchal 1969: F. Souchal, 'Jean Aubert, architecte des Bourbon Condé', *Revue de l'Art*, no. 6, 1969, pp. 29–38

Souchal 1980: F. Souchal, *Les Frères Coustou*, Paris 1980

Sourches 1882–93: L.-F. Du Bouchet, Marquis de Sourches, *Mémoires*, eds. G.-J. de Cosnac et al., 13 vols., Paris 1882–93

Stafford 1981: B.M. Stafford, 'Towards Romantic Landscape Perception: Illustrated Travels and the Rise of "Singularity" as an Aesthetic Category', *Studies on the Eighteenth-Century*, vol. x, 1981, pp. 17–75

Standen 1975: E. Standen, '*The Memorable Judgement of Sancho Panza*: A Gobelins Tapestry in the Metropolitan Museum', *Metropolitan Museum of Art Journal*, vol. x, 1975, pp. 97–106

Standen 1976: E. Standen, 'The Story of the Emperor of China: A Beauvais Tapestry Series', *Metropolitan Museum of Art Journal*, vol. xi, 1976, pp. 103–17

Standen 1977: E. Standen, '*Fêtes Italiennes*: Beauvais Tapestries after Boucher in the Metropolitan Museum of Art', *Metropolitan Museum of Art Journal*, vol. xii, 1977, pp. 107–30

Standen 1977²: E. Standen, 'Some Notes on the Cartoons used at the Gobelins and Beauvais Manufactories in the Eighteenth century', *J. Paul Getty Museum Journal*, vol. iv, 1977, pp. 25–8

Standen 1984–5: E. Standen, 'The *Amours des Dieux*: A Series of Beauvais Tapestries after Boucher', *Metropolitan Museum of Art Journal*, vol. xix–xx, 1984–5, pp. 63–84

Standen 1988: E. Standen, 'Ovid's *Métamorphoses*: A Gobelins Tapestry Series', *Metropolitan Museum of Art Journal*, vol. xxiii, 1988, pp. 149–91

Stanton 1980: D.C. Stanton, *The Aristocrat as Art. A Study of the Honnête Homme and the Dandy in Seventeenth and Nineteenth-Century French Literature*, New York 1980

Starobinski 1964: J. Starobinski, *L'Invention de la liberté, 1700–1789*,

Geneva 1964

Stephens 1978: F.G. Stephens, *Catalogue of Political and Personal Satires Preserved in the Department of Prints and Drawings in the British Museum*, vol. ii *1689–1733*, London 1978

Stern 1930: J. Stern, *A l'ombre de Sophie Arnould. François-Joseph Bellanger, architecte des Menus Plaisirs, premier architecte du comte d'Artois*, 2 vols., Paris 1930

Stewart 1992: P. Stewart, *Engraven Desire. Eros, Image, and Text in the French Eighteenth Century*, London 1992

Stoloff 1978: B. Stoloff, 'Role Sociale et fonction économique de l'architecture française sous l'ancien-régime', Thèse d'Etat, Université de Strasbourg, 1978

Strandberg 1962: R. Strandberg, 'Jean-Baptiste Bullet de Chamblain, architecte du roi', *B.S.H.A.F.* 1962, pp. 193–255

Strandberg 1963: R. Strandberg, 'Le château de Champs', *G.B.A.*, vol. lxi, 1963, pp. 81–100

Strandberg 1965: R. Strandberg, 'Les dessins d'architecture de Pierre Bullet pour la place Vendôme et l'hôtel Reich de Pennautier-d'Évreux', *G.B.A.*, vol. lxv, 1965, pp. 71–90

Strandberg 1982: R. Strandberg, 'Dessins et documents inédits concernant les constructions de Jean-Baptiste Colbert, marquis de Torcy pour son hôtel de Paris et ses châteaux de Croissy, Sablé et Bois-Dauphin', *G.B.A.*, vol. xcix, 1982, pp. 131–46

Stryienski 1913: C. Stryienski, *La Galerie du regent Philippe d'Orléans*, Paris 1913

Stuffmann 1964: M. Stuffmann, 'Charles de La Fosse et sa position dans la peinture française à la fin du XVIIᵉ siècle', *G.B.A.*, vol. lxvi, July–Sept. 1964, pp. 1–121

Stuffmann 1968: M. Stuffmann, 'Les Tableaux de la collection de Pierre Crozat', *G.B.A.*, vol. lxxii, July–Sept. 1968, pp. 11–114

Stürmer 1979: M. Stürmer, 'An Economy of Delight: Court Artisans of the Eighteenth Century', *Business History Review*, vol. liii, no. 4, Winter 1979, pp. 496–528

Styles 1988: J. Styles, 'Design for Large-scale Productions in Eighteenth-century Britain' *Oxford Art Journal*, vol. xi, no. 2, 1988, pp. 10–16

S.V.E.C.: *Studies on Voltaire and the Eighteenth Century*

Swarte 1893: V. de Swarte, 'Samuel Bernard, peintre du Roi, académicien, et Samuel Jacques Bernard, surintendant de la Maison de la Reine, amateur d'art', *Réunion des Sociétées des Beaux-Arts des Départements*, vol. xvii, 1893, pp. 287–304

Szambien 1986: W. Szambien, *Symétrie, Goût, caractère. Théorie et terminologie de l'architecture à l'âge classique, 1550–1800*, Paris 1986

Tadgell 1978: C. Tadgell, *Ange-Jacques Gabriel*, London 1978

Talbot 1974: W.S. Talbot, 'Jean-François De Troy: *Pan and Syrinx*', *Cleveland Museum of Art Bulletin*, Oct. 1974, pp. 250–59

Tallard 1756: *Catalogue raisonné des tableaux, sculptures, tant de marbre que de bronze, desseins et estampes de plusieurs grands maîtres, porcelaines anciennes, meubles précieux, bijoux et autres effets qui composent le cabinet de feu Monsieur le duc de Tallard*, Remy & Glomy, Paris 1756

Taralon 1974: J. Taralon, 'Le château de Champs-sur-Marne', *Monuments Historiques de la France*, vol. xx, no. 4, 1974, pp. 49–65

Tate 1968: R.S. Tate, 'Petit de Bachaumont: His Circle and the *Mémoires Secrèts*', *S.V.E.C.*, vol. lxv, 1968, pp. 11–211

Taylor 1982: O. Taylor, 'Voltaire iconoclast: An Introduction to the *Temple du Goût*', *S.V.E.C.*, vol. ccxii, 1982, pp. 7–81

Tellier 1987: L.-N. Tellier, *Face aux Colbert, les Le Tellier, Vauban,*

Turgot et l'avènement du libéralisme, Quebec 1987

Terrasson 1715: J. Terasson, *Dissertation critique sur l'Iliade d'Homère*, 2 vols., Paris 1715

Terrasson 1720: J. Terrasson, *Lettres sur le nouveau système des finances*, Paris 1720

Tessé 1888: M.J.B. René de Froullain, comte de Tessé, *Lettres du maréchal de Tessé*, Paris 1888

Testelin 1853: H. Testelin, *Mémoire pour servir à l'histoire de l'Académie Royale de Peinture et Sculpture depuis 1648 jusqu'en 1664*, ed. A. de Montaiglon, 2 vols., Paris 1853

Teynac-Nolot-Vivien 1982: F. Teynac, P. Nolot, J.-D. Vivien, *Wallpaper. A History*, London 1982

Teyssèdre 1965: B. Teyssèdre, *Roger de Piles et les débats sur le coloris au siècle de Louis XIV*, Paris 1965

Thiery 1986: L.-V. Thiery, *Guide des amateurs et des étrangers à Paris*, 2 vols., Paris 1786–7

Thirion 1895: H. Thirion, *La Vie privée des financiers au dix-huitième siècle*, Paris 1895

Thiry-Druesne 1979: A. Thiry-Druesne, 'L'hôtel Peyrenc de Moras, puis de Boullogne, 23, place Vendôme. Architecture et décoration intérieure', *B.S.H.P.*, 1979, pp. 51–84

Thompson 1967: E.P. Thompson, 'Time, Work-discipline, and Industrial Capitalism', *Past and Present*, vol. xxxviii, 1967, pp. 56–97

Thompson 1974: E.P. Thompson, 'Patrician Society, Plebian Culture', *Journal of Social History*, vol. vii, no. 4, Summer 1974, pp. 382–405

Thompson 1986: M.P. Thompson, 'The History of Fundamental Law in Political Thought from the French Wars of Religion to the American Revolution', *The American Historical Review*, vol. xci, 1986, pp. 1103–28

Thornton 1965: P. Thornton, *Baroque and Rococo Silks*, London 1965

Thornton 1981: P. Thornton, *Seventeenth-century Interior Decoration in England, France and Holland*, New Haven and London 1981

Thrale 1932: *The French Journals of Mrs Thrale and Dr Johnson*, ed. M. Tyson and H. Guppy, Manchester 1932

Tocqueville 1961: A. de Tocqueville, *De la démocratie en Amérique*, ed. H.G. Nicholas, London 1961

Todd 1989: C. Todd, 'French Advertising in the Eighteenth century', *S.V.E.C.*, vol. cclxvi, 1989, pp. 513–47

Toledo 1985: *The Age of Louis XV. French Painting, 1710–1774*, Toledo, Oh., 1985

Tours 1962: *Peintures du XVIIIᵉ siècle au musée des beaux-arts de Tours*, by B. Lossky, Paris 1962

Troyes 1977: *Charles-Joseph Natoire, 1700–1777*, Musée des Beaux-Arts de Troyes, Troyes 1977

Tuck 1979: R. Tuck, *Natural Rights Theories, Their Origin and Development*, Cambridge 1979

Turner 1986: V. Turner, *The Forest of Symbols. Aspects of Ndembu Ritual*, Ithaca 1986

Tyvaert 1974: M. Tyvaert, 'L'image du roi: légitimité et moralité royale dans les histoires de France au XVIIᵉ siècle', *R.H.M.C.*, vol. xxi, Oct.–Dec. 1974, pp. 521–47

Valence 1989: *Hubert Robert et la Révolution*, Musée de Valence 1989

Van Kley 1975: D. Van Kley, *The Jansenists and the Expulsion of the Jesuits*, New Haven 1975

Van Kley 1984: D. Van Kley, *The Damiens Affair*, New Haven 1984

Verlet 1958: P. Verlet, 'Le Commerce des objets d'art et des marchands-merciers à Paris au XVIIIᵉ siècle', *Annales E.S.C.*,

1958, pp. 10–28

Verlet 1965: P. Verlet, *Le Grand Livre de la tapisserie*, Paris 1965

Verlet 1982: P. Verlet, *The Savonnerie: Its history. The Waddesdon Collection*, London 1982

Verlet 1982²: P. Verlet, *Les Meubles français au XVIIIᵉ siècle*, Paris 1982

Verrue 1737: *Catalogue des tableaux de feue Madame la comtesse de Verrue*, Paris 27/iii/1737

Vertot 1720: A. Abbé de Vertot, *Histoire des révolutions arrivé dans le gouvernement de la république romaine*, 2nd edn. 3 vols., The Hague 1720

Vial-Marcel-Girodie 1912: H. Vial, P. Marcel and A. Girodie, *Les Artistes décorateurs du bois*, 2 vols., Paris 1912

Vicherd 1986: C. Vicherd, 'Mazarin ou la tyrannie. Le rejet des pratiques politiques "italiennes" par les Frondeurs', in *La France et l'Italie au temps de Mazarin*, ed. J. Serroy, Grenoble 1986

Vidal 1992: M. Vidal, *Watteau's Painted Conversations*, London 1992

Vitet 1880: L. Vitet, *L'Académie royale de peinture et sculpture, étude historique*, Paris 1880

Vizthum 1966: W. Vizthum, 'La galerie de l'hôtel La Vrillière', *L'Oeil*, vol. cxliv, Dec. 1966, pp. 24–32

Voltaire 1733: F.-M. Arouet de Voltaire, *Le Temple du goût*, Amsterdam 1733

Voltaire 1816: F.-M. Arouet de Voltaire, *Dictionnaire philosophique*, 7 vols., Paris 1816

Von Stackelberg 1970: Von Stackelberg, 'Le "Télémaque travesti" et la naissance du réalisme dans le roman', in *La Régence*, Colloque, Centre Aixoix d'Etudes et de Recherches sur le Dix-Huitième Siècle, Paris 1970, pp. 206–12

Vovelle 1974: M. Vovelle, 'L'élite, ou le mensonge des mots', *Annales E.S.C.*, 1974, pp. 49–72

Ward-Jackson 1972: P. Ward-Jackson, 'Some Mainstreams and Tributaries in European Ornament from 1500 to 1750', *Victoria and Albert Museum Bulletin Reprints*, no. 3, 1972

Ward-Perkins 1956: J.B. Ward-Perkins, 'Nero's Golden House', *Antiquity*, vol. xxx, 1956, pp. 209–19

Washington 1973–4: *François Boucher in North American Collections: 100 Drawings*, National Gallery of Art, Washington 1973–4

Washington 1984: *Antoine Watteau, 1684–1721*, National Gallery of Art, Washington; Grand Palais, Paris; Schloss Charlottenburg, Berlin, 1984–5

Watelet-Levesque 1792: H. Watelet and P.-C. Levesque, *Dictionnaire des arts de peinture, sculpture et gravure*, 3 vols., Paris 1792

Watin 1773: J.F. Watin, *L'Art du peintre doreur, vernisseur*, Paris 1773

Watson 1965: F.J.B. Watson, 'The Paris *Marchands-merciers* and French Eighteenth-century Taste', *Antiques*, vol. lxxxvii, 1965, pp. 347–51

Watson 1969: F.J.B. Watson, 'Recent Museum Acquisitions: A French Eighteenth-century Room for Jerusalem', *Burlington Magazine*, vol. cxi, Dec. 1969, pp. 758–61

Watson 1939: E.C. Watson, 'The Early Days of the Académie des Sciences as Portrayed in the Engravings of Sébastien Le Clerc', *Osiris*, vol. viii, 1939, pp. 556–75

Weigert 1931: R.A. Weigert, 'Les travaux décoratifs de Jean Bérain à l'hôtel de Mailly-Nesles', *B.S.H.A.F.*, 1931, pp. 167–74

Weigert 1937: R.A. Weigert, *Jean I Bérain, dessinateur de la chambre et du cabinet du roi, 1640–1711*, 2 vols., Paris 1937

Weigert 1937²: R.A. Weigert, '*La Tenture des Triomphes Marins* d'après Jean Iᵉʳ Bérain', *B.S.H.A.F.*, 1937, pp. 17–18

Weigert 1950: R.A. Weigert, 'Quelques travaux décoratifs de Claude III Audran', *B.S.H.A.F.*, 1950, pp. 85–93

Weigert 1952: R.A. Weigert, 'Un collaborateur ignoré de Claude III Audran: Christophe Huet décorateur (1700–1759)', *Etudes d'Art du Musée d'Alger*, vol. vii, 1952, pp. 63–78

Weigert 1955: R.A. Weigert, 'L'art décoratif en France: les groteschi ou grotesques, leur adaptation et leur évolution, Jean I Bérain', *L'Information Culturelle et Artistique*, vol. i, 1955, pp. 100–6

Weigert 1960: R.A. Weigert, 'Claude III Audran, père de l'art décoratif', *Médecine de France*, no. 115, 1960, pp. 17–32

Weigert 1967: R.A. Weigert, 'En marge des proverbes de Lagniet', *G.B.A.*, vol. lxx, 1967, pp. 177–84

Weigert-Dupont 1960: R.A. Weigert and J. Dupont, 'Une œuvre de Claude III Audran à Clichy', *Revue des Monuments Historiques de la France*, vol. vi, 1960, pp. 223–32

Weigert-Hernmarck 1964: R.A. Weigert and C. Hernmarck, *L'Art en France et en Suède, 1693–1718. Extraits d'une correspondance entre l'architecte Nicodème Tessin le jeune et Daniel Cronström*, Stockholm 1964

Whitman 1969: N.T. Whitman, 'Myth and Politics: Versailles and the *Fountain of Latona*', in *Louis XIV and the Craft of Kingship*, ed. J.C. Rule, Englewood Cliffs 1969, pp. 286–301

[Wicquefort] 1673: A. van Wicquefort, *Avis Fidelle aux veritables Hollandois. Touchant ce qui c'est passé dans les villages de Bodegrave & Swammerdam, & les cruautés inouïes que les français y ont exercées*, The Hague 1673

Wiebenson 1978: D. Wiebensen, *The Picturesque Garden in France*, Princeton 1978

Wildenstein 1966: D. Wieldenstein, *Documents inédits sur les artistes français du XVIIIᵉ siècle*, Paris 1966

Wildenstein 1982: D. Wildenstein, 'Les tableaux italiens dans les catalogues de ventes Parisiennes du XVIIIᵉ siècle', *G.B.A.*, vol. c, 1982, pp. 1–48

Wildenstein 1921: G. Wildenstein, *Rapports d'experts, 1712–1791. Procès-verbaux d'expertises d'oeuvres d'art extraits du fonds du Châtelet, aux Archives Nationales*, Paris 1921

Wildenstein 1924: G. Wildenstein, *Lancret*, Paris 1924

Wildenstein 1956: G. Wildenstein, 'Le goût pour la peinture dans la cercle de la bourgeoisie parisienne autour de 1700', *G.B.A.*, vol. xlviii, 1956, pp. 113–20

Wilhelm 1967: J. Wilhelm, 'Le grand cabinet chinois de l'hôtel de Richelieu, place Royale', *Bulletin du Musée Carnavalet*, 1967, pp. 2–15

Wilhelm 1975: J. Wilhelm, 'Deux plafonds peints par Hugues Taraval à l'hôtel Grimod d'Orsay', *B.S.H.A.F.*, 1974 (1975), pp. 123–30

Wilhelm 1975²: J. Wilhelm, 'Le Salon du graveur Gilles Demarteau peint par François Boucher et son atelier avec le concours de Fragonard et de J.-B. Huet', *Bulletin du Musée Carnavalet*, 1975, no. 1, pp. 4–20

Wilson 1983: G. Wilson, 'Postscript: The Recent History of the Panelled Room from the Hôtel Herlaut', *J. Paul Getty Museum Journal*, vol. xi, 1983, pp. 86–8

Wrigley 1983: R.B. Wrigley, 'Criticism of Contemporary Art in Eighteenth-century France (1737–1789): A Thematic Study', PhD Thesis, Oxford University 1983

Yarendi 1973: M. Yarendi, 'Journalisme et histoire contemporaire à l'époque de Bayle', *History and Theory*, vol. xii, 1973, pp. 208–

Yates 1947: F. Yates, *The French Academies of the Sixteenth Century*, London 1947

Young 1769: A. Young, *Letters Concerning the Present State of the French Nation*, London 1969

Zafran 1984: M. Zafran, *European Art in the High Museum*, Atlanta 1984

Zeller 1957: G. Zeller, 'Une notion de caractère historico-social: la dérogeance', *Cahiers Internationaux de Sociologie*, vol. xxii, 1957, pp. 40–74

Zukin 1977: S. Zukin, 'Mimesis in the Origins of Bourgeois Culture', *Theory and Society*, vol. iv, 1977, pp. 333–58

Index

332

Photograph Sources and Credits

Angers, Musée des Beaux-Arts   126, 221 (photo: Pierre David)

Atlanta, The High Museum   28

Baltimore, Walters Art Gallery   268

Berlin, Kunstbibliothek, Staatliche Museen   136, 188, 205, 208

Besançon, Musée d'Art et d'Archéologie   257

Boston, Museum of Fine Arts   162 (bequest of the Maria Antoinette Evans Fund)

Chicago, The Art Institute   30

London, copyright of The British Library   16, 17, 18, 54, 67, 85, 87, 88, 105, 108, 167, 182, 186, 187, 204, 252, 270

London, The British Museum, reproduced by permission of the Trustees   47, 68, 96, 97, 139, 150, 191, 192, 193, 221, 243, 244, 254, 255, 256, 258, 259, 266

London, by courtesy of Christie's   44, 110, 122, 198, 199

London, The Conway Library   3, 14, 15, 19, 20, 70, 86, 90, 92, 94, 100, 109, 112, 118, 120, 124, 180, 219, 226, 228, 229, 230, 231, 233, 234, 271, 272

London, Courtauld Institute of Art, Book Library   51 a–d, 121, 296

London, Hazlitt, Gooden and Fox   129 a–b

London, The Heim Gallery   141, 251

London, The Royal Academy   36

London, by courtesy of Sotheby's   116, 250

London, The Victoria and Albert Museum   77, 78, 107, 143, 276, 283, 290, 291, 292, 293, 295

London, The Wallace Collection, reproduced by permission of the Trustees   170, 173, 286, 289

London, The Witt Library   51, 121, 135, 138, 154, 161, 169, 200, 250

Malibu, J. Paul Getty Museum   43

Meudon, Musée d'Art et d'Histoire   123

Montpellier, Musée Fabre   220, 222

Neuchâtel, Musée d'Art et d'Histoire   262, 263, 264, 265

New Haven, Beinecke Rare Book and Manuscript Library, Yale University   202

New Orleans, New Orleans Museum of Art   29

New York, The Cooper Hewitt, The Smithsonian's Museum of Design/Art Resource   74, 83, 93, 111, 197, 240, 269, 280

New York, The Metropolitan Museum of Art   37, 39, 40, 41, 59, 61, 131, 214, 215, 216, 217, 218

Orléans, Musée des Beaux-Arts   260, 261

Paris, Archives Nationales   168, 174, 235

Paris, Arch. Phot. S.P.A.D.E.M.   102 (photo: Atget), 117, 151, 153, 171, 172, 178 (photo: Atget), 180 (photo: Atget)

Paris, Artephot, frontispiece, 227, 232

Paris, Bibliothèque Nationale   21, 24, 35, 46, 47, 48, 58, 60, 62, 63, 66, 79, 80, 81, 82, 101, 103, 106, 113, 157, 158, 159, 163, 164, 165, 184, 190, 195, 203, 209, 236, 249, 294

Paris, Bulloz   210

Paris, Jean-Loup Charmet   5, 26, 64, 65, 73, 89, 98, 99

Paris, Ecole Nationale Supérieure des Beaux-Arts   267, 275

Paris, Fondation Jacques Doucet   38, 56, 57, 71, 183, 189, 196, 274, 278, 281, 282, 284, 285

Paris, Galerie Cailleux   166

Paris, Giraudon   32, 33, 49, 119, 128, 130, 175, 176, 207, 210, 211, 212, 241, 242, 267

Paris, Musée des Arts Décoratifs   2, 4, 6, 11, 12, 17, 75, 152, 160, 239, 246

Paris, Mobilier Nationale   45

Paris, Réunion des Musées Nationaux   23, 31, 53, 69, 72, 114, 140, 147, 148, 149, 155, 156, 201

Russborough, Sir Alfred Beit Foundation   181, 185

St Petersburg, The Hermitage   34, 224

San Francisco, Fine Arts Museum   115, 287 (Mildred Anna Williams Collection)   288 (Mildred Anna Williams Collection)

Stockholm, Nationalmuseum   7, 8, 9, 10, 25, 76, 95, 125, 127, 133, 134, 137, 142, 144, 145, 146, 177, 206, 237, 238, 245, 247, 248

Troyes, Musée des Beaux-Arts   223, 225

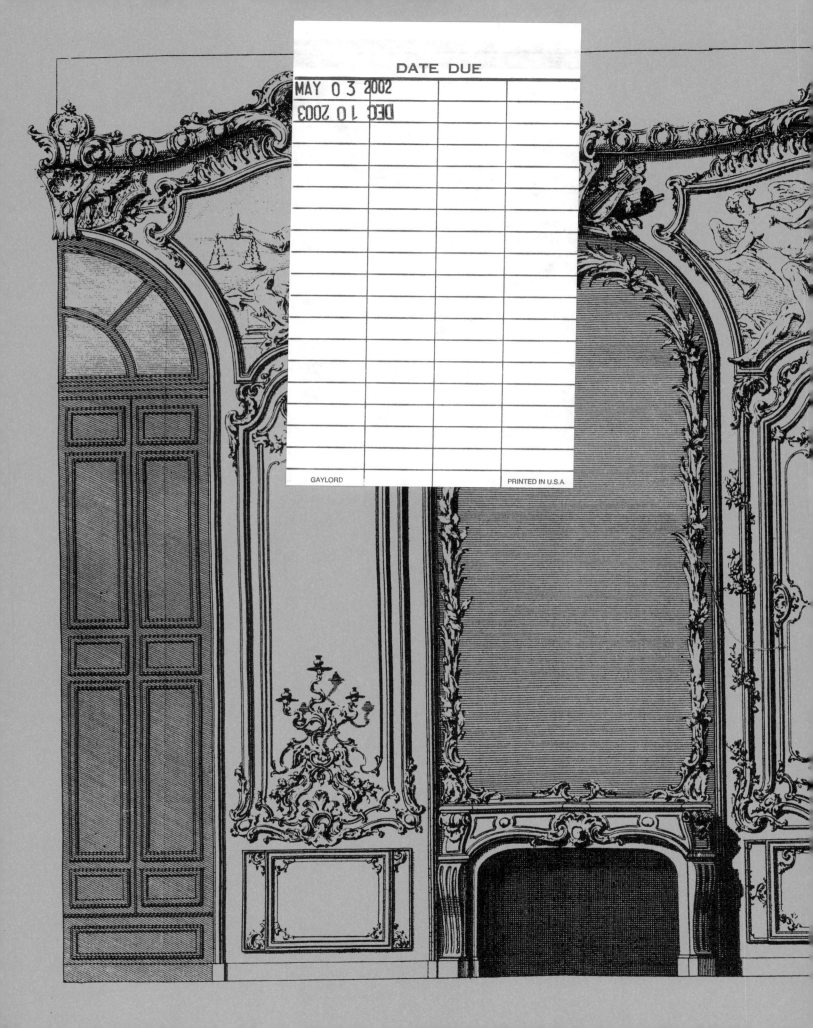